Communication in Everyday Life

Communication in Everyday Life

Steve Duck • David T. McMahan

University of Iowa   Missouri Western State University

Los Angeles | London | New Delhi
Singapore | Washington DC

For information:

SAGE Publications, Inc.
2455 Teller Road
Thousand Oaks, California 91320
E-mail: order@sagepub.com

SAGE Publications Ltd.
1 Oliver's Yard
55 City Road
London EC1Y 1SP
United Kingdom

SAGE Publications India Pvt. Ltd.
B 1/I 1 Mohan Cooperative Industrial Area
Mathura Road, New Delhi 110 044
India

SAGE Publications Asia-Pacific Pte. Ltd.
33 Pekin Street #02–01
Far East Square
Singapore 048763

Printed in Canada

Library of Congress Cataloging-in-Publication Data

Duck, Steve.
Communication in everyday life / Steve Duck, David T. McMahan.
    p. cm.
Includes bibliographical references and index.
ISBN 978-1-4129-6957-4 (pbk.: alk. paper) 1. Communication. I. McMahan, David T. II. Title.
P90.D8333 2010
302.2—dc22   2009022999

Printed on acid-free paper

09   10   11   12   13   10   9   8   7   6   5   4   3   2   1

Acquiring Editor:	Todd R. Armstrong
Editorial Assistant:	Aja Baker
Production Editor:	Sarah K. Quesenberry
Copy Editor:	Melinda Masson
Proofreader:	Gail Fay
Indexer:	Kathy Paparchontis
Typesetter:	C&M Digitals (P) Ltd.
Book Designer:	Ravi Balasuriya
Cover Designer:	Janet Kiesel
Marketing Manager:	Jennifer Reed Banando

Brief Contents

Chapters 15 and 16 can be
found on the companion Web site,
www.sagepub.com/ciel.

Detailed Contents

Engaged and Relational Listening

Recognizing and Overcoming Listening Obstacles

Critical Listening

Chapter 10 ■ Health Communication   261

Chapter 15 ■ Histories of Communication

Chapter 16 ■ Interviewing

Chapters 15 and 16
can be found on the companion
Web site, www.sagepub.com/ciel.

Preface

Communication in Everyday Life grew out of discussions with basic course directors, instructors, and students throughout the United States and other countries during the creation of and following the publication of our previous book, *The Basics of Communication: A Relational Perspective* (2009). It became clear that basic communication courses continue to play a central role in the discipline by attracting new majors, providing a foundation for the study of upper-level courses, and supporting the entire academic community as important general education requirements and preparations for life in the future. These conversations also revealed a shared belief that the basic course is not just about simply training students in a discipline but educating them more broadly for life beyond college and instilling within them an inquisitive curiosity that will serve them throughout their lives. It also became clear that instructors of the basic course are among the most dedicated professionals in this or any academic discipline. With this dedication comes a passion for improving the basic course and strong beliefs concerning what material should be included in these courses.

It further became obvious through these discussions that there exist two views regarding the content of hybrid basic communication courses. One view maintains that public speaking *should* be included in these courses as a defining and substantial element, and the second view maintains that public speaking *should not* be included in these courses as a primary component. At no time did those suggesting the exclusion of public speaking discount its importance or its historical position in the development of the communication discipline. Rather, their concerns largely involved the amount of class time required for the performance of public presentations, the inclusion of public speaking as a separate course in many departments, and the growing importance of other topics within the discipline which are not being incorporated in basic courses but should be included.

Consequently, *Communication in Everyday Life* was written to meet the needs of basic course instructors who desire a hybrid textbook that does not include multiple chapters on public speaking but instead includes chapters on topics equally important to students' lives but frequently missing from other textbooks. In addition to traditional topics found in hybrid textbooks, this book includes chapters on (a) identities, (b) family communication, (c) communication in the workplace, (d) culture and society, (e) technology, (f) media, and (g) public and personal influence.

A Relational Perspective

As with *The Basics of Communication,* the material is presented with a thematic integration to everyday life that allows all of these topics to cohere and coalesce by pointing out the *relational* basis of all communication as a major feature of students' lives. By "relational basis" we mean the influences created by and upon relationships during the course of activities *other than* relational development, management, or intimacy creation—for example, the effects of a personal relationship on one's ability to persuade a person with health advice, the role of media messages as topics of discussion in everyday talk between acquaintances, or the effects of the use of cell phones and the Internet as relational tools in everyday life. In short, we deal not only with the creation of relationships but also with the way relationships flow into many other daily experiences as mediators and moderators. We then apply this perspective to basic issues in communication.

The key feature of this text, then, is its basis in the idea that relationships make, are present in, modify, and create all communication. Our coverage of relationships is not as containers created by emotions; instead, we stress the importance and implications of the fact that they are perpetually *managed and enacted* daily experiences. In short, we emphasize the vital intersection of communication with relational contexts. We believe that this point provides both insight and coherence with reference to the topics normally covered in a basic text and simultaneously integrates such material with the increasingly popular and important, but previously independent, research on relationship communication. Relational communication is gradually refining or even replacing the traditional concept of "interpersonal communication" previously represented in basic texts. All of our coverage of traditional topics is extended and developed from this point of view.

We believe that our relational approach makes the importance and operation of communication more understandable through direct connections to student experience and therefore will facilitate classroom discussion while channeling and capitalizing on students' natural interests. We use this idea to illuminate the daily lives of students, and we offer the pedagogical purpose of showing how the students' experiences can be clarified through the principles of communication theory. Our goal is to help students understand their own daily lives by increasing the analytic awareness of their experiences and showing how communication theory and research can illuminate them. We further emphasize the social context of everyday experience, not only at the level of dyadic relationships and membership of networks of other people but also by noting that people's interactions with one another create the location of society's influence on the individual: Social partners are the human face of such abstract notions as "society" and "culture." Our relational approach helps pedagogically by showing how much of life's experience (even our experience of "society at large") is in fact perceived through the direct social connections that we have with other people. Only through our direct experience of others who represent the abstractions, "culture" and "society," do we feel their influence at all.

Given the variety of their educational backgrounds, demographic characteristics, and experiences, all students share the fact that their understanding of the world has been formed and influenced by relationships, through which people engage one another and which themselves lay the groundwork for much else that occurs in social life. Therefore, we focus not on the traditional approaches based on intimacy development but instead on the ways relationships create epistemics and rhetorical visions—that is, ways of understanding and (re)presenting the world—and we interweave this claim into traditional topics in interpersonal communication and media to show how much of life's apparently personal experience is in fact processed through the social connections that we have with other people.

By adopting an overall coherence of approach, it is possible to prevent segmentation of separate topics from one another by use of the guiding overarching theme and hence to tie together several previously—but to us always artificially—separate aspects of communication, which will help communication majors develop further as their courses proceed and allow them to see connections between presently disparate areas of communication study. This basic hybrid text will therefore lay the groundwork for a lifetime of learning, as well as present a strong overview of communication for those people whose only exposure to the work of communication scholars will be this book. In this way, we hope to make the book relevant to business majors, to those in training for the health professions, and to many other students with an interest in communication studies merely as a sideline or as a minor part of their degree.

Pedagogical Features

We view the pedagogical features within textbooks as fundamental elements in the comprehension and incorporation of the material being presented. Unfortunately, chapter boxes and other pedagogical elements, often sidebar features, are frankly overlooked by students and instructors alike. Accordingly, we have purposefully included pedagogical features with a fundamentally integrative and summational force, which will add to students' learning by giving them an immediate and visible structure for what they study in the text. These pedagogical tools are located throughout, as well as at the end of, each chapter.

To help guide the students, each chapter begins with a pedagogical overview: "These are the key things you need to know about this topic. Now let's look at them in more detail and go on to extrapolate and develop the complexities." **Focus Questions** are then posed to further direct students through the chapter. These questions are purposefully positioned after an opening narrative rather than at the very beginning to increase the likelihood that students will use them.

The main body of the chapters includes the following pedagogical boxes: (1) Make Your Case, (2) Strategic Communication, (3) Listen In On Your Life, and (4) Contrarian Challenge. **Make Your Case** boxes provide students with opportunities to develop their own positions or to perform an exercise about the material, which then can be used as a basis for class discussion in which students compare their experiences. Within the nonverbal communication chapter, for example, students are asked to consider a situation where they felt uncomfortable in the presence of another person. **Strategic Communication** boxes present students with guides to integrate the material into their lives when influencing others. For instance, the technology chapter asks students to consider how the purpose of their messages and the technological preferences of the person they are contacting will determine the appropriateness of face-to-face, telephone, or computer-mediated interaction. **Listen In On Your Life** boxes ask students to consider the material in relation to their own lives and lived experiences. Specifically, this feature will sensitize students to issues and encourage them to become careful observers of the activities and events going on in their own lives, compelling them to examine and apply the material. For example, the listening chapter asks students to consider friends, family, classmates, or coworkers they would label as *good* and *bad* listeners. Students are then asked to consider what behaviors lead them to these evaluations and then to determine measures to enhance others' listening skills. Finally, **Contrarian Challenge** boxes encourage critical thinking by asking students to consider positions which counter or contest those presented by us in the text or those commonly held in society. In the family chapter, for example, students are asked to contemplate the prevalent social view that genetic relationships are more significant than other ways of viewing "family."

Margin notes are also included in each chapter to provide students with additional information about the material or with open-ended questions to ponder as they study the material. Accordingly, some margin notes serve to enhance student interest in the material by providing unique information, such as when the first "smiley face" emoticon was sent or who invented the Internet. Other margin notes urge students to reflect upon the material by posing such questions as whether families would be considered groups.

Pictures included in each chapter also serve as pedagogical tools rather than as mere illustrative distractions. Each picture caption is stated in the form of a question that corresponds with material being discussed. Students will be asked to examine the picture and answer the accompanying question based on their understanding of the material. Not open-ended, these questions have specific answers that appear at the end of each chapter.

Each chapter also ends with pedagogical materials that bring the overview and focus questions full-circle. **Focus Questions Revisited** is implemented as a way of summarizing chapter material via pedagogical structure rather than as a simple (and usually ignored) chapter summary. Also, instead of including review questions, which often serve only to establish lower levels of comprehension, each chapter also includes the following features: (a) Ethical Issues, (b) Media Links, and (c) Questions to Ask Your Friends. These features enable students to further examine how the chapter material fits within their communicative lives as a whole. **Ethical Issues** urge students to contemplate and develop a position regarding ethical quandaries that arise in communication. For example, the technology chapter asks students to consider whether employers should use material on social networking sites, such as Facebook or Twitter, when making hiring decisions. **Media Links** lead students to draw from media in order to further explore the issues discussed in each chapter. For example, the relationships chapter instructs students to examine the Sunday newspaper section of marriages, engagements, and commitment ceremonies to check for similarities in attractiveness. Finally, **Questions to Ask Your Friends** provide students with questions to ask their friends in order to further increase their awareness of the material and integrate it into their lives. In the culture and society chapter, for example, students are urged to ask their friends about favorite children's stories and to connect themes to cultural ideals.

To further assist student learning, we have adopted an informal tone in our writing. This writing style is intended not only to invite students into the conversation about the issues that we present as basics of communication but also to engage their capacities to reflect about a problem and work through it with us, leaving them with a greater sense of having mastered the material by thinking through it for themselves, under guidance. We continually refer to everyday issues that students may have encountered or heard about from others, and we challenge them from time to time to reflect on and apply to their own lives what they have been reading about here.

Instructor Support

Although a fundamental feature of the book is, of course, to update discussion of topics by integrating the latest research while providing a new relationally based perspective on the material normally included in traditional texts, this is a two-edged sword. A challenge associated with developing a new textbook—especially one offering an original approach and addressing more up-to-date issues of communication—is that many instructors already have their courses in good shape and do not need the extra burden of rewriting those courses to fit a completely new text. We have therefore sought to add in new material in a way that supplements and develops rather than replaces traditional material. By this means, we seek to support those teachers who have developed courses on the basis of older material and who want to add some spice from the newer research without having to completely revise their existing lectures and notes. Thus, although the present text updates much of the theory and research included in other, older-style texts, we have constructed this book to reflect the traditional design for the basic text. A host of ancillary materials are also available that would benefit both new and experienced instructors of the basic course.

In sum, we see the advantages of this book as fourfold:

1. It presents a coherent reformulation of communication around the theme of relational and everyday experience.

2. It recognizes transformations within the discipline of communication and covers material increasingly relevant to students' lives.

3. It has strong self-reflective pedagogical features applied to students' own personal experiences and is thus different from many of the older texts.

4. It can be readily adopted without major restructuring of existing courses because it adds, we think, a more interesting approach to existing topics rather than entirely redrawing the map.

See if you agree.

_____

Communication in Everyday Life is accompanied by the following supplements, tailored to match the content of the book.

Student Study Site

This free student study site provides additional support to students using *Communication in Everyday Life.* Each chapter in the text will be accompanied by a self-quiz on the Web site, which includes 10 to 15 true/false and multiple-choice questions. Students will be able to check their answers to the questions immediately. E-flashcards, Internet exercises and resources, links to video and audio clips, and a link to the book's Facebook group are also included on this site to provide students with additional information and support. Also included are SAGE journal articles with discussion questions to get students into original research. Visit the study site at **www.sagepub.com/ciel.**

Instructor's Resources Materials

Protected Instructor Site

This Web site is a helpful teaching aid for professors new to teaching the course and to using *Communication in Everyday Life.* Included on the Web site are PowerPoint slides, suggested class activities, sample syllabi, suggested Web resources, and teaching tips. Visit the instructor site at **www.sagepub.com/ciel.** If you are a qualified adopter and have your email address and password on file with SAGE, you may log in to the site and begin accessing the instructor materials immediately. If you are not yet a qualified adopter with SAGE, you will need to register on the site.

Computerized Test Bank on CD

A computerized Diploma test bank on CD is available with this text. Qualified adopters can contact Customer Care at 800-818-7243 to request a CD.

Acknowledgments

A book such as this is a far larger undertaking than we realized when first proposing it. Although our two names appear on the front cover, many other people contributed to its final form and shape. Chief among these and to whom we owe the largest debt is the inestimable Todd Armstrong, our editor for this volume. Working with Todd has been and remains a real pleasure, and this project benefited enormously from his experience, wise guidance, and flexibility—a really helpful and constructive combination of knowing when to insist and when to think again. He was ably assisted by associate editor Deya Saoud, editorial assistant Aja Baker, and a production team led most capably by Sarah Quesenberry, among whose team Melinda Masson stands out as an exceptional developmental and copy editor. Michele Sordi has also been of great help to us. We also want to extend our heartfelt thanks to Carmel Schrire and her marketing team for their exceptional work and for the enthusiasm they bring to our projects. Carmel has proven time and again to be without equal through her keen insight and expertise. Our work with everyone at SAGE Publications has made this project a most pleasurable experience.

We are grateful to those colleagues and friends who took the time to read drafts and redrafts of the manuscript at all stages, from initial outline to re-revised "final" manuscripts. Without their wisdom and suggestions, many of the elements of the book would be less interesting and exciting than we believe they are now. We would also like to thank those students, both graduate and undergraduate, who knowingly or unknowingly provided observations, examples, and thoughtful discussion of some of the ideas under development, whether in or outside of class, in particular Ryan Gourley, Chitra Akkoor, and Kristen Norwood. We would also like to thank Dr. Charles McMahan, David's first communication instructor both formally as his professor and informally as his dad, for his valuable suggestions based on over 40 years of teaching in the discipline of communication.

Involvement in a book such as this takes an enormous toll on family life, and we are grateful to our respective spouses and families that we have managed to complete the project and still remain married. Their forbearance provided a supportive atmosphere for us to manage the long hours and extended absences required to bring such a project to completion.

Finally, we would like to thank all of our parents, siblings, nieces and nephews, extended families, friends outside academics, acquaintances, strangers we have encountered, people we like, and people we do not like, all of whom have provided us with ideas for a relational perspective on communication and an appreciation for the importance of everyday life.

They, of course, communicate without the expert knowledge that reviewers can bring to the venture, and we are indebted to the following for their unstinting generosity in commenting on the textbook in spite of their incredibly busy schedules and making many brilliant suggestions that we were all too happy to borrow or appropriate without acknowledgement other than here. They generously contributed to whatever this book in its turn contributes to the growth and development of the field. We could not have developed the relational perspective without their professionalism and thoughtfulness.

Matt Abrahams
De Anza College

Brent E. Adrian
Central Community College–Grand Island

Allison Ainsworth
Gainesville State College

Carlos Alemán
James Madison University

Melissa W. Alemán
James Madison University

Alicia Alexander
Southern Illinois University–Edwardsville

Karen Anderson
University of North Texas

Christine Armstrong
Northampton Community College

Bryan H. Barrows III
Lone Star College–North Harris

Sally Bennett Bell
University of Montevallo

Keith Berry
University of Wisconsin–Superior

Robert Betts
Rock Valley College

Robert Bodle
College of Mount St. Joseph

David M. Bollinger
University of North Carolina at Wilmington

Deborah Borisoff
New York University

Jay Bower
Southern Illinois University–Carbondale

Kathy Brady
University of Wisconsin–Whitewater

Michele Bresso
Bakersfield College

Paulette Brinka
Suffolk County Community College

Stefne Lenzmeier Broz
Wittenberg University

Dale Burke
Hawai'i Pacific University

Linda Cardillo
College of Mount St. Joseph

Sheena M. Carey
Marquette University

Anna Carmon
North Dakota State University

Laura Cashmer
Joliet Junior College

Yvonne Yanrong Chang
University of Texas–Pan American

April Chatham-Carpente
University of Northern Iowa

Denise M. Chaytor
East Stroudsburg University

John Chetro-Szivos
Fitchburg State College

Daniel Chornet-Roses
Saint Louis University–Madrid Campus

Carolyn Clark
Salt Lake Community College

Brian Cogan
Malloy College

Sarah Cole
Framingham State College

Janet W. Colvin
Utah Valley University

Anna Conway
Des Moines Area Community College

Gil Cooper
Pittsburg State University

Lisa Coutu
University of Washington

Miki Crawford
Ohio University Southern Campus

Alice Crume
Kent State University

Kevin Cummings
Mercer University

Kimberly M. Cuny
University of North Carolina at Greensboro

Roberta A. Davilla
Western Illinois University

Quinton D. Davis
University of Texas at San Antonio

Jean Dewitt
University of Houston–Downtown

Linda B. Dickmeyer
University of Wisconsin–LaCrosse

Aaron Dimock
University of Nebraska at Kearney

Marcia D. Dixson
Indiana-Purdue University–Fort Wayne

Shirley K. Drew
Pittsburg State University

Michele Rees Edwards
Robert Morris University

Michael Elkins
Indiana State University

Larry A. Erbert
University of Colorado–Denver

Billie Evans
Graceland University

Lisa Falvey
Emmanuel College

Jeanine Fassl
University of Wisconsin–Whitewater

Sarah Bonewits Feldner
Marquette University

Jerry Fliger
Toccoa Falls College

Sherry Ford
University of Montevallo

Jil M. Freeman
Portland State University

John French
Cape Cod Community College

Tammy French
University of Wisconsin–Whitewater

Todd S. Frobish
Fayetteville State University

Beverly Graham
Georgia Southern University

Darlene Graves
Liberty University

Dawn Gully
University of South Dakota

Suzanne Hagen
University of Wisconsin–River Falls

Martin L. Hatton
Mississippi University for Women

Thomas Edwards Harkins
New York University

Patrick J. Hebert
University of Louisiana at Monroe

Susan Hellweg
San Diego State University

Valerie Hennen
Gateway Technical College

Annette Holba
Plymouth State University

Lucy Holsonbake
Northern Virginia Community College

Sallyanne Holtz
University of Texas at San Antonio

David Hopcroft
Quinebaug Valley Community College

Alec R. Hosterman
Indiana University South Bend

Gayle E. Houser
Northern Arizona University

Rebecca Imes
Carroll University

Ann Marie Jablonowski
Owens Community College

Amir H. Jafri
Davis and Elkins College

Lori Johnson
University of Northern Iowa

Michelle Johnson
The College of Wooster

Bernadette Kapocias
Southwestern Oregon Community College

Jim Katt
University of Central Florida

William M. Keith
University of Wisconsin–Milwaukee

Doug Kelley
Arizona State University

Elizabeth Kindermann
Mid Michigan Community College

Branislav Kovacic
University of Hartford

Shelley D. Lane
University of Texas at Dallas

Rachel Lapp
Goshen College

B. J. Lawrence
Bradley University

Kathe Lehman-Meyer
St. Mary's University

Nancy R. Levin
Palm Beach Community College

Kurt Lindemann
San Diego State University

Judith Litterst
St. Cloud State University

Deborah K. London
Merrimack College

Karen Lovaas
San Francisco State University

Louis A. Lucca
F. H. LaGuardia Community College (CUNY)

Julie Lynch
St. Cloud State University

Valerie Manusov
University of Washington

Lawrence M. Massey
Spokane Falls Community College

Masahiro Masuda
Kochi University

Marie A. Mater
Houston Baptist University

Nelya McKenzie
Auburn University at Montgomery

Bruce McKinney
University of North Carolina at Wilmington

Shawn Miklaucic
DeSales University

Jean Costanza Miller
George Washington

Yolanda F. Mitchell
Pulaski Tech

Thomas Morra
Northern Virginia Community College

Kay E. Neal
University of Wisconsin–Oshkosh

John Nicholson
Mississippi State University

Carey Noland
Northeastern University

Laura Oliver
University of Texas at San Antonio

Rick Olsen
University of North Carolina at Wilmington

Susan Opt
Salem College

Nan Peck
Northern Virginia Community College

Lynette Sharp Penya
Abilene Christian University

Frank G. Perez
University of Texas at El Paso

Jeffrey Pierson
Bridgewater College

Jon Radwan
Seton Hall University

Rita L. Rahoi-Gilchrest
Winona State University

Pravin Rodrigues
Ashland University

Tracy Routsong
Washburn University

M. Sallyanne Ryan
Fairfield University

Erin Sahlstein
University of Nevada, Las Vegas

David P. Schultz
Trinity Lutheran College

Pamela Schultz
Alfred University

Pam L. Secklin
St. Cloud State University

Marilyn Shaw
University of Northern Iowa

Tami Spry
St. Cloud State University

Gina Stahl-Ricco
College of Marin

Suzanne Stangl-Erkens
St. Cloud State University

John Stone
James Madison University

John Tapia
Missouri Western State University

Avinash Thombre
University of Arkansas at Little Rock

Amy Torkelson Miller
North Dakota State University

April R. Trees
Saint Louis University

David Tschida
St. Cloud State University

Jennifer Tudor
St. Cloud State University

Jill Tyler
University of South Dakota

Ben Tyson
Central Connecticut State University

Michelle T. Violanti
University of Tennessee

Catherine E. Waggoner
Wittenberg University

John T. Warren
Southern Illinois University–Carbondale

Sara C. Weintraub
Regis College

Scott Wells
St. Cloud State University

Richard West
University of Texas at San Antonio

Bruce Wickelgren
Suffolk University

Sarah M. Wilde
University of North Carolina at Greensboro

Daniel Wildeson
St. Cloud State University

Richard Wilkins
Baruch College

Bobette Wolensenky
Palm Beach Community College South

Sarah Wolter
Gustavus Adolphus University

Yinjiao Ye
University of Rhode Island

Lance Brendan Young
University of Iowa

We would also like to extend our deep appreciation to the following student reviewers for their keen insight as those for whom this book is truly intended.

Fayetteville State College: Katrina Faison, Kristy Mitchell, Jourdan Scruggs, Elvia Stangle, and Desiree Thomas; *Lone Star College–North Harris:* Lyndi Bryson and Beverley Church; *Malloy College:* Karenlyn Barone; *University of Nevada, Las Vegas:* Jenny Farrell; *Owens Community College:* Stephen Traxel; *University of Wisconsin–Milwaukee:* Angela McGowan; *Washburn University:* Lisa Bellanga, Garrett Bendure, Adam Forbes, Andrew Foxhoven, Blaine Grooms, Kari Hadl, Janelle Hill, Kaitlin Marsh, Tessa Okruhlik, Elise Richardson, Carmen Romero-Galvan, Lindsey Scott, Daniel Usera, Talia Van Anne, Cassandra Wall Gaddis, and Shannon Ware; *Winona State University:* Jana Heydon, Chris Johnsen, Jennifer Lamont, McKenzie Larson, Kate Perardi, Amanda Peters, Brad Reiter, Erin Rieckenberg, Paul Rohde, Emily A. Schultz, Katrina Theis, Danielle Topka, and Brent Vyvyan.

About the Authors

Steve Duck taught at two universities in the United Kingdom before taking up the Daniel and Amy Starch Distinguished Research Professorship in the Communication Studies department at the University of Iowa in 1986, where he is also an Adjunct Professor of Psychology. He was recently promoted to Collegiate Administrative Fellow and works with the Deans' Caucus in the College of Liberal Arts and Sciences. He has taught several interpersonal communication courses, mostly on interpersonal communication and relationships but also on nonverbal communication, communication in everyday life, construction of identity, communication theory, organizational leadership, and procedures and practices for leaders. Always by training an interdisciplinary thinker, Steve has focused on the development and decline of relationships from many different perspectives, although he has also done research on the dynamics of television production techniques and persuasive messages in health contexts. Steve has written or edited 50 books on relationships and other matters and was the founder and, for the first 15 years, the editor of the *Journal of Social and Personal Relationships*. His 1994 book *Meaningful Relationships: Talking, Sense, and Relating* won the G. R. Miller Book Award from the Interpersonal Communication Division of the National Communication Association. Steve cofounded the series of International Conferences on Personal Relationships that began in 1982. He won the University of Iowa's first Outstanding Mentor Award in 2001 and the National Communication Association's Robert J. Kibler Memorial Award in 2004 for "dedication to excellence, commitment to the profession, concern for others, vision of what could be, acceptance of diversity, and forthrightness." Able to play the recorder by ear (no small achievement, although he has big ears), he wishes he could play something a bit more complicated like the piano, the guitar, or the violin.

 **David T. McMahan** has taught courses that span the discipline of communication, including numerous courses in interpersonal communication, media, communication education, theory, and criticism. David's research interests also engage multiple areas of the discipline with much of his research devoted to bridging the study of relationships and media. This work includes examining the discussion of media and the incorporation of catchphrases and media references in everyday communication. A great deal of research has been derived from his experiences in the classroom and his commitment to education. His early work in this area focused on communication competence, self-conception, and assessment. His focus has since shifted toward topics that include both media and relationships, such as contradictions within advisor-advisee relationships and discussions of media in the classroom. His diverse research experiences include studies on symbolic displays of masculinity and violence in rural America, media-based political transformations of the world's nation-states, *The New York Times*' reporting of mass-murder suicide, and primetime animated series. His work has appeared in such journals as *Review of Communication, Communication Education,* and *Communication Quarterly,* as well as edited volumes. A member of the National Communication Association, Central States Communication Association, Eastern Communication Association, Iowa Communication Association, and Speech Communication Association of Puerto Rico, David has served numerous roles within these organizations. He has received multiple awards for his work in the classroom and has been the recipient of a number of public service and academic distinctions, most recently being named a Centennial Scholar by the Eastern Communication Association. He hopes to someday become a game show host.

1

An Overview of Everyday Communication

I f you think there is anything important in your life that does not involve communication, leaf idly through this book and see if it makes you challenge your first thought. It will take only a couple of minutes, and then you can put the book back on the shelf. However, we do not think you will be able to come up with very many activities in life that are not improved by communication and that would not be made better by your ability to understand communication more thoroughly. We wrote this book partly because we believe that everyone needs to know something about communication. Especially if you are a student, *Communication in Everyday Life* will help you improve your life through understanding communication, whether you are headed off to become a dental hygienist, a researcher, a preacher, a businessperson, a nurse, a physician, a member of a sales force, a parent, or just somebody's good friend.

We are passionate about the study of communication because it has so many obvious uses and influences in everyday life, and we believe very strongly that you too can benefit from knowing more about how communication works. We have never met anyone who did *not* want to understand more about his or her everyday life and, in particular, about his or her relationships. We have tried to bind together these interests by writing this book, which answers questions about how communication and relationships hang together and connect with other parts of life, such as listening, culture, gender, media, giving presentations, or merely being you. We cover all of this with a particular theme in mind—the way you carry out your everyday life through your relationships with other people—and how the above are relevant to our theme.

The phrase *relationships with other people* draws your attention not only to how your relationships work and can be improved but also to how they affect you during the course of other activities that happen in your life. Your relationship with someone affects your ability to persuade that person to take your health advice, for example, or the media that you use can become topics of discussion between acquaintances. Cell phones and Facebook are forms of communication that have become relational tools in everyday life, especially if you are in long-distance relationships. So, in this book, we deal not just with the creation of relationships but with the way relationships flow into many other daily experiences as effects not only on those experiences themselves but also on everyday life communication.

We sincerely believe that your daily life as a student, friend, romantic partner, colleague, and family member can be improved through the principles of communication theory. One of our purposes is to help you understand your daily life by making you more aware of how everyday life works through communication. We believe that all students desire to see, recognize, and understand their many instances of daily contact with communication research and theory. Another purpose is to develop your studies by encouraging more eager and independent thinking about research into such topics as conflict, relationship development, gender, culture, technology, and business and professional speaking.

Whatever your purpose in reading this book, and whatever your ultimate goal in life, we hope that it will enrich your experience, sharpen your abilities to observe and analyze communication activity, and make your life a little bit more interesting because you can understand the processes going on around you. So take us up on our challenge. Thumb through the contents and look at a few of the pictures to see if you now "get" what we think is important about communication and why you need to learn about it.

Focus Questions

- What is communication, and how does it work in your everyday life?
- How does communication create worlds of meaning?
- How do the assumptions in a culture affect communication?
- What are the properties of communication?
- What does it mean to say that communication is both representational and presentational, and why is the difference important?
- What is a "frame," and how is communication framed?
- What is a working definition of communication for this book?

How This Book Is Structured to Help Your Learning

Because we are convinced of the importance of the topic and because we are passionate about helping people learn about it, we have used some special features designed to make it particularly interesting and relevant to you. First of all, the tone of this book is somewhat different from other textbooks you may have come across. We have deliberately adopted an informal and conversational tone in our writing, and we even throw in a few jokes. We are not attempting to be hip or cool: Trust us; we are far from either, so much so that we are not even sure if the words *hip* and *cool* are used anymore. Instead, we use a conversational voice because we believe that it makes this book more engaging to read. Plus, we genuinely like and have a good time talking about this material, so we want to share our enthusiasm in a way that we hope is infectious. We have become used to seeing the significance of communication as if it speaks for itself, but we realize that not everybody else takes that view. Because we are also deeply committed to the importance of studying communication, we want to discuss it all in such a way that is clear, understandable, and applicable to your life. We hope that this will make it as exciting to you as it is to us.

Everything that appears in this book—even every picture—does so for a reason, and that reason centers on increasing your understanding, your application, and even your enjoyment of the material. For example, the pictures do not have standard captions, but each asks a question that you can answer for yourself, although we provide possible answers at the end of each chapter. The pictures are here not just to make the book look pretty, but they serve the purpose of teaching you something and making you think for yourself.

Instead of beginning each chapter with questions to focus on before you know what the chapter is about, our **Focus Questions** follow an opening narrative for each chapter. They are so positioned because we want to ensure that you read them after you have seen the basic issues with which the chapter deals. We personally skipped them when we were in school: They appeared at the very beginning of the chapter, and we did not yet know what they were about. We strongly encourage you to read them. Because they come after the narrative that sets up the questions in each chapter, they will guide you through the chapter and provide you with insight as to what you should focus on as you read. Because they are important, we will also revisit and answer them at the end of each chapter so that you can see if your answers match ours. In fact, we do this instead of summarizing the chapter in the conventional way. The end of every chapter is therefore directly connected to the beginning.

Although we wanted to limit the number appearing in each chapter, boxes can have a great deal of value for your learning. Each chapter includes the following four types of boxes: (1) Make Your Case, (2) Strategic Communication, (3) Listen In On Your Life, and (4) Contrarian Challenge. **Make Your Case** boxes provide you with opportunities to develop your own positions or to perform an exercise about the material that might be used during class discussion. In the language chapter, for example, you are asked to find out the secret languages that you and your friends speak without realizing it. **Strategic Communication** boxes help you integrate the material into your life when influencing others. For instance, the technology chapter asks you to consider how the purpose of a message and the technological preferences of the person you are contacting will determine the appropriateness of face-to-face, telephone, or computer-mediated interaction. **Listen In On Your Life** boxes ask you to consider the material in relation to your own life and lived experiences. We want you to start recognizing communication in your life and how the discussed material applies. For example, the listening chapter asks you to consider friends, family, classmates, or coworkers you would label as *good* and *bad* listeners. You are then asked to analyze what behaviors led to these evaluations and to determine measures to enhance the listening skills of others. These exercises, therefore, will also serve to further your understanding and comprehension of the material. Finally, **Contrarian Challenge** boxes invite you to think more carefully about what you have read and see if we have persuaded you or if you can see another side to what we have written. For example, although this chapter will present communication in a logical way, as do other textbooks, we invite you to answer the challenge of whether communication in everyday life is actually quite messy and disorganized and much less clear and clean than the theories present.

Also included in each chapter are **margin notes,** which provide additional information about the material or open-ended questions to ponder as you study it. Accordingly, some margin notes provide unique information, such as when the first "smiley face" emoticon was sent, who invented the Internet, or what percentage of people believe that they are shy enough to need treatment. Other margin notes urge you to reflect on the material by posing questions, such as whether or not families would be considered "groups."

The very end of each chapter includes features to further enhance your mastery and comprehension of the material. Once again, we thought very carefully about what to include here. We did not want questions that ask you to merely memorize and repeat what you read in this book; rather we wanted those that ask you to *think* about it outside of class as you carry out the rest of your life. We wanted to include features that ask you to go beyond each chapter's contents and engage in higher levels of thinking.

Accordingly, each chapter also includes the following features: (a) Ethical Issues, (b) Media Links, and (c) Questions to Ask Your Friends. **Ethical Issues** urge you to contemplate and develop a position regarding ethical quandaries that arise in communication. For example, the technology chapter asks you to consider whether employers should use material on social networking sites, such as Facebook, when making hiring decisions, and the relationships chapter asks if it is ever ethical to have two romantic relationships going on at the same time and why (or why not). **Media Links** ask you to draw from media in order to further explore the issues discussed in each chapter. You are asked to watch a TV newscast and discover ways in which the newscasters establish a relationship with the audience, for example, and to read a newspaper article looking for examples of logical fallacies. The relationships chapter invites you to examine the Sunday newspaper section of marriages, engagements, and commitment ceremonies for similarities in attractiveness. Believe it or not, romantic partners often look alike! Finally, **Questions to Ask Your Friends** provide you with questions to ask your friends in order to further increase your awareness of the material and integrate it into your life. In the culture and society chapter, for example, you are urged to ask your friends about favorite children's stories and connect themes to cultural ideals. It may initially seem strange to drag your friends into your own learning, but in fact, just as in everyday life itself, you will learn from them, and you will be teaching them a thing or two as well. Plus, this activity will help underscore the significance of relationships in your life. As with the boxes, we are serious about having you try out these instructional tools to improve your study of the material.

A **Student Study Site** is also available to improve your study of the material. It includes electronic flashcards to check your knowledge of key terms and concepts, study quizzes, Internet activities and resources, links to video and audio clips, and a link to the Facebook group we've created for the book. You can access the site for free at www.sagepub.com/ciel.

Ultimately, we want to invite students—you and others you know—into the conversation about the issues we present as basics of communication. As part of that, we are trying to stretch your capacity to think about a problem and work through it with us, leaving you with a greater sense of having mastered the material by thinking through it for yourself, under guidance. Because we want to increase the discussion of communication generally, we continually mention everyday issues so that you can talk about them with your friends and become more helpful to *them* too. You should be able to reflect on your friends' and your own lives from time to time and apply to them what you have been reading about here. "You know, funny you should say that because I've just been reading about that exact same thing, and what the book said was . . ." Which leads us neatly into the first issue to consider: the way communication is so intricately tied up with relationships.

Communication and Relationships

Communication and relationships are intertwined processes. Not merely speaking into the air, *communication is speaking into relationships,* whether you are speaking to your best friend about something personal, signaling your membership with fellow citizens by honoring the flag, or presenting a talk to an audience of complete strangers. Furthermore, "communication" is not simply messages sent from one person to another; communication *does* something: It causes a result, creates an atmosphere, manages an identity, and, for example, reveals your age, gender, race, or culture. That is, any type of communication you ever participate in has a relationship assumed underneath it and also does or achieves something for you as a result; namely, communication creates a world of meaning. These two themes—that communication is based in the relationships of everyday life and that it creates more than it appears to—are the themes of our approach. Therefore, this book takes a *relational* perspective to communication, and the constant guide in understanding everyday communication will be the relationships that you have with other people.

Not only, like all other basic communication books, will *Communication in Everyday Life* teach you what communication is, but it will also continually interconnect with your *everyday experience* of relating to and with other people. Defining communication turns out to be difficult, and it will take the whole chapter to conclude what it means. Within this chapter, we invite you to start thinking more carefully about everyday communication and how it works. We will teach you how to break down its components and assumptions and see why communication is not as simple as it looks. In the rest of the book, we will show you how to connect and use these components and assumptions, thus allowing you to apply them to all sorts of communicative activity, such as giving a friend some advice about health, acing an interview, making a toast at a wedding, persuading a friend to do you a favor, or making someone feel comfortable talking with you. You will also learn how to deal successfully with a relational conflict that could lose you a friend if you do not handle it effectively and with sensitivity.

What Is Communication Anyway?

Y ou send "messages" not only by words or gestures but also by the clothes you wear and your physical appearance, which is why you dress carefully for an interview to make a good first impression and send a good message.

At this point, you may be asking the "big deal" questions: What is so problematic about everyday communication? Why bother to explain it? Don't people know what it is about and how it works? Communication is just about sending messages, right?

True: Most of the time, people communicate without thinking, and it is not usually awkward. But if communicating is so easy, why do people have misunderstandings, conflicts, arguments, disputes, and disagreements? Why do people get embarrassed because they have said something thoughtless? Why are people misunderstood, and why do people misunderstand others? If communication is simple, how do people know when others are lying if all that matters is listening to their words as a straightforward representation of a situation? Why would anyone be agitated or anxious about giving a public talk if talk is just saying what you think? Why is communication via e-mail so easy to misinterpret? People would never disagree about what happened in a conversation if the students who asked the above "big deal" questions were right. Why, then, are allegations of sexual harassment sometimes denied vigorously, and how can there ever be doubt whether one person intentionally touched another person inappropriately? Why are coworkers so often a problem for many people, and what is it about their communication that makes them "difficult"?

Many students assume that communication means the sending of messages from one person to another through e-mails, phone calls, gestures, instant or text messages, or spoken word. They often assume that communication informs other people about what they are thinking, where they are, or how to do stuff or else, like text messages between cell phones, that it transmits information from Person A to Person B. That basic view has some truth to it, but communication involves a lot more than simply sending messages as if they are tennis balls hit to an opponent. Students also need to know more about "messages": Like tennis balls, they can bounce oddly, spin off, or miss their target. We'll explain how contexts modify messages: Meeting a person in class, for example, is different from meeting the same person at a party.

Even if communication were just about messages, the notion of "messages" would need a closer look. The meaning of messages—not simple in the way that instant messages contain certain unchangeable words—is modified by the person who says them. For example, consider the phrase "I love you" said to you by your mother, your brother, your friend, your priest, your instructor, the president of the United States, or your physician. See how messages get more complex even when the words ("I love you") are the same? Also think of "I love you" said by the same person (e.g., your mother) on your birthday, after a fight with her, as you leave home for school, on her deathbed, at Thanksgiving, or at the end of a phone call. Would it *mean* the same thing? Finally, think of "I love you" said by your romantic partner in a short, sharp way; in a long, lingering way; with a frown; with a smile; with a hand on your arm as you get up to leave; or with a hesitant and questioning tone of voice. The same words send a different message depending on the context and the style of delivery.

Thinking More Carefully About Everyday Communication

Let's start by examining our first two claims: Not just emotional connections, relationships create worlds of meaning for people through communication, and communication produces the same result for people through relationships. As one example, group decision making is accomplished not just by the logic of arguments, agenda setting, and solution evaluations but also by group members' relationships with one another outside the group setting. Groups that meet to make decisions almost never come from nowhere, communicate, make a decision, and then go home. The members

Photo 1.1 Many conversations between close friends are "framed" by previous experiences and conversations—hence, the phrase "frame of reference." In what ways can you work out that these two women are friends and that they therefore share some history together that frames their interaction? (See page 25.)

know one another, talk informally outside the group setting, and have personal likes and dislikes for one another that will affect their discussions about certain matters. Many decisions that appear to be made during an open discussion are actually sometimes tied up before the communication begins. Think about what generally happens in Congress. The politicians often know how the vote will go *before* the debate actually happens. Words have been dropped in ears, promises made, factions formed, and relationships displayed well in advance of any discussion. This striking but everyday example might make you think of others from your life: How does *influence* work in your family? Is everyone equal? What about interactions with friends and enemies? Do you *believe* them equally, as if they are independent and pure sources of truthful messages? How about TV shows and news channels? Does it make a difference whether you *like* the newscaster or not, or do you *trust* all newscasters equally?

Paul Watzlawick and his colleagues (Watzlawick, Beavin, & Jackson, 1967)[1] put it a little differently, suggesting that whenever you communicate with anyone, you also relate to him or her at the same time. All communication contains both a content (message) level and a relational level, which means that, as well as conveying information, every message indicates how the speaker and listener are socially and personally related. In the United States, for example, you say, "Excuse me, sir…" when addressing a stranger rather than "Hey, jerk…" But there are other, less obvious relational cues in speech about who is the boss and who is the employee, who is a professor and who is the student, who is the parent and who is the child, or who is the server and who is the customer. For example, "Come into my office! Now!" indicates a status difference just through the *style* of the communication. Because the relationships between people most often are not openly expressed but subtly indicated or taken for granted in most communication in any particular culture, the content and relational components of messages are not always easy to separate. You must pay careful attention to learn how it is done. We'll start with a familiar experience and work through it as a means to get your brain tuned up: a restaurant server speaking to customers.

What Do You Do Through Communication?

"Hi! My name is Roberta, and I'll be your server today. Our special is witchety grub stewed in yak fat with broccoli sautéed in mushroom sauce at $24.95. If you have any questions, let me know. May I get you anything to drink while you read the menu?" Look at the above server introduction and its contents:

A greeting: "Hi!"

An introduction to the person: "My name is Roberta."

A direct statement of the person's relationship to you: "I'll be your server today."

A list of particular foods

If you do not recognize "witchety grub," it may be because you are not an Australian for whom this is a food delicacy, but the rest probably makes sense even if you do not know that a yak is a species of livestock cattle in China. These details are known in their original culture, but you belong to a different culture in which they are strange. Other cultures make different assumptions than your culture makes and take different knowledge for granted. Communication scholars talk about culture "getting done" or "being performed" in relationships through assumptions taken for granted between two communicators. Each time you talk to someone, from your culture or another, you are taking knowledge for granted, doing what your culture expects, and treating people in ways the culture acknowledges. You are doing, performing, and enacting your culture through communication; you are not just making sound waves but speaking into the relationships recognized by your culture.

---

1. You will notice as we go through the book that when we refer to someone else's work or ideas, we will use this kind of format, with the authors' surnames and a date. The date gives the year in which the original paper or book was published. Look for the full reference at the end of the chapter; this format is used in most social science textbooks and professional writing. You may also be asked to use this format when you write your own papers.

In our example, the server's introduction makes sense because the speaker splits the world up in much the same way that you do, and you also know how to "do/speak restaurant" and what a "menu" is, for example. Most people understand how communication points out particular objects in this way ("menu," "server," "broccoli," "our special"). But notice also how the communication makes the interaction work in a particular way, setting up one person (server) in a particular kind of *relationship* with the other person (customer) while setting that relationship up as friendly and casual ("Hi," not "A thousand welcomes, princely masters"). You have built-in expectations about the relationship between a server and a customer. You already know and take for granted that these relational differences exist in restaurants and that restaurants have "servers" who generally carry out instructions of "customers." Therefore, you expect that you as the customer will be greeted, treated with some respect by the server, told what the special is, and asked to make choices. You know that you will eventually pay for your food and that the server is there not only to bring you food, water, the check, and your change but also to help if you have difficulties understanding the menu. Roberta will answer any questions about the way the food is prepared or help if you need to find the restrooms. Both you and your server take this for granted; it is a cultural as well as *relational* element of your communication. All of this is included in the idea of "doing culture" or "doing relationships" in communication.

We asked you earlier to think about whether communication is just about sending and receiving messages. Now ask yourself how many messages the server is sending in this relatively brief encounter. There seem to be just four: her name and job, her relationship to you, the nature of the special on the menu, and the greeting. On deeper inspection, you might find such others as status, culture, and politeness—all relational in their own ways. Also note that the comments are appropriate only in some places and at some times—in restaurants but not at your graduation ceremony as you shake hands with the president to get your diploma. Communication scholars would say that the introduction also "does various work," for example, to structure time. Notice how the words make sense only as the *beginning* of an interaction. If Roberta said them when you were leaving her restaurant, you'd think she was nuts. The comments also use codes; that is, they use one idea to stand in for others. Roberta says "menu" rather than "a list of all the food that we prepare, cook, and serve in this restaurant for you to choose for your meal" because she assumes you will know the code word *menu* and its meaning in a restaurant as opposed to on a computer screen.

Make Your Case

Do you think someone from another culture might be confused about Americans' love of buffalo wings? What are some other food names that might confuse a visitor to this country? Have you ever sampled (or seen on TV) an unfamiliar food from another culture? Describe the experience. Was there anything about the name or type of food that shocked or surprised you or challenged your assumptions about what "food" is?

In Japanese, there are more than 200 ways for one person to address another according to protocols of respect and status differences recognized by the participants. Pretend you are going on a business trip to Japan; what could you do to prepare yourself and ensure that you do not insult your customers/clients?

This simple example from everyday life experience in our culture underlines the point that when you communicate with other people, many assumptions are made—sometimes about *meaning* or *power* or *relationships* or *gender* or *race* or the *culture* in which the communication occurs. Whether or not you know it, all of those assumptions—and much else besides—happen whenever you communicate, steering and shaping the interaction. Indeed, one fundamental aspect of speaking is built on the fact that you and your audience—whether a wedding group, a political rally, your boss, or your friend—know what you mean when you use certain words. Remember that in Japan, Mexico, China, or Zimbabwe, people take for granted not only different assumptions about words but also different rules about respect, greeting rituals, rank, and relationships between people.

So, if upon beginning this chapter a definition of communication seemed obvious to you, that was partly because you may not yet recognize all the assumptions that you take for granted in your cultural experience. At this point, you may not question or even notice communication in your everyday life, yet every time you talk to someone else, you are doing/speaking your culture, doing/speaking your relationship with that person, and doing/speaking your identity. Communication does more than send a simple message; it builds a world of meaning on one person's relationship with another.

Stating this idea more technically, communication not only describes the world but also sets it up in a particular way, makes interactions happen in a particular form, and directs how we deal with other people. Part of this creative element of communication shows up as a way of establishing the relationship between you and the server, but the same formative and relational messages are conveyed in all interactions. The way you speak to someone tells him or her and everyone else whether the two of you are close; whether you are strangers; whether you are equals; which one of you is respectful, anxious, or shy; who commands a relationship; or who is rude.

Listen In On Your Life

After your next conversation with someone, take note of two or three key things that were said. What was taken for granted, and what did you need to know in order to understand these things? Would a random stranger have understood you? Why or why not?

Three Ways to Think About Communication

By now, you know that communication takes a lot for granted and is affected by context, relationships, and culture. You also know that it creates worlds of meaning. So now let's look at these properties and effects of communication a little more deeply and systematically. In everyday life, people use the term *communication* in

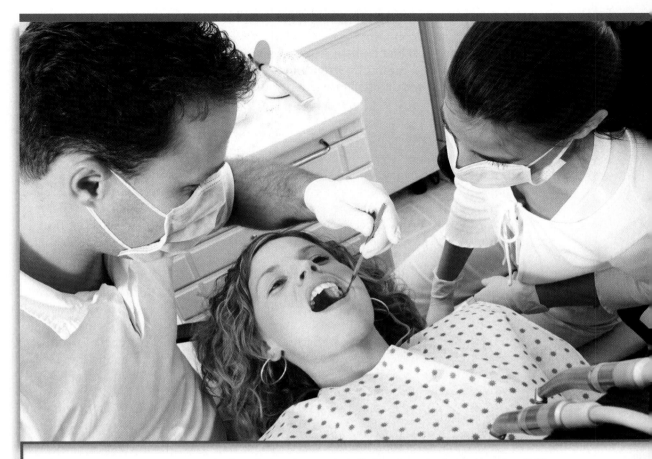

Photo 1.2 What are some ways, both verbal and nonverbal, that communication takes place? (See page 26.)

three ways, often without realizing the importance of the differences between the uses. Each usage assumes something different about how communication works and whether or not it has even really happened.

Communication as Action

If you see **communication as action**, you see it as a sender sending messages whether or not they are received. Communication as *action* occurs when someone leaves a message on your voicemail, posts a message on your desk, or puts a message in a bottle in the ocean—that is, when someone transmits information through words or gestures and their accompanying meaning. So if Carlos sends an e-mail to Melissa, communication has occurred. But what if Melissa doesn't read her e-mail? Has communication truly occurred? According to the definition of communication as action, the answer is yes, but really all you know is that there has been an attempt to communicate.

Communication as Interaction

Let's look at a different way of thinking about communication—namely, **communication as interaction**, which counts something as communication only if there is an exchange of information between two (or more) individuals. Using the previous example, communication exists between Carlos and Melissa if Carlos sends Melissa an e-mail and Melissa replies. This exchange represents a much more typical perception of communication. In fact, people tend to use the term *communication* for communication as both action and interaction, but the two are actually very different.

Communication as Transaction

An even more sophisticated way to see communication is **communication as transaction,** or the construction of shared meanings or understandings between two (or more) individuals. For example, communication exists between Carlos and Melissa if, through their e-mail messages, they both arrive at the shared realization that they understand/love/know/need each other or their communication results in a deal. In other words, the interaction results in more than the exchange of literal messages. They get more out of it, and extra meanings (e.g., about the relationships between the people) are communicated above and beyond the content of the messages exchanged. A pair of messages, such as "Please get some milk" and "OK," also produces a result: Someone gets some milk because both participants realize that was the transaction's intended result. The communication, then, is interesting not because simple messages were exchanged but because something magical and extra happened. Two people speak and trust is built (transacted); two people touch one another and love is realized (transacted); two people argue and power is exerted (transacted); someone calls a grown man "Boy" and racial bigotry is transacted; a man holds the door open for a woman and either sexist stereotyping or politeness is transacted, depending on your taken-for-granted assumptions. In all cases, the communication message (the actual words, gestures, or actions) transacts or constitutes something above and beyond the words, gestures, or actions.

Although it is possible to see communication as action, interaction, or transaction, in this book, our relational perspective makes transaction the most interesting, and it draws our attention to the fact that communication creates more than reports, especially in everyday communication between people who know one another. This **constitutive approach to communication** pays close attention to the fact that communication can create or bring into existence (**constitute**) something that has not been there before. From the transactional/constitutive point of view, in all communication we go beyond what is happening in the talk itself to create something new.

Properties and Effects of Communication

The ability to constitute, transact, or create a world of meaning gives communication its power, allowing you to "go beyond" the obvious to the hidden meaning. For example, you see a symbol (e.g., "the finger") and "go beyond" to what it stands for (you are being insulted). To fully understand what all of these ideas mean, we must explore the properties and effects of communication. After examining symbols, the fundamental elements of communication, we can then discuss such issues as (a) meaning, (b) representation and presentation, (c) what is taken for granted in the use of symbols, and (d) intentionality. These items will be crucial in realizing all the ways you "go beyond" in, as well as in leading us to our definition of, communication.

Communication Involves the Use of Symbols

All communication is characterized by the use of symbols, a topic that has a very long tradition in the history of our discipline (Griffin, 2006; Saussure, 1910/1993). A **symbol** is an object or idea whose meaning is more complicated than it looks: For example, "the finger" is an abusive symbol of rejection, the Stars and Stripes is a symbol of the United States, $ is a symbol for dollar, and a red light is a symbol for "Stop." A more complicated example is a police officer's uniform, which is a symbol not only for "power," "official," and "law and order/law enforcement" but also for more taken-for-granted knowledge, such as "I have been trained" and "I will serve and protect." In all of these cases, the symbols (and a person using them) are understood because the audience can "go beyond" the visible object or symbol and understand the intention or meaning beneath it.

Whether verbal or nonverbal, a symbol's meaning is not always simple. In fact, you can go beyond the symbols described above. For instance, if you look at a red light on top of a yellow light and a green light, you can go beyond to recognize that you are looking at an organized system of lights that is different from a red light on its own. You can even go beyond that to realize that the three lights organized together are arranged in a particular combination that makes this "a traffic light." You can go beyond that to realize that the traffic light controls traffic. This examination of a traffic light might strike you as so obvious that you don't see why it matters, but it is very important that you have learned that the three lights in particular order at particular places convey very specialized meanings to particular beings (to drivers but not to birds, for example). In fact, the ability to recognize such orders and symbolic arrangements is fundamental to communication. Traffic lights do not in any sense at all communicate messages to birds about stopping and going, even if they might provide convenient perches. Birds just don't get it; they don't understand the symbols that humans understand in the traffic signal. As drivers, you see the red light and halt your car because you have already made several "going beyond" computations: red light → traffic signal → traffic signals have legal force → traffic signals control traffic → red traffic signal means stop your car because it is dangerous to proceed → other drivers now have priority → you could get a ticket if you don't stop. If the drivers in front of you stop at a red traffic light, you don't honk at them; you know why they stopped: They understood the red light in the same way you do.

Symbols Versus Signs

The terms *symbols* and *signs* are sometimes used interchangeably, but we will draw a broad technical differentiation and then stick to the term *symbol* as used below. A **sign** (also called an indexical sign) in this technical sense has a causal connection to

Figure 1.1 The insignia for the rank of General, U.S. Army versus British Army.

something. For example, a weather vane is a sign of the direction of the wind; wet streets are a sign that it has rained; smoke is a sign of fire. However we argue about it, we cannot make smoke *not* happen when there is a fire or make streets *not* get wet when it rains. There is a direct causal connection between them. Signs are always consequences and indicators of something specific, which human beings cannot change by their arbitrary actions or labels.

Symbols, on the other hand, are arbitrary representations of ideas, objects, people, relationships, cultures, genders, and races—to name only a few. For example, the shape of a heart is a symbol of love; a star on the shoulder is a symbol of rank and power; a touch on the arm could be a symbol of sympathy or love; a large car could be a symbol of wealth, power, and status. The exact meaning of the representation or the best way to represent what we mean can be something that we can change or that a society (or partners in a relationship) can argue about, or it can be something where different cultures make different arbitrary choices (e.g. as shown in Figure 1.1, the U.S. Army and the British Army indicate the rank of General by different symbols on the shoulder). A symbol can be a movement, a sound, a picture, a logo, a gesture, a mark, or anything else that represents something other than itself—but its meaning is always made up. You already know lots of symbols that communicate—for example, the hand sign for "call me" or the picture that indicates a restroom.

Symbols can be split into those that are iconic and those that are not. Both are representations of ideas as indicated above, but icons look like what they represent—for example, the stick figures used to indicate men's and women's restrooms or the airplane sign used to indicate the way to the airport. Other symbols do not have the pictorial connection to what they represent. The dollar sign does not look like a dollar; the heart shape symbolizes love but is not a picture of love so much as a picture of the place where you sometimes say, metaphorically, you *feel* the love.

Because symbols are arbitrary, made-up conventions for representing something, they can be different in different cultures, and strangers need extra help. When Steve's mother first came to the United States, for example, she could find directions not to "toilets" but only to "restrooms," and she did not want a rest. Eventually, she had to ask someone. The euphemism *restroom* is not immediately obvious to cultural outsiders as a reference to toilet facilities. In

Make a list of symbols you encounter in your everyday life that communicate strategically and purposefully. Which of these symbols might be confusing for someone from another culture? Explain why.

other cultures—for example, in England—they may be referred to as conveniences or by a sign saying WC (meaning water closet). Even some indicators for restrooms within U.S. culture are quite confusing, as they very clearly require a shared understanding of cultural reference points (e.g., we have seen indicators for Does and Bucks, Pointers and Setters, Lads and Lasses, and Knights in Need and Damsels in Distress).

Where cultures meet—for example, in airports—this shared understanding cannot be presumed. Where travelers are from several different countries and may speak different languages, there tends to be greater use of icons and pictures that people from different nations can recognize as meaning "men" or "women." In some places, the words *men* and *women* convey to us that we will find things useful for men and women, but we need not only the ability to read English but also the knowledge to assume something about the facilities that will be provided. We need to know, for example, not to enter these places merely because we want to be in the company of men or women. We also have to know that the icons or other symbols mean "for women *only*" or "for men *only*." As one of the assumptions made in our society, the "only" part of the message normally goes unstated.

Because symbols may have different meanings in different cultures, one of the difficulties in creating universal road warnings is finding a picture that everyone in all cultures will recognize as having the same meaning. Most of the diagrams that we call road "signs" are actually symbols, in the sense that they are arbitrary but agreed upon: for example, a picture of an airplane that means "to the airport." To find them useful, it is really important to know what specific symbols mean in particular cultures or in particular contexts in your own culture. In this sense, then, symbols, whether iconic or not, *do* culture, because you have to understand the culture, at least in part, in order to know what the symbol means there.

Words as Symbols

You may now realize that words are symbols too. Language is a *symbolic* form of communication similar to the other symbols just discussed: Language uses words to stand for objects or ideas. One of the assumptions we make about language is that it is intended to communicate, to make the listeners go beyond the sounds themselves. You probably first thought of symbols in terms of just pictures that represent something else, but obviously the word *chair* does not look, feel, or even sound like what you sit on. The word *chair* has been arbitrarily chosen to

Photo 1.3 How many symbols are there in the picture, and what do they illustrate? (See page 26.)

represent the objects on which we sit, and other languages present the same item in different symbolic ways (*sella, chaise, stoel,* and *zetel,* for example).

Communication Requires Meaning

Communication requires that symbols convey **meaning** or, as we have termed it, that they permit a communicator to "go beyond" one item to another. What a symbol represents is said to be its meaning; particular meanings, however, are not tied to only one symbol but can be conveyed in multiple ways using different symbols. For example, happiness can be conveyed by the words "I'm happy," by a thumbs-up sign, or by waving a flag and jumping up and down when your team scores. A friend of yours may indicate "I'm happy" just by talking more frequently than otherwise. Over the course of the relationship, you have learned that her frequency of talk is a meaningful indicator of her emotional state.

Furthermore, because they are completely arbitrary, symbols have the potential for multiple meanings subject to change, as shown by the example in Figure 1.2. If such a change can occur, any meaning attached to a symbol has been arbitrarily constituted and socially constructed, and it varies according to culture, context, and the relationship between the interactants.

Let's look at what is meant by "socially constructed." Symbols take on meaning in a social context or society as they are used over time. Communication scholars Hopper, Knapp, and Scott (1981) pointed out this context in personal relationships, such as when romantic couples develop code words and phrases ("personal idioms"), secret ways to refer to other people or to discreetly tell each other that it is time to leave a party early. You could quite easily say openly to your partner, "My left foot itches" as a code phrase for "I'm very bored; let's get out of here," but the second phrase would be very impolite to say in front of others. The meaning of symbols within a society or relationship does not develop overnight but instead results from continued use and negotiation of meaning within that society or relationship, as in the example of the yellow ribbon.

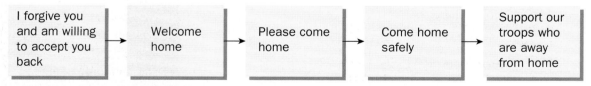

Figure 1.2 Symbols such as the yellow ribbon tied around a tree have held multiple meanings over time.
Source: Griffin, 2006.

Multiple Meanings

A single symbol can also have multiple meanings when used in different contexts. For example, the physical context, or the actual location in which a symbol is used, will impact its meaning. If you said, "There is a fire" while in a campground, it would mean something entirely different than if you said those exact same words while in a crowded movie theater. The situational context will also impact the meaning of a symbol. Asking someone out on a date would mean one thing when uttered at a bar on singles' night and something else entirely if the question were asked of someone recently widowed—and at the spouse's funeral.

> Did you know that the thumbs-up symbol does not mean OK in all cultures? In some cultures, it is a crude sexual insult.

The same symbols will also differ in meaning according to the interactants' relationship. Look again at the earlier example of saying, "I love you." It means something vastly different when spoken to a person you have been dating for more than a year than it does when spoken to a blind date you met just 3 hours ago. Saying it to the first person would probably elicit a smile, while saying it to the second might lead to embarrassment, in the United States at least—some cultures do not either recognize or encourage "dating" in the first place (Chornet-Roses, 2006)!

Communication Is Both Presentational and Representational

Your use of symbols indicates not only what is true (the facts) but also what you would like people to think (your personal view of the facts). This is true whether you look at nonverbal behavior or verbal behavior, but let's take language first. Communication can be representational and presentational; that is, although it normally describes facts or conveys information (**representation**), it also presents your particular version of, or "take" on, the facts or events (**presentation**). In short, you must stop seeing communication as simply a neutral way of reporting the objective world and start looking for ways in which people communicate strategically or put a rhetorical "spin" on their reports of events, people, and objects.

So used to thinking that language just describes facts (representation), people sometimes find this distinction hard to grasp. But you may recognize that when a conservative news channel reports political events, it picks up on different aspects of the news than a liberal news channel does, and it also explains, analyzes, and evaluates them differently. Each channel presents reality in the way it wants you to understand it. When the two sides in a court case tell their stories, they are not representing reality but presenting two different ways to think about an event. When you give a persuasive speech, you do not just give the facts (representation); instead, you carefully select those facts that will make your presentation more persuasive.

Contrarian Challenge

Communication is presented in the chapter as quite orderly and systematic, built on logical use of symbols, and so on. But isn't communication really quite a messy business in everyday life? Does everything you say or hear make absolute sense? And is it not possible to send a message without wanting to (e.g., nervously licking your lips when being quizzed by your partner about why you have shown up late). Would that count as "communication"?

Students do not always recognize at first that the same presentational processes go on in informal, everyday speech. For example, if you say, "My boss is an SOB," it is not an objective comment (representation) but a strategic communication of a personal view of the boss (presentation). If you say, "This class stinks," it is an opinion (presentation), not a fact (representation), and other people may disagree with you. If reviewers give a movie four out of five stars, that too is an opinion, a presentation rather than a representation, as some may find the movie disappointing.

The same kind of distinction between representation and presentation can be made about nonverbal behavior. Have you ever seen people at football games wearing huge sponge hands with the index finger pointing up to indicate "We're number one"? The team may not actually be number one, but the people wearing the sponge fingers—doing a presentational form of nonverbal behavior—would like it to be. If, on the other hand, someone asks you where the nearest restaurant is located and you point directly toward it, your nonverbal behavior is representational and indicates the position of something real.

In all of your everyday talk, then—a vital point for you to understand for the rest of this book—your communication with other people *presents* them with a way of looking at the world that is based on how you prefer them to see it. Your talk is not a neutral descriptive representation; it is always presentational and intended to persuade (Hauser, 1986). Keep in mind what we said earlier: Think of representation as "facts" and presentation as "spin" (or strategic communication), and listen for how your words often put a lot more of your personal perspectives into what you say than they seem to do at first glance.

Communication Takes Much for Granted

If communication uses arbitrary symbols whose meaning can vary between occasions, differ between cultures and persons, alter according to circumstances, and be presented with "spin," isn't it a miracle that people ever understand one another at all? How on earth do they do it? Wood and Duck (2006) point out that talk is used in social frames. **Frames** are basic forms of knowledge that provide a definition of a scenario, either because both people agree on the nature of the situation or because the cultural assumptions built into the interaction and the previous relational context of talk give them a clue. Think of the frame on a picture and how it pulls our attention into some elements (picture) and excludes all the rest (the wall, the gallery, the furniture). In similar fashion, a conversational frame draws a boundary around the conversation and pulls our attention toward certain things and away from others. When we talk in the "frame" of a communication class, we can discuss communication in a special, focused, and expert way, but in the "frame" of TV news or business management, good communication might just refer to the way a president gets a political point across or to the style of management employed by a boss to her employees.

In interviews, one person talks to run the show, and the other one talks to play a secondary part by answering rather than asking questions. Understanding the interview frame helps you understand your role in the conversation and what is expected of you. Likewise, understanding the restaurant frame helps you understand why one person is talking about specials and insisting that you make decisions based on a piece of laminated cardboard that lists costs of food. In any social frame, you also understand rules about turn taking: When you talk, you hope that the other person will listen, and you both know you should not talk at the same time, in White U.S. culture at least—Latino

Photo 1.4 We often realize that people put a presentational "spin" on their talk to influence the way we understand what they say. One of these customers appears a little more skeptical than the other and seems to be evaluating what the salesman has said. How can you tell? (See page 26.)

and African American cultures often encourage and expect simultaneous speech as a sign of involvement and attention ("Amen!"). If your instructor says something and then pauses, it may indicate to you that you are expected to reply (e.g., "Oh yes, Professor, I certainly agree. You are 100% right; very good point"). In this case, the nature of the social and relational frame says more than the pure content of the text. This set of assumptions helps you act appropriately by answering questions, filling pauses, taking turns, or regulating the interaction so it moves forward in ways suited to that situation. Also notice that although instructors may call on students to participate in discussion, students rarely call on instructors in the same way: The frame of expectations is simply different.

When communicating with others, you make other framing assumptions about how they might interpret and understand the terms used. The assumptions made when communicating in a relationship often mean that a great deal can be left unsaid. Think about your own life where you and your friends take a lot for granted and don't say everything explicitly. Having both taught at the University of Iowa, when your authors talk with one another, we can include words or terms that presume knowledge of the university (such as Hawkeyes, Pentacrest, and LR1-VAN). These terms require a background of knowledge built into the interpretation of the words themselves, some of which depends specifically on knowing about the University of Iowa (e.g., that University of Iowa students are nicknamed "Hawkeyes," that the Pentacrest is the administration center, and that LR1-VAN is a particular lecture hall). Each term would not need to be explained in our conversation because both authors know that the other one understands what those symbols/words mean.

Another assumption that gets made when communicating is that the other person will be able to *recognize* the presentational nature of communication. He or she will recognize that the symbols being used not only convey but also make reference beyond their literal meaning. An instructor's comment, "This is on the test," for instance, usually creates an energetic frenzy in students. "This is on the test" is a 5-word sentence, but students will read it as 28 words: "This is on the test, and if you want a grade better than a C, you must take particular note of what I am going to say next." In other words, much of what we say means *more* than what we actually say. Of course, you also have to know what "C" means, both as a symbol of your performance and as something interpreted in the context of an education system that uses a sequence from A through F as a grading scale, where A is good and F is bad.

When people ask you whether they did a good job on a project, for example, they also want you to go beyond the literal question and recognize that they are rarely looking for an absolutely honest response. Instead, they expect a compliment of some sort, and should your response fall short of this expectation, you could be in for trouble. They assume that you know what they really mean and that your response will be tactful and courteous but not necessarily brutally frank.

Listen In On Your Life

Check out the number of ways in which relationships are presented to other people in your everyday talk. For example, how often do you draw people's attention to the fact that someone is "your friend"? How often do you indicate your relational status by references to your significant other? Also analyze an interaction between you and your instructor, and point out some of the ways in which power is hidden in the talk taking place.

Communication Involves Intentionality

One more idea for you to think about is intentionality. Before you treat another person's behaviors as symbolic and therefore meaningful, you normally first assume that the behavior was produced consciously and deliberately. However, an accidental burp can "communicate" (as action), as can a blush, so should you treat as "communication" only those messages sent intentionally? If you are at an intersection wishing to make a left-hand turn into traffic and you see a car approaching in the opposite lane with its left-turn signal light flashing, you have to be sure that it is intentionally activated before you can interpret the meaning of that signal. In this case, your determination of intentionality could prevent a nasty accident.

In light of our relational perspective on communication, you can usually make assumptions about the level of intentionality of people you know, and you make these assumptions from what you know about them personally. But you also know that, in general, people like to look good, and an intended nasty remark is taken as worse than a simple thoughtless mistake or accidental affront ("Oops…" and "Sorry…" tend to take the sting out of an act by identifying it as mistaken or accidental and not intended to be *meaningful*). But does it work in such cases as "I'm sorry if this offends you, but you are really ugly," "I'm not coming to your party tonight because it is sure to be really boring," or "Professor, are we going to do anything important in class today?" Think about why or why not.

You can learn from these examples that there has to be an underlying background of social practices and norms in a particular culture, group, or friendship. Most of what you do makes sense (or allows us to go beyond the literal message) because of what you take for granted about the relationship or the society in which you communicate. You make taken-for-granted assumptions about the other person and what he or she knows. All the same, you realize that there can be many arguments about intentionality and whether someone really meant to do what he or she did ("You deliberately touched my knee, you pervert!" "No, I accidentally brushed up against it") or really intended the consequences of what he or she did ("How could you have done that? You must have known it would hurt me!" "No, I was just very thoughtless, and I apologize").

Given what we have just written, you can reflect on the recent suggestion by Laura Guerrero and Kory Floyd (2006) that there are really four types of communication all of which are forms of communication as interaction since they involve both the sending and the receiving of messages:

1. *Successful communication:* sent intentionally and interpreted accurately (i.e., in the way the sender intended)

2. *Miscommunication:* sent intentionally but interpreted inaccurately (i.e., not as the sender intended)

3. *Accidental communication:* sent without intent but interpreted accurately as meaning something that the "sender" was truly feeling (e.g., all students' constant fear that they will be caught yawning during a boring talk by an instructor)

4. *Attempted communication:* messages sent intentionally but not received (e.g., imagine that your partner leaves a note on your door asking for a meeting today at the Java House at 3:00 P.M. to talk about your relationship with the caveat that if you do not show up the relationship will be over, but you do not get the message)

Strategic Communication

We have begun to unfold applications to your own life in terms of new ways to analyze the situations that you experience. Now go out for a meal in a restaurant, and take notes about the server/customer relationship and how it gets "done." What elements of taken-for-granted cultural assumptions do you think we did not discuss here but could have? For example, what is communicated (transacted) by a server's uniform, style of speech (bubbly or bored), friendliness, or aloofness? What deeper impressions did you form about the server's personality? What were they based on, and why?

There is a fifth type of communication too—a very dangerous one in relationships—where a *message is sent unintentionally and interpreted inaccurately* (e.g., a woman smiles at a casual thought passing through her mind, but a man in her presence takes it as a "come on" directed at him).

Conclusion: Communication Is . . .

We rest our case. Even if we focused this chapter only on everyday talk of the kind introduced by the nice server with the witchety grub, you now have seen just how much more there is to communication than just one person producing and sending a message to another like we do with texts on cell phones. Everyday communication goes beyond the literal message in all sorts of ways. For example, we saw that context and relationship affect (and so "go beyond") literal messages, and vice versa. Also, communication itself transacts or constitutes something—creates, by itself, something that wasn't there before (trust, love, respect, dislike, commitment)—and goes beyond the literal. Your words are by no means the only messages; nor are they the more important element of communication—an inseparable combination of the verbal and nonverbal components. Furthermore, communication sends both content and relational information simultaneously, requires a special cultural knowledge built into the meaning and attributed to the symbols used to communicate, is organized by the shared understandings that constitute a culture, is socially constructed, and is framed by the social contexts and backgrounds of information. Communication, then, takes a lot for granted, builds a set of assumptions into messages, and demands enormous amounts of simultaneous thinking, processing, and integration by speakers and audience alike. It is personally biased, spun, or turned in a way that makes all communication into a personal rhetorical presentation of a view of reality, not by any means an objective description or representation.

Taking all this into account, then, an essential feature of communication is that it goes beyond the literal translation of messages; in fact, communication puts a lot more mess into messages. Not simply a description of events or things in the world, and not a simple transmission of a message from one person to another, communication instead involves the creation and/or sharing with at least one other person meaning that is not only contained in the literal message but associated with it by the people involved and brought in from other sources, such as culture, memory, and the past history of the relationship between the communicators.

Rephrasing this in terms we will continue to unpack, concepts to include in the definition of communication are presented in Table 1.1. We must also include in our definition of communication the concepts of intentionality and nonverbal communication.

For now, then, we will point all these elements out and offer a temporary, working definition that we will fill out and explore: *Communication is the transactional use of symbols, influenced, guided, and understood in the context of relationships, taken-for-granted understandings, meanings, and reality that it presents and creates as ways for people to share an understanding of the world that they inhabit together.*

Table 1.1 Concepts to Include in the Definition of Communication

Presentation	Communication is a presentation of a preferred way of knowing or understanding the world.
Relational	All communication is speaking into relationships.
Going beyond	Communication steps out of the present and points somewhere else, referring to objects, people, or ideas not actually in the interaction, such as things in the future, the past, or the history of a relationship or drawn from the imagination of the speaker and the audience.
Taken for granted	Communication builds in and assumes certain ways of looking at the world as preferred by your culture, your relationship partner, or yourself.
Shared assumptions	Communication involves sharing viewpoints, vocabulary, and meaning, or it would not be possible for people to communicate as interaction or transaction.

Communication in everyday life involves not only words but the way we speak them, as well as such nonverbal accompaniments as gestures, body posture, facial expressions, and tone of voice (rather than content of speech). In everyday communication, verbal and nonverbal communication often overlap and cannot really be separated. A medical student must learn about the muscle system, the blood, the lungs, and other systems that can be conceptually separated, but you cannot have a living body without all the parts together. Similarly, we must separate verbal and nonverbal communication to help your learning, but it makes no sense to separate them in real life. They make the whole communication package work when they are understood together, but for the purposes of this book, we must at least begin by discussing them separately, in Chapter 2 and Chapter 3, respectively.

Focus Questions Revisited

What is communication, and how does it work in your everyday life?
We have taken a constitutive/transactive view of communication in this book, and by this we mean that communication is more than the passing of messages from one person to another. It creates something above and beyond the specific words spoken. In everyday life, communication is influenced particularly by the relationships that exist between conversational partners. These relationships and other taken-for-granted assumptions allow people to "go beyond" the literal sense of their speech and transact or constitute worlds of meaning that bind them together.

How does communication create worlds of meaning?
Communication is built on the recognition of shared assumptions that require the two partners to understand and take for granted certain beliefs about how the world operates. Every culture and relationship has built into it such assumptions, revealed and drawn upon in communication.

How do the assumptions in a culture affect communication?

Every culture has built-in assumptions about how people should be treated, activities performed, practices carried out, and emotions displayed. The assumptions about the proper and correct way to interact with other people, the behaviors that constitute rudeness or respect, and the manner in which individuals should communicate with one another all influence what is said in interaction.

What are the properties of communication?

Communication involves meaning, representation or presentation of facts and viewpoints, taken-for-granted assumptions, the use of symbols, and intentionality.

What does it mean to say that communication is both representational and presentational, and why is the difference important?

Communication can simply represent something that exists in the world, or it can present the speaker's viewpoint about something. The difference between these two elements of communication is important to recognize when what are offered to us as representations of fact are indeed presentations of a viewpoint hidden in communication. Students of communication must learn to recognize the difference and be aware of how presentation occurs in what appears to be representation.

What is a "frame," and how is communication framed?

Like a frame on a picture, a frame in communication is a basic form of knowledge that provides a definition of a scenario either because the people agree on the nature of the situation or because the cultural assumptions taken for granted give them a clue. We can frame communication as being of a particular type—for example, an informal or a formal situation. The frame in which communication occurs will influence what is said and how.

What is a working definition of communication for the book?

Communication is the transactional use of symbols, influenced, guided, and understood in the context of relationships, taken-for-granted understandings, meanings, and reality that it presents and creates as ways for people to share an understanding of the world that they inhabit together.

Key Concepts

communication as action   (p. 11)
communication as interaction   (p. 11)
communication as transaction   (p. 12)
constitute   (p. 12)
constitutive approach to
   communication   (p. 12)

frames   (p. 18)
meaning   (p. 16)
presentation   (p. 17)
representation   (p. 17)
sign   (p. 13)
symbol   (p. 13)

Questions to Ask Your Friends

- What is "good communication," and what is "bad communication"? What do your friends think are the main characteristics of each, and where do they believe such ideas came from in the first place?

- Listen to a friend telling a story about an interaction in everyday life, and take special note of his or her method. Why did the story start the way it did, and what was taken for granted in that beginning? How did the "setup" help the story unfold and make the outcome feel "right"?

- Ask your friends to talk about an occasion when they used strategic communication/presentation. How do they think the story might have been told differently by one of the other people involved in the interaction?

Media Links

- In what ways do song lyrics, for example, not merely entertain us but *present* particular ways of living, particular attitudes, and particular styles?

- How do media ads encourage us to be satisfied with what we already have, and how do they present a need to acquire more?

- Do news stories represent or present facts, and how is their presentation made important (with words? images? frames?)? Find some examples, and bring them to class.

Ethical Issues

- What assumptions appear to be built into other people's speech concerning race, sex, age, power, and justice?

- What assumptions about these things can you now discover in your own talk?

- In what ways might it be unethical to use some of what you have learned in this chapter?

Answers to Photo Captions

Photo 1.1 ▪ The women are probably old friends as demonstrated by their physical closeness, close gaze, mirroring of posture (both holding their cup with both hands at about the same height), and obvious enjoyment of the conversation. The fact that the speaker is looking at the listener while talking from such a close distance is a sign of intimacy.

Photo 1.2 ▪ When you are seated in a dentist's chair at first, you can communicate with the dentist about where there is pain or what problems you are experiencing. Once the examination begins, however, there is very little opportunity for intelligible speech. You can indicate discomfort by wincing, or acceptance by nodding, or signaling too much pain by raising your hand as a signal.

Photo 1.3 ▪ The white dress symbolizes a bride, the striped uniform symbolizes a convict, and handcuffs symbolize imprisonment (but notice that one of the cuffs is not connected to anything, which symbolizes escape). The man is embracing the woman, symbolizing both power and affection, but is looking away from her as she is from him, symbolizing distance and disinterest. The overall effect of the picture is to symbolize marriage as an imprisonment, or is it an escape from imprisonment and loneliness?

Photo 1.4 ▪ Both of the customers are looking skeptical, the woman with a slightly dropped jaw and raised eyebrows, the man with a questioning glance. The salesman looks defensive and is attempting to indicate honesty by his open palm gesture ["Look, I'm being open with you"]. From his focus on the woman we can infer that she is the one whom he sees as more skeptical of what he has been saying.

Student Study Site

Visit the study site at **www.sagepub.com/ciel** for e-flashcards, practice quizzes, and other study resources.

References

Chornet-Roses, D. (2006). *"I could say I am 'dating' but that could mean a lot of different things": Dating in the U.S. as a dialogical relational process.* Unpublished doctoral dissertation, University of Iowa–Iowa City.

Griffin, E. (2006). *Communication: A first look at communication theory* (6th ed.). New York: McGraw-Hill.

Guerrero, L. K., & Floyd, K. (2006). *Nonverbal communication in relationships.* Mahwah, NJ: Lawrence Erlbaum.

Hauser, G. (1986). *Introduction to rhetorical theory.* New York: Harper & Row.

Hopper, R., Knapp, M. L., & Scott, L. (1981). Couples' personal idioms: Exploring intimate talk. *Journal of Communication, 31,* 23–33.

Saussure, F. (1993). *Saussure's third course of lectures on general linguistics (1910–1911).* London: Pergamon. (Original work published in 1910)

Watzlawick, P., Beavin, J., & Jackson, D. (1967). *Pragmatics of human communication: A study of interactional patterns, pathologies and paradoxes.* New York: Norton.

Wood, J. T., & Duck, S. W. (Eds.). (2006). *Composing relationships: Communication in everyday life.* Belmont, CA: Thomson Wadsworth.

2

Verbal Communication

A man walked into a bar. A second man walked into a bar. A third one didn't, because he ducked. You know the word *bar*, and you know that in our culture jokes and stories often start with the phrase "A man walked into a bar…" Such cultural knowledge frames your expectations about the story you are being told. A *frame*, you recall, is a context that influences the interpretation of communication. However, the word *bar* has different meanings, and if you were faintly amused by the opening sentences here, it is partly because the word is used in the first sentence differently than you expected on the basis of the form of the story. The punch line works only because you are misled—twice—into thinking of a different kind of "bar." Familiarity with the story's cultural form frames your expectations in a way that pulls the last sentence right out from under you.

Whenever you speak, you *use* language in ways that take much for granted, and the study of *language use in talk* is the subject of this chapter. Not only does language have a grammatical structure, but when used in conversation, it also brings into use cultural and relational assumptions represented by symbols, frames, and meanings. In this chapter, then, you will learn more about how frames, symbols, and meanings work in the spoken language of everyday life and how they serve to build and sustain relationships.

In everyday talk, words weave together seamlessly within a context that includes nonverbal communication (NVC), or symbolic activity, such as facial expressions, hand gestures, movements, changes in posture, and pacing or timing of speech. In practice, nonverbal aspects of communication help you frame your expectations and interpretation of what someone else means. To make this book usable, though, we have to separate verbal and nonverbal communication into two parts: language in Chapter 2 and, in Chapter 3, the NVC system of meaning and how it connects with the words people speak (for example, how a smile frames a comment as friendly, not as hostile). Keep in mind that this split is artificial when it comes to understanding everyday life.

Focus Questions

- What are the differences between grammatical language and talk in everyday use?
- What frames your understanding of talk and gives it meaning?
- What values are hidden in the speech you use?
- How does everyday talk make use of relationships to frame meanings?
- How do different types of talk work, and how do they connect to relationships?
- What is talk style, and how does it frame meaning?
- What are the key elements of stories?

How Do You Know What Talk Means?

When you use the word *cat*, everyone assumes you are referring to an animal. You know what animals are and, specifically, what a cat looks like. When you started to learn to read, "The cat sat on the mat" may have been one of the first sentences you ever came across. In everyday life talk, however, if you say to a person, "You really are catty" (Norwood, 2007), you are speaking not literally but relationally or metaphorically. A listener would understand what you mean, even though the words are simply not true: He or she is not a cat. This example emphasizes an important point: The formal grammar of a language is different from how that language is used in everyday chitchat.

When considering how people actually talk to one another, linguists like Ferdinand de Saussure (1910/1993) draw a distinction between langue and parole. **Langue** is the formal grammatical structure of language that you will read about in books on grammar. **Parole** is how people actually use language, with informal and ungrammatical structure that carries meaning to us all the same. "Git 'er done!" is an example of parole but would earn you bad grades in an English grammar course (langue). When people feel relaxed in a close relationship, they are much more likely to use parole that deviates from strict grammar, whereas people in a formal setting are more likely to use a closer reflection of the langue. Communication is used loosely in relationships as they are quite informal in the context of everyday life. Relationships frame both what gets said and how it gets understood.

Language and your use of talk are also based on other frames of familiarity and other sets of assumptions—some to do with the way words get used and some with the relational messages sent by the words you pick out. Some have to do with the times that you live in and the items that are familiar to you, whereas others have to do with how you know that the strict rules of grammar may be bent when you speak language out loud. We are sure that our readers normally speak in perfectly polished grammatical sentences; after all, you are educated people. However, quite probably you also know that in everyday talk you often speak in ungrammatical ways that everyone else understands. For example, "Ain't no way I'm gonna do that!" does not make a lot of sense from a strictly grammatical point of view, but it sends messages of defiant resistance to anyone who speaks a current modern form of English. "A plague on both your houses" means something when you are reading Shakespeare, but you would be unlikely to say it in everyday life.

Multiple Meanings: Polysemy

Words, gestures, and symbols can have their meanings altered on different occasions or in circumstances according to the particulars that frame the talk. Communication scholars and philosophers call this **polysemy**, multiple meanings for the same word (Ogden & Richards, 1946). Even though you already knew that the same word could carry multiple meanings, knowing the academic term for it becomes important for deepening your insights into the way that everyday conversation actually works because you need to know how, in a particular sentence, you work out which meaning a person is using. If every communication—whether words, facial expressions, or gestures—can have several different meanings, each time you receive a message, you must determine which meaning applies.

Polysemy exists as a feature of all communication, and we must always deal with the ambiguities that it necessarily creates. Being able to deal with this ambiguity is especially important in everyday communication because it comprises many types of talk (both formal and informal): technical jargon, ordinary slang, put-downs, boasting, euphemisms, and even occasional cursing. In the course of a single conversation, the partners can switch between styles and vocabularies, which means they need to ensure that the context clarifies to both of them what is going on when these switches occur.

> Did you know that a "cat" is not only an animal but a kind of whip (cat-o'-nine-tails), a movable penthouse to protect soldiers besieging a medieval castle, a jazz fan (a "cool cat"), and a brand of tractor (Cat, short for Caterpillar)?

If a friend moves from informal to formal talk, suddenly curses, or switches from slang to technical talk, is he or she angry with you, or is there another explanation? Look at it the other way, too. If an acquaintance switches from formal to informal talk, might he or she be expressing the intention to develop a friendly relationship in place of a previously more formal one? The most important point in this chapter, then, is that relationships frame the meaning of talk. A strong and close connection exists among language, talk, and relationships.

Uncertainty about meaning decreases the more you have the useful frames that relationships and other contexts give you. Ultimately, the best and most helpful guide to a person's meaning is the personal knowledge you have from a close relationship with him or her. People tend to hang around with others who share their general system for understanding meanings (Duck, 2007), so that familiarity helps narrow down the choices. You are better able to communicate with another person when both of you can assume you are in the same frame and know what you are talking about. You make assumptions about the likely best choice of meaning based on what you know about the frame you are in. You signal the frames you are using via various relational, cultural, and personal cues. For example, "Let's not be so formal" is a direct way of saying that you are in the "friendly frame," but "Take a seat and make yourself comfortable" has the same effect. More subtly, the fact that therapists have cozy offices with comfortable furniture, rather than hard benches, sends the same framing message in a different (nonverbal) way. Such cues place an interaction into a frame of informal relaxation rather than emphasizing toughness, distance, business, or threat.

People can work out what you mean on a given occasion by reading these broad cues. The more familiar you are with the meanings available in a culture, the easier it is to read these general cues. But the key to deeper understanding—the crucial guide to interpreting what someone means—is your relationship to others and how well you know them and their thinking styles. Talk is more than just language: It is the *use* of language, and the use of language can be personalized. In fact, the more closely two people get to know each other—what they know, how they think, how they talk—the more personal their talk becomes.

Photo 2.1 Why might this pairing of street signs be amusing to a citizen of the United States, and what is taken for granted by those people who understand the joke? (See page 52.)

Conversational Yellow Pages: Categories That Frame Talk

Having culture or relationships is like having the Yellow Pages for conversation in a particular language. There are lots of phone number categories, so it helps if you know you are looking for a plumber and can find the page with the plumber numbers listed. So, too, with talk: It helps if you know that when your partner talks about love, you are on the "romance" page, not the "tennis" page. Probably the strongest clue in language is provided by naming.

You already learned that language splits our world in many ways, dividing it into those items for which there are names. **Naming** is an important process because it seems both *arbitrary* ("It doesn't matter if you call it salad or dessert; it's still just Jell-O") and *natural* ("What do you mean, 'What's Jell-O?' It's Jell-O. Everybody knows Jell-O"). The naming process involves another, quite subtle, process too: distinguishing items from other items for which we also have (different) words. Several thinkers from both rhetorical studies (Burke, 1966) and psychology (Kelly,

1969) have observed that definition involves negation or contrasting. That is, whenever you say what something is, you also say either explicitly or implicitly what it is not. When a behavior is named as "sexual harassment," it is not "a joke" or "flirting." Some thinkers even suggest that you cannot know some concepts without knowing their opposites (for example, the concept of light makes no sense without the concept of darkness).

An even stronger version of this idea was proposed by Edward Sapir and Benjamin Whorf (Sapir, 1949; Whorf, 1956). The **Sapir/Whorf hypothesis** proposes that "you think what you can say." In other words, the names that make verbal distinctions also help you make conceptual distinctions rather than the other way around. The words that a person or culture uses will have a direct influence on how the person or culture understands the world: The words make the world rather than the opposite, as you might typically think. Although it turns out not to be actually true that they have a *huge* number, you have no doubt heard that the Eskimos have some different words for snow because people in that part of the world want to be able to differentiate between sorts of snow that "mean" or carry different connotations for their activities in life. For example, assume that *snow1* indicates a kind of snow that means the coming of a storm, and *snow2* indicates a kind of snow that means the coming of spring. Using different words (*snow1*, *snow2*) helps the Eskimos make this and other important distinctions that matter in their lives.

Naming something not only sticks a label on it but also differentiates it from the rest of the world; your name tag, for example, goes on only *your* stuff. So, although language has several functions, a major function is to separate the world into different categories of objects and concepts (chairs, dogs, ideas, papers, professors, students, taxes, death, justice, freedom). Phrased in a more academic way, language—and, in particular, the names we use in talk—will classify our world by giving things separate identities and properties. These serve to structure our worlds into *thought units* or items that we consider quite different from each other. Naming is incredibly powerful, and it makes a huge difference, for example, whether you name someone an "insurgent" or "a freedom fighter." Because there are two subtypes of meaning, we can connect them to the distinction we made in Chapter 1 concerning representation and presentation.

Types of Meaning

It is traditional for communication studies to draw a distinction between *denotative* and *connotative* meaning as a way of splitting the world into finer thought units. **Denotative meaning** refers to the identification of something by pointing it out. If you point at a cat and say, "Cat," everyone will know that the sound denotes the object that is furry and whiskered and currently eating your homework. **Connotative meaning** refers to the overtones, implications, or additional

Contrarian Challenge

We have a word for the front of the hand (*palm*), but no single word for the back. According to the Sapir/Whorf hypothesis this should mean that we can't tell the difference, shouldn't it?

meanings associated with a word or an object. For example, cats are seen as independent, cuddly, hunters, companions, irritations, allergens, stalkers, stealthy, and incredibly lucky both in landing on their feet all the time and in having nine lives. If you talk about someone as a "pussycat," you are most likely referring to the connotative meaning and implying that he is soft and cuddly and perhaps stealthy, companionable, and lucky. You are unlikely to be referring to the denotative meaning and warning people that he is actually, secretly a cat and has fur and eats homework.

A handy way of thinking about this distinction is that "denotative meaning" basically identifies something, and "connotative meaning" gives you its overtones. Connecting these meanings with the ideas in Chapter 1, you can see that denotative meaning roughly corresponds with representation/facts and connotative meaning roughly corresponds with presentation/spin.

Denoting

Once you understand this distinction, you can see how important it is in the way you use language in everyday life talk. You can work with other people in conversation only when you can assume that they split the world by using the same words to denote and connote items that you do. Denoting the same object or idea by the same words is an obviously fundamental requirement for communicating; if you point to something and use the applicable word (*bar*, *cat*, *food*, *witchety grub*), but the other person does not understand what you're pointing to, the communication is not effective. As we phrased this idea in Chapter 1, what occurs is action, not interaction; that is, the message is sent but not received. When parents teach their children to communicate, they spend lots of time pointing out objects and repeating the correct words (communication as action) so the child learns to connect the object with the label ("Look at the cat." "Yes, that's a cat"). At the moment where the child gets what is going on, communication as interaction begins (message sent and received). Something even more magical begins to happen as the child starts to understand his or her world more effectively and to see connections and meaning and learns to *go beyond*. "That's a fire. It's hot. Don't touch it, or you will hurt yourself" turns the communication into transaction, and constitutive activity occurs as the child learns to associate fire as an object with the possibility of heat and therefore pain.

Connoting

On the other hand, connoting is about understanding the implications and background behind the same words. For example, some words carry baggage that makes you feel good, and some do not. Consider the different emotions stirred up by the words *patriot* and *traitor*. The first connotes many good feelings, based on implications of loyalty, duty, and faithfulness. The second connotes bad qualities like deceit, two-facedness, untrustworthiness, and disloyalty. These connotations are extra layers of meaning atop the denotation of a person as one kind of citizen or the other. You would feel proud to be called a patriot but ashamed to be called a traitor.

Such words carry these strong connotations in your particular culture as a whole, but connotations can be more personal and complex the better you know someone. You expect to share more meanings and connotations with friends or people with whom you share a history or a bit of common understanding and experience. You have learned their preferences, the overtones they associate with simple words, and their connotative meanings. For example, you know whether "Go Hawks!" would carry a positive, negative, or neutral overtone to them—that is, whether your use of the phrase would excite, annoy, or leave them dispassionate. An important element of talk, therefore, is that the more personally you know people, the more confident you can be that you understand their deeper meanings and, in particular, the connotations that they associate with particular objects or ideas.

A consequence of this association is that your ability to understand people improves as you know more about their minds, because that information helps you understand their specific intentions on a particular occasion. If you know where someone's "buttons" are, you know whether he or she responds irritably to an exclamation ("Go Hawks!") because he or she is feeling defensive, just tired, or not particularly playful.

Intentionality

As we noted in Chapter 1 communication scholars have spent considerable time discussing the notion of **intentionality,** a basic assumption in communication studies that messages indicate somebody's intentions or that they are produced intentionally or in a way that gives insight, at the very least, into the sender's mental processes. For example, if someone says something apparently insulting ("You dork!"), it makes a great deal of difference whether you believe he or she did it intentionally or thought the comment was funny and didn't mean it to be hurtful (for example, if he or she said it with a smile or a joking tone of voice).

You normally assume that people send messages intentionally, and therefore the messages tell you something about their motivation and underlying personality. A meaningful message must have intention behind it, or the receiver must be able to assume that it did. Indeed, people usually assume that communication cannot happen unless someone sends an intentional message. It is more accurate, however, to say that you assume his or her intentions were present and that he or she did something because he or she wanted or meant to. Note that, in general, the apologies "I'm sorry; I didn't mean that the way it sounded" and "I don't mean to be rude, but . . ." are both ways of clarifying the speaker's intent. These apologies soften or clarify the message and indicate how the speaker wishes the intent behind it to be "read." However, the issue of intentionality is not whether it was actually present but whether you *assume* that it was (for example, you might not believe that the apology is sincere). It is not an objective issue about what is on the other person's mind but a subjective issue about what an observer attributes to and projects onto the other person. To interpret messages more accurately, you must develop a good feel for the speaker's intentions.

Culture, context, past history, and your relationship to the other person in a conversation help you know what meanings are listed on the relevant Yellow Page, as it were. Otherwise, you'd end up having constant arguments and conflicts where one person keeps assuming that the other person meant something other than intended, and there would be nothing but confusion, ill will, and suspicion, which would threaten the development of relationships. Interactions between enemies and rivals or conversations based on mistrust show exactly this characteristic: that people are always looking for, or suspecting, a hidden meaning or agenda. Communication scholar Dan Kirkpatrick and colleagues (Kirkpatrick, Duck, & Foley, 2006) noted that enemies do not trust each other to mean what they say, always suspecting a lie or a "setup." This suspicion makes the conversation unproductive and very difficult to handle. The deeper and more trusting your relationship with someone, the more likely you are to understand his or her intentions and nuances. Once again, the close connection among relationships, communication, and meaning solves social dilemmas for you and helps you understand someone's meaning.

Relationships and Connotation

Your ability to understand people's intentions and meanings increases hugely the more personal your relationship is with them. A vast part of becoming closer to other people is getting to know them better and learning how they tick—an informal way of saying that you understand their worlds of meaning. When you know people better, you also know better than strangers what they mean when they make certain comments. Suppose Larry and one of his friends have a running joke about "tiramisu," which refers to a situation where something funny happened in a restaurant when one of them ordered tiramisu for dessert. Mentioning the word *tiramisu* is a shorthand way of saying, "This person has made a very weird response in a funny way." Larry knows that; his friend knows that; but other people are not in on the joke. If they ever heard Larry use the word, they would never know what he meant and would be completely unable to interpret any intention behind it.

In a relationship context, your assumptions, shared understandings, and forms of speech encode/transact the relationship by means of shared understanding. The understandings shared by you and your friends represent not only common understanding but also your relationship. No one else shares the exact understandings, common history, experiences, knowledge of the same people, or assumptions that you take for granted as not needing to be explained at any length.

Think for a minute about what happens when a friend from out of town comes to visit, and you go out with your in-town friends. You probably notice that the conversation is a bit more awkward even if it is still friendly: You do a bit more explaining, for example. Instead of saying, "So, De'Janee, how was the hot date?" and waiting for an answer, you throw in a conversational bracket that helps your friend from out of town understand the question. For example, you may say, "So, De'Janee, how was the hot date?" and follow it with an aside comment to the out-of-towner ("De'Janee has this hot new love interest she has a *real* crush on, and they finally went out last night").

When you talk to people, you use words that refer to your shared history and common understandings that represent your relationship or shared culture. As you talk, you monitor that knowledge

Make Your Case

You and your friends probably have several examples of shorthand terms and phrases for reminding one another of events, feelings, or people who populate your relational history. You may also have special nicknames for people known only to you and your partner or close friends. Come up with some examples, and bring them to class.

Photo 2.2 Two people's conversation may be affected by the context, their relationship, and their age, culture, and experience, among other things noted so far. What might these friends be talking about? (See page 52.)

and occasionally must explain to outsiders, but the very need for explanation—particularly important when you are giving a speech to an audience that does not know what you know—indicates a level of relationship, not just a level of knowledge. Relationships presume common, shared knowledge.

Words differentiate the world into objects and thought units and then name them. Talk does this relationally, too: With friends, we draw on words differently than we do in work relationships, family relationships, enemy relationships, or competitive relationships. Although, whenever you talk, you use language (enshrouded in NVC) to denote something in the world, it is very important to recognize that there is more to talk than that. You do not just do things with words when you talk. You do things with *relationships* too, and a lot of the words you use in conversation demonstrate and transact your relationships. Therefore, over and above the differentiating that *language* does, people adopt different styles of *speaking* according to their relationship. Restaurant servers, for example, identify items strictly relevant to their task, such as broccoli, witchety grubs, and prices. Friends can refer to their previous experience together, their common history, their knowledge of particular places and times, and other experiences they both understand ("Remember when we went to

Jimmie's . . ."). Because both of you know what is being referred to, neither of you needs to explain.

Words and Hidden Values

Let's take this a little further and show how words also make value judgments and how these judgments are built into the talk that happens in relationships, and vice versa. A society or culture not only uses different words from those current in another language, obviously, but also prefers some subjects to others. For example, how do you react to the words *spider, ice cream, class test, Porsche, sour, Republican, liberty, death,* and *justice?* Communication philosopher Kenneth Burke (1966) made a distinction between **God terms** and **Devil terms** in a particular culture. God terms are powerfully evocative terms that are viewed positively in a society, and Devil terms are equally evocative terms that are viewed negatively. The obvious difference is that both are powerful, but each in a different way; terms like *justice* and *liberty,* for example, are seen very positively in U.S. society (God terms), whereas *Osama bin Laden* may be a Devil term (see Table 2.1 for some other examples). Depending on your political point of view, such words as *Bush* or *Clinton* may be one or the other, so you can see that God and Devil terms are not absolutes for everyone in the same society, although some terms are equivalent for everyone. The terms apply in relationships, too, because the partners in a relationship will have special references for people and events that may or may not be mentioned or topics that you know your partner is sensitive about—his or her Devil terms—and that you therefore steer away from. Sometimes your partner may act on behalf of society: "Oh! You shouldn't say such things! You're bad!" In such a statement, he or she is reminding you about the norms of society and its God and Devil terms.

We noted previously that symbols indicate not only what is true but also what you would like people to think, and we used the terms *presentation* and *representation* to describe this difference. At times, your speech is persuasive or preferential; it makes distinctions that you want your audience to accept as valid. Kenneth Burke's point about the value judgments built into words is very similar—namely, that your words encode your values and you see some concepts as good (communication studies) and some as bad (pedophilia). Every time you talk, you are essentially using words to argue and present your personal preferences and judgments, as well as simply describing your world. Your

Table 2.1 God and Devil Terms

God terms in the United States	Liberty, Freedom, Justice, American Dream
Devil terms in the United States	Communism, Torture, Inequality, Prejudice, King George III
Challenge: *How would you classify the following terms? What are some other terms that you consider God or Devil terms?*	C (course grade), Abortion, Banker, Politician, Raw Food, Cigarettes, Exercise, Natural, Facebook

culture has a preference, as do you and your friends, and your communications express that in both obvious and hidden ways. Start paying more attention to those expressions of the values embedded in the words that you use to talk in your everyday lives. If you tell your instructor about your grade and say, "I think I deserved a B–, but you gave me a C+," you and the instructor both recognize that a B– is "better than" a C+ in the framework of meaning taken for granted in school. Your words are *going beyond* what they seem to be saying and are taking for granted the context, the relationship, and the culture in which the conversation occurs.

> Keep in mind that nonverbal communication is a constant context for all talk. Not only the words themselves but also how you choose to utter them will differ and serve as frames. Frames can also be created by the style in which something is said. If talk is friendly, chances are that an ambiguous comment is friendly and not hostile, so previous context helps you make the decision about its meaning.

Everyday Life Talk and the Relationships Context

Duck and Pond (1989), apart from being our favorite combination of authors' names, came up with some interesting ideas about how relationships connect with talk in everyday life. They pointed out that talk can serve three functions for relationships: It can make something happen in relationships (instrumental function), can indicate something about the relationship (indexical function), or can amount to the relationship and make it what it is, creating its essence (essential function). Although these functions might sound complicated at first, you practice each of them every day without knowing it. Let's take a closer look.

Instrumental Functions

Whenever you ask someone out for a date, to a party, to meet you for a chat or a coffee, to be your friend, or to be just a little bit more sensitive and caring, you are performing an **instrumental function of talk** in relationships. What you say reveals a goal that you have in mind for the relationship, and talk is the means or instrument by which you reveal it. Anything you say that serves the purpose of bringing something new to or changing anything about the relationship is an instrumental function of talk in relationships. A proposal of marriage, a request that a relationship be put on hold, an announcement to a work group that you have been promoted and your relationship is now different, and "I never want to see you again" are all examples of the instrumental function of talk.

Indexical Functions

An **indexical function of talk** demonstrates or indicates the nature of the relationship between speakers. You index your relationship in the *way* that you talk to somebody. If you say in a sharp tone, "Come into my office; I want to see you!" you are not only being discourteous, but you are indicating that you are superior to the other person and have the relational right to order him or her around. The content and relational elements of the talk occur together.

There are other ways of indexing a relationship too. Two friends talk intimately, for example, using language that they know they both understand but other people might not. To pick up the example from Chapter 1, saying to your friend "Let's meet at the LR1-VAN after I have seen Jim about his foot" contains so much coded information that anyone listening to the sentence would know you two share lots of understanding about each other's lives. You would need to explain to an outsider what the "LR1-VAN" is, who "Jim" is, and why he would be talking to you about his foot, but a close friend would not need the explanation. In your talk with other people, you constantly weave in clues about your relationships, and that is what the indexical function of talk is all about. Talk is relational, and how we use it tells people about the relationship we have with our audience.

Conversational Hypertext and Hyperlinks

We have already mentioned, without formally naming or describing it, one form of indexical function in talk: hyperlinks. Duck (2002) noticed that lots of talk involves a kind of **conversational hypertext.** You know what hypertext is from your use of computers and the Internet, and how you talk to people works the same way. In conversation, we often use a word that suggests more about a topic and would therefore show up on a computer screen in blue, pointing you to a hyperlink. For example, you might say, "I was reading Duck and McMahan, and I learned that there are many more extra messages that friends pick up in talk than I had realized before." This sentence makes perfect sense to somebody who knows what "Duck and McMahan" is, but others may not understand. On a computer, they would use their mouse to find out more about Duck and McMahan by going to www.sagepub.com/ciel, but in a conversation, they would "click" on the hypertext by asking a direct question: "What's Duck and McMahan?"

Conversational hypertext, therefore, is basically the idea that all of our conversation contains coded messages that an informed listener will effortlessly understand. In relationships, the shared worlds of meaning and the overlap of perception make communication special and closer. Uninformed listeners, however, can always request that the hypertext be unpacked, expanded, or addressed directly.

You and your friends talk in coded, hypertextual language all the time. Only when you encounter someone who does not understand the code do you need to further explain. In the previous example, "De'Janee" is hypertext until you have been introduced to her, and the "hot date" is hypertext until you learn that De'Janee has a new love interest. After that initial explanation, the term *hot date* might become a shared reference; even the friend from out of town now knows to what it refers. If, later in the conversation, someone starts to talk about "De'Janee's hottie," the out-of-town friend will be included in the shared knowledge, and, at that point, the group of friends will have created a new hypertext to the conversation and the relationship that even the out-of-town friend understands.

Research shows how you can tell, just from their talk, whether people know one another because of the way they treat conversational hypertext as needing no further explanation. Planalp and Garvin-Doxas (1994) reported a number of studies where they played tapes of talk to an audience and asked the listeners to say whether the people on the tape were friends. Listeners were very skilled at making this identification and could easily tell whether two conversational partners were acquainted or merely strangers. What made the difference was whether or not the talkers took information for granted or whether they explained the terms used. Said without explanation, "Jim was worried about his foot again" identified the two conversers as friends. On the other hand, the following showed them to be unacquainted: "Jim—that's my friend from high school—was worried about his foot again. He has gout and has to be careful about setting it off; it is a problem that keeps coming back. It worries him a lot, so he usually calls me when it flares up, and I have to deal with it."

Strategic Communication

We want you to think about a situation where you overheard two people talking and you could tell—you just *knew*—that they were not close but that one of them was trying to impress the other and get into a relationship with him or her. What did you notice that made you sure you were right about the person doing the "impressing," and how did you know whether or not the other person was impressed? Come to class prepared to share that experience and to talk about what you can tell from what people say—in particular from the way things are said.

Essential Functions

People very easily underestimate the extent to which talk and its nonverbal wrapping *are* a relationship. Of course, even when you are in a relationship, you and your partner do not spend every moment with each other. You experience absences, breaks, and separations: They may be relatively short (one person goes shopping), longer (a child goes to school for the day), or extended (two lovers get jobs in different parts of the country, go on vacation separately, or are involved in a commuter relationship). Because these breaks in sequence occur, there are many ways you indicate to one another that, although the interaction may be over, the relationship itself continues. For example, you might say, "See you next week," "Talk to you later," or "Next week we will be discussing the chapter on health communication." All of these phrases are examples of the **essential function of talk**—namely, a function of talk in making the relationship real and talking it into being by simply assuming that it exists. The above examples, talking about the continuance of the relationship beyond an upcoming absence, demonstrate that the relationship will outlast the separation.

Most of the time, however, talk creates and embodies relationships in other ways, both implicitly ("I've got you, babe") and explicitly ("You're my friend"). There can be direct talk that embodies the relationship ("I love you") or indirect talk ("What shall

Spend some time listening for different types of talk that occur in everyday life and the corresponding ways in which relationships are essentialized or transacted.

Up to this point, we have not said a lot about how "talk" can be divided into different categories, and we have treated "talk" as a unitary and consistent "thing." But it is not. How many different types of "talk" can you identify?

we do this Friday night?") that recognizes the relationship's existence but does not mention it explicitly. The essential function of talk operates in hidden ways as simple as more frequent references to "we" and "us" or inclusion in talk where joint planning is carried out or nicknames are used. Linguistic inclusion ("Let's...," "we," "us"), also known as **immediacy**, is a seemingly small but nevertheless powerful way to essentialize the relationship in talk. Nicknames, even as obvious as "Honey" or "Jimbo" rather than "James," clearly show familiarity, whereas inclusion in planning ("Let's do something really special tonight") signals the essentializing of the relationship as a taken-for-granted part of the speaker's life.

Politeness and Facework

Different kinds of talk essentialize relationships in different ways. For example, a polite conversation is different in style from an impolite one and essentializes a different type of relationship. Of course, other frames may indicate whether the impoliteness results from dislike or the informality that characterizes close friendship.

Let's start with politeness, since in one way or another, most of our everyday talk is polite even with strangers. In this context, communication scholars Bill Cupach and Sandra Metts (Cupach & Metts, 1994; Metts, 2000) speak of **facework**, a term that refers to the management of people's face, meaning dignity or self-respect. When people are ashamed or humiliated, you might talk of them "losing face," and although that is a metaphor, it is worth noticing how often people who are embarrassed or who feel foolish cover their faces with their hands. An almost automatic reaction to shame or to the recognition that we have done something foolish, it makes our point that "face" is connected to moral appearance in the social world as a composed and centered social being. You might also think about the term *boldfaced lie*, used for a particularly daring falsehood. Doing facework or presenting a strongly favorable image of yourself, a particularly important aspect of giving talks, speeches, or interviews, is even more important in the everyday conduct of life.

Sociologist Erving Goffman (1971) promoted the notion that "face" is something managed by people in social interactions, noting that you do it for yourself and other people. Many times, for example, you try to save someone else's face by trivializing an embarrassing mistake ("Oh, don't worry about it; I do that all the time"; "Think nothing of it"; "No big deal"). In effect, you are saying that you don't see the person's behavior truly as an indication of who he or she really is: You are trying to let him or her off the hook as a person and are distinguishing his or her momentary *actions* from his or her deep, true *self*.

Photo 2.3 Talk in friendships or relationships can be described in terms of three functions: instrumental, indexical, or essential. Which function of talk would you use to describe the two men in this photo? (See page 52.)

Face Wants

People have positive face wants and negative face wants: **Positive face wants** refer to the need to be seen and accepted as a worthwhile and reasonable person; **negative face wants** refer to the desire not to be imposed upon or treated as inferior. The management of this type of face want is perhaps the most familiar: "I don't mean to trouble you, but would you . . ."; "I hope this is not too inconvenient, but would you mind . . ."; "Sorry to be a nuisance but . . ."; and our personal favorite from students, "I have a *quick* question" (implying that it will not be a lot of trouble or a big imposition to answer it). Although this management of people's negative face wants is quite common, positive face wants are also dealt with quite frequently, and you often hear people pay compliments like "You are doing a great job!"; "How very nice of you"; or "You're too kind."

Use of either type of behavior allows you to manage your relationships by paying attention to the ways people need to be seen in the social world. The behaviors are therefore a subtle kind of relational management done in talk and one that may not have been obvious—or at least not obviously connecting talk to relationships.

Ways of Speaking

In everyday conversation with people you know, other aspects of talk are worth noticing as ways of transacting relationships. The form or style of language through which you choose to express your thoughts carries important relational messages, and sometimes you use that knowledge as part of what you choose to say on a particular occasion. When people talk to very young children, they tend to adopt baby language; when students or employees talk with professors or supervisors, they try to sound "professional." When talking with friends, you use informal language, but in class or in conversation with your boss, your language may be a bit more complicated. Think about the difference between saying, when you're hungry, "I'm so hungry I could eat a horse" and "My state of famishment is of such a proportion that I would gladly consume the complete corporeality of a member of the species *Equus przewalski poliakov*." The first example is written in what communication scholars call **low code**, and the second is written in **high code** (Giles, Taylor, & Bourhis, 1973). Low code is an informal and often ungrammatical way of talking; high code is a formal, grammatical, and very correct—often "official"—way of talking. You might be able to look around your lecture hall and see a sign that says something like "Consumption of food and beverages on these premises is prohibited." That is a high-code way of saying the low-code message "Do not eat or drink here."

By now, then, you can see that not just individual words are polysemic; so is the whole structure of language and the *way in which* you speak. Let's spend some time elaborating on this so that you come to understand how it plays out in relationships with an audience, whether public or intimate.

The language you use contains more than one way of saying the same thing—a sort of stylistic polysemy. Although this may not have struck you as particularly important yet, the form of language you use to express essentially the same idea conveys its own messages about something other than the topic you're talking about. In fact, it connotes and essentializes the relationships between you and your audience, as well as conveys something about you as a person. A high form is formal, pompous, and professional; a low form is casual, welcoming, friendly, and relaxed. By choosing one form over another at a particular point of speech, you are therefore not just sending a message but doing three things: delivering *content* about a particular topic, *presenting* yourself as a particular sort of person (projecting identity), and *indexing* a particular sort of relationship to the audience. Part of your connotative meaning at a given time is always an essentializing commentary about "the state of the relationship" between the speaker and the audience, whether a large or small group or an individual. Just as public speakers adopt particular ways of talking depending on the group with which they strive to identify, so too a person can choose a friendly, informal style or a more distant, formal style with a stranger, according to his or her desire for a close or distant relationship.

Just as you can set the frame, you can change it. You can choose a particular way to say something, but you may change or adapt it either to suit an audience or to see changes in feelings or in the relationship that occur during the course of the interaction. Giles and his colleagues (1973) have shown that people will change their accent, their rate of speech, and even the words they use to indicate a relational connection with the person to whom they are talking. They called this process **accommodation** and identified two types: convergence and divergence. In **convergence**, a person moves toward the style of talk used by the other speaker. For example, an adult converges when he or she uses baby talk to communicate with a child, or a brown-nosing employee converges when he or she uses the boss's company lingo style of talk. In **divergence**, exactly the opposite happens: One talker moves away from another's style of speech to make a relational point, such as establishing dislike or superiority. A good example is how computer geeks and car mechanics insist on using a lot of technical language to customers, instead of giving simple explanations that the nonexpert could understand. This form of divergence keeps the customer in a lower relational place.

We have not indicated who is more likely to converge or to diverge. Would you predict that a high-status person would be more likely to converge or diverge?

The different ways of sending the same content in a message are another instance of how meaning and relationships are inextricably tied together. Talking conveys content and something about your identity. It conveys even more about your sense of the ongoing changes in your relationship with others and how it may be altered by the course of an interaction.

Narration: Telling Stories

The multilayered framing aspect of talk is especially noticeable when people tell stories. Communication scholars use the term *narrative* to cover what is involved when we say *what* people are doing and *why* they are doing it, whether talk includes funny events, tragic events, significant emotional experiences, or relational stories (meeting new people, falling in love, breaking up). You may not always notice that talk has the features of a story, but you have heard many examples—"How we met," "How my day was," and even "I couldn't do the assignment," which may not at first strike you as a story. A **narrative** is any organized story, report, or prepared talk that has a plot, an argument, or a theme. In a narrative, speakers do not just relate facts but also arrange the story in a way that provides an account, an explanation, or a conclusion—often one that makes the speakers look good or tells a story from their own particular point of view (i.e., when they are making their talk not only representational but also presentational).

Much of everyday life is spent telling stories about yourself and other people, whether or not they walk into bars. For example, you may tell a story about when you went into a shop and something funny or unexpected happened, or you may tell your friends how when you were working in the pizza parlor, some guy came in and couldn't, like, make his mind up about whether he wanted, like, double cheese or pepperoni, and you stood there for, like, 5 minutes while he made up his mind. Communication scholar Walter Fisher (1985) pointed out how much of human life is spent telling stories and coined the term *homo narrans* (Latin for "the person as a storyteller or narrator") to describe this tendency. Indeed, he suggested that storytelling is one of the most important human activities. Stories are also a large part of relating, so we need to spend some time exploring how people narrate and justify their action in stories.

Stories or narratives often appear to be straightforward talk, but very often they are elaborate frames, too, and can frame up excuses for your actions. For example, in the cheese and pepperoni case, the end of your story might be "I was so mad," and the details about the person making the decision might be used to justify (frame) the fact that you felt irritated. People often give excuses and tell stories that help explain their

Photo 2.4 People tell stories every day, whether about the crazy commute that made them late to work or a funny interaction with a bank teller. How do you know that one of the people in the photo is telling a story, and what role does storytelling seem to play in their relationship? (See page 52.)

actions within a set of existing frames. This section looks at how stories use, and also provide, frames for your talk to present you incidentally as a relationally responsible and attractive person (facework).

Burke's Pentad

All stories have particular common elements known as **Burke's pentad** (Burke, 1966); *pentad* is a word derived from the Greek for "five" (see Table 2.2 for a listing of the elements).

Table 2.2 Common Elements of Burke's Pentad

1. Scene (setting)	*Where* it happened
2. Agent (character)	*Who* was involved
3. Act (single event or sequences of events)	*What* (facts) unfolded in time
4. Agency (plotline)	*How* (the way in which) acts happened
5. Purpose (outcome)	*Why* (What was the result or goal?)

The outcome usually offers a moral result (the moral of the story). The next time you hear people telling stories in everyday life communication, you can recognize that their reports fit this particular theoretical framework for justifying and explaining their actions.

Stories start out with a scene involving people (agents) in which something happened (act) ("I was working in a pizza parlor last night, and this guy came in…"; "My professor told me yesterday during office hours that…"; "My mom was driving home from work last night and realized…"; "I was talking with my boyfriend yesterday, and we decided to break up because…"). These elements of talk introduce the main characters (agents), often yourself and someone you know ("I was working…this guy came in…"). Stories involve the interaction and intersection of characters (agency)—"He couldn't make up his mind…"; "I stood there for 5 minutes waiting…"—and their plotlines are based on a sequence of events that result in an outcome ("I was so mad"). Although the pizza story may not have sounded quite so complicated at first, you may now be able to see, if you look hard enough, that almost all stories and conversations fit this kind of structure—with which you are actually very familiar, although you may not previously have been able to name the terms it encompasses.

The important point is not just that you could learn to identify the specific elements (scene, act, etc.) but also how the story is used to frame its outcome as reasonable and inevitable. Take a look at the examples in Table 2.3; you probably get the point that the punch lines of stories—even news stories and scientific reports or tales of people walking into bars—are reasonable and acceptable according to how they are set up in such ratios of justification and presentation.

Table 2.3 How a Story Is Used to Frame Its Outcome as Reasonable or Inevitable

Agent:act ratio	• Uses a person's character to explain actions. • For example, "He's the kind of guy who does that."; "Friends don't let friends drive drunk."
Scene:act ratio	• Uses a situation or circumstances to justify action. • For example, "Desperate times call for desperate measures."; "This is war and we need to use harsh methods to obtain the truth from prisoners."
Scene:agent ratio	• Uses a situation to explain the kinds of characters who are found there. • For example, "Politics makes strange bedfellows."; "Miami is a sunny place for shady people."
Scene:agent:act ratio	• Uses a situation or circumstances (e.g., a disintegrating parental marriage) to explain a person's actions. • For example, "Children of divorced parents are more likely to be insecure in relationships and get divorced themselves later in life."

It is worth paying attention to the elements of the pentad that show up in a person's typical accounts of everyday life experience, because it gives insight into how the person thinks. The terms of the pentad used by a narrator tend to transact or present certain aspects of the world in the communication. When a person highlights a specific element of the pentad, that gives insight into the way he or she thinks about the world. From this point of view, stories are not simply narrations of events but personalized ways of telling: The narration indicates presentation of a perspective.

One significant frame that sets the scene for all narratives comes from two sources: (1) the character of the agent telling the story, making the speech, giving a toast, reporting the gossip, or talking the talk, and (2) the relationship between the speaker and the audience (a latent agent:agent ratio). Formal speakers are often introduced in ways that frame them as important for their audience by listing their rank, their accomplishments, or the reasons the audience should pay attention to them ("I am pleased to present the president of the corporation..."; "We are very honored to have with us today the Secretary of State..."; "Today's speaker has for a long time been a leading member of our community..."). In formal settings a toastmaster may wear a uniform, a priest who is speaking may wear the clothes of office, or speakers may wear business clothes to clarify their importance, professionalism, and seriousness. However, even in informal settings all speakers invite you to accept the important frame that they *matter* whether or not they are giving a formal presentation. The bottom line of many stories in everyday life really comes down to "I'm a decent person, and what I'm telling you is essentially a good idea/I did the right thing, didn't I?" Outside of therapy, you rarely meet anyone who does not, at root, think he or she is an essentially good person, perhaps misunderstood and undervalued but essentially decent and OK. Now you may recognize that these story "bottom lines" are not only offering justifications and accounts for acts but also using the features we have talked about in this chapter to relate the speaker and the audience. Speaking to any audience is always an act set in a relational scene.

A speaker's character frames what he or she says and justifies his or her attempts to persuade an audience, whether a formally seated audience at a political rally or business speech or simply someone listening to a friend. All speakers try to make relational partners, potential friends, and other audiences appreciate or even like them, but in most everyday life conversations, the chances are that you are already speaking to friends, family, and people who like you quite a bit to begin with. Your relationship then frames, or sets the scene for, what you are going to say, just as much as your argument and your words do.

Other scenes also exist. Narratives, stories, and all daily talk occur within a set of assumptions about the culture and what works within it; about justice, responsibility, and free will; about personality; about "speaker truth"; and about audience. A speaker who believes it will be a problem to convince the audience will adopt different strategies than will someone who assumes that whatever is said will be readily and unquestioningly accepted. When you talk with your friends, you most likely do not find it necessary to keep convincing them that you are speaking the truth. You assume that *they* assume that you speak the truth. In other circumstances, it may be more important for you to tell stories in a way that assumes a particular version of the facts or set of hypertextual assumptions based on your own particular reasons. For example, if you are talking about the terrible character of a person who just broke off a relationship with you, the frame is that you are a decent person while the other person is a jerk.

At other times, you may want to describe yourself in a way that helps other people understand how you "tick," or you may want to reveal personal information that helps them understand you better. Again, remember that you do this very much from your own point of view and personal motives. Don't ever believe that when someone tells you a story, it is a neutral and simply representational view of the world: All stories and speech are presentational. When listening to politicians, you can expect them to present events in a way that suits their personal interests best. You have to learn to recognize that *everyone* is a politician for his or her own party: the "vote-for-me-because-I-am-a-good person" party.

Giving Accounts

Although narratives appear on the surface just to report (represent) events, they frequently account for (present) the behaviors. **Accounts** are forms of communication that offer justifications ("I was so mad"), excuses ("I was really tired"), exonerations ("It wasn't my fault"), explanations ("...and that's how we fell in love"), accusations ("But he started it!"), and apologies ("I'm an idiot"). In short, accounts "go beyond the facts." How narratives are structured will often give a clue as to the motives of people involved or perhaps to the teller's understanding of the world. In fact, you should be noticing what you can learn about a storyteller from how he or she tells the story. Everyday communication involves different ways of narrating stories, and many give revealing insight into the thought frames of the person doing the telling.

Psychologists, communication scholars, and sociologists would talk about the above pizza parlor story as "giving an account" (Scott & Lyman, 1968), or telling a story in a way that justifies, blames, or calls for someone to account for what happened. The purpose of representational elements (or "facts") in reports can actually turn out to be presentational; that is, your description of something is not simply a report of facts but contains "spin" and therefore explains the "facts" you are reporting. For example, if you tell your friend, "I just failed a math test. It was way too hard," both of these statements appear to be facts, but one is actually an explanation for why you failed (the test was too hard) and is a personal view about the reason for your failure. It is therefore a *presentational* account and not simply a statement of fact. Your teacher may think you failed because you did not do the work, for example.

If you listen to everyday conversation, you will start to hear these sorts of framing justifications much more often now that you know what to listen for. Once you recognize their frequency, you can begin to understand something about their structure and what it tells us about communication and the implied relationship between the speaker and the audience. For example, you don't bother to justify yourself to people whose opinions you do not care about, and furthermore, you would not justify yourself to an enemy in the same way you would to a friend. You expect the friend to know more about your background and to cut you some slack. This familiarity would influence the style of your report, once again connecting talk to relationships.

Remember what we wrote at the start of this chapter: that a whole system of NVC frames what we say, too. If I say "I love you" but grimace when I say it, that frames the words in a different way than if I smile and look all gooey when I say it. The next chapter covers NVC on its own and then reconnects it as a frame for interpreting talk. Although we have separated talk from its real behavioral context so that you can understand features of talk itself, it never happens in practice in a way that is separated from nonverbal behavior. The next chapter shows you how nonverbal behavior works and how it is used not only to send messages on its own but also to affect how the messages in talk are modified or understood.

Focus Questions Revisited

What are the differences between grammatical language and talk in everyday use?

Grammatical language has a formal structure (langue), whereas talk in everyday use tends quite frequently to disregard the rules of grammar (parole). Langue is used in formal settings, and parole, often a mark of the fact that the people know one another well, tends to be used in less-formal settings.

What frames your understanding of talk and gives it meaning?

Context, situation, language structure, culture, and the task at hand all give you clues about the frame you are in for a given conversation. The previous talk also gives lots of clues. Likewise, you draw clues about relationships and appropriateness of talk directly from context: In restaurants, you talk to servers about food; in a romance, you talk about love, but at work, you do not—unless you are a therapist or are giving a colleague some personal advice.

What values are hidden in the speech you use?

Many cultural and personal values are hidden in the speech used between persons in everyday life. Cultures recognize certain kinds of relationships but not others and manage the degree of respect shown by one person to another in different ways. Other values may be hidden in a particular society's use of God and Devil terms. Your speech often also contains codes that indicate the depth of relationship you have with the person to whom you are speaking.

How does everyday talk make use of relationships to frame meanings?

Everyday talk draws on the relationship that exists between two people in a conversation to indicate what is appropriate or inappropriate for them to do and say to one another. Friends who know one another well may talk in ways that are inappropriate between strangers.

How do different types of talk work, and how do they connect to relationships?

We already pointed out politeness, conflict, and rudeness, but other types of talk could include information, questions, argument/persuasion, jargon, euphemism, instructions, assignments, profanity, rituals, catch-up talk, hostility, harassment, bullying, comforting, social support, advice, small talk, planning, speechmaking, confession, and forgiveness. Many of these forms of talk represent ways to keep a relationship together; others are ways of keeping people away.

What is talk style, and how does it frame meaning?

The style of talk can be carried out in high code or low code. High code is appropriate for formal settings, and low code is appropriate for informal settings. The choice to use one or the other frames the meaning of the interaction, and switching between the two types of code is a way of creating greater closeness or distance, depending on which direction the switching takes place in. Convergence is when two people speak in the same style and indicates closeness or liking, but divergence is when they speak in different styles and indicates distance or disliking.

What are the key elements of stories?

According to Burke's pentad, the key elements of stories are scene, agent, act, agency, and purpose/outcome. The act is what is done, the scene is where it takes place, the agent is the person performing the act, the agency is how the act is done, and the purpose or outcome is basically the result or endpoint of the story, often tinged with moral judgment.

Key Concepts

accommodation   (p. 45)
accounts   (p. 49)
Burke's pentad   (p. 46)
connotative meaning   (p. 33)
convergence   (p. 45)
conversational hypertext   (p. 40)
denotative meaning   (p. 33)
Devil terms   (p. 38)
divergence   (p. 45)
essential function of talk   (p. 41)
facework   (p. 42)
God terms   (p. 38)
high code   (p. 44)

immediacy   (p. 42)
indexical function of talk   (p. 39)
instrumental function of talk   (p. 39)
intentionality   (p. 35)
langue   (p. 30)
low code   (p. 44)
naming   (p. 32)
narrative   (p. 45)
negative face wants   (p. 43)
parole   (p. 30)
polysemy (p. 31)
positive face wants   (p. 43)
Sapir/Whorf hypothesis   (p. 33)

Questions to Ask Your Friends

- Try conducting a conversation with one of your friends where you use only high code. Take note of how long it is before your friend senses something wrong or inappropriate in the situation, and then ask him or her what he or she thinks is happening.

- Ask your friends if they ever find it hard to know when you are kidding and what makes it hard.

- Have your friends report an occasion when they caught someone in a boldfaced lie and how they knew. How did they handle it (thinking of facework)?

Media Links

- Listen for how news stories are structured in ways that illustrate the pentad.

- How do news anchors introduce stories intended to be seen as "not serious" as compared to those regarded as serious and important?

- What techniques do news anchors use on television in order to relate with their audience and seem friendly, likeable, and credible?

Ethical Issues

- Note how sexist, racist, and heterosexual (marking) language is relational and always places one group of people in an inferior position relative to another group of people. Is it ever ethical to use this kind of language?

- Should the stories you tell always be true? Why or why not?

- Should you always be polite and save people's face when they do something embarrassing?

Answers to Photo Captions

Photo 2.1 ▪ The U.S. Constitution stipulates the separation of church and state, but this pair of street signs indicates that this is the point where Church and State intersect. Someone who finds it amusing would have to know about the U.S. Constitution and the fact that Americans do not say the word *street* when talking about the intersection of two roads.

Photo 2.2 ▪ Since they are quite young they are likely to be excited about the seaside, observing waves and events out of the ordinary experience of their everyday lives, like seagulls and ships. As children they are likely to find the difference of the seaside from their normal living experience intriguing, and one is obviously pointing out a source of interest and excitement to the other. Perhaps there is talk of a pirate from one of their children's books and the shared experiences that they have had in being scared by such sea stories!

Photo 2.3 ▪ Indexical or essential function; they seem very at ease and familiar in speaking with each other; the talk is occurring in a kitchen at night, which suggests that they are friends and must be relaxed by the atmosphere because the chairs certainly wouldn't help.

Photo 2.4 ▪ The individuals are relaxed, indicating a friendship and shared bond. Everyone is looking at the person on the right gesturing with the red implements, perhaps "props" in the story. The two men and one of the women seem amused, but the woman on the right seems a little concerned. Amusement and concern about the narration/storytelling serve to bond the friendship.

Student Study Site

Visit the study site at www.sagepub.com/ciel for e-flashcards, practice quizzes, and other study resources.

References

Burke, K. (1966). *Language as symbolic action: Essays on life, literature and method.* Berkeley: University of California Press.

Cupach, W. R., & Metts, S. (1994). *Facework.* Thousand Oaks, CA: Sage.

Duck, S. W. (2002). Hypertext in the key of G: Three types of "history" as influences on conversational structure and flow. *Communication Theory, 12*(1), 41–62.

Duck, S. W. (2007). *Human relationships* (4th ed.). London: Sage.

Duck, S. W., & Pond, K. (1989). Friends, Romans, Countrymen; lend me your retrospective data: Rhetoric and reality in personal relationships. In C. Hendrick (Ed.), *Review of social psychology and personality: Close relationships* (Vol. 10 pp. 17-38). Newbury Park, CA: Sage.

Fisher, W. R. (1985). The narrative paradigm: An elaboration. *Communication Monographs, 52,* 347–367.

Giles, H., Taylor, D. M., & Bourhis, R. Y. (1973). Towards a theory of interpersonal accommodation through language use. *Language in Society, 2,* 177–192.

Goffman, E. (1971). *Relations in public: Microstudies of the public order.* New York: Harper & Row.

Kelly, G. A. (1969). Ontological acceleration. In B. Mather (Ed.), *Clinical psychology and personality: The collected papers of George Kelly* (pp. 7–45). New York: Wiley.

Kirkpatrick, C. D., Duck, S. W., & Foley, M. K. (Eds.). (2006). *Relating difficulty: The processes of constructing and managing difficult interaction.* LEA Series on Personal Relationships. Mahwah, NJ: Lawrence Erlbaum.

Metts, S. (2000). Face and facework: Implications for the study of personal relationships. In K. Dindia & S. W. Duck (Eds.), *Communication and personal relationships* (pp. 72–94). Chichester, UK: Wiley.

Norwood, K. M. (2007). *Gendered conflict? The "cattiness" of women on "Flavor of Love."* Paper presented at the Organization for the Study of Communication, Language, and Gender, Omaha, NE.

Ogden, C. K., & Richards, I. A. (1946). *The meaning of meaning* (8th ed.). New York: Harcourt Brace Jovanovich.

Planalp, S., & Garvin-Doxas, K. (1994). Using mutual knowledge in conversation: Friends as experts in each other. In S. W. Duck (Ed.), *Dynamics of relationships* (Understanding relationship processes 4, pp. 1–26). Newbury Park, CA: Sage.

Sapir, E. (1949). *Selected writings in language, culture and personality* (D. Mandelbaum, Ed.). Berkeley: University of California Press.

Saussure, F. (1993). *Saussure's third course of lectures on general linguistics (1910–1911).* London, Pergamon. (Original work published in 1910)

Scott, M. B., & Lyman, S. M. (1968). Accounts. *American Sociological Review, 33,* 46–62.

Whorf, B. (1956). *Language, thought, and reality: Selected writings of Benjamin Lee Whorf* (J. Carroll, Ed.). Boston: MIT Press.

3

Nonverbal Communication

Nonverbal communication is inseparable from talk in normal interaction and carries messages over and above the words you speak. For example, a smile makes your words seem friendly, but a sneer makes the same words seem sarcastic. Nonverbal communication most often goes along with and supports talk, although not always. You might say, "I'm *not* angry" but look as if you are really angry, or you might say, "I love you" and only have to exchange a glance with your partner for him or her to see that you really mean it. Not only does nonverbal communication frame talk, but it can also frame other people's assessments and judgments of you before you even speak, and it can indicate how you feel about other people. The way you move, look, and sound and the speed and pitch of your voice convey relational messages to others—whether with friends as you're chatting in a lounge or with an interviewer considering you for a job or with patients as you're about to tell them bad news. All nonverbal communication conveys something about your sense of relaxation and comfort with the person(s) with whom you're speaking. Nonverbal communication also indicates your *evaluation or assessment* of that person. In short, nonverbal communication is an essential *relational* element of all interaction, and you cannot have interactions without nonverbal communication; nor can you have interactions without the *relational messages* that nonverbal communication sends.

Nonverbal communication, or NVC, has been tied up with your communication all of your life, which can make it difficult for you to appreciate its importance because it is too obvious. But is NVC something worth understanding and learning about? You bet!

- What is nonverbal communication?
- How does nonverbal communication work, and what work does it do in communication?
- How does nonverbal communication regulate (e.g., begin and end) interactions?
- What are the elements of nonverbal communication, and how do they interconnect?
- How can you improve your use of nonverbal communication?

What Is Nonverbal Communication?

Nonverbal communication is everything that communicates a message but does not include words. This definition covers a very wide range of topics: facial expression, hand movements, dress, tattoos, jewelry, physical attractiveness, timing of what happens, position in the interaction (for example, the professor always stands at the front of the class), tone of voice, eye movements, the positioning of furniture to create atmosphere, touch, and smell—and that is not an exhaustive list.

Photo 3.1 What features of nonverbal behavior can you use to draw inferences about this person, and what is your impression? (See page 81.)

The Two Sides of Nonverbal Communication: Decoding Versus Encoding

It is important to distinguish between **decoding** and **encoding** of NVC. Decoding a nonverbal message is exactly like decoding anything else—you draw meaning from something you observe. For example, if somebody blushes unexpectedly, you might decode that as meaning he or she is embarrassed. On the other hand, when you encode a nonverbal message, you put your feelings into behavior through NVC; for example, if you are feeling happy, you *look* truly happy. A good *de*coder can work out sensitively what is going on inside another person, but if you're a good *en*coder, you put your feelings "out there" well and help other people "get" what is going on inside you. Skillful actors, teachers, and public speakers are good encoders; effective therapists, advisors, and interrogators are good decoders. Good encoding helps your listeners understand what you feel about your subject; good decoding helps you figure out what the speaker is trying to tell you.

Encoding is important when you go on a job interview, give speeches, or go on a first date because you need to display confidence rather than anxiety, and the more confident you are, the more people will attend to what you say. Decoding is important when you're chatting with a friend: You need to be able to notice if your friend is anxious or having a hard time but not telling you directly, for example, or even lying.

> Nonverbal communication conveys both intentional and unintentional messages. Consider these examples: During a call to a computer technical support line, you hear a distinct sigh. Does this make you think that person wants to help you? You walk into a professor's office and see that the furniture is arranged in a way that "walls" you off from her or him. Is this professor approachable?

The Two Modes of Nonverbal Communication: Static Versus Dynamic

Communication scholars traditionally divide the many kinds of NVC into two aspects (Manusov & Patterson, 2006): **static** (fixed) and **dynamic** (changeable). The color of someone's eyes is static NVC; a change in the size of his or her pupils is dynamic NVC.

Static NVC refers to those elements of an interaction that do not change during its course. For example, the arrangement of furniture in a particular room can send nonverbal messages about status and power or about comfort and informality, and it is unlikely that the furniture itself will be moved around during the course of the interaction. A judge's power in the courtroom is symbolized by the fact that the judge sits higher up than all the other people in the court. A shop assistant going behind the cash register to complete your purchase is using a static aspect of the design of the shop that separates out "customer areas" from "shop assistant areas." Customers can go into one part of the shop but not into the other part without permission. If you followed the assistant behind the cash register, you might be suspected of intending a robbery.

The room in which you interact also counts as a static nonverbal cue (Duck, 2007). An interaction in a friend's bedroom is conducted in a different static environment from one in a public lounge and frames the interaction with a different context. How you interact at home may be influenced by the lighting and décor (static nonverbal cues) that make the environment relaxing, as opposed to those cues present when you're speaking in the static environment of a large lecture hall.

Other examples of static nonverbal cues are body piercings, military uniforms, the clothes you wear into an interaction, the color of your hair, your sex, your age, your tattoos, your height and build, your ethnicity, or whether you are wearing sunglasses, pajamas, a sexy outfit, or jewelry. Although some of these things *may* change during the

Think about a situation where you felt uncomfortable in the presence of another person. Inside, you may have been filled with anxiety. How do you think the other person could have known that you were anxious? Were you sweating, blushing, agitated, speaking too fast, or jumpy? What did you do to try to conceal your nerves? Have you ever seen other people trying to appear calm, but you weren't fooled? What were they doing? What were their bodies saying to you in these languages of NVC? What behaviors gave away their anxiety? Think about this issue (and write some notes if you care to), and come to class ready to talk about it.

course of an interaction, most often they don't; they can, however, send signals about your relationship to another person or to society at large. For example, Seiter and Sandry (2003) showed people photographs of job applicants with different numbers of body piercings. They found that reviewers did not give different physical attractiveness ratings according to the type of jewelry the applicants wore, but the applicants' credibility was rated much lower when they were wearing jewelry. In particular, applicants' likelihood of being hired significantly decreased when they were wearing a nose ring.

Dynamic NVC involves movement and change during the course of the interaction—behaviors closely watched by poker players. Most dynamic NVC relates to bodily activity or position. Facial expressions, gestures, postures, the pitch and tone of the speaker's voice as she relates a story, the way someone's eyes move, and the amount of touching that takes place during the course of conversation are all dynamic aspects of NVC and can be broken down into several different parts. Don't forget as you go through all these parts that each of them can convey emotional and relational messages separately and together. As you will see later in the chapter, NVC also serves a second, extremely important relational function: It regulates (e.g., starts and stops) interaction. It also helps maintain emotional flow.

How Nonverbal Communication Works

Having discussed the two sides and the two modes of NVC, we can now discuss the operation of nonverbal symbols to give you a better understanding of how they are used in your everyday experiences. Verbal and nonverbal communication are both symbolic and share many of the same characteristics, such as being personal, ambiguous, guided by rules, and linked to culture. As we discuss the nature of NVC, we address the characteristics it shares with verbal communication as well as how they materialize. We will also discuss characteristics unique to NVC, such as its continuous nature and that it is often beyond your full control. This comparison will help you develop insight into the nature of NVC and, while you're at it, give you an even clearer understanding of verbal communication (Knapp & Hall, 2002; Remland, 2004).

Symbolic

Nonverbal and verbal communication are both symbolic. The key difference between them is that verbal communication involves the use of language and NVC involves the use of all other symbolic activity.

Like verbal symbols, nonverbal symbols can be described as polysemic; that is, a single nonverbal symbol can have multiple meanings. The highly ambiguous nature of nonverbal symbols often makes it quite difficult to ascertain their intended meanings. For example, what does a stare mean: affection, anger, hostility, interest, longing, or "Be quiet!"? Like that of verbal symbols, the meaning of nonverbal symbols depends on the *context* of the interaction and the relationship of the interactants. Is your arriving 20 minutes late to class impolite? What if your instructor does it?

Guided by Rules

Nonverbal communication is guided by rules. As in verbal communication, rules guide the choice of nonverbal symbols that should be used in specific situations and with certain people. You would probably shake your instructor's hand rather than give him or her a high five. The appropriateness of greeting someone with a kiss changes depending on whether he or she is your romantic partner, an attendant behind the counter at a gas station, or someone from a culture where a kiss on the cheek is an accepted greeting even between persons of the same sex (Russia or Italy, for example).

Rules also guide your understanding of how to evaluate nonverbal behavior. For instance, you know that nonverbal expressions of gratitude include shaking a person's hand, smiling, and talking in an appreciative tone of voice as opposed to avoiding eye contact, pouting, and talking in a surly tone of voice. You also measure the extent to which a person is thankful through his or her nonverbal behaviors. A brisk handshake is evaluated differently than a hearty handshake; a slight smile is evaluated differently than a broad smile. You can even gauge the extent of a person's degree of appreciation through slight alterations in his or her tone of voice.

As opposed to those guiding verbal communication, the rules guiding NVC have been learned more indirectly and primarily through your interactions with others (Remland, 2004). This course may be the first time you have ever formally studied NVC, but you have been studying verbal language in school for years. In your English classes, for example, you learned the difference between nouns, verbs, adjectives, and adverbs and about proper sentence structure. In grade school, you learned vocabulary skills and the meanings of certain words. With NVC, you have learned nearly everything, from the meaning of particular nonverbal symbols to the structure of their use, informally throughout your lifetime as you have interacted with other people.

There is actually a diagnosable disability called NLD (nonverbal learning disorder; http://www.nlda.org/) where people fail to understand NVC. They may stand too close to you, get in your way when you try to get past them, or fail to read your tone of voice correctly or to differentiate anger from nonanger. Sometimes, this disability will cause misunderstanding of others' intentions; for example, a person with NLD may wrongly assume that someone looking at him is intentionally threatening. A child with NLD who is told with a glare "I wouldn't do that if I were you" will not correctly interpret the glare but will take the words literally—not as a command to stop—thinking the speaker means, "In your position, my choice would, as a matter of fact, be not to do what you have chosen to do." Adults often consider such children insolent or inattentive, but in fact, their understanding of NVC rules is impaired. A particularly frustrating disability for everyone, NLD doesn't count as bad enough to require medical treatment, yet it is socially disruptive to have people stand too close to you or fail to recognize your boundaries. If you suspect somebody has this problem, it is of course important to recognize that his or her behavior is caused not by rudeness but by an inability to understand the rules. Several otherwise high-functioning intelligent people (including Albert Einstein, some believe) suffered from this particular disorder, showing that it is possible to be both extremely intelligent and nonverbally disabled.

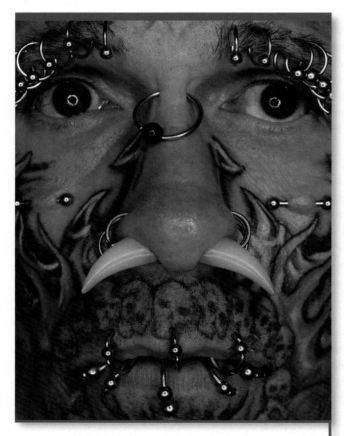

Photo 3.2 How does static NVC work, and what work does it do in communication? (See page 81.)

Cultural

Nonverbal communication is highly linked to culture. The appropriateness of certain nonverbal behaviors changes according to culture (Knapp & Hall, 2002). In the United States, eye contact is often viewed as a display of courtesy, honesty, and respect. In other countries, making eye contact, especially with a superior, is considered improper and highly disrespectful. Meanings of nonverbal messages depend on culture, including address, use of space, touch, and time. Dialect and accent can also indicate that a person comes from a particular country or region, and particular cues may be associated with stereotypes—for example, sexiness (French accent), slowness (Southern drawl), or cheeky friendliness (Irish accent). Also, many gestures are acceptable in some cultures but impolite or offensive in others (although in our culture the forefinger-to-thumb "O" means "perfect," in other cultures it is an offensive sexual suggestion). While many nonverbal behaviors and symbols are perhaps universally recognized (the smile, for example), they do not necessarily have universal meaning and understanding in the same contexts (Remland, 2004).

Personal

Nonverbal communication can be very personal in nature (Guerrero & Floyd, 2006). Similar to verbal communication, you develop your own personal meanings and use of nonverbal symbols. A person's use of some nonverbal symbols may even become idiosyncratic over time. You also respond positively or negatively to certain nonverbal symbols. Some people may not like to hug or be hugged, for example. One person may view the peace sign (shown in Figure 3.1) as cliché and may look at celebrities flashing the peace sign at cameras with disdain. Another person may view this sign as still having great meaning and value and may regard its use with admiration. Others still may cover themselves with tattoos (see http://www.bellaonline .com/articles/art37314.asp for the Leopard Man).

Figure 3.1 The Sign for Peace. Note that as presented it means "Peace" in the USA, "Victory" for Winston Churchill. If reversed so that the back of the hand is shown to someone, it is the UK equivalent of "the finger."

Ambiguous

The meaning of NVC is highly ambiguous, even more than the meaning of verbal communication. You are often uncertain what another person's NVC actually means, unless you have clear signals from context. You often use the physical or situational context, along with your relationship with that person, to assign meaning and understanding, but you may never know for certain whether it is accurate.

The ambiguous nature of NVC is largely why it is so valuable when flirting with someone. Nonverbal behaviors associated with flirting can mean so many different things. You could use eye contact, a quick or sustained glance, a smile, or even a wink either to flirt with someone or just to be friendly. Here, ambiguity is useful because it releases the pressure of not receiving the desired response. If the other person is interested, the response transacts your ambiguous message (for example, a long and perhaps longing stare) as a come-on; if the other person is not interested, the response transacts your ambiguous behavior as "just friendly." Always remember the ambiguous nature of NVC and heed this piece of advice: Another person may receive your friendly glance as a sexual provocation.

Less Controlled

Nonverbal communication is less subject to your control than is verbal communication. In the presence of someone you dislike, you might be able to keep from calling that person a jerk, but nonverbally you may be expressing your displeasure unknowingly through dirty looks or changes in pupil size. Nonverbal behaviors often occur without your full awareness and very often reveal how you really feel. This betrayal of your internal feelings, known as **leakage**, refers to the fact that NVC allows you to "leak" your true feelings. Because your spontaneous NVC is more difficult to control than your verbal

Contrarian Challenge

We have said that spontaneous NVC is hard to control, but can't people train themselves to appear cool and even to control their heart rate? Does this show that NVC is hard to control or not?

communication, people are more likely to believe your nonverbal over your verbal messages—especially when they are contradictory. Audiences rely more on what you do than on what you say.

Continuous

Nonverbal communication is continuous and ongoing. You will always be communicating nonverbally through your physical appearance; furthermore, in face-to-face speaking situations, you begin communicating nonverbally before you start talking and will continue communicating after you stop. For example, if you do not want to give a speech, you may convey this message nonverbally by having a look of dread on your face before you begin speaking. Afterward, this look of dread may be replaced by a look of relief as you say your final words.

The Functions of Nonverbal Communication

Nonverbal communication, whether static or dynamic, has several different functions in everyday life, some of which reinforce verbal behavior, some of which regulate interactions, and some of which serve to identify people. Nonverbal communication also registers people's emotional states or displays their attitudes about themselves, the other person in the interaction, or their comfort level. One of the clearest indicators of liking and disliking, for example, is registered by NVC: Pupil size, an uncontrollable activity, indicates the degree to which someone likes the person or idea that he or she is considering. If you look at a person you like very much, your pupil size will increase, whereas if you look at someone you dislike, your pupil size will decrease.

Interconnects With Verbal Communication

One function of NVC involves its interconnection with verbal communication. Your interpretation of a verbal message's meaning is often framed by accompanying nonverbal elements, such as tone of voice, facial expression, and gestures.

Quite often your NVC will *repeat* your verbal communication. When you send a verbal message, you often send a corresponding nonverbal message. For example, when you say hello to someone from across the room, you might wave at the same time.

Alternatively, nonverbal messages can *substitute*, or be used in place of, verbal messages. For example you might just wave to acknowledge someone and not say anything.

Nonverbal communication is often used to *emphasize* or highlight the verbal message. If you have ever gone fishing and described "the one that got away" to your friends, you have no doubt used NVC to emphasize just how big that fish really was by holding your arms out wide to indicate its gargantuan length. A verbal message can also be emphasized through your tone of voice. When you tell someone a secret, for example, you may use a hushed voice to emphasize its clandestine nature.

When NVC is used to *moderate* verbal communication, it essentially tempers the certainty of a verbal message. For instance, a doubtful tone of voice and the slight scrunching of your face and shoulders could indicate uncertainty. If your supervisor did this while saying, "I may be able to give you a raise this year," you would probably not anticipate an increase in pay. By moderating the verbal message nonverbally, your boss is letting you know there is uncertainty in that statement.

Your NVC can also *contradict* your verbal communication— sometimes intentionally, such as when you are being sarcastic. Contradiction may occur unintentionally as well—for instance, when someone charges into a room, slams the door, sits down on the couch in a huff, and, when you ask what is wrong, says, "Oh, nothing." Contradiction is not always this obvious, but even when it is more subtle, you are generally skilled at detecting it—especially when you share a close, personal relationship with the speaker. In situations of contradiction, you will be more likely to believe the person's nonverbal over verbal communication, because, as we discussed earlier, spontaneous NVC is less subject to your control than is verbal communication.

Regulates Interactions

Another function of NVC is to help regulate your interactions. Nonverbal communication informs you how you should behave and conveys how you want others to behave especially in starting or ending interactions. Used to determine whether you should actually engage in interactions with another person, NVC helps you know when to send and when to receive verbal messages.

Regulators are nonverbal actions that indicate to others how you want them to behave or what you want them to do. A classic regulator occurs at the end of most college classes: Students begin closing their books and gathering their belongings to signal to the instructor that it is time to end class. Other regulators include shivering when you want someone to close the window or turn up the heat, a look of frustration or confusion when you need help with a problem, and a closed-off posture (arms folded, legs crossed) when you want to be left alone.

Nonverbal communication is often used to determine whether you will actually engage in conversation. If one of your friends walks past you at a rapid pace with an intense look on his or her face, it may be an indication that he or she is in a hurry or not in the mood to talk. In this case, you might avoid interacting with your friend at this time. If someone looks frustrated or confused, however, you may decide to interact with him or her because the nonverbal behavior signals a need for help.

Nonverbal communication also serves to *punctuate* how you talk to other people; it starts and ends interactions and keeps them flowing. Specifically, NVC creates a framework within which interaction happens in proper sequence. Most of the time it is perfectly effortless and unconscious, but you must *act* to get in and out of conversations: For example, you must "catch the server's eye" to start ordering in a restaurant.

Photo 3.3 How does NVC regulate (begin, maintain, and end) interactions? (See page 81.)

You follow elaborate nonverbal rules to begin and to break off interactions. Consider what happens when you see someone walking toward you in the distance and wish to engage in conversation. Kendon and Ferber (1973) identified five basic stages in such a greeting ritual, as shown in Table 3.1.

Nonverbal communication is also used to signal the end to an interaction. You may, for example, stop talking, start to edge away, or show other signs of departure, such as looking away from the other person more often or checking your watch. You might also step a little farther back or turn to the side. Most people will pick up on the fact that the interaction is coming to an end and will join in rituals of ending, such as stepping back, offering a handshake, or stating directly that it's time to go.

Identifies Others

Nonverbal communication also functions to identify specific individuals. Just as dogs know each other individually by smell, humans use basic olfactory recognition but can also recognize one another specifically from facial appearance. You also use such additional physical cues as muscles, beards, skin color, breasts, and the whiteness of a person's hair to identify him or her as a particular sex, age, race, or athletic ability.

Clothing, also an identifying signal, can be used to identify someone's sex (men rarely wear dresses), personality (whether they wear loud colors, sedate business attire,

Table 3.1 Kendon and Ferber's (1973) Five Basic Stages of a Greeting Ritual

1. Sighting and recognition	Occurs when you and another person first see each other.
2. Distant salutation	Used to say hello with a wave, a flash of recognition, a smile, or a nod of acknowledgement.
3. Lowering your head and averting your gaze (to avoid staring)	Done as you approach the other person, which breaks off your visual connection while you get close enough to talk and be heard.
4. Close salutation	Most likely involves some type of physical contact, such as a handshake, a kiss, or a hug, which brings you too close for a comfortable conversation.
5. Backing off	For example, taking a step back or turning to the side to create a slightly larger space, the actual size of which is dictated by the type of relationship you share with the other person.

or punk clothing), favorite sports team, and job (police, military, security). Clothing can also identify changes in people, such as whether they have a special role today (prom outfits, wedding wear, gardening clothes), or indicate specific differences about their lives (casual Friday).

People can also distinguish others' scents: What perfume or cologne do they wear? Do they smoke? Are they drinkers? You may not comment on these kinds of clues because they are very often noticed with lower levels of awareness. If your physician smells of alcohol, however, you may well identify him or her as professionally incompetent to deal with your health concerns.

Transmits Emotional Information

An additional function of NVC is to convey emotional information. When you are angry, you scowl; when you are in love, you look gooey; when you feel happy, you smile. Nonverbal communication actually allows you to convey three different kinds of emotional information as follows.

Attitudes Toward the Other
First, NVC conveys your *attitudes toward the other person* in an interaction. If your facial expression conveys anxiety, viewers assume you are frightened. If your face looks relaxed and warm, viewers assume you are comfortable. If you care about what your professor has to say, you fall silent when a lecture begins; talking in class (professors' biggest complaint about students) makes it difficult for people to hear and shows lack of respect.

Attitudes Toward the Situation

Second, NVC conveys your *attitudes toward the situation*. For example, rapidly moving about while talking conveys a message of anxiety. Police officers often see fidgeting and an inability to maintain eye contact as indicators of a person's guilt.

Attituded Toward Yourself

Third, NVC conveys information about your *attitude toward yourself*. If a person is arrogant, confident, or low in self-esteem, it is expressed through nonverbal behaviors. An arrogant man may not express verbally how highly he thinks of himself, but you can tell he holds himself in high regard through his nonverbal actions, such as facial expression, tone of voice, eye contact, and body posture. If someone stands up to her full height and faces you directly, you might assume that she is confident. Conversely, if she slouches and stares at the ground, you might assume that she is shy, diffident, and insecure.

Establishes Relational Meaning and Understanding

Your relationships with others guide and inform your everyday communication, and your everyday communication develops these relationships. Nonverbal communication not only regulates social interaction, but it also acts as a silent *relational* regulator. Regulation of interactions serves to regulate engagement, politeness, coordination of action, and sense of pleasure in the interaction—all of which are ultimately relational in effect. The appearance of others enables you to distinguish and make judgments about them, as well as forms the basis of relational attraction. In fact, you often are attracted to people with facial and bodily features very similar to your own.

Relational meaning and understanding can be gained from all of the aforementioned functions of NVC, especially the expression of emotional information, and you will see more examples as we next work through the types of NVC. When we write about the function of NVC in the establishment of relational meaning and understanding, think specifically about how it establishes rapport, connection, engagement, responsiveness, liking, and power.

The Elements of Nonverbal Communication

So far we have discussed NVC as if it is a single thing, but it is actually made up of many different elements used collectively in the construction and interpretation of meaning, the development of identity, and the enactment of relationships. We discuss them individually to provide a more detailed explanation, but keep in mind that NVC works as a system comprising all these elements. Accordingly, we put them back together again at the end of this section.

Proxemics: Space and Distance

Proxemics is the study of space and distance in communication. Using space in different ways conveys different meanings: You lay it out as living rooms, bedrooms, offices, or bus shelters, and you decorate, rearrange, and occupy it. You often mark and establish it as your own even when you do not have exclusive control over it: sitting in your favorite chair at school or laying your books on a table to indicate its occupation. Countries possess space and usually mark it with a flag to indicate ownership and control. Both countries and people get quite upset if space regarded as theirs is invaded in some way. If somebody sits in your favorite chair or moves the books you placed on a table, you will probably be irritated. If a person you have just met stands mere inches away and stares at your face, you may feel uncomfortable. Of course, a romantic partner standing that close to you may be more than welcome. The occupation of space and the distance you maintain from others conveys messages about control, acceptance, and relationships.

Territoriality is the establishment and maintenance of space that you claim for your personal use. Knapp and Hall (2002) point out three types of territory that you may establish: primary, secondary, and public. Primary territory is space that you own or have principal control over and that is central to your life, such as your house, room, apartment, office, or car. How you maintain and control this space conveys a great deal to those around you. Decorating your home in a particular fashion not only provides you with a sense of comfort but also informs others about the type of person you may be or the types of interests you may have. Even in dorm rooms, though they are generally less than spacious, roommates find a decorative way to assert ownership of "their" areas.

You establish secondary territory, or space that is not central to your life or exclusive to you, as your own through repeated use. A good example of secondary territory is the room where your class is held. Chances are pretty good that you and your fellow students always sit in the exact same location that you sat in on the first day of class. Even though this space does not belong to you, others associate it with you because of repeated use. Accordingly, if you came to class one day and someone was sitting in "your" seat, you would probably get a little upset or at minimum be uncomfortable during class if you were forced to sit elsewhere.

Public territory is space open to everyone but available for your sole temporary occupancy, such as park benches or

Photo 3.4 From how many types of NVC can you tell that these two people like each other? (See page 82.)

seats in a movie theater. Secondary and public territory can involve the same type of physical space, such as a table at a restaurant, so consider this: If you go to the same restaurant every day for lunch and always sit at the same table, eventually it will become your secondary territory. Although it is open to everyone, once you claim that space for your temporary use, you assume exclusive control over it for the time being and would not expect anyone to violate that. Of course, there are cultural variations in the use of public territory. In the United States, for example, if you and your date went to a restaurant and were seated at a table for four, the two additional seats would remain empty regardless of whether other people were waiting to be seated. In many European countries, however, it would not be surprising if another couple you do not know were eventually seated at your table.

Markers, used to establish and announce your territory, are usually quite effective. People generally mark space by putting their "stuff" on it. Markers are especially common when using public territory because of its seemingly open and unrestricted nature. For example, when you lay a jacket over the back of a chair, you have claimed that chair. Should someone want to move the chair, he or she would probably ask your permission rather than simply removing the jacket and taking the chair. Markers are often used to indicate privacy and control, and you feel uncomfortable if someone else enters the space without permission. People meet this "invasion" with varying degrees of disapproval, but blood pressure frequently goes up (Guerrero & Floyd, 2006).

Personal Space and Distance

In addition to establishing territory as your own, you carry around with you an idea of how much actual space you should have during an interaction, and it will be affected by your status, your sex, and your liking for the person with whom you are talking. It also will be affected by the situations in which you find yourself.

Personal space refers to that space legitimately claimed or occupied by a person for the time being. Close friends are literally closer in the sense that you permit them to be in closer proximity than you do other people. You generally tend to stand closer to the people you like. In fact, if you look around, you can tell whether people are friends or strangers according to the amount of space between them.

All of us have a **body buffer zone**, a kind of imaginary aura around us that we regard as part of ourselves. People differ in the size of their body buffer zone, and if you step into the body buffer zone that someone feels is "their space," even if it is beyond what you would normally expect, you may be in for trouble. Your friends and family can enter your body buffer zone more freely than other people. You react to space and its use depending on the kind of situation in which you find yourself. An early pioneer of personal space research, E. T. Hall (1966) distinguished among intimate distance (contact to 18 inches), personal distance (18–48 inches), social distance (48–144 inches), and public distance (12–25 feet) (see Figure 3.2). Although valuable, this early research does not account

In what ways could you rearrange the space in your interaction to make another person feel more comfortable, and how would you most easily convey to that person that you are interested in what he or she is saying?

for cultural differences, and it has become accepted that people from Latino and Arab cultures require less space for each of these types of encounters than do Northern Europeans and North Americans.

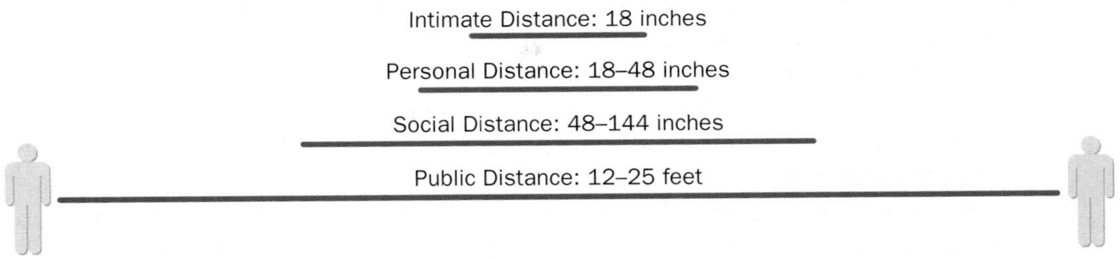

Intimate Distance: 18 inches

Personal Distance: 18–48 inches

Social Distance: 48–144 inches

Public Distance: 12–25 feet

Figure 3.2 Hall's (1966) Four Types of Personal Space

Proxemics and Everyday Life

The actual meaning of space and distance is framed by your relationships with others. What it means for someone to stand mere inches away from you could vary a great deal depending on whether he or she is a friend, an adversary, or a complete stranger. A friend moving the backpack you placed on a table in order to sit near you would mean something entirely different than if a complete stranger did it.

Your use of space and distance actually signifies or enacts these particular relationships. Individuals in subordinate roles tend to give more space to individuals in leadership positions. An employee, for example, would stand at a greater distance when talking with an employer than he or she would with a coworker, indicating the superior-subordinate nature of that relationship and enabling both interactants to perform their respective roles. Actual physical space is often laid out to indicate and perform leadership or power roles. For example, a formal chairperson of a meeting sits at one end of the table, usually in a special seat, and everyone else lines up along the length of the table at right angles to the chairperson; in contrast, a more secure or less formal leader might sit anywhere at the table. From seemingly minor physical facts about the distribution and use of space, then, you can determine relational information about the people in a setting—who is in charge and who is not—as well as the leader's preferred style of interaction, formal or informal.

Your use of space and distance is also where relational negotiation takes place. For instance, a friend who desires a more intimate relationship with you may begin standing a bit closer to gauge your reaction. Similarly, a subordinate decreasing the amount of space given to a superior may be indicating a desire for an advanced role or a more

Get into an elevator and notice how people react to being in a public space that is confined. How close do the people stand? Which way do they face? Do they make eye contact with one another? Where do they look?

equal relationship. Either attempt could be accepted or rejected depending on the other person's view of the relationship. Such relational negotiation frequently takes place in families, with adolescent sons or daughters wanting their parents to stay out of their bedrooms.

The use of space and distance will also guide your actual interactions with others and how you might approach them. If your friend has books, papers, and other material spread out over a large space, it could indicate that he or she prefers to be alone. In this case, you might ask your friend before you move these items to the side, or you might avoid going over altogether. Your instructor working in his or her office with the door wide open could be indicating that he or she is available to see students. Still, you would probably attempt to knock or at least announce yourself before entering the office, because you are essentially invading the instructor's primary space. The reactions of your friend sitting at a table or your instructor working in the office—looking up and smiling or with a harried expression—will probably dictate what you do next, which brings us to the next element of NVC.

Kinesics: Movement

Kinesics refers to the movement that takes place during the course of an interaction. While interacting, you may move around quite a bit, shift position and walk around as you talk, cross and uncross your legs, or lean forward on a table or sit back in a chair. Kinesics can be broken down into posture, gesture, and eye contact/gaze. In every case, whether separately or in combination, these cues once again convey messages about your relationship to the speaker or your audience, to the subject you are discussing, or to the situation as a whole. Often, movement is seen as either very intimate or very aggressive, especially if you move into somebody's space as we discussed with proxemics.

Posture

Posture refers to the position of your body during the course of an interaction; it may be relaxed and welcoming or tense and off-putting. For example, someone draping him- or herself over a chair will look very relaxed, and someone sitting up straight or standing to attention will not. You can probably look around the room now and see people with different postures. Even during class, you likely draw conclusions about whether people are interested just from the posture they adopt.

In an open posture, the front of the body is observable, and in closed posture, the front of the body is essentially shut off, usually because the arms are folded across the chest or the person is hunched over. Both types of posture convey the three attitudes we noted before: (1) attitudes about self (confidence, anxiety, shyness, a feeling of authority), (2) attitudes about others (liking, respect, attention), and (3) attitudes about the situation (comfort, ease). An open posture conveys positive messages, and a closed posture conveys negative messages. When someone feels "down," he or she tends to look "down," slumping over, slouching, and generally being depressed (depressed—pressed down). These postures send messages to others about a person's relaxation, attention, confidence, comfort, and willingness to communicate.

Gesture

Gesture can be defined as a movement of the body or any of its parts in a way that conveys an idea or intention or displays a feeling or an assessment of the situation. Suppose you were in a foreign country, one of your friends suffered heatstroke, and no one knew the word for *dehydrated* in that country's language. You would likely indicate your needs for water by making a "drinking" gesture.

When people think of gestures, hand or arm movements most often come to mind, but facial expressions also count as gestures for our purposes. Quite frequently, your face and the rest of your body work together to express meaning. For instance, when a person is expressing an emotion, his or her face will provide information about the exact emotion being expressed or experienced, and his or her body will provide information about its extent. You could, for example, be angry and scowling while your body is fairly loose and fluid, indicating low-intensity anger. However, you could be scowling, holding your body tight and rigid, and almost shaking, which would indicate great anger and tell others to use their knowledge of proxemics to give you plenty of space!

Gestures can be split broadly into two sorts: those that signal a feeling not expressed in words (emblems) and those that signal something said in words (illustrations). Emblematic gestures are not related to speech in the sense that they do not help illustrate what is being said, although they may clarify what a person means. Consider conductors directing bands and orchestras, police officers directing traffic, and coaches signaling plays. Emblems can nevertheless be translated into verbal expressions; for example, you recognize that bouncing the palm of your hand off your forehead means, "How stupid of me! Why didn't I think of it before?"

Illustrators

Illustrators are directly related to speech as it is being spoken and are used to visualize or emphasize its content. For example, turning your palm down and then rotating it as you describe how to unscrew a bottle cap is an illustrator, and screwing up your face while saying "This tastes disgusting" is an illustrator using facial expression. Like other NVC, gestures can also regulate interaction, and some gestures that relate to speech regulate its pace or emphasis. While making a speech, you might raise a finger to draw attention to the fact that you wish to make a key point.

Eye Contact Versus Gaze

Eye contact refers to the extent to which you look directly into the eyes of another person and how that person looks back at you. Someone who "looks you in the eye" while talking is generally seen as reliable and honest; someone with shifty eyes is treated as suspicious and untrustworthy.

Gaze—distinguished from eye contact, where both interactants look at each other—describes one person looking at

Richard Nixon and Winston Churchill each used versions of the emblematic "V is for victory" to denote different political messages. Nixon's use indicated his personal victories, and Churchill's use related to the British people's fight against Germany in World War II. Can you think of a female historical figure who used an emblematic gesture?

another and, most of the time, is seen as rewarding. Most people generally like to be looked at when they are talking to someone else. In fact, if you gaze at a speaker and smile or nod approvingly, you will probably find that the speaker pays more attention to you, looks toward you more often, and engages in eye contact with you. Try this with your instructor the next time you are in class, and see if he or she responds to you personally in this way.

Starting with the broad generalization that gaze and eye contact convey mostly positive messages, note that eye contact indicates engagement in interactions, and eye contact and orientation can start conversations or establish the likelihood of interaction. A continued positive pattern of eye contact shows that you are paying attention to someone and are interested in what he or she is saying.

Although most eye contact is positive, it can also convey negative messages. A wide-eyed stare can mean a disbelieving "Excuse me?!" or be a threat. Years ago, Ellsworth and her colleagues (Ellsworth, Carlsmith, & Henson, 1972) stood at the intersections of roads and stared at some drivers and not others. Those who were stared at tended to drive away more speedily, suggesting that a stare is a threatening stimulus to flight. Gaze can therefore be threatening and negative as much as it can be enticing and positive. Something for you to think about, then, is how this particular element of NVC helps you determine whether a positive or negative message is being sent (hint: NVC is a system of different parts that interrelate).

Eye contact or gaze is often used to gather information or acquire feedback from the speaker as you are listening and from the listener when you are talking. If you are looking at someone, you can see how he or she is doing and get a better idea of what is going on for him or her. If you are talking, this allows you to assess whether another person is paying attention, how he or she responds to what you are saying, and how he or she evaluates you.

Some people (shy people, for example), afraid that others will evaluate them negatively, tend to decrease eye contact (Bradshaw, 2006), which cuts out negative inputs from other people. For shy people, this is a distinct advantage, but it also reduces the amount of information they can gather about a listener's reaction to what they say. Many outsiders assume that decreased eye contact is evidence of other social flaws, such as deception, so a shy person who avoids eye contact through fear of feedback may eventually create an impression of being shifty and unreliable. Burgoon and colleagues (Burgoon, Coker, & Coker, 1986) found that gaze aversion produces consistently negative evaluations of interviewees. Typically, unconfident behavior (as in shy people) involves not only low eye contact but also nervous speech, poor posture, tendency for long silences in conversation, and lack of initiative in discussion.

Eye contact is also used to regulate interactions. Some characteristic patterns of eye movements go along with talk in conversations to regulate its flow. The speaker, for example, tends to look at the listener at the start and end of sentences (or paragraphs, if the speaker is telling a longer tale) but may look away during the middle parts. A listener who wishes to speak next will tend to look hard at the present speaker, and a person asking a question will look right at the person to whom it is directed, maintaining his or her gaze while awaiting a reply. Listeners tend to look at speakers more consistently than speakers look at listeners in everyday speaking. When giving a speech to a group or large audience, however, it is important that you not only look at your audience (rather than at your notes) most of the time but also distribute your gaze around the room or the group.

Interaction is further regulated through use of eye contact to manage the turn taking noted earlier, a kind of eye-based "over and out." In cultures where simultaneous speech is taken as a sign of impoliteness, rather than of active and desirable involvement in the interaction, eye contact is used to end or yield a turn (a speaker looks longer toward the audience at the end of sentences), as well as to request a turn (a listener establishes longer eye contact with a speaker in order to signal willingness to enter conversation). You leave conversation by breaking off eye contact (typically 45 seconds before departure) and then, when the talking stops, turning toward an exit.

Strategic Communication

Try to give someone directions using absolutely no gestures (you can move your lips and blink your eyes only; pretend you have a heavy shopping bag in each hand and a stiff neck). How successful were you in conveying the directions? Do you think the person could find the location you described? How did you feel while you were trying to convey the directions?

Vocalics: Voice

Vocalics, sometimes called paralanguage, refers to vocal characteristics that provide information about how verbal communication should be interpreted and how you are feeling. For example, the tone of your voice can be strained when you are angry or high-pitched when you are anxious, and your talking speed may be fast when you are excited. Vocalics indicate your degree of comfort in an interaction and whether you like the person to whom you are talking or feel upset by him or her. You can also signal to other people how you feel about what you are saying. You must manage your paralanguage when giving a speech, for example, to let people know you're interested in your topic. In contrast to verbal communication, vocalics involves the voice rather than the content of speech, referring not to what you say but to how you say it.

A main element of vocalics involves the sound of your voice (voice quality) and how it can change during the course of an interaction or a speech. Sometimes you can tell who is calling on the phone just by the way a call begins; some people do not need to identify themselves directly to you since you just know how their voices sound. Even people who do not know you can tell something about you from your accent and tone of voice. For example, your accent can give people information about where you come from (the deep South as opposed to Minnesota, for instance). The sound of your voice alone can indicate your age

What do you think when you hear a person with a Southern accent, a New York accent, or a British accent? How do you think people perceive you based on your accent?

and sex. Also, some people make decisions about your attractiveness on the basis of the sound of your voice, with some accents preferred over others.

You often use the tone or pitch of your voice to emphasize parts of the sentence that you think are the most important. A loud scream or a shout of "Fire!" or "Help!" conveys the situation as urgent in a way that a simple conversational tone would not. These aspects of vocalics are used to emphasize elements of an interaction to which an audience must pay more attention. You can make a speech more interesting, for example, by varying vocalic pitch and tone in a way that keeps the audience attentive and helps the audience identify the most important parts of the speech. Tone of voice also enables you to determine what someone really means by the words coming out of his or her mouth and is especially important when trying to determine whether or not a person is being sarcastic.

Another aspect of vocalics is speech rate, or the speed at which someone talks. When a teacher wants you to pay special attention to what is being said, he or she will sometimes slow down so you realize the importance of the point. Someone who speaks too fast is likely to be treated as nervous or stressed or possibly shy or uncomfortable in the situation. In everyday life, where people are relaxed among friends, their speech rate tends to be lively and fluent rather than stilted or halting. In stressful circumstances, however, their speech rate may be hesitant or uneven.

One surprising part of vocalics is silence. You have likely heard the seemingly contradictory phrases "Silence is golden" and "Silence is deadly." Tending to differ on the extent to which they view silence as one or the other, people evaluate silence depending on contextual and relational factors surrounding its use. Most people in the United States—especially on a date or in an interview—meet silence or a prolonged break in conversation with discomfort. Actually able to convey many messages, however, when someone does not know what to say or cannot take a turn in a conversation, silence could indicate embarrassment, anxiety, or lack of preparation as well as shyness, confusion, or disrespect. Silence can also be used to show anger or frustration, such as when you are mad at someone and give him or her the "silent treatment," or relational comfort, in that people do not feel pressured to keep the conversation going. "Shared inactivity" can be an indication of the absolute comfort in one another's presences as when you and a partner just veg out in front of the TV.

Giles (2008) shows that people can indicate their membership in a particular group or their relationship to other people by the way they use vocalic nonverbal behavior. For instance, if you are from the South, you might use a heavier accent in your conversation with others from your state or region, but you might tone down your accent when talking to people from the Northeast. Where people wish to maintain a distance from the person they are talking to, they will diverge, or hang on to differences in accent, but when they want to become closer to the other person, they will tend to converge, or match their way of talking to the other person's. You may notice yourself copying the speech styles of people you like.

Vocalics and Regulation

In addition to sending relational messages, people also use vocalics to regulate their interactions. A sharp intake of breath indicates shock, pain, or surprise; "uh-huh" or "um," known as **backchannel communication** (vocalizations by a listener that give feedback to the speaker to show interest, attention, and/or a willingness to keep listening) may be used either to encourage someone else to keep talking or to indicate that a speaker does not want to yield the floor, still has something to say, but has not yet decided what.

The most common use of vocalics in regulating your interaction is with **turn taking**, which is when you hand over speaking to another person. This hand-over happens much less obviously than does a radio form of communication, where an airline

Contrarian Challenge

Classic research claims that about 80% of the meaning of the message is conveyed nonverbally. How does "I sentence you to 5 years in jail" fit such a claim?

pilot or a trucker, for example, says "over" or "comeback" to indicate that he or she has finished speaking and wants another person to respond. In your normal interactions, you don't need to say "over" because you can tell from the speaker's tone of voice or eye movements (referring back to kinesics) that he or she wants you to begin speaking, but you still need to signal a hand-over. For example, when someone asks a question, raising the pitch of his or her voice afterward serves to prompt you that the questioner now expects an answer. You also know when people are coming to the end of what they want to say because they will generally slow down somewhat and drop the pitch of their voice. That is how students know when a lecture is coming to an end and that they can start closing their books!

Chronemics: Time

Chronemics encompasses use and evaluation of time in your interactions, including the location of events in time. For example, the significance of a romantic encounter can often be determined by when it occurs. You might see a lunch date as more informal and less meaningful than a late-night candlelit dinner. Whether you are meeting for lunch or dinner, however, your meal will have a time structure and pattern. You probably have the salad before the ice cream.

Chronemics also involves the duration of events. You have probably noticed that boring lectures seem to last forever. You may also have had the experience that people often end their college romances after about 18 months or during the spring semester, when one partner might be graduating or going away for the summer. You are quite likely to comment if you run into someone whom you have not seen for "a-a-a-ges." Also, you would probably feel the need to apologize if you left an e-mail unanswered for too long or were late for an appointment. Cultural differences in attitudes toward time also exist; some cultures especially value timely completion of tasks over attention to relationships, respect, or status, while others place the priorities exactly in reverse, feeling that it is discourteous to get down to the task before taking plenty of time to create a good relational atmosphere first.

Chronemics and Regulation of Interaction

Chronemics can affect the structure of interactions. You all have an expectation about the number of milliseconds that are supposed to elapse between the time when one person finishes speaking and when the other joins in. When this timing gets disrupted, interaction becomes uncomfortable for everybody—one reason why people who stammer or are very shy create difficulty for other people in interaction by not picking up the conversational baton when they are expected to (Bradshaw, 2006). You also recognize that when someone is really paying attention to you and is interested in what you are saying, he or she will tend to be engaged and maintain "synchrony." He or she will not allow too much time to elapse between utterances and try to synchronize his or her interaction and behavior with yours. In addition, you can indicate interest in somebody else by answering his or her questions promptly, a chronemic activity. You also convey information about your knowledge and expertise by keeping your talk flowing freely and not allowing yourself too many hesitations. Fluency and the absence of hesitation both count as chronemic elements of nonverbal communication since they are about the timing of speech.

Another important element of the timing of speech is whether or not your speech overlaps someone else's, which encompasses relational themes of the interaction. In the United States, White culture assumes that it is rude to interrupt someone, without making an apology, when he or she is talking, and interruption is often seen as a power/dominance ploy. By contrast, in African American and other cultures, it is simply rude and uncaring not to respond to someone else's talk when it is offered, and backchannel communications, such as "Amen to that," "Go on," "Then what?" "Oh yeah!" and "Is that right?" are expected. Of course, you also know that sometimes you interrupt somebody else without intending to and that overlapping of speech is sometimes just a demonstration of excitement and interest. Friends do it all the time, and it seems to be an index of the informality of their conversations. Some researchers distinguish between *interruption,* where you stop the flow of the other person speaking, and *overlap,* where you talk at the same time as the other person. In White United States culture, friends tend to overlap more often than interrupt, but in other cultures, too, overlap is a sign of involvement in close relationships. Unlike strangers, friends can in fact interrupt one another relatively freely without anyone taking offense. Some kinds of interruption simply indicate the informality and friendliness of the interaction.

Haptics: Touch

Haptics is the study of the specific nonverbal behaviors involving touch. When people get into your personal space, they will likely make actual physical contact with your most personal possession, your body. Touch is used not only as a greeting to start an interaction (a handshake or a kiss) but also in ceremonies, whether baptism, the confirming laying on of hands, holding a partner's hands while making wedding vows, or as a means of congratulation from a simple handshake to a pat on the back to those piles of players who form on top of the goal scorer in sports.

Psychologist Sidney Jourard (1971) observed and recorded how many times couples in cafés casually touched each other in an hour. The highest rates were in Puerto Rico (180 times per hour) and Paris (110 times per hour). Guess how many times per hour couples touched each other in the mainland United States? Twice! (In London, it was zero. They never touched.) Jourard also found that French parents and children touched each other three times more frequently than did American parents and children.

Heslin (1974) noted that touch, of which there are many different types, has many different functions, as shown in Table 3.2. These forms of touch show positive feelings, but each could also produce negative feelings: Someone you feel close to shakes your hand instead of hugging you, or someone you are not close to tries to hug you. Touch can also indicate influence. Have you ever seen a politician who places one arm on the back of a visiting foreign dignitary to indicate a place to which the person should move? The two actions together serve to indicate politely to the other person where the next stage of a discussion or proceedings will take place. Touch can also serve as a physiological stimulus, for example in sexual touch or from a reassuring back rub.

As with all other NVC, touch can play a role in interaction management. For example, you can touch someone on the arm to interrupt the flow of conversation. Also you both begin and end encounters with handshakes on many occasions, indicating that the beginning and ending of the interaction have essentially relational consequences because you imply, through touch, continuance of the relationship beyond the specific interaction.

Table 3.2 Heslin's (1974) Functions of Touch

Functional/ professional	Touch is permitted by the context—for example, during a medical exam, someone you hardly know may touch parts of your body that even your best friend has never seen.
Social/polite	Touch is formal—for example, a handshake.
Friendship/warmth	Touch is an expression of regard.
Love/intimacy	Touch is special, permitted only with those with whom you are close.

The Interacting System of Nonverbal Communication

In the last few pages, we have split NVC into separate parts to give a better understanding of the complicated system that makes it work, but we promised to reassemble them at the end. It has probably struck you that elements of NVC carry double messages or, at least, that they can be "read" in more than one way. A stare can be a threat or a sign of longing; a touch can be an intimate caress or a sexual harassment violation; a move toward someone can be loving or aggressive. Same behavior, different meaning! How do you know what to make of the behavior and how it should be understood?

Essentially, you can discern the meaning of NVC in four ways that recognize that it occurs as part of a system and is related to other parts of an interaction:

1. Nonverbal communication has a relationship to the words used with it. It can affect how words are understood, and words can affect how NVC is understood. Someone caressing your thigh and saying "I love you" is doing something different from someone touching your thigh and saying "Is this where it hurts?"

Listen In On Your Life

Look out for how your nonverbal behavior mirrors the behavior of people you are with. People often find that they unconsciously adopt a similar posture to another person in an interaction (for example, they fold their arms when the other person does). How often do you act the same as another person you like, and how often do you consciously differentiate yourself from someone you dislike, using nonverbal means alone?

2. Any NVC has a relationship to other NVC that happens simultaneously. If someone is staring at you with a scowl and clenched fists, you can assume that the stare is intended as a threat; if the stare is accompanied by a smile and a soft expression, it is intended as friendly. Likewise, a smile accompanied by agitated gestures, sweating, or blushing probably means the person is nervous, but someone smiling and looking relaxed with an open posture is probably feeling friendly and confident.

3. The interpretation of NVC depends on its context. If someone stares at you in class, it feels different from a stare across a crowded singles bar; a scream at a sports match probably means your team just scored, but a scream in your apartment could indicate the discovery of a spider.

4. How NVC is interpreted is also affected by your relationship to another person. If the person caressing your thigh is a nurse, you're probably right to assume that the touch is part of a treatment or medical exam, so stay there and get well. If the person is your instructor, it's time to leave—and leave quickly.

We have referenced a few of the errors and violations that can occur in NVC (such as sitting in someone else's special chair or touching someone when he or she does not want to be touched), but we have not given you direct guidance for how it can be improved. The preceding four guidelines should generally help you avoid serious errors, but we can go further and address specific ways to improve NVC overall.

Improving Your Use of Nonverbal Communication

Let's start with what you already know. People can be poor at encoding their intentions or at decoding others' meanings. The goal of improving NVC suggests immediately that you can identify errors that need to be improved or avoided.

Errors and NVC mistakes occur as part of life and cannot be avoided altogether, but violations can. A violation is a serious breach of a rule of NVC, such as invading someone's territory or personal space in the ways discussed earlier. In general, a violation openly breaks a rule that ignores the four guidelines in the previous section that help interpret the interacting system of NVC. All the negative interpretations that follow violations of NVC rules derive from the fact that the violations are taken to *indicate a negative attitude or relationship* toward the other person, usually of dislike or disrespect. Although any NVC rule can be violated, the most fateful are often violations of touch since the body is the most personal and primary area of space, and invasion of someone's body or personal space is a deeply disrespectful act.

Successful conversation and use of NVC depend in large part on how people tune in to one another and respond appropriately. Recall the earlier distinctions between encoding and decoding. Someone who is socially skilled is a good encoder *and* a good decoder, but you tend to notice more obviously when someone is bad at encoding and continually producing inappropriate NVC. For example, some very young children do not yet understand the rules and often need to be told directly, "Don't stare; it's rude" or "Look at me when I am talking to you." It is harder to notice when someone is a poor decoder and just "doesn't get it."

One way to become a better decoder is to make sure that you *attend* to whether other people pay attention to NVC and seem to understand it. A good decoder also *bonds* with the speaker and watches out for the signals that the speaker sends about comfort in the situation. A good decoder will notice when the speaker is anxious and will smile more often or reward the speaker with head nods and encouraging NVC to put him or her at ease. A good listener also *coordinates* with the speaker and responds to his or her cues so the interaction runs smoothly with no awkward silences. Skilled listeners should also *detect/decode* the undercurrents of a speaker's talk by attending carefully to eye movements and gestures that "leak" what the speaker truly feels. Finally, a good listener is *encouraging* and invites the speaker to continue, shows interest, looks at the speaker directly, is focused, and makes the speaker the center of attention in the conversation.

What about skilled encoding? A good speaker will *affirm* the listener by encoding approval and liking while talking—that is, as we have noted, by smiling or good eye contact. Good speakers also *blend* their NVC together with the talk to allow for *consistency* between what is said and what is delivered in the NVC channels. *Directness* is achieved by making sure that NVC is done clearly and unambiguously, and *emotional* clarity is presented by good signaling of what is felt. Good speakers and good actors are able to convey the emotions of their words by matching their nonverbal expression of emotion to the meaning of the words.

The skills listed in Table 3.3 can be broadly summarized by saying that two people in an interaction should not disrupt the usual patterns of normative interaction, and hence, they show the importance of NVC in regulating interaction while also sending positive messages about the other person and yourself—in short, about the relationship between the two people.

Table 3.3 Encoding and Decoding Skills

Speaker/Encoder	Listener/Decoder
Affirming	Attending
Blending	Bonding
Consistency	Coordinating
Directness	Detecting/Decoding
Emotional Clarity	Encouraging

Focus Questions Revisited

What is nonverbal communication?
Nonverbal communication is everything that communicates a message but does not include words. We looked, among other things, at space and distance, movement, vocal tone and pitch, time, gestures, touch, eye movements, and posture.

How does nonverbal communication work, and what work does it do in communication?
Nonverbal communication serves to convey attitudes about self, others, and interaction and to illustrate speech and regulate interaction.

How does nonverbal communication regulate (e.g., begin and end) interactions?
Nonverbal communication regulates interaction by initiating conversation, regulating the turns with which people speak, and defining when interactions have reached their end. It does this through eye movements, vocalics, and gestures, among other things.

What are the elements of nonverbal communication, and how do they interconnect?
Elements of NVC are proxemics, kinesics, vocalics, chronemics, and haptics. They work as an interacting system so a particular cue (for example, a stare) can be interpreted in the context of other cues (for example, a grim or friendly expression). The overall meaning of communication is determined by the combination within the system and by the frame of the relationship in which it happens.

How can you improve your use of nonverbal communication?
There are two sides of NVC that can be improved: encoding and decoding. Improvement of encoding involves better projection of your emotions and feelings; improvement of decoding involves paying more attention to the other person in an interaction and fully understanding what he or she means.

Key Concepts

backchannel communication   (p. 74)
body buffer zone   (p. 68)
chronemics   (p. 75)
decoding   (p. 56)
dynamic   (p. 57)
encoding   (p. 56)
haptics   (p. 76)
kinesics   (p. 70)

leakage   (p. 61)
personal space   (p. 68)
proxemics   (p. 67)
regulators   (p. 63)
static   (p. 57)
turn taking   (p. 75)
vocalics   (p. 73)

Questions to Ask Your Friends

- How good are your friends at telling when you are not speaking the truth?

- How good are your friends at telling when you're embarrassed, when you wish you did not have to tell them something, or when you feel uncomfortable?

- Ask your friends whether they think they could get away with telling you a lie.

Media Links

- Look for TV news stories involving police putting people into cars. What percentage of police touch the person's head? In what other circumstances, if any, do people open the car door for someone else and then touch the head of the person getting in? What do you think is being conveyed?

- How many news stories can you find where a fight got started because someone felt another person was "looking at him in a funny way" or infringing upon his personal space?

- How do TV shows use the placement of furniture to add something to the story (look at *The Office, The Cosby Show,* or *Friends*)?

Ethical Issues

- Now that you know more thoroughly some of the behaviors involved in NVC, would it be ethical for you to use this information to deceive other people?

- Would it be unethical for you to use your knowledge to reveal when other people are being deceptive?

- If a member of another culture is breaking a nonverbal rule in your culture, should you tell him or her? Why or why not?

Answers to Photo Captions

Photo 3.1 ■ There are static cues and dynamic cues: Static cues include the hairstyle, wrist band, chain, necklace, and tattoo, all identifying him as a "punk." Although this is a still photo, he has taken a posture that in everyday conversation would be part of a dynamic system of movement. His posture is somewhat defiant, his expression somewhat condescending or possibly threatening or hinting at menace.

Photo 3.2 ■ Bodily adornment can create images of power and intimidation in enemies. People sometimes adopt body modifications in order to raise their status or inspire fear.

Photo 3.3 ■ Nonverbal communication regulates interaction first through recognition (we recognize someone as the individual he or she is by sight, by touch, or in the case of animals and human beings by smell/fragrance), and then there are various rituals of behavior that begin interactions (catching someone's eye, handshakes, bowing, or sniffing) and behaviors that are used to end interactions, such as a handshake, a bow, a wave, or a wag of the tail.

Photo 3.4 ▪ You can tell they like each other from at least the following: physical closeness, touching together parts of the body not normally touched with strangers (thighs and calves), and smiling at an intimate distance. Their similar dress codes and open postures indicate comfort with each other; the woman's body (her left shoulder) and head lean toward the man. There are also static cues: Where they are sitting is an intimate place.

Student Study Site

Visit the study site at **www.sagepub.com/ciel** for e-flashcards, practice quizzes, and other study resources.

References

Bradshaw, S. (2006). Shyness and difficult relationships: Formation is just the beginning. In C. D. Kirkpatrick, S. W. Duck, & M. K. Foley (Eds.), *Relating difficulty: The processes of constructing and managing difficult interaction* (pp. 15–41). Mahwah, NJ: Lawrence Erlbaum.

Burgoon, J. K., Coker, D. A., & Coker, R. A. (1986). Communicative effects of gaze behavior: A test of two contrasting explanations. *Human Communication Research, 12,* 495–524.

Duck, S. W. (2007). *Human relationships* (4th ed.). London: Sage.

Ellsworth, P. C., Carlsmith, J. M., & Henson, A. (1972). The stare as a stimulus to flight in human subjects: A series of field experiments. *Journal of Personality and Social Psychology, 21,* 302–311.

Giles, H. (2008). Communication accommodation theory. In L. A. Baxter & D. O. Braithwaite (Eds.), *Engaging theories in interpersonal communication* (pp. 161–173). Thousand Oaks, CA: Sage.

Guerrero, L. K., & Floyd, K. (2006). *Nonverbal communication in relationships.* Mahwah, NJ: Lawrence Erlbaum.

Hall, E. T. (1966). *The hidden dimension.* New York: Doubleday/Anchor.

Heslin, R. (1974). *Steps toward a taxonomy of touching.* Paper presented at the meeting of the Midwestern Psychological Association, Chicago.

Jourard, S. M. (1971). *Self-disclosure.* New York: Wiley.

Kendon, A., & Ferber, A. (1973). A description of some human greetings. In R. P. Michael & J. H. Crook (Eds.), *Comparative ecology and behavior of primates* (pp. 591–668). New York: Academic Press.

Knapp, M. L., & Hall, J. A. (2002). *Nonverbal communication in human interaction* (5th ed.). New York: Holt, Rinehart, and Winston.

Manusov, V., & Patterson, M. L. (2006). *Handbook of nonverbal communication.* Thousand Oaks, CA: Sage.

Remland, M. S. (2004). *Nonverbal communication in everyday life* (2nd ed.). New York: Houghton Mifflin.

Seiter, J. S., & Sandry, A. (2003). Pierced for success? The effects of ear and nose piercing on perceptions of job candidates' credibility, attractiveness, and hirability. *Communication Research Reports 20*(4), 287–298.

4

Listening

What if we told you that we could provide you with the secret to academic success, career advancement, and improved relationships? It does not involve giving copies of this book to your instructors, employers, friends, and family—although that is a tremendous idea! Imagine the look of joy on their faces when they open the package and see their very own copy of Duck and McMahan, the perfect gift for the young and young at heart! OK...sorry for the shameless self-promotion. The truth is, though, we can tell you the secret to these things, and it is something many people rarely consider: listening.

Effective listening entails more than merely going through the motions of the listening process. Effective listening means being an active, engaged, critical, and relationally aware listener who recognizes and overcomes the many obstacles to listening encountered in everyday communication.

In this chapter, we discuss the objectives for listening, such as relational development, gaining and comprehending information, critical evaluation, enjoyment, and therapeutic goals. We also address the process of active listening and discuss how listening and hearing are not the same thing, even though the terms *listening* and *hearing* are often used interchangeably. Discussions of listening frequently do not go beyond the active listening process, but communication involves more than simply listening carefully and intently. We specifically examine engaged listening and relational listening as we discuss how people may go beyond active listening in the communication process.

You do not have to read this book to realize that people listen more effectively on some occasions than on others; however, you may not be fully aware of the many obstacles that people actually face when listening. Accordingly, we address these obstacles and discuss how you might overcome them. You may very well be a listening champion once you finish studying this chapter! Even if you do not receive an award for listening, your listening skills will significantly improve, assisting you in school, your career, and your relationships.

The final part of this chapter is dedicated to critical listening. Being critical does not necessarily entail finding fault or disagreeing with messages, but it does involve determining their accuracy, legitimacy, and value. This process may lead just as often to a positive evaluation of a message as to a negative evaluation of a message. We discuss the prevalence of critical evaluation in everyday life and examine the four elements of critical evaluation. We also explore the use of fallacious arguments, those that seem legitimate but are in reality based on faulty reasoning or insufficient evidence. Fallacious arguments, actually quite evident in everyday communication, appear in many of the commercials and advertisements you come across each day. After reading this chapter, you will be better equipped to recognize—and not be fooled by—these arguments.

Focus Questions

- Why is listening important enough to have an entire chapter devoted to it?
- What are the objectives of listening?
- What does it mean to listen actively?
- What are engaged and relational listening?
- Why do people sometimes struggle when listening?
- What is critical listening, and why is it so important?
- What are fallacious arguments?

What Is the Importance of Listening in Everyday Communication?

Listening is the communication activity in which people engage most frequently. In fact, studies conducted over the past 80 years have consistently ranked listening as the most frequent communication activity (Barker, Edwards, Gaines, Gladney, & Holley, 1980; Janusik & Wolvin, 2006; Rankin, 1928; Weinrauch & Swanda, 1975). One of the most recent studies examining the amount of time spent listening found that people dedicate nearly 12 hours daily to listening-related activities, such as talking with friends, attending class, participating in a business meeting, or listening to music on an iPod (Janusik & Wolvin, 2006). In other words, you probably spend half of each day listening!

As frequently as people engage in listening, its significance in daily life is not always given a lot of consideration. Since listening is so pervasive, people may tend to take this essential communication activity for granted. Perhaps the most mundane of all everyday relational activities (Halone & Pechioni, 2001, p. 60), listening is nevertheless crucial to everyday interactions in a number of important contexts.

For example, listening—often the primary channel of instruction at all levels of education—is a fundamental element in instruction and key to academic success.

One study revealed that student listening accounted for 90% of classroom time at the secondary and college levels (Taylor, 1964). If you are enrolled in a number of lecture-based courses, this finding is probably not surprising. Beyond the sheer bulk of time dedicated to listening in instruction, effective listening can be directly linked to academic achievement (Conaway, 1982). Listening is also a critical component in the relationships that develop between students and their instructors and between students and their academic advisers. Both instructor-student and adviser-advisee relationships demand effective listening by everyone involved. Ironically, while listening is the primary method of instruction and is so fundamental to academic achievement, it remains the least-taught type of communication skill. Listening has been described as "the most neglected [communication] skill at all educational levels" (Wolvin & Coakley, 1996, p. 33).

Effective listening skills are also crucial to career success and advancement. Employers frequently rank listening as one of the most sought-after skills (Curtis, Winsor, & Stephens, 1989; Maes, Weldy, & Icenogle, 1997; Winsor, Curtis, & Stephens, 1997; Wolvin & Coakley, 1991). Surveying the importance of listening in all professions and its significance in developing occupational areas, one listening scholar concluded "job success and development of all employees, regardless of title, position, or task will continue to be directly related to the employees' attitudes toward, skills in, and knowledge about listening" (Steil, 1997, p. 214).

Effective listening also plays a fundamental role in relationship development and maintenance. Those relationships in which both partners engage in effective listening tend to be successful, long lasting, and positive, while relationships in which one or both partners fail to engage in effective listening tend to struggle and provide less satisfaction and enjoyment. Effective listening is an essential component of every action that takes place within relationships at all stages of development.

Listening Objectives

People generally have reasons for listening. While they may have a primary objective for listening, a single communicative exchange can have multiple listening goals. We discuss these listening goals in isolation, but keep in mind that all listening situations may entail more than one objective.

Relational Development and Enhancement

You may engage in listening for the development and enhancement of relationships. Actually, you can gain a greater understanding of your relationship with another person even when it is not being discussed directly. When the relationship is being discussed, however, listen carefully. Granted, deep relational discussions are not as common as the everyday interactions that develop and enhance relationships, but they are certainly not absent from relationships. In these cases, careful listening is required to better understand yourself, your partner, and the relationship.

Gaining and Comprehending Information

People also listen to gain and comprehend information. As a student, you are likely well aware of this listening objective as you listen to lectures during class or to a classmate during a class discussion. Other examples include listening to someone on a help line explain how to retrieve a lost computer file, listening to a salesclerk describe the difference between two products, and listening to a friend provide directions to a party.

Critical Listening

The goals of critical listening include evaluating the accuracy of a message as well as its value in a given situation. For example, you may listen critically when someone is trying to sell you an automobile, offering career advice, or justifying his or her actions within your relationships. Critical listening may, but will not always, lead to negative evaluation or dismissal of a message. You may decide, for example, that the automobile offer is good, the career advice is beneficial, and the behavior taken within a relationship was justified. We discuss critical listening and the evaluation of fallacious arguments later in this chapter. It is included briefly here because of its position as not only a type of listening but also an objective of listening. Furthermore, placing critical listening and listening to gain and comprehend information together highlights the probability of multiple listening objectives occurring within the same communicative event. During class lectures and discussions, for example, you listen to gain information at the same time you evaluate that information using what you have already discussed in class and what you already know about communication and relationships.

Enjoyment and Appreciation

People also listen for enjoyment or appreciation: listening to a friend tell a story about a recent trip, listening to songs on an MP3 player or a radio, listening to the dialogue of a favorite movie, or listening to crickets chirp and birds sing while you walk through a wooded area. The objective of these listening experiences is to gain pleasure, for example by listening to music: A particular song may always cheer you up when you are sad, may remind you of an enjoyable past experience, or may just make you smile when you hear it on the radio. Music, nature sounds, and other aural stimuli are often used as part of relaxation processes. Sometimes the enjoyment experienced is derived from appreciation of the message. Carefully selected words can enhance the value of a message and increase the pleasure derived from your communication with others (Baxter & DeGooyer, 2001).

Listening to a favorite song from the past can often evoke memories of sights and smells. Which of your favorite songs has this effect on you? Why do you think music affects people?

Therapeutic Listening

Another listening objective surrounds therapeutic listening, or enabling someone to talk through a problem or concern (Wolvin & Coakley, 1996). Examples of therapeutic listening include listening to a coworker complain about a customer or client, listening to a sibling's concerns about a parent, listening to a friend's

Photo 4.1 What type of environment should be developed for therapeutic listening? (See page 114.)

concerns about an upcoming examination, and listening to neighbor talk about financial difficulties.

Therapeutic listening necessitates the creation of a supportive listening environment in which the sender becomes aware that he or she can speak openly and feels comfortable about expressing him- or herself. In addition to verbal encouragement and approval, positive non-verbal behaviors can be used to provide the sender with a sense of comfort and acceptance.

Therapeutic listening also requires you to listen with **empathy**, which entails viewing a problem from the perspective of another person to understand his or her thinking and how he or she is feeling. Empathy is not the same thing as **sympathy**, or expressing an awareness of another person's difficulty or concern. Providing empathy involves not only sympathy but also an attempt to understand and feel another person's experience. Empathy does not mean you must possess the same feelings of sorrow or concern as the other person; it means attempting to put yourself in his or her situation and viewing things from that perspective. If a family member of someone you know dies, you will not necessarily experience the same feelings of loss or pain. However, you may have felt a similar loss in the past and, as a result, be able to conceive of what that person is experiencing and feeling.

Also required of therapeutic listening is that you determine what another person desires from an interaction. The person might simply be needing to express certain anxieties or frustrations, might be seeking approval or justification for feelings, or might be seeking advice and counsel about appropriate actions. Determining what another person actually desires from an exchange is sometimes difficult. Generally, expressing an understanding of his or her situation would be a minimum response. Whether he or she wants additional input, such as approval for his or her feelings or advice about potential actions, may be gleaned from the conversation. The person may say such things as "Do you think I am just being silly?" "Would you see it this way?" or "What would you do if you were in my situation?" This type of conversation, of course, requires that you listen carefully throughout the interaction to determine what the person actually desires from the exchange.

As a final note, therapeutic listening requires recognizing your limitations. In dire situations or moments of deep despair, people may require more help than you can provide. In such cases, you might encourage and assist them in finding more-appropriate and better-equipped support, such as from a professional counselor or an assistance organization. Sometimes offering such guidance is the most helpful and appropriate action you can take.

The Process of Active Listening

Many people use the terms **hearing** and **listening** interchangeably. Although connected, they are not the same. Hearing is the passive physiological act of receiving sound that takes place when sound waves hit your eardrums. If someone starts beating on a desk, the resulting sound waves will travel through the air and hit your eardrum, the act of which is an example of hearing. As a passive act, hearing does not require much work or energy to occur; you can hear without really having to think about it. Listening is the active process of receiving, attending to, interpreting, and responding to symbolic activity. As opposed to hearing, listening is active because it requires a great deal of work and energy to accomplish. It is also referred to as a process rather than an act, since multiple steps or stages are involved.

Receiving

The first step in the listening process is the act of **receiving** sensory stimuli as sound waves travel from the source of the sound to your eardrums. As mentioned above, listening and hearing are connected, and receiving is the point at which that connection is established. As you continue reading, keep in mind that the entire listening process is not limited to only aural stimuli. Multiple sensory channels, including taste, touch, smell, and sight, can be used to make sense of a message you have received.

Attending

Attending to stimuli, the second step in the listening process, occurs when you perceive and focus on stimuli. Just because stimuli are received does not mean that you will recognize their presence or direct your attention to them. Imagine approaching a friend whose concentration is on a book (newspaper, television program, computer screen, ballgame, or any other object or activity). Although you greet him by saying hello or his name, he does not seem to recognize you are speaking and continues to focus solely on the book. You speak again, a little louder this time, and still receive no response. You may have to tap him on the shoulder, hit him over the head, or practically scream to get his attention away from that book. You are not being ignored; he just does not realize you are speaking to him. The sound waves are hitting his eardrums, but he is not attending to them.

You are constantly being inundated with competing stimuli, only some of which you pick up. The stimuli that receive your attention are generally those you deem most necessary to accomplish the task at hand. In a conversation with your boss about an important project that must be completed by the end of the day, for example, you will probably attempt to concentrate on what she is saying rather than on competing stimuli, such as other conversations taking place nearby or music playing in the background.

Although you may attempt to focus primarily on those stimuli that enable you to complete your task, it is sometimes difficult to maintain your focus. Imagine you are listening to a lecture in class and attempting to focus on your instructor's message. Two people sitting in the row behind you start talking about an upcoming assignment while the instructor is still delivering the lecture, and you begin to focus less attention on the instructor's message and more attention on the disturbance behind you. A car playing loud bass music then passes by the building and also competes for your attention. The air conditioner or heating unit kicks on, and the hum of the air briefly distracts you from the lecture. All of these stimuli are now competing for your attention, and attending to the lecture becomes increasingly difficult. The truth is, listening is not easy but takes a great deal of work and effort. There is a reason it is referred to as an active process!

Interpreting

The third step in the listening process, known as **interpreting**, is when you assign meaning to sounds and symbolic activity. You use multiple sensory channels and accompanying stimuli when listening, especially sight and visual stimuli. Returning to the earlier example of a person beating on a desk, if you see his or her hand hitting the desk each time that sound is received, this cue will assist you in making sense of what you hear. Likewise, visually perceiving a smile or a scowl when a person is speaking to you will help determine whether he or she intended a caustic remark as a sarcastic joke or as a serious retort.

Responding

An additional step in the listening process, **responding** is essentially your reaction to the message or communication of another person. Your response, or feedback, to messages occurs throughout the entire communication process and not just after a message has been received. Reacting while receiving a message is an example of the continuous nature of nonverbal communication. Even though you may not express yourself verbally while another person is speaking, you may express yourself nonverbally as you react to a message being received.

Responding to a message while it is being received shows another person you are indeed listening to what he or she is saying. Imagine the difficulty of talking with someone who does not react to your message. Instead, this person simply stares back at you with a glazed look in her eyes and no change in facial expression or body posture. You would probably decide to either stop talking or provide this person with immediate medical attention.

In addition to letting someone know you are listening, responding while a message is being received enables the sender to know how you feel about the message. Traditional positive feedback or response to a message includes leaning forward, smiling, and nodding your head in agreement, while negative feedback or response includes leaning away from the source, frowning, and shaking your head in disagreement. Feedback can also include looks of shock, excitement, boredom, and confusion—all of which will impact what comes next in the message. Your instructors rely on such feedback during class to determine the development and path of lectures and discussions. If students appear intrigued by a particular topic, the instructor may choose to spend a bit more time addressing it in class than originally planned. If students appear confused, the instructor may offer additional examples or explain the topic in another way. These same behaviors occur during public presentations as speakers respond relationally to the audience.

After receiving a message, you may respond with verbal feedback in which you explain your interpretation of the message. **Reflecting**, sometimes referred to as paraphrasing, involves summarizing what another person has said in your own words to convey your understanding of the message ("I understand you to mean that our team has until the end of the week to finish the project"). Sometimes these reflections or paraphrases are accompanied by requests for clarification or approval ("Do you mean it will be impossible to receive my order by the first of the month?"). Reflecting primarily assists in ensuring accurate understanding of the message, but it serves the secondary function of exhibiting attentiveness to the message and concern about its accurate interpretation.

Engaged and Relational Listening

For quite some time, the process of active listening described above has been viewed as the ideal method of listening. It has been included in many communication textbooks and corporate training sessions throughout the years. Acknowledging the responsibilities of both the source and the listener in the communication process, active listening demands that the listener fully take part in the communication process by attempting to accurately interpret a message as it was intended and by responding to the message source. This description is correct for the most part; however, participating in the communication process involves more than listening carefully to what is said, even if you listen intently and can repeat it. A tape recorder can accomplish both of these things. We are not saying that active listening is wrong; we are saying that it is not enough. Two other types of listening are necessary for truly effective communication to take place: engaged listening and relational listening.

Engaged Listening

Engaged listening entails making a personal relational connection with the source of a message that results from the source and the receiver actively working together to create shared meaning and understanding. Not just listening actively, engaged listening involves caring, trusting, wanting to know more, and feeling excited, enlightened, attached, and concerned.

Disengaged Listening

Perhaps the best way to explain what we mean by engaged listening is by first demonstrating what it is *not*—for example, that irritating little animated character that comes with some computer operating systems and keeps showing up and asking you dumb questions about what you are doing. Usually, it appears when it is least wanted, shows no personal interest in your activity, and lacks any recognizable form of social skills. Many people turn it off (and are turned off by it). The character does not *engage* you, though it appears to be actively listening ("Hi! I see you are writing a breakup letter. The format for a breakup letter is…").

Other examples of disengaged listening come from standard attempts to be friendly and positive in boilerplate responses to technical support questions, apologies from the bank/airline/hotel, and recorded telephone messages while you are on hold. Most of these responses start off saying how important you are while the rest of the message in both form and content conveys a contrasting meaning. For example, if your call is really so important, why have you been on hold for 20 minutes? If technical support providers really spend their lives hoping to provide you with personalized service as you wrestle with a problem, why do they simply add your name to a generic, prewritten response already given to thousands of other people?

Perhaps the most obvious example of being actively involved but not engaged emerges in the nonverbal attentiveness that managers and other customer service providers learn during training courses. Taught many of the active listening response behaviors described earlier, such as eye contact and displays of warmth and understanding, the really bad managers and customer service providers learn to do this without ever learning engagement. They simply go through the motions, with no real meaning underlying their behaviors.

Engaged Listening for a Transactional World

Engaged listening accompanies the view of communication as a transaction rather than a mere action or interaction. If communication were merely an action or interaction, active listening would be more than sufficient; however, communication, more than the sending or exchanging of symbols, involves the construction and negotiation of shared meaning between

Make Your Case

Recall an experience with a customer service representative in which you felt that you were not listened to. What about the customer service representative's responses made you feel this way? If you were training customer service providers, how would you prepare them to be good listeners?

people and the personal connections that they subsequently develop. Communication is a transactional process that demands engaged listening to be effective.

Engaged Listening and Deeper Levels of Understanding

Engaged listening enables you to grasp a deeper understanding of the message that goes beyond what can be achieved through mere active listening. Take reflection, the routine approach to active listening described earlier. While you may be able to paraphrase or repeat what you hear, this ability does not guarantee you will actually understand the overtones of what is said. The *gist* can be formulated in a reflection (what is actually said), but that is not necessarily the *upshot* (key part or importance of what is said). For example, active listeners may be able to understand and "reflect" that when someone says, "As a father, I am against the occupation of Iraq," he is stating opposition to the situation in a foreign country. Active yet disengaged listeners, however, may miss the deeper significance of the first three words. Apparently irrelevant to the rest of the sentiment expressed, they were probably uttered because they are central to *the speaker's view of self* and to *the speaker's view of his relationship with others* and therefore constitute a major part of what he wants to tell the world. Engaged listeners would be able to pick up on this additional meaning.

Relational Listening

Relational listening involves recognizing, understanding, and addressing the interconnection of relationships and communication. Vital to understanding how your personal and social relationships are intrinsically connected with communication,

Photo 4.2 What must be considered when engaging in relational listening? (See page 114.)

listening relationally will also enhance your understanding of your personal relationships and the meaning of communication taking place. When engaging in relational listening, you must address two features of communication and relationships: first, how communication impacts the relationship and, second, how the relationship impacts communication.

All communication between people in a relationship will impact that relationship somehow. Some exchanges may have a greater impact than others, but all communication will exert influence on the relationship. Relational listening entails recognizing this salient feature of communication, considering how a given message impacts the relationship, and addressing this impact in an appropriate manner. The relationship people share will also influence what is (or is not) communicated, how it is communicated, and its meaning. Relational listening when receiving a message would thus entail addressing the questions listed in Table 4.1.

Table 4.1 Questions to Consider When Receiving a Message

1.	What impact does this message have on my understanding of the relationship?
2.	What impact may this message have on the other person's understanding of the relationship?
3.	Does this message correspond with my understanding of this relationship?
4.	Is something absent from this message that would correspond with my understanding of this relationship?
5.	Is this message being communicated in a manner that corresponds with my understanding of this relationship?
6.	What does this message mean based on my understanding of this relationship?
7.	What does this message tell me about the other person's understanding of this relationship?

How you answer these questions will determine the actions that result from the message you receive. First, these questions will guide your actual response to the message, given your relational understanding of its meaning and its impact on your relationship. Second, your answers to these questions will change your perception and understanding of the relationship. Sometimes these changes in perception and understanding will be quite profound, while other times your perception and understanding will be only slightly modified. All communication will change your relationship, once again underscoring the importance of listening.

Recognizing and Overcoming Listening Obstacles

Effective listening is fundamental in the development of shared meaning and understanding, allowing you to comprehend and appreciate the perspectives of others and providing others with insight about you. It accounts for many of the positive attributes

Strategic Communication

Listening has a profound impact on classroom performance. As you explore obstacles to effective listening, consider how you can enhance your listening abilities in the classroom by recognizing and overcoming these obstacles.

derived from our interactions with others. Yet, while effective listening can lead to many positive outcomes, ineffective listening (frequently resulting from obstacles inherent in and associated with listening) can lead to equally negative outcomes and cause problems in your relationships.

Difficulties in communication and disagreements occurring in relationships can often be attributed to ineffective listening, a result of the many obstacles to listening that people may encounter in everyday life. Listening obstacles and the consequence of ineffective listening are just as much a part of everyday communication as effective listening. In this section of the chapter, we discuss listening obstacles along with suggestions for overcoming them. Recognizing these obstacles and the detrimental impact they have on everyday communication is the first step in overcoming them, so let's get started.

Environmental Distractions

Environmental distractions—probably a listening obstacle with which you were already familiar before reading this book—result from the physical location where listening takes place (Wood, 2009). If you have ever tried listening to a friend when loud music is playing at a bar or restaurant, for example, or if people are whispering in class while you are attempting to listen to your instructor, you already know well that the environment can hinder effective listening.

However, a host of environmental distractions can obstruct listening, and these distractions go beyond competing sounds that make it difficult to hear and pay attention. The temperature of a room can distract you from fully listening if it happens to be uncomfortably warm or cool. Activity and movements of people not involved in a conversation can also distract you from focusing on a message being received. Consider what happens when you eat at a restaurant with someone and you sit facing a wall and your friend sits facing the entire restaurant. You generally find it much easier to focus on the conversation because you are less distracted, but your friend finds it more difficult to focus on the messages because of competing stimuli—watching other diners coming and going, watching the servers milling about, and even eavesdropping on the conversations of others (Gumpert & Drucker, 1997).

Medium Distractions

Medium distractions result from limitations or problems inherent in certain media and technology, such as mobile phones or Internet connections. You have probably needed to include the phrases "Are you still there?" and "Can you hear me now?" in a conversation with someone when at least one of you was using a cell phone. You also likely have continued talking long after a call has been disconnected only to realize the disconnection when your phone starts ringing in your ear. Such distractions make it very difficult not only to pick up on the words being spoken but also to fully concentrate on the message. Similar to problems encountered with cell phones, a slow Internet connection can also make listening problematic during a videoconference or link-up in which there are extended delays or the sounds and images do not correspond. Problems involving poor connections and delays also occur when using instant and text messaging, making it very difficult to concentrate on the messages being exchanged.

Source Distractions

Source distractions result from auditory and visual characteristics of the message source. Vocal characteristics—for example, an unfamiliar or uncharacteristic tone and quality of voice, extended pauses, and such repeated nonfluencies as *um, uh,* or *you know*—can distract you from listening to someone's message. A person's physical appearance, nonverbal behavior, and artifacts, such as clothing or jewelry, may also serve as distractions. You might find it difficult to listen to someone who is overly animated or insists on standing too close to you. Particularly loud or flashy outfits may also distract you from focusing on a person's message.

Factual Diversion

Often a problem students experience when taking notes while listening to a lecture in class, **factual diversion** occurs when so much emphasis is placed on attending to every detail of a message that the main point becomes lost. In fact, one study found students cite this problem as the most frequent listening obstacle (Golen, 1990). They become so intent on documenting every single detail that they lose the main point of the discussion. Imagine you are in a history course studying the American Revolution. The instructor is discussing Paul Revere's "midnight ride," which just so happens to be her area of expertise. As a result, throughout the discussion she offers multiple details about this infamous ride, including the type of buttons on Revere's jacket, the color and name of his horse, the temperature, and even what he ate for breakfast that morning. You begin to furiously write them all down in your notes. In fact, you note every single detail but one—the purpose of his ride! You know the color and name of his horse but not what he was doing on top of it. When you focus too much on every detail of a message, you very likely will miss the main idea.

Semantic Diversion

Semantic diversion takes place when people are distracted by words or phrases used in a message through negative response or unfamiliarity. People tend to respond positively or negatively to words they encounter. The intensity of this response will vary, with some words eliciting a strong or weak response in one direction or the other (Osgood, Suci, & Tannenbaum, 1957). Semantic diversion occurs when your response to a certain word used during a message causes you to focus unnecessary attention on that word or prevents you from listening to the rest of the message. For example, you may hear a word that elicits a strong negative response, such as a racial or sexual slur, and focus on your feelings about that word rather than fully attend to the message.

Semantic diversion also involves letting unfamiliar words or phrases cause us to stop listening to or shift our attention away from the message. People often encounter unrecognizable words in a message; for instance, during a lecture your instructors may occasionally use a word with which you are unfamiliar. At this point in the lecture, you may focus undue attention on that word by becoming preoccupied with determining its meaning, wondering why it was used in the message and whether you should be familiar with the term. You spend so much time pondering that single word or phrase that you do not attend to those that follow and thus miss a great deal of the message.

Content (Representational) Listening

Content (representational) listening occurs when people focus on the content level of meaning, or literal meaning, rather than the social or relational levels of meaning. The presentational nature of the symbols takes them beyond mere representation; that is, words should not always be taken literally. Instead, your words and actions often have an underlying meaning. The social and relational meaning of words and other symbols can be derived from the relationships of the interactants along with the interactional context and other factors. Content listening occurs when you focus solely on the surface level of meaning and fail to recognize or engage in determining deeper levels of meaning. A colleague may remark, "This project I have been working on is more difficult than I anticipated." If you listen only at the content level, you may see this statement as straightforward; however, it may very well have a deeper meaning: Listening at a deeper level may uncover that your colleague needs your assistance, seeks words of motivation, or is determining if your relationship is one that would provide such support. Content listening does not engage in seeking the deeper levels of meaning inherent in most messages and only focuses on surface-level meaning.

Selective Listening

Selective listening occurs when people focus on the points of a message that correspond with their views and interests and pay less attention to those that do not. The old saying "You only hear what you want to hear" may sound familiar. After reading the earlier part of this chapter, you of course want to change it to "You only *listen* to what you want to *listen* to," but this version admittedly does not strike the same chord as the original. This old saying essentially encompasses what is meant by engaging in selective listening: People pick up on the parts of a message that correspond with their views or that they find most interesting and disregard the rest. Imagine meeting a friend for lunch when you are particularly hungry. Upon meeting your friend, she begins telling you about her morning. You drift in and out of the conversation until she asks what restaurant you prefer. At that moment, you become very interested in the conversation and focus on what is being discussed.

Selective listening quite often occurs during disagreements with other people. Envision a discussion with a romantic partner during which you are presented with a series of mistakes that he or she perceives you as having committed during the course of your relationship. We know you are probably an innocent little lamb, but let's pretend you are guilty of many of the transgressions of which you stand accused but still do not view yourself as a bad partner. You let many of the

Photo 4.3 Why are wandering thoughts so common? (See page 114.)

accusations pass without much consideration until one of which you are innocent comes along. Suddenly, you become quite engaged in the conversation and proclaim your innocence and goodness in the relationship. In doing so, you focus on the area of the message that corresponds with your point of view and that you can most efficiently defend, and you ignore the areas of the message that counteract your particular view and cannot be adequately defended.

Egocentric Listening

Egocentric listening occurs when people focus more on their message and self-presentation than on the message of the other person involved in an interaction. This type of listening is frequently observed during disagreements or arguments when people concentrate so much on what they are going to say next that they fail to listen to others. Perhaps you are in the middle of a heated discussion with a rival coworker and have just come up with a brilliant line that will put him in his place. Thinking about how great this line will be, you cannot wait for his lips to stop moving so you can nail him. The problem is that you have stopped listening to your coworker. You are so absorbed in developing and presenting your own message that you have failed to listen to his.

Wandering Thoughts

Wandering thoughts occur when you daydream or think about things other than the message being presented. This lack of attention happens to everyone from time to time. No matter how intent you are on focusing on a message, your mind wanders and you start thinking about other things. Consider listening to a lecture in class when your mind starts to wander. You think about a high school classmate, a pet you used to own, the great parking space you found last week, whether or not you have received any new e-mail messages, and a scene from *High School Musical* that you have seen at least 20 times. Wandering thoughts are caused not necessarily by lack of interest in the topic but rather by the connection between the rate of speech and the ability to process information, which can directly impact listening comprehension (Preiss & Gayle, 2006). People speak on average between 100 and 150 words per minute, but listeners process information at a rate of between 400 and 500 words per minute. You can process a speaker's words faster than they can come out of his or her mouth! An effective way to overcome this obstacle is to take advantage of the extra time by mentally summarizing what the speaker is saying. This strategy will enable you to remain focused, as well as increase your understanding of the message.

Experiential Superiority

Experiential superiority takes place when people fail to fully listen to someone else because they believe that they possess more or superior knowledge and experience than the other person (Pearson & Nelson, 2000). If you have worked at the same job for a number of years, you might choose not to listen to a recently hired employee's suggestion about your work. You might feel that because you have more experience in the position, you do not need to listen because you will not hear anything new. Unfortunately, the new hire's suggestion might be good, but you will never know because you did not listen.

Status of the Other

Status of the other becomes an obstacle to listening when a person's rank, reputation, or social position leads people to dismiss or fail to critically examine a message. The status of the other as an obstacle to effective listening may be associated with experiential superiority, but the distinction is that the status of the other does not deal with *your* knowledge or experience but that of others. If someone does not have favorable credentials, you may dismiss his or her message without fully listening to it, feeling that the message will not have value or may be erroneous. The status of the other person will also impact the extent to which you critically engage a message. People tend to be more critical of messages from individuals of equal status than of those from higher-status individuals. For instance, you may not critically evaluate a message from your supervisor because you assume he or she will be correct (Pearson & Nelson, 2000).

Past Experience With the Other

Past experience with the other becomes an obstacle to listening when previous encounters with a person lead people to dismiss or fail to critically examine a message. You may know people who habitually lie or who seem to be wrong about nearly everything they say, and your past experience with these individuals may compel you to not listen to them. Although they may have something worthwhile to say, you will never know because you decided not to listen. Of course, the opposite holds true as well. Perhaps you know someone who always seems to provide you with good information and strong advice. Similar to listening to someone of a higher status, you may accept this person's message without any critical thought or evaluation. The message could have problems, but you do not engage in its critical evaluation because you assume it is sound and worthwhile.

Message Complexity

Message complexity becomes an obstacle to listening when a person finds a message so complex or confusing that he or she stops listening (Wood, 2009). At times, you may listen to a person discussing a topic that you feel is beyond your grasp. You may try to listen intently to comprehend what is being discussed, but you just find it too confusing and difficult to understand. In this situation, you feel tempted to stop listening because you believe you cannot glean anything valuable from paying further attention. You might, however, actually gain some understanding from continuing to listen, and the discussion might actually start making sense. Unfortunately, you will lose this understanding if you continue to ignore the remainder of the message.

> **Listen In On Your Life**
>
>
> Which of your friends, family members, classmates, or coworkers would you consider *good* listeners? What behaviors do these people enact when interacting with others? In what ways could their listening still improve?
>
> Which of your friends, family members, classmates, or coworkers would you consider *poor* listeners? What behaviors do these people enact when interacting with others? In what ways could their listening improve?

Critical Listening

Critical listening involves analyzing and evaluating the accuracy, legitimacy, and value of messages and is part of the more general process of critical evaluation of everything in life. Being critical does not necessarily mean being negative or finding fault with a message. Students often see the term *critical* and initially believe that critical listening entails disagreement or disapproval. However, critical listening can just as easily result in a positive evaluation of a message. Much like movie critic Roger Ebert, who rates movies with either a "thumbs down" or a "thumbs up," as a critical listener, you may evaluate messages positively or negatively. In addition, a message will likely have both positive and negative qualities, in which case you must decide whether the positive attributes outweigh the negative ones or vice versa. Few messages can be evaluated as entirely negative or entirely positive, with the actual evaluation ranking somewhere in between. Rather than "thumbs up" and "thumbs down," perhaps "thumb slightly askew upward" and "thumb slightly askew downward" are more appropriate.

Critical Evaluation in Everyday Life

Critical evaluation encompasses every aspect of daily life and all symbolic activity. One communication scholar examined the function of evaluation in his life throughout the course of a single day, discovering, consequently, that it is an ever-present requirement (Pelias, 2000). People are constantly being called to make critical evaluations and judgments as they encounter others' messages and general life experiences. Your critical choices can range from major life-altering decisions, such as deciding to attend college, to seemingly less important but still significant decisions, such as which television program to watch or where to meet a coworker for lunch. The need for critical listening pervades your daily life, as is especially evident in your personal relationships, your academic life, and your role as a consumer.

Personal Relationships

Critical listening is fundamental to personal relationships. Parents, for example, must critically analyze the messages of children who desire to stay out past curfew. Children may then critically evaluate their parents' reasoning as to why they may or may not stay out after curfew. Romantic partners critically examine each other's assessments of the relationship, perhaps needing to evaluate reasons to either maintain or dissolve it. Friends often critically evaluate one another's listening when asked for advice about a decision to be made. All relational decisions and interactions demand the presence of critical evaluation.

Photo 4.4 Are there some types of relationships or areas of life that do not require critical evaluation? (See page 114.)

Academic Life

As a student, engaging in critical evaluation is consistent with higher levels of
learning and understanding the material.
Critical evaluation, going beyond mem-
orizing facts and definitions and then
regurgitating them on an examination,
means questioning and evaluating the material to determine its accuracy and legitimacy. Only by doing so can you truly understand and comprehend the material. We
encourage you to critically evaluate all that you hear in the classroom and all that you
read in your textbooks—including this one. Through this evaluation, you will gain a
better understanding of the material, be able to utilize and synthesize it more fully, and
increase your overall ability to learn.

> Estimates of the number of
> advertisements people are generally
> exposed to in a single day range from
> around 300 to more than 3,000.

Consumers

Consumers are bombarded with advertisements throughout the day that demand critical evaluation. They appear in newspapers and magazines. You see them on billboards,
on buses and cabs, on park benches, on T-shirts, and occasionally being pulled behind
a plane. Commercials play between television programs and songs on the radio. Pop-up
advertisements appear when you visit your favorite Web site. Engaging in critical evaluation enables you to determine the legitimacy of these messages and allows you to make
better decisions when making a purchase. As a consumer, you must frequently interact
with a salesperson whose job often depends on the ability to sell you a product or service. Sometimes, salespeople's messages are completely accurate and legitimate; sometimes, they are flawed. Critical listening may mean the difference between getting a
good deal on a used car and getting a good deal on a used car with the additional charge
for the undercoating that the salesperson urged you to buy.

Elements of Critical Listening

Now that we have introduced critical listening and discussed the pervasiveness of critical evaluation in everyday life, we can examine the four elements that compose it.

Evaluation of Plausibility

Some messages seem legitimate and valid whenever you first listen to them. When
encountering other messages, however, you immediately get the feeling that something is just not right. Even if you cannot immediately pinpoint the problem with these
messages, you feel as if something is amiss. When you experience these feelings, you
are evaluating the **plausibility** of the message, or the extent to which it seems legitimate (Gouran, Wiethoff, & Doelger, 1994). You might not believe that diaper-wearing
winged monkeys were spotted flying over campus because this event is implausible. The
plausibility of other messages might not be as obvious, but something might still strike
you as problematic. For example, an automobile dealership guaranteeing "free maintenance for life on all new cars sold this month" may strike you as plausible but problematic. You may feel that the message does not provide sufficient information or is not
entirely genuine. When you are unsure of a message's legitimacy, it is best to follow your

instincts. The evaluation of plausibility is your first line of defense as a critical listener, and often your first impression of a message is accurate.

Evaluation of Source

When critically examining a message, you must evaluate its source. You may know people who never provide you with good advice or who always seem to be wrong about everything. While you should still listen to these people in case they offer a worthwhile message, your past experiences with them may dictate the degree of belief and value that you place on their messages. Of course, you need not know someone personally to evaluate his or her messages. You make judgments about a source's credibility based on such factors as trustworthiness and expertise in a particular area. For example, you are likely to believe information provided by an astrophysics scholar about the requirements of naming a planet. You would not necessarily believe an astrophysicist's advice, however, about the best way to sell an item on eBay.

Evaluation of Argument

Sometimes the message you critically evaluate will be in the form of an argument, which consists of a claim and evidence to support it. You must examine the following three criteria when critically evaluating an argument: (1) consistency, (2) appropriate support, and (3) adequate support. **Consistency** concerns whether the message is free of internal contradiction and in harmony with information you already know is true (Gouran et al., 1994). Earlier in this chapter, we mentioned the importance of listening. If we contend later in the chapter that listening is not very important in your everyday life, this contradiction should strike you as problematic. One of these two statements is obviously wrong or misrepresented, and this contradiction might lead you to question the information being provided. (Incidentally, you do not need to search for that statement later in the chapter. We have a great editor who would prevent such a situation, and we really do believe in the importance of listening.) Consistency also entails whether the information provided agrees with information you already know as true. If someone is describing the best route to travel through the Midwest and mentions that "once you enter Missouri, just keep driving south until you reach Iowa," you might question the message given your previous knowledge that Iowa is actually located north of Missouri. The information being offered is not consistent with previous information you know to be true.

The evidence and support material provided to back a claim must also be appropriate. In other words, it must directly support and uphold the claim. For instance, a coworker might attempt to convince you that you should purchase a home in California. When providing support for this suggestion, he notes that housing prices must be reasonable because a friend just purchased a home in West Virginia and got a great deal. Of course, providing average purchase prices throughout the state of California would be more appropriate, since this would support the claim being made.

There must also be an adequate amount of evidence to support the claim proposed. We cannot, however, tell you exactly how much evidence is sufficient because the amount will vary with each message. It also varies according to other aspects of critical evaluation. For example, if you find a message or claim implausible, you may require more evidence. If you find the source of a message highly credible on the topic being discussed, you may require less.

Evaluation of Evidence

As a critical listener, you must also evaluate the evidence by considering the following criteria: verifiability and quality. **Verifiability** indicates that the material being provided can be confirmed by other sources or means (Gouran et al., 1994). If someone tells you during the day that the sky is blue, you can verify this by going outside and looking for yourself. If someone tells you Abraham Lincoln was assassinated by John Wilkes Booth, you can verify this by confirming the information in a book about President Lincoln. Some material may be more difficult to verify, in which case you must evaluate other aspects of the message.

The quality of the evidence encompasses your perceived credibility of the source, lack of source bias, and timeliness. Part of a speaker's credibility is derived from the sources that he or she uses to develop a message. Evaluating the evidence used is another way to evaluate the source of a message. When first looking at the evidence itself, however, you must determine a message's believability based on its source. If you talk with someone about a medical procedure and she provides you with information she read in a book authored by an expert in that area, you might determine this evidence as credible. If she provides you with information gathered from someone she sat next to on the bus that morning, you might determine this evidence as not credible. The evidence should also be free of bias or partiality. Would the source of the evidence benefit from this information if it were true? For instance, as a critical listener, you would likely doubt evidence of health benefits gained from soft drinks if a soft drink manufacturer provided the information. Finally, the information provided should also be timely and up-to-date. Engaging in critical evaluation would compel you to question the use of statistics gathered in 1985 when addressing current issues.

Critical Listening and Fallacious Arguments

Engaging in critical listening requires the recognition of **fallacious arguments**, or those that appear legitimate but are actually based on faulty reasoning or insufficient evidence.

Argument Against the Source

Argument against the source occurs when the source of a message, rather than the message itself, is attacked. This fallacy is traditionally known as *argument against the person* or *ad hominem (to the human being) argument,* but we prefer to call it *argument against the source* to recognize the growing trend in attacking not only people but also media sources. Political analysts are often guilty of this fallacy. For instance, you might hear a political analyst say, "The senator's latest proposal is not acceptable because she is nothing but a pathological liar." Rather than critically evaluating the actual proposal, the analyst attacks the source of the proposal instead. Challenging the source of a message instead of the message itself may indicate the message as sound; otherwise, the flaws of the message would be challenged. Attacks on people rather than messages are usually quite spiteful and have little or nothing to do with the actual message.

Contrarian Challenge

Arguing against the source rather than the message is considered a fallacious argument. However, are there times when it would be appropriate to question the source of the message?

Sometimes actual media sources or systems are challenged. For instance, when discussing a television news segment you just watched with a friend, he might say, "That cannot be right because television news is biased against the current administration," challenging not the information within the segment but the media source of the information. Once again, the source, rather than the message itself, is challenged.

As a critical listener, you should not avoid questioning the credibility of a source to avoid this fallacy. Source credibility does factor into the critical analysis of a message, but just make sure you critically examine both the source and the message. Further, avoid personal attacks toward the message source. Any challenge of the source must relate to the message itself.

Appeal to Authority

Appeal to authority happens when a person's authority or credibility in one area is used to support another. Sports heroes and actors, for example, have been used to sell everything from magazine subscriptions to underwear. However, just because a person has particular knowledge or talent in one area does not mean he or she is knowledgeable or talented in all areas. Ask most doctors of philosophy to change the oil in an automobile and see what happens!

Appeal to People (Bandwagon Appeal)

Appeal to people (bandwagon appeal) claims that something is good or beneficial because everyone else agrees with this evaluation. Appeal to people can often be found in discussions between parents and children. A child might say, "I need this new phone because everyone at school has one" or "I want to go to this party because everyone is going to be there." In these cases, the time-honored parental response is something along the lines of the following: "If your friends jumped off a bridge/cliff/skyscraper, would you do the same thing?"

While you may learn of this fallacy early in life, you are not necessarily susceptible to its charms. Consider the many products that boast their own popularity in advertisements: "Squeaky Clean is the nation's top-selling brand of dish soap" or "See *Bonaparte Firecracker,* the movie that audiences have made the number-one comedy for 2 weeks in a row." No mention is made of dexterity in removing grease from pans or of wonderful acting. These products' popularity is offered instead, and you are asked to join the crowd. As a critical listener, you should recognize when the appeal to people fallacy is being used and question why other evidence was not provided. Is Squeaky Clean the number-one dish soap because it gets dishes cleaner than other brands or because it is cheaper? Has *Bonaparte Firecracker* been the top comedy for 2 weeks in a row because it is a good film or because the available movie selection has been particularly poor? Does the specification of the movie's genre mean it is not as popular as you are led to believe? If the top seven films of the last 2 weeks were all dramas or action movies, *Bonaparte Firecracker* could be the most popular comedy but the eighth most popular film overall.

Appeal to Relationships

Appeal to relationships occurs when relationships are used to justify certain behaviors and to convince others of their appropriateness. Communication scholar Erin Sahlstein (2000) has noted

> Sometimes it is not the messages of others that make people susceptible to the appeal to people fallacy but rather their own intrapersonal communication, or communication with the self. They convince themselves of the value of an object or a behavior because of the actions of other people. Making a decision based on what you perceive others to be doing is referred to as *social proof* (Cialdini, 1993).

that people often refer to the relationship they share with another person in an interaction when attempting to convince him or her to behave a certain way. When someone says, "Could you be a friend and give me a ride to the library?" the inclusion of the relational term *friend* underscores the existence of the relationship and reminds the other person of behaviors and duties associated with that sort of relationship. You might expect a "friend" to provide transportation when requested, but not an "acquaintance." The use of relational terms also justifies requests being made. A "friend" *could make* and *be asked to make* this sort of request without great loss of face by either interactant. Appealing to a relationship may be somewhat legitimate but also fallacious. Asking a friend for a ride to the library is one thing; asking a friend to drive the getaway car while you rob a convenience store is another. Certain obligations are associated with each type of relationship, but each responsibility also has limitations. As a critical listener, you must determine when the use of relational terms is legitimate and when it is unreasonable.

Post Hoc Ergo Propter Hoc *and* Cum Hoc Ergo Propter Hoc

Latin for "after this; therefore, because of this," **post hoc ergo propter hoc** argues that something is caused by whatever happens before it. According to this logic, the following statement is true: A man kissed a woman, and two weeks later she was pregnant; therefore, the kiss was responsible for her pregnancy. You likely see the inherent problem with this statement. Admittedly, the above example may seem a bit obvious. However, the use of this sort of reasoning is actually quite common and frequently evident in advertising. Consider commercials you may have seen in which a person eats sandwiches at a fast-food restaurant and then loses an incredible amount of weight. Did eating the sandwiches cause the weight loss, or were additional exercise and other lifestyle changes that accompanied this eating habit responsible for the dramatic loss in weight? Another commercial may boast an individual who used the Ab-Buster-Flab-Cruncher-3000 for just 6 minutes each day and lost 7 inches from his waist in just 2 weeks. Was the Ab-Buster-Flab-Cruncher-3000 responsible for the loss of mass around the middle, or were additional variables working to produce this result (eating a certain type of fast food sandwich, perhaps)?

Cum hoc ergo propter hoc argues that if one thing happens at the same time as another, it was caused by the thing with which it coincides. Once again, we are dealing with a Latin phrase. *Cum hoc ergo propter hoc* translates into "With this; therefore, because of this." As with its *post hoc* companion, this fallacy argues that one event causes another due to their association in time. While *post hoc* argues that something occurring *before* something else is the cause, *cum hoc* argues that something occurring *at the same time* as something else is the cause. Someone might remark, "I wore a new pair of socks on the day of my communication midterm and earned an A on the test. Wearing new socks must have been the reason I scored so high. From now on, I'm going to wear a new pair of socks each time I take a test." If this were all it took to score well on an examination, life would be pretty sweet! Wearing new socks at the same time you ace an examination, however, will not guarantee you a high score on your next exam. If you really want to improve your exam scores, try visiting **www.sagepub.com/ciel**. Another example of *cum hoc ergo propter hoc* follows: "Since my sister started dating her new partner, she does not call me on the phone as often. This must be because of her new partner." A drop in the frequency of calls coinciding with dating a new partner does not mean the new partner caused the drop.

Although quite common and often very convincing, these fallacies are difficult to prove when challenged. Upon recognizing them, as a critical listener, you may question and expect the speaker to prove two things: First, does a direct link actually exist between what is deemed the cause and what is deemed its effect? This link is often very difficult to prove, even when it does exist. Using the previous example, a great deal of evidence would be needed to prove that the Ab-Buster-Flab-Cruncher-3000 can reduce inches around a person's waist. Second, if a link between the cause and its effect exists, did any additional variables work to produce the effect? Using another earlier example, your sister's new romantic partner may be partially responsible for reducing the amount of times she calls you. Your sister could, however, be working more hours at her job, be upset about something you said during a previous conversation, or be having difficulties with her telephone. A number of additional factors apart from dating a new partner could also have caused the decrease.

Hasty Generalizations

Hasty generalization arises when a conclusion is based on a single occurrence or insufficient data or sample size. Asked about where to purchase a new car, someone might remark, "My coworker bought a car at that dealership east of town, and it broke down a week later. If you buy a car at that dealership, it will probably be a lemon." Just because the dealership sold a faulty car once does not mean it will sell another defective car. Hasty generalizations are quite common in the political realm, especially when advice is offered to politicians: "In 1992, Benjamin Hill was elected governor by pledging to change the state song to 'Yakety Sax.' Pledging to change the state song will lead to an election victory." Regardless of how endearing and infectious songs like "Yakety Sax" might be, just because this event happened one time does not mean it will happen again.

Sometimes, the hasty generalization is based on a small sample size. In other words, the people involved or questioned are not significantly representative of a given population. When defending a new policy on campus, someone might say, "I asked people in my algebra class, and they all agreed that a campuswide attendance policy is a good idea. So I guess the policy is a good one that the students like." Simply because a few people agreed with this policy in one class does not mean it is good or that the majority of students agree with the policy. When listening to advertisements throughout the day, you are likely to hear one accompanied with numbers: "The results are in, and 75% of individuals surveyed prefer the taste of Fizzo over the competitors. Fizzo is the soft drink consumers prefer." Drinking Fizzo may be like having a party in your mouth to which everyone is invited, but what if only four people were surveyed? As a critical listener, you also have to question who the "individuals asked" really were. They could very well be Fizzo board members, and the one who preferred a competitor's soft drink may no longer be employed with the company.

Red Herring

Red herring describes the use of another issue to divert attention away from the real issue. This fallacy is especially common when someone wishes to avoid a particular topic. When talking about the cost of higher education, you might hear "I find it difficult to fathom that you insist on addressing higher education funding when the spotted pygmy squirrel is on the verge of extinction" or "Sure, the cost of higher education is staggering, but so is the cost of health care, which has become a major burden on millions of people." During an argument between romantic partners, you might hear the following use of a red herring: "Why are we talking about me going out with my friends when we should be talking about your inability to commit to this relationship?" This example contains a strategic attempt to divert attention away from the issue of going out with friends by dragging commitment to the relationship across the conversational trail. You may also notice that it attempts to shift focus away from not only the original topic but also the individual accused of transgression in the relationship.

> The name "red herring" comes from the phrase "draw a red herring across the trail," derived from the practice of 17th-century dog trainers. They would drag a smoked herring across the trail of a fox to determine how well dogs could remain focused on the original scent (Urdang, Hunsinger, & LaRouche, 1991).

False Alternatives

False alternatives occur when only two options are provided, one of which is generally presented as the poor choice or one that should be avoided (Pearson & Nelson, 2000). One flaw in this reasoning is that there are usually more options than the two provided. Traveling by plane, for example, comes with the likelihood of delays caused by mechanical problems and the always kind and supportive airline personnel who have been known to use false alternatives by explaining, "You can either endure a delay while we find a plane that is functional, or you can leave as scheduled and travel in a plane that is not working correctly." Waiting for a functional plane seems much better than facing possible mechanical problems after takeoff; however, this overlooks the other equally probable option: having a functional plane available to begin with by ensuring proper maintenance is accomplished well before the flight is scheduled to depart. As a note of caution, pointing out this option to airline personnel at the gate will severely decrease your chances of receiving a seat upgrade on that particular flight!

In addition, quite possibly the option deemed less favorable is not as negative as it is portrayed, and the preferred option is not as beneficial. Furthermore, it is possible that neither option is entirely accurate. For instance, a politician may insist, "You can either vote for me and lower your taxes or vote for my opponent whose budget proposals will likely double the amount of taxes you pay each year." A vote for the opponent may not lead to an increase in taxes at all, and voting for this particular candidate does not guarantee lower taxes.

Likewise, an auto mechanic may explain, "You can either replace the serpentine belt in your car now or face being stranded should it end up breaking at one of those cracks." It is possible that the serpentine belt does not need immediate repair, as well as that you would not be stranded somewhere should it actually break. Such claims and options often go unchallenged unless a person recognizes this fallacy is being utilized and critically examines the statements being made.

Composition and Division Fallacies

Composition fallacy argues that the parts are the same as the whole (Pearson & Nelson, 2000, p. 118). According to this fallacy, any student at your school could be picked at random to represent all students at your school. You had better hope a decent student is selected, because he or she will be representing you personally! Common sense tells you that one person cannot accurately represent an entire group of people, but this fallacy nevertheless remains pervasive in our daily lives. Consider how often entire populations are represented in newspaper articles by one person or perhaps a few people. An article might say, "Students on campus are in favor of the tuition increase to pay for the new sports complex. When asked about the increase in tuition, sophomore Emalyn Taylor noted, 'If it takes an increase in tuition to replace the old sports complex, that's what needs to be done.'" This report essentially says that if one student (part) is in favor of the tuition increase, all students (whole) are in favor of it as well.

Division fallacy argues the whole is the same as its parts (Pearson & Nelson, 2000, p. 118). For instance, when being set up on a date by a friend, you might argue, "Everyone you have ever set me up with has been a loser, so this person is going to be a loser too." This statement essentially reasons that if previous dates have been losers (whole), this date (part) will also be one. Another example could happen when deciding which movie to see at the theater, in which case someone might remark, "I do not want to see that director's new movie. All of his movies are terrible," once again arguing that what is true of the whole must be true of its parts. In this case, if all of a particular director's movies (whole) stink, his latest movie (part) will stink as well.

Equivocation

Equivocation relies on the ambiguousness of language to make an argument. A friend may urge, "We should eat at that new pizza restaurant because it is the *best*." Does this mean it is the best restaurant, the best pizza restaurant, or the best new pizza restaurant? Is it the best new pizza restaurant in your city, the nation, or the world? Why is it the best? Is this ranking based on selection, service, price, or taste?

The equivocation tactic is frequently used in commercials. You might hear an announcer proclaim, "Squeaky Clean dish soap is *better!*" This sounds good, but you cannot be certain what Squeaky Clean is actually better than. Is it better than using no dish soap at all or washing dishes by dropping rocks into the sink? Is it better than other brands of dish soap? The use of equivocation leaves such questions unanswered, often the point of this fallacy. When ambiguous words and phrases, such as *improved, bargain, good value, delicious,* or *soothing,* are used, listeners must fill in the context on their own, which often results in a product or an idea being received in a much more positive manner than warranted. Individuals or advertising agencies are then able to legitimately assert that they never made such a claim. The makers of Squeaky Clean dish soap could say, "We never said *it was better than all other brands;* we just said it was *better.*" While this tactic is tricky, this statement would be absolutely true. The good news is now that you are able to recognize the use of equivocation, you will be well equipped to find the best dish soap—whatever *best* means!

Focus Questions Revisited

Why is listening important enough to have an entire chapter devoted to it?
Listening is not only the communication activity in which you engage most frequently but is also fundamental to success in education, careers, and relationships. Often the most common activity in classrooms, listening has been directly linked to academic achievement, is one of the most sought-after skills by employers, and is critical to success and advancement in the workplace. Effective listening in relationships leads to greater satisfaction and is essential for successful relational development.

What are the objectives of listening?
There are five objectives of listening:

1. Relational development and enhancement

2. Gaining and comprehending information

3. Critical listening

4. Enjoyment and appreciation

5. Therapeutic listening

Even though these objectives were discussed in isolation, remember that a single communicative exchange can involve multiple listening goals.

What does it mean to listen actively?
Active listening is a process of receiving, attending to, interpreting, and responding to symbolic activity. Receiving auditory stimuli is the first step in the listening process. Attending occurs when you perceive and focus on stimuli. Interpreting involves assigning meaning to sounds and symbolic activity. Responding, the final step in the active listening process, entails reacting to this symbolic activity.

What are engaged and relational listening?

Engaged listening and relational listening are advanced types of listening that demand more of the listener than active listening. The engaged listening process entails making a personal relational connection with the source of a message that results from the source and the receiver actively working together to create shared meaning and understanding. Relational listening involves recognizing, understanding, and addressing the interconnection of relationships and communication.

Why do people sometimes struggle when listening?

You may encounter a number of obstacles to listening. Recognizing and overcoming these obstacles is crucial to effective listening.

What is critical listening, and why is it so important?

Critical listening is the process of analyzing and evaluating the accuracy, legitimacy, and value of messages. Involving the evaluation of a message's plausibility, source, argument, and evidence, critical listening has a profound impact on personal relationships, learning, and the evaluation of persuasive messages.

What are fallacious arguments?

Fallacious arguments are those that appear legitimate but are actually based on faulty reasoning or insufficient evidence. The ability to recognize fallacious arguments will enable you to become a more critical listener.

Key Concepts

appeal to authority   (p. 106)
appeal to people (bandwagon appeal)   (p. 106)
appeal to relationships   (p. 107)
argument against the source   (p. 105)
attending   (p. 90)
composition fallacy   (p. 110)
consistency   (p. 104)
content (representational) listening   (p. 98)
critical listening   (p. 101)
cum hoc ergo propter hoc   (p. 108)
division fallacy   (p. 110)
egocentric listening   (p. 99)
empathy   (p. 89)
engaged listening   (p. 93)
environmental distractions   (p. 96)
equivocation   (p. 110)
experiential superiority   (p. 100)
factual diversion   (p. 97)
fallacious arguments   (p. 105)
false alternatives   (p. 109)

hasty generalization   (p. 108)
hearing   (p. 90)
interpreting   (p. 91)
listening   (p. 90)
medium distractions   (p. 96)
message complexity   (p. 101)
past experience with the other   (p. 100)
plausibility   (p. 103)
post hoc ergo propter hoc   (p. 107)
receiving   (p. 90)
red herring   (p. 109)
reflecting (paraphrasing)   (p. 92)
relational listening   (p. 94)
responding   (p. 91)
selective listening   (p. 98)
semantic diversion   (p. 97)
source distractions   (p. 97)
status of the other   (p. 100)
sympathy   (p. 89)
verifiability   (p. 105)
wandering thoughts   (p. 100)

Questions to Ask Your Friends

■ Ask a friend to recall a time when he or she misunderstood someone else. Have your friend describe the situation and determine if problems with listening had anything to do with the misunderstanding. If so, how could the misunderstanding have been prevented through effective listening behaviors?

■ Evaluating your listening, in what ways do your friends consider you a good listener? What suggestions do they have for improving your listening?

■ Ask a friend to describe a time when he or she made a purchase based on the recommendation of a salesperson that he or she later regretted. Was a lack of critical listening partially responsible? What suggestions could you offer your friend when making future purchases?

Media Links

■ Watch television and pay close attention to the commercials being aired. What fallacious arguments are evident in these commercials? Are some forms of fallacious arguments more prevalent than others? How effective are these commercials? Having studied this chapter, do you notice a difference in how you listen to these commercials?

■ Watch a political talk show, such as *Fox News Sunday, Meet the Press, The Rachel Maddow Show,* or *The O'Reilly Factor.* What obstacles to listening are evident during interviews and panel discussions on these programs?

■ Concurrent media exposure occurs when two or more media systems are used simultaneously. For example, you may be using the Internet while listening to the radio or reading a newspaper at the same time you are watching a movie on television. What impact might concurrent media exposure have on listening to media?

Ethical Issues

■ When would you consider the appeal to relationships fallacy *appropriate?* When would you consider this fallacy *inappropriate?*

■ We mentioned that you should be aware of your limitations when engaged in therapeutic listening. When would you consider it appropriate to suggest that a friend seek professional assistance?

■ Consider a situation in which you were engaged in therapeutic listening and a friend told you in confidence that he or she was doing something harmful or dangerous. Would it be appropriate to tell someone else if you believed it would prevent your friend from being harmed or harming others? If you believe it would be proper to tell someone else, in what circumstances would this behavior be appropriate?

Answers to Photo Captions

Photo 4.1 ▪ Therapeutic listening requires a supportive environment in which a person feels comfortable speaking openly and expressing him- or herself.

Photo 4.2 ▪ When engaged in relational listening, a person must consider (a) how communication impacts the relationship and (b) how the relationship impacts communication.

Photo 4.3 ▪ Listeners are able to process information at a faster rate than people generally speak.

Photo 4.4 ▪ No. All relationships and even the most mundane parts of life require critical evaluation.

Student Study Site

Visit the study site at **www.sagepub.com/ciel** for e-flashcards, practice quizzes, and other study resources.

References

Barker, L., Edwards, R., Gaines, C., Gladney, K., & Holley, F. (1980). An investigation of proportional time spent in various communication activities by college students. *Journal of Applied Communication Research, 8,* 101–109.

Baxter, L. A., & DeGooyer, D., Jr. (2001). Perceived aesthetic characteristics of interpersonal conversations. *Southern Communication Journal, 67,* 1–18.

Cialdini, R. B. (1993). *Influence: The psychology of persuasion.* New York: Morrow.

Conaway, M. S. (1982). Listening: Learning tool and retention agent. In A. S. Algier & K. W. Algier (Eds.), *Improving reading and study skills* (pp. 51–63). San Francisco: Jossey-Bass.

Curtis, D. B., Winsor, J. L., & Stephens, R. (1989). National preferences in business and communication education. *Communication Education, 38,* 6–14.

Golen, S. (1990). A factor analysis of barriers to effective listening. *Journal of Business Communication, 27,* 25–36.

Gouran, D. S., Wiethoff, W. E., & Doelger, J. A. (1994). *Mastering communication* (2nd ed.). Boston: Allyn & Bacon.

Gumpert, G., & Drucker, S. J. (1997). Listening as an indiscreet act: Or eavesdropping can be fun. In M. Purdy & D. Borisoff (Eds.), *Listening in everyday life: A personal and professional approach* (pp. 163–177). Lanham, MD: University Press of America.

Halone, K. K., & Pechioni, L. L. (2001). Relational listening: A grounded theoretical model. *Communication Reports, 14,* 59–71.

Janusik, L. A., & Wolvin, A. D. (2006). *24 hours in a day: A listening update to the time studies.* Paper presented at the annual meeting of the International Listening Association, Salem, OR.

Maes, J. D., Weldy, T. G., & Icenogle, M. L. (1997). A managerial perspective: Oral communication competency is most important for business students in the workplace. *Journal of Business Communication, 34,* 67–80.

Osgood, C. E., Suci, G. J., & Tannenbaum, P. H. (1957). *The measurement of meaning.* Urbana: University of Illinois Press.

Pearson, J. C., & Nelson, P. E. (2000). *An introduction to human communication* (8th ed.). New York: McGraw-Hill.

Pelias, R. J. (2000). The critical life. *Communication Education, 49,* 220–228.

Preiss, R. W., & Gayle, B. M. (2006). Exploring the relationship between listening comprehension and rate of speech. In B. M. Gayle, R. W. Preiss, N. Burell, & M. Allen (Eds.), *Classroom communication and instructional processes* (pp. 315–327). Mahwah, NJ: Lawrence Erlbaum.

Rankin, P. T. (1928). The importance of listening ability. *English Journal, 17,* 623–630.

Sahlstein, E. M. (2000). *Relational rhetorics and RRTs (Relational Rhetorical Terms).* Unpublished manuscript. Iowa City, IA.

Steil, L. K. (1997). Listening training: The key to success in today's organizations. In M. Purdy & D. Borisoff (Eds.), *Listening in everyday life: A personal and professional approach* (pp. 213–237). Lanham, MD: University Press of America.

Taylor, S. E. (1964). *What research says to the teacher; listening.* Washington, DC: National Education Association.

Urdang, L., Hunsinger, W. W., & LaRouche, N. (1991). *A fine kettle of fish and other figurative phrases.* Detroit: Invisible Ink.

Weinrauch, J. D., & Swanda, R., Jr. (1975). Examining the significance of listening: An exploratory study of contemporary management. *Journal of Business Communication, 13,* 25–32.

Winsor, J. L., Curtis, D. B., & Stephens, R. D. (1997). National preferences in business and communication education: Survey update. *Journal of the Association for Communication Administration, 3,* 170–179.

Wolvin, A., & Coakley, C. (1991). A survey of the status of listening training in some fortune 500 corporations. *Communication Education, 40,* 152–164.

Wolvin, A., & Coakley, C. G. (1996). *Listening* (5th ed.). New York: McGraw-Hill.

Wood, J. T. (2009). *Communication in our lives* (5th ed.). Boston: Wadsworth Cengage Learning.

5

Self and Identity

W e don't know you and you don't know us, but from reading this book, you probably have some impressions of us. You know who *you* are, though, don't you? Not just name and address but the kind of person you are. You have an **identity**, and we don't just mean an ID that you show people to prove your age. You are an individual, and you are friends with other individuals, each perhaps quirky in his or her own way and with a unique personality and identity. You might see these individuals and yourself as persons deep inside, with a history, a childhood set of experiences that made you who you are. You know things about yourself that no one else knows. You are you, you-nique!

This chapter will teach you that you have multiple layers to your identity—not just in the obvious way that some of your own private thoughts are secret, some are revealed in intimate moments of talk, and some are performed as roles ("I'm your classmate/ sister/boss"). We look at these but also show how layers of identity come out through communication in relationships. Some are brought forth and created by the situation in which you find yourself or in the company of certain people but not others. (Do you really behave the same way with your mother as you do with your best friend?) Some others are the result of cultural symbols attached to "being gay or lesbian" or "being a go-getter or a team player," and some are performed for an audience. In intimate relationships, you can perform and express most of your true self; in a police interview, you may want to conceal some of what you are; in a hospice at the end of your life, you may want to hang onto a little *dignity* as the skills, performances, and parts of your body and self that used to compose your identity have ceased to work so well, and you are now physically more dependent on others.

Identity in all of these forms is partly a characteristic (something that you possess), partly a performance (something that you do), and partly a construction of society. For example, society tells you how to be "masculine" and "feminine" and indicates that "guys can't say that to guys" (Burleson, Holstrom, & Gilstrap, 2005), thus restricting the way in which men can give one another emotional support. Society also provides you with the categories for describing a personality, and the media cause you to focus on some traits more than others. Categories like gluttonous, sexy, short, slim, paranoid, and kind are all available to you, but they are not all equally valued.

Thus, the ways you express yourself in talk or nonverbal communication and the way you respond to other people in your social context *transact* part of your identity, so your identity is partly constructed through your interactions with other people. Have you had the experience of being with someone who makes you nervous when you normally aren't nervous or who helps you feel comfortable and relaxed when you feel tense? In these instances, your identity is molded and transacted by the person, situation, or communication—all features that we will explore. You'll get used to a rather odd phrase that is used in communication studies: "*doing* an identity," which is sometimes used instead of "*having* an identity," because communication scholars now pay close attention to the ways in which people's behavior carries out, enacts, transacts, or *does* an identity in talk with other people.

Focus Questions

- Is a person's identity like an onion, built layer by layer and communicated slowly as intimacy increases?
- How do daily interactions with other people form or sustain your identity?
- How much of your "self" is a performance of social roles where you have to act out "who I am" for other people?
- What is meant by a symbolic self, and why do we have to account to other people for who we are?
- What is the role of culture in your identity experiences?

Who Are You?

Consider this example. A young man kissed his grandmother on the cheek as he left home one evening to join his friends waiting in a car. As he took his place in the front seat, he waved good-bye and promised not to stay out too late. The car made its way up the block; he and his friends laughed as they recounted one friend's recent date with a girl from the neighborhood. The laughter stopped suddenly when they noticed a younger boy standing on the corner. This boy, a member of a rival gang, hoped to gain a higher rank by hanging out in enemy territory. The young man in the passenger seat glared at the boy, pulled out a gun from underneath the seat, and began shooting. One bullet struck the boy in the chest, killing him instantly. Another bullet hit a nearby elderly woman walking home from the store. The car sped off as she fell to the ground. His friends in the car congratulated him on defending the block and then casually returned to their conversation. When the young man returned home later that evening, he kissed his grandmother on the cheek, checked Facebook, went into his room, and then drifted peacefully to sleep.

How could he have done that? How can anyone do something so vile as to shoot two people in cold blood? Your first thought may be to blame his personality: He was an evil person, per-

On October 26, 2007, a keen soccer fan was sent to jail in the United Kingdom for killing a father of two by stabbing him 29 times after the man had joked that he hoped the killer's favorite team (England) would lose a soccer game against Brazil ("Football," 2007).

haps with psychopathic tendencies. Or you could put it down to the identity that had been constructed during his initiation into the gang when he was trained to accept the importance of defending gang territory. On the other hand, he probably saw himself in personality terms too, but more favorable ones—as a good grandson, a loyal person, devoted to his gang, and someone unafraid of doing what is necessary. He may have felt a twinge of guilt when the elderly woman got hit, or he may have shrugged and thought, "Well, that stuff happens in [gang] wars." Worse atrocities happened in the Holocaust, in Bosnia, and in Iraq. Hannah Arendt (1963) pointed out how banal and routine such atrocities become in wars. The routines of gang membership, war, or bureaucracy make it all too easy to come to see real human beings (other gang members, Serbs, Jews, Shias, Sunnis, American soldiers) as *just* targets, numbers, insurgents, subjects, or prisoners. They become anonymous elements of the daily routine, part of the job that needs to be done, dehumanized "others" who just need to be counted, sorted, and cleaned away. The people lose their personal identity, but so too in a strange way does the perpetrator (who becomes "just" a gang member, prison guard, or rifle sharpshooter).

What Arendt missed in her analysis of such perpetrators, however, is the importance of their daily *communicative* relationships with other people who act and think in the same way about these "others." Comrades implicitly accept the way that "others" are treated and reinforce the identity of gang member, guard, or assassin as "OK." Arendt saw the problem as getting so used to cruel acts because they happened all the time and became just part of doing the job. Communication scholars can look deeper and see that all ongoing relationships between people are what make it easier to carry out bad deeds or to perform an identity that we would regard as unacceptable from another vantage point.

Of course, *you* (or your friends) have never done anything that dehumanizes, stereotypes, or depersonalizes others, have you? You have never called anyone "a cheese-eating surrender monkey" or taken away a person's uniqueness by calling him or her "an illegal" or "a frat boy" or lumped someone together with all other "college kids" or chanted, "Oh, how I hate Ohio State."

Earlier chapters talked about frames for situations and thinking. Shotter (1984) sees identity as a frame for interpreting other people's actions, and Burke (1962) also saw motives and personality language as nothing more than helpful frames for interpretation (see Chapter 2). In short, your identity is going to be revealed in a language that reflects the priorities of a particular culture or relationship and its frames for thinking about how humans should act and describe themselves. The first point to recognize, then, is that human beings talk about their identities in ways that are steered by social norms and conventions in their society and that they expect other people to present such narratives and behaviors. Your culture also frames identity as a sense of a stable inner self; it therefore feels quite normal for you to think in those terms, and you can easily understand the idea that someone could let you know about his or her private self by revealing its layers. However, you would be thought crazy if you said, "My identity is blue with an elephant spirit inside." You'd soon be locked up. You have to use terms and phrases that your audiences recognize as symbolically meaningful in the culture: "I'm a go-getter but quite private, ambitious yet introverted." In other words, you *frame* your talk about yourself and your identity in the language that your culture has taught you to use.

Identity as Inner Core: The Self-Concept

Listen In On Your Life

How would you describe yourself? National identity? Ethnic identity? Gender identity? Sexual identity? Age identity? Social class identity? Religious identity? What else?

Now check the categories that you can use to personalize your profile on Facebook or MySpace. Are they the categories you would use to describe yourself to a child, an employer, or a new neighbor? People actually are encouraged—perhaps even required—to identify themselves by association with particular categories and such items as favorite videos and music, hobbies, and sexual orientation. How would you feel if your instructor composed a slideshow of all the Facebook profiles of the people in your class and showed it to everyone?

Finally, a deeper question: How do the categories that you are offered relate to products sold by the larger companies that own these sites, such as music, DVDs, MP3s, and movies?

Although we will start with the common-sense idea that you have a true inner self, by the end of the chapter, we will show that communication studies can teach you much more about how personal identity is built by relationships with other people. The chapter should make you think about ways in which identity is connected to language; to other people; to the norms, rules, and categories in society/culture; and to narratives of origin and belonging to other relationships. This identity may be represented by such statements as "I'm an African American" or, on a bumper sticker, "Proud parent of an Honor Roll student at City High." Both of these examples make statements of identity yet are claiming it through relationships with other people or membership in groups. Of course, the gang member may not have thought about any of this when he pulled the trigger, but after reading this chapter, you might see his actions in some new ways.

Psychic/Reflective Self

You usually think about persons as having some true inner core self that stays

Photo 5.1 How do daily interactions with other people form or sustain your identity? What is being communicated here about gender, identity, and culture? (See page 141.)

the same and makes them who they are—a personal, private, and essential core, covered with layers of secrecy, privacy, and convention. This is known as a **self-concept** and is the point of view from which you talk about people *having* an identity. Consequently, you are alarmed by people who have multiple personalities or are bipolar because you believe that someone should have only one consistent personality and that people who have more parts are disturbed or psychologically irrational. Your personality or identity may be hard for other people to reach, but according to many self-help books and celebrity biographies, it is reachable. Communication serves merely to help people *talk about* or *express* what is inside, perhaps doing so in greater depth as you get to know one another better. Communication scholars can teach you the skill of expressing yourself well or helping you be open and honest and let the real you be heard.

You recognize the usefulness of this idea of self-concept and represent it normally as a consistent inner self made up of the person's broad habits of thought (e.g., someone is kind, outward-looking, introverted, or self-centered). You might see that self revealed communicatively in styles of behavior (e.g., someone is aggressive, calm, ambitious, reliable, hardworking, or manipulative) or in characteristic styles of perception (e.g., someone is paranoid, trusting, insightful, or obstinate). *Personality* is the label that you would first use to describe someone's *identity* if you were asked about it casually in a conversation by someone who wanted to know what that person was like.

All the same, it's a very odd idea indeed, given the fact that people are so complex. A person can simultaneously be many identities depending on your focus. For example, a person can simultaneously be a loving parent, a loyal friend, a vegetarian, a conservative, quick-tempered, a good dancer, a bad cook, business savvy, and a team player. Furthermore, you have a choice in the type of identity that you describe, and you can focus on a relational identity (friend/parent), an interactional identity (worker/customer/server), a sex or gender identity (male/female/masculine/feminine/GLBT), a racial/ethnic identity (the boxes to check on government forms), or a behavioral identity (extrovert/introvert). You have a choice, then, about where to begin your description of your identity.

Actually, you already know another key point about identity from your everyday experience. People not only are multilayered but also can have different moods and be good company on one day and bad on another. You also recognize that people can fluctuate during the course of the day and that events may happen to them that cause them to act "out of character." These fluctuations help demonstrate that it's a peculiar idea that somebody could have a *fixed* inner identity if it can also be so variable and complex over time. The best you can hope for, then, is that the more you get to know someone through talk, the more you can understand the person's usual self and the events or people that trigger it to spin off into different styles and forms. You need all the help you can get for such a task, so, right or wrong, you tend to view it as an especially valuable form of information when other people give you inside scoop about their identity or self-concept, as if they were peeling away layers. Indeed, psychologists Irwin Altman and Dalmas Taylor (1973) used the analogy of peeling an onion to describe the way we get to learn about other people's identities.

The upshot, though (and we are sorry to spoil it for you), is that all the magazine articles that offer to tell you about "the real [Brad Pitt/Beyoncé/Jennifer Lopez/Hillary Rodham Clinton/Adolf Hitler]" are always going to be nonsense. The notion that someone has a real single inner core is suspect for communication scholars from the get-go.

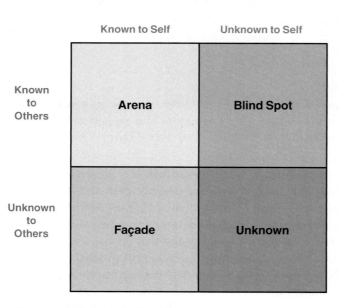

Figure 5.1 The Johari Window

Source: From "The Johari Window: A Graphic Model of Interpersonal Awareness," by J. Luft and H. Ingham, 1955, proceedings of the western training laboratory in group development, Los Angeles: UCLA. Reprinted with permission.

Also, if identities could not be changed or reviewed, there would be no therapists or communication textbooks with advice on how to develop your communication and presentation skills.

The Johari window, developed in 1955 by two guys called Joe (Luft) and Harry (Ingham)—and we're not kidding—distinguishes between the things that a person knows about self and the things that others know about the person. As you can see in Figure 5.1, people have blind spots—that is, everyone but the person in question can see a particular thing about him or her (for example, that he or she is "a pain")—and there are cases where we pretend (façade), concealing from people something that we know about ourselves (guilty secrets and so forth). The arena is basically where we openly act out a public identity that everyone else knows and recognizes.

Describing a Self

If you ask people to tell you who they are, they will tell you their name and start unfolding their self-concept, usually with a narrative that places their self in various contexts. "Steve Duck" indicates to someone in your culture that the person is male and has had to put up with many entirely predictable and very unoriginal jokes about his name. Although he has lived in the United States of America for more than 20 years, he is a Brit, and his family comes from Whitby in North Yorkshire, England, where the first recorded Duck (John Duck) lived in 1288. John Duck and Steve Duck evidently share the same skeptical attitude toward authority figures, since John is in the historical record because he sued the Abbot of Whitby over ownership of a piece of land. John was descended from the Vikings who sacked and then colonized Whitby in about 800 AD, and we know this because "Duck" is a Viking nickname-based surname for a hunchback. (Have you ever ducked out of the way of anything? If so, you have crouched like a hunchback.)

Steve Duck is also relatively short for a man, is baldheaded but bearded, likes watching people but is quite shy, and can read Latin, which is how he found out about John Duck while researching his family tree. Steve likes the music of Ralph Vaughan Williams, enjoys doing cryptic crosswords, knows about half the words that Shakespeare knew, and has occasionally lied. He resents his mother's controlling behavior, was an Oxford college rowing coxswain, loves reading history (especially Roman history), and is wheat/gluten intolerant. He thinks he is a good driver; is proud of his dad, who was a Quaker pacifist (that antiauthority thing again); and has lived in Iowa for 23 years. He has had two marriages and four children, carries a Swiss Army knife (and as many other gadgets as will fit onto one leather belt), and always wears two watches.

Notice that some of this information about his identity is *self-description*. That is, these words describe him in much the same way that anyone else could without knowing him personally (for example, short, bald, two watches). Self-description usually involves information about self that is obvious in *public* (or on your résumé). If you wear your college T-shirt, talk with a French accent, or are short, this evidence about you is available even to strangers who can see your physical appearance or hear how you sound. "Identity" in this sense, then, is communicated publicly by verbal and nonverbal means, including skin color and physique, and it parks the individual in categories or national, racial, or ethnic groups or else lumps them in stereotypes. It isn't really an individual identity but is more a group membership.

Self-Disclosure

Some points in Steve's description of himself count as **self-disclosure**—that is, the revelation of personal information that other people could not know unless Steve *made* it known. In the above example, these are the points that describe particular feelings and emotions that other people would not know unless Steve specifically disclosed them. The "resents," "is proud of," "enjoys," and "thinks" parts give you a view of his identity that you could not directly obtain any other way, though you might work them out from what Steve says or does. These parts, since they are openly stated as insights into his thinking, would count as self-disclosure rather than as self-description. The term *self-disclosure,* then, is specifically limited to revelation of private, sensitive, and confidential information that is relevant to identity, such as your values, fears, secrets, assessments, evaluations, and preferences, usually revealed to one or two other persons at a time.

Jourard (1964, 1971) wrote about self-disclosure as making your identity "transparent" to others. He felt that people who made the most disclosures were acting in the most psychologically healthy manner. Early research connected self-disclosure not only with healthy psychology but also with growth in intimacy. Indeed, classic reports (e.g., Derlega, Metts, Petronio, & Margulis, 1993) found that the more people become intimate, the more they disclose to each other information about themselves that is both broad and deep. Also, the more you get to know someone's inner knowledge structures, the closer you feel to him or her. This closeness generally develops only if the information is revealed in a way that indicates you are receiving privileged information that other people do not know. For example, if a man lets you (and only you) know the secret that he has a serious invisible illness (such as diabetes, lupus, or prostate cancer), an unusually strong fear of spiders, or a significantly distressed marriage, you may feel valued and trusted as a result of that disclosure, because he let you into his inner life.

But there is an important relational process going on here: When someone tells you about his or her inner identity, you may feel you are being honored and valued by someone's revelation of the inner self, or you may actually not care for what you are hearing. The important point, then, is that the disclosure itself does not make a difference to a relationship; the relationship, rather, makes a difference to the value of the self-disclosure. If you feel the relationship is enhanced by self-disclosure, it is; if you don't, no matter how intimate the disclosure, the relationship does not grow in intimacy. Later research has refined this idea (Dindia, 2000; Petronio, 2002). For example, too much disclosure of identity is not necessarily a good thing at all times. You've probably been bored by somebody constantly telling you more than you wanted to know about herself—TMI! On the other hand, people who are closed and don't tell anything about themselves are usually regarded as psychologically *un*healthy in some way.

In addition, communication scholar Kathryn Dindia (2000) points out that the revelation of identity is rarely just a simple progression and is certainly not just the declaration of facts and then—bam!—intimacy. Self-disclosure is a dynamic process tied to other social processes that relate to your identity and how you want to disclose yourself over time. It is a process that can be continued through the life of relationships and is not a single one-time choice: to disclose or not to disclose. Indeed, part of your identity is the skill with which you reveal or conceal information about yourself and your feelings, as any good poker player knows.

In fact, the revelation of your identity, like identity itself, is an open-ended process that continues indefinitely in relationships even after they have become deeply intimate. It is dynamic, continuous, and circular so that it is hard to say where self-disclosure or identity begins or ends. It is also influenced by the behavior and communication of the other person(s)—the audience. Self-disclosure and identity both occur in the context of a relationship that has ups and downs, and all of these elements are interdependent. For example, José learns more about Juanita's identity when he hears her disclose something about herself that makes him feel more positive about her and their relationship. It also makes him nervous because, in the past, he did something that her disclosure shows she would not like. So he tells her what he did and how sorry he is about it. Juanita likes the fact that he confides in her and feels better about the relationship as a result, but she wonders if José is still the same person he was when he did the bad thing or if he is genuinely sorry and has changed . . . and so on. Thus, identity, self-disclosure, and relationships are mutually connected transactions, not just simply the peeling away of layers.

Dialectic Tensions

People also place a limit on the amount of information that they reveal to others, and some choose to remain private, even in intimate relationships. Baxter and Montgomery (1996) identify a push-pull **dialectic tension** of relationships. Dialectic tensions occur whenever you are in two minds about something or feel a simultaneous pull in two directions. Some communication scholars (e.g., Baxter, 2004; Baxter & Braithwaite, 2008) suggest that there simply is no singular core of identity but a dialogue between different "voices" in your head. For example, in relationships, you want to feel connected to someone else, but you do not want to give up all of your independence. You can see how you—and your identity—can grow by being in a relationship, but you can also see that this comes at a simultaneous cost or threat to your identity, independence, and autonomy. The autonomy-connectedness dialectic is one dialectic tension, but another is openness-closedness, where people feel social pressure to be open yet also want to retain control over private information. This tension leads to people sometimes giving out and sometimes holding back information about self. Even in the same relationship, a person can feel open and willing to reveal information sometimes but crowded and guarded at other times. These tensions are simply part of being in a relationship that has its own flow: A personal relationship is not a consistent or simple experience any more than identity is. Each affects the other over time.

In fact, people in relationships negotiate boundaries of privacy (Petronio, 2002). For example, part of the difference between friendship and mere acquaintance is that you have stronger boundaries around your identity for acquaintances than you

Self-disclosure reacts to a **norm of reciprocity** (i.e., an unspoken rule about fairness and giving back about as much as you receive). If I say something self-disclosing to you in everyday life, you should tell me something about yourself in return. If one person keeps telling information but gets nothing back, the person will stop doing it. Oddly enough, the norm of reciprocity can actually be used to interrogate people or find out information about them indirectly. If you say something personal about yourself, that loads an obligation on the other people to respond by saying something equally personal about themselves.

do for friends. Also, as Jon Hess (2000) notes, you simply don't like some people, so you don't want them to know personal stuff about you, and you may actively try to limit what they find out about you. Caughlin and Afifi (2004) have shown that even intimate partners sometimes prefer to completely avoid topics that may annoy or provoke the other person. Petronio (2002) deals with the inconsistencies in the revelation of information by pointing to the importance of boundary management of the topics that have specific meanings within different relational settings. People experience a tension between a desire for privacy and a demand for openness differently in different relationships. Couples make up their own rules for controlling the boundaries of privacy based on the particular nature of their relationship. So, for example, a couple may define, between themselves, the nature of topics that they will mention in front of other people and what they will keep private. A married couple may decide what topics they can discuss in front of the children, for instance, and these topics may change as the children grow older. In other words, people show, employ, and work within different parts of their identity with different audiences at different times.

One of the important points that Petronio (2002) makes, then, is that the suitability of something for disclosure is itself affected by relational context and by agreement between the partners. She also draws attention to the ways in which a couple can decide how much to disclose. Amount, type, or subject of self-disclosure can be topics for discussion (often called *metacommunication* or communication about communication). In short, in contrast to Jourard's (1964, 1971) idea that there are absolute rules about self-disclosure of identity, Petronio strongly indicates that it is often a matter of personal preference or is worked out explicitly between the partners in a relationship through communication.

The upshot of this discussion of self-disclosure as a revelation of layers of self, then, is that your identity is not just a straightforward, layered possession of your own inner being. Neither is your self-disclosure of that identity just your decision alone but something jointly owned by you and a partner, so to speak. By now you are recognizing that there is more to identity than just *having* or *revealing* one, then. The norms of appropriateness and reciprocity and the rules about amount of information and the revelation of negative information show that there is a social context for communication about identity. Identity is revealed within that set of social rules, cultural norms, and contexts.

Identity and Other People

Saying that there is a social context for identity is basically making two points:

1. Society as a whole broadly influences the way you think about identity in the first place.

2. The other people who meet a person may influence the way that person's identity is expressed.

When you reveal your identity, you often use stories to tell the audience something about yourself and help them shape their sense of who you are. As with self-disclosure, so too with stories: They are influenced by both society/culture and the specific persons or audience to whom you do the telling.

Photo 5.2 How much of your "self" is a performance of social roles where you have to act out "who I am" for other people? (See page 141.)

Narrative Self and Altercasting

People tell stories about themselves and other people all the time and often pay special care to what they will say, particularly for occasions like job interviews, sales pitches, and strategic communication of all sorts. You may have noticed that you tell stories of your identity for consumption by other people in a social context involving key features of all human stories (see Chapter 2). A report about an identity often characterizes the self by means of a memory or history in its narrative or a typical or an amusing instance that involves character (your identity), plot, motives, scenes, and other actors (see Chapter 2). Therefore, even when you reveal an internal model of self, it organizes your identity in ways other people understand in terms of the rules that govern accounts, narratives, and other social reports. As Kellas (2008) has pointed out, narratives can be an ontology (how I came to be who I am), an epistemology (how I think about the world), an individual construction, or a relational process, such as when a couple tells the story about how they first met.

Reports about an identity have a narrative structure that builds off both the sense of origin derived from early life and a sense of continuity. The self comes from somewhere and has roots—"I'm Hispanic," "I'm a true Southerner," "I'm a genuine Irish McMahan." Identity comes in part from narratives of origin, whether personal, cultural, or species. ("Where did I come from?" "Where did our culture come from?" "How did humans get started?") A sense of origin leads, for most people, straight back to their family, the first little society that they ever experienced. The specific context of family experience is a major and first influence on a person's sense of origin and identity, and it gives the person a sense of connection to a larger network of others; indeed, in African American cultures, "the family" can be seen as a whole community that goes beyond the direct blood ties that define "family" for some other cultures. The earliest memories from which you build your sense of origin are represented in your experiences in childhood in some form of family or family-like environment.

However, your early memories are not neutral facts. They are loaded, like dice, by the experiences you had in your family. A horrible childhood can make a person absorb an identity that gives him or her low self-esteem, for example. People who learn from their childhood *experiences* with parents, teachers, and peers that they are essentially worthless tend to develop a low self-esteem and therefore to treat the later relational world a lot more cautiously and with greater anxiety than do people who are treated in childhood as interesting, worthy, and good. The latter end up confident and secure about themselves, whereas those treated by their parents or caretakers as nuisances not only come to see themselves that way but also become anxious in relationships or avoid them altogether. A key point, then, is that by both direct and indirect means, your interactions and communication with other people shape your views of yourself even when you don't realize it or necessarily want it to happen— and this influence is not automatically something you just grow out of.

Early experiences with other people influence your later life significantly, as a result of their impact on the thought worlds/worlds of meaning that you develop and the sense of identity that they create through narratives that you form about yourself and your history. The ways they do this range from effects on the way a person ends up feeling about self and worth as a person, to the goals that people set for life, to the levels of ability that they feel they have in particular areas, to the ways they relate to other people, to the dark fears that they hoard all their lives, to their beliefs about the way to behave properly and appropriately (religious beliefs, rituals about birthdays, who cares for people emotionally, whether sports "matter"), to whether life is peacefully cozy or violently conflicted. Early experiences in "the family" lay down many of the tracks upon which your later life will run.

In part, what you identify as true about yourself relies on you reporting in a way your audience believes to be coherent and acceptable. It is not just that you *have* a self but that you shape the *telling* of your identity in a way that your culture, your friends, and your audience will accept. This distinction is like the difference between the words in a joke and the way someone tells it: The telling adds something performative to the words, and a person can spoil a joke by telling it badly. Likewise with identity, it has to be performed or told in appropriate ways. When the gang member, Purdue fan, or frat boy brags about his achievements to friends, he probably tells it differently than he would to the police, Indiana University fans, or the dean of students.

Labeling

Another way to create and publish an identity is through **labeling**—that is, by adopting a particular style of name that labels the characteristics you want to stand out. If a faculty member refers to himself as "Dr. Pat," that creates a certain kind of image, a mixture of professionalism and accessibility and also an amusing cross-reference to the cultural icon Dr. Phil. These nicknames and labels for the self and others can be used for creation or reinforcement of a type of identity. In the case of *other people*, a technical term used in discussion of communication and identity is **altercasting**. Altercasting refers to how language can force people into a certain identity and then burden them with the duty to live up to the description, which can be positive or negative (Marwell & Schmitt, 1967). For example, you are altercasting when you say, "As a good friend, you will want to help me here" or "Only a fool would . . ." These direct statements involve a labeling of the listener as a certain kind of person (or not). The labels position the person to respond appropriately (as a friend or not as a fool). More subtly, people can be altercast by some of the language tactics discussed in Chapter 2. If a mechanic or computer geek uses technical language (divergence), this altercasts the other person as "nonexpert." You could respond by accepting the "one-down" role of a nonexpert and feeling like a fool, or you could resist by saying something that reasserts your expertise. Even such small elements of communication transact your identity and the identities of those people around you.

The idea that you have this onion self revealed in layers is all very well, then, until you stop to think that you would hardly bother to speak your identity at all—in fact, there would be no shared language in which to do it—if there were no other people to be your audience. One absolute requirement for communication is that someone else hears and understands what you say. When you communicate about yourself, therefore, it must be because you assume that the audience will understand you, so you must assume a shared basis for understanding other people. On top of that, you must assume that some special people—friends, for example—not only understand your "self" but also do reality checks for you. When people talk about themselves, then, they assume you, their audience, will be able to comprehend, interpret, and probably support it to some extent. The earlier description of Steve, for example, mentions a Swiss Army knife because that particular item is assumed to be known in your culture. That means, however, that any description of an identity is not just a revelation of an inner core but is steered by beliefs about the criteria, categories, and descriptions that will matter to, or even impress, the relevant audience. For example, people project a professional identity by wearing smart business clothes to a job interview, and people can communicate their culture through their accent and behavior. You have some idea from your own personal experiences about the ways and categories in which other people experience and expect you to communicate "who you are"—and that is a *relational* point.

Symbolic Identity

You can already glimpse ways in which your sense of self is influenced by language frames, culture, origin, membership, and other people's thoughts about you. But are you really "who you are" without specific interactions with specific other people? Don't you actually *do* a lot of your identity for other people? You probably do not behave exactly the same way with your best friend as you do with your mother, your instructor, or a traffic cop. Most people have a range of identities that they can turn on as necessary according to circumstances and the other people in the interactions with them. In that case, identity is not so much something that you have as it is something that you *do* and communicate to other people in ways that they recognize. For example, you do not have "Indiana University fan" carved on your inner core, but you *do* "Indiana

University fan," for example, by wearing Indiana University clothing, going to Indiana University games, and making jokes to your friends about Purdue.

Do you feel like a different person when you are with your friends than when you're talking to your mother? Are you the same person all the time, or do you have good and bad days, and do you ever do things you regret or regard as not typical of you as a person? Most people have protested that someone has misrepresented them (and so *resisted* or *contested* an altercasting by refusing to accept it). A hostile or negative person can make you feel very bad about yourself. Have you ever met anyone who didn't really "get" what you are about? On the other hand, you may have had a close relationship with a partner that felt good because you were able to be your *true self* around the other person or because the person helped bring out sides of you that other people could not. Did you struggle to assert an identity independent from your parents when you were a teenager? If you have had any of these experiences, you must already be asking yourself how that is possible if "you" are really one identity. You may also have started to think about how advertising, religion, and social fashions influence the ways you dress and act. Other people can affect what you regard as important, the values you aspire to, the choices that you make, and how these feed into your sense of identity. Your culture and your identity at the very least interact with one another, and at most culture accounts for quite a lot of who you are and how you act.

Symbolic Self

The lesson is simple: Your identity is shaped by the people you interact with because you can reflect that your "self" is an object of other people's perceptions and that they can do critical thinking or listening about you as well. In short, your identity is a **symbolic self**, a self that exists for other people and goes beyond what it means to you; it arises from social interaction with other people. As a result, when and if you reveal yourself, you do so in the terms that society at large uses to explain behavior. We fit identity descriptions into the form of narratives that your society and your particular acquaintances know about and accept. Hence, any form of identity that you present to other people is partly connected to the fact that you buy into a bank of shared meanings that the particular audience or community accepts as important in defining a person's identity.

For example, part of the gang member's identity is a result of the fact that he talked with his gang every day, greeted them each day, asked about their families, and joked around with them. He also probably discussed rival gangs with them, saw himself as dutiful and good by his/their standards, and knew that his fellow gang members, at least, would be people he would meet again the next day for conversation and laughter. In short, he was living in a cultural context that tolerated his actions and, more important, was in a series of repeated relationships with the same people who shared his values. Tomorrow he would have to preserve and project his identity to his gang, and he would do this in his conversation, his everyday connections with them, and the sheer banality of his everyday experience of being alive in their

Contrarian Challenge

If you do not have a central core that is "you," then how come people who know you well can apparently predict what you will do and know how you should be dealt with?

company—just being the sort of dutiful gang member that he was in his own eyes and the sort of reliable guy he was in their eyes. If you cheer for Purdue or Indiana University, you do it in a group of people who share your views and probably are your friends, people you talk to. You act out your loyalty to your team among your fellow fans.

Another way of thinking about someone's identity, then, is in terms of how broad social forces affect or even transact an individual's view of who he or she is, a set of ideas referred to as **symbolic interactionism**. In particular, George Herbert Mead (1934) suggested that people get their sense of self from their dealings with other people and from being aware that other people observe, judge, and evaluate one's behavior. Think of how many times you have done or not done something because of how you would look to your friends if you did it. Has your family ever said, "What will the neighbors think?" Mead called this phenomenon the human ability to adopt an **attitude of reflection**, to think about how you look in other people's eyes or to reflect on the fact that other people can see you as a social object from their point of view. Guided by these reflections, you do not always do what you want to do but what you think people will accept. Or you may end up doing something you don't want to do because you cannot think how to say no to another person in a way that looks reasonable to other people ("SHAN'T!" won't do). Your identity, then, is not yours alone. Indeed, Mead also saw self as a transacted result of communicating with other people: You learn how to be an individual by recognizing the way that society treats you. You come to see yourself (your identity) as representing someone who is a meaningful object for other people. People recognize you as who you are and treat you differently from other people, so you come to see yourself as distinct not only in their eyes but also in your own. For example, physically attractive people often act confidently because they are aware of the fact that other people find them attractive. On the other hand, unattractive people have learned that they cannot rely on their looks to make a good impression and may therefore adapt and develop other ways of impressing other people (for example, by developing a great sense of humor; Berscheid & Reis, 1998). You come to see yourself, to some extent, as others see you. You come to see yourself as having the characteristics that other people treat you as having, and in many cases you play to those social strengths.

You can, therefore, go further in connecting identity through relationships to communication. If other people treat you with respect and you come to see yourself as a respected individual, self-respect becomes part of your inner being. If your parents treat you like a child even though you have now grown up, they evoke from you some sense that you are still a child, which may cause you to feel resentment. If you are intelligent and people treat you as interesting, you may come to see yourself as having different value to other people than does someone who is not intelligent.

You get so used to the idea that it gets inside your "identity" and becomes part of who you are, but it originated from other people, not from you. If you are tall, tough, and muscular (not short, bald, and carrying a Swiss Army knife), perhaps people habitually treat you with a bit of respect and caution. Over time, you get used to the idea, and identity is enacted and transacted in communication as a person who

> When you go home from college where you are "an adult," you may end up being treated in the family back home as "a kid" or, at the very best, "a grown-up kid." What communicative styles and techniques can you identify as bringing this about?

Photo 5.3 What is meant by a symbolic self, and why do we have to account to other people for who we are? (See page 141.)

expects respect and a little caution from other people. Eventually, you will not have to act in an intimidating way in order to make people respectful. Your manner of communicating (whether in talk or nonverbal behavior or both) reflects their approach to you, and their way of communicating reflects it back. Yet, your identity began in the way you were treated by other people, and it eventually becomes transacted in communication.

Another way of thinking about this is to see how "society" gets your friends to do its work for it. You have never met a society or a culture, and you never will. You will only ever meet people who (re)present some of a society's or a culture's key values to you. This contact with other folks puts them in the role of *Society's Secret Agents*. These people you meet and talk with are doing your culture's and your society's work and are enacting the way in which that culture represents the sorts of values that are desirable within it. In short, when you communicate with other people in your culture, you get information about what works and what doesn't, what is acceptable and what isn't, and how much you count in that society—what your identity is "worth." For example, the dominant culture in the United States typically values ambition, good looks, hard work, demonstration of material success, and a strong code of individuality, and people stress those values in their talk with one another or else feel inadequate because they don't stack up against these values.

Of course, you cannot escape the influence on your self-concept of people with whom you are forced to interact whether you like them or not (coworkers, professors, or relatives, for example), but the principle is the same even though you most often think of the influence of your friends and relatives or key teachers on yourself. Nonfriends may challenge aspects of your sense of identity and make you reflect on the question, "Who am I?" Sometimes this reflection results in your confidence in your opinions being reinforced, and sometimes it results in them being undermined, reconsidered, or modified, but even the challenges and discussions of everyday communication transact some effect on your view of self, your identity. Your sense of self/identity comes from interactions with other people in society as a whole.

Transacting a Self in Interactions With Others

In keeping with this book's theme, you can't have a self without also having relationships with other people—both the personal relationships you choose and the social relationships you reject. More than that, it's impossible for a person to have a concept of self unless he or she can reflect on identity via the views of these other people with whom he or she has social or personal relationships. Your identity is *transacted* or constituted in part from two things: First, you take into yourself—or are reinforced for taking into yourself—the beliefs and prevailing norms of the society in which you live. Second, you are *held to account* for the identity that you project by those people you hang out with. The gang member would have lost status in the gang if he had not shot his target. As an Indiana University fan, you lose face if you don't know the score during your game with Purdue or cannot name your own team's quarterback. As a student, you are expected to know answers about the book you are reading for your class.

Let us rephrase this point: Because individuals acquire individuality through the social practices in which they exist and carry out their lives, they encounter powerful forces of society that are actually enforced on the ground by Society's Secret Agents, their relationships with other people that affect their identities. (That "raised eyebrow" from your neighbor/instructor/team fan was actually society at work!) Your "self" is structured and enacted in relation to those people who have power over you in formal ways, like the police, but most often you encounter the institutions within a society through its secret agents: public opinion and the people you know who express opinions about moral issues of the day and give you their judgments. You, too, are one of Society's Secret Agents, guiding what other people do and thinking just as they do.

Again, your identity is a complex result of your own thinking, history, and experience and of your interaction with other people and their influence on you, both as an individual and as one of Society's Secret Agents. Behind all those things that you think of as simply abstract social structures, like "the law," individuals are acting in relation to one another (you and the police officer). These social relations

Strategic Communication

Look at your Facebook profile. How do you think you look? Take a closer look, this time at the profiles of the members of your class. How do you think they are trying to present themselves as individuals? Take notes and discuss this issue in class.

get internalized into yourself, and you slow down at speed-limit signs not because you want to but because you saw the police car and don't want a ticket.

It is important to note how the routine banality of everyday life talk with friends who share the same values and talk about them day by day actually does something for society and helps make you who you are. Such routines reinforce people's perspectives and put events in the same sorts of predictable and routine frameworks of meaning through trivial and pedestrian communication with one another in everyday life (Wood & Duck, 2006). But—here's the point of this section, so remember it well—you *do* your identity in front of the audiences, and they might evaluate and comment on whether you're doing it right. Although we used the extreme case about the gang member as an attention grabber, the same kinds of processes are going on in interaction when you profess your undying allegiance to one football team and your supposed hatred of the opposing team. The people around you do not resent it but actually encourage you and reinforce your expression of that identity. They share it and support it. Just as the gang member accepted his identity with all its disturbing implications, so do you when you categorize the opposing team as some kind of enemy. The underlying idea—that a group of people can be treated as nothing more than depersonalized, dehumanized others—runs through team loyalty and rivalry, town versus college kids, and any other kind of stereotyping.

Performative Self

So now that you know the importance of other people in influencing who you are, you are ready to move on to look more closely at the curious idea that you don't just *have* an identity; you actually *do* one. Part of an identity is not just *having* a symbolic sense of it but *doing* it in the presence of other people and doing it well in their eyes. This is an extremely interesting and provocative fact about communication: Everyone *does* his or her identity for an audience, like an actor in a play. Facework is part of what happens in everyday life communication (Chapter 2), and people have a sense of their own dignity and image—the person they want to be seen as. That is part of what gets transacted in everyday communication by the person and by others in the interaction who politely protect and preserve the person's "face." We can now restate this idea for the present chapter as being the performance of one's identity in public, the presentation of the self to people in a way that is intended to make the self look good.

Erving Goffman (1959) dealt with this particular problem and indicated the way in which momentary social forces affect identity portrayal. Goffman was particularly interested in how identity is performed in everyday life and how people manage their image in a way that makes them "look good" (Cupach & Metts, 1994). You will already have worked out for yourself that the concept of "looking good" means "looking good *to other people.*" It is therefore essentially a relational concept, but it takes you one step closer to looking at the interpersonal interaction that occurs on the ground every day. Rather than looking at society in the generalized and abstract way that George Herbert Mead did, Goffman focused on what you actually do in conversations and interactions.

As you recall, your portrayal of yourself is shaped by the social needs at the time, the social situation, the social frame, and the circumstances surrounding your performance. Remember the server from Chapter 1? She does not introduce herself that way to her *friends* ("Hi, I'm Roberta, and I'll be your server tonight . . .") except as a joke, so her performance of the server identity is restricted to those times and places where it is called for and appropriate. Goffman differentiated a **front region** and **back region** to social performance: The front region/front stage is where your professional, proper self is performed. For example, a server is all smiles and civility in the front stage of the restaurant when talking to customers. This behavior might be different from how he or she performs in the back region/backstage (say, the restaurant kitchen) when talking with the cooks or other servers and making jokes about the customers or about being disrespectful to them. That means the performance of your identity is not sprung into action by your own free wishes but by social cues that this is the right place and time to perform your "self" in that way.

An identity is a person making sense of the world not just for him- or herself but in a way that makes sense within a context provided by others. Any identity connects to other identities. You can be friendly when you are with your friends, but you are expected to be professional when on the job and to do student identity when in class. An individual inevitably draws on knowledge that is shared in any community to which he or she belongs, so any person draws on information and knowledge that are both personal and communal. If you change from thinking of identity as about "self as character" and instead see it as "self as performer," you also must consider the importance of linguistic competence in social performance, and that includes not doing or saying embarrassing or foolish things.

Embarrassment and Predicaments

Embarrassment is one of the big problems of social life and involves you actually performing a behavior that is inconsistent with the identity or face that you want to present. Cupach and Metts (1994; Metts, 2000) have done a large amount of research on this topic. Someone who wants to impress an interviewer but instead spills coffee on her lap will be embarrassed because her "face" of professional competence is undercut by clumsiness; someone who wants to present a "face" of being cool but who suddenly blushes or twitches will probably feel embarrassed because the nonverbal behavior contradicts the identity of being cool. In both cases, the actual *performance* of an identity (face) is undercut by a specific behavior that just does not fit that presentation of face.

People can be embarrassed by dumb acts that undercut their **performative self**, the doing of the identity that they have claimed for themselves (such as professional competence), momentarily like this, or they can get into longer-term **predicaments** that present a greater challenge to the performative self. Think of predicaments as extended embarrassment. If you go to a job interview and your very first answer makes you look stupid, you know you are still going to have to carry on through the interview anyway, with the interviewers all thinking you are a hopeless, worthless, and unhireable idiot. You'd rather jump into a vat of boiling sulfur right now, but you cannot; you have to sit it out watching their polite smiles and feeling terrible.

Predicaments, like standing up to give a speech and realizing you brought only page 1 of your 10 pages of notes can be a real test of character (it was for one of us authors, anyway), but predicaments test the performative self and challenge the person to live up to the claims presented in the symbolic identity that the face set up. Of course, predicaments are modified by relationships. As people become closer and more intimate, they are allowed to breach the presentation of one another's face to a greater degree than strangers may do (Metts, 2000). Part of knowing someone well is that you can cross the normal social,

Make Your Case

What was your most embarrassing experience, and why was it embarrassing? What did it say about you? What did you do about it?

physical, or psychological boundaries that exist for everyone else who does not know him or her so well.

Mock put-downs are quite a common form of intimate banter in English-speaking countries but not in Eastern cultures, which suggests that the notion of face and identity is a culturally influenced one on top of everything else that influences it. However, the idea that people work together in relationships to uphold one another's face through politeness is an important one, called **teamwork** by Goffman (1971). Direct challenges to another person's competence ("You are a failure!") are openly offensive in most circumstances, although the more intimate the relationship is, the greater the degree to which they are tolerated. Friends are permitted a great deal more latitude in making such comments than strangers are, and less offense is taken when a friend says such a thing than would be taken if a stranger or relatively distant and unknown colleague at work said it. Bosses may say it directly to an inferior because they have social power to break normal social rules, but it can still hurt. A worker who said it to a boss would be seen quite unambiguously as stepping outside the proper relational and hierarchical boundaries. This very fact makes a point that both context *and* relationships serve to define the sorts of communication about identity that are accepted, and vice versa. Except in live standup comedy shows where audience members attend expecting to see someone (preferably someone else) humiliated, the open attack on someone's identity management is a relational communication with great power and shock value.

Self Constituted/Transacted in Everyday Practices

Although this chapter has been about personal identity, we have seen that identity is molded by the ways in which the surrounding culture influences its expression, the way that you *do* your identity and are recognized as having one. Once you recognize that your identity is not just an internal structure but also a practical performance, the relevant communication involved in "being yourself" is affected by the social norms that are in place to guide behavior in a given society. People judge your identity performance and expect you to know about the same practical world and explain or account for yourself.

Practical Self

Your identity is done in a material world that affects who you are. For example, the fact that you can communicate with other people more or less instantaneously across huge distances by mobile telephone materially affects your sense of connection to other people. This practical self—and how the ability to do practical things affects your sense of self—is illustrated by the importance to many young people of learning to drive a car. When you can drive, not only do you go through the transformation of self as "more of a grown-up," but you can actually do lots of things when you have a car that you cannot do when you do not have one, so your sense of identity expands. Part of your *performance* of self is connected to the practical artifacts, accompaniments, and "stuff" that you use in your

Photo 5.4 How is your identity transacted in everyday practices? (See page 141.)

performance. If you have the right "stuff" (professional suit, bling, or a sports car), the self that you project is different from the self you perform when those things are not influencing your performance.

Accountable Self

An important element of doing an identity in front of an audience is that you become an **accountable self**, which essentially allows your identity to be morally judged by other people. What you do can be assessed by other people as right or wrong according to existing habits of society. Any practical way of performing identity turns identity itself into a moral action—that is, identity as a way of living based on choices made about actions that a person sees as available or relevant but that others will judge and hold to account. This point moves the discussion about social construction of identity on from interaction with other people through the force of society and its value systems. Society as a whole encourages you to take certain actions (do not park next to fire hydrants, protect the elderly and the weak, be a good neighbor, recycle!).

Moral accountability (which is related to the moral context for narratives) is a fancy way of saying that society as a whole makes judgments about your actions and choices and then holds you to account for the actions and choices that you make, but it also forcefully encourages you to act in particular ways and to see specific types of identity as "good" (patriot is good, traitor is bad; loyalty is good, thief is bad; open self-disclosure is good, passive aggression is bad, for example).

Improvisational Performance

The identity that you thought of as your own personality, then, is not made up of your own desires and impulses but is formed, performed, and expressed within a set of social patterns and judgments built up by values and practices in a community or culture through the relationships that people have with one another in it. The gang members did not call the shooter to account; the Indiana University fan is not asked why she is cheering for Indiana University by other Indiana University fans.

For all of these reasons, it makes sense to see a person's identity as a complex and compound concept that is partly based on history, memory, experiences, and interpretations by the individual, partly evoked by momentary aspects of talk (its context, the people you are with, your stage in life, your goals at the time), and partly a social creation directed by other people, society and its categories, and your relationship needs and objectives in those contexts. Your performance of the self is guided by your relationships with other people, as well as your social goals. Even your embodiment of this knowledge or your sense of self is shaped by your social practices with other people and your sense of their valuing your physical being. Your self-consciousness in their presence and the ways you deal with it also influence the presentation of yourself to other people. Although a sense of self/identity is experienced on the ground in your practical interactions with other people, you get trapped by language into reporting it abstractly as some sort of disembodied "identity," a *symbolic* representation of the little practices and styles of behavior that you actually experience in your daily interactions with other people. Once again, then, another apparently simple idea (identity, personality, self) runs into the relational influences that make the basics of communication so valuable to study.

Table 5.1 summarizes what you've learned in this chapter about identity and relationships.

Table 5.1 Some Ways to See Identity Communication and Relationships

Psychic/ reflective self	***Habits of thought/of behavior/of perception/identify a person's "personality."*** What you normally think of as identity a priori: Your communicative behavior just expresses the inner self.
Symbolic self	***Broad social forces affect self differentiation/characterization.*** Self arises out of social interaction and not vice versa; hence, it does not "belong to me." You are who you are because of the people you hang out with, interact with, and communicate with; you can be a different identity in different circumstances.
Performative self	***Present social situation affects self-portrayal.*** Selves act themselves out in a network of social demands and norms; you do your identity differently in front and back regions and try to present the right "face" to the people you are with.
Practical self	***Material world affects self/how you think of self.*** Practical aspects of materiality transform the concept of self. Your identity is represented by objects that symbolically make claims about the sort of person you are.
Accountable self	***Social context influences broad forms of portrayal.*** Personality is just an abstract concept. People act within a set of social ideas and habitual styles of thinking, allowing other people to comment and steer how we behave.
Improvisational performance	***There is a rhetorical spin to this and how "self" is presented.*** Ideology affects the manner of presentation of terms, characteristics, and so on. We try to narrate ourselves in the way that our society expects us to represent identity.

Focus Questions Revisited

Is a person's identity like an onion, built layer by layer and communicated slowly as intimacy increases?

For some reasons and purposes, it makes sense for us to see identity this way, but it really is not the only way that "identity" actually works in the everyday encounters of relationship life.

How do daily interactions with other people form or sustain your identity?

In at least two ways: Their responses to us affect the way we feel about ourselves; also, they act as Society's Secret Agents by innocently enforcing society's norms and beliefs through their comments on our own styles of behavior and identity performance.

How much of your "self" is a performance of social roles where you have to act out "who I am" for other people?

Much of what you do in everyday life is steered by your awareness of yourself as a social object for other people—hence, your performance for them of the roles and styles of behavior that are appropriate in the circumstances. Your "inner self" may be constrained by this awareness.

What is meant by a symbolic self, and why do we have to account to other people for who we are?

Your "self" is presented to other people as a symbol, and you have to describe yourself in terms and phrases that your audiences recognize as symbolically meaningful in the culture. You are also able to take an attitude of reflection that recognizes that you are an object of other people's perceptions and judgment. You will remember from Chapter 1 that people can observe your behavior and "go beyond" it to its symbolic meaning.

What is the role of culture in your identity experiences?

Culture has multiple roles in identity experience. For one thing, cultures regard "individuality" differently; for another thing, your origin from a particular culture steers the way you think about people and their styles of behavior; for still another thing, your culture is part of your identity, and people proudly claim their cultural heritage as part of "who they are."

Key Concepts

accountable self   (p. 137)

altercasting   (p. 129)

attitude of reflection   (p. 131)

back region   (p. 135)

dialectic tension   (p. 125)

front region   (p. 135)

identity   (p. 117)

labeling   (p. 128)

moral accountability   (p. 137)

norm of reciprocity   (p. 125)

performative self   (p. 135)

predicaments   (p. 135)

self-concept   (p. 121)

self-disclosure   (p. 124)

symbolic interactionism   (p. 131)

symbolic self   (p. 130)

teamwork   (p. 136)

Questions to Ask Your Friends

- Discuss with your friends or classmates the most embarrassing moment that you feel comfortable talking about, and try to find out what about the experience threatened your identity. What identity were you projecting at the time, and what went wrong with the performance?

- Look at how advertisers sell the *image* of particular cars in terms of what they will make you look like to other people; the advertisers recognize that your identity is tied up in your material possessions. Include in this consideration the following topics: How is your identity affected by your preferences in music, the Web, fashion magazines, resources, or wealth?

- Get a group of friends together and ask them each to write down what sort of vegetable, fish, dessert, book, piece of furniture, style of music, meal, car, game, or building best represents their identity. Read the responses out loud and have everyone guess which person is described.

Media Links

- Watch the movie *Sideways* (Payne, 2004) and fast-forward to the veranda scene during which Miles talks to Maya about his preference for wine and it becomes apparent that he is using wine as a metaphor about himself. He projects his identity through his interest in and knowledge about the subtleties of wines, and he uses it to describe himself and his hopes that Maya will learn to understand him.

Maya: You know, can I ask you a personal question, Miles?

Miles: Sure.

Maya: Why are you so into Pinot?

Miles: [*laughs softly*]

Maya: I mean, it's like a thing with you.

Miles: [*continues laughing softly*] Uh, I don't know, I don't know. Um, it's a hard grape to grow, as you know. Right? It's, uh, it's thin-skinned, temperamental, ripens early. It's, you know, it's not a survivor like Cabernet, which can just grow anywhere and, uh, thrive even when it's neglected. No, Pinot needs constant care and attention. You know? And in fact it can only grow in these really specific, little, tucked away corners of the world. And, and only the most patient and nurturing of growers can do it, really. Only somebody who really takes the time to understand Pinot's potential can then coax it into its fullest expression. Then, I mean, oh its flavors, they're just the most haunting and brilliant and thrilling and subtle and . . . ancient on the planet.

- Bring examples to class from magazines or TV shows that demonstrate how media representation of ideal selves (especially demands on women to be a particular kind of shape, but try to be more imaginative than just these images) are constantly thrown in our path.

- How do media shows encourage us to be open, honest, and real? Do television programs such as *The Jerry Springer Show* teach us anything about the "right" ways to be ourselves?

Ethical Issues

- If your identity is partly constructed by other people, how does this play out in relation to diversity, cultural sensitivity, and political correctness versus speaking the truth?

- Analyze the difficulties for someone "coming out" in terms of performance, social expectations, norms, and relationships with those around the person.

- If you have a guilty secret and are getting into a deep romantic relationship with someone, should you tell him or her early on or later? Or should you not tell him or her at all?

Answers to Photo Captions

Photo 5.1 ▪ There are messages about identity both "inside" the picture and "outside" it: The performance of femininity and womanhood are being communicated to the girl, a sense of the importance of looks and the enhancement of natural appearance in private. The picture also communicates to outsiders the role of personal hygiene in personal identity.

Photo 5.2 ▪ On special occasions we adopt prescribed roles, dress in prescribed ways, and enact prescribed rituals and behaviors in order to "do the right thing." A graduation is a good example of a time when individuals can temporarily lose control over their presentation of self as other people expect them to dress in particular ways and perform particular behaviors.

Photo 5.3 ▪ Your identity represents something symbolic to other people, and they may unjustly respond to aspects of your self by attempting to trivialize or humiliate you. The African Americans are being driven off a "Whites only" beach in 1963.

Photo 5.4 ▪ Interactions and experiences with other people give us a sense of our own identity and what it means to hold certain values and carry out certain types of action. This boy is learning how to "be a man" in his local community.

Student Study Site

Visit the study site at **www.sagepub.com/ciel** for e-flashcards, practice quizzes, and other study resources.

References

Altman, I., & Taylor, D. (1973). *Social penetration: The development of interpersonal relationships.* New York: Holt, Rinehart, and Winston.

Arendt, H. (1963). *Eichmann in Jerusalem: A report on the banality of evil.* Harmondsworth, UK: Penguin Books.

Baxter, L. A. (2004). Distinguished scholar article: Relationships as dialogues. *Personal Relationships, 11*(1), 1–22.

Baxter, L. A., & Braithwaite, D. O. (2008). Relational dialectics theory: Crafting meaning from competing discourses. In L. A. Baxter & D. O. Braithwaite (Eds.), *Engaging theories in interpersonal communication.* (pp. 349–361). Thousand Oaks, CA: Sage.

Baxter, L. A., & Montgomery, B. M. (1996). *Relating: Dialogs and dialectics.* New York: Guilford Press.

Berscheid, E., & Reis, H. T. (1998). Attraction and close relationships. In D. T. Gilbert, S. F. Fiske, & G. Lindzey (Eds.), *The handbook of social psychology* (4th ed., pp. 139–281). Boston: McGraw-Hill.

Burke, K. (1962). *A grammar of motives and a rhetoric of motives.* Cleveland: World Publishing Co.

Burleson, B. R., Holmstrom, A. J., & Gilstrap, C. M. (2005). "Guys can't say that to guys": Four experiments assessing the normative motivation account for deficiencies in the emotional support provided by men. *Communication Monographs, 72*(4), 468–501.

Caughlin, J. P., & Afifi, T. D. (2004). When is topic avoidance unsatisfying? Examining the moderators of the association between avoidance and dissatisfaction. *Human Communication Research, 30*(4), 479–513.

Cupach, W. R., & Metts, S. (1994). *Facework.* Thousand Oaks, CA: Sage.

Derlega, V. J., Metts, S., Petronio, S., & Margulis, S. T. (1993). *Self-disclosure.* Newbury Park, CA: Sage.

Dindia, K. (2000). Self-disclosure, identity, and relationship development: A dialectical perspective. In K. Dindia & S. W. Duck (Eds.), *Communication and personal relationships* (pp. 147–162). Chichester, UK: Wiley.

Football jibe killer sent to jail. (2007, October 27). *BBC.* Retrieved March 12, 2008, from http://news.bbc.co.uk/1/hi/scotland/glasgow_and_west/7063686.stm

Goffman, E. (1959). *Behaviour in public places.* Harmondsworth, UK: Penguin.

Goffman, E. (1971). *Relations in public: Microstudies of the public order.* New York: Basic Books.

Hess, J. A. (2000). Maintaining a nonvoluntary relationship with disliked partners: An investigation into the use of distancing behaviors. *Human Communication Research, 26,* 458–488.

Jourard, S. M. (1964). *The transparent self.* New York: Van Nostrand Reinhold.

Jourard, S. M. (1971). *Self-disclosure.* New York: Wiley.

Kellas, J. K. (2008). Narrative theories: Making sense of interpersonal communication. In L. A. Baxter & D. O. Braithwaite (Eds.), *Engaging theories in interpersonal communication* (pp. 241–254). Thousand Oaks, CA: Sage.

Luft, J., & Ingham, H. (1955). *The Johari window: A graphic model of interpersonal awareness.* Proceedings of the western training laboratory in group development, Los Angeles, University of California at Los Angeles.

Marwell, G., & Schmitt, D. R. (1967). Dimensions of compliance-gaining behavior: An empirical analysis. *Sociometry, 30,* 350–364.

Mead, G. H. (1934). *Mind, self, and society.* Chicago: University of Chicago Press.

Metts, S. (2000). Face and facework: Implications for the study of personal relationships. In K. Dindia & S. W. Duck (Eds.), *Communication and personal relationships* (pp. 74–92). Chichester, UK: Wiley.

Payne, A. (Director). (2004). *Sideways* [Motion picture]. United States: Fox Searchlight Pictures.

Petronio, S. (2002). *Boundaries of privacy.* Albany: State University of New York Press.

Shotter, J. (1984). *Social accountability and selfhood.* Oxford: Basil Blackwell.

Wood, J. T., & Duck, S. W. (Eds.). (2006). *Composing relationships: Communication in everyday life.* Belmont, CA: Thomson Wadsworth.

6

Talk and Interpersonal Relationships

Wwe want you to rethink relationships: They're not just about emotion. Instead, they are about knowledge, ways of understanding the world, ways of connecting symbols, and ways of connecting symbolically to other people. Of course, we are going to stress just how much communication helps you make connections between people and knowledge and that you really cannot have one process without the other. Communication and relationships, as well as what you know and how you know it, are directly connected.

Previously, we noted that everyday talk is done in an evaluative context involving critical thinking and (moral) judgment about what you hear and say. Critical thinking applies not only to stories told in politics or to persuasive appeals but also to listening to other people talk about themselves and their relationships. Furthermore, critical thinking can be stimulated by, or can focus on, nonverbal communication: "Why did she blush when she told me that bit of the story? Something fishy there…" Critical thinking about relationships can be based on the internal coherence of a breakup story, for example—whether it all seems to hang together and make sense—or the plausibility of the talk. You have heard friends tell a story about how they acted well in a romance or a friendship and, while listening politely and smiling pleasantly, privately thought skeptically to yourself, "Yeah, right!"

This chapter covers four topics:

1. How communication in relationships ratifies/supports your knowledge base by providing for your psychological and other needs,

2. How everyday communication increases intimacy level or moves relationships through positive stages,

3. How everyday communication decreases intimacy level or moves relationships through negative stages, and

4. Critical evaluation of the whole concept of relational stages.

Focus Questions

- How does your everyday communication with other people transact your relationships?
- How does your talk compose your relationships during everyday conversation?
- How do relationships grow or change, and how does this show up in speech?
- What are the different types of communication that take place when a relationship is coming apart?
- Do relationships develop and break down in a linear fashion?

What Is the Best Way to Connect Talk, Relationships, and Knowledge?

How many of your present beliefs do you discuss and debate with your friends and family? Have you ever considered how much of *what* you know depends on *who* you know? You may discuss your life, current news, the nature of the outside world, and how to interpret the events that happen in it with, for example, people at work or school. Researchers from different disciplines have shown over the years that you typically prefer to hang out with people with whom you share similar attitudes and general beliefs (Byrne, 1997; Kerckhoff, 1974; Sunnafrank, 1983; Sunnafrank & Ramirez, 2004). Thus, you tend to respect their judgments and enjoy talking to them because they often reinforce what you believe (Weiss, 1998)! Of course, you will occasionally disagree, but by and large, the friends you prefer to hang out with let you talk about yourself in ways you like. In turn, they talk about themselves in ways you like, adopt the attitudes and beliefs you like, and see the world in broadly the same way you do. Also very likely to have similar social, religious, racial, economic, and educational backgrounds, your friends, in short, live in worlds very like your own, and when you communicate with them in everyday life, you feel broadly supported and validated as a person who lives in a similar world of meaning.

Just think how much of your daily talk involves comparison of ideas with someone else ("What do you think of the way she's dressed?" "I didn't like that lecture, did you?" "I forgot to check Facebook this morning. What's new?"). Even such small talk and casual chatter serve to compose our experience of life and our relationships (Wood & Duck, 2006). Your interactions with friends may often seem light and unimportant—not, in fact, very productive. On the contrary, even small talk serves to reestablish the relationship, provide you with reality checks, give you information,

Think of a time when you asked a female friend for advice; then recall a situation where you asked a male friend for advice. What was different about how they encouraged or comforted you?

transmit news, bring you up to date, and, most important of all, make you feel included. That is a relational outcome: Inclusion is a relational term, and any talk, however small, that acknowledges and includes you serves a relational purpose.

Your everyday communication reinforces both your relationships and what you know, as well as makes you rely on the opinions of people you like, and thus you run the risk of dulling your critical thinking a little. You are more likely just to take their word for it. In Chapter 2, we discussed other ways relationships are established and represented in talk. The key point is that all talk performs a relational function, and we need to explore that process in detail. All forms of friendly and supportive communication actually show how you rely on your connections with other people to filter your knowledge and help you critically evaluate events, people, and situations. Because communication is about the distribution of knowledge, the people you know and with whom you spend your time affect your knowledge. They influence/steer/select the messages you send or attend to, the information you believe, the type of critical thinking you do, and how you evaluate the outcomes. So, not just a *result* of communication, relationships are also significant in the opposite process, the formation and transaction of knowledge—the creation of the world of meaning you inhabit.

Relationships also exert influence on the distribution of information. You tell secrets to your friends that you would not tell to strangers, and news travels through networks of folks who know one another (Bergmann, 1993; Duck, 2007). Relationships also affect what you believe or challenge about the world in general, how you think about other people, and how you evaluate their behavior (whom you gossip about and why, for example). The marketing world knows about the power of the connection among relationships, information flow, critical thinking, and "knowledge." Marketers use WOM (word of mouth) campaigns that exploit the fact that we respect our friends' opinions about the right purchases to make and what is "cool." In the latest marketing fad, "buzz agents" are paid to tell their friends about particular products, thereby creating "buzz" and influencing people to buy them (Carl, 2006).

Listen In On Your Life

Go to a busy public place (such as the student union, a shopping mall, or a coffee shop), and pay attention to the conversations going on around you. What percentage of the conversations involve people talking about themselves? How do you think the location you chose affected this percentage?

Building and Supporting Relationships

Robert Weiss (1974) identified six specific areas where relationships provide us with something special, needed, or valued. These six **provisions of relationships** are as follows:

Belonging and a Sense of Reliable Alliance

The major benefit that people desire from relationships is *belonging and a sense of reliable alliance:* You like to feel that someone is "there" for you. Quite often, you state this desire explicitly, but more often you just learn from daily interaction with somebody that he or she looks after your interests, cares for you, inquires about your state of mind/health, and can usually be relied upon to help when asked—and sometimes even without being asked. That's what Weiss meant by "reliable alliance," and it comes over in talk not only directly ("I'm here for you") but also indirectly as you listen to another person and realize (transact) from the talk that he or she really is reliable and interested in your welfare (Leatham & Duck, 1990).

Emotional Integration and Stability

The second of Weiss's provisions of relationships is *emotional integration and stability*. Other people provide you with emotional support in the form of a shoulder to cry on, and, in your daily communication, your friends often offer you comfort and support in gender-specific ways (Burleson, Holmstrom, & Gilstrap, 2005). They also, however, support your knowledge base. Carl and Duck (2004) indicated how much people rely on each other to verify, support, or do reality checks on the world in their everyday communication. Drawing on the previous work by Weiss (1974), they indicated the importance of using other people as sounding boards for emotions or responses to situations. For example, people often ask friends, "Did I do the right thing?" "Do you think I should believe what this person says?" or even "Should I take this job?" Friends also give you information about the rules for conducting relationships (Baxter, Dun, & Sahlstein, 2001) and offer you advice about other problems in life (Goldsmith & Fitch, 1997). Human beings find these commentaries emotionally fulfilling and valuable, of course, but they support your world of meaning in a deeper way, too.

Opportunity to Talk About Yourself

Opportunity to talk about yourself not only is enjoyable but subtly gives you extra chances to derive the above provisions from other interactions. People like to put themselves into their talk, offer their opinions and views, be important in stories they tell, and otherwise be part of a narrative of their own lives that makes them appear valuable and good. Indeed, one of the main things that makes a relationship more rewarding to people, according to Robert Weiss, is a sense of being known, so it is hardly surprising that self-disclosure (talking openly about oneself and revealing one's inner layers, discussed in Chapter 5) largely comprises what happens in relationship growth and maintenance.

Opportunity to Help Others

Humans also like the feeling of being there for others, which is Weiss's fourth provision: *opportunity to help others*. You like to be asked for advice because such a request values your way of looking at the world and recognizes your world of meaning. It also allows you to talk about yourself and thus simultaneously fulfills another provision noted above. Manusov, Kellas, and Trees (2004) examined how friends told and listened to one another's stories about a failure in their life and explored the facework (making someone "look good") done in the accounts. People who asked about the event and then received a very long and complex explanation felt more burdened, despite the fact that the speakers imagined such accounts were more acceptable from the listeners' points of view. So, although those who took the opportunity to help others actually ended up feeling burdened by an overlengthy response, at least the speakers appreciated the chance to talk about themselves!

Provision of Physical Support/ Reassurance of Worth and Value

A final set of ways relationships ratify and gratify your world is by providing support when you need it. Weiss divided this support into two provisions: the *provision of physical support* and the *reassurance of worth and value*. If you have to move a heavy piano, you need other people, for example, or you might need someone to drive you to the airport or look after your cat while you are on vacation. Relationships provide you with opportunities for such physical support from friends and relatives. You may feel valued by someone giving up his or her time for you in this way, but you certainly find it confirming when someone says, "Good job!" "Sure! Drop that jerk. You deserve better anyway," or "I'd love to help solve that with you." More important, relationships show you how other people see the world, how they represent/present it, what they value in it, what matters to them, and how your own way of thinking fits in with theirs. In such talk and action, they reassure your worth and value as a human being.

Everyday communication provides reassurance and the other provisions of relationship needs seamlessly. People advise, seek advice, help, seek help, encourage, reveal things about themselves, and talk to one another in ways that offer the above provisions all the time, often without being obvious. In the course of everyday life, you communicate with people who offer you ways to check your knowledge of the world, and you share knowledge about other people in return. Suppose someone praises you ("Great job!" "I love your outfit," "You did well on the test—and you are making great comments in class. You are obviously a good learner"). The speaker not only establishes the relational right to make comments about you but also shows a desire to connect positively with you and make you feel good about yourself. Organizing, reaffirming, correcting, or otherwise presenting a view of you that affects your knowledge of self and how you appear to other people, the person emphasizes those parts of the world in which you do things right and perform commendably. Thus, he or she communicates to you support for an area of your knowledge about yourself, transacting validation for that part of your identity. In contrast, criticism can upset your knowledge and confidence about yourself and your performances while also acknowledging the other person's relational rights to comment on you (or else you resent that the person claims such a right: "Who does he think he is?"). Whether the relationship or communication validates and supports your world or challenges and undermines it, the connection remains tight between relationships and what you know and believe.

Composing Relationships Through Talk

Talk transacts knowledge and relationships. Part of what is composed during the tight connections among talk, relationships, and knowledge is a range of different

Photo 6.1 How does your everyday communication with other people transact your relationships? How are the relationships between the people here conveyed and transacted in talk? (See page 168.)

relationships. These relationships are composed of and sustained by different styles of talk. Every culture has its own way of thinking about relationships, so the transactions of culture and relationships connect very directly in this chapter. For example, Japanese language differentiates more than 200 ways of indicating a speaker and listener's relationship, and whenever two Japanese speakers converse, they inevitably and directly signal their status relationship at very complex levels. By contrast, American culture often splits up relationships into a very basic distinction between "formal" and "informal." This broad differentiation includes important subtleties (e.g., hookups, cross-sex nonromantic relationships, speed dates, nonresidential parents, in-laws, buddies, "the 'rents").

Types of Relationships Recognized in Talk

People in Western culture also differentiate among strangers, neighbors, friends, family, and romantic partners, sometimes within categories (for example, among romantic partners, we differentiate between dates and spouses). Our language is not subtle enough to denote the level of differentiation in Japan, even though we might decide we need to reflect carefully on how we sign off on an e-mail or a letter, recognizing that "yours," "love," "see ya," and "cordially" each connotes a different relational message.

Western scholars make a distinction between social and personal relationships: In **social relationships**—for example, your relationships with servers (including those selling yak fat), store assistants, bus drivers, and prison guards, all of whom may change shifts with other individuals who continue to perform the same tasks and social functions—people are interchangeable. Only specified and irreplaceable individuals (e.g., your mother, father, brother, sister, or very best friend), on the other hand, may engage in **personal relationships** with you. You can't just pick a random person off the street and make him or her instantly into your best friend—and certainly not into your father or sister. You could in time attempt to turn servers, bus drivers, or checkout clerks into acquaintances, dates, or lovers. You cannot, however, just switch people around in personal relationship roles in the way that you could pick one cashier over another and still get served politely in an interchangeable social relationship.

Just as cultures denote different relationship types, so too do they value certain types of relationships over others. Some cultures notice "friends, acquaintances, and romances"; others attend more closely to relationships with parents and are deeply concerned about the management of respect. Confucian philosophy in Chinese culture represents six basic types of relationships, all of which center on men and five of which are essentially structured as superior-subordinate relationships: emperor-subject; father-son; husband-wife; elder brother–younger brother; teacher-student; and one of equality, friend-friend. In the United States, you may use titles in talk, such as "Professor," "sis," "pal," and "Mom," that directly indicate the status relationship of one speaker to another.

Keeping Relationships Going in Talk

Communication theorist Stuart Sigman (1991) considered how even small talk can keep relationships going. He wrote about **relational continuity constructional units (RCCUs),** or a means of recognizing and recording the fact that the relationship is still continuing even when the partners are *not* face-to-face and may be apart from one another. RCCUs are symbols that indicate that you expect the relationship will exist in the future even when you are not actually conducting it or that recognize that a separation or absence has ended and the relationship is still in place. Sigman divided them into *prospective, introspective,* and *retrospective* types.

Prospective Units

Prospective units provide recognition that an absence is about to begin. In essence, prospective units refer to the future while recognizing that, for the time being, the relationship's interaction will be suspended. Prospective units include "Let's set the agenda for next time" and "When shall we three meet again, in thunder, lightning, or in rain?" Any other form of communication—even nonverbal communication—that suggests the likelihood of the partner's return is also a prospective unit. For example, if one partner leaves a toothbrush in the other's apartment, the toothbrush indicates the missing partner will likely return and offers a recognition that the absence is purely temporary. Sigman referred to such nonverbal evidence as "spoors," like the track marks made by deer in snow, that indicate the partner's previous physical presence (and expected return).

Make Your Case

Listen to how you talk with friends differently from strangers during a chosen day. Note the kinds of differences in the relationships involved. How many relationships are with intimate strangers or, more accurately, with familiar acquaintances (people you talk to and whom you know well enough not to ignore but do not feel close to)? Look at the lists you have created in this exercise, and identify the differences between communication with friends and communication with strangers. What topics do you talk about with friends but not strangers? What range of topics do you talk about in each type of relationship? Does the topic, style, or range of topics make a difference between the relationships, or is it something else? Talk to your class about these differences.

Introspective Units

By contrast, *introspective units* are direct indications of a relationship's existence during the physical absence of one partner. The difference between introspective units and prospective units is that prospective units recognize that the absence is about to happen whereas introspective units acknowledge it as already happening. Examples include wedding rings worn when away from the spouse, greetings cards, phone calls, mediated contact, and, of course, e-mail messages.

Retrospective Units

The final category—namely, *retrospective units*—directly signals the end of an absence. The most familiar examples of retrospective units are a kiss upon greeting or a handshake upon reunion, and the most common forms of conversation that fit this category are catch-up conversations and talk about the day (Vangelisti & Banski, 1993). By reporting on their experiences during the day, partners emphasize their psychological togetherness, as well as a shared interest in one another's lives and the events that happened in those lives during their physical separation. Hence, in these communicative moments, or "end-of-the-day talks," with your partner or friends, you relate to each other as well as simply report what happened.

Notice again, then, how even little bits of small talk often serve relational purposes and how even such phrases as "talk soon" do something to compose relationships in everyday life: They essentialize your relationships and establish you as connected with other people because they are important to you and you want them to know how you feel and what you did. This connection is the essential function of talk (Chapter 2). People's favorite complaint when they miss someone they know well is that they cannot talk to that person as frequently as they wish. If you have ever been in a long-distance relationship, you know what we mean (Sahlstein, 2004, 2006); it's just not the same when you cannot talk to people when you feel like it or as frequently. *What* is just not the same, however, is that the relationship is essentialized differently because the patterns of talk are different.

Your normal daily conversations compose and essentialize relationships in a stronger way than do long-distance relationships, and much of the casual conversation you have with the people you know is a steady, if overlooked, reinforcement of your relationships. Frankly, many of your conversations with friends are probably not big slices of intimacy, just a lot of small stuff that makes you feel connected—the "essential function" of talk.

Talk and Relational Change

Any relationship between people is partly indexed and essentialized (see Chapter 2) by the kinds of talk that they do—either the contents of their talk or how they talk. But how does your talk with someone change your relationship—turning a casual friend into a best friend, for example—or how do you get acquainted with people in ways that increase intimacy? The hypertext (Chapter 2) in your conversation helps you both identify and maintain your intimacy level, and your willingness to tell each other your private thoughts helps you recognize your deeper connection to one another as individuals. More important than such relationships being *indexed* in talk is the fact that friendships are based on increased personal knowledge about someone else. Your talk changes as it essentializes a growing understanding of another person and a greater ability to move around in the map of his or her psyche and way of being. Once again, knowledge, communication, and relationships interconnect.

A less obvious relationship change is how degrees of intimacy are altered as relationships grow; even talk about oneself can alter the form (or comfort level) of the relationship. As a relationship becomes more intimate, partners must change the ways they talk with one another (otherwise you would not be able to distinguish close friends from acquaintances), and you may recall from Chapter 2 that Planalp and Garvin-Doxas (1994) showed that people are actually quite skilled at differentiating between friends and acquaintances in speech they overhear. Therefore, it must be true that as a relationship grows in intimacy, someone (at least one partner) is driving it forward by opening up intimate topics or changing to more relaxed styles of talk.

Moving Between Types of Relationships

Now stop and think about the following. If you know there are different kinds of relationships, it must also be true that we can transition from one kind to another. Under the right conditions, you can cross the boundaries between "not allowed" and "allowed" or "inappropriate" and "appropriate" behaviors as the level of appropriateness changes to suit the new relationship. Any development of relationships must involve *crossing boundaries* between one level and another, between one set of permitted behaviors and another, and between one definition of the relationship and another. When you move from acquaintances to friends, dates to partners, lovers to enemies, or spouses to divorcés, you are moving across the boundaries between different types of relationships in your culture, and you say and do different things together.

Most of what we say—and what relationship research has typically presumed—about crossing boundaries, particularly in romance, reflects the idea of a progression from "no emotion" to "intimacy" and then to "greater intimacy." Of course, in today's world, relational technologies such as the Internet, cell phones, and Twitter have altered how people experience romance, and hookups occur without any traditional relationship development (Paul, 2006). This new approach to romance necessarily invalidates much of the old research that was based on outdated romantic practices inappropriate to the experience of people now in college; it does not, however, invalidate the thesis of this book that relationships of all sorts are reflected in talk, communication, and two people's knowledge base about one another, rather than in some abstract emotions. If you see people in public these days, at least a third of them will be *relating*—such as, talking on their cell phones (see Chapter 12). When you see them, they will be conducting and performing relationships in talk, not in any traditional sense transacting relationships in emotion.

In any culture, the connection between relationships and communication is inescapably built into other sorts of talk that occur, how "respect" for a superior might be transacted in communication, and the acceptable ways in which closeness can be spoken. Think about going up to your instructor and saying, "I love you" or "I hate you." How do you think he or she would respond? Why?

So how do people signal or bring about change in relationships through communication? Because most research on romantic relationships has been carried out on college students, some in the 1980s and 1990s before cell phones or the Internet, relational development from initial contact to romantic involvement is often represented as a developmental progression driven by a simple growth of personal/internal emotions, from first impression to long-term affection. Forget for the moment that this scenario does not necessarily represent the experience of older people, those with lives outside college, or those not involved in a romantic relationship. Note instead that it underestimates how often networks and people introduce partners to one another (which actually happens approximately 60% of the time; Parks, 2006) and the extent to which people connect on the Internet before ever meeting face-to-face. Yet, the development of romance is reported in most books as something that two people do for themselves on the basis of individual and internal feelings of love and initial attraction that they express and communicate in affectionate ways. It is all too rarely seen as a change in talk based on the information individuals know (or have inferred) about each other's ways of thinking about the world. Because talk essentializes relationships rather than merely indexes them, any change in a relationship involves real change in talk or mode and style of communication.

The interesting point here is how talk and communication connect at these different levels to relating and hence to emerging differences in relationships. We can change relationships by the subtle things already written about or by direct talk intended instrumentally to change them.

Direct and Indirect Talk to Change Relationships

Direct talk about relationships is something people do in special ways, on special occasions, and with very special care. For one thing, any direct talk about a relationship forces the partners to focus on its explicit definition or type, which can involve immediate definition of the relational state in a way that they had not foreseen or do not find truly welcome.

In 1985, Baxter and Wilmot pointed out the difficulties people have when they raise certain topics for discussion in a relationship. It is actually quite difficult to make the relationship itself a topic of discussion, and the phrase "Let's talk about our relationship" sends chills down the spine of most people, particularly men (Acitelli, 1988). There is no escape once the topic comes up. You cannot talk about the relationship without ending up somehow defining it and its meaning to the two partners involved. For at least one of them, the result may be unwanted. He or she may have hoped that the relationship would be defined as something stronger and with a better future than the other person is willing to accept. The best outcome is that the two people agree to see the relationship in a particular way that they both accept. All other outcomes are bad for at least one of the people involved.

Perhaps partly for this reason, talk that develops or restrains movements between relationship types tends to be indirect. Asking someone "Will you have sex with me?" is a direct and very high-risk strategy, whereas many indirect strategies are more effective without being threatening (e.g., a warm kiss, a bunch of flowers, a deep sigh, a longing look, or even a smart or sexy outfit). For this reason, flirtation is one of the key ways people push the envelope in relationships through *indirect* communication.

Flirtation is a safe way to propose relationship growth for two reasons: First, it generally serves as an indirect form of relationship question, and second, it can be taken as either a simple statement of fact, a friendly joke, or something more sexually or relationally loaded. Because it is ambiguous in this way, flirtation is deniable—you can always claim you were "just teasing." If the person you flirt with is interested in a relationship, his or her response will accept the relationally loaded reading of the message; if the person is not interested, he or she can "read" the message as fun or fact and nothing more. For example, a friend of ours was interested in a cashier at a local supermarket, and when he paid by check, the cashier asked, "Is everything current?" He replied, "Yes, especially the phone number." This could be read as a statement of fact or as an invitation to call. Actually, the cashier did call him, and they became lovers for 10 years.

> **Contrarian Challenge**
>
> We have noted that talk changes as relationships change, but is this a chicken and egg problem? Which comes first?

Stages in Relationship Development

An all-too-easy assumption, backed up by popular cultural beliefs, is that relationships go through stages, from initial contact to strong attachment. Honeycutt (1993) has questioned whether the stages actually exist or are merely assumed to exist in our culture. True: You can identify stages in relationships (dating, engagement, and marriage, for example), but the progression is rarely simple, and many an engagement has had a rocky road or been called off temporarily. Sometimes, the relationship reverts to a previous and less intimate form. Couples sometimes revert from engagement to dating, to just being friends, or even to being enemies. None of these tracks really follows a true progression, does it?

Even in the development of a relationship, one person might not want it to move ahead too fast and may resist his or her partner's attempts to make it grow, or some people might be wary of letting others into their lives and will try hard to keep them—the intrusive neighbor, the undesirable coworker, or the unwanted romantic who won't take no for an answer—at a distance. Hess (2000) indicated that people have an extensive range of communicative strategies for keeping disliked people at a distance, from simply ignoring them to treating them as objects to direct and open hostility and antagonism. In normal life, however, people know that unwanted relationships happen and have strategies to deal with it, so the rosy assumption that all relationships develop positively is too simplistic.

All the same, relationship development is often treated in research as if it is based on individual feelings or attitudes toward the other person that are assumed, as emotions deepen, to lead to a progressive relationship. This theory assumes that as feelings intensify, they are just worked out unproblematically and translated into behavior, and the relationship develops more or less straightforwardly from emotions without the involvement of—and certainly not with any particular behavioral effort from—the individuals concerned. How the relationship actually develops in behavioral or communicative

Photo 6.2 How do relationships grow or change, and how does this show up in speech? (See page 168.)

terms is often not explained but merely measured as an increase in intimacy assessed by means of scales and self-reports. If people report steadily increasing "intimacy," they must have a steadily deepening relationship, and it must have become progressively deeper as their intimacy grew. In fact, this theory is often called the evolutionary course of personal relationships. Think, though: Is it all that realistic? Not at all for those shy, awkward, or inept people who desperately want to relate to others but cannot summon the courage to develop their relationships.

The theory may not be real in other ways, either. In fact, as Jesse Delia pointed out in long-ago 1980, most of our relationships are quite shallow and do not really develop at all, even with frequent contact. How much deeper is your "relationship" with your regular supermarket checkout clerk than it was the first time you went to the grocery store? Also,

Did you know that 41% of people describe themselves as shy, and 24% feel it is a serious enough problem that they should seek help to overcome it (Pilkonis, 1977)?

many relationships are deliberately kept at a careful distance, and there are many people you don't ever want to get to know in great and intimate depth (such as your defense attorney, your boss, your professor, or even, in some cases, your roommate). By far, the majority of your relationships in everyday life are weak ties of this loose and distant nature (Granovetter, 1973). Can you generalize about the development of relationships, then? The next section explores a different model for relationship progression.

The Relationship Filtering Model

Duck's (1988, 1999) Relationship Filtering Model suggests that people pay attention to a number of different cues used in sequence as they try to form an impression of another person's underlying thought structure. The sequence in which you pay attention to characteristics of other people is basically the sequence in which you encounter them: physical appearance, behavior/nonverbal communication, roles, and attitudes/personality. At each point in the sequence, people are filtered out, and only those who pass all filters become friends or lovers. The model follows the intuitive process through which you get to know people layer by layer and assumes your basic goal is to understand them on the basis of whatever cues are available at the time. At each deeper level, you get a better understanding of how they tick, and you let them deeper into your world (Figure 6.1).

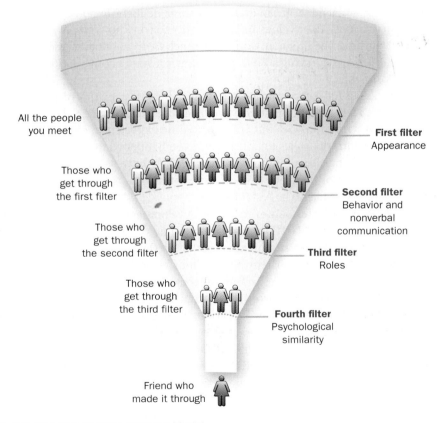

Figure 6.1 The Relationship Filtering Model

Think about meeting and getting to know strangers. When you meet obvious members of your culture, it is reasonable to assume you share common language and probably a set of beliefs about your culture's workings. Typically careful of strangers, however, newly acquainted people engage in safely noncontroversial small talk: You never know if someone is an ax murderer and just hasn't told you yet. The conversation normally stays on safe topics unless you meet in a singles' bar, on a speed date, or in a context clearly intended to promote relational growth (such as "welcome to the neighborhood" events or orientation weeks).

When you meet strangers, all you have to go on initially is how they look and sound. In everyday life when basic personal information is missing, you seek it out; interactions with strangers focus on information gathering, asking questions, and providing information about self, such as where you come from, your general background, and perhaps some of your personal views. Mostly, this information appears inconsequential: Who really cares which high school you attended? Well, the answer is that this sort of trivial information provides evidence about your background—even your religion, socioeconomic class, or style of thinking—that can be useful to your "audience." If you go on to make evaluative remarks about the school itself, you could give your audience helpful insights into your general attitudes, ways of thinking, and values. These pieces of information might be important in building a picture of yourself that will help other people make a decision about whether they are interested in allowing you through to the next filter to become their acquaintance or friend. You can even make some deductions about strangers' looks that might help you judge their values and personality so you know how to talk to them. If someone is young, he or she probably won't have much to say about arthritis, and if someone is wearing a suit and carrying a Bible, you might not start a conversation with him or her about Darwinism.

The more you get to know people—whether colleagues at work or people in your classes—the better the map of their world of meaning. Most of your classmates are, at best, little-known acquaintances, but you share some experiences and knowledge and would have some common topics to talk about if you happened to get stuck in an elevator or had to sit together on a long bus journey. You'd have some common topics of knowledge and an idea of their position on issues but perhaps not the depth of understanding that talk with a friend has established.

As Duck (2007, p. 80) notes, however, "[T]he development of relationships is not simplistically equivalent to the revelation of information nor to the decrease of uncertainty. The process of relationship development is created by the *interpretation* of such things by the partners, not by the acts themselves." In other words, the relationship grows not from the information that you learn about the other person but from how you "go beyond" it. Physical appearance, nonverbal communication, roles, and attitudes are *information loaded,* and you can "go beyond" them to make inferences about a person's worlds of meaning. You are much more likely to meet people of the same race, educational background, socioeconomic status, and religion as you, leading to a tendency to assume, when you meet such people, that you share common values at some level. Later interaction may prove that you share fewer values than you first thought, but at least you began the relationship with a good working hypothesis.

When you first meet people, therefore, the Relationship Filtering Model asserts that you will *assume,* unless they demonstrate otherwise, they are similar to you but that your goal is ultimately to understand them. The same principle applies to all other "stages" of the Relationship Filtering Model; namely, your goal is to understand more accurately how the other person thinks—and sees the world.

When you first see people, even from a distance, you may make assumptions about them just on the basis of their appearance. You can observe their age, race, sex, dress, number of tattoos and body piercings, height, and physical attractiveness and any marked social stigmas, such as extremely unusual hairstyles or disfigurements, visible disabilities, or physical peculiarities. Although these cues do not necessarily provide accurate information about people, they nevertheless allow you to make inferences about their inner world of meaning. The Relationship Filtering Model assumes that you filter out people who do not appear to support

Strategic Communication

An interview is a special situation where the interviewer has more personal information about you than you have about him or her. How do you think this inequality affects your ability to build a relationship with this person? What could you do to gain knowledge about the interviewer?

your ways of seeing the world or confirming self and thus are not prospects for the kind of relationship you like or are seeking. As you begin to interact more, you can make more accurate judgments about whether people are likable or unlikable and whether they support your worldviews. If they pass the filter, you may begin to take extra efforts to include them in your social circle. In all of your filtering interactions, you are really trying to find out what people are like at the level of their deeper psychology, so you aim all the questions you ask and all the communication strategies you adopt toward finding these deeper selves. The more fully you understand somebody, the more you understand how he or she thinks. The Relationship Filtering Model proposes this ultimate goal of understanding people's thinking as the goal of all communicative activity in relationship development. The more you understand someone and the more he or she appears to support your world of meaning, the more you want to hang out with him or her and the more you use emotional labels like "friendship" and "love" to represent this connection.

The Serial Construction of Meaning Model

The Relationship Filtering Model later developed into a model of the **serial construction of meaning** (Duck, 1994, 2007). This model specifically deals with how two individuals come to understand and appreciate one another through talk, which reveals their shared experiences and leads to a larger understanding that they use the same frameworks/worlds of meaning. The basic idea of this model is the same as the filtering model with the added indication of four steps in which this process can be developed by talk. In the first step, two people have had the same experience but do not know it because they have not talked about it (*commonality*). Suppose that both have been skiing in Montana but don't know it because it has not come up in a conversation. Although they have an experience in common, they do not yet have any reason to believe it. What if they then move on to discuss either skiing or Montana and come to realize that they have had the same experience (*mutuality*)? They now both know something about each other that suggests they have something in common. Of course, however, one of them may have loved the experience while one had a terrible time. The next thing they need to

In this model, two people A and B have feelings about an experience X. In the final step (shared meaning), they realize that they share meanings and evaluations of other things too (M, N, O, Y, Z), and the model represents the way in which they gradually connect to one another and finally see each other as a unit that shares evaluations of several different experiences.

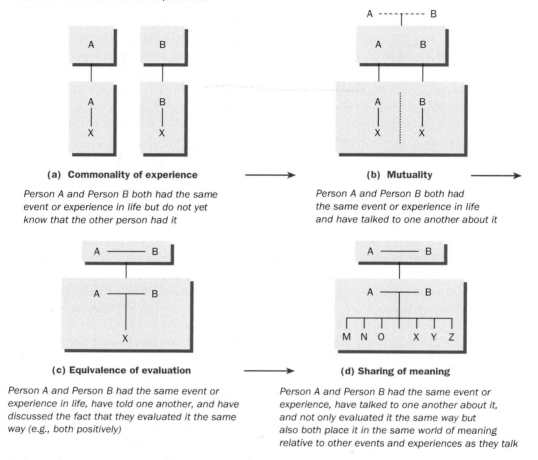

(a) Commonality of experience ⟶

Person A and Person B both had the same event or experience in life but do not yet know that the other person had it

(b) Mutuality ⟶

Person A and Person B both had the same event or experience in life and have talked to one another about it

(c) Equivalence of evaluation ⟶

Person A and Person B had the same event or experience in life, have told one another, and have discussed the fact that they evaluated it the same way (e.g., both positively)

(d) Sharing of meaning

Person A and Person B had the same event or experience, have talked to one another about it, and not only evaluated it the same way but also both place it in the same world of meaning relative to other events and experiences as they talk

Figure 6.2 A Model of the Serial Construction of Meaning

know, then, is whether they evaluate the whole experience in the same way (*equivalence of evaluation*). As they discuss what they made of their respective trips, they may come to see that they both enjoyed it and that it meant the same to both of them. The deeper final step is placing the Montana skiing experience in the context of lots of other experiences and evaluations or attitudes. In this step of the conversation, the two people come to understand that the skiing trip meant the same to them not just as an experience but also in relation to their broader worlds of meaning. For example, they may see that they both love the outdoors, believe in the importance of fitness and exercise, and delight in visiting the mountains in particular (*shared meaning*). This final step in realizing a larger shared world of meaning represents a magical moment, a kind of Holy Grail of relating: realizing how another person's mind works, that it is very similar to yours, and that you like each other. Figure 6.2 illustrates the serial construction of meaning model.

Coming Apart

Unfortunately, not all relationships work, and some come apart at the seams. Duck (1982) and Rollie and Duck (2006) have proposed a basic model to explain the workings of relational breakup—in particular, the conversational changes that take place at different points in the process. The original model (Duck, 1982) proposed five stages, moving from the negative thoughts inside an individual's head to how the broader social network eventually becomes involved with the final story about ending a relationship.

Duck's (1982) model focuses on the uncertainties surrounding the end of relationships, which involve the partners and others in the network. In the **intrapsychic process**, an individual simply reflects on the strengths and weaknesses of a relationship and begins to consider the possibility of ending it. At this stage, the person often highlights in his or her mind the advantages of leaving over the disadvantages, as well as the disadvantages of staying over the advantages.

Next, the **dyadic process** involves confronting the partner and openly discussing a problem with the relationship. This confrontation may be unpleasant or lead to greater mutual understanding and reconciliation. If reconciliation does not occur here, the process goes on.

In the third phase, the **social process**, the person tells other people in his or her network about the relationship problem, seeking either their help to keep the relationship together or their support for his or her version of why it has come apart. You would like people to hear your side of things. What's more, you would like them to agree with your presentation!

Fourthly, the **grave dressing process** involves creating the story of why a relationship died and erecting a metaphorical tombstone that summarizes its main points from birth to death.

More recently, Rollie and Duck (2006) added a further **resurrection process**, which deals with the ways people prepare themselves for new relationships after ending an old one. The end of a particular relationship is not the end of all relational life, and one of people's major tasks once any single particular relationship has finished is to begin seeking a replacement. The Rollie and Duck model is strongly focused on the types of communication that occur during each process.

Rollie and Duck (2006) discuss the talk topics and patterns of communication that go with each process. For example, in the intrapsychic process, the

Photo 6.3 As relationships come apart, people, especially couples, find it harder to interact and tend to become more hostile and unsympathetic in their behaviors toward each other. What are the signs that this couple is in distress about their relationship? (See page 168.)

person withdraws and reflects alone and thus pulls back somewhat from the partner—a form of "leakage" in behavior rather like the leakage in nonverbal activity discussed in Chapter 3. In the dyadic process, the person speaks specifically with the partner and focuses on the relationship itself ("Our Relationship Talks"). Because these discussions take time from other activities, friends may notice they do not see as much of the person as before and suspect something is wrong. In the social process, the person actively seeks greater contact and communication with third parties—not with the partner—to get advice, to cry on someone's shoulder, to get supportive commentary, or even to have his or her evaluation of the partner confirmed ("I always told you he was a jerk!").

The grave dressing process involves storytelling, and you've probably heard a lot of breakup stories yourself. The most usual form of breakup story follows a narrative structure that portrays the speaker as a dedicated but alert relater who went into the relationship realizing it was not perfect and needed work. After all, the speaker wants to look like a good person, not a fool! The speaker then tells of all the work that went into the relationship but how the partner was unresponsive or unhelpful, or perhaps both partners were mature enough to realize their relationship was not going to work out, so they made the tough but realistic decision to break it off. Such a narrative is advantageous in its representation of the person not as "damaged goods" but as perfectly reasonable, a good relational worker ripe and ready for a resurrection and a new healthy relationship. So this kind of breakup story, therefore, projects a person's identity as attractive to other people looking for relationships.

Other sorts of relationship breakup stories normally indicate how a partner betrayed the speaker, but all these accounts follow a basic narrative form (Chapter 2) and make the speaker look OK, if somewhat shocked. Listen for such stories. You can learn a lot about human nature and about particular people by listening to the stories they tell about relationships. Figure 6.3 shows the breakdown process model.

So Are There Stages in Relationship Development or Not?

In our experience, students find the linear progression idea built into "stages" both informative and frustrating. Although familiar with the idea that relationships take steps, grow, or pass from one stage to another, they recognize the messiness of life: that it does not easily fall into such rigid steps and stages. In part, student dissatisfaction comes from seeing that the different types of relationships are not so similar. One date is not necessarily like another, every engagement has unique features, and all personal relationships are importantly different. Life is just too complex to fit into simple boxes, categories, stages, and progressions.

You have probably also experienced relationships that have not moved smoothly from one stage to the next. Sometimes you may be hard put to say what stage a relationship is at—or even whether it is "on" or "off" (remember junior high school?). In particular, stage models tend to underestimate the extent of individuals' resistance to progression. In the case of a declining relationship, people very often try hard to stop the decline and

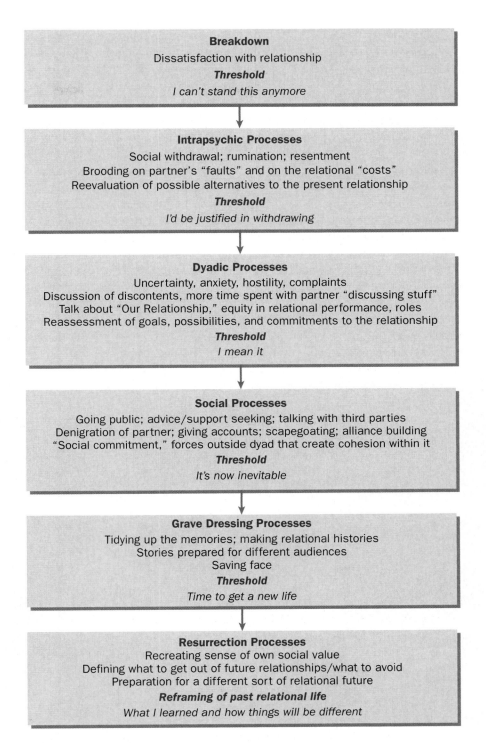

Breakdown
Dissatisfaction with relationship
Threshold
I can't stand this anymore

Intrapsychic Processes
Social withdrawal; rumination; resentment
Brooding on partner's "faults" and on the relational "costs"
Reevaluation of possible alternatives to the present relationship
Threshold
I'd be justified in withdrawing

Dyadic Processes
Uncertainty, anxiety, hostility, complaints
Discussion of discontents, more time spent with partner "discussing stuff"
Talk about "Our Relationship," equity in relational performance, roles
Reassessment of goals, possibilities, and commitments to the relationship
Threshold
I mean it

Social Processes
Going public; advice/support seeking; talking with third parties
Denigration of partner; giving accounts; scapegoating; alliance building
"Social commitment," forces outside dyad that create cohesion within it
Threshold
It's now inevitable

Grave Dressing Processes
Tidying up the memories; making relational histories
Stories prepared for different audiences
Saving face
Threshold
Time to get a new life

Resurrection Processes
Recreating sense of own social value
Defining what to get out of future relationships/what to avoid
Preparation for a different sort of relational future
Reframing of past relational life
What I learned and how things will be different

Figure 6.3 Breakdown Process Model

When searching for a "breakup" photo for this page, the only photos we could find featured women who were brokenhearted rather than men. Even though the picture we finally selected includes a man who appears to be upset, a woman is clearly at the forefront. What does this tell you about cultural views of relationships?

do not want it to happen. It hurts! So they often propose to reconcile or make up and stop things from falling apart. Much of their activity seems to suggest that they do not—as the stage models might suggest—see a breakup as inevitable.

Not always obvious to the partners at the time, the breakup of a relationship could be the beginning of the end or simply a blip on the graph. It is not as unavoidable or programmatic as researchers assume. You may already have seen one reason why: Researchers tend to ask people to report on what has happened to them, which of course focuses them on reports of the past ("retrospective reports"). When people give retrospective reports, they fit everything into a narrative structure in the form discussed in Chapter 2. Because they already know what happened, they can shape their reports in a way that makes sense of events—even those that may have been messy or uncertain at the time. Because our culture sees relationships as developing in terms of stages and steps, people therefore tend to report this relational activity in such terms, which researchers then eagerly fit into models that show stages and steps. Retrospective reports also accentuate the notion that relationships are plainly goal oriented even when life is less clear cut.

Photo 6.4 Do relationships develop and break down in a linear fashion? (See page 168.)

The possibility that relationships are redefined quietly and almost thoughtlessly during the progress of talk and are not relentlessly progressive is ignored in such models. In reality, it is important to focus on relational change as a whole—not just big changes but the little ones too—and not just on conscious and directed linearity but on the uncertainty that surrounds the future outcome of relationships and the different ways they are essentialized in the talk of everyday life. These bits of talk can lead to questions about the nature and form of the relationships, which is how change occurs. Is dissolution a special case of human processing or just an extension of these processes? It is one more example of how talk changes relationships in the context of uncertainty about the future. People talk, things happen, and relationship consequences arise. In short, your talk reflects cultural expectations and can lead to self-fulfilling prophecy. Processes of change may be connected to everyday experiences in complex ways and are not necessarily different just because researchers (and particularly researchers' methods) treat them as such. If you listen critically to how talk makes relationships work, we hope you will agree.

You have probably noticed that every relationship that benefits you also brings you difficulties, what Jackie Wiseman (1986) elegantly referred to as the bond/bind dilemma. To be in a successful relationship with someone, you must give something up or be prepared to make sacrifices. If you want to benefit from a bond with another person, you must also be prepared to put up with the binds, such as driving him or her to the airport, and to supply the other provisions of relationship that we discussed at the beginning of the chapter. We humans do not simply *need* these provisions for ourselves but also *supply* them for others, so the provisions of relationships are a two-way street.

A more complicated illustration of this idea by Baxter and Montgomery (1996) pays attention to the dialectic tensions present in relationships that people have to manage day-to-day. A dialectic tension is essentially a built-in contradiction between two aspects of the same dimension, such as **autonomy-connectedness** or **openness-privacy.** Everyone wants to be autonomous and independent; everyone simultaneously wants to connect with someone else. For that reason, from time to time you experience the tension between autonomy and connectedness and must make choices about how to handle it. In the same way, you recognize that you must be open and honest with your partners in relationships, but you also need some privacy and do not always wish to tell them everything. The operation of these two dialectics, demonstrated in the talk that individuals have with one another, is often very significant in relationships. The simultaneous push/pull that individuals experience in negotiating their relational activities tends to show through in their talk. Once again, it seems that stages are not clearly laid out in relationships but rather that you experience ups and downs, pushes and pulls, and tensions and countertensions in almost all of your relational experiences. If your talk reflects a degree of ambivalence about what is happening in a relationship, that is because relationships are very complicated to conduct successfully.

Given all these pieces of evidence, then, it is not surprising that relationships are often turbulent and that stage models of relationship growth and decline can be viewed as too simplistic in the real world. Certainly, as we indicated at the beginning of the chapter, relationships are not simply driven by emotions but are the result of complex management of competing forces handled in both direct and indirect talk.

Focus Questions Revisited

How does your everyday communication with other people *transact* your relationships?

Everyday communication with other people transacts your relationships by supporting your knowledge base and providing some of the psychological and other needs for support and understanding. Several forms of communication serve to include people in relationships, thus transacting the intimacy between them. There are several forms of communication that build support and sustain relationships, ranging from direct intimacy talk to indirect discovery of similarity.

How does your talk compose your relationships during everyday conversation?

Talk composes your relationships both directly (for example, through requests for friendship and connection or requests to end a relationship) and indirectly by demonstrating social and personal relationships in the kind of talk two persons engage in. Everyday chitchat can show that a relationship still exists between two people, and friends as compared to acquaintances tend to take much more for granted and do less explaining in their conversations. Relationships are also sustained by relational continuity constructional units, or small-talk ways of demonstrating that a relationship persists through absence.

How do relationships grow or change, and how does this show up in speech?

Relationships grow and change in several ways, as people become more knowledgeable about one another and more relaxed in each other's company. In the early stages of a relationship's development, conversation tends to be about broad and uncontroversial topics, where people need to fill in details about themselves and their past history so the other person can understand. As the relationship becomes more developed, individuals need to fill in less background information and are able to take much more for granted.

What are the different types of communication that take place when a relationship is coming apart?

The breakdown of relationships is marked by changes in both the topic of conversation and the audience to which the person communicates. In the early parts of a breakup when an individual is simply contemplating ending a relationship, he or she tends to withdraw from social contact and become very brooding. The second phase of a breakup is characterized by confrontation with a relational partner and less time spent with other friends. A third phase develops where the person decides to tell friends and associates about the breakup and to enlist their support. In the fourth phase, the person develops and tells a story to the world at large, explaining how the breakup occurred and making him- or herself "look good." The final (resurrection) phase is characterized by communication aimed at developing new relationships and letting go of the past.

Do relationships develop and break down in a linear fashion?

No. There are many cultural reasons why people would like to believe that there are stages in relationships, but these cultural beliefs tend to force their narratives of relationship into a pattern that conforms with their beliefs and therefore creates a self-fulfilling prophecy. People can make sense of both the development and the breakup of relationships, often a messy process, only retrospectively, and it is easy to make a relationship look as if it moved in linear fashion even when it did not.

Key Concepts

autonomy-connectedness   (p. 165)
dyadic process   (p. 161)
grave dressing process   (p. 161)
intrapsychic process   (p. 161)
openness-privacy   (p. 165)
personal relationships   (p. 150)
provisions of relationships   (p. 147)

relational continuity constructional
   units (RCCUs)   (p. 151)
resurrection process   (p. 161)
serial construction of meaning   (p. 159)
social process   (p. 161)
social relationships   (p. 150)

Questions to Ask Your Friends

- Write the story of your most recent breakup. Does it follow a neat progression? Have a friend read it and ask you questions about particular details. Does this questioning make you want to revise your narrative in any way?

- What turning points are there in relationship growth or decline that you and your friends believe you can identify through talk?

- The next time your friends ask, "How was your day?" ask them what they think they are doing and enter into a broad and fulfilling discussion about the nature of retrospective RCCUs and how even small talk serves to maintain relationships during absence.

Media Links

- Look at several Sunday paper sections on marriages and engagements. Check for similarities in attractiveness level between the people involved. Next take these pictures and cut them down the middle. How easy is it to reconnect the right people?

- Take any movie where a romance develops between two main characters. Does it either develop or dissolve according to the proposal made in this chapter, and if not, how?

- What models of "true romance" are presented in different kinds of movies? Is the romance depicted in action films, if any, the same as or different from that presented in romantic comedies? In what ways?

Ethical Issues

- Do you think that someone who is ending a relationship with someone else has an ethical duty to explain to the other person why?

- What is unethical about having two romantic relationships at the same time?

- Can you think of a time when the autonomy-connectedness dialectic presented you with an ethical dilemma (e.g., made you think about lying in order to maintain your freedom without losing a relationship)? Don't use that example, but try to find others.

Answers to Photo Captions

Photo 6.1 ▪ Parents talking to children during the performance of household chores might demonstrate an element of teaching that would show the power relationship between them.

Photo 6.2 ▪ People self-disclose their inner thoughts, secrets, worries, and concerns as they become closer. This conversation between friends (look at the distance between them, the place where the talk is happening, and their postures) is obviously very intense and deep, not shallow and uninvolving.

Photo 6.3 ▪ The expressions—hostile resentment and dejected resignation—on the two people's faces are clear, and the woman has literally turned her back on the man and is looking upward, as if for help from the skies, while close to tears. The man's closed posture shows difficulty, but the surroundings are comfortable and the man and woman are sitting close to one another, suggesting that they are either at home or in counseling.

Photo 6.4 ▪ No, relationships do not break down linearly, though people often report as if they do.

Student Study Site

Visit the study site at **www.sagepub.com/ciel** for e-flashcards, practice quizzes, and other study resources.

References

Acitelli, L. K. (1988). When spouses talk to each other about their relationship. *Journal of Social and Personal Relationships, 5,* 185–199.

Baxter, L. A., Dun, T. D., & Sahlstein, E. M. (2001). Rules for relating communicated among social network members. *Journal of Social and Personal Relationships, 18,* 173–200.

Baxter, L. A., & Montgomery, B. M. (1996). *Relating: Dialogs and dialectics.* New York: Guilford Press.

Baxter, L. A., & Wilmot, W. (1985). Taboo topics in close relationships. *Journal of Social and Personal Relationships, 2,* 253–269.

Bergmann, J. R. (1993). *Discreet indiscretions: The social organization of gossip.* New York: Aldine de Gruyter.

Burleson, B. R., Holmstrom, A. J., & Gilstrap, C. M. (2005). "Guys can't say that to guys": Four experiments assessing the normative motivation account for deficiencies in the emotional support provided by men. *Communication Monographs, 72*(4), 468–501.

Byrne, D. (1997). An overview (and underview) of research and theory within the attraction paradigm. *Journal of Social and Personal Relationships, 14,* 417–431.

Carl, W. J. (2006). What's all the buzz about? Everyday communication and the relational basis of word-of-mouth and buzz marketing practices. *Management Communication Quarterly, 19*(4), 601–634.

Carl, W. J., & Duck, S. W. (2004). How to do things with relationships. In P. Kalbfleisch (Ed.), *Communication Yearbook* (Vol. 28, 1-35). P. Thousand Oaks, CA: Sage.

Delia, J. G. (1980). Some tentative thoughts concerning the study of interpersonal relationships and their development. *Western Journal of Speech Communication, 44,* 97–103.

Duck, S. W. (1982). A topography of relationship disengagement and dissolution. In S. W. Duck (Ed.), *Personal relationships 4: Dissolving personal relationships* (pp. 1–30). London: Academic Press.

Duck, S. W. (1994). *Meaningful relationships: Talking, sense, and relating.* Thousand Oaks, CA: Sage.

Duck, S. W. (1998). *Human relationships* (3rd ed.). London: Sage.

Duck, S. W. (1999). *Relating to others* (2nd ed.). Milton Keynes, United Kingdom: Open University Press.

Duck, S. W. (2007). *Human relationships* (4th ed.). London: Sage.

Goldsmith, D. J., & Fitch, K. (1997). The normative context of advice as social support. *Human Communication Research, 23,* 454.

Granovetter, M. S. (1973). The strength of weak ties. *American Journal of Sociology, 78,* 1360–1380.

Hess, J. A. (2000). Maintaining a nonvoluntary relationship with disliked partners: An investigation into the use of distancing behaviors. *Human Communication Research, 26,* 458–488.

Honeycutt, J. M. (1993). Memory structures for the rise and fall of personal relationships. In S. W. Duck (Ed.), *Individuals in relationships [Understanding relationship processes 1]* (pp. 60–86). Newbury Park, CA: Sage.

Kerckhoff, A. C. (1974). The social context of interpersonal attraction. In T. L. Huston (Ed.), *Foundations of interpersonal attraction* (pp. 61–77). New York: Academic Press.

Leatham, G. B., & Duck, S. W. (1990). Conversations with friends and the dynamics of social support. In S. W. Duck with R. C. Silver (Eds.), *Personal relationships and social support* (pp. 1–29). London: Sage.

Manusov, V., K., Kellas, J. K. & Trees, A. R. (2004). Do unto others? Conversational moves and perceptions of attentiveness toward other's face in accounting sequences between friends. *Human Communication Research, 30*(4), 514–539.

Parks, M. (2006). *Communication and social networks.* Mahwah, NJ: Lawrence Erlbaum.

Paul, E. L. (2006). Beer goggles, catching feelings and the walk of shame: The myths and realities of the hookup experience. In C. D. Kirkpatrick, S. W. Duck, & M. K. Foley (Eds.), *Relating difficulty: Processes of constructing and managing difficult interaction* (pp. 141–160). Mahwah, NJ: Lawrence Erlbaum.

Pilkonis, P. A. (1977). The behavioral consequences of shyness. *Journal of Personality, 45,* 596–611.

Planalp, S., & Garvin-Doxas, K. (1994). Using mutual knowledge in conversation: Friends as experts in each other. In S. W. Duck (Ed.), *Dynamics of relationships: Understanding relationship processes* (Vol. 4, pp. 1–26). Newbury Park, CA: Sage.

Rollie, S. S., & Duck, S. W. (2006). Stage theories of marital breakdown. In J. H. Harvey & M. A. Fine (Eds.), *Handbook of divorce and dissolution of romantic relationships* (pp. 176–193). Mahwah, NJ: Lawrence Erlbaum.

Sahlstein, E. M. (2004). Relating at a distance: Negotiating being together and being apart in long-distance relationships. *Journal of Social and Personal Relationships, 21*(5), 689–710.

Sahlstein, E. M. (2006). The trouble with distance. In C. D. Kirkpatrick, S. W. Duck, & M. K. Foley (Eds.), *Relating difficulty: Processes of constructing and managing difficult interaction* (pp. 119–140). Mahwah, NJ: Lawrence Erlbaum.

Sigman, S. J. (1991). Handling the discontinuous aspects of continuous social relationships: Toward research on the persistence of social forms. *Communication Theory, 1,* 106–127.

Sunnafrank, M. (1983). Attitude similarity and interpersonal attraction in communication processes: In pursuit of an ephemeral influence. *Communication Monographs, 50,* 273–284.

Sunnafrank, M., & Ramirez, A. (2004). At first sight: Persistent relational effects of get-acquainted conversations. *Journal of Social and Personal Relationships, 21*(3), 361–379.

Vangelisti, A., & Banski, M. (1993). Couples' debriefing conversations: The impact of gender, occupation and demographic characteristics. *Family Relations, 42,* 149–157.

Weiss, R. S. (1974). The provisions of social relationships. In Z. Rubin (Ed.), *Doing unto others* (pp. 17–26). Englewood Cliffs, NJ: Prentice Hall.

Weiss, R. S. (1998). A taxonomy of relationships. *Journal of Social and Personal Relationships, 15,* 671–683.

Wiseman, J. P. (1986). Friendship: Bonds and binds in a voluntary relationship. *Journal of Social and Personal Relationships, 3,* 191–211.

Wood, J. T., & Duck, S. W. (Eds.). (2006). *Composing relationships: Communication in everyday life.* Belmont, CA: Thomson Wadsworth.

7

Family Communication

Societies treat the family as so important an institution that they give it special tax breaks, emphasize it in religion, and tend to idealize it in the media and even fairy tales. On this view, divorce is a bad thing (Devil term) and family is a good thing (God term). *Family communication* has recently become a hot topic, partly because the family is a primary source for all your early socialization. Your parents or guardians are the first of Society's Secret Agents to shape the ways in which you think about almost everything, from your own Self to your views about the world in general. Family communication instills and frames cultural values from the beginning and is a key starting point for your sense of self and identity (Chapter 5). However, for good or ill, you mostly can't choose your family members, and they are yours forever.

But what exactly *is* "a family"?

Think about two puzzling recent news stories before you get going. First, although it proved to be false, there was a news story in 2008 that raises some interesting questions. It claimed that a happily married couple, both given up for adoption at birth, later discovered to their horror that they were in fact twins, and their marriage, even though it was a happy one with children, was forcibly terminated by the law. OK, it turned out not to be true, but what if it had been? The couple had not known that they were genetically related, and the marriage was a successful one up to that point. Why could they not be "a family"?

A second, definitely true story was reported in October 2006 on the BBC (http://news.bbc.co.uk/1/hi/world/asia-pacific/6052584.stm). In this case a Japanese woman in her 50s gave birth to her own grandchild, having acted as a surrogate mother for her daughter whose womb had been removed as a result of cancer. The daughter had donated her own eggs, the eggs had been fertilized in vitro using the daughter's husband's sperm, and the fertilized egg had then been transplanted to the grandmother to carry through term to birth. Just after the birth, the daughter and her husband formally and legally adopted the child, and the grandmother/birth mother formally and legally renounced any rights to the child as her own. Physically the "grandmother" was the mother; genetically she was the grandmother. What do you see as her role in "the family"?

As the chapter progresses, we'll teach you to focus less on family structure and more on the communication that makes the structure work. A deeper and more revolutionary question left for the end of the chapter is whether you should classify people as "family" according to some social structural categories that are used by lawyers and demographers or according to the communication styles that members use to *transact* family life and share worlds of meaning. As Kathleen Galvin (2007) notes, "The greater the ambiguity of family form, the more elaborate the communicative processes needed to establish and maintain identity" (p. 1). We will teach you in this chapter that "a family" essentially depends on a set of interconnected *communicative* relationships.

Focus Questions

- What is a family, and how should people specifically interested in family communication start to define what counts and what does not?
- What sorts of diverse forms of "family" are recognized in different societies/cultures?
- What are the possible ways in which "a family" may be defined, and which one is best for a communication scholar?
- What types of everyday communication in a family *transact* the nature of family life?

What Are the Functions and Structures of Families?

Families as Social Ideals

Because the family is seen as the root of socialization and a small form of "society" itself, it is given special attention in modern life. However you think of "a family" there is a strong tendency to (a) separate it from other forms of relational interaction and also (b) idealize the concept. Politicians, religious officials, and tax collectors all like the idea of the family, and most religions have something explicit and direct to say about the importance of the family in the belief system (e.g., there is some version of "Honor thy father and thy mother," or respect is due particularly to your parents and elders).

The media and politicians also bombard you with images of *good* families, and there are debates about the way a family may be constituted and how important families are in society. There is a strong hetero-normative pressure; there is a suspicion of countries or religions that permit polygamous relationships. Bigamy is illegal, and adultery—which threatens the family bonds—is disapproved; partners without children are not seen as "a family"; there is a discussion in society whether biological parents separated from a child at birth are "the true family" as compared to the child's lifelong foster caregivers or adoptive parents.

These views are essentially positive, conservative, and static: They see "a family" as a stable structure, usually with a definite power hierarchy and usually a traditional one with husband and wife plus 2.4 kids and a quartet of silver-haired grandparents somewhere in the background. This traditional group is represented in advertising as happy, supportive, quite comfortably wealthy, and harmoniously understanding—usually eating a Thanksgiving turkey or driving around in a newly purchased automobile—while the older generation is usually represented as advice givers. You are also subtly influenced in other ways: for example, to get family calling plans for your phones, a cultural fact that emphasizes the people you *should* be calling.

> According to Mr. Justice Coleridge, "We are experiencing a period of family meltdown as catastrophic as the meltdown of the ice caps," and its effects "pose as big a threat to the future of our society as terrorism, street crime or drugs. . . . almost all of society's social ills can be traced directly to the collapse of the family life . . ." (BBC News, 2008, ¶ 8).
>
> Interestingly similar statements can be found from the time of Abraham Lincoln, from the time of the Plymouth Pilgrims, and even by the Roman poet Horace.

Families are therefore supposed to be good for us. Le Poire, Hallett, and Erlandson (2000) identify two key defining functions as *nurturing* and *control:* A family nurtures, supports, and sustains its members, not only emotionally and educationally but also financially. The family also exerts control over their behavior (often thought of as parental control over children but actually much more than that, since it teaches children about the nature of society and the world—**socialization**). There is a large set of social **rules** and norms for "family" that monitors the way in which family life should be carried out. Many of these are similar to the issues discussed in Chapter 5, where individual identity is responsive to larger social pressures. The labeling of a particular set of people as "a family" is a powerful way to establish *expectations* about how people should feel about one another and should communicate affection, loyalty, or membership.

All the same, the fact is that families often present very negative experiences for people at least some of the time (Coleman & May-Chahal, 2003; Klein, 2004). Many teenagers come to dislike their parents (for either a short or a long period) as part of the process of establishing an independent identity. Early experiences with parents can lead to decreased self-esteem or to insecurities in later life relationships. Warm and accepting parents typically produce secure children comfortable with their later adult relationships, whereas distant and aloof parents tend to produce children whose later personal relationships are characterized by distance, aloofness, persecuted vigilance, and insecurity (Rowe & Carnelley, 2005).

Although rates are declining, the family is, outside of the military, the most violent social institution, and by no means are all families functional or even fun. People are more likely to be assaulted, abused, or even murdered by a family member than by a random stranger (see Figure 7.1). Most people's personal acquaintance with violence is represented by, and restricted to, their interactions with family members (Coleman &

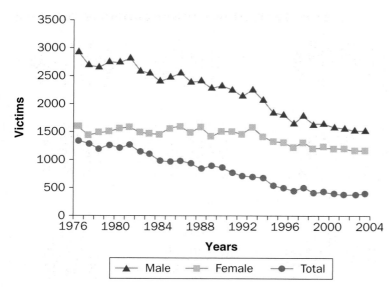

Figure 7.1 Murder by intimate partner, 1976–2007

Source: http://www.silentwitness.net/sub/violences.htm.

May-Chahal, 2003). In part this is simply a consequence of the fact that, being close and intense, families tend to communicate all the extremes of emotion. Their everyday communication may convey at one time or another both love and hate, peaceful coexistence and outright open conflict. They also provide plenty of opportunities for a very rich range of emotional experiences to be demonstrated and manifested toward one another.

Types of Families: Families as Frames

Segrin and Flora (2005) identify three ways of defining "family": structural, functional, and transactional. *Structural methods* define "a family" as those who are related by blood, law, or adoption; *functional definitions* focus on the behaviors that make a family work well, such as mutual support, socialization, and financial assistance; *transactional definitions* are based on the communication that takes place within a group in a way that builds a sense of family identity. This last definition is of course the most appealing definition for communication scholars.

For many purposes, families are seen primarily as social or demographic *structures* that contain and connect particular individuals (for example, two parents and a child, mother and partner, father and son, daughter and aunt, stepparent and stepchild). This way of seeing "family" is structural or genetic: who is in it, who is biologically or legally related to whom, who is older, who is a parent, who is offspring. You could map that structure by indicating dates of adoptions, deaths, births, marriages, and so forth as a way to depict who was in the family at a particular time, essentially representing the family as an interconnected group of individuals. This is the information, after all, that most people use when they construct a family tree—for example, names, dates, relationships, and events that specify inclusion or exclusion from the group.

Le Poire (2006) notes that this particular structure of a family can be defined according to (a) *biological ties* (genetics, bloodlines, or biological connectedness), (b) *legal definitions* based on a person's suitability to be a parent or the person's right to have custody of the children after divorce, or (c) *sociological definitions*. This third set is based not only on the two foregoing kinds of category but also on those groups that self-define themselves as families with an expectation of future functioning as "a family." Many African Americans, for example, define "family" to include **kin networks** (cousins, second cousins, children of cousins, uncles, aunts, and even long-term friends who are considered family, too).

Different Family Structures

If you see families as structures, then your first representation of a family is likely, in this society, to be a **nuclear family** (i.e., just the parents plus their children) (Le Poire, 2006). Importantly, however, every nuclear family also is a small family subgroup within a larger family conceptual group. Two parents and the kids are nested within a wider group of the grandparents, cousins, broader families of both parents, and many more strange add-ons of aunts, uncles, in-laws, and many relatives you may never even meet—the **extended family**. In Japan, an extended family includes ancestors long since dead, whom the living have a duty to honor and worship. The living accept a strong responsibility to procreate in order to continue to produce future honor and worship for this group and for themselves after their own death (Golliher, 2006). You can also consider **family of origin** (the parents you were born to) and the **family of descent** (the clan or historical family tree that you branch from), the **family of generativity** (the one you may start for yourself), or the **family of choice**.

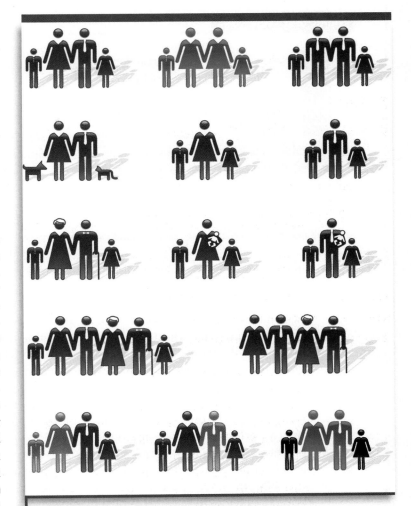

Photo 7.1 How many different types of family can you identify in this illustration? Are there any that are omitted, and would you have included all the ones that are illustrated here? (See page 199.)

This latter may be one created through adoption, for example, or may simply be the group of people you decide is your "true" family even though there is no genetic connection. When parents adopt nongenetic offspring, divorce, or remarry other partners, then so-called **blended families** are the result (Afifi & Hamrick, 2006). This means that one parent's children may spend at least some of their time in a family where children of another adult are present as "brothers or sisters." The creation of one blended family can sometimes mean that the children of divorced parents experience daily life in two "families." This is described as a **binuclear family**—that is, two families based on the nuclear form (for example, the children's father, their stepmother, and her children, if any, as well as the children's mother and their stepfather and his children, if any).

Make Your Case

What is your "family" structure? How does communication in your family (e.g., at family get-togethers) indicate the patterns of intimacy that exist in the family? Would an outsider be able to draw an intimacy map of your family, and do you know the map of your friends' families?

The one defining feature of such traditional views of "a family" is a transgenerational concept that involves the existence of at least one member of one generation who is the responsibility of at least one member of another generation (Duck, 2007). This structural arrangement can take many shapes. The traditional heterosexual nuclear family of one male and one female and their offspring has now been supplemented by many other diverse possibilities, such as families we choose (Weston, 1991) or even one adult and a dog. An incomplete list of possibilities is two same-sex parents; communal rearing groups; fostering; adoption; grandparents, aunts, or uncles raising their direct or indirect descendents; and single-parent families.

Single-parent families can arise from several circumstances. For example, singleness may be a choice, a preference, or an unwanted outcome (e.g., as a result of an undesired divorce or unexpected death). A person may not wish to be encumbered with a permanent partner even after having a child or children. You can therefore distinguish those single-parent families where there has never been more than one parent from those single-parent families where there was previously more than one parent. In the latter case, one of them chose to leave for whatever reason or has been involuntarily removed from a direct parental role by divorce, death, or other circumstances such as serious chronic incapacitating illness or incarceration. Many military families operate effectively this way even though both partners are still alive but one is away on active service. In addition any couple may choose to have no children of their own, but the traditional definition of family means you will not count them as a family unless the couple is looking after their own parents instead.

Now consider other increasingly prevalent forms of family, whether resulting from different original pairings of parents or from reconnection of different parents into a blended family. As Suter (2006) indicates, forms of family that have two same-sex parents are increasingly frequent. Obviously everything that can happen to heterosexual parents can happen there too, including socialization, love, caring, support, separation, blending, abuse, self-sacrifice, and family stress. In the case of two men acting as parents, they may adopt unrelated children, may parent the existing genetic offspring of one or both of them, or may newly generate children from one father and a willing or paid female surrogate and then bring those children up with two fathers. In the case of two women acting as parents, again they may adopt unrelated children, may parent the existing genetic offspring of one or both of them, or may newly generate children from one parenting mother and a willing or paid male sperm donor often known to them or selected from a sperm bank and then bring those children up with two mothers. In these cases as in the others, the "structure" suffers all the same stresses of aging, development, and interaction that occur as the family adjusts to the passage of time and the alterations to family members' expectations and behaviors that follow as a result.

Photo 7.2 Families come in many forms. What three forms of family are depicted in this photograph? (See page 199.)

Structures and Communication Systems

The difficulties for communication scholars of using such structural definitions are now obvious. A family tree would not tell you anything about the *personal and communicative relationships* between the people in the family structure. What if you are incredibly close to one parent but feel distant from the other one and so do not talk with that parent as much as with the other? What if your family structure was disrupted (by death or divorce, for example), and you feel really bad about the fact that you never get to see your kids? What if one of your parents or siblings abused you physically, sexually, or verbally, and you are now almost terrified of intimacy with anyone else? What if your family was so happy that you enter every relationship feeling very self-secure, with total confidence and self-respect, and you find it easy to trust everyone else you meet (or what if they treated you so badly you can never trust anyone)?

How would any of that show up in a simple structural representation like a family tree? Clearly, it would not, but it might show up in the patterns of communication. Some of these feelings and experiences are more than likely to affect family communication, self-concept, identity, relationships with other people, and life goals in ways not registered on the simple diagram of family structure. Also intergenerational communication is important in the way families see themselves (Huisman, 2008).

Contrarian Challenge

Concepts like "separated at birth," "blood is thicker than water," and "brothers reunited after 60 years" suggests strongly that people see genetic relationships as more significant than other ways of viewing "family." At the same time, politicians and others often treat the family as the bedrock of society. Is this essentially saying that genetics matters more than experience, and you should stay in a family with an abusive and violent parent?

Structure and Communication

There actually is a method—the genogram—for representing some of these details, and it can be found at http://www.genopro.com/genogram/. In a genogram the basic family tree structure is embellished with various emotional and historical information that helps both the person and (say) a therapist make more sense of the communication that is going on in the family or in the individual than the family structure does alone. You may want to try creating one, either as a class exercise or purely for your own pleasure or enlightenment. Basically, instead of just looking at the names and their relationship to one another, you start to ask questions about the emotional connections instead. First you draw a picture of the family structure, but then you add to it an emotional map as well and one that shows communication patterns. For example, "X was Y's sister, but no one in the rest of the family except Y would talk to her because X had once insulted their mother very nastily" or "B's father would never speak to him after he came out." Not all fathers like all of their daughters equally well, not all siblings like one another equally strongly, and the mere existence of membership in a family is not a guide to the strength of feelings between the members. Figure 7.2 is a genogram for Harry Potter that clearly illustrates his biological and relational ties. Hence we emphasize how the relationships are transacted through communication.

Several scholars have identified the ways in which family communication can be broken into different categories. Although this is still an essentially structural approach to families, it nevertheless represents the structure in terms of the style of communication that is adopted there. Koerner and Fitzpatrick (2002), for example, described family communication along two dimensions: *conformity orientation* and *conversation orientation*. Conformity orientation describes "the degree to which family communication stresses a climate of homogeneity of attitudes, values, and beliefs," whereas conversation orientation describes "the degree to which families create a climate in which all family members are encouraged to participate in unrestrained interaction about a wide array of topics" (pp. 85–86).

These two dimensions create a four-category typology of family communication that can be used to typologize families by comparing their positions on each dimension, whether high or low on each: (a) *Protective* families are high in conformity orientation and low in conversation orientation. Family members place a value on conformity to family norms and do not permit or expect discussion of alternatives. (b) *Pluralistic* families are the opposite on both dimensions: high in conversation orientation but low in conformity orientation. Such families encourage conversation about rules and enjoy discussion, innovation, and diversity of lifestyle, so it is not

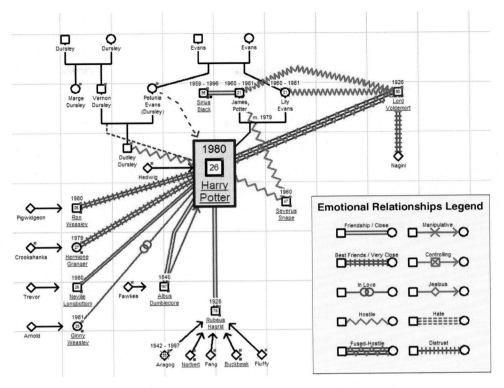

Figure 7.2 Genogram example for Harry Potter

Source: http://www.genopro.com/genogram/

Note: Names and descriptions have been collected from the Harry Potter books written by J. K. Rowling and from Wikipedia, the free online encyclopedia (www.wikipedia.org).

offensive to break family rules if it raises a worthy issue for discussion. (c) *Consensual* families are high in both conformity and conversation orientation. In these families, parents expect children to obey rules but provide opportunities to discuss and question these rules, as long as there is ultimately agreement about how the rules should be followed in the future. (d) *Laissez-faire* families are low in both conformity and conversation orientation. These families have lax rules and do not talk about them much. One consequence is that members of such families are somewhat emotionally distant from each other (Koerner & Fitzpatrick, 2002).

Systems Theory

Some scholars moved to a different theoretical approach that sees families (however defined structurally) as *systems*. **Systems Theory** is an important way to understand families—as something made up of parts but operating as a whole system that can achieve functions that individuals alone cannot and that also creates an environment in which those individuals must exist (Griffin, 2009). The original notion of Systems Theory was developed by Von Bertalanffy (1950). Although he was a biologist, he foresaw the value of conceiving of many things as systems, whether machines, human interactive systems, or ecosystems. In some disciplines the study of systems is called *cybernetics,* and in the case of a machine there are several components that work together in order to produce something more than the sum of its parts (*nonsummative wholeness*). A great example is a motor car, which is made up of individual nuts, bolts, pipes, computer chips, cogs, levers, and wheels, which altogether can end up producing and transacting something greater than the sum of its parts, namely motion toward a destination.

Characteristics of Systems

Many cybernetic systems are also *goal-oriented* and *self-regulating;* that is, they keep a check on their own activity and adjust what they do in response to input from the environment in order to achieve a particular objective. The classic example of this is the thermostat, which reads the temperature and turns on a heating or cooling device whenever the temperature gets out of range. As soon as the temperature is restored to the desired level, the thermostat serves to turn off the heating or cooling device but continues to read the environment in order to discover when it should reactivate the appropriate device. Such systems show *hierarchy* among component parts and environment, in that one component tends to be in charge of others (e.g., the engine drives the wheels). Yet the parts are also *mutually interdependent,* and the performance of one influences the success of the total system. If one part of the motor car ceases to function (e.g., if a wheel falls off), then the system (motor car) will no longer be able to achieve its objectives (going to a destination) until the part is repaired.

Viewing Families as Systems

Using the same sorts of key terms (nonsummative wholeness, goal orientation, self-regulation, hierarchy, interdependence, and common fate), several family scholars began to apply Systems Theory to families (Bateson, 1972; Watzlawick, Beavin, & Jackson, 1967). Such researchers (Bosticco & Thompson, 2005) have pointed out that families are like systems in many ways, particularly in terms of their *mutual interdependence, hierarchy, common fate,* and *self-regulation.* Most families have a power hierarchy, and all members share a common fate and depend on one another for their outcomes and performance to some extent. For example, if one member of the family becomes ill, then the performance of the other members at various tasks—like going to work—may be influenced (in this instance a parent may have to take a day off work in order to look after a sick child). This kind of *interdependence* can work in different ways too, and a classic example is where one parent is an abuser or an alcoholic and the behavior of other members of the family is forced to adapt to this (Wright & Wright, 1995). The whole system of the family is affected by the one individual having an alcohol dependency or being abusive. The children may learn to be very cautious around a drunken parent who could become violent. Their behavior is influenced by the behavior of another part of the "system" not only in the present but it may cause them to become hypervigilant in all future relationships.

As Systems Theory would predict, it sometimes turns out to be difficult to cure an individual alcoholic in a family, because over time the family members come to find creative ways to deal with

If you have any experience in your family with alcoholism or the effects of alcohol or drug dependence on the operation of your family system, then take a look at Le Poire et al. (2000).

Photo 7.3 What impact does reading storybooks have on the socialization of children? (See page 199.)

the alcoholism, and they get locked into using them. A classic example is the case where a family prefers the drunk parent to be incapably drunk, because that way he or she is not as dangerous to other people as when in a state of a more capable alertness. It has also been reported that some spouses prefer their partners when drunk because they are funny. Somewhat surprisingly, then, it is rather hard to cure alcoholism if you do not treat the family as a system but merely treat the individual as an alcoholic with an individual problem. Indeed, family systems therapists often will not work alone with children in therapy as they see no purpose to that. If they take the child out of the system and try to help the child as an individual but then put the child back into exactly the same unchanged system, the child will not have the power to change it, and the symptoms will recur.

Family Structures and Other External Forces

Even though the above describes families as systems internally (the dynamic family is itself a system), families also exist within other connections of people and can be characterized as "systems" from that point of view—wheels within wheels. Any family system can also be seen as placed in networks of other structures, systems, and social connections that affect its experience also. A network is a complex set of groups to which any individual belongs. For example, two parents may have different sets of friends and

One of the major influences on children's development of smoking habits and attitudes toward drugs is the sort of influence that happens not only in the family but also in the adolescent peer group. Many adolescents reported that they were pressured by their peers into taking up smoking or drugs, and some influential communication programs have been developed to help children resist such pressures (Lloyd & Anthony, 2003; Miller-Day, Hecht, & Marks, 2000).

may work in different places where they know different sets of people as well as those people whom they know in common. Their children play with children from other families, they go to school and meet peers, and as adolescents they will certainly communicate with a **peer culture** that may influence their behavior. In short, the family does not live in isolation but has connections with other groups, and these networks can influence the way in which family life is experienced. Galvin (2007) notes that redeployed families (our term) face a problem of presenting their identity as a family group to the outside world that sees them as not "normal."

This faces the family with the issue of "discourse dependency"—that is, a way in which they frame and represent themselves to one another and to the outside world through their communication. For example, Suter (2006) analyzed the way in which children may be faced with explaining to their friends why they have two mommies, and so their family structure is not simply a personal matter between them and their two parents. The effects of peer culture can also wash back into the family, as when children bring their friends home or adolescents adopt the styles and habits of their peer group in contrast to those usually adapted within the family. This often generates a familiar and predictable form of adolescent rebellion against the previously experienced family norms and practices.

Children, Rules, and the Outside World

Children have multiple models in the complex, interconnected, networked world that we are talking about here. Parents are not the only influence to which children are accountable: First of all, the school system calls them to account, but increasingly as they age through teenage years, adolescents' peer groups become more influential in their decisions. As the children develop, their social world begins to extend beyond the parenting and family group to a wider world of schoolteachers, friends, and peers, all of whom can influence the way in which the children learn and behave whether outside or inside the "family structure." As children get old enough to become active outside their home family environment, so too they discover that there are different ways to do and perform a family life. Your family and your friends' families do many things, like celebrating birthdays and holidays and even everyday living, in different ways, as you will know if you have ever been to a sleepover at a friend's house.

However, the peer group does not simply communicate influence but is also most often the group that is consulted when an adolescent has questions about sexuality, in particular in seeking information about sexual experiences. Teenagers tend to ground their information about morals from their parents or family groups, but their communication about actual sexual practices is much more likely to be derived from the adolescent network (Lloyd & Anthony, 2003).

As children grow older, the family's influence on them changes. Schools exert an influence on family activities and the timetabling and priorities given to family experience. This means that childhood evening time spent together is now exchanged for separate time as the child does homework or school-related activities, and various kinds of "spillover" enter family life. This spillover is not only from school and the child's wider network. Parents' work organizations may require them to do assignments that cut into family time, or adolescents may want their peers to stay out late when their parents want them home. Of course, this changes the nature of communication within the family. So with the family, it is important to consider not only its structure, its members, and the interaction of its parts but also how these all work to transact an experience of family life.

More subtly, each of these groups has a thought world/world of meaning attached to it, and these may be in conflict in various ways. For example, your friends and your family may have different attitudes toward achievement in school or toward sexual relationships outside of a marriage. Although family and parents start out being the most powerful influences on children, as the children grow up, their exposure to other sources of information and to other people provides them with new and often competing ideas and values.

Families as Transacted Relationships

We noted that family communication seems to be both a hot topic and an interesting one with lots of clear connections to your own personal life. It is hardly surprising that family communication is a growing area over and above its familiarity to students, because the family context is one that exemplifies many of the issues we have previously discussed. First, a family offers most of the provisions of relationship that friendship and romance supply. In Chapter 6, we noted that relationships provide such resources as reliable alliance, emotional integration, and support, and the same is true of the family. A family also tends to have its own styles, rituals, and practices—for example, its own norms and rituals that represent a shared world of meaning, which distinguishes it from other families and their worlds of meaning. **Norms** are the habitual rules for conducting any family activity, and **rituals** are particularly formalized ways for handling, say, the routines of mealtimes or birthday gift giving. There are many other issues of family dynamics, for communication with stepchildren or siblings and family rituals that represent classic instances of basic forms of communication. For example, dialectics influence what a given family believes is "private" information. As another example, patterns of support, argument, and conflict in families may be different from one another even if the underlying forms are similar to those in dyads.

The four different styles of family communication that were reported earlier (protective, pluralistic, consensual, laissez-faire) suggest different responses by parents to a child's increased access to peer networks, which these days are increasingly conducted through such relational media as cell phones, Facebook, Twitter, and Internet social sites. Whereas permissive parents are unlikely to show much interest in their child's access to such media, protective parents are much more likely to take control and to restrict their child's use of such relational technologies. This in turn is likely to influence the child's access to peers who make frequent use of those technologies and therefore transacts a different form of social life for the child.

Strategic Communication

Look at any of your family's rituals and analyze the ways in which it communicates something centrally important to the identity of the family. How does the ritual "perform" family life, and what central features of that family does it tend to emphasize?

Transacting Family Life

The move to considering behaviors, rituals, and norms means that you are no longer looking at families as groups (i.e., *institutions* or *structures*) so much as performances or sites of communication, and that is an important shift of emphasis. You might recognize that family communication provides a link to our previous discussion in Chapter 5 on the influences of interaction with significant individuals on your identity as well as to the coming discussion of patterns of influence in larger groups (Chapter 8). On the whole, however, the topic of family communication has no clearly established placement in communication texts.

The omission of family communication from most textbooks is odd because many scholars recognize the ways in which media communication influences our views of family. Relevant and interesting though such aspects of our media experience and culture are, however, they do not focus on the issue of how communication acts as a transaction of family or on how families act as dynamic collectivities. In such collectivities, communication connects these individuals' experiences and meaning systems. That is, as you have seen in other chapters, the interactions in a family do more than just send messages: *They convey both content and relational components.* In moving from seeing a family only in terms of its structure or its closeness as a group, then, you start to look more closely at the way in which communication *works* in the family. Can't different forms of the same basic structures differ in their patterns of interaction and communication? Some families are peaceful and cooperative whereas others may involve conflict very frequently. A family, of whatever type, necessarily has a number of competing and complicating processes and activities to negotiate, over and above simple decisions such as who should do the dishes or whether it can afford to go on vacation.

Authority and Power

First, families are more than categories: They have communicative practices and norms and power structures within them. There is, especially when children are young, a firm authority structure in a family that means that decisions are not effectively made between equal beings. There is, at least at first sight, an **authority structure** in a family, one more firmly enforced in some families, religions, and cultures than others. Some stress the role of one parent as head of the family; others stress equality of all the mature members. However, there is an unstated structure also. If your parents decide that the toddling young members of the family will go with them to the Ozarks for the weekend, then they do: The toddlers don't get to vote; they're just taken to the place, willingly or not.

As the younger family members mature, then the family communication may become increasingly inclusive and consultative about some activities, though most middle-class parents seem to press their children involuntarily to accept opportunities that involve piano lessons, dancing, or sports. In the teen years, the "children" become more independent and make a lot of their own choices, so the notion of family decision making gets quite differently executed anyway. It is important, then, not to transfix "the family" as only one sort of entity. Its styles of communication are constantly changing as the family members grow older. It grows, changes, and develops in form and style, as its component members all age and mature or decline with the passage of time. Therefore you miss something important

> I n the 16th century English children were expected to stop what they were doing and to stand in silence, as a mark of respect, when their father came into the room whether or not they were grown adults themselves (Stone, 1979).

if you do not look within the category ("family") and explore the way this is transacted in communication.

Consider how the above definition of family authority is too simplistic and too inclined to overlook the way in which authority is not a simple rigid hierarchy but a communication practice. Can't a child exert power over a parent by throwing a tantrum or being obstinate? Who has the power then? Isn't every screaming child basically letting the neighbors know how wicked and incompetent the parents really are? That's a kind of communicative power, and it certainly affects family experience. So power can be *formally* structured in a family, but it can also operate *informally* or bidirectionally. The **bidirectionality hypothesis** (Pettit & Lollis, 1997) recognizes that power can work in two directions. That is, at some points and times it works one way when parents control or influence their young kids, but power also goes the other way and sometimes kids can control or influence parents.

Norms and Rituals

Families have their own specific norms and rituals. The norms may be based on family beliefs about the proper way of indicating respect for elders, for example. They may also relate to equality of members where everyone must be heard as equal and having the same value, especially as the children are old enough to make real contributions to discussions and decisions. Also families have rituals. Think about the ways in which your family works. Take a moment to think about the ways in which your family *does* routine events and celebrations. How do you "do dinner" or "do vacations" or "do birthday parties"? Are these rituals organized in the same way that they are done in your friends' families? Probably not. There are no standard ways for families to conduct their lives, though there will be some sort of broad agreement in a given culture about how a set of family activities should occur, the events they recognize and celebrate, and the ways in which they carry out their rituals of life.

Carol Bruess and Anna Hoefs (2006) describe an amusing family ritual concerning gift giving at Christmas, where one person always ends up with a wooden cat puzzle that was once given to a member of the family. It was a surprisingly odd gift, so it ended up becoming a family joke. Instead of throwing away an unwanted gift, the family turned it into a ritual where the last person to be given the cat puzzle one year always gives it as "the gift" to another member next year. The ritual of discovering who got stuck with it this year is part of the family enjoyment of gift giving at Christmas that adds to the fun and makes the family reconnect with its history, hypertext, and private knowledge as family members relationally connected by this shared joke. The ritual serves to remind the family of a playful way in which it transacts and enjoys something within its structure as a set of members. The ritual reestablishes the "we-ness" of the family group. In short, the ritual re-creates and reestablishes the relational reconnection of the family. Once again, then, if you see a family as only a structure, then you miss the symbolic importance of such communicative rituals in transacting relationships within the original structure.

Take the blended family again as a specific case. It has to create its own new rituals and norms, just like any other family, but these are most likely somewhat different from the practices of each of the separate preblended arrangements. Baxter, Braithwaite, Bryant, and Wagner (2004) studied the quiet tensions and difficulties created within blended families and how they show up in the communication of the family, especially as it handles boundaries of privacy and disclosure with a new member (the new stepparent, for example). Baxter et al. explored the communications between a stepchild and a stepparent and the difficulty in handling the question of closeness and distance (which the authors describe as the *dialectic of integration*). Galvin (2007) also notes that integration often involves negotiations and significant implications for the family, especially in the different levels of commitment acceptance and connection implied by whether a child refers to his or her stepfather as "my mother's husband," "Brad," "my stepfather," "my other Dad," or even just plain "Dad."

The communication between the stepparent and stepchild also showed a problem based on the stepchild's (un)willingness to grant the stepparent any kind of legitimacy in a parent role. Finally, as a special case of the privacy-openness dialectic that we have noted before, the stepchild-stepparent relationship was particularly sensitive to the issue of candor and discretion. Both participants were very much aware of the eggshells upon which they would be walking if they were to talk about any personal or private material, at least until they had established a reliable level of relationship where complete trust existed. Once again, then, the experience of a blended family is determined very largely by the communication patterns that take place within it.

In both cases, people find it very difficult to adjust communicatively to the structural changes although many make the transition very successfully. A remixed family, like a remixed music track, has some of the features of the original but may have significant differences that make it original in its own way. The communication processes change, and the family transacts itself differently. The key issues are not just to do with the structure of the newly created unit. Sometimes there are power issues and different ways of living life in the new structure from what was done in the old ones, but these are also connected to routine and organizational issues in the "structure." Both children and adults feel a sense of loss of the old relationship as well as recognizing the challenges of the new one. In the case of adoptees, there are also issues of "loss" felt as they reach adulthood and wish to know more about their biological origin (Powell & Afifi, 2005).

We could again treat these merely as structural issues and look at the size of the group or the power changes in a structure that modify its form. Indeed there are occasions where this is truly relevant, as when two families blend and so have to live in the same accommodation that used to house only one of them, with children sharing bedrooms that used to be their own personal space, for example. More interesting for our purposes, however, is the issue of how the communication changes as a result of, or along with, the other changes.

Tamara Afifi (2003) discovered something very similar when she explored foster families and found that children experienced considerable tension in dealing with communication with their custodial parents on the one hand and their noncustodial parents on the other. There is a tendency for each person to feel triangulated—that is, set at odds with one of the other persons in the family—whenever he or she discusses anything that might be considered private from the point of view of the other person.

All of these studies suggest that it is extremely difficult for people who move between one form of family and another to negotiate what the privacy boundaries are and what information counts as secret, private, or personal. It is the creation of some sort of sense of specialism about the information that is transmitted in family communication that creates these difficulties and has nothing to do with the structure/membership of the family itself.

Sandra Petronio (2002) noted that all family members, not just members of blended families, must negotiate quite frequently about *privacy* and its violation. This is particularly important during the years when children become adolescents who might now expect parents to respect their rooms as private areas, for example. Furthermore, there are questions as to whether parents should open children's e-mail, eavesdrop if they are offered the chance, or go through an adolescent's personal possessions looking for such things as drugs (Petronio & Durham, 2008). Occasionally parents use direct invasion tactics like this or sometimes provide unsolicited advice, which may also be a violation of privacy on some level.

That people are in the same family does not mean they necessarily agree about the preferences and decisions that should be made on a particular occasion. There are often issues of communication **boundary management** and **privacy management** to be dealt with in a way that we discussed in Chapter 6. These are, in everyday communication, most often related to personal information that specific persons or members may have and that others do not know. For example, one parent may allow a child a special secret treat on the condition that the other parent is not told—we know a family where there are "DTMs [Don't Tell Moms]" where the other members carry out an activity, such as eating candy, knowing that the mother might have preferred it not to happen. Other examples come from the ways in which siblings may work together to defeat parental control, backing one another up in ways that resist parental authority, such as "covering" for one another during absences or when challenged by the parent (Nicholson, 2006).

Family Secrets

In addition, there may be family secrets that the members agree to conceal from other people outside the family group, such as alcoholism in one parent, a teenager's fight with a drug problem or anorexia, the fact that an uncle is confined in a mental institution, or the fact that one person committed a serious misdemeanor that has not yet been detected. The keeping of such secrets can be either toxic or bonding. Anita Vangelisti and her colleagues (e.g., Vangelisti & Caughlin,

Listen In On Your Life

What is the authority structure in your family, whether formal or informal, and are these two forms the same? How has that changed as you have aged? What have been the influences upon it and its changing?

1997) have reported many studies of this form of communication in families and the ways in which families transact the concealment of such secrets. The fact that such communication not only protects the family reputation in the outside world but also serves to bind the members together through the playing out of their shared secret as private knowledge holding them together is part of the important dynamic of family secrets (as is the DTM—it bonds together the father and the children by creating a relational boundary that encloses and connects them).

Family Storytelling

A final important communicative aspect of families is the process of **family storytelling**, which acts as an important mechanism for the creation of a sense of **family identity**. A family identity is an important aspect of an individual's connection to the world and image of self, and as Huisman (2008) showed, it revolves around intergenerational storytelling, where the elders talk about dead relatives or relate stories about particular

Photo 7.4 What could children learn from the stories told by their father about his experiences in the military? (See page 199.)

family characters who defined the essence of being "a Threlkeld" or "a Lawson." Jody Koenig Kellas and April Trees (2006) have shown the importance of **family narratives** in this process, not only in indicating a family's sense of what it is like in general but also in indicating how it deals with difficult and traumatic experiences. In the process of telling stories about their significant events, families create a shared sense of meaning about the family experience, whether it is something positive like a birth or an adoption or something negative such as a death or divorce. The point is that when a family starts to develop a common story about such events as these, the members blend their own individual and personal experiences together into a shared story that marks and creates—and hence transacts or constitutes—the family history in a particular way. In particular, in extended families in the United States, the elders often describe the way in which immigration and inclusion into the American culture were negotiated in their early days as settlers (Huisman, 2008).

Information Flow: Kin Keeping and the Communication of News

Long-distance relationships (LDRs) apply to families as well, once the children have left the nest. When children move away from home, many issues arise, and the empty-nest parents are left conducting the relationship with their offspring at a distance. Erin Sahlstein (2006) has noted that this brings out one particular function of certain members of the family who serve to do "**kin keeping**"; that is, they act as a reservoir for information about members of the family, and they pass the information to the other members of the network. For example, one person could end up being told everything that happens in the lives of everyone else in the family and then act as a central hub-and-spoke system for passing the information along to everyone else. Sahlstein uses the example of her mother, who keeps her up to date about what has been happening to her brother and other members of the family whom Erin does not contact so often. Her mother always knows what is going on and so helps keep the family together through the passing around of information about everyone else. In this way, she still keeps the family together, and this is what is meant by the "kin-keeping function."

However, there is another aspect of information flow that does not make you stop and think because it seems so normal and natural that it is simply taken for granted. But just give some thought to the way in which you would spread the news that you have found a new romantic partner and are thinking of moving in with him or her or that you are about to become engaged or married or are expecting a child. Whom would you tell first about such news (or, in the case of an unexpected and unwanted pregnancy, from whom might you wish to keep the news)? Most of you have an understanding that if you are close to your parents they would be told before other people find out. Family members might have a right to expect to be told. In other words, such communication is not just about messages

Consider the following dialogue from the movie *My Big Fat Greek Wedding* (Zwick, 2002):

Toula Portokalos: Ma, Dad is so stubborn. What he says goes. "Ah, the man is the head of the house!"

Maria Portokalos: Let me tell you something, Toula. The man is the head, but the woman is the neck. And she can turn the head any way she wants.

but is about the relational priorities that are indicated by the way in which information is spread around. Information flows through the family system in a way that reflects the closeness of the relationships that people have with one another and operates in a way that sustains the hierarchy or the strength of the particular relationships (Duck, 2007). In short, the transmission of information is done in a way that supports (or at least represents the strength and nature of the bonds in) the family system. Information flow does not just happen randomly: It serves a transactive function in the maintenance of family and personal relationships.

Change and Development in Family Processes

Whatever form a family takes, its structure—and hence the influence of structure on the family processes and communication patterns—will change with the passage of time. Some of these changes are seen as normal growth—new children are born; children go to school; children become more independent, turn into adolescents, leave home, and start families of their own; the parents age and need to be looked after and eventually die. Other changes are seen as fractures in the surface of normality: divorce, separation, chronic illness of one adult, death of a relatively young parent in an otherwise still intact family. Other forms of fracture in the family are also transacted in discourse. Buzzanell and Turner (2003) found that traditional (husband breadwinner) family roles tend to be underscored within discourse used to describe job loss, financial strain, and necessity of dual incomes. The wife supports the family, but their communication maintains the husband as financial leader and primary decision maker.

Both big and gradual changes are accompanied by or transacted in dynamic patterns of communication. These too are not only are changing all the time but occasionally respond to dramatic events such as family members' need to console one another during unexpected grief. For example, although some couples don't have kids, the original pair-bond couple is responsible for the formation of a nuclear family, and the addition of children will change the dynamics of the communication in a number of ways as a result of the transition to parenthood or the decision to adopt. The addition of a (first) child brings significant difficulties/differences in the communication patterns and relational behaviors that follow the decision. Indeed, the transition to parenthood is a very significant stressor for couples: Satisfaction with the marital relationship tends to decrease sharply soon after this point (Kayser & Rao, 2006).

Although you can see the addition of children as a simple structural change, it is the communicative consequences that are the most interesting here. When there are children present, the focus of attention and the nature of tasks about which the couple communicates will necessarily change too (Yingling, 2004). No couples spend their dating or romantic time together talking about diapers and sleep patterns, but the couple with a new baby does that far more often than it might want. When there are no children to consider, the couple can act much more spontaneously than when it must consider the children as well. The need to arrange babysitters so that the couple can have some "alone time" is not something that romantic couples ever have to take into account when they are youthful and hormonally inclined. After commitment to a long-term partnership and the addition of children, however, romantic talk tends to get pushed aside in favor of discussion of practical childrearing tasks, and this in part accounts for the decreasing couple satisfaction that is associated with the addition of children (Rholes, Simpson, & Friedman, 2006). The couple gains new topics for conversation (feeding schedules, the dangers of electric sockets, and the most desirable sorts of fluffy toys). Its communication also loses some of the old styles (especially romantic and relaxed topics and the chance to have spontaneous and uninterrupted talk). In both cases the dynamics of communication transact the changes in family structure.

Although this is a quite striking example, less extreme changes to everyday communication happen all the time in any family "structure" as the participants grow up or get old or become ill or are faced with the decisions of life that arise in any family. Communication topics change from issues of schooling, job choice, instruction, and discipline to appropriateness of rules for "child" behaviors as the child grows older. Parents will talk between themselves and with the child about play possibilities (is the child old enough for a sleepover yet?). Also talk will turn to permissions or disputes about dating, and there are many communicative changes when the children become teenagers and establish their independence or eventually leave home.

Also consider the changes that are continuous, long term, and two-sided in family life. In addition to the sudden and drastic changes when children are added, relationships within a family change relentlessly with age across the life course (Pearson, 1996).

Photo 7.5 What might the children be learning from seeing their parents fight like this? (See page 199.)

There are alterations to the dependency structures that exist as parents and children age. Your parents may be fit and well right now, but give it another 40 years and you may be looking after your parents in the same sorts of ways they looked after you when you were merely a dependent and inept bundle. The helpless babies who were looked after by parents eventually find, as adults, that the roles are reversed, and they end up caring for their relatively helpless elderly parents in return (Blieszner, 2006).

How will communication change, do you think, when your parents cannot move about on their own, cannot hear what the doctor says, or cannot remember medical instructions given by health professionals? The *structure* of the family will be the same as before (the same people are in it, the same ones are parents, the same ones are children). However, you can expect the *communication dynamics* to change as the elder members become more, not less, dependent on the younger ones and the younger ones become more, not less, responsible for caring for the older members. For example, Petronio, Sargent, Andea, Reganis, and Cichocki (2004) note that elderly patients often ask to be accompanied by family member "advocates" during visits to a physician. This raises numerous privacy dilemmas, as the advocates necessarily violate the privacy boundaries while protecting the health of their parent. This situation can also unwittingly lead to the dialogue with the physician being directed more in their direction than in the direction of the patient, who is typically treated as superfluous to the dialogue. All the same the elderly parent relies heavily on his or her family member to make decisions on his or her behalf. This is just one example of the ways in which the same basic family structure communicatively transacts alterations over time to fundamental family matters, to power, to dependency patterns, and to family life itself.

In short, a family is always dynamic and changing; something is usually going on in it. When you look at it as a structure or as a group of members, the nuclear family is the same right through until someone is added to it or someone is taken away. Viewed more dynamically as a communication system, family communication is obviously always changing within that basic framework, even when the membership stays the same.

Redeployment of Families and Their Communication

Any form of family redeployment is tough to handle for everyone concerned, whether occasioned by addition of children, divorce, or empty nesting. The divorced or separated partners experience many difficulties and strains about their own personal experiences as they enter negotiations about ownership of property and maintenance payments. They may struggle to make joint decisions about the children's future when they may have experienced loss of trust in the relational partners with whom they are required to discuss it all. These kinds of communications are particularly difficult. Separated parents often also experience subsequently poor relationships with their own children, partly as a result of difficulty in maintaining contact and sometimes because their ex-partner undermines them in the minds of the children.

Although you may normally think of the difficulties that happen between the adults or the consequences for the children when a divorce occurs, consider the special case of divorced parents who are separated from their children. Stephanie Rollie

Photo 7.6 What problems might "weekend dads" experience in handling their kids? (See page 199.)

(2006) wrote about the particular case of NRPs—nonresidential parents (those divorced parents who live away from their kids and see them only on weekends, for example). She was interested in their strategies for maintaining relationships with their children. She pointed out a particular difficulty that they have in negotiating the absence-presence-absence cycle that is an essential part—indeed, the defining characteristic—of their relationship with the child. It is obviously extremely stressful for both the NRP and the child to keep being reminded that they must once again be separated. It is important for the parent, as the older person with more insight and control over such behaviors, to be able to remind the child of the continuing existence of the parent-child relationship during the periods of separation. It turns out that the parents use the same sorts of relational continuity constructional units (RCCUs) discussed in Chapter 6—the small-talk means of recognizing and recording the fact that the relationship is still continuing even when the partners are *not* face-to-face and may be apart from one another.

Most NRPs are able to do this by giving the children photographs or toys that remind them about the absent parent (these would be **introspective units**). Sometimes the residential parent with custody has such a bad experience with the divorce that he or she will not let these items be taken into the house, so the child is deprived of the various ways to be reminded about the absent parent. NRPs make a lot of use of **prospective units** about future meetings, even laying out ideas for future behavior in order to show their continued interest in the child ("Be good" or "Don't forget to do your homework" are examples here).

These examples from NRPs are special and lively instances where talk is used to continue family relationships that are otherwise difficult to maintain, but they exemplify the same principles that are used in all forms of relationships. When people say, "See ya later" or "What time shall we meet tomorrow?" this everyday method of sustaining relationships conceals a simple mechanism for continuing relationships in their present form, even in the family, reconfigured family, or disassembled family, even if this particular interaction is ended.

Families Communicate!

Given what is included in the previous chapter about friendships, you will not be surprised that our general idea is the same as the one we spelled out before. Relationships even in the family are always under the influence of other relationships and respond to the direct personal inputs of other people and the activities of other SSAs (Society's Secret Agents) to support social norms and conventions. The nested groups of networks, neighbors, and extended family within which a nuclear family exists are not simply a convenient academic idea. They represent and carry out the living interactions of society as its Secret Agents—the people who live in it—act to reinforce their habits, actions, and opinions for one another.

When you are thinking about "family communication" you must recognize that within any given family there occur different networks of connection. You might think of "family communication" as one sort of animal, and in many ways, you have found that it is. For example, the family may have secrets, like an alcoholic parent, that everyone in the family treats as private information together, and such secrets can be bonding or toxic. However, the different pairs of people in the family may talk to one another in different ways that are by no means common to everyone. We'd expect the adults to talk to one another in ways different from the communication that occurs between a younger brother and sister, but each child may talk to each of the parents differently, feeling preferred by one rather than the other, for example. That is, communication within the family will always depend on the specific relationships of the particular people involved at the time. For example, you and your brother, you and your father, and your mother and your sister may talk to each other differently, and this cannot be characterized as "family communication" as a whole.

Families communicate between parents and child(ren) and among siblings but also are influenced by and responsive to the forces outside the family itself. You are particularly shaped by society's views about what "family" looks like. For example, you may argue whether "gay marriage" creates a family, whether lesbians may adopt children, or about the role that "natural parents" may have in rearing a child if those natural parents are teenagers themselves. Note then that the family, whatever form you envision, is not only a system of its own but a system within a system of other influences and networks.

Although our first thoughts were about the structure of a family, you end up where this book always ends up: The family is another instance where relationships between people are done communicatively and dynamically and in important ways that show bidirectionality of influence and mutual interdependence. These are instances of the essential and inescapable effects of relational forces on all types of communication wherever you look.

Focus Questions Revisited

What is a family, and how should people specifically interested in family communication start to define what counts and what does not?

Although a family tree can indicate who was whose parent/cousin/grandparent, it does not indicate anything about the dynamics of communication that occurred within the family; nor does it indicate who hated whom or who preferred whom. Yet families have specific ways of communicating, and often the closeness of the personal relationships between people is not simply and well reflected by the structural or genetic connections that the individuals have to one another. By placing greater emphasis on the communication patterns that occur within the family we were able to demonstrate that families transact their relationships with one another in important ways that are not predictable simply from structure alone. Galvin (2007), in particular, has pointed out the ways in which families are discourse dependent.

What sorts of diverse forms of "family" are recognized in different societies/cultures?

Different sorts of families (as structures) are nuclear families, extended families, kin networks, families of origin, families of descent, families of generativity, families of choice, blended families, stepfamilies, single-parent families, and same-sex families.

What are the possible ways in which "a family" may be defined, and which one is best for a communication scholar?

From the point of view of communication studies, the analysis of the messages that people send one another in a family structure is merely a starting point that represents communication as just action (the messages send information but do not actually change or transform anything). More sophisticated views pay attention to bidirectional aspects of family communication and treat the communication as interaction, where the response of one person to another is relevant to the "meaning" of the communication. However, we have taught you that families actually transact themselves through communication, and this indicates that the interaction of people itself transacts a feeling of connectedness among them. In short, the ways in which a family communicates are themselves ways of being/creating/making a family what it is.

What types of everyday communication in a family transact the nature of family life?

Everyday communication in families can be about something or nothing. There are many little ways in which families conduct their norms and customary patterns of behavior. There are also such things as family secrets, the importance of managing boundaries around the privacy of the individuals involved, dialectics, family storytelling, and information flow. These all are also relevant to the understanding of a family as is the kind of style of communication that each individual shows in the presence of the others. The structure—the family tree alone—does not tell you whether the mother was secretive, dominating, or fun to be with; nor does it show the brutality or selfishness of a father—it shows merely that he was the father. Yet the communication that transacts family life is exactly of this emotional and relational sort. To understand family life, you need to know how its members interacted, what identity was transacted, and who they were in each other's eyes before you know what it was like to be in that family.

Key Concepts

authority structure   (p. 186)
bidirectionality hypothesis (p. 187)
binuclear family   (p. 177)
blended family   (p. 177)
boundary management   (p. 189)
extended family   (p. 177)
family identity   (p. 190)
family narratives   (p. 191)
family of choice   (p. 177)
family of descent   (p. 177)
family of generativity   (p. 177)
family of origin   (p. 177)
family storytelling   (p. 190)
introspective units   (p. 195)

kin keeping   (p. 191)
kin networks   (p. 176)
long-distance relationships   (LDRs)   (p. 191)
norms   (p. 185)
nuclear family   (p. 177)
peer culture   (p. 184)
prospective units   (p. 196)
privacy management   (p. 189)
rituals   (p. 185)
rules   (p. 175)
single-parent family   (p. 178)
socialization   (p. 175)
Systems Theory   (p. 181)

Questions to Ask Your Friends

- Does family conflict matter more than conflict at work?

- How do your friends' family members do Thanksgiving or other holiday rituals?

- How do your different friends do their family life in ways that (a) correspond with or (b) are different from the others? For example, what do friends with same-sex parents call their moms and dads?

Media Links

- In what ways are unity and harmony in the family depicted? Do you find that the family is shown as essentially stable and comforting even if there are hiccups (even in comedy shows)?

- Can you find TV shows that debunk the idea that families are happy functional units? See the film *Loverboy* or watch *Family Guy* or *The Simpsons*.

- How has the representation of the family changed in the media over the last several decades? Compare the film *Pleasantville* and the old TV show *Leave It to Beaver* with *Family Guy* or *The Simpsons*. What's different?

Ethical Issues

- What forms of connectivity between people should be regarded as "family"? Check with class members from different cultures about how family is defined from different points of view.

- Should people be free to choose their own marriage partners, or should the family make the decision for them (in order to uphold family honor, for example)?

- What are the different ethical consequences of classifying families according to the kinds of communication that occur instead of in terms of only genetic and biological relationships?

Answers to Photo Captions

Photo 7.1 ▪ Notice that one of the families contains no children but two pets, whereas another contains two adults with their senior parents, none of whom is a child. All of these represent families as structures rather than communicating or transacted groupings, and the rest of the text here challenges that view.

Photo 7.2 ▪ The three forms of family shown are nuclear; nontraditional family with two same-sex parents, possibly blended; and family of choice.

Photo 7.3 ▪ The family is acting as a socializing agent using cultural stories to teach the kids about the values of society, the joys and rewards of reading, the value of learning, and the advantages of connected involvement during the learning process. You may have come up with other answers also.

Photo 7.4 ▪ They learn to value the world in a way that the father does (service, duty, and allegiance to the country), but they also learn how "to be a man." Look at the hairstyles of the three individuals in this photo and how two converge and one diverges, subtly expressing the difference between masculinity and femininity.

Photo 7.5 ▪ The children may be learning about the instability of marriage, they may be learning about power struggles within a relationship, or they may be learning about what is appropriate and not appropriate to see, hear, or say in a family environment (note that the three children are adopting the positions of the famous monkeys: "See no evil; hear no evil; speak no evil").

Photo 7.6 ▪ They may have to live in a place that is too small to accommodate a whole family; they may have different rules about behavior; they may not want to be painted as the "bad guy," so they let the kids get spoiled; and they may have parallel lives that involve them with other people or with work that distracts them from their parental role on weekends.

Student Study Site

Visit the study site at **www.sagepub.com/ciel** for e-flashcards, practice quizzes, and other study resources.

References

Afifi, T. D. (2003). "Feeling caught" in stepfamilies: Managing boundary turbulence through appropriate communication privacy rules. *Journal of Social and Personal Relationships, 20*(6), 729–755.

Afifi, T. D., & Hamrick, K. (2006). Communication processes that promote risk and resiliency in postdivorce families. In M. A. Fine & J. H. Harvey (Eds.), *Handbook of divorce and relationship dissolution* (pp. 435–456). Mahwah, NJ: Lawrence Erlbaum and Associates.

Bateson, G. (1972). *Steps to an ecology of mind.* New York: Ballantine Books.

Baxter, L. A., Braithwaite, D. O., Bryant, L., & Wagner, A. (2004). Stepchildren's perceptions of the contradictions in communication with stepparents. *Journal of Social and Personal Relationships, 21*(4), 447–467.

BBC News. (2006, October 15). *Woman gives birth to grandchild.* Retrieved May 4, 2009, from http://news.bbc.co.uk/2/hi/asia-pacific/6052584.stm

BBC News. (2008, April 5). *Families in meltdown, judge says.* Retrieved May 2, 2009, from http://news.bbc.co.uk/1/hi/uk/7331882.stm

Blieszner, R. (2006). A lifetime of caring: Dimensions and dynamics in late-life close relationships. *Personal Relationships, 13*(1), 1–18.

Bosticco, C., & Thompson, T. (2005). The role of communication and story telling in the family grieving system. *Journal of Family Communication, 5*(4), 255–278.

Bruess, C. J. S., & Hoefs, A. (2006). The cat puzzle recovered: Composing relationships through family rituals. In J. T. Wood & S. W. Duck (Eds.), *Composing relationships: Communication in everyday life* (pp. 65–75). Belmont, CA: Wadsworth.

Buzzanell, P. M., & Turner, L. H. (2003). Emotion work revealed by job loss discourse. Backgrounding—foregrounding of feelings, construction of normalcy, and (re) instituting of traditional masculinities. *Journal of Applied Communication Research, 31,* 27–57.

Coleman, S., & May-Chahal, C. (2003). *Safeguarding children and young people.* London: Routledge.

Duck, S. W. (2007). *Human relationships* (4th ed.). London: Sage.

Galvin, K. M. (2007). Diversity's impact on defining the family: Discourse-dependence and identity. In L. H. Turner & R. West (Eds.), *The family communication sourcebook* (pp. 1–27). Thousand Oaks, CA: Sage.

Golliher, R. (2006). *Relationships with the dead in Japan.* Unpublished manuscript, University of Iowa, Iowa City.

Griffin, E. (2009). *Communication theory: A first look* (7th ed.). New York: McGraw-Hill.

Huisman, D. (2008). *Intergenerational family storytelling.* Unpublished PhD thesis, Communication Studies, University of Iowa, Iowa City.

Kayser, K., & Rao, S. S. (2006). Process of disaffection in relationship breakdown. In M. A. Fine & J. H. Harvey (Eds.), *Handbook of divorce and relationship dissolution* (pp. 201–221). Mahwah, NJ: Lawrence Erlbaum and Associates.

Kellas, J. K., & Trees, A. R. (2006). Finding meaning in difficult family experiences: Sense making and interaction processes during joint family storytelling. *Journal of Family Communication, 6*(1), 49–76.

Klein, R. C. A. (2004). Sickening relationships: Gender-based violence, women's health, and the role of informal third parties. *Journal of Social and Personal Relationships, 21*(1), 149–165.

Koerner, A. F., & Fitzpatrick, M. A. (2002). Toward a theory of family communication. *Communication Theory, 12*(1), 70–91.

Le Poire, B. A. (2006). *Family communication: Nurturing and control in a changing world.* Thousand Oaks, CA: Sage.

Le Poire, B. A., Hallett, J., & Erlandson, K. T. (2000). An initial test of inconsistent nurturing as control theory: How partners of drug abusers assist their partners' sobriety. *Human Communication Research, 26,* 432–4547.

Lloyd, J., & Anthony, J. (2003). Hanging out with the wrong crowd: How much difference can parents make in an urban environment? *Journal of Urban Health—Bulletin of the New York Academy of Medicine, 80*(3), 383–399.

Miller-Day, M., Hecht, M., & Marks, S. (2000). *Adolescent relationships and drug resistance.* Mahwah, NJ: Lawrence Erlbaum.

Nicholson, J. H. (2006). "Them's fightin' words": Naming in everyday talk between siblings. In J. T. Wood & S. W. Duck (Eds.), *Composing relationships: Communication in everyday life* (pp. 55–64). Belmont, CA: Wadsworth.

Pearson, J. C. (1996). Forty-forever years? In N. Vanzetti & S. W. Duck (Eds.), *A lifetime of relationships* (pp. 383–405). Pacific Grove, CA: Brooks/Cole.

Petronio, S. (2002). *Boundaries of privacy.* Albany: State University of New York Press.

Petronio, S., & Durham, W. T. (2008). Communication privacy management theory: Significance for interpersonal communication. In L. A. Baxter & D. O. Braithwaite (Eds.), *Engaging theories in interpersonal communication* (pp. 309–322). Thousand Oaks, CA: Sage.

Petronio, S., Sargent, J. D., Andea, L., Reganis, P., & Cichocki, D. (2004). Family and friends as health-care advocates: Dilemmas of confidentiality and privacy. *Journal of Social and Personal Relationships, 21*(1), 33–52.

Pettit, G., & Lollis, S. (1997). Reciprocity and bidirectionality in parent-child relationships: New approaches to the study of enduring issues. *Journal of Social and Personal Relationships, 14,* 435–440.

Powell, K. A., & Afifi, T. D. (2005). Uncertainty management and adoptees' ambiguous loss of their birth parents. *Journal of Social and Personal Relationships, 22*(1), 129–151.

Rholes, W. S., Simpson, J. A., & Friedman, M. (2006). Avoidant attachment and the experience of parenting. *Personality and Social Psychology Bulletin, 32*(3), 275–285.

Rollie, S. S. (2006). Nonresidential parent-child relationships: Overcoming the challenges of absence. In C. D. Kirkpatrick, S. W. Duck, & M. K. Foley (Eds.), *Relating difficulty: Processes of constructing and managing difficult interaction* (pp. 181–202). Mahwah, NJ: Lawrence Erlbaum and Associates.

Rowe, A. C., & Carnelley, K. B. (2005). Preliminary support for the use of a hierarchical mapping technique to examine attachment networks. *Personal Relationships, 12*(4), 499–519.

Sahlstein, E. M. (2006). Relational life in the 21st century: Managing people, time and distance. In J. T. Wood & S. W. Duck (Eds.), *Composing relationships: Communication in everyday life* (pp. 110–118). Belmont, CA: Wadsworth.

Segrin, C., & Flora, J. (2005). *Family communication.* Mahwah, NJ: Lawrence Erlbaum and Associates.

Stone, L. (1979). *The family, sex, and marriage in England 1500–1800.* New York: Harper Colophon.

Suter, E. A. (2006). He has two mommies: Constructing lesbian families in social conversation. In J. T. Wood & S. W. Duck (Eds.), *Composing relationships: Communication in everyday life* (pp. 119–127). Belmont, CA: Wadsworth.

Vangelisti, A. L., & Caughlin, J. P. (1997). Revealing family secrets: The influence of topic, function and relationships. *Journal of Social and Personal Relationships, 11,* 679–705.

Von Bertalanffy, L. (1950). An outline of general systems theory. *British Journal for the Philosophy of Science, 1*(2), 63–79.

Watzlawick, P., Beavin, J., & Jackson, D. (1967). *Pragmatics of human communication: A study of interactional patterns, pathologies and paradoxes.* New York: Norton.

Weston, K. (1991). *Families we choose: Lesbians, gays, kinship.* New York: Columbia University Press.

Wright, P. H., & Wright, K. D. (1995). Co-dependency: Personality syndrome or relational process? In S. W. Duck & J. T. Wood (Eds.), *Confronting relationship challenges: Understanding relationship processes 5* (pp. 109–128). Thousand Oaks, CA: Sage.

Yingling, J. (2004). *A lifetime of relationships.* Mahwah, NJ: Lawrence Erlbaum and Associates.

Zwick, J. (Director). (2002). *My big fat Greek wedding* [Motion picture]. United States: Gold Circle Films.

8

Small-Group Communication and Leadership

Scholars, including many communication researchers, have been writing about small groups for years and years and years. Small groups (say, fewer than 15 people)—from committees in Congress to juries to college admissions committees to job interview panels—can affect our lives in multiple ways. Juries, for example, can deprive us of life, liberty, and the pursuit of happiness, so we want to be sure that groups make good decisions—or at least do not make bad ones. Many questions arise about how group members communicate with one another when they are making decisions and what communicative mistakes they make. Also interesting is whether a group leader communicates differently from nonleaders (and, if so, in what ways). Feminist scholars have recently drawn attention beyond the different communicative styles of men and women in groups to marginalization in groups and the effects of group composition on group communication and behavior.

Communication students find a host of other questions about groups interesting. For example, why do groups sometimes make bad decisions even though they have talked about all the issues very thoroughly? Why is group conflict such a common experience? What about group discussions and meetings often makes them so tedious and boring? You also probably want to know how to communicate well in and make good presentations for strategic involvement in community activism, and we deal with that in Chapter 14, since nowadays the corporate world expects all college graduates to know about communicating in groups, especially in teams. (Consider the difference between a group and a team. Note the rhetorical spin that makes "team" sound more cohesive, coordinated, and united than a mere "group.")

Communication scholars Poole and Hollingshead (2005) have produced a volume that discusses different theories about these questions, including psychodynamic perspectives seeking to understand the psychological forces that lead group members and leaders to act how they do (McLeod & Kettner-Polley, 2005). Other scholars deal with social identity and how groups (try to) make themselves coherent and at the same time distinctive from other groups (Abrams, Hogg, Hinkle, & Otten, 2005). Some look at a network perspective on groups and explore the connection of one group to another (especially in a larger organization—say, "sales" in relation to "marketing") and of the relationship of one group member to another, whether familiar with each other or not (Katz, Lazer, Arrow, & Contractor, 2005). Others take a temporal perspective on groups and look at how they form, develop, and change and how communication between members changes in style and form during these processes (Arrow, Bouas Henry, Poole, Wheelan, & Moreland, 2005).

Too little attention, however, is paid to the *relationships* that exist behind the communication that takes place in groups. For example, conflict that happens in groups can be seen as a battle of *ideas*. It makes more sense, though, to see it as a battle between *people who have ideas* and relationships with one another, whether hostile or friendly before the conflict began. If you have ever been involved in group conflict in class or with people in your friendship network, you know how painful and difficult it is to deal with, because, not really about ideas, arguments, and abstractions, group conflict is about emotions, feelings, and relationships—and the *people* who *hold* the ideas and *make* the arguments.

Focus Questions

- What exactly is a "group," and what makes it different from an assembly, a collective, or a team?
- Can you define groups only in terms of the kinds of communication that take place between members, or must you look at the relationships that lie behind the communication? Does communication transact the existence and nature of the group?
- How do groups form, and what changes in their communication?
- What communicative and relational skills make a leader into a good leader?
- In what ways are discussions of team-based organizing and communication different from traditional approaches to small-group communication?
- How can a group promote its own decision-making capacities in more effective ways?

What Makes a Group?

Before we can tackle any of the above questions about communication in a group, we first must decide what "a group" is and is not. Is a group just one more person than a dyad and

one person short of a crowd? Or should communication scholars look beyond the numbers
to the activities that "groups" carry out and how
they communicate or transact their "group-
ness"? In this section, we give you some pointers. Think of any group you belong to, and not
in the standard way used in most research, you
have already answered the question "What is a
group?" by referencing your sense of *membership*. The standard answer to the question walks
through a bunch of other criteria without stressing the key point that essentially a collective
becomes a group once it recognizes itself as one
and its members identify themselves as such.

Defining a Group

Beyond the recognition of membership, scholars traditionally agree that a simple assembly or
collection of people is not really a "group" unless
they have a **common purpose**; that is, they
share a goal or objective, are working toward the
same end, or are collected as a group to achieve
a particular result (such as a sales group wanting
to find ways to increase sales). Beyond that minimum requirement, however, people in groups
are *organized*, have *awareness* of one another
as *members* of the same group, and carry out
communication among themselves. For exam-

Photo 8.1 What exactly is a group, and what makes
it different from an assembly, a collective, or a
team? How many of each of these can you see in
this picture? (See page 227.)

ple, you would not necessarily count a collection of cancer patients visiting a hospital for
chemotherapy as a "group"; nor would you count the stay-at-home dads waiting outside
to pick up their children from school, although such people may arrive at the same place
at the same time. Once they get to know one another and start to talk routinely, however,
they become "a group" because their communication transacts them into one (their talk
not only creates an interchange of information but also makes a set of random people
into a "group"). At that particular point, they develop a recognized, organized, social, or
even personal relationship with each other: They shared a purpose all along, but once they
started to recognize one another and to communicate, they became more than just a collection of bodies waiting for something else to happen.

Different groups have different kinds of communication (some very formal, some
quite casual), and everyone in a group does not necessarily have to talk to everyone else
for it to count as a "group." For example, in a college discussion section, the students may
all talk to the discussion leader but not to one another. A discussion section still counts as
a group rather than a random collection of students because there is a common purpose,
a set time to meet, some rules, and a leader (i.e., an implied organizational structure).
Most important, the people see themselves as more than just a bunch of folks but as
members of something shared.

Regular "friendship groups" or "social networks" are not included in Table 8.1 on the next page. Why do you think researchers would see a friendship group as different from the other types of groups, and does it matter? One obvious point is that friendships have very little structure and are based on the notion of equality, whereas many other groups have a formal structure that gives people different rank or powers. What other differences do you notice between the "groups" you belong to and the "friendships" you have?

In the present chapter, we discuss the small groups that might occupy part of your experience (for example, Bible study groups, board meetings, sorority committees, friends deciding what kind of pizza to order on Friday night, chat rooms, focus groups, or sets of roommates working out a cooking roster). In each of these groups, when decisions are made, someone essentially persuades someone else, in the context of the rules that govern the relationship. Everyday life relating involves informal persuasion of people in a group just as persuasive speeches to large audiences have an underlying set of assumptions about the relationship of speaker to audience (Chapter 14). Here we look only at the processes by which decisions get made by small interactive groups, but by and large we will say that the principles—the transactive principles of communication now familiar to you—are broadly similar in all of these cases: They depend on relationships.

In the long history of research into communication in groups, scholars have most often looked at group decision making in terms of quality of information and message transmission. Notice how much information transfer and decision making takes place relationally—you listen to complaints, give advice, carry out tasks, and do favors for friends without really giving the prospect much thought. It's what friends do for one another, offering advice, knowledge, information, help, and support. The *kind* of communication and how it is carried out makes the group the sort that it is (see Table 8.1). Although many communication courses focus exclusively on deliberate and purposive persuasion, especially in groups that make formal decisions or in public presentations and speeches, there is a relational basis to this kind of communication, too. Discussion of group decision making usually involves looking at the most effective forms of communication that help groups reach decisions, often because groups have a set task, purpose, or objective (such as a team responsible for deciding whether to launch a space shuttle, a business meeting deciding a sales plan, or a jury deciding on guilt or innocence). Most people have been in such decision-making groups or meetings, but most of your decision making does *not* occur in such groups. Rather, group decision making happens between people in longer-term relationships. Essentially, communication between people transacts group membership, not the other way around, and some obvious relationship issues arise that will affect and be affected by communication.

Formation of Groups

Groups created for experimental purposes and those in real organizational settings develop their own ways to conduct business. Bruce Tuckman (1965), a psychologist,

Table 8.1 Types of Groups

Type of Group	Primary/ Fundamental Purposes	Features	Examples
Formal groups	Task oriented, general management oversight, outcome focused, often legislative or formally structured to run an organization	Membership is restricted or delegated; attendance is expected. There is a clear structure; power is vested in the chair; there is an agenda. There may be formal rules for speaking/turn taking; there may be voting.	Congress, congressional committees, debate clubs, shareholder meetings, annual general meetings of organized bodies, executive committees of unions, student government organizations, legislative assemblies
Advisory	Task specific, usually evidentiary or evaluative, with the intention of producing an outcome that is a focused "best solution" to a specific problem or arrangement of an event	Membership is specific and restricted; there may be a chair, there may be structure, and there may be an agenda. Discussion is usually open, informal, and focused on the weighing of evidence or alternatives. Critical and evaluative argument of different proposals is encouraged.	Sorority and fraternity social affairs committees, homecoming committees, juries, accident investigation boards, review boards for awards and prizes
Creative	Evaluation of concepts or creation of new products or approaches to complex problems	Membership is usually invited. There is lack of structure, absence of critique of members' ideas, and generativity; individuals are discouraged from critical comment on the ideas generated by others. The point is to generate as many ideas as possible and evaluate them later.	Brainstorming; consciousness raising; creativity groups; focus groups; test-bed groups for developing specifications and criteria for complex projects, such as the beta versions of new software, advertising logo development teams
Support	Advising, comforting, sharing knowledge, spreading information, and raising consciousness about specific issues	Membership is loosely defined; members come and go as needed; participation is voluntary as and when desired.	Alcoholics Anonymous, breast cancer survivors, grief support groups, study groups, PFLAG (Parents, Families and Friends of Lesbians and Gays)
Networking	Obtaining, building, or sustaining relationships, usually online	Membership is not defined; members join and leave as desired.	Chat rooms, social networking groups, MySpace, Facebook

proposed five stages of group development, and another similar phase model was proposed by communication scholar Aubrey Fisher (1970).

Tuckman's Five Stages of Group Development

1. *Forming:* The group begins to come into existence and seeks guidance and direction from a leader concerning the nature of its task and procedures.

2. *Storming:* The group starts the creative process of focusing on its goals but may become entangled in socioemotional and relationship storms and interpersonal conflict between individuals.

3. *Norming:* The group starts to define its purposes, roles, and procedures and begins moving more formally toward a solution of its task.

4. *Performing:* Having established how it will perform its task, the group now does so, with members not only seeking solutions to their problems but being careful about one another's feelings and roles in the group.

5. *Adjourning:* Having performed its functions, the group reflects on its achievements, underlines its performative accomplishments, and closes itself down. There is a certain amount of self-congratulation at this stage: "Good job, everyone."

Fisher's Model of Group Progression

- *Orientation:* The group members get to know one another—assuming, of course, they do not already—and come to grips with the problems they have convened to deal with.

- *Conflict:* The group argues about the possible ways of approaching the problem and begins to find solutions.

- *Emergence:* Developed from the previous stage, emergence occurs when some daylight of consensus begins to dawn and the group starts to move toward agreement.

- *Reinforcement:* The group recognizes that it is reaching consensus and explicitly consolidates that consensus to complete the task.

Fisher supposed that the types of communication going on in a group would serve to identify as well as promote the particular stage. Thus, the model has the advantage of helping researchers watch a decision-making group to see where it is headed or to identify issues that might prevent it from moving successfully toward the final conclusive stage. Notice the assumption of the model, however, that the stage of the group produces certain identifying types of communication, not vice versa.

> Is your family a group? If so, is it the same or different from the other groups you belong to?

We have emphasized the importance of everyday communication throughout this book, and you can immediately recognize that groups, whether or not they change their speech styles in the exact stages proposed by Fisher, certainly speak differently than when friends chat. One feature that makes formal groups feel different is that they constrain everyday speech by adopting rules that affect the patterns of speaking from those that happen in everyday speech. "Will the senator yield?" and "If it please the court" are not remarks you often hear outside of formal decision-making groups!

What are the effects of the differences between everyday communication and the corralling and formalizing of speech that happen in group decision making? For one thing, you must know the right language to belong to a group: The Speaker of the House of Representatives does not begin the business of the day by announcing "Yo, dogs, wassup?" but uses a prescribed formula, not widely known to outsiders. One element of group membership, then, is created by *knowledge of the styles and rules governing talk* in the group and the differences between them and everyday life conversation. For this reason, seeing "the composition" of groups as just a counting of heads and characteristics is a mistake. If one sees groups just as structures rather than as communicatively related membership systems, it only makes sense to identify the composition of a collective in terms of names, ranks, sex, age, and other general information. *Groups* interact not because of their "composition" (numbers of females or males, old or young) but because of the communicative relationships developed and the kinds of talk shared between specific people involved.

Primary and Secondary Groups

It is also customary to divide group structures into **primary groups** (those that share close personal relationships, such as friends) and **secondary groups** (those that represent casual and more distant social relationships, such as the people you meet for discussion section but not for other purposes or at other times). Primary and secondary groups, however, do not have strict boundaries; individuals can belong to both and can move back and forth. A group of regular customers at a supermarket represents an example of a secondary group unless they know one another on a personal level; such groups as political caucuses would also count as secondary groups because they get together as formal institutions and then disband once the task is completed. Yet, some members of a secondary group, such as a political caucus, may also be personal best friends, which puts them in a primary group at the same time. So the labels of primary and secondary groups are helpful in categorizing people only when you see the distinction structurally. *Transactively*, however, how the members of a collectivity treat or communicate with one another brings them out as one type of group or another.

It is easy to overlook two facts: (1) that most everyday groups are not simply brought together for a researcher to study (as are many groups discussed in research reports) and (2) that everyday real group members' lives operate in customary everyday ways within an enduring larger structure. New members enter an existing structure and most often have very little or no influence on its development. For example, a sales group is ultimately responsible to a head office; "the faculty" in a particular department ultimately must follow the dean's directions and university procedures correctly; a professional football team is ultimately responsible to a group of owners and directors. However a small group acts on a particular special occasion, such as a sales meeting, the larger organization probably continues both its structured existence and its personal relationships, much more likely to be conducted in the looser styles of everyday talk than in the stricter forms of talk used in meetings.

It is all very well to look at groups in theoretical structural ways, as bodies, numbers, and depersonalized decision makers, but within that generalized structure sit real human beings who have relationships with one another. The "board of executives" may make a decision that may be influenced by the friendship between Alina and Sangeet; the mutual dislike between the meeting chair, Christina, and John; and so on. A business board meeting can be looked at as a formal structure created by the organization with the task of making top-level decisions, but the real people put into it by the organization will develop personal relationships with one another. Within the board, Jim may be friends with Sarah; Sarah trusts Chitra; Juanita resents Jamaal... and the formal and informal relationships can clash. For example, Sarah trusts Chitra interpersonally,

Make Your Case

Consider in class or by yourself whether these count as groups: a family; an audience of people watching a football game in a sports bar; an audience at a public lecture on campus; the people watching a movie at the cinema; witnesses to a car accident talking to one another as they watch the police take notes. You might also reflect on whether or not you are in a group when you use the speaker phone feature on a mobile/cell phone in a public place. Who is in the group, and who is out? What communicative features are different in the above cases?

but in a board setting, they are both constrained to act not on their personal feelings but in the service of group goals, where consensus of the group is seen as a more important objective than is Sarah's personal trust for Chitra. Sarah and Chitra may have to carry out tasks for the group that strain their personal trust: For example, they may be asked to decide which employees to fire so the business can cut costs, yet they may have personal relationships with the individuals being discussed for "letting go."

So, although a "group" can be just a set of friends talking to one another and making a decision about where to go for dinner, it is more important to see *all* groups not just as structures but as dynamic, communicative, relationally transacted entities that are more than the sum of their parts.

Features of Groups

Let's now look at some of the characteristics used in the past to single out groups for study. We'll apply our relational transactional lens to these characteristics as we go along. The above discussion already identified a few key features of groups that come to the forefront when you treat them as structures without attending to the dynamic interpersonal relationships between members. We did not give them their technical terms, however, so we will do that now to connect you with traditional research before offering our new perspective.

Togetherness

The members of a group are first defined by their common motives and goals (Thibaut & Kelley, 1959). For example, an advisory committee shares the task of coming up with a thoughtful report, and a homecoming committee shares the goal of making this the best homecoming ever, with the smartest ideas and themes. A related feature of groups is that they divide the labor in a way that leads to **interdependence**; that is, everyone relies on everyone else to do his or her part of the job well, and the team cannot function properly if its members do not work interdependently. For example, members of a football team are interdependent because the performance of the whole team depends on the coherent yet distinct performance of each of its members. Not everyone can be a quarterback; people in the offensive lineup have different jobs than those in the defensive lineup. The work is divided even though the team as a whole shares a purpose: namely, winning the game. The ultimate success of the group/team as a whole will depend in part on whether every member does an assigned job. If everyone tried to do the same task (all tried to throw the ball, all tried to block the other team, all tried to catch passes), the whole enterprise would be ineffective because the other jobs would be neglected. In this way, interdependence often involves the division of labor into particular jobs so the members can better achieve their goals. Interdependence works as a transacted outcome of the communication between team players! The coaches and the captain have the job of coordinating the other members' performances in a way, through communication, that hangs it all together.

Group members usually show commitment to each other and to their group's goals when it is working well (Harden Fritz & Omdahl, 2006). One transactive feature that makes a group a "group" is that individual members share a commitment to the overall group goals, want to be team players, and communicate that desire by their talk and behavior. The members may also show commitment to one another, watch each other's backs, and look out for one another, particularly in effective groups. The more people share commitment to one another as members of a group, the more they help the whole group move forward toward its goals. The group may show commitment to individual members through caring for their welfare, as well as aiming to achieve the goals of the group.

Groups, particularly effective groups, also manifest synchrony as they work together. **Cohesiveness**, essentially another word for *teamwork*, describes people working in unison (Hogg, 1992). You have probably seen a motivational poster that shows a rowing team all pulling together. They are synchronously cohesive. If every member pulled the oar whenever he or she felt like it rather than all pulling at the same time, the members would show low cohesiveness and keep getting in each other's way. Their oars would clash, and the boat would go nowhere (take it from an Oxford college rowing coxswain!). Another goal of many groups is to maintain high morale and civility by making sure that members do not disrespect each other. Maintaining good relationships between members, another example of cohesiveness, is a goal of any group that seeks to be effective. Cohesiveness, however, or the degree to which members are attracted and committed to one another, is a primary output of groups' social emotional exchanges in talk and thus is a transactional and relational consequence of communication.

Expectations About Performance

Groups usually expect particular behavior from members. We covered this in the context of the larger society as a whole in Chapter 5 on identity, where we saw that others' expectations influence our own behaviors and the performance of our identity. Small groups have more specific expectations about behavior and influence the group itself. Correct behavior elicits a reinforcing response, which then

How do various groups to which you belong show their commitment to membership? Don't just list your college "fight song" but report on specific examples of communication that transact commitment.

influences further expectations of and for other people, providing, therefore, another example of the constitutive and transactive way in which communication sustains behavior.

Group Norms

In the context of groups, for example, **group norms** involve established status relationships, values, and sanctions; that is, rules and procedures occurring in a group but not necessarily outside it are enforced by the use of power or rules for behavior. A group norm may be that everyone should speak in turn and that all voices should be heard, as is common in meetings in the Netherlands, for example; that everyone should speak in terms of seniority, follow the leader, or speak his or her mind creatively without fear of being criticized; or, alternatively, that "nobody rocks the boat and everyone should be a team player." Most groups have a norm that requires mutual respect. Some therapy groups purport, however, to break down people's defensiveness about their egos, so people are encouraged to make honest, even if negative, comments about each other with no attempt to dress them up politely (T-groups, encounter groups, and EST groups; Weigel, 2002). A stronger version of this norm is also evident in military training groups whose purpose, in part, is to break down the recruits' individuality by insulting them and getting them used to the idea of doing whatever they are told without objecting or answering back. In all of these cases, though, the group sets its own norms and ways of ensuring their enforcement. Most groups have their own **group sanctions**, or punishments for "stepping out of line," speaking out of turn, or failing to accept the ruling of the chair or leader. For example, an unruly member—one who persistently violates the norms—may be thrown out of a meeting and hence be denied any voice in what happens later in that meeting. More subtly, everyone else in the group may shun a dissenter and classify him or her as to be avoided outside and ignored inside the meetings.

Group Roles

Another form of expectation about performance has to do with roles. You know about roles from movies: A role is when someone acts out a part that fits in with parts other people play in "the drama." Erving Goffman (1959) pointed out that people perform a lot of life as if it were drama, and in Chapter 5, we discussed the *performance* of identity. Other roles come into play in groups, such as the role of leader, but groups with a continuous existence tend to mark out other roles as well. In formal organizations, these roles have titles, like sales director or manager. If you have ever bought a car, you know that one dealer will often play the role of "the friendly guy" while another one will play the role of "hard-nose" so they can soften you up first and then play hardball in the negotiations over price. Groups that meet more than once and interact frequently with an expectation of continued future existence also develop roles.

> If two friends are also in a sales-team group decision-making situation where one is "the leader," which role should the leader adopt if the friend says something funny but irrelevant—the "stay-on-track leader" role or the "have-fun-with-friends" role?

In groups of coworkers, "the sales team," or a college discussion section, roles not only evolve for the people involved; patterns of interaction that repeat themselves and reinforce these roles evolve as well. People in that group likely will be categorized and informally assigned particular roles ("the Joker," "the Grinch," "the loose cannon," or "the rising star," for example).

The identification of members' roles and leadership in groups, an early hope of research in group processes (e.g., Hollander, 1958), largely stemmed from the research done in World War II intended to identify future military leaders early in their careers and give them fast-track promotion to particularly suitable leadership roles. Even today, the military identifies individuals as "flyers" or even "no-hopers" and places some recruits on the fast track to promotion as a result of abilities demonstrated on tests early in their enlistment. This style of research in groups, however, has largely run into the objection that it takes too little account of how people adapt to situations and circumstances and that the communication occurring in group interaction can generate unexpected skills or adaptations in people.

Group Culture

A **group culture**, another form of expectation set that affects groups, can take many forms and may be evident in how members talk to one another, the clothes they wear while working as a group, or the special terms and language or jokes they use. For example, an organization may have a formal dress code in the workplace except on "casual Friday," or group members may talk in ways that reflect an organizational hypertext language specific to their particular organization and that would not be understood outside it (for example, the language codes discussed in Chapter 2). Workers on a construction site may have a group culture that particularly values physical strength rather than managerial thinking and thus may tend to play down any evidence of thoughtfulness. Dennis Mumby (2006) illustrates a similar kind of culture in a group when he writes about his experiences as a college student working in a manual labor job where the other workers tended to mock the fact that, with all his "college boy" intelligence, he could not drive some of the machinery as effectively as they could. The very use of the term *college boy* to describe him represents, in talk, the group culture that intelligence was less important in its work than other skills. In the film *Office Space,* one element of group culture in the restaurant where the Jennifer Aniston character ("Joanna") works is the wearing of "flair" (badges and decorations on the servers' uniforms). In one scene, a manager points out that Joanna is wearing only the *minimum* amount of flair and therefore is not demonstrating adequate commitment to the group culture.

All of these forms of expectation in groups (norms, roles, culture) are important ways of stressing communicatively the fact that a person belongs to a group and must play particular parts in its performances. They all communicatively transact the relationships between people that make groups into the sort they are (revisit Table 8.1).

> Listen for the norms, roles, and culture of two or three of the groups you belong to and identify their differences in terms of the kind of group you are thinking about.

Leadership

Most groups are formally structured in a way that grants someone leadership (though research has been conducted on leaderless groups). **Leadership** is the formal position where a specific person has power over the others in the group: a boss in the workplace, a team leader in a task group, a chair of any committee, or an elder of a religious community. Such people are required to communicate authoritatively, to run the agenda, and to move the group forward in particular ways that others should follow. Looking at how talk is actually conducted, however, you can see that conflicts sometimes arise between the structure and the exercise of informal power, making power itself a transactive result of communication. A particular group's power holder has **formal power** (is the group's designated leader), but the group may communicate in a way that this power means, in effect, very little. For example, the designated chair of a committee may actually be very ineffective at leading a discussion, and another member of the committee (emergent leader) may be better at communicating and may be more respected than the chair. This situation leads in the group to a kind of **informal power** essentially based on liking, relationships, and communication competence rather than on formality.

Power and Leadership

In a very striking example of how this power structure works, John Hepburn and Anne Crepin (1984) studied the relationships between prisoners and guards in a state penitentiary, where the formal structure of power fairly clearly is that the guards are in control and the prisoners are not. Important factors need to be taken into account, however, when evaluating whether the system is structured along the formal lines as expected. The system cannot work in some important ways if only formal power is taken into account. First, the prisoners outnumber the guards very significantly, and at any time, if they acted together, they could probably overpower a single guard, whether or not the guard is carrying weaponry. Second, the guards' superiors take note of how they handle prisoners. Particular guards get a reputation for being good with prisoners, while other guards are seen as incompetent. The good ones receive bigger pay raises than the others, so it turns out once again that the prisoners can influence the outcomes for the guards in unexpected ways. If the prisoners choose to communicate cooperatively with a particular guard, the superiors will see that guard as doing his or her job well. If the prisoners decide to make a particular guard's life difficult by disobeying orders or showing disrespect in their talk, he or she will be frequently

Contrarian Challenge

Most research on group decision making assumes that the structure and the style of communication are more important than the personal relationships between members. Which do you think is more important?

pulled into conflicts in a way that his or her superiors will eventually see as evidence of inability to get the job done well. Hence, the guards need to play along, communicating with prisoners in a constructive and amiable fashion that helps them develop decent working relationships so they can do their job at all. So who *really* has the power? As you can tell, power is always a transactional concept and is always related to relationship dynamics.

An informal system of relative power among the prisoners also develops within a penitentiary, and some prisoners are top dogs while others are not. The guards must learn to pay attention to this informal hierarchy among the prisoners and not simply treat them all equally, or

Photo 8.2 What communicative and relational skills make a leader good? (See page 228.)

eventually the prisoners will stir up trouble for the guards. Again, power is transacted into being by how two parties relate and communicate.

Power in groups, then, is not always as clear as it seems from the structure of groups. You can probably think of examples from your own life where a person who appears powerful over you might find things turning around unexpectedly. For example, your instructors appear to have power over you, yet you get to rate them at the end of their courses in a way that may influence their careers or pay status.

Leadership as Transacted

Given these points, you nevertheless normally think that the formal group leader has power over the other group members, and researchers tend to look at the role of leadership in small groups in terms of *functions* and *types* or *styles* of leadership. Typically differentiated into socioemotional and task leaders (Bales, 1950), as discussed below, more recently leaders have been regarded as group stewards or *team* leaders (Northouse, 2007).

Task Leaders

A task leader stresses the activity of the group and keeps members on topic, makes sure decisions get made and the agenda gets followed, is responsible for defining the group's intended accomplishment, and is charged with directing what happens to fulfill the set tasks of the group. For example, a committee chair is supposed to keep the group on track, know what its agenda is, and make sure it reaches a conclusion at the end of its allotted meeting time. The task leader may be charged with summarizing what got done in a meeting and setting the agenda for the next one. This kind of leader also often is responsible for procedural activities and ensuring that proper procedures are followed during the course of discussion. The chair of a committee of Congress, for example, must know the proper rules of parliamentary procedure encoded in Robert's Rules of Order. These procedures may involve such matters as who may propose a motion, the form in which a motion may be proposed, how amendments may be discussed, and the order in which motions must be considered. In the film *Apollo 13,* the task leader is the flight controller (nicknamed "Flight" and played by Ed Harris), who supervises the whole mission and makes the team all work together to bring back the stranded astronauts. He defines what different members of the ground team should do, gives them objectives, delegates specific responsibilities, and devises an overall strategic plan for saving the mission.

Socioemotional Leaders

By contrast, a socioemotional leader pays attention to how everyone feels in the group, ensuring that all members feel comfortable with what happens in the decision-making process, get their turn in the discussion, and are relatively happy with the outcome. Of course, the task leader and the socioemotional leader can be one and the same (as indeed turns out to be the case in *Apollo 13,* where Flight manages to rally his team by calming them down and forcing them to be realistic). Much early research in groups shows that quite different forms of communication are involved in the two tasks (Parsons & Bales, 1955) and that a person may be good at one element of the group process (keeping people on task, for example) but relatively poor at another (keeping everyone happy). When the two roles are performed by different people, most often the task leader focuses on goals at the expense of the feelings of the people involved. The socioemotional leader is better at keeping the personal relationships between group members on an even keel or in the right emotional arena, managing people's "face" and handling their feelings well rather than evaluating their performance on the task as the only goal.

The identification of such stylistic differences depends on the assumption that the communication happening in a group results from the leaders' individual character or the sorts of roles that members get allocated (leaders, followers, secretaries, and organizers, for example). Once again, then, any analysis of group activity in these terms presupposes a model of communication as action, with the communication produced by a particular person generated by his or her character or role in the group (McLeod & Kettner-Polley, 2005). Although individuals have their own ideas about what needs to be said and done when they occupy certain roles in a group (task leader, for example), how they actually do it will be shaped, steered, and focused by other people's communication, group processes themselves, and other influences from culture and society—just as you saw occurring in Chapter 5 about the performance of a person's "identity."

Such social influences from others really mean that leadership is a *process,* not a trait or a characteristic. Leadership is transacted communicatively between one person and others such that when one gives a direction and another gladly carries it out, leadership has been successfully transacted in the interchange. Leadership is not *in a person* but *between people.* When someone is assigned to be a leader, manager, director, or department head, certain expectations result from the appointment, and usually such a person has real control over resources that other team members need. As we saw in the case of the prisoners and guards, however, an emergent leader may actually run the show without having the title. Sometimes, particular members of decision-making groups come up with consistently better ideas than the designated leader, and eventually people start to see those members as the true influencers.

Much previous research has looked for leadership traits (the "born leader," if you like), where other research has sought the skills that can be taught to make anyone an effective leader. For example, managers may need certain levels of knowledge and technical skill to lead a team: They cannot guide and correct other people if they do not know how to do it correctly (Mumford, Zaccaro, Harding, Jacobs, & Fleishman, 2000). Leaders also require skills in problem solving and social judgment, ability to see things from other perspectives, and "people skills" (Argyle, 1983).

More recent work on leadership (Northouse, 2007) has emphasized leaders' roles as "stewards" of either people or resources during their tenure at the helm. It also emphasizes that the burden rests not with the leader alone but also with the rest of the group as a team that should still be coherent and effective once a new steward takes over. As noted early in this chapter, the term *team* has a rhetorical spin that signifies interdependence, cooperation, effective division of labor, common goals, coordination, and mutual respect, suggesting that relational aspects of an effective team are at least as important as the group's task outcomes. Hence, research on teams places emphasis on making people feel valued as well as getting the job done (Clampitt, 2005). Any old despot can force slaves to build pyramids, but very few leaders can make their underlings feel important afterward. Julius Caesar's leadership qualities included that he made a point of knowing the names of as many of his men as humanly possible—he had a staggering memory—and addressing each one personally as often as he could. By paying attention to their feelings as people, he built his legions into formidable teams that would do for him what they would do for no one else.

Effective teams and their leaders are therefore interdependent partly as a result of the fact that they attend to personal relationships and carry out the friendly and respectful communication necessary for truly "personal" relationships. Personal communication transacts a collaborative climate, strong personal commitment, high regard for other team members, and a unified commitment to excellence that enables the group to achieve its goals as clearly articulated by a good leader (Northouse, 2007). Clarity and purposefulness, two extra features of a leader's communication, thus help the team once interpersonal trust and mutual respect have been built.

Group Decision Making

Groups make decisions all the time, and television and movies show these decisions very frequently. In order to make decisions, group members sit around a table in high-glass towers using flip charts and tapping their pencils or using highly sophisticated electronic equipment. Hugely important managerial decisions are made by unusually powerful people in suits with unlimited resources and teams of heavies to back them up. Often, however, a subplot emerges: Someone in the group is a traitor.

The Informal Side of Group Decision Making

In real life, groups of different types make decisions all the time in ways that this formal, stilted, and illusory way does not adequately represent. Most everyday life groups are not made up of extremely powerful people, and most decisions are not based on the availability of unlimited resources. When the ground flight team in Houston in *Apollo 13* frantically but effectively makes decisions about "the problem" on the spacecraft, it has clear goals but very limited ways to work toward them. Keep in mind that when you and a group of friends decide which movie to see, not only are the stakes a lot lower than in the earlier examples, but the range of options and outcomes is accordingly of a completely different order of magnitude.

Even formal groups can come to conclusions and make decisions in a variety of ways, such as voting, consensus, straw polls, or mandates from the boss. They use these mechanisms particularly when in session "as a group"; however, in the informal meetings outside of these structures, business is conducted in different ways that could nevertheless influence the outcome of a group deliberation. For example, what happens in a formal committee session may be influenced by a private discussion between the chair and a committee member before the meeting. Likewise, how faculty members vote on a particular issue may be influenced by concerns about tenure, promotion, and future consequences. These kinds of informal meetings and personal concerns for consequences outside of formal sessions are significant and meaningful for the people involved. Incidentally, such secret discussions often happen in politics where two rival political parties cannot agree on a piece of legislation at first but manage to come up privately with a toned-down compromise version outside the formal meeting that both sides can then publicly accept in the meeting itself.

Group Goals and Functions

In formal groups that make decisions about particular topics, it is important to have a number of objectives very clearly worked out beforehand. Much research in communication studies has looked at the best way groups can be sure to make effective decisions. A primary consideration for a group faced with a particular set of issues is as basic as making an agenda that specifies a time and place to meet to discuss the problems and then using that time to actively discover the logistical solutions available. Groups must take many other steps, however, to be—and for their decisions to be—effective.

A particularly influential approach to this question is the functional theory of group decision making (Gouran & Hirokawa, 1996). This approach suggests that the most effective sequence in group decision making is to define the problem, analyze the issues, establish the criteria, generate solutions, evaluate solutions, choose and implement the best solution, and then develop an action plan to monitor the solution. It is most important for a group to start with problem analysis; that is, a group must first decide what requires improvement or change in a situation, and to do so, the members must analyze the problem carefully and thoughtfully to ensure that they understand it fully before trying to solve it. An effective problem-solving or decision-making group will do a good problem analysis as its first communicative venture in the process, thoroughly considering the nature of the question and making sure it has a good grasp of what is at stake.

Having understood the nature of the problem, the group's next task is goal setting, or what it needs to do to solve the problem. The group must establish criteria by which it can work out whether the problem has been solved and then effectively evaluate whether its solution is better than other possibilities. To do this evaluation, the group must identify and discuss alternative ways to solve the problem and then evaluate effectively whether each will work. Assessing and evaluating the positive and negative consequences of each possibility are important in order to see whether the solution is better than the problem. For example, a medical team that decides to cut off a patient's hand because his or her palm constantly itches has probably not thought the problem through properly or evaluated alternative solutions effectively.

There are three forms of communication that can help a decision-making group achieve its goals, divert from its goals, and get back on track, respectively: (1) **promotive communication**, (2) **disruptive communication**, and (3) **counteractive communication**, as described in Table 8.2.

Table 8.2 Three Forms of Communication in Decision-Making Groups

Promotive communication	• Helps a decision-making group achieve its goals by specifying them • Works toward moving the agenda along and keeping people on track (i.e., serves their objectives in effective ways) • For example, a person may help the group focus by telling a story about how he or she solved a similar problem (Glidewell, Tucker, Todt, & Cox, 1982).
Disruptive communication	• Diverts the group from its goals and takes it down side alleys • Does not push the group forward toward achieving its goals • Does not help the group toward goals but may raise morale or lower tension • Somebody who tells an amusing story from his or her own life that has very little connection to the group's goals would be a disruptive communicator.
Counteractive communication	• Gets the group back on track by reminding its members of its purposes • For example, in *Apollo 13,* Flight reminds the team members that they are telling him *what they need* to solve the problem of how to return the space capsule safely to Earth, and he is telling them *what they have* to work with. In short, he uses counteractive communication to bring them back to reality and to tell them that resources are limited and unalterable—they simply *must* work within the available means.

Group Decision Making Is About Relationships

In discussing the group decision-making process, we have pointed out that such considerations as group culture, group history, group future, group norms, and cohesiveness or conformity are all in their own way relationship concepts (see Table 8.3).

Table 8.3 Relationship Concepts in Group Decision Making

Group culture	The relationships that exist between the people in a group.
Group history	A sense of collectivity and common origin, which, as you recall from Chapter 5 on identity, is important in how people and groups enact themselves. Groups are often aware that they have to live up to their own history and not let down those who have gone before them.
Group future	Indicates that the members of a group feel they will still be connected and committed in the future (many lab research groups lack this sense).
Group norms	Defined ways of behaving that set the standard for that behavior.
Cohesiveness/ conformity	Going along with the group even if you disagree; refers to how people treat one another and regard the group as an important relational component of their common life irrespective of the achievement of other goals.

An attempt to be cohesive at the expense of anything else, however, can sometimes get in the way of a group's effective functioning if everyone wants to keep everyone else happy rather than make tough decisions. Sometimes, people would rather preserve good relationships than make good decisions. Irving Janis (1972) famously referred to this negative kind of consensus-seeking cohesiveness as "groupthink," where members place a higher priority on keeping the process running smoothly and agreeably than they do on voicing opinions that contradict the majority opinion. The group thus prefers the well-being of its members and the morale and teamwork of the group at the expense of proper critical evaluation of the ideas expressed. Groupthink can result in faulty decision making because a group prefers to be a *happy* ship rather than a ship going in the right direction. Although usually a good thing, cohesiveness can lead to negative consequences.

Persuasion, whether purposive or incidental, is most often based on relationships, even in groups. Your friends persuade you and you persuade them, but very often people meet in groups to reach decisions in a more formal way than friends do day-to-day. The question looked at here is really whether the formality of groups changes how persuasion works or whether relationships lie at the bottom of it all. Even in a formal group, your standing will influence whether people do what you want. Formally, because bosses control resources (such as pay), agenda, policy, and other norms to do with dress code and organizational expectations, they have power in an organization that others do not. Incompetent, bullying, and authoritarian bosses can rule with a stick, but everyone still hates them and often takes any quiet chance to undermine them in everyday chatter around the water cooler and in privately circulated e-mail exchanges. By contrast, popular and inclusive or supportive bosses and leaders can get people to do more than absolutely required and encourage greater efforts without force. In these cases, people do what their bosses ask because they like them and do not resent the request.

Group decision making (especially small-group decision making) is normally presented as a formal, semirational interaction, where groups sit around and work through decisions. On the other hand, a lot of everyday persuasion is often masked, unnoticed. When you separate decision making into the activities of groups in meetings, you tend to overlook just how much persuasion of group members actually occurs in other settings for other reasons. Sometimes, people vote for a proposal not because it is compelling but because they like the person who proposed it or dislike the person who opposed it, for instance. Although it is important to understand group features and processes, especially when considering how talk styles change the way people otherwise operate (e.g., if they have to follow formal rules for turn taking in speech), don't forget that groups are made up of *people.* Members (e.g., members of a work team) have relationships with one another *outside* as well as *inside* their meetings. After the formal discussion, when the group splits up, the members go on with the rest of their lives, which can mean chatting to other group members in places outside the group. Real-life groups exist continuously both as groups

Photos 8.3a and b In what ways are discussions of team-based organizing and communication different from traditional approaches to small-group communication? (See page 228.)

(e.g., "The work team meets every Friday," "Bible study group is Wednesday night," "The book club meets every Thursday") and as individuals whose lives may be connected outside the group (e.g., two members of the same work team may be friends, Bible study group members may also be neighbors, book club members could be in the same family).

All your lives, you are embedded in various groups—families, workplace groups, friends, servers/diners, sales/shoppers—and the overall processes reflect a little group decision making but a lot of other processes that generally occur in conversation. So our point is not so much that group decision-making literature can apply to other forms of interpersonal communication in the outside world but that these outside-world processes of interpersonal communication can apply even to formal, small-group decision making. Instead of isolating group decision making like a big animal in a zoo that needs its own diet and treatment, it makes more sense to see all human communication as part of the same interdependent ecosphere where creatures (like family communication or persuasive speeches) roam in different spaces but, as it were, essentially share about 99.9% of the common communication DNA. We believe that interpersonal communication as a whole operates with basically the same principles and that they apply across the board with minor variations in specific cases.

Sometimes people sit down and make actual decisions about what to do, but often the banal routine of everyday life does it for them. If you know it is your job to clean up the dishes after a meal on Wednesday night, the group does not have to keep deciding it, though it may occasionally remind you about an existing decision still in force. A group can also, of course, sit down and make a decision again and change the roster. Most of the time, however, previous decisions are assumed to still be in force and have power, unless they are explicitly brought up for reconsideration.

Thus, a lot of what groups and individuals do is defined by preexisting decisions. If your group has a ritual way of "doing Friday night," few actual decisions are needed on any particular Friday, and everything just follows the regular path. People show up at the expected time and place without being reminded, and then the Friday runs the same course as always. Everyone is happy and does not sit down to decide to change the ritual. All the same, you are influenced by your groups whether you notice it or not, just as your interaction with specific people (as we saw in Chapter 5 when thinking about symbolic interaction) brings out your identity in interesting ways.

What we have written about good decision making draws on the existing research literature about it, but a tension exists between treating group decision making as a special case of human behavior or seeing it merely as a species of behavior that has more in common with the rest of life than it is distinct and different. In this textbook, we emphasize the relational underpinnings of every aspect of life, and we see this underpinning as the core of most behavior that happens during communication episodes—whether or not they happen in groups.

Strategic Communication

The research literature in interpersonal communication concerning group decision making is most often attentive to formal groups that have power and resources. Although the studies that have been done to test theories of group decision making were often based on more limited types of groups with few resources, the intention was always for the results to apply to those groups in the outside world that are more fully endowed with importance and possibility. The question that we want you to consider is the extent to which this literature on group decision making actually applies to real life as you know it.

Focus Questions Revisited

What exactly is a "group," and what makes it different from an assembly, a collective, or a team?

A group may be regarded as an organized structure composed of individuals having a common purpose, interdependence, and division of labor. The key elements that make a "group" different from a random collection of people, however, are that group members are aware of one another as such and communicate it through their talk. Groups are different from teams in that teams are more concerned with the strength of the relationships among members and involve mutual respect and concern among members. Team members want to avoid anyone in the group feeling bad about a particular outcome or decision.

Can you define groups only in terms of the kinds of communication that take place between members, or must you look at the relationships that lie behind the communication? Does communication transact the existence and nature of the group?

Group communication is all about everyday talk and relationships, especially the relationships between people who have, hold, and use different sorts of information in the group. Indeed, it is not so much that groups transact communication as that, when communication and relationships are seen as interconnected, the very notion of a group is a transacted and symbolic concept. Through communication, the group members see themselves as belonging to a group, and the group sees itself as an entity with meaning sustained and created by its own symbolic actions. Groups are not structures or composites but dynamic human relationships and processes transacted within and by means of norms and roles.

How do groups form, and what changes in their communication?

The formation of groups has most often been studied in experimental settings, and how they form in normal life has been less clearly understood. Where formation of groups has been studied, it appears that changes in the nature of talk occur, with the first stages being general orientation toward one another and the later stages representing discussion or conflict, which resolves itself in the solution of a task and is followed by mutual congratulation. In longer-term groups, not simply focused on the completion of a particular task in a specific time frame, people will more likely move from formal and superficial talk toward deeper and more meaningful personal talk, much in the way that self-disclosure occurs, though they will also focus their talk on any tasks or objectives the group has in front of it.

What communicative and relational skills make a leader into a good leader?

Leaders need to focus on the task and have knowledge that allows them to direct and guide other people toward its completion. A good leader is also able to handle the socioemotional activity in a group and make people feel they are valued members of a team. A really good leader has a combination of communicative skills that help solve problems and present judgment clearly, listens carefully to understand other people's perspectives, and is able to reflect the value of their contribution to the team. Frequent communication with team members and openness of communication that lets people know what is going on helps sustain members' sense of value to the group. Clarity and purposefulness are also communicative features of a good leader.

In what ways are discussions of team-based organizing and communication different from traditional approaches to small-group communication?
Team-based organization and communication differ from traditional approaches to small-group communication in that they place much more emphasis on the value, personal feelings, mutual respect, and internal cohesiveness of the members of the team. The division of labor, and the interdependence of team members specifically, builds bonding among them that can outlast the tenure of a particular steward of the team. The team, therefore, does not fall apart once the leader is changed, and the emphasis of team-based organization is to sustain the team as a coherent, self-respecting, and mutually respecting unit, irrespective of the specific problems it is dealing with at a particular time and of the leader nominally in charge for the moment.

How can a group promote its own decision-making capacities in more effective ways?
A group can promote its own decision-making capacities by setting a definitive agenda, doing a thorough problem analysis, assessing its goals, and thoroughly assessing alternative possibilities. The group should establish its goals explicitly and realistically, setting goals that are attainable within a specified timeline and have clear criteria by which it can evaluate the outcomes. Promotive communication and counteractive communication are ways to keep groups on task.

Key Concepts

cohesiveness   (p. 213)
common purpose   (p. 207)
counteractive communication   (p. 221)
disruptive communication   (p. 221)
formal power   (p. 216)
group culture   (p. 215)
group norms   (p. 214)

group sanctions   (p. 214)
informal power   (p. 216)
interdependence   (p. 212)
leadership   (p. 216)
primary groups   (p. 211)
promotive communication   (p. 221)
secondary groups   (p. 211)

Questions to Ask Your Friends

■ How does your group of friends decide what to do on Friday night? What processes discussed in this chapter can you see at work there?

■ Who do you and your friends think is a good leader, and what makes a person so?

■ What group norms and rituals can you identify in the small groups and organizations to which you belong?

Media Links

- The following three movies offer good instances of groups in action and cover some of the concepts discussed in this chapter: *Office Space, Apollo 13*, and *12 Angry Men*. Each movie demonstrates something different about groups: The opening sequence of *Office Space*, for example, gives you a good idea of a group culture, and some of the characters represent different leadership styles (analyze Lumbergh's—ugh!—power and leadership style). *12 Angry Men* demonstrates how a task leader can bring emotionally led individuals back on track by promotive communication while also handling the socioemotional concerns of different members. What aspects of leadership and group norms can you identify in the group communication that takes place in *Apollo 13*?

- The next time you are in a group, pay attention to any discussions about media that take place. For instance, someone might bring up a television program viewed the previous evening or a newly discovered Web site. In what ways could such discussions be considered disruptive communication? In what ways could such discussions actually enhance group cohesion and relationships?

- In any reality shows you watch, how do groups form, what are their dynamics and transactions, and what are their weaknesses?

Ethical Issues

- Some say that leaders must use authority to mobilize people to face tough decisions when the followers are struggling with change and personal growth. Others stress that leaders should take care of and nurture their followers. What do you think?

- Should groups and organizations do what is right even if it results in lower dividends to stakeholders to help finance their operations? For example, should oil companies make more real and substantial contributions to environmental protection even if it means that shareholders receive no dividend in a particular year? Should Big Tobacco stop selling cigarettes?

- What conditions would make it wrong, and what conditions would make it right, to blow the whistle on your group irrespective of the consequences to you personally?

Answers to Photo Captions

Photo 8.1 ▪ A group has a common purpose, and members are aware of each other, have organization, and communicate with one another. All the basketball players and the referee are members of a "basketball group." A collective may have a common purpose but lacks organization, so the audience is a collective. Each side in the game is a team as well as a group, since the members (presumably) care for one another's welfare and play together more effectively by creating chances for each other or not trying to do it all on their own.

Photo 8.2 ▪ The ability to identify with the audience shows understanding of their concerns, a sharing of their feelings, and having answers that will work. A good leader focuses people on issues, motivates them to address solutions, and helps achieve their goals. Leadership is not in a person but is transacted between people, as the leader acts as steward of their interests, for the moment.

Photo 8.3a and b ▪ Traditional approaches are structured and formal (Table 8.1). Team-based communication allows members more freedom and creativity. The important thing, however, is the *style of communicating* in the group. People in suits can have informal conversations, whereas people with coffee mugs and baseball caps can have highly structured communications. So, although the differences in the pictures probably led you to assume that they are based on structure, they will in fact be based on the types of communication transacted in each example.

Student Study Site

Visit the study site at **www.sagepub.com/ciel** for e-flashcards, practice quizzes, and other study resources.

References

Abrams, D. B., Hogg, M. A., Hinkle, S., & Otten, S. (2005). The social identity perspective on small groups. In M. S. Poole & A. B. Hollingshead (Eds.), *Theories of small groups: Interdisciplinary perspectives* (pp. 99–137). Thousand Oaks, CA: Sage.

Argyle, M. (1983). *The psychology of interpersonal behaviour* (4th ed.). Harmondsworth, UK: Penguin.

Arrow, H., Bouas Henry, K., Poole, M. S., Wheelan, S., & Moreland, R. (2005). Traces, trajectories and timing: The temporal perspective on groups. In M. S. Poole & A. B. Hollingshead (Eds.), *Theories of small groups: Interdisciplinary perspectives* (pp. 313–367). Thousand Oaks, CA: Sage.

Bales, R. F. (1950). *Interaction process analysis.* Cambridge, MA: Addison-Wesley.

Clampitt, P. G. (2005). *Communicating for managerial effectiveness.* Thousand Oaks, CA: Sage.

Fisher, B. A. (1970). Decision emergence: Phases in group decision making. *Speech Monographs, 37,* 53–66.

Glidewell, J. C., Tucker, S., Todt, M., & Cox, S. (1982). Professional support systems— The teaching profession. In A. Nadler, J. D. Fisher, & B. M. DePaulo (Eds.), *New directions in helping 3: Applied research in help-seeking and reactions to aid* (pp. 163–184). New York: Academic Press.

Goffman, E. (1959). *Behaviour in public places.* Harmondsworth, UK: Penguin.

Gouran, D. S., & Hirokawa, R. Y. (1996). Functional theory and communication in decision-making and problem-solving groups. In R. Y. Hirokawa & M. S. Poole (Eds.), *Communication and group decision making* (2nd ed., pp. 55–80.). Thousand Oaks, CA: Sage.

Harden Fritz, J. M., & Omdahl, B. L. (2006). Reduced job satisfaction, diminished commitment, and workplace cynicism as outcomes of negative work relationships. In J. M. Harden Fritz & B. L. Omdahl (Eds.), *Problematic relationships in the workplace* (pp. 131–151). New York: Peter Lang.

Hepburn, J. R., & Crepin, A. E. (1984). Relationship strategies in a coercive institution: A study of dependence among prison guards. *Journal of Social and Personal Relationships, 1,* 139–158.

Hogg, M. A. (1992). *The social psychology of group cohesiveness: From attraction to social identity.* London: Harvester Wheatsheaf.

Hollander, E. P. (1958). Conformity, status and idiosyncrasy credit. *Psychological Review, 65,* 117–27.

Janis, I. (1972). *Victims of groupthink.* Boston: Houghton Mifflin.

Katz, N., Lazer, D., Arrow, H., & Contractor, N. (2005). The network perspective on small groups: Theory and research. In M. S. Poole & A. B. Hollingshead (Eds.), *Theories of small groups: Interdisciplinary perspectives* (pp. 277–312). Thousand Oaks, CA: Sage.

McLeod, P. L., & Kettner-Polley, R. (2005). Psychodynamic perspectives on small groups. In M. S. Poole & A. B. Hollingshead (Eds.), *Theories of small groups: Interdisciplinary perspectives* (pp. 63–97). Thousand Oaks, CA: Sage.

Mumby, D. K. (2006). Constructing working-class masculinity in the workplace. In J. T. Wood & S. W. Duck (Eds.), *Composing relationships: Communication in everyday life* (pp. 166–174). Belmont, CA: Wadsworth.

Mumford, M. D., Zaccaro, S. J., Harding, F. D., Jacobs, T. O., & Fleishman, E. A. (2000). Leadership skills for a changing world: Solving complex social problems. *Leadership Quarterly, 11*(1), 11–35.

Northouse, P. G. (2007). *Leadership: Theory and practice.* Thousand Oaks, CA: Sage.

Parsons, T., & Bales, R. F. (1955). *Family, socialization and interaction process.* Glencoe, IL: Free Press.

Poole, M. S., & Hollingshead, A. B. (2005). *Theories of small groups: Interdisciplinary perspectives.* Thousand Oaks, CA: Sage.

Thibaut, J. W., & Kelley, H. H. (1959). *The social psychology of groups.* New York: Wiley.

Tuckman, B. W. (1965). Developmental sequence in small groups. *Psychological Bulletin, 63,* 384–399.

Weigel, R. G. (2002). The marathon encounter group—vision and reality: Exhuming the body for a last look. *Consulting Psychology Journal: Practice and Research, 54,* 186–198.

9

Communication in the Workplace

hen we ask students to tell us what their workplace is like, they say things like "My restaurant is very upscale, and I really like the people and the customers I work with"; "I work in a fitness center, and the manager is a control freak"; or "I used to work at a corporate head office before I came back to college, and the people really got on my nerves, which is why I decided to come back to college." They also tell us stories about the way a colleague had advised them not to pay too much attention to one particular company rule because nobody ever really enforced it but that they should always be sure to show up early when one particular shift manager was on duty because she was very strict about timekeeping. They also get plenty of advice from older employees about how to get bigger tips or what to do if a customer complains.

When we ask the broader and more abstract question "What comes to mind when you think about work or the workplace in general?" they envision something different from their own personal experiences and instead talk of leaders and followers/ employees, managers and peons, law offices with strict lines of report, corporate businesses where sales departments and marketing departments are often in conflict, nonprofit organizations with specific rules and cultures, and other arrangements of management. They tend to think, in short, in terms of *structure*.

In the case of corporate organizations, they talk about the corporate head office, managerial hierarchies, vice presidents and middle management, chain of command— the sort of structure that is often represented in organizational flowcharts that you can look up in most computer word processing programs. These are hierarchically organized charts that show who reports to whom. Although most students do not experience their workplace quite that way, they do recognize it as a general way of thinking about the workplace as an organization. Yet in their own experience, they notice how work is a place that makes meaning between people, where a particular culture exists, and where "the way things get done around here" is passed on to new employees not only by instructions from the boss but by individuals telling one another stories about how they dealt with a difficult situation that might arise in the new employee's interactions with customers.

Accordingly, we will start by looking at organizations in this familiar structural way and move on to show a better and more recent approach for understanding organizations. You have already learned from the family chapter to make this move: to see structure (official formal structures) as *transacted* (brought into being) in interpersonal communication (who knew?). In this same way, "the workplace" and "organizations" are transacted in communication through relationships. The goal of this chapter is to teach you how to move from the traditional structural views of organizations toward the communicative approach that is based on the ways and types of communication that make a workplace what it is. Interestingly, this same move is happening in management and business schools where leadership is now seen as a relational skill rather than as the use of structural power to get people to do your will (Northouse, 2009). Democracy and civil mutual respect are also regarded as essential to good workplace ethics nowadays (Northouse).

A moment's thought will make it clear to you that relationships do not exist in an organization between faceless structural units called "Sales" and "Marketing" but rather exist between individuals or members of such groups who know one another and have long-term relationships with one another (Chapter 8). In fact *workplace* is a misleading term in some respects as it directs your attention away from (long- or short-term) personal relationships and toward places and impersonal structures between abstract organizational units. Members of a sales "team" know one another; members of a marketing "team" know one another; people in an organization deal face-to-face in the workplace or through relational technology with other individuals from different organizations in order to do the business that they engage in; their business is *transacted* through communication in the relationships that exist between the people involved.

Surprise! "The workplace" is (and organizations generally are) best viewed as a relational enterprise that involves meaning making, rhetorical visions, and everyday communication. This fact is often disguised by abstract terms like *conflict management* (which, of course, happens between individuals) or *leadership* (of individuals by other individuals) or *decision making* (by individuals interacting face-to-face or through relational technology). Corporate organizations project an identity by having employees in their workplace organization wear identifying uniforms, or they conduct business with customers face-to-face, giving away pens with company logos and often much more substantial company gifts. They often have special jargon for communication in the workplace, while they project themselves to the public by the same means we have already discussed in the identity chapter (Chapter 5) and will tie here specifically to the workplace. These terms, however, also connect to what we have said about concern culture and speech codes. Organizations and workplaces are, in effect, small cultures after all. (Note from your culturally diverse authors: The British English word here for "coworkers" is *workmates,* making them sound friendly and connected rather than simply people who show up at the same place and work together like cogs in a system. One culture assumes that they will bond together; the other assumes that they will have to be *made* to.)

Organizations handle their public image through communication (public relations) and often try, where appropriate, to establish loyalty to their brand by calling their workers not "employees" but "associates" and to present their "valued customers" as loyal allies of their organization (so they don't go and buy someone else's product instead!). Organizations try to present themselves as individual entities, just like individuals themselves do, and try to be your friend. They have public relations offices not only to project a good image to the public but also to prepare corporate rhetorical strategies for dealing with catastrophes and are judged by the way they handle them in public (whether with an apology or with a defensive response) (Ice, 1991).

There is one final point to set you thinking. Hierarchy is a defining characteristic of organizations, and any organization has top people and bottom people, those who command and those who obey, those who make decisions and those who carry them out. It is hardly surprising that if you view an organization as a structure you will find that this leads to a significant managerial bias in much research. The research is geared toward the power structure and established order, where "workers" have no real power. Where organizations seek ways to maximize output and profit they may not care if the result does not involve making the company more enjoyable for the workers. Organizations, which often sponsor such research, believe that the power lies in management and leadership, so they are most interested in improving those aspects of organizational operations. This sort of formal power structure, however, sometimes can be undermined and undercut by the informal relationships between participants. A poor boss may in fact inspire no confidence or respect among subordinates, who undermine authority by disobedience, resistance, or private jokes about the jerk who is supposed to be "Our Dear Leader." The chapter, then, incorporates our general attempt to reconceptualize all traditional phenomena in interpersonal communication texts as about, driven by, and carried out through interpersonal relationships. The topics in the traditional books (like the nature of work, leadership, the culture of the workplace, and relationships between people in organizations) can be reconceptualized as based on the relational perspective we have taken throughout the book so far.

This chapter essentially provides you with an increasingly popular and ultimately more accurate view of organizations and the workplace in general as driven by and carried out through interpersonal relationships.

Focus Questions

- Where do people get their ideas about the workplace?
- What is an organization—a structure or a transacted set of communication activities?
- How are organizations constituted by the interaction and relationships between members?
- What types of personal relationships can exist between individuals and affect organizational effectiveness?

In What Ways Do People Think of the Workplace?

One very influential approach to leadership and organizations proposes that they are sites of meaning making (Weick, 1995). We will look at Weick's specific approach in detail later on, but you will already know that his general idea fits very well with what we are saying in this book. People develop understanding, rhetorical visions, and predispositions or expectations about how to behave and perform in specific frames, and other people help them do it. If this were not a general principle of communication in everyday life, then it would not apply to the workplace, but it does. We get our ideas about work from Society's Secret Agents right out of the crib and are conditioned by TV, movies, and other experiences to accept what "work" is like and how "professionals" look, act, and operate. In what ways do we come to understand the meaning of work and how we should perform our roles within it?

There are many ways in which people tend to think of the workplace, some driven by language as it structures thought (Chapter 2), developed in childhood and reinforced in later life; some derived from practical experience with the norms and organizational culture of the company or business; and some refined by the relational interactions that occur among the specific people who work there. If we invited you to join the Suck/Cess Team at Duck & McMahan's Drain Cleaning Company ("We can even unclog memories"), you would already have expectations about how to dress, how to behave in a professional manner, and how to think about rising to the top (it's not the sort of company where you want to stay at the bottom very long).

Accordingly, these three strands (language and socialization, culture, and the relational practicalities of conducting the business) will provide the structure for this chapter.

Language and Socialization About Work

Because this is a book about communication, it is important to see how communication contributes to your understanding of organizations and also to see how your socialization teaches you to treat the workplace as a special kind of *frame* your thinking. Much of your thinking about organizations is created by the language that you use to describe it (Chapter 2) and also by your learning before you ever enter the workplace. After all, there is something like 15 years of childhood and socialization that can form the basis for your expectations about what "work" is all about before you ever get there.

Metaphors of Organization

One strong influence on both relationships and thinking in general is the use of metaphors (Chapter 2), and there are many different metaphors for organizations. In this chapter, we will focus on metaphors of organizations as machines; organizations as cultures; and organizations as instruments of domination.

Gareth Morgan (2006) specifically points out the importance of the metaphors that structure ways of seeing and thinking about organizations that guide the ways in which managers and members of organizations think particularly about change and development within an organization. A *machine metaphor* represents organizations as standardized by repetition, specialization, or predictability.

Modern management techniques that were previously guided by this metaphor have sought to escape from it and seek to change the workplace to make it more welcoming and inviting. There has been much more emphasis on the fact that workers are also stakeholders in an organization because of their membership within it. Their voices should be listened to so that they do not simply feel like cogs in a machine or anonymous numbers on a list. Their value to the company or the organization is something that must be recognized and valued by management (Sias, 2009). That is why there are now endless (and often detested) "bonding weekends" and "team-building exercises."

As far back as early cinema or even the silent era (Charlie Chaplin in *Modern Times* [1936] or the silent movie *Metropolis* [1927]), movies represent the metaphor of organizations as machines and suggest that the machine has the effect of turning workers into robots, a fear that was very real in society in those days as mechanization of jobs on the assembly line began to occur more frequently (and nowadays those jobs very often are done by robots or computers). In a more recent example, if you have seen *Office Space* you will recall the receptionist who spends the first 5 minutes of the movie routinely and sequentially (and in a chirpy mechanical voice) repeating robotically, "Corporate Accounts Payable . . . Nina speaking . . . Just a moment."

Other metaphors focus on *organizations as cultures* based on shared meaning, and the notion of "sharing" presupposes relationships between people. We will return to this possibility several times during the course of the chapter because it is a metaphor that much more strongly emphasizes the transactions of communication that we wish to stress. However, the concept of *organizational culture* is one that readily springs to mind, and the atmosphere in particular organizations can be very different; "atmosphere" is very apparent to people who work in different organizations and may even come across to the customers themselves. Most organizations try to create an atmosphere of friendliness and the valuing of customers by the use of such phrases as "Your call is very important to us," as you sit there listening for 20 minutes to the music of Vivaldi. Some companies even go so far as to say, for example, "Univision™ doesn't just have viewers. We have relationships. Relationships with millions of people who say they simply cannot live life without us" (Univision, 2008).

For most people, however, organizations are not seen as friends but are more likely to be seen metaphorically as *instruments of domination* that shape and control not only the workers' behavior but even their thoughts and ideologies. This metaphor is extremely commonly used because most people feel that work is not only undesirable but actually oppressive. Most people would rather be out fishing or shopping or bicycling than trundling containers of trash from place A to place B or sitting in boring meetings or driving delivery trucks. It is very clear that in order to become a member of any workplace you are faced with *autonomy-connectedness* (see Chapter 6). You give up lots of your freedom in order to devote most of your time to working for your employer,

Photo 9.1 What is this picture telling us about the nature of work and the glossy expectations of professional success? How is it sending messages of what professionals look like and what they do? (See page 257.)

when you would probably rather be doing something else. However, in the early part of your life you learned that work is unavoidable, unless you happen to be extremely wealthy, and you need to aim for success.

Learning About the Workplace

Vocational anticipatory socialization is the preparation for becoming a worker in the form of socialization that takes place in a child's early life though family interaction and through exposure to the media. You first learned about the nature of work and the workplace through socialization in your families, during your childhood. Cockburn-Wootten and Zorn (2006) note that many families tell stories about the nature of work experiences, some of them funny, some of them poignant, but all conveying to young children something about the nature of work. As children you heard adults talking about the work that they do, and you were able to gain some sense of whether they see it as important or simply something that they reluctantly do in order to feed the family. A child's attitude toward the workplace can be affected by these ordinary comments, whether they are about the nature of particular professions or the nature of the colleagues with whom the adult individual lives life during the long daily period of absence from the family. For children who have not yet experienced the workplace, these kinds of stories, comments, and conversational pieces can be quite formative.

Family stories about work, of course, are often structured to express and emphasize certain values such as the payoffs of hard work or the ways to break the rules and get away with it (Cockburn-Wootten & Zorn, 2006). Each conveys something to the child about the mysteries of the workplace. Such stories may emphasize the swirling together of the leisurely "true" individual self and the necessarily but reluctantly "working self." The workplace may be described by a parent as a source of stress or as a source of income (or both) but as something for which the growing child must prepare and for which a so-called "Protestant Work Ethic" is often induced—the drive to achieve and succeed through hard work (Allen, 2006).

Children also see the workplace depicted and sometimes satirized or mocked on TV and in the media. Programs may indicate that work is an exciting life-or-death environment (*CSI, House, World's Wildest Police Videos,* and *Deadliest Catch*) or some dull and chaotic tedium (*Office Space, The Office,* and *The Drew Carey Show*). A quite characteristic way of representing the workplace is through one of the show's main stars—particularly in detective and hospital shows—who goes out on a limb on a hunch, argues with the boss about the fact that this involves breaking certain rules, and is ultimately vindicated. This, of course, is the underlying plotline of almost every episode of *House*. In such shows, the role of the boss is to enforce the organizational culture of the workplace yet quietly support the individual who is known to be something of a maverick but who is generally right in the end! You are possibly seeing the obvious connection between this representation of work and the notion of shared rhetorical visions that we have previously covered in earlier chapters. Society's Secret Agents do their work in many different ways.

Other stories stress the dangerous nature of, say, a firefighter's job and extend that fact to the identity that encompasses the individual and admirable heroes who perform the work. The ultimate media message of *World's Wildest Police Videos* is that the police always catch criminals, who are frequently described as "punks" and often presented as inept and hopeless losers. In its own way, this program conveys messages about the value of police work to society and the ultimate folly of breaking the law. As well as being engaging and informative about police work, it serves as yet another example of Society's Secret Agents at work, infiltrating and reinforcing society's values into our ordinary life.

Through such socialization, people develop shared cultural understandings of work and its place in society and personal life. There is often, for example, a straightforward identity connection between job and person through the God term (Chapter 2) of one's profession (doctor, nurse—to say nothing of professor!) or the status and social structure associated with other kinds of workers such as dentists, janitors, lawyers, or meatpackers. Identity becomes embedded in these stories in important ways by showing us that people derive much of their sense of identity from their job or that much of their social identity is established by the workplace to which they belong and the function they perform there (see Chapter 5). So also do relationships and a sense of the role of "the boss" as compared to that of "the workers" become instilled in the child's mind. Bosses tell you what to do, and you are supposed to do it. Your goals as an individual may be placed alongside those of the organization itself, and your success or failure may be judged according to your success in "climbing the ladder" and other social goals implanted in young minds. You are taught that it is better to be a boss than a peon and you should aim to progress through promotion or else you will be seen to have failed.

Such vocational anticipatory socialization instills dominant beliefs like TGIF (thank goodness it's Friday) or "a case of the Mondays" that reinforce the idea that for many people work is simply a necessary evil between weekends. In this way people may draw the conclusion that there is a difference between "work" and "relationships" and certainly a tension between "work" and "family" (Totten, 2006). Work happens when you are constrained by the organization; "relationships" happen in the evening or on weekends when you are relaxing. On the other hand, you are presented with many glossy images of the positive side of work—and particularly of success at work. In both cases,

> When Steve's father brought his boss home to dinner when Steve was 7 and his younger brother was 5, it was presented as a very significant event where they had to dress up smartly and be on their absolute best behavior. Although they did not realize what was at stake about the importance of behaving well in the presence of a boss, as a matter of fact they soon realized—even at their young ages—why their father hated his work so much.

shared rhetorical visions and the influence of societal rhetorical visions about work are consistent with our general "take" on the world in this book.

Going to Work: The Workplace as a Special Frame

There are important differences between the workplace and the kind of normal everyday life experiences that we have with friends and associates—at least on the surface—and it is these differences upon which much research has focused (Sias, 2009). Indeed, a workplace is different from everyday life in many important respects, and this is largely the result of how the workplace is framed through learning, language, and life. Furthermore, these are developed in large part through the communicative efforts of managers or leaders within an organization (Fairhurst & Sarr, 1996). In the terms used in Chapter 2 (to describe presentation versus representation), this means that a leader or a manager or an organization or a workplace itself presents (rather than represents) certain options of meaning and interpretation as acceptable over and above others. This is an important principle in understanding the way in which workplace practices frame, operate, and allow us to extend to the workplace in new terms our perspective concerning talk and relationships. Of course, although the workplace has special practices and codes, it is also important to recognize that these overlie the normal and usual practices and codes of everyday life.

In what follows, we will extend to the workplace what you have learned about relational narratives and sense making in other chapters. In doing so, we will first explore the direct continuation of aspects of interpersonal communication into the new frame of the workplace. Second, we will apply some of our analysis of transaction of communication to the workplace itself. We will begin by looking at what people import into the workplace, and then we will examine the workplace as a place in itself and look at the talk there, asking what workplace talk does to sustain and transact the organization. This is another way of asking how people "perform" and also transact the workplace. We will then apply the transactional nature of communication to the workplace itself, examining how workplace talk sustains and transacts organizations.

Developing Work Identities

When you are at work, you are of course in a different *frame,* but in that particular work frame you perform identities connected to work, leaving aside those transacted in your existing network of relationships, your personal goals, and the personal moral context by which to judge your performance. Everyday life patterns and practices are extended into the new context and frame the workplace. However, these can be constrained or even altered by the workplace frame.

Going to Work: What Is Different, and What Is the Same?

Continuation of identity imports your normal practices of everyday talk into the workplace. Since everyday talk is usually recreational or relational, the *instrumental purpose* of the workplace affects the nature of talk at work and so can reshape the way in which talk operates to transact your identity (Mokros, 2006). For example, the workplace constrains the kinds of identity you can perform (Chapter 5) and requires that you adopt a professional working identity. A striking example is in the armed forces when the first part of boot camp training is to break down an individual's sense of personal identity and to replace it with a highly trained, disciplined, unquestioningly obedient uniformity as one of a team of people who carry out automatically whatever orders may be given (almost as if they were in college!).

In less extreme cases, you share the rhetorical vision that you will be expected to dress in a particular way (a suit, a uniform, overalls, a logo shirt) and will be introduced to the organization in a less dramatic fashion. For example, organizations usually require you to dress differently from the way you dress at leisure. The nonverbal communication (Chapter 3) that takes place through these styles of dress carries messages of connection to the organization and requires you to perform roles not done elsewhere. Dress may also indicate your position in the organization, whether you wear a certain kind of military insignia on your sleeve or whether you have a peaked cap and epaulets (pilot) or an apron (flight attendant). The organizational relationship between one person and another is conveyed by nonverbal cues. Management is referred to as white-collar workers while laborers are described as blue-collar workers—don't forget. The symbolic distinctions of workplace dress are well built into our language and our ways of understanding hierarchy in relationships (Chapter 6).

You will also be expected to adopt a new "working identity" and adapt to that culture. This may involve learning new *speech codes,* jargon, and idioms that are appropriate to a particular workplace (remember the server in Chapter 1) and adapting your speech to represent your **professional face**. In many professional settings, you will be required to learn the jargon that is appropriate to the job and will be expected to adopt high code (Chapter 2) when interacting with customers, clients, or other people involved in the same organization. You may be able to express your own personality in particular ways that fit with this professional face; servers, for example, can often project their personal style into the role of server in a way that maximizes their tips. However, in a wholesale produce market, the interpersonal performance of relational preferences (liking, disliking) can affect whether a given merchant gets a good or bad deal on the produce that he or she wishes to purchase (Mokros, 2006), and this, of course, is based on interpersonal relationships.

Performance of Work Identities

On top of whatever you take into the workplace, the organization attempts to overlay special and different formats of identity constructed in the workplace and for the conduct of workers' relationships not only with one another but with customers and clients. Although Chapter 5 focused on the personal identities that we perform, the workplace requires conflicting sets of performances. The workplace has some influence on the way talk molds identity at work, partly through power dynamics that are built into the workplace, making some people officially powerful and some less powerful, at least in terms of formal

In the movie *Waiting . . .* , the boss is presented as an idiotic and ineffective jerk whom the workers despise along with the diners. The cooks and servers play tricks on diners by spoiling the food of people who complain. They also play an obscene game in the kitchen in order to distract themselves from the boredom of the job. Two memorable (bottom) lines from the movie are "Never [mess] with the people that serve you food!" and "What happens in the kitchen ends up on the plate."

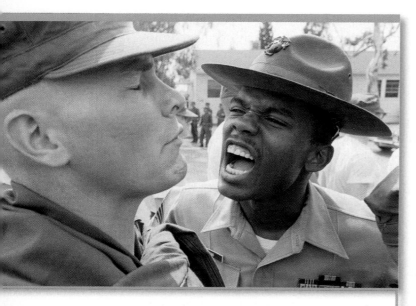

Photo 9.2 Is this sergeant "only doing his job"? What is happening to the recruit and his sense of identity? (See page 258.)

power. For example, the server in Chapter 1 has less power than the diners in that she is expected to carry out their instructions. Relationally, however, she has informal power and can at any time decide to delay the serving of their order or place other people ahead of them in her list of service. We pointed out also that she has to adopt a stylized form of greeting required by her role and that she is identified as a server by the clothing that her organization requires her to wear in order to indicate that she is someone on duty to perform roles for the customer (asking questions related to food, taking orders, delivering food). Her working identity requires her to be polite but not overly chatty and to focus rapidly on the task of taking diners' orders and, ultimately, their money.

In the workplace, interactions are also subject to language performances that facilitate the completion of the organization's tasks. Talk tends to be formal and structured and to focus on the professional deportment of the person involved. Police officers say, "10-4," not "Yep" or "Got it." Airline pilots address the control tower in special codes that are meaningless outside the organizational frame in which they work. When an alarmed pilot shouts, "No gear, no gear!" to the control tower when lined up to take off and observing another plane coming in to land with its landing wheels not properly down, he prevents a catastrophe (e.g., National Transportation Safety Board, 1993). Outside of that special context his shout would mean nothing. In short, there often is jargon and special language to be learned for the workplace (see Table 9.1). The point is that special language gives you special positioning and expert involvement in the workplace and identifies you as a special person within an organizational frame and also as an expert who knows special terms that outsiders do not.

From your performances in the workplace you also learn that it is inappropriate to play around in ways that are entirely appropriate in friendships. When one is in the front region of performance in the workplace it is inappropriate to behave sloppily or unprofessionally. On the other hand, in the back region, where there is more of a relaxed atmosphere, playfulness may be encouraged as a way of building a sense of community and team membership (Mokros, 2006). You learn to distinguish very clearly between the front and back regions here also.

Negotiating Relational and Work Goals

One clear difference between work and everyday life is that **instrumental goals** are predominant at work whereas **relational goals** are predominant outside work. This can

Table 9.1 Examples of Workplace Jargon and Special Language

Profession	Jargon	Translation
Police officer	1. "10-4" 2. "MO"	1. "Yes," "got it" 2. "Modus Operandi"—a criminal's typical pattern of behaviors when conducting a crime
Airline pilot	1. "No gear!" 2. "Roger"	1. "A plane's landing gear has not descended." 2. "I understand."
University teacher	1. "TA" 2. "Midterm"	1. "Teaching Assistant" 2. A method of assessing student progress
Marital therapist	1. "Borderline" 2. "Intake"	1. A client with a particular personality disorder 2. A special form for admitting a new client to the practice

involve direct delegation of duties. It can also involve a direct assessment of performance in ways that are not expected in everyday conversation with friends. Typical *relational goals* involve intimacy and support, and by contrast goals at work are more focused on instrumental activity and the achievement of organizational objectives. Since everyday talk is usually recreational, the instrumental purposes required at work will affect the nature of talk and reshape the way in which talk operates. You are focused on issues of task management.

Another clear difference at work is that the talk tends to construct distance and **formality/hierarchy** in certain parts of the organization (e.g., between management and workers). Thus, work represents a strain or restraint on relationships as an individual is forced to adopt a professional face rather than a personal identity (Chapter 5) when dealing with people at work. For example, it is essential in a working environment that the tasks of the workplace are performed adequately and efficiently. This may involve the clear explanation of a particular task to subordinates and the delegation of specific activities to those who must carry them out. By contrast, in your friendships, the delegation of tasks and the spelling out of particular activities that must be performed are relatively small parts of your conversational life ("Hey, Joy, don't forget to order the pepperoni toppings!").

Although there are instrumental goals in our everyday relationships such as asking someone out on a date, the *essential function of talk* (Chapter 6) is much more to the front and center of your conversations outside of the workplace. The conflict between essential goals in relationships and predominantly instrumental ones in the workplace may be difficult for people to manage, and this may strain their performance of their usual identity, as there is a conflict between the role of worker and the role of friend.

Outside of the workplace, people may have the purpose of developing their relationships and may make use of self-disclosure in a way that develops intimacy (Chapter 6). However, at work, the development of long-term intimacy is not one of the purposes of conversation. A salesperson working in a large department store simply needs to present and project a friendly face rather than one that leads to the development of intimacy with customers. Relationships at work don't develop in intimacy, and at work they are often specifically prohibited from doing so (even *consensual* sex can lead to dismissal).

The Workplace as a Culture

Socialization into the workplace is done most often through special, if occasionally very brief, training that involves at least being shown the ropes by another employee. Although the organization expects that this will involve watching corporate videos, attending management team training sessions, going to retreats, and doing bonding exercises, individuals may form relationships with others in the organization that undercut these things. Such socialization also involves the instillation of the organizational culture into its newest members. Organizational culture is a popular notion, but it is a difficult one to pin down. It is important to recognize the fundamental truth that *people* are part of, not detached from, systems that influence them. People carry around their history in any organization or group—as a structure; as agreed memory; as meaning; as narrative; as persuasive practices, then. Their relationships to one another are key to the understanding of the workplace.

Organizational Culture and Routines

Bastien, McPhee, and Bolton (1995) reported a longitudinal case study of an administrative unit of a large nonfederal government organization following the election of a new chief executive officer (CEO). They were interested in the ways that attempts to change the climate become the dominant characteristic of the emerging situation as a new CEO begins to impose a character on the organization. For example, if a new CEO wants people to treat one another differently, it is not as easy as just making a decree about it. People have long-standing relationships with each other that the new ordinance may undermine.

In most cases, of course, such changes are minor or illusory, and much that has gone on before continues to go on the way it always has—partly because the workplace consists of existing relationships between people who have had long-term histories of interactions with each other in particular roles. These patterns of interaction emphasize that people are neither purely free co-constructors of social reality nor simple pawns moved around by abstract social structural forces. In fact, their existing

To prevent the bonds that develop between people who work together continually, including trust and the relaxation of attention to the rules, communist East Germany used to change the pairings of its patrolling border guards every day so that no one ever worked with the same person twice or long enough to build up mutual trust. That way, the guards were more willing to follow the "shoot to kill" rules more dutifully, even if it involved shooting a fellow guard who was trying to escape to the West.

interpersonal relationships with each other produce and reproduce social systems and their structures through social interaction and long-term relations, much as Society's Secret Agents reinforce our views about what is acceptable behavior in public.

Structuration Theory

Giddens's (1991) **Structuration Theory** points to the regularities of human relationships that act as rules and resources drawn on to enable or constrain social interaction. Examples are norms or habitual expectations of how to communicate and relate to one another. You can certainly reinterpret structures as essentially relational expectations that transact and create "the workplace" and its structures of organization, leadership, and performance—a complex way of saying what we just said! The relationships and expectations become a context for future interaction. Giddens smartly changes the notion of *structure* in organizations from static or objective hierarchies into something *structured by the transactions* themselves and the communication between people in everyday life relationships within the organization.

In essence the distinction between structure (rules, policies, and resources) and systems (patterns of relations) amounts to a *duality of structure*—two different ways of creating the same eventual actual outcome. Also vital to this theory are *organizational production and reproduction* over time (including specific organizational practices as communicative behavior and material reality). It is no surprise that organizations produce and reproduce themselves over time through conversations between the individuals within the organization. For example, people refer to previous experiences or decisions that have been made; people remember the way things used to be done; and as each new person enters and older people leave, passed down from one workplace generation to the other is a system of beliefs and practices about how the organization works.

In the workplace, then, there are certain things that get *done* in the relational talk more noticeably than in other places, and these create the kinds of repetition of structure that Giddens (1991) emphasizes. They all take their force from the way they are repeatedly enacted in talk and relationships, however, and not from the formal structures that exist as abstract forms. For example, if your instructor tells you to answer a question and you do so, then you have transacted the power of your instructor over you. There is no *abstract structure* that forces you to answer. Instead you do so because you understand the norms and customs of the organization and you transact that in your behavior, based on knowledge of proper relationships with the instructor.

This means that organizational climate is not a property of organizations but an interpersonally and relationally *transacted* product of communication based on the relationships between people and what they talk about and how they do so. By constantly referring to a particular theme (customer satisfaction, for example), workers in the workplace make it a theme of the organization's culture. It therefore experiences **sedimentation,** or is laid down into the organization by the workers' talk and everyday relational practices: The repetitive structuration of talk/repetitive patterns of communication and relationships gradually drop to the bottom like sediment in a river and so affect the future course that the river takes, as it were. In other words, the "structures" that matter in an organization are not physical buildings or the formal hierarchical organization "reports to" charts but derive from the sedimented ways in which the people have repeatedly reinforced their relational and conversational interactions. It is these repetitive conversational patterns and topics that create any sedimented structures

In any organization to which you belong, listen for the number of times somebody says "That's the way we do things around here" or makes an equivalent claim. In what way do such statements establish and continue the norms of an organization and invalidate anybody raising questions or new ways of doing things? How do you hear people counteracting such a claim, and what is the outcome?

that an organization has in its practices of work. This suggestion is referred to as a "**structurational approach**" and serves to create those structures that we see as organizations. It is very much like saying that a village is not simply the buildings but the people and the interactions that they have with one another: It is more of a community than a set of houses.

Structurational approaches therefore offer basically a social constructivist and critical approach looking at how people enact and enable or contain future interactions through their talk. Surprise! "Structure" is all about communication and *relationships!* Workplace culture, workplace groups, and workplace communities consist of thinking, relating, reflective people who monitor their own behavior and tend to repeat it rather than reinvent a new style each day (who has time?). It is easier to take the path of least resistance—the way we have always done things around here, the way you and I interacted yesterday, or the way our relationship was before today (take another look at relational continuity constructional units, Chapter 6). Thus a daily routine relational interaction in the workplace ultimately becomes the basis for future interaction. The format into which new recruits are introduced and the patterns of existing relationships into which they must fit become key—perhaps individuals may get minor things to change a little bit, but ultimately the organization continues through its existing patterns of talk and relationships between the individuals who exist and live their lives within it. Thus the appearance of "structure" in an organization really depends entirely on the existing relationships and familiar patterns of communication that repeat themselves in everyday life, even in the workplace.

Meaning Making

We mentioned earlier Weick's (1995) notion that meaning making lies behind the activities of organizations and people at work. He interprets such "organizing" of expectations as a result of the human search for meaning in the attempts to make sense of a stream of events by using recipes, guides, norms, or selective attention to events as a means of reducing equivocality or uncertainty. He does not emphasize the preexisting relationships between people and their rhetorical visions as we do, however.

Most often the means by which people do this organizing of experience is through interpersonal communication about what is going on or through framing the situation in particular ways that allow good contexts for expectations to be discussed (Fairhurst & Sarr, 1996). Fairhurst (2007) extends this notion to the idea that norms and other meaning systems are transacted in the discourse between people in an organization—again, though not stated directly by Fairhurst, this is a relational point. In other words, it is talk between people who have existing relationships with one another that creates and reinforces frames and norms rather than vice versa. To this we would add that the continuity of relationships between people over time tends to reinforce both talk and norms. Since discourse presumes that at least a basic relationship exists between the speakers—otherwise it could not occur—it is relationships that lie at the base of all organizational "structures."

The workplace can be placed in a frame of *moral ordering* and a social ordering or an *interaction order;* that is, the workplace is understood within a particular sequence and structure for behavior that is particular to the place where it is done (scene: act ratio) so that judgments can be made about people's performance. The performance of a work identity is discussed relative to the norms of the workplace and also relative to relational needs where the two conflict.

The Organization and Its Norms

Your school probably has a document called something like "The Code of Student Life," and this describes behaviors that the school expects you to carry out and those it expects you to avoid. For example, it will talk about civility in the classroom and the punishment that you can expect for plagiarizing or copying other people's work. Just as in groups (Chapter 8), organizations develop *norms* that establish and clarify the expectations that will apply while you are a member of the organization. Norms are parts of structures as traditionally perceived, and so are rules and resources. A norm is an unstated rule that is understood to be represented in a pattern of behavior, whereas rules and resources are more formally available. These appear to represent formal power or at least resources to which someone can refer in order to exert power. "It says here in paragraph 9 subsection 2a that you must not [do what you did], so you're fired." The real question is how this works relationally and the extent to which such organizational norms are actually about relationships, as we have constantly reiterated throughout the book.

Frames and Hierarchies: Formal Versus Informal Power

One evident norm or rule in an organization is expectation of hierarchy—indeed hierarchy is a defining characteristic of organizations. Organizations offer guidelines but also constrain the activities of individual workers by insisting that messages work through the chain of command, for example. Employees often compensate for weaknesses in the chain of command by forming informal communication networks and resistance ("Let's work more slowly for Duck & McMahan Drain Cleaning Company until they fire the terrible supervisor. That'll clog 'em up!"). However, as we have noted, these actually come down to relational activities.

So before you get carried away with the mistaken notion that we are talking about structures in a traditional sense, let's take another look at how norms and rules actually work in an organization through relationships and talk. We already wrote in Chapter 8 about the differences between formal and informal power. In any organization there are people designated as the powerful and the powerless, but even norms and documents can be challenged or amended when they create relational tensions. In fact, positions can be reversed when the powerless activate the key buttons in the whole enterprise: acceptance and deference. If the powerless refuse their deference to those who are placed in authority over them, then those people have no authority over them. Slaves can revolt like Spartacus (and threaten the society as a whole) or workers can strike, and the basic operation of the business itself is placed at risk.

Workers may refuse to obey or may choose to resist management and its instructions (Mumby, 2006). Resistance may be done in talk or behavior that shows a worker's lack of respect for the management (for example, Mumby reports one of the workers in his organization made a point of reading the newspaper when he was supposed to be working and of talking negatively about the management and its inability to stop him from doing so). Other forms of resistance to management may be captured in talk that shows reluctance to do the work or actual withdrawal of effort that involves individuals taking longer to do the job than they know they actually need. Those who read newspapers when they should be working or who talk disrespectfully about management are projecting personal identities as resistant and uninvolved relative to the norms that are expected in the workplace. In their own way, through their everyday communication practices, they are doing their own tiny but personal "identity thing" to resist an organizational culture.

Stereotyping can also be used to resist membership or inclusion of particular individuals in the organization, and its stereotyping can be reflected in talk. Mumby (2006) reports on a job he took as a student in an organization that involved large amounts of manual labor. His inclusion in the organization was initially resisted by the permanent employees who resented college students being allowed to take temporary positions in a job where they were experts and permanently employed. As part of their working banter, they performed "working-class masculinity," which involves demonstration of physical strength but also knowledge about technical machinery, which would be lacking in someone with a college education who had only "book learning" at his or her disposal, not practical skills (Mumby).

They continually referred to his inability to operate machinery that they easily and effectively used day-to-day and were particularly overjoyed when he drove a large tractor into a ditch and had to be pulled out by others who were more used to operating the machine. From that point on, they referred to him as "College Boy," which is a tactic for excluding him from membership with the other manual laborers in the group, who did not go to college. Ultimately, however, they began to accept him because he passed or avoided other tricks and traps that they set for him, so he earned their ultimate respect and was eventually included in their relationships (Mumby, 2006).

Industrial Time

One feature of the workplace, which is characteristic of that set of circumstances and different from others, is that people there, as in any other culture, have a specific approach to time—in this case "industrial time." Before clocks were accurate, the predominance of agricultural work led to a vague approach to time based on the seasons, crop cycles, and the availability of daylight, so there was very little need for punctuality as we understand it today (see Chapter 11 on polychronic and monochronic societies). Once clocks had been introduced and industry had turned to a more repetitive performance of specific kinds of work using machines, it became important for employers to count the number of minutes when a worker was actually doing work for which he or she was paid by the minute or the hour. This introduced the notion of **industrial time**, which is the time a person is actually counted as being at work and therefore is paid for doing such work. In the same way that individuals are able to show resistance to other work ethics, they resist the management's control over their time at work and become clock-watchers, downing tools at exactly 5:00 P.M. when their shift ends. This is a form of resistance that is obviously based on relationships of solidarity/connection with other workers as opposed to management. The workers also talk about time and the amount of time that it should take to do a job. Workers often set about covering for one another during absences or periods of lateness—for example, "clocking in" to work for someone who has not arrived on time and will otherwise be penalized by the managers if they find out. These kinds of interpersonal favors for one another make the workplace operate through a relational base that brings workers together in a sense of community that resists management that otherwise would have perfect control over workers' personal time.

Contact With the Public: Customer-Client Relationships

First, it is necessary to distinguish between customer *relations* (customer service) and customer relation*ships,* which are defined by the boundary between the workplace and its external environment. In the first case, the customer is part of the work environment for the time when the customer is receiving service. In the second case, an attempt is made to establish a relationship that outlasts the temporary connection between customer and server. In the 1980s it was realized that it is far more expensive for an organization to acquire new customers than it is to retain old ones. At that point, Berry (1983) coined the term *relationship marketing* and emphasized the value to organizations of building constructive and long-term relationships with their clients.

A number of techniques have been used to retain customer loyalty even to the extent of an organization claiming to be friends with its customers as noted above in the case of Univision™. However, the differences between friendship in the real world and the kinds of friendship an organization attempts to establish with its customers are many and important. For example, self-disclosure is an important element of friendship development in the real world as we saw in Chapter 5. However, no organization is going to disclose its business plans to its customers even though it might want to obtain as much of your personal information as it can extract from you without seeming intrusive. So you can bet your bottom dollar that the self-disclosure between a large organization and yourself will never be equalized or reciprocal: In fact, your bottom dollar is what the organization wants.

Equally important are such elements as trust and commitment in everyday relationships. It can take a very long time for two individuals to build up a sense of mutual trust, and it is difficult for organizations to shortcut this process. However, the concept of relationship marketing is an interesting confirmation of the breadth that can be developed from the perspective we are taking in this book (Carl, 2006). Organizations attempt to reproduce friendships in their customers even though this rarely works in the same ways as relationships between individuals in real life (Chapter 6).

Susan Fournier (1998) demonstrated that many people define themselves in terms of brands to which they feel particularly loyal and even see themselves in terms of such products as shampoo or motorcycles (Harley rider) as defining characteristics of their identity. She showed the validity of the relationship premise of the level of consumers' lived experiences with their brands. Consumers simply see themselves in terms of the products that they consume and often feel loyal to the brands that "make them who they are."

Photo 9.3 What seems to be going on in this photograph, and what would you say is the problem with what is happening? (See page 258.)

The Workplace as Relationships

People have traditionally confused "organization" with physical and hierarchical structure rather than considering it as something, like families and groups, that is *transacted* in discourse. Yet relationships are the true driving force of any organization. Relationships and relating are built into any existing organizations that have long-term histories, memories of working together in the past, and/or recollections of how things were done last time that a similar problem arose. Indeed the cyclical rhythms of the workplace exist only in memories and talk about memories. All of these factors are overlooked in traditional ways of seeing organizations as physical or bureaucratic structures, which are as natural as ways to think of organizations as they are traditional.

As Sias (2009, p. 1) notes, "The daily activities in a typical organization . . . occur in the context of interpersonal relationships" (see Table 9.2). The relationships at work are usually *involuntary,* and people do not usually choose their coworkers: They are just there when you are hired. If you're lucky, you'll find them friendly and welcoming, and you may even become friends—or more—with them.

The converse of that, however, is often a problem in organizations: You cannot always get away from your coworkers even if you don't like them. However, the same point is true in both cases: Problems and successes in the workplace both have a relational basis. This is usually celebrated in organizational communication literature as a relatively novel approach these days and also as obvious. "Good working relationships" like "good communication" generally are accepted as the panacea for organizational ills and as the basis for all organizational successes. Managers are encouraged to become friendly with their workers, up to a point, and certainly to nurture and mentor them rather than just order them about. The problem is that it is all too easy to regard such terms as *leader, manager, worker,* and others that operate in organizations in the workplace as generalized abstractions rather than as *real face-to-face interaction between real people.*

We have said that relationship processes are the basis for the workplace, but we have not talked about friendship and romance in the workplace—or even strong hatreds. What happens when relationships at work get personal? The workplace contains many different kinds of relationships, some of which are good and some of which are bad. Some people get along well; some do not. Some relationships get very close, and that can create suspicions and political issues for the other workers in the same place. Likewise, if you are friends with someone who then gets promoted, what happens to the relationships?

Table 9.2 Some Daily Activities of Organizations That Occur in the Context of Interpersonal Relationships

1.	directing
2.	collaborating
3.	information gathering
4.	information sharing
5.	rewarding
6.	punishing
7.	conflict
8.	resolution of conflict
9.	controlling
10.	feedback
11.	persuasion
12.	interviewing
13.	reporting
14.	gossiping
15.	debating
16.	supporting
17.	selling
18.	buying
19.	ordering
20.	managing
21.	leading
22.	following

Source: Sias, 2009, p. 1.

Relationships as Workplace Challenges

Parts of an organization do not always act in concert and occasionally attempt to undermine one another. Sales teams sometimes promise the impossible in order to make a sale, and the technicians who have to actually make the product as specified simply cannot live up to the promise. A product may look good to the designers, but the bean counters in accounting are not able to find the dollars to make it happen.

Of course, every introductory textbook with a chapter on organizational communication deals with these issues and with the conflict that is based on differences in the

Make Your Case

Do you think that people in an organization should not be allowed to have consensual relationships with one another, or is it an unfair restriction on their freedom if an organization bans such relationships? What sorts of circumstances might alter your judgment? Make an argument that supports your opinion.

internal communication between managers and workers in the workplace. These issues should not be ignored, but we are more interested in the problems of communication that arise from the relationships between people there rather than the managerially biased issues of how "an organization" (seen as a structure) communicates down its "structural" chains of command and lines of management. There are other books where you can read about that if it interests you. Here we will give it all a very quick summary before moving on to what we think really matters: relationships between the people in the workplace.

Common Causes of Problems in Internal Communications

The standard problems within organizations are assumed to result from managers' failure to "communicate" properly with their workers. For example, it tends to be an assumption by the manager that "if I know it, then everyone must know it," and this leads to a series of difficulties for the workers who simply do not know what the manager or leader knows and yet require it in order to operate effectively. It is therefore incumbent on managers to make their staff openly aware of what they know and everything relevant to the workers' performance. The problem is that people say such things without defining what "communication" means. You now know that communication as action can be entirely ineffective, like posting company policies on a notice board and hoping people read them. Communication must be at least interactive, where the two sides interact and do active and critical listening (Chapter 4). Best, however, is if it is communication as transaction, such that the interaction builds trust, confidence, a sense of membership and belonging, and mutual interest.

Another common belief is that everybody hates bureaucracy and that leaders should not burden themselves or their workers with bureaucratic written policies and procedures. However, such a refusal to clarify policies and procedures can lead to confusion. When something is written down, at least everyone can refer to the same document in order to resolve confusion. This is compounded when managers fail to understand the importance of communication or else assume that it just happens. It is very important that managers ensure that communication has actually taken place with those people who need to know the information and the policies are enforced.

As you learned in Chapter 4, active listening is an extremely important part of communication in everyday life, and it is a significant contributor to good working relationships. Many managers believe that it is their job to tell employees what to do and that employees have no place in directing the enterprise. However, many employees have important things to say, and a good manager will be willing to listen in the ways that we indicated in Chapter 4. Managers need to listen to their workers, and personnel need to listen to one another before it is too late and the communication problems result in a catastrophe. Personal communication between managers and employees or among employees can use an existing relational base between the people in order to separate from a collection of data that information which is important and that which is not.

Proper—that is, interactive and transactive—communication in an organization is made more effective when group members question one another and ask pertinent questions in order to avoid groupthink (see Chapter 8). It is important for good managers and effective workers to respect and value what they hear other people saying and to clarify that they have correctly interpreted it. Each person in an organization needs to take responsibility for speaking up when he or she doesn't understand a communication and for making suggestions about ways to improve the communication that is taking place in his or her organization.

Legitimate and Illegitimate Organizational Interference in Life

In everyday relationships you recognize limits on the questions that you can ask people without breaking relational rules. In the workplace, however, these rules may be different. The workplace occupies a legitimate place in people's lives but sometimes spills over into the parts of life that used to be private, nonwork areas, at least while you are at work. The frequent use of the Internet, cell phones, and various technologies that blur the difference between workspace and home space, for example, means that we are often unable to draw sharp distinctions between whether someone is at work or whether someone is at home. This can lead to some negative consequences for the home life, whereas the developments of technology can lead to some interesting relational consequences for the workplace itself. Workers are often expected to be available by e-mail 24/7, and they accept calls on their BlackBerrys even during weekends. In essence, these come down to the question of your rights to keep the workplace out of your home and your rights over your privacy at work. What, then, are your relational rights in connection with other people in the workplace, and what legitimate limits are there that you can expect to be honored?

Spillover From Work Into Daily Life

Like a family or a friendship, no organization exists alone in the social world; instead one has multiple points of contact with other organizations and people and their lives. One obvious problem is that people may bring home their work problems and be preoccupied during family time. A corresponding problem that goes the other way is that a personal problem at home can have a negative impact on someone's performance at work (Crouter & Helms-Erickson, 2000). If my partner is sick, then I will be anxious to check frequently that things are not getting worse, or I may not be able to concentrate on the project. These are known as "spillover effects," and although apparently they occur in unrelated spheres of life, they demonstrate that the different relational worlds in which a person moves cannot be so easily separated.

Totten (2006) noted that there is also a difficulty in negotiating the familial and professional roles. Role negotiation occurs when a person has two competing roles to enact at once, such as representing oneself as both a responsible employee and a caring parent if a child is sick at home. There are many occasions when an individual is faced with a choice between doing the work of the workplace and doing the work of parenting. The spillover of one kind of caring may spoil one's attention to the other. A sick kid can mean you have to cancel clients, take a day off work, or eat into your holiday or sick time, let alone seeing the key project you were working on fall slowly past its deadline. Although one has a clear duty to attend to the needs of one's family and particularly young children, it is also clear that an organization has certain rights to expect an employee to perform roles that are required as part of the job he or she is paid to do.

Surveillance in an Organization

Organizations have a legitimate right to expect not to be the victim of theft by their employees and vice versa. By the same token, they may have a right that you do not use your personal computer in the office for playing Internet war games during office hours, a point of view shared by some fellow workers who otherwise feel cheated by their coworkers (Zweig & Webster, 2002). Misuse of employer resources, whether physical resources or time that is being paid for, is a serious problem, and the issue comes down to a relational one because the employer's response amounts to an invasion of personal privacy and a breach of relational trust. Zweig (2005) explored surveillance and electronic performance monitoring and noted that these cross the basic psychological spaces and boundaries between the employer and the employee—and hence create a different type of relationship between them.

Most workers accept that it is legitimate for an organization to keep an eye on what its workers do and carry out other practices that are related to the efficient completion of work. For example, it is reasonable for employers to expect that someone who is contracted to work for a certain number of hours per day at a particular place should actually do so, that he or she should not call his or her family and have extended chats instead of working (perhaps except in the case of family emergencies), and definitely that he or she should not bring in a camp bed and take a deep sleep during work time. All of these things would be seen as unreasonable by coworkers.

Zweig (2005) showed that some forms of "intrusion" are regarded as acceptable, even if not desirable, within the parameters of the employer-employee relationship. Some supervision is seen as a violation of personal liberty—for example, the opening of employees' mail or unreasonable searching of bags and clothing. On the other hand, it is regarded as an acceptable part of the duties of the job that one may be timed and observed or told what to do or moved from one task to another at the will of the manager. Would you accept the same rules if your friends proposed them?

Why would you resent secret company surveillance? If your boss is looking over your shoulder and catches you writing personal e-mails during company time, you would probably accept it as your fault. On the other hand, if the organization routinely monitors your e-mail—which it probably does—you might feel that your privacy is being invaded. Why might this be so? Reflect on nonverbal communication in Chapter 3 and consider whether there are any parallels in the situations of nonverbal violation and electronic violation.

Just as in other relationships, people regard themselves as having charge of certain kinds of private information in the workplace—that is, information over which they have ownership and control (Petronio, 2002). There is a certain boundary within which people will tolerate intrusions by an employer as long as this is done with one's express or implicit permission. When permission has not been given, a psychological and relational barrier gets crossed, and this changes the nature of the relationship between employer and worker. Reconsider Chapter 6 and what was acceptable as self-disclosure and what was not. Does this apply equally to relationships at work? What questions about your private life is it legitimate for your boss or coworkers to ask?

Although such issues are realistic in organizations that take a traditional and managerially focused approach to the workplace, the issues that concern the majority of workers in the workplace are based on interpersonal matters: communication in everyday life and relationships.

The Downside of Good Relationships at Work

So far we have focused on the importance of relationships, essentially distinguishing members from nonmembers (by jargon or clothing, for example), the differences in number of participants and interactions in any given organization and knowledge of membership that individuals in an organization have, and the different sorts of membership that are possible in an organization. Now we will turn to the interpersonal issues in the workplace, and we will of course emphasize communication and relationships.

We noted earlier in the chapter that there is a distinction between relational goals and the instrumental work goals of the workplace. This raises a number of questions for you to think about concerning cases where work spills over into relational life or where relational life spills over into work. In the previous section, we looked at work spilling over into your private life, and in this section we will look at the opposite: What happens when friendship or romance spills over into the workplace?

Love and Hate in the Workplace

You may have noticed that we have written so far as if the workplace contains only particular types of interactants and they are basically limited to customers and salespersons, leaders and followers, or members of sales and marketing. We have emphasized the individual nature of relationships that occur when salespeople and marketing people hold meetings with one another, but it is obvious that the workplace can contain a number of different levels of relationship from friendship to outright hostility.

In extremely broad terms, the types of relationships in the workplace can be strict, formal, hierarchical, collegial, or a mix of the four. In the cult movie *Office Space* the creepy manager, Lumbergh, attempts in an ingratiating way to be overly friendly and informal while still exercising power and authority. The mismatch between the two is part of the problem that makes the workplace so unpleasant for his subordinates, and he is judged as insincere because of this discrepancy.

The problem that we identified at the beginning of the chapter is that there is a natural in-born conflict between the demands of the workplace and the demands of

Photo 9.4 Relationships at work: In what ways might personal relationships at work have a negative effect on productivity? (See page 258.)

Table 9.3 The Three Types of Friendly or Collegial Relationships Between People in an Organization

Information peer relationships	• Low on personal self-disclosure, but information about the task is freely and openly discussed • Civil and cordial but not close
Collegial peer relationships	• Individuals at work regard one another as friends and act in all respects in ways indistinguishable from friends outside the workplace; that is, they self-disclose and joke around and arrange to meet outside the workplace for social events
Special peer relationships	• Characterized by very high openness, self-disclosure, and intimacy • Virtually indistinguishable from best-friend relationships outside of the workplace

Source: Kram & Isabella, 1985.

relationships. The workplace represents an interaction order—that is, it is based on rules. Every workplace has its own norms and behaviors that emphasize the team and the cooperative performance of teamwork in order to fulfill instrumental goals most enjoyably for those involved. On the other hand, friendship is not supposed to be instrumental. What happens, then, when people who work together become friends, and is it good for them or for the organization or not?

Kram and Isabella (1985) identified three different types of friendly or collegial relationships between people in an organization. All three types—*information peer relationships, collegial peer relationships,* and *special peer relationships*—are described in detail in Table 9.3.

There is particular suspicion when two members in the same place become romantically involved (Dillard & Miller, 1988), and a fear may exist that information shared with one person will be automatically transmitted to the second. Therefore in the workplace caution can develop if a budding romance is suspected. Workers not only expect the productivity of the lovers to go down as they spend more time adoring one another but also tend to be careful in their dealings with members of a romantic couple or others who are known to be close friends (Sias, 2009).

Contrarian Challenge

We have been writing as if the workplace and the rest of life are distinct and separate areas of life, as do many other authors. Does this make sense, or do the two forms of life basically intersect in the modern world? Is the notion of "spillover" from work to home just a simplistic idea now that work and the rest of life are so closely interwoven anyway?

Favors for Buddies

One of the ways in which organizations and workplaces operate is through the interpersonal relationships among the people in those places and organizations. As a sales manager, you may be prepared to cut a special deal for someone in another organization because you know him or her personally. Therefore your organization benefits from a sale it otherwise might not make while the other organization benefits from the relationship that you have with its buyer and therefore gets something it wants at a cheaper rate than it could get from the competition. In the supply side of an organization (the sources from which it buys the parts to make the product that it then sells to other customers), these sorts of favorable relationships are vital ways for the organization to cut its costs (C. Heal, personal communication, May 23, 2008). Although it appears on the surface that commercial transactions are carried out between one organization and another, in fact they are done through the personal relationship between one member (or several members) of one organization and those of another over the phone, in group meetings, on e-mail, or by other interpersonal means. It is vital for organizations to maintain good personal relationships among the individuals who do this sort of business on their behalf. Once again, then, "organizational work" is done at the relational level.

You're My Boss, but You Were My Friend

Many people in the workplace develop friendly relationships with one another when they are at the same level because it makes their work easier. However, it can create problems when one of them is promoted over the other (Zorn, 1995), assuming that friends at work are freely chosen and real. However, the expectations of friendship require the revelation of self and perhaps secrets, and this may pose no threat to anyone while the two individuals remain at the same level in the hierarchy of the organization. However, if one of them is promoted to a rank higher than the other, then the information acquired during the friendship may become a source of conflict, particularly if the information leads to a negative assessment of a person's capacity to fulfill the job properly (Zorn).

Secondly, the knowledge that a person is friends with the boss on a personal level can have an adverse effect on the other members of the same team, who naturally enough expect that the friends will look after one another and may even act as a team in the political arena of the organization. Workers tend to become suspicious that the boss will show favoritism toward friends, and this of course has an undesirable effect on morale.

Employee-Abusive Communication

Sometimes workers are not nice to one another, and it is only recently that communication researchers have begun to understand the frequency of hostile workplaces and bullying. It is not just a question of personal criticism or attacks on appearance but "emotional tyranny . . . of the weak by the powerful" (Waldron, 2000, p. 67). Backstabbing gossip and derogatory talk about other employees are also examples of employee-abusive communication. In fact, there are many forms of contemptuous or discounting messages that are available in the workplace just as they are in other places. The workplace has often been the home to hostile interviews, but in the everyday running of an organization, the kinds of talk that go on and count as abusive would run

Strategic Communication

The research literature in interpersonal communication concerning the workplace is most often biased toward hierarchies, structures, and a managerial point of view, as stated earlier. The question that we want you to consider is the extent to which the literature on "organizations" actually applies to real life as you know it from any workplace you have ever experienced.

from offensive jokes to shunning and ostracism to the ignoring of an individual's requests or withholding important information that the person needs in order to complete the job properly (Lutgen-Sandvik & McDermott, 2008).

Focus Questions Revisited

Where do people get their ideas about the workplace?
People's ideas about the nature of work and the workplace are obtained early in childhood through family stories and discussions with others at school or through the media, which present certain professions and jobs as more or less valuable than others and stress the importance of work as part of identity or the value of "success."

What is an organization—a structure or a transacted set of communication activities?
An organization can be viewed as a simple structure as in an organizational chart or as a sedimented set of practices that are transacted through repetitive communication, memory, narrative, and routine daily discourse. A better way of looking at the workplace, however, is as a set of interpersonal relationships between specific individuals.

How are organizations constituted by the interactions and relationships between members?
Although we often talk about organizations transacting business with other organizations, in fact these transactions occur at the face-to-face interpersonal level between individuals or groups of individuals who know one another, and this is a relational activity. It is important to focus away from looking mostly at the managers in the situation and to look at the everyday discourses between other employees who transact their relationships within the organization.

What types of personal relationships can exist between individuals and affect organizational effectiveness?
Since the workplace is another frame for real interactions and although it has hierarchical structures, there is no reason to suppose that relationship types there are different from those anywhere else, especially as these may be transacted in communication.

Key Concepts

continuation of identity   (p. 238)
formality/hierarchy   (p. 241)
industrial time   (p. 246)
instrumental goals   (p. 240)
professional face   (p. 239)
relational goals   (p. 240)

sedimentation   (p. 243)
structurational approach   (p. 244)
Structuration Theory   (p. 243)
vocational anticipatory
   socialization   (p. 236)

Questions to Ask Your Friends

- Ask your friends if they get offended by other students in a large lecture class listening to an iPod through the whole lecture. Does it disrupt your learning in the lecture or not? Are colleges right to assume that it does?

- Ask your friends if they would find it offensive if you recommended a particular product to them and they later discovered that you had been paid by a large organization in order to make the recommendation. Would they assume that you were acting in their best interests and really believed in the product (Carl, 2006)?

- What is the most interesting example that you and your friends can produce about the way in which front and back regions operate in the workplace?

Media Links

- There are several movies that depict organizations and behavior in the workplace that could help illustrate ideas presented in this chapter—for example, *Office Space, In the Company of Men, Wall Street,* and *Waiting. . . .* Even *Titanic* is an example, since the CEO's concerns over publicity provoke the captain to exceed the safe speed limits of the ship.

- Occasionally, organizations fall over their own rules or objectives and make serious errors because of disobeying their own rules or following them too closely. Watch *Titanic* for examples of organizational hierarchy tripping itself up.

- What organizational cultures exist, and what is the difference between them as represented by *NYPD Blue* versus *Hill Street Blues* or *Grey's Anatomy* versus *House?*

Ethical Issues

- Is it "stealing" if you take paper home from work to do work-related activities (with most of it, at least)? If you catch someone taking paperclips from work, should you tell on him or her?

- Corporate surveillance: Where are the limits, and what are the rights of organizations to oversee the behavior of their employees? Is it OK for organizations to ban employees from making personal phone calls on company time? What about opening their personal mail? Body searches? Where would you draw the line?

- The Eichmann defense: In 1961 Adolf Eichmann, one of the Nazis responsible for the concentration camps in World War II, offered in his defense at trial in Israel that he was only obeying orders from his superiors in the organization and that he therefore should not be held responsible for the murders that he organized in the Holocaust. He was convicted and subsequently executed in 1962. When and under what circumstances is it legitimate to argue that you were "only obeying the orders" of your superiors in the workplace/organization or are "only doing your job"?

Answers to Photo Questions

Photo 9.1 ▪ This picture tells us that real professionals are young and good looking and well dressed. They also wear spectacles (did you spot them on the top of her head?—but she would look less attractive with the glasses actually in place). Success is about rising sales and a clear vision of the future (notice that we are looking at her through clear glass, so this is a metaphorical way of indicating clarity of purpose).

Photo 9.2 ▪ The sergeant's job in this situation is to reduce the recruit's sense of personal identity and make him conform to the required military identity that demands immediate response to commands without thought. The recruit is having his personal identity reduced and altered into one that conforms with the requirements of military discipline.

Photo 9.3 ▪ Clearly there is an argument going on in this photograph, and you will have noticed the two raised fingers of accusation from the man and one of the women. It looks as if there is a conflict about somebody's performance, and that is not being handled in a way that best preserves the face of everyone involved.

Photo 9.4 ▪ Relationships at work can be engrossing to the extent that they take people away from their main tasks; when one of the people feels bad, the other may also feel bad, so the effect is doubled; the people in a relationship may become suspects to their coworkers who may know about an affair but be unsure whether to tell the management. Finally, if the relationship breaks up, then both people may lose their ability to concentrate on their work or get on collegially, especially if they have to stay working in the same workplace.

Student Study Site

Visit the study site at www.sagepub.com/ciel for e-flashcards, practice quizzes, and other study resources.

References

Allen, B. J. (2006). Communicating race at WeighCo. In J. T. Wood & S. W. Duck (Eds.), *Composing relationships: Communication in everyday life* (pp. 146–154). Belmont, CA: Wadsworth.

Bastien, D., McPhee, R., & Bolton, K. (1995). A study and extended theory of the structuration of climate. *Communication Monographs, 62*, 87–109.

Berry, L. L. (1983). Relationship marketing. In L. L. Berry, G. L. Shostack, & G. D. Upah (Eds.), *Emerging perspectives on service marketing* (pp. 25–28.). Chicago: American Marketing Association.

Carl, W. J. (2006). What's all the buzz about? Everyday communication and the relational basis of word-of-mouth and buzz marketing practices. *Management Communication Quarterly, 19*(4), 601–634.

Cockburn-Wootten, C., and Zorn, T. (2006). Cabbages and headache cures: Work stories within the family. In J. T. Wood & S. W. Duck (Eds.), *Composing relationships: Communication in everyday life* (137–144). Belmont, CA: Wadsworth.

Crouter, A., & Helms-Erikson, H. (2000). Work and family from a dyadic perspective: Variations in inequality. In R. M. Milardo & S. W. Duck (Eds.), *Families as relationships* (pp. 99–115). Chichester, UK: Wiley.

Dillard, J. P., & Miller, K. I. (1988). Intimate relationships in task environments. In S. W. Duck (Ed.), *Handbook of personal relationships* (pp. 449–465). New York: John Wiley & Sons.

Fairhurst, G. T. (2007). *Discursive leadership.* Thousand Oaks, CA: Sage.

Fairhurst, G. T., & Sarr, R. (1996). *The art of framing: Managing the language of leadership.* San Francisco, CA: Jossey-Bass.

Fournier, S. (1998). Consumers and their brands: Developing relationship theory in consumer research. *Journal of Consumer Research, 24,* 343–373.

Giddens, A. (1991). *Modernity and self-identity: Self and society in the late modern age.* Cambridge, UK: Polity Press.

Ice, R. (1991). Corporate publics and rhetorical strategies: The case of Union Carbide's Bhopal crisis. *Management Communication Quarterly, 4*(3), 341–362.

Kram, K. E., & Isabella, L. A. (1985). Mentoring alternatives: The role of peer relationships in career development. *Academy of Management Journal, 28*(1), 110–132.

Lutgen-Sandvik, P., & McDermott, V. (2008). The constitution of employee-abusive organizations: A communication flows theory. *Communication Theory, 18*(2), 304–333.

Mokros, H. B. (2006). Composing relationships at work: Three minutes at a wholesale produce market. In J. T. Wood & S. W. Duck (Eds.), *Composing relationships: Communication in everyday life* (pp. 175–185). Belmont, CA: Wadsworth.

Morgan, G. (2006). *Images of organizations.* Thousand Oaks, CA: Sage.

Mumby, D. K. (2006). Constructing working-class masculinity in the workplace. In J. T. Wood & S. W. Duck (Eds.), *Composing relationships: Communication in everyday life* (pp. 166–174). Belmont, CA: Wadsworth.

National Transportation Safety Board. (1993, November 15). *Tall strike during go-around, Boeing 727–227* [Report No. CHI94FA039]. Retrieved May 11, 2009, from the Flight Simulation Systems Web site at http://www.fss.aero/accident-reports/look.php?report_key=817

Northouse, P. G. (2009). *Introduction to leadership concepts and practices.* Thousand Oaks, CA: Sage.

Petronio, S. (2002). *Boundaries of privacy.* Albany: State University of New York Press.

Sias, P. M. (2009). *Organizing relationships: Traditional and emerging perspectives on workplace relationships.* Thousand Oaks, CA: Sage.

Totten, L. D. (2006). Who am I right now? Negotiating familial and professional roles. In J. T. Wood & S. W. Duck (Eds.), *Composing relationships: Communication in everyday life* (pp. 186–193). Belmont, CA: Wadsworth.

Univision. (2008, April 21). [Advertisement]. *The New York Times,* p. C10.

Waldron, V. R. (2000). Relational experiences and emotions at work. In S. Fineman (Ed.), *Emotion in organizations* (pp. 64–82). Thousand Oaks, CA: Sage.

Weick, K. (1995). *Sense-making in organizations.* Thousand Oaks, CA: Sage.

Zorn, T. (1995). Bosses and buddies: Constructing and performing simultaneously hierarchical and close friendship relationships. In J. T. Wood & S. W. Duck (Eds.), *Under-studied relationships: Off the beaten track [Understanding relationship processes 6]* (pp. 122–147). Thousand Oaks, CA: Sage.

Zweig, D. (2005). Beyond privacy and fairness concerns: Examining psychological boundary violations as a consequence of electronic performance monitoring. In J. Weckert (Ed.), *Electronic monitoring in the workplace: Controversies and solutions* (pp. 37–52). Hershey, PA: Idea Group.

Zweig, D., & Webster, J. (2002). Where is the line between benign and invasive? An examination of psychological barriers to the acceptance of awareness monitoring systems. *Journal of Organizational Behavior, 23,* 605–622.

10

Health Communication

ealth communication is not something that is confined to visits to a doctor's office or a hospital but instead occurs in communication and everyday life. It comprises lifestyle choices people make, how they talk with their friends and families about illness and health, the kinds of social support that they give and receive, decisions to reveal or conceal private information about pain or fear, media images and appeals splashed over billboards or the sides of buses and on TV, and Internet activity. In short, health communication is very much built into both everyday communication and relationships. Indeed, life expectancy and disease survival rates are surprisingly highly correlated with the number of friends that you have and how much you talk to people every day (Duck, 2007).

Emphasizing the role of communication in health may seem somewhat curious at first. Many people may consider that health issues are confined to the physical or biological and not connected to the symbolic or relational. However, communication scholar James W. Chesebro (1982) has maintained that health and illness are not just physical experiences but also socially symbolic and relational experiences. Talcott Parsons (1951), for example, noted that sickness is not simply a physical experience but a social one. It allows people to enter a "sick role" that automatically excuses them from social and work obligations or other people's expectations about behavior ("He's not lazy or incompetent; he's actually quite ill"). Health and illness are very much physical, but how we think about them and respond to them is very much symbolic and relational. This shift in thinking may be a bit confusing, so let's consider the example of cancer. From a physical or biological standpoint, this disease involves the abnormal activity or breakdown of cells within a body. However, what it *means* to have cancer or what it *means* for a friend, romantic partner, or family member to have cancer is symbolic, and cancer has relational effects. For example, it may restrict movement, reduce energy, decrease sociability, increase tiredness, and make people feel uncomfortable "being seen like this." How societies or cultures *respond* to cancer is symbolic and relational. How people *deal* with the disease is symbolic and relational, and many chronic diseases (e. g., epilepsy, cancer, or multiple sclerosis) affect the sufferer's social life, while even a cold or a headache can make you feel temporarily unsociable ("not tonight, Josephine . . .").

Such issues are very complex and interwoven not only with each other; they are connected to everyday life in numerous ways. To teach you how to get a feel for the full range in a single chapter, we will focus on three key areas of health communication: (1) patient-provider relationships, (2) social networks, and (3) media and technology.

Although health communication is not confined to medical settings, patient-provider relationships and their corresponding interactions have a tremendous effect on everyday experience and health decisions. Unfortunately, communication between patients and providers is often problematic and counterproductive, with many patients feeling treated dismissively by doctors who think they are gods. On the other hand, many doctors feel frustrated that patients cannot remember simple instructions on how to take their pills. We will examine typical patient-provider interactions and discuss suggestions for developing more effective patient-provider relationships. We will then explore the impact of social networks on health, examining the influence of friends, families, and others on lifestyle choices or willingness to accept health advice and the influence of everyday communication on social support. Since health issues are often considered very personal and private, we will also discuss how people decide whether to share this information with others. Finally, we will examine how media and technology influence health communication and what people make of government health campaigns. We will explore how entertainment and news/health media impact people's lifestyle choices, their understanding of health and illness, and their expectations of treatment. Then, we will discuss the use of the Internet when searching for health-related information and when seeking social support and ask you to think about the way in which the availability of health Web pages on the Internet may have made a physician's job easier or more difficult.

Focus Questions

- How do patients and providers generally communicate (relationally), and can it be improved?
- What are the benefits of effective patient-provider relationships?
- How do social networks influence lifestyle choices through everyday communication?
- How do people manage their privacy with health-related issues?
- In what ways do different media influence lifestyle, distribute health-related knowledge, and stimulate everyday communication about it?
- How does direct-to-consumer advertising impact health communication?
- What influence does the Internet have on health communication?

How Do Patients and Providers Interact?

Patients and providers meet in a variety of circumstances. Patient need for expert help runs the whole gamut from "Stop me dying when I don't even know where I am and have no control over anything at all" (Secklin, 2001) to "I've got this embarrassing itch, and all I want is for you to fill out a form prescribing the best cream for it, because the over-the-counter stuff that I can get for myself doesn't work." Expectations of the proper or ideal relationship between patients and providers, the actual development of their relationship, the construction of relational identities, and the nature of their interactions will be guided by these situations and cultural expectations surrounding health.

Patient-Provider Relational Prototypes

As with all relationships and relational identities, those created during patient and provider interactions are co-constructed. As such, both parties are responsible for the relationships and identities created during the interaction. However, interactants may not always approve of the relationships and relational identities being created. As we discussed in Chapter 5, altercasting involves the ways in which a person's communication influences the identity of another person. Altercasting can work in two related ways. First, a person's communication can force a particular identity on another person. A patient saying to a provider, "Well, you are the expert, so what do you suggest I do?" positions the provider a certain way and compels him or her to live up to that label. Second, as a person attempts to create a particular identity, the communication of another may either affirm or negate that identity. If a patient suggests a particular treatment option to a provider, who in turn replies, "I am the expert, so you had better let me decide what is best for you," then the provider is combating the identity being created by the patient.

Based on cultural and individual expectations, Athena du Pre (2005, pp. 222–227) has noted the following relational identities created in patient and provider interactions: (a) machines and mechanics, (b) children and parents, (c) consumers, and (d) partners.

In transacting a **machines-and-mechanics** relationship, providers are viewed as competent experts analytically diagnosing a physical problem and then fixing it. Patients are passive and allow the expert mechanic to give them a proper tune-up with little or no input or objection. Minimal personal involvement is conveyed throughout the interaction, which can be less emotionally taxing on providers but discomforting for patients, who most likely view themselves as more than simply a collection of parts. However, if a patient is unconscious or temporarily disoriented by a motor accident, for example, then this pairing of roles works to the patient's advantage.

As **children-parents**, patients and providers may display more emotional and personal involvement compared with the mechanistic view; however, the provider clearly portrays a dominant role of expert while the patient assumes a submissive and dependent role. This view of provider and patient relationships is the most traditional and still most common. Patients view providers as knowing what is best for them and believe that they should go along with whatever providers ask of them (Beisecker & Beisecker, 1993).

Photo 10.1 How might the development of each patient-provider relational identity facilitate this patient's disclosure about her concerns to her therapist? What are the risks of each approach? (See page 288.)

Patients are increasingly viewing themselves as **consumers**, paying providers for specific information and expecting them to carry out their wishes. This view transacts the patient role as an increasingly dominant one within interactions with providers, which could be seen as an improvement over patients' more traditionally passive role. However, just as patients may not desire to be treated as machines, providers often view themselves as more than a clerk carrying out the exact wishes of a paying customer (Beisecker & Beisecker, 1993). This consumer-oriented mentality is similar to that expressed by some college students who expect a high grade simply because they are paying to take a class (Wright, Sparks, & O'Hair, 2008). Like most providers, however, instructors are frequently unwilling to play the role of willing clerk. Instead of viewing them as customers who are always right, it is better to view patients and students as clients. Sometimes clients have to be told things they do not want to hear! An important issue here is just how much the "consumer" really does understand about the situation and how "a *little* information is a dangerous thing."

Patients and providers may also *transact* the relational roles of **partners** during their interactions. Patients and providers work together to solve a problem and are viewed as equals, each bringing special knowledge to the interaction. The provider possesses unique medical knowledge, and the patient possesses unique knowledge about his or her physical and emotional state. Although this view is increasingly supported by medical professionals and patient groups, it is sometimes difficult to achieve due to preconceived notions of the patient and provider relationship along with unwillingness or inability on the part of both patients and providers.

How Patients and Providers Communicate

Patient and provider interactions most often transact relationships that place the patient in a passive role and place the provider in a dominant role, as outlined in the machine-mechanic relationship and the child-parent relationship, both of which require a large degree of trust of the physician by the patient. Driven by traditional and cultural norms, such interaction styles can interfere with the communication and wellness processes in certain circumstances.

Providers tend to dominate interactions with patients through questions and directives. Through directives, or commands, the dominant position of providers is further substantiated. Of course, a provider telling a patient to breathe deeply, cough, open wide, or sing a chorus of "Moon River" may have legitimate medical backing. At the same time, it clearly places the provider in a dominant position and may consequently hinder a patient's ability to question the provider and to participate in decision making regarding his or her treatment, with such participation clearly being best when the patient is informed, is knowledgeable, and understands the situation to the fullest.

Providers also focus most often on establishing a patient's physical problems rather than psychosocial problems (social and relational issues accompanying or even causing illness). This approach likens patients to machines and gives no account to relevant emotional and relational needs. When patients attempt to incorporate such issues into the interaction, providers tend to interrupt them and refocus on physical symptoms. Consequently, providers may miss opportunities to discover the actual cause of a patient's problem or miss relevant treatment opportunities. For example, a patient's high blood pressure may be caused by stress at work, trouble at home, financial difficulties, or the fact that the patient was recently arrested for shoplifting. The physician may not ask the right questions to find out this complex picture, and if the patient clams up from embarrassment, the truth will never show up to help the physician make the right diagnosis.

Additionally, providers limit personal disclosure and avoid engaging in other behaviors that may serve to increase the closeness of their relationship with patients. Providers rarely share personal information other than that which is connected to their professional experiences ("Yeah, I had a boil right there once myself. Don't they hurt? Ha ha ha!"). Strict focus on the physical symptoms neglects other aspects of a patient's life that may be relevant to the symptoms, and this will go undetected by an insensitive provider, especially since patients rarely challenge the dominant position of providers so that they can insist on introducing their original thoughts and instead continue to be directed by the provider.

Further complicating matters is an unwillingness of some patients to fully disclose their medical concerns to providers. Especially when dealing with personal or embarrassing issues, patients tend to avoid disclosing information that would be pertinent to providers. In fact, patients undergoing a medical examination sometimes delay disclosing the real reason for their visit until a provider is getting ready to leave the room. These "doorknob disclosures" generally result in another medical evaluation or interview being conducted, resulting in further delay for the next patient (du Pre, 2005).

Variables Related to Patient-Provider Communication

Characteristics of patient-provider interactions are influenced by a host of variables. Chief among these are the actual expectations of a given patient and a given provider, often based on the experience of their past relationship together. However,

Contrarian Challenge

Television shows like *House* and *Grey's Anatomy* have made viewers more aware that physicians are human and make mistakes. This does not mean that physicians *always* make mistakes, but shouldn't an intelligent patient do homework before visiting a physician so that he or she is ready to disclose all the relevant information in order to facilitate the right treatment?

many other variables have been discovered to affect relationships and communication between provider and patient.

For example, a patient's *age* relative to a provider affects patient-provider interactions. Older patients seem to adhere more strongly to traditional roles of patients and providers. Consequently, older patients tend to be less expressive when interacting with providers and less willing to challenge their authority (Street, 2003). Further, psychosocial issues are less likely to be provided by older patients or addressed by their providers.

Patient-provider interaction styles also appear to be influenced by *gender*. Female providers tend to be more supportive and to provide more information (both psychosocial and medical) than male providers (Street, 2003). Female patients tend to be more explicit and more emotionally expressive than male patients, consequently receiving more information from providers than male patients (Hall, Irish, Roter, Ehrlich, & Miller, 1994; Hall & Roter, 1995).

Ethnicity may also play a role in patient-provider interactions. Reviewing several studies, Roter and Hall (2006) concluded that "Caucasians receive care that is of higher interpersonal quality than Blacks or Hispanics receive, as well as more positive talk and more information, even within the same medical practices" (p. 67). These authors attribute such findings to negative stereotypes and believe providers are unaware of how these stereotypes impact their interactions with patients.

Finally, interactions among patients and providers may differ based on the *education level* of patients. For instance, patients with higher levels of formal education tend to be more expressive than patients with less formal education (Street, 2003). Beyond the fact that people with more formal education tend to be more verbally expressive than those with little or no formal education, it is possible this finding can be attributed to different perceptions about the patient-provider relationship. People with more formal education may see less of a power difference between themselves and providers. They may consequently expect to be more involved in the health care process and may be more confident in their contributions to the interaction. It is also possible that providers may also perceive a more equivalent relationship with patients possessing more formal education (Kaplan, Gandek, Greenfield, Rogers, & Ware, 1995).

Improving Patient-Provider Communication: Developing Effective Relationships

A patient's physical appearance may also impact his or her interaction with providers. Well-dressed patients experience fewer interruptions from providers, while disheveled-looking patients are given fewer opportunities to talk (Hooper, Comstock, Goodwin, & Goodwin, 1982). Wearing formal attire to your next visit to the doctor may be overkill, but it might not hurt!

A number of health communication scholars have noted the importance of a patient-provider relationship based on partnership or mutuality, in which the interactants share control of the interaction and equally negotiate an understanding of patient needs and treatments (e.g., du Pre, 2005; Roter & Hall, 2006; Wright et al., 2008). Such a relationship can only be established through extensive transformations of existing patient-provider communication patterns. Debra Roter and Judith Hall (2006, pp. 6–20) have outlined seven communication principles that would vastly improve existing interactions among patients and providers. In Table 10.1, we examine the primary ideas behind these seven communication principles, whose recognition and subsequent incorporation could assist in the development of effective patient-provider relationships.

Table 10.1 Patient-Provider Communication Principles

Patient-provider communication should acknowledge . . .
Patient Stories Stories reveal what people perceive as the most important details or elements of a situation. They hold crucial information pertaining not only to physical symptoms but also to the psychological and relational issues connected with a specific patient's illness.
Patient Expertise Patients should be considered experts about their unique situation, regardless of how common the illness or medical concern. As such, their expertise and contributions should be valued as greatly as those of providers.
Provider Expertise Beyond utilizing specialized medical knowledge to confirm illness and to set forth treatment options, providers should use their knowledge to educate patients. Sharing their expertise with patients in a manner that is clear and understandable can enhance patient-provider relationships and improve the health and healing process.
Physical and Psychosocial Connections There exists a powerful connection between health and everyday life. Both patients and providers do not always recognize the importance of everyday life experiences and instead focus their attention on biological causes. A holistic understanding of patient experiences can improve diagnoses and treatment options.
Emotions The expression, recognition, and subsequent transacted meaning of emotion impact patient-provider relationships just as they do other relationships. Patients and providers should recognize the profound influence of emotion and their mutual emotional investments.
Reciprocity As with any relationship, patients will act in accordance with provider interaction styles (positive or negative) and vice versa. Both patients and providers must recognize the influence of reciprocity on their relationship, treating each other with respect and recognizing the concerns and needs of each other.
Roles and Expectations Patients and providers should recognize the influence of traditional roles and expectations while attempting to establish a more constructive relationship and more effective communication styles. They must clearly express their expectations of the relationship, the interaction, and each other.

Benefits of Effective Patient-Provider Relationships

We can now examine the positive outcomes resulting from effective patient-provider relationships. These benefits include satisfaction with the encounter, greater

We have championed the need for a reciprocal relationship between patients and providers. Can you see any drawbacks to this type of patient-provider relationship? Do you believe a different type of relationship would be more advantageous such as providers having a dominant role or patients having a dominant role? If so, what would be the advantages of such a relationship, and what would be the disadvantages?

likelihood of adherence to treatments (taking the pills as prescribed, giving up all alcohol for 7 days, eating no crunchy foods for a week, not eating grapefruit while taking the medication, and suchlike), improved physical and psychological health, and even a decrease in malpractice lawsuits.

Satisfaction

Effective patient-provider relationships enhance feelings of patient satisfaction, which is increasingly recognized as an important goal in addition to the traditional goal of patient recovery or survival (Wright et al., 2008). Examining studies of patient satisfaction since the 1960s, J. B. Brown, Stewart, and Ryan (2003, p. 144) discovered five key elements of patient-provider interactions that impact satisfaction. First, providers should express concern for patients and an acceptance of their situation. A second key element of patient satisfaction is a perception of medical competence. A doctor might be very kind, caring, and understanding, but if he or she says, "Well, let's break out those leeches and take care of that athlete's foot," a patient may become less than satisfied with the overall interaction. This element of patient-provider interactions underscores the importance of not overlooking the need for a strong medical knowledge base while recognizing the need for improved patient-provider interaction. Third, patients are more satisfied when there exists a balance between discussions of psychosocial needs and concerns and discussions of biomedical needs and concerns. Patient satisfaction thus increases when providers recognize that physical ailments are not the only concerns experienced by patients and that social and psychological well-being may be equally important (Roter et al., 1997), especially in respect to what will happen to them during treatment, how it will feel, what obstacles there may be, and how their social and family life could be affected. An additional element in patient satisfaction is a continuity of the patient-provider relationship. Continuing to use a particular provider for health needs is naturally connected with past satisfaction. Continuity in patient-provider relationships makes a patient feel as if a provider is knowledgeable about his or her specific needs. Furthermore, like many positive relationships, trust is likely to increase overtime, which may increase patient disclosure and thereby increase

A point rarely researched and recognized by practitioners is that the relationships and communication established by front-office staff can greatly influence overall patient satisfaction. The health care providers can be very good in themselves, but the patient may already feel badly treated or disrespected by a dismissive or overhasty office staff before the physician even shows up.

a provider's ability to successfully treat the patient, which would increase patient satisfaction, and so on. Finally, patient satisfaction is linked to the full expression of patient and provider expectations. Effective patient and provider communication cannot be fully achieved unless the expectations of both are clearly expressed. Of course, expectations may not always be agreeable or realistic and must thus be discussed by the patient and provider in attempt to reach some sort of agreement.

Adherence to Treatments

Effective patient-provider relationships also increase the likelihood that patients will adhere to treatments and lifestyle recommendations established by providers (Wright et al., 2008). Naming patient-provider interaction as the most important variable in adherence to treatment, J. B. Brown et al. (2003, p. 146) have noted four components of patient-provider interaction influencing patient adherence. First, the relationship between patients and providers is generally one in which providers are expected to give patients clear information about treatment options and procedures. Such explanations enable patients to gain a sense of co-ownership of the problem and its solution, help them recognize their importance, and ensure that they understand exactly what the treatment entails. Intricate treatments may be especially unclear to patients. It is a fairly obvious point that people who are sick and confused, old and confused, in such pain that it reduces their concentration, or simply not being addressed in familiar speech codes may not be best placed to fully understand procedures and their own responsibilities.

Photo 10.2 Elderly patients or those undergoing complex treatments sometimes have difficulty remembering the regimen of pills and medications they should take. How could a physician facilitate a patient's adherence to the prescribed treatment? (See page 288.)

Second, patients and providers must reach agreement about treatment expectations. Patient expectations are not always realistic, and providers must understand patient perspectives. Once these expectations are established, decisions must be made about the actual treatment. Accordingly, the third component influencing adherence involves patient activity in deciding what treatment options to establish. When patients feel as though they have contributed to the development of their treatment, this increases their perceptions of personal investment and accountability, resulting in increased adherence to the treatment.

Finally, a provider's ability to empathize with and encourage a patient also increases adherence to treatments. A given treatment may be more or less of a burden depending on a particular patient's situation. For instance, some people may struggle with the cost of medication, or limited transportation access may hinder the ability to engage in regular rehabilitation appointments. Elderly people in particular may find it hard to remember complex instructions about when to take medication or may become confused about what they have been told. Feeling as though a provider has taken their personal situation into account and has offered encouragement will increase the likelihood that patients will adhere to treatments. Providers can encourage elderly patients to bring along a "listener" to take notes or help remind them about what to do when they leave the doctor's office.

Physical and Psychological Health

Effective patient-provider relationships also enhance the physical and psychological health of patients (Wright et al., 2008). It is fairly easy to understand how effective patient-provider communication can enhance patient physical and psychological health, since it increases adherence to treatments. If the physician is right, then this will increase the likelihood that patients will overcome a particular ailment and feel pretty darn good about it as a result. Beyond adherence, however, effective communication increases the chances that providers will ask the right questions during evaluations and that patients will be willing to be forthcoming, freely supplying providers with information that they do not otherwise know and that could speed their arrival at a proper diagnosis. Effective patient-provider communication will also decrease patient anxiety and stress related to the interaction and overall medical concerns, because the patient feels accepted, understood, and safer.

Malpractice Claims

And now, one for the medical providers out there: Effective patient-provider relationships may decrease malpractice lawsuits (J. B. Brown et al., 2003; Wright et al., 2008). Medical providers do not often get sued when a patient's health improves. However, overall communication patterns of providers influence the likelihood that a malpractice claim will or will not be filed. Positive communication behaviors such as smiling, eye contact, appropriate touch, and a courteous voice *decrease* the chance of lawsuits, while not smiling, no eye contact, inappropriate touch, and a discourteous voice *increase* the chance of lawsuits (Lester & Smith, 1993).

Social Networks and Health Communication

Social networks have a profound influence on health. Social networks influence many of the lifestyle choices people make, from eating and exercising to smoking, drinking, and taking drugs. Social networks also provide various forms of support. In what follows, we will examine the influence of social networks on health and lifestyle. We will then look at the support provided by social networks, secondary goals of social support, and how everyday communication serves as a foundation for social support. Finally, we will explore the communication privacy management theory to better understand how people manage private health information.

Social Networks and Health and Lifestyles

Social networks influence the decisions people make regarding health-related issues and overall lifestyles. The nature of health, its importance, the evaluation of health advice, and the meanings of health and lifestyle choices are all transacted in interactions with others. Beyond genetic predispositions, your family members have an incredible influence on your food consumption, your exercise habits, whether or not you drink or smoke, and other health and lifestyle choices through both their actions and the ways in which they talk about these things. Food is often ritually connected with celebrations and momentous occasions in your family (such as birthday cakes and Thanksgiving turkeys), and it is possible that you associate food with joy and happiness. Alcohol consumption may be viewed in the same manner by some families for some occasions ("And now, a toast to the bride and groom"). Of course, just because your family does something does not mean that you will do the same thing, whether it is positive or negative. However, family members do have a strong foundational influence, and your decisions and behaviors will often be based on the views cultivated within your family's communication.

Friends also have a profound influence on your health and lifestyle decisions. Research indicates that people with overweight friends tend to be overweight themselves, although the direction of causality is hard to establish: Do overweight people choose overweight friends, or do people who choose overweight friends become larger themselves afterward? While it may be an epidemic, obesity cannot be caught like a cold, but it can be influenced by your friends' rhetorical visions about fitness, food, and size. Behaviors and talk about food and exercise influence people's attitudes and the decisions that are made about diet, exercise, and ordering the super-sized meal. Your friends' eating habits and exercise routines may influence or set the standards for your own. Part of the reason people are influenced in this manner is through comparing themselves with others. Restaurant employees indicate that if one person at a table orders dessert, the likelihood that others will greatly increase. Beyond this reason, however, are the meanings attached to food and to exercise that have been transacted though interactions. As with family, just because your friends do something does not mean that you will follow along. Selecting only skinny friends is not the way to lose weight or stay thin. However, recognizing the symbolic influence of your friends' rhetorical visions may explain your attitudes toward diet and exercise.

Health and lifestyle behaviors are frequently shared relational activities. For instance, smoking might be a way to forge and maintain relational connections with colleagues and classmates through bonding activities like sharing cigarettes or lights or the fact that smokers must meet outside in the "smokers' hole." Of course, a person passing a construction crew placing tar on the road and thinking "I would sure like to inhale some of that along with some tasty nicotine and other carcinogens" must have an addiction. However, relationships with others through the social bonding and companionship provided by commonly shared smoking or food and drinking habits have consistently been listed as one of the perceived benefits of smoking (Balch, 1998). Further, adolescents report negative relational consequences when attempting to stop smoking such as a decrease in the number of (smoking) friends (Pingree et al., 2004).

People's talk about their smoking also serves to minimize the perceived risks and influences the likelihood that a person will continue the behavior. In case you have not heard, SMOKING WILL KILL YOU. Most people have heard the warnings, but many otherwise intelligent people continue this behavior. Alan DeSantis (2002) has examined the ways in which talk among a group of smokers collectively crafts and reinforces *pro*smoking arguments that refute established findings, decrease the impact of anti-smoking messages, and minimize cognitive dissonance and anxieties connected with the activity. For example, the patrons of a particular cigar shop tended to discuss the unreliability of government health advice; tended to take a view that there was a government conspiracy to conceal the truth from the public; and tended to identify other causes of death, which could happen unexpectedly at any moment and were unrelated to smoking. By talking about such things fairly frequently, they managed to reinforce each other's rhetorical vision that the dangers of smoking have been misrepresented by evil statisticians or lying governments. DeSantis's work is an extremely strong example of the ways in which relationships and the interactions that transact relationships influence health and lifestyle decisions.

Alcohol consumption is another lifestyle behavior associated with relationships. In fact, drinking alone has been listed as a potential sign of alcoholism! Drinking among college students continues to be a problem on many campuses, resulting in physical, academic, relational, and legal problems for many students. The pressure to drink is often based on relational obligation, and those who try to avoid the consumption of alcohol often experience relational distress as a result (Seibold & Thomas, 1994).

A final area of health and lifestyle decision making and behavior we can discuss is the use of "recreational" drugs. As with tobacco and alcohol, initial drug use often involves those with whom we share a close personal relationship. Relational connections—and accordingly perceived obligations—embedded in the offer of drugs makes prevention strategies particularly difficult. Whether or not someone complies with an invitation to take drugs is influenced by relational ties, relational history, relational goals, relational consequences of compliance or noncompliance, and relational power. Accordingly, it is easier to refuse offers from certain relational partners than others (e.g., mere acquaintances compared with best friends) (Trost, Langen, & Kellar-Guenther, 1999). Once again, relationships and the everyday communication that transacts them are inherent factors in the health and lifestyle decisions and the behaviors that are enacted.

Types of Social Support

The support received from social networks takes numerous forms but generally involves two basic types, which can be further broken down into two subtypes of support. The two primary types of social support are (1) action-facilitating support and (2) nurturing support (du Pre, 2005). **Action-facilitating support** involves providing information or performing tasks for others. **Nurturing support** involves helping people feel better about themselves and the issues they are experiencing. Although we have separated them into two types of support, action-facilitating support and nurturing support are often connected in their application as you will see as we go along.

Action-Facilitating Support

Action-facilitating support includes informational support and instrumental support. **Informational support** involves providing someone with information in order to increase his or her knowledge and understanding of health issues. For instance, someone dealing with hypertension may be provided with information found online by a friend. As we will discuss later in this chapter, 48% of those seeking health information on the Internet do so for someone else. An additional 8% are seeking information for others along with answering their own questions (Fox, 2006). Providing someone with information not only increases his or her understanding of the situation and ability to make informed decisions but also increases his or her feelings of competence and value, issues related to nurturing support. Accordingly, when you provide someone with a piece of information, you are doing more than just that. You are reinforcing the existence of the relationship, you are reinforcing his or her importance, and you are validating his or her ability to make his or her own decisions. As with most actions, additional symbolic meaning is inherent in the provision of information as relational support.

These same meanings are evident with **instrumental support**, which involves performing tasks for someone. For instance, you might perform tasks around the home when a friend is too sick to do them for him- or herself, or you might give someone a ride to the doctor. Doing such things, once again, goes beyond the mere completion of tasks and additionally entails personal and relational reinforcement.

Nurturing Support

Nurturing support includes emotional support and esteem support. **Emotional support** enables people to express their feelings and to have those feelings validated by others. Some people are reluctant to express their emotions for cultural, personal, or relational reasons. This reticence is especially true when experiencing fear, anger, or depression. Providing people with the opportunity to express their emotions can prove very beneficial in the coping and healing process. Emotional support frequently entails therapeutic listening, which, as discussed in Chapter 4, requires not only empathy but also the ability to determine what a speaker desires from a situation. People seeking emotional support frequently desire to simply express their emotions and are not necessarily seeking advice or to be cheered up. Especially before a person takes the step to consult a physician, such support may be a key way in which decisions are made as to whether a condition is serious enough for a visit to the doctor or is just something that he or she should allow to run its course.

Although it may seem like positive emotional support, telling someone that he or she is going to be just fine and that there is nothing to worry about is not always beneficial or welcomed. While perhaps meant as encouragement, such assertions may appear to imply that the recipient's fears and concerns are unjustified and inappropriate. It may

Photo 10.3 In what ways can social support help improve a patient's health? (See page 288.)

seem as though he or she is being patronized instead of encouraged. In Western cultures such as the United States, people in dire sickness greatly prefer being told the truth rather than being told that everything is going to be fine. Such findings, of course, do not mean that someone should never be encouraged. Rather, providing emotional support demands recognition that encouragement is not always what a person desires or needs from a friend in everyday communication.

Emotional support also involves making people feel valued by letting them know that they are needed and that others care for them. Health problems may lead people to view themselves as a burden to others. Their worth and value need to be validated to prevent or overcome these feelings. This form of support also entails reinforcing relational connections by letting those experiencing health problems know that others will stick around even when things get rough.

Esteem support involves making someone feel competent and valued. Health problems are often accompanied by a perceived lack of control, which is often increased by well-meaning assistance and advice from others. Consequently, people may begin to feel as though they are incapable of normal activities or of making their own decisions. This form of support promotes feelings of competence and ability by allowing and encouraging people to act on their own and to take part in decision making related to their care.

Secondary Goals of Social Support

While the goals of social support just discussed frequently receive the most attention, there exist secondary goals of both those seeking and those providing social support. These secondary goals are just as significant as the primary goals, and in fact, it could be argued that fully understanding the primary goals would be impossible without them. These secondary goals involve identities and relationships.

Identity Goals of Social Support

Identity goals inherent in social support are connected with face wants discussed in Chapter 2. People desire to be seen as worthwhile and as decent overall (positive face wants) and do not wish to be imposed upon or treated in a negative manner (negative face wants). The possibility of negative face arises with every request for or offer of social support. Asking for a ride to the hospital, for example, may place a person in an inferior position and may also be seen as imposition of a burden on the person being asked. Accordingly, people must manage their interactions in a way that ensures the prevention of negative face or in a manner that minimizes negative face. ("Pardon me. I hate to bother you, but I seem to have stapled my eyelid to my knee. Could I trouble you for a ride to the hospital? I would drive myself, but if I did, I'd likely pass out and crash.")

Providing or receiving social support can be consistent or inconsistent with transacted identities. Consequently, people may struggle with the desire to create particular identities that may be hindered through support actions. Of particular concern for those providing social support is a desire to be viewed as competent and reliable. A lack of autonomy or independence is a key concern for those seeking or receiving social support.

Relational Goals of Social Support

Closely associated with identity goals, relational goals also guide social support. Of primary concern are the expectations surrounding relationships. Although the communication transacting relationships is a more important indicator of potential social support than the actual type of relationship, certain relationships are expected to fulfill social support functions. Furthermore, certain relationships are expected to fulfill *specific* social support functions. A friend would usually be expected to provide support in times of need whereas an enemy would not be. However, the number of friends you have does not correlate to the amount of social support you have available just as the number of enemies does not correlate to the lack of social support you have available. Again, the important point is not the absolute number but the quality of the communication taking place and transacting the relationships.

Nevertheless, there are expectations that support will be available from certain types of relationships (Carl & Duck, 2004). When a relationship provides the support expected, this reinforces the relationship and may very well make both relational partners feel better about themselves and the relationship. The person seeking support may have improved feelings about the problem she or he is experiencing and may perceive a reinforced source of support. The person providing support may feel worthwhile and may perceive a potential source of support should he or she need support in the future. On the other hand, when a relationship does not provide the support expected, a person might experience disappointment and rejection along with feeling even worse about the situation than before. If the person expected to provide support is unable, he or she may experience feelings of disappointment and failure and feel as if a potential source of support has been lost (Burleson, 1990).

Certain relationships may also be expected to provide certain types of social support (for example, some social relationships may provide instrumental support while other closer relationships may provide comfort). The types of issues someone is dealing with may also dictate whose support is sought and whose support is most effective. Once again, when a person is unwilling or unable to provide necessary support when expected, relational and personal problems may arise.

Everyday Communication and the Foundation of Social Support

The foundation of social support is established in everyday communication with others. It is here in everyday communication where people establish their beliefs about the likelihood of receiving support from members of their networks along with expectations surrounding how support will be potentially acquired and fulfilled when needed. Everyday communication in general serves to underscore the existence and continuance of a relationship, thereby establishing the possibility that someone could serve as a resource for support if the occasion arises.

Of course, it is important to recognize that it is not the existence of a relationship itself that guarantees the probability of support but rather it is the communication that transacts that relationship. A person may be considered a friend, but this does not ensure that he or she would be able and willing to provide you with the right kind of support you might seek when dealing with health issues or that the support provided would be accurate and appropriate. That person might be great to go shopping with on the weekend or to discuss sports with but would not be someone you would seek out in times of emotional or health need. On the other hand, another person you consider a friend may be someone you would seek out in times of need, someone you are confident would be willing and able to provide you with competent support.

What this ultimately means is that beyond the instrumental and relational objectives fulfilled through everyday communication, there are inherent supportive functions of everyday communication as well, and every time you speak with someone you are establishing a basis for support in the future. As discussed in Table 10.2, there is a total of six supportive functions of everyday communication: (1) information, (2) perpetuation, (3) detection, (4) ventilation, (5) distraction, and (6) regulation (Barnes & Duck, 1994).

Table 10.2 Supportive Functions of Everyday Communication

Information

Everyday communication with members of a social network enables people to determine who might be a reliable source of support when needed. It also provides insight into the nature of social support. Observing how such support actions as advice giving, resource granting, and others are constructed and evaluated allows people to develop proper frames to better understand and enact social support.

Perpetuation

Perpetuation is concerned not with *determining* potential sources of support but rather with *maintaining* sources of support. Everyday communication serves to sustain relationships and enable their continuance. It helps ensure that sources of support are readily available when necessary.

Detection

Everyday communication provides a baseline from which people may perceive the communication of others. There exist certain patterns of interaction that people come to expect from those in their social networks (such as being talkative or subdued). Purposefully or not, changes in these patterns could be a signal that someone is in need of support.

Ventilation

Everyday communication allows for the ventilation of stress and worries, allowing people to feel better and preventing stress and worry from becoming a major problem. Talking about problems with others can be a productive way of managing concerns and anxieties.

Distraction

Sometimes the best way to deal with a problem is by not dealing with it—at least for a while. Since everyday communication is often viewed as mundane, routine, trivial, and light, it is often a welcome alternative to discussions of major health issues and problems.

Regulation

Everyday communication serves a regulation mechanism in two ways. First, since everyday communication is often viewed as trivial or mundane, social support can be sought and provided with seemingly less consequence when compared with social support sought and provided during moments of deep discussion. Second, everyday communication can also serve as a precursor to deeper discussions. Broaching the topic during the course of everyday communication allows people to evaluate another person's response and determine whether or not a more in-depth discussion or increased disclosure of the issue would be warranted and worthwhile.

Communication Privacy Management

Health is among the personal and relational topics that people may consider private information. Accordingly, even within your social network, there are some people with whom you will disclose such information and some people with whom you will not. Teenagers dealing with sexual issues or pregnancy may turn to their friends before seeking assistance from their family. Further, some information will be shared while other information will remain hidden. A person may reveal an anxiety disorder to a romantic partner but not fully reveal the extent of the problem. As we discussed earlier, issues of disclosure even impact discussions with medical providers, who are not always provided with pertinent information from patients. When it comes to social support, who is provided with such information and the extent to which that information is disclosed become important factors. Disclosing private information of any type is a perilous activity on many levels, and disclosing private health information even more so. For instance, Cline (2003) has noted that people revealing HIV infection often face threats to lifestyle and well-being, identity, and relationships.

Sandra Petronio's (2002) **communication privacy management theory** explains how people create and manage privacy boundaries in their relationships, and her approach can enable you to better understand how health information may or may not be revealed. Since it deals with private information, *self-disclosure* rests at the heart of this theory. As we discussed in Chapter 5, self-disclosure deals with the revelation of private, sensitive, and confidential information. Telling someone standing in front of you that your hair color is brown would be not self-disclosure but self-description. On the other hand, telling someone that you have recently been diagnosed with fibromyalgia would be self-disclosure since that would be private information that could not be discovered just by looking at you.

Private information comes with perceived *ownership*. A person's private information is considered something that is owned and, consequently, something that one can control. This control entails determining who is given access to information and the right to keep some information private. Ownership can be personal or collective. Personally, someone may keep his or her depression hidden from coworkers. Collectively, a family may choose to keep a mother's alcoholism hidden from those outside the family.

Of course, what one person considers private information may not be considered private information by another person. You may know some people who share quite a bit of private information and other people who may reveal very little. These people have erected different *privacy boundaries,* or borders between what is considered private and what is not.

Once erected, these privacy boundaries will vary in their degree of *permeability*. We will discuss criteria for privacy rules below, which often dictate the extent of permeability. However, relationships often determine the actual permeability of these boundaries. Depending on the degree of closeness and relational type, some people will be allowed access to information while other people will be denied access.

Briefly stepping away from health issues (although all can certainly be linked to health issues), consider the following topics: romantic relationships, sexual experiences, traumatic or regrettable events, dangerous behavior, financial issues, everyday experiences. Which of those topics would you generally avoid discussing with the following: a parent, a coworker, a romantic partner, a best friend? The topics avoided most likely varied according to the relationship. When we ask our students to consider these options in class, they generally reveal that a best friend is given the most access to private information. However, the degree of permeability will always vary. A parent may be denied access to certain information when a person is younger but allowed access to that information when a person grows older. Access to information may also change as relationships become more intimate or experience change. For instance, a marriage or commitment proposal may necessitate the revelation of financial issues that were once hidden.

Returning fully to discussions of health, depending on the degree of permeability, some people will be provided with access to that information, and some people will be denied access to that information. Certain information will be revealed while other information will remain concealed from others.

Access to private information demands *coordination* by those involved. People must cooperate to keep boundaries intact and to ensure that information revealed is not misused by the recipient. Whether or not explicitly stated, certain topics may be avoided in a relationship. For instance, a friend may know that a person does not like talking about his or her excessive drinking and avoids that topic. Both people thus work together to keep some private information from view (even when it might be obvious to everyone). Coordination also entails ensuring that when private information is shared, it is not used against the person or spread to others who were not intended to receive the information. When private information is disclosed, there may be an implicit understanding that it is not intended for further transmission. However, private information shared in confidence is sometimes revealed to others, either maliciously or because the recipient did not realize it was not to be shared with others. *Boundary turbulence* occurs when people struggle to coordinate privacy rules and boundaries.

Criteria Impacting Privacy Rules

The question remaining pertains to what factors impact the development of privacy rules and boundaries. Petronio (2002) has offered five key criteria beyond the relational aspects that guide them: (1) culture, (2) gender, (3) motivation, (4) context, and (5) risk-benefit.

Cultures vary according to beliefs in what information should be disclosed and who should or should not be the recipients of that information. Given the sometimes dramatic differences in how cultures view health and illness, this criterion is an especially powerful determinant in deciding whether or not to disclose health information and to whom.

Gender also informs the erection of privacy rules and boundaries but is not as powerful as many people may believe. Analyzing over 200 studies dedicated to gender and self-disclosure, Dindia and Allen (1992) discovered that while women tend to disclose more than men, the differences are extremely small.

Listen In On Your Life

Consider a time when you struggled with determining whether to reveal or conceal private information. What factors did you consider when making your decision? What impact did your decision have on your relationship with the person to whom you revealed or from whom you concealed the information? What impact did your decision have on you personally? Would you have made the same decision given a second chance?

Motivation deals with the need to satisfy the equally strong need to both reveal private information and conceal private information. Revealing and concealing information is a necessary interplay of any relationship and will influence the boundaries and rules guiding privacy. A person may also be motivated to increase the intimacy level of his or her relationship with another person through self-disclosing private information and the possibility that his or her disclosure could compel the other person to reciprocate. Doing so could possibly even develop an additional outlet for social support. However, as we discussed in Chapter 5, disclosure itself does not lead to increased intimacy but rather leads to the meanings people attribute to that disclosure.

Context of events is a strong criterion influencing the disclosure of private information. Receiving devastating health news may result in a need to share that information with others in order to receive social support. Likewise, making decisions about treatment options may necessitate sharing private information with others in order to obtain guidance. Of course, dealing with health-related concerns does not mean that people will automatically begin sharing private information with others. Some people may actually decrease the amount of private information shared when dealing with such concerns.

When deciding whether to reveal or conceal private information, people compare the *risks and benefits* involved. Disclosure can result in many benefits and in many negative consequences. For instance, disclosure can lead to rejection by the other person. A person can potentially incur personal and relational distress as a result of disclosure. There are also identity concerns. For example, someone who generally attempts to create a dominant persona may not wish to express fears and apprehensions to others. Furthermore, when private information is revealed, a degree of privacy and autonomy is lost. We do not want you to think disclosing private information will lead to horrible consequences. However, it is important to recognize the risks and challenges associated with disclosure. Doing so impacts the construction and permeability of privacy boundaries and the rules guiding the revelation or concealment of this valuable personal information.

Media, Technology, and Health

Media and technology are fundamental components of everyday life and greatly influence health communication. As we will discuss in Chapter 12, media and technology are ubiquitous parts of everyday experience—in other words, they are a nearly constant presence. Health issues make up a great deal of media and technology content, including television programs, newspaper and magazine articles, advertisements, and Internet sites. This content influences people's lifestyles, awareness of health issues, understanding of health issues, and how people talk about health both with their social network and with their health provider. In what follows, we will examine the impact of media and technology on health communication. First, we will examine the impact of entertainment and news programming on health communication, including awareness, expectations, and lifestyles choices. Next, we will explore advertising of lifestyle choices through both advertisement and general media content. We will then examine commercials and print advertisements for prescription drugs. Finally, we will explore the use of the Internet and its impact on health communication.

Entertainment Media

Health care has long been a staple of entertainment programming. Since the introduction of television, a vast number of television dramas and comedies have focused on medical professions (Turrow, 1989). These health-related offerings increase an awareness and understanding of medical issues, but they may lead to inaccurate perceptions of health care and unrealistic expectations.

Entertainment programming can increase awareness of medical issues and procedures. Although certain health-related topics are given priority over other topics (Signorielli, 1993), media are nevertheless a rich source for learning about health. Indeed, much of the information people possess about health and wellness has come from media. Even when health information is gained through talking with other people, the original source of the information likely came from media.

However, such programming may lead to inaccurate perceptions and expectations of health. Thus, media may increase people's awareness and understanding of health-related issues, but this awareness and understanding may not be entirely accurate. When it comes to television portrayals of illness, the focus tends to be placed on acute illness that can be cured rather than chronic illness, which often must be endured (Turrow & Coe, 1993). Accordingly, the prevalence of chronic illness tends to be understated and perhaps engenders a sense that many illnesses can be readily cured and that physicians and drug companies have all the answers.

Television programs also tend to portray medical miracles much more often than they occur in physical reality. For instance, survival rates of patients receiving CPR (cardiopulmonary resuscitation) on television were found to be significantly higher than those found in medical literature (Diem, Lantos, & Tulsky, 1996). Such medical miracles are often the result of heroic efforts on the part of medical providers, which also serves to place them in a dominant position during patient-provider interactions. There is a sense that *real* health care providers should be assumed to know all the answers since they seem to know them all on television.

A final element of television programming that may lead to unrealistic perceptions is a focus on the individual nature of illness rather than societal, political, or relational factors (Signorielli, 1993). When someone gets sick on television, rarely is it due to inadequate housing, a lack of nutritious food, environmental conditions, or unavailable preventative care. Psychosocial and relational concerns also tend to be ignored, with emphasis placed primarily on biological symptoms and causes. Once again, this may lead both patients and providers to minimize the psychosocial and relational when evaluating and treating illness.

News and Health Media

Television news programs, newspapers and magazines, and general health programming are also sources of information and misinformation about health. Television news frequently features stories about health-related issues. Entire cable networks such as Discovery Health are dedicated to issues of health and wellness. Furthermore, newspapers and magazines frequently feature health-related articles and information. Health magazines themselves are among the fastest growing categories of magazine. Like entertainment programming, news and health programming can lead to increased awareness and understanding of health-related issues, which can be very beneficial, but this information may also be inaccurate and misleading.

Certain health and illness issues are more frequently addressed in news and health media than others. The number of reports on certain illnesses is often in negative correlation to their actual prevalence (Kline, 2003). Sensationalized health stories such as violent deaths tend to receive more attention than more common deaths such as those as a result of heart disease and cancer (Frost, Frank, & Maibach, 1997). Parrott and Condit (1996) have maintained that newspapers in particular tend to display a protechnology bias and dramatization when reporting on women's health issues. Such reporting reinforces the expectation of medical miracles like that created by entertainment media.

When health and illness issues are included in news and health media, many inaccuracies and contradictions are often reported. A study of breast cancer and mammography reports in print media found that of 113 citations to scientific studies, only 60 of them could actually be traced to the original source. Of these 60 citations, 42 content-based inaccuracies were subsequently discovered (Moyer, Greener, Beauvais, & Salovey, 1995). Also, much of the "advice" presented in newspaper articles pertaining to pregnancy and prenatal development was found to be in conflict (Daniels & Parrott, 1996).

Furthermore, health and illness issues are often framed in ways that may be misleading. James Kinsella (1989) argues that news media tended to avoid coverage of AIDS early on due to viewing it primarily as a disease affecting gay males. When coverage of the epidemic eventually increased, little attention was given to transmission of the disease, which mischaracterized the actual risks for the entire population. Just as certain illnesses will receive more attention than others, the reporting of illnesses will be conducted in a manner that suits the perspective and agenda of media outlets.

Lifestyles

Media have long promoted unrealistic and unhealthy body images and the glorification of drinking, smoking, and sexual promiscuity. As we discuss the promotion and portrayal of lifestyles, we will examine both advertisements and general media content. Keep in mind that media do not directly cause people to develop unhealthy body images, drink, smoke, and engage in sexual promiscuity. Many people would like to blame media for these and other negative behaviors to simplify these problems and to reduce personal responsibility. However, there are many contributing factors to people's lifestyle choices, most notably social networks as discussed earlier and personal responsibility. At the same time, media do influence people's perceptions and understanding of the world, and it is important to recognize the potential influence on lifestyles.

In a case of tragic irony, media seem to engender negative body images while promoting unhealthy nutrition. While the average woman wears a size 12 dress in America, many of the models on television, magazines, and billboards are a size 0. One study discovered that almost all *Playboy* centerfolds and around 75% of fashion models had a body mass index of 17.5 or below, which places them within the American Psychological Association criteria for anorexia nervosa (J. D. Brown & Walsh-Childers, 2002). Many of the advertisements found in magazines are dedicated to weight loss or muscle gain, urging people to succumb to unrealistic and unhealthy ideals. Wright et al. (2008) have noted an increased emphasis on plastic surgery through such television shows as *Nip/Tuck, Extreme Makeover,* and *The Swan.* The latter program clearly connected cosmetic surgery to self-esteem and happiness. After contestants underwent extensive cosmetic surgery, a "beauty contest" was staged in which all but one contestant discovered they were still not attractive enough!

Media may also promote unhealthy nutrition. In spite of media personalities and characters being substantially below weight, they are frequently portrayed eating unhealthy foods and unhealthy proportions (Signorielli, 1993). Television commercials often feature highly caloric foods of little nutritional value rather than healthier food options. The same holds true for many magazine advertisements, especially those aimed at African American audiences. Less than 3% of the advertisements in *Ebony* and *Essence* magazines featured fruits and vegetables while alcoholic beverages were featured in 46% and 62% of the advertisements, respectively (Pratt & Pratt, 1996).

Alcohol consumption also seems to be promoted by media. Alcohol consumption is usually portrayed in a positive manner with few negative or sickening consequences materializing as a result. According to Nancy Signorielli (1998), alcohol is generally consumed by media characters more than any other beverage—twice as much as coffee and tea, 14 times more than soft drinks, and 15 times more than water. As noted above, alcoholic beverages are frequently included in magazine advertisements (Pratt & Pratt, 1996) and are prominently featured in television commercials with little mention of negative consequences that could result from the consumption of alcohol.

Although there have been changes in tobacco use and restrictions when advertising through the years, smoking is still being promoted through media. In the past, many television characters and personalities were seen smoking. For members of young generations, this may seem as difficult to fathom as passengers smoking on an airplane and instructors and students smoking in classrooms—which were once both common occurrences. At the present time, few media characters and personalities smoke, but those who do are often portrayed in a positive manner (Signorielli, 1998). Smoking, especially cigars, is often portrayed in media as sophisticated and worldly, while the negative effects are downplayed or challenged. Alan DeSantis and Susan Morgan (2003) have examined the ways in which the magazine *Cigar Aficionado* connects cigars to the "good life" and provides readers with strategies to combat antismoking sentiments.

Cigarettes have not been advertised on television since the early 1970s, but they are still advertised in magazines and billboards. A particularly interesting study found that between 1987 and 1994, African American women's magazines featured nine articles about tobacco-related cancers and 1,477 advertisements for tobacco products (Hoffman-Goetz, Gerlach, Marino, & Mills, 1997). These advertisements seem to have a tremendous impact on smoking behaviors of both adults and children. Joe Camel, a sunglasses-wearing cartoon mascot used to promote Camel cigarettes and introduced in 1987, was featured in some of the most famous cigarette advertisements. Although the makers of Camel cigarettes denied children were being targeted, a study found that children were able to recognize Joe Camel at similar levels as Mickey Mouse (Fischer, Schwartz, Richards, Goldstein, & Rojas, 1991). Furthermore, Camel's share of illegal cigarette sales to children rose from 0.5% to 32.8%, representing close to $500 million in the early 1990s (DiFranza et al., 1991). Following years of public outcry and government scrutiny, Joe raised a final cigarette with his nicotine-stained hooves and took his last smoke-filled breath in 1997.

Sex is incredibly prevalent in media, but its consequences are rarely included. Sexual promiscuity is portrayed as commonplace and as positive rather than negative in spite of associated problems. As Signorielli (1993) notes, media portrayal of sex "does little to enhance sexual identities or to provide viable and/or adequate information about sex. Contraception is rarely mentioned, yet few characters worry about becoming pregnant. Similarly, sexually transmitted diseases are rarely examined . . ." (p. 60).

Once again, media do not necessarily cause harmful lifestyle choices, but they do influence people's perceptions, understanding, and acceptance of these behaviors. Recognizing the potential influence of media, you will now be better able to understand images people encounter when making choices.

> Joe Camel was not the first cartoon character to promote cigarettes. Winston was an original sponsor of *The Flintstones*, which aired in prime time before making its way to Saturday morning and after-school timeslots (Hilton-Morrow & McMahan, 2003). There were even commercials featuring Fred and Barney enjoying and extolling the virtues of the cigarettes. Somewhat ironically, the other original sponsor was vitamin manufacturer Miles Laboratories. Perhaps you or someone you know took Flintstones Complete vitamins as a child. Now you know why—even though the original omission of a Betty-shaped vitamin remains a mystery.

Advertising Medications

Got a hangnail? Have we got the drug for you! Duck and McMahan Hangnail Fixer-Upper is all you need to rid yourself of fingernail frustration. Warning: May cause dizziness, irregular heartbeat, shortness of breath, weight gain, weight loss, nausea, uncontrollable itching, putrid odors emanating from the body, increased and uncontrollable bowel movements, loss of teeth, impaired vision, paranoia, and death. Put an end to your hangnail worries with Duck and McMahan Hangnail Fixer-Upper, a SAGE Publications product.

Before you look for this product at your local pharmacy, we can reassure you that it does not really exist. However, the wording of this advertisement may sound familiar to you given the dramatic increase in direct-to-consumer advertising of medications. Billions of dollars are spent each year on the promotion of prescription drugs (Rosenthal, Berndt, Donohue, Frank, & Epstein, 2002). In case you are wondering why drug manufacturers would list all of the horrible side effects of their medication, the reason is FDA (Food and Drug Administration) compliance. When the benefits and virtues of a drug are included in an advertisement, the side effects must be included as well. When only the name of a drug is mentioned and you are simply encouraged to ask your doctor about it, the side effects do not have to be included. Ask your doctor about Duck and McMahan Hangnail Fixer-Upper and see what he or she recommends!

Three types of direct-to-consumer advertisements exist. One type of direct-to-consumer advertisement discusses the illness but never mentions the name of the drug. Patients viewing the advertisement may be compelled to seek treatment for the illness, which would increase the chances that a particular drug would be prescribed. A second type of direct-to-consumer advertisement mentions the drug but does not make any claims concerning its effectiveness. As above, these advertisements are not required to

Appearing in 1708, an advertisement for Daffy's Elixir Salutis was the first advertisement for a patent medicine in an American newspaper (Young, 1992).

discuss potentially negative side effects. The third type of direct-to-consumer advertisement is the most common and features the name of the drug along with its uses and benefits. Once again, potential side effects must be included in these types of advertisements (Wilkes, Bell, & Kravitz, 2000).

Beyond fodder for comedians (would-be and actual), direct-to-consumer advertising impacts health communication in a number of ways, with both positive and negative outcomes (Hoek, Gendall, & Calfee 2004; Wilkes et al., 2000). First, it increases patient awareness of illnesses treated by the medications. This increased awareness could be beneficial if a patient recognizes legitimate symptoms from the commercial or advertisement and seeks medical treatment, but it could very well lead to unnecessary treatments and overmedication. Much of the direct-to-consumer advertising includes symptoms that everyone has occasionally.

Second, it increases patient awareness of an available treatment option. Once again, this increased awareness could be beneficial but has potentially negative outcomes. Drug treatments focus on physical elements of illness and tend to overlook psychosocial and other factors contributing to the illness as well as nonmedicinal treatments. Further, such advertising increases the prescription of certain medications even though other medications may be just as if not more effective.

Third, direct-to-consumer advertising increases the likelihood that patients will take a more active role in discussions with providers. An increased awareness may encourage patients to feel more equivalent to providers. However, information gleaned from a brief commercial or print advertisement is usually quite limited, and the potential problems caused by the drug are generally not fully realized. Accordingly, providers must spend time reeducating patients, limiting time available to discuss other issues and concerns about a patient's illness and treatment options.

Health Communication and the Internet

The Internet has had a tremendous impact on health communication in recent years. In what follows, we will examine the use of the Internet when searching for health-related information and the use of the Internet for coping and support.

Searching for Information

Research conducted by the Pew Internet & American Life Project indicates that 80% of Internet users, nearly 113 million adults, have searched for health information online. Those Internet users most likely to seek online health communication are women, college graduates, and younger than 65 years. Not surprisingly, those with home broadband access and more online experience are also more likely to search for health information using the Internet. Underscoring the relational components of health, of those people seeking online health information, 48% searched for information on behalf of someone else, while 36% searched for information connected to their own health questions.

Eight percent searched for information on behalf of themselves and others. Over half of those searching for information noted that their last search impacted how to treat an illness, changed their overall approach to health, and resulted in asking new questions of their providers or seeking additional treatment, respectively. Of those people seeking health information online, 44% indicated their lifestyle perspectives had changed, 39% indicated their coping behaviors had changed, and 35% indicated the information had impacted their decision about seeking medical treatment (Fox, 2006). Gaining information online also helps prepare people for interactions with providers both beneficially (it makes them more aware of what they need to tell the physician) and negatively (it can make them feel that they know as much as the physician does, if not more) (Diaz et al., 2002).

Internet users seeking medical information online search a variety of topics. With 66% of those individuals seeking health information indicating they had searched for this topic, the most sought-after health topic involved a specific disease or medical condition. Medical treatments and procedures came in second; diet, nutrition, vitamins, or supplements came in third; exercise and fitness came in fourth; and prescription or over-the-counter drugs rounded out the top five (Fox, 2005). Although they may search for drug information online, the majority of Internet users are still not buying medication online. Only 4% have purchased drugs online, with 62% believing that purchasing drugs online is less safe than purchasing them at a pharmacy. Regardless of these numbers, 63% indicate they receive spam e-mail advertising sexual health medication (Fox, 2004).

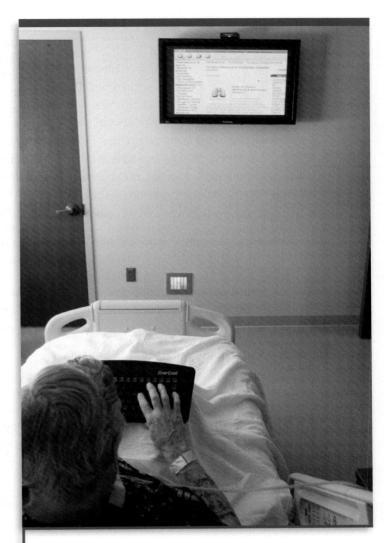

Photo 10.4 In what ways do people use the Internet in connection with health issues? (See page 289.)

Coping and Support

The Internet is also used to cope with health-related concerns and as a way to seek out support. Related to the above use of the Internet, seeking information about health

concerns often enables people to cope with worries and concerns they may have (Brashers, Goldsmith, & Hsieh, 2002). Seeking information enables people to feel empowered or have control in what may seem an uncontrollable situation. As noted above, many of the searches for information occur on behalf of others, underscoring the fact that coping does not just involve personal medical concerns but involves relational concerns as well.

The Internet is also being used as a support mechanism. Many support groups are now available online in such forms as asynchronous discussions (in which interactions do not occur at the same time), as formal synchronous meetings (in which interactions occur at the same time), and as informal chats (VanLear, Sheehan, Withers, & Walker, 2005). Online support groups are beneficial for their convenience and relatively easy access along with providing an outlet for people physically unable to attend formal support group meetings or people who choose not to attend face-to-face meetings for personal reasons.

Online support appears to be very beneficial. Reeves (2000, p. 47) maintains that the Internet promotes empowerment, augments social support, and facilitates helping others. Online support groups have been found to foster empathic communication and trust (VanLear et al., 2005, p. 24) and impact emotional outcomes for their users (Shaw, Hawkins, McTavish, Pingree, & Gustafson, 2006). The number of Internet users seeking online support will likely increase as familiarity with and access to the Internet continue to increase.

Focus Questions Revisited

How do patients and providers generally communicate (relationally), and can it be improved?

Often based on traditional expectations and relational prototypes, patient-provider communication generally transacts relationships that place the patients in a passive role and place the provider in a dominant role. Acknowledging factors such as patient stories, patient expertise, provider expertise, physical and psychosocial connections, emotions, reciprocity, and roles and expectations can improve patient-provider relationships.

What are the benefits of effective patient-provider relationships?

Effective patient-provider relationships can result in increased patient satisfaction, greater adherence to treatments, improved physical and psychological health, and a decrease in malpractice lawsuits.

How do social networks influence lifestyle choices through everyday communication?

The nature of health, its importance, the evaluation of health advice, and lifestyle choices are all transacted in communication with others. For instance, obesity can be influenced by your friends' rhetorical visions about fitness, food, and weight. Further, certain lifestyle behaviors such as smoking and drinking are shared relational activities.

How do people manage their privacy with health-related issues?

The management of privacy can be explained using the communication privacy management theory. People create and manage privacy boundaries (borders between private and nonprivate information) with varying degrees of permeability. Such factors as culture, gender, motivation, context, and risk-benefit influence what information is shared and with whom.

In what ways do different media influence lifestyle, distribute health-related knowledge, and stimulate everyday communication about it?

Entertainment media can increase awareness of medical issues and procedures but may lead to inaccurate perceptions and expectations of health and medical procedures. News and health media tend to focus on certain health and illness issues while neglecting others. Both entertainment media and news and health media also feature medical miracles that may lead to unrealistic expectations. Media in general have long promoted unrealistic and unhealthy body images and the glorification of drinking, smoking, and sexual promiscuity.

How does direct-to-consumer advertising impact health communication?

Direct-to-consumer advertising increases patient awareness of illnesses treated by the medication, increases patient awareness of available treatment options, and increases the likelihood that patients will take a more active role in discussions with providers. The factors have both positive and negative outcomes.

What influence does the Internet have on health communication?

The Internet serves as a source of information about a variety of health issues. It is also used to cope with health-related concerns and as a way to seek out support.

Key Concepts

action-facilitating support   (p. 272)

children-parents (patient-provider relationship)   (p. 263)

communication privacy management theory   (p. 277)

consumers (patient-provider relationship)   (p. 264)

emotional support   (p. 273)

esteem support   (p. 274)

informational support   (p. 272)

instrumental support   (p. 273)

machines and mechanics (patient-provider relationship)   (p. 263)

nurturing support   (p. 272)

partners (patient-provider relationship)   (p. 264)

Questions to Ask Your Friends

- Have a friend describe his or her most recent visit to a doctor's office. What key elements are included in the story? What do these key elements tell you about how your friend perceived the visit?

- Ask your friends to describe the ideal relationship between patients and providers. What do their responses tell you about how people view patient-provider relationships and what people want these relationships to be like?

- Have a friend tell you about a time that he or she received support from someone in his or her social network that was very beneficial. Why would your friend characterize the support as beneficial?

Media Links

- Watch a fictionalized medical comedy or drama on television. How might the portrayal of health and illness influence people's expectations of medical treatment?

- Read a newspaper article about health issues or medical concerns. What support, if any, does the author provide? Given our discussion of evaluating evidence in Chapter 4, do you find the information provided in the article to be credible?

- Search online for information about a health question you may have or can come up with (say, leprosy). What information is available to you? Do you find the information helpful? If so, how might the information be incorporated into your life? If not, how might the information be improved?

Ethical Issues

- Cultures and people differ on the extent to which medical information should remain private. Do you consider your health information to be private? Who should have access to that information? Who should be denied access to that information? If your condition is genetic, should your family be told?

- Some health issues could hinder a person's performance on a particular job. Should employers be provided with relevant health information during the hiring process?

- Should a person posting health information online be held accountable if someone uses the information and is harmed as a result?

Answers to Photo Captions

Photo 10.1 ▪ A machine-mechanic relationship may allow the therapist to quickly narrow in on the patient's concerns, but minimizing patient activities may overlook deeper or even the actual problems. A children-parents relationship may provide comfort to some patients but again may cause a provider to miss fundamental problems. A consumer relationship will increase patient activity and involvement, but sometimes providers know best. A partner relationship will allow patients and providers to work together to solve the problem. It may take additional time and work but is often worth the extra efforts.

Photo 10.2 ▪ Effective patient-provider relationships increase the likelihood that patients will adhere to treatments. Specifically, patient-provider interactions that include clear treatment information, agreement about treatment options, patient participation, and provider empathy and encouragement will increase the likelihood that patients will follow treatment regimens and other lifestyle recommendations.

Photo 10.3 ▪ Benefits received through social support can be linked to specific types of support. Action-facilitating support can provide information to increase knowledge and understanding of health issues as well as assistance with tasks. Nurturing support can enable people to express feelings and have those feelings validated as well as enhance self-image and esteem.

Photo 10.4 ▪ The Internet is used to seek out information regarding health issues, as a coping mechanism, and as a source of support.

Student Study Site

Visit the study site at www.sagepub.com/ciel for e-flashcards, practice quizzes, and other study resources.

References

Balch, G. I. (1998). Exploring perceptions of smoking cessation among high school smokers: Input and feedback from focus groups. *Preventative Medicine, 27,* A55–A63.

Barnes, M. K., & Duck, S. W. (1994). Everyday communicative contexts for social support. In B. R. Burleson, T. L. Albrecht, & I. G. Sarason (Eds.), *Communication of social support: Messages, interactions, relationships, and community* (pp. 175–194). Thousand Oaks, CA: Sage.

Beisecker, A. E., & Beisecker, T. D. (1993). Using metaphors to characterize doctor- patient relationships: Paternalism versus consumerism. *Health Communication, 5,* 41–58.

Brashers, D. E., Goldsmith, D. J., & Hsieh, E. (2002). Information seeing and avoiding in health contexts. *Human Communication Research, 28,* 258–271.

Brown, J. B., Stewart, M., & Ryan, B. L. (2003). Outcomes of patient-provider interaction. In T. L. Thompson, A. M. Doresy, K. I. Miller, & R. Parrott (Eds.), *Handbook of health communication* (pp. 141–161). Mahwah, NJ: Lawrence Erlbaum.

Brown, J. D., & Walsh-Childers, K. (2002). Effects of media in personal and public health. In J. Bryant & D. Zillman (Eds.), *Media effects: Advances in theory and research* (pp. 389–415). Mahwah, NJ: Lawrence Erlbaum.

Burleson, B. R. (1990). Comforting as social support: Relational consequences of supportive behaviors. In S. W. Duck (Ed., with R. C. Silver), *Personal relationships and social support* (pp. 66–82). London: Sage.

Carl, W. J., & Duck S. W. (2004). How to do things with relationships. In P. Kalbfleisch (Ed.), *Communication yearbook* (Vol. 28, pp. 1–35). Thousand Oaks, CA: Sage.

Chesebro, J. W. (1982). Illness as a rhetorical act: A cross-cultural perspective. *Communication Quarterly, 30,* 321–331.

Cline, R. J. W. (2003). Everyday interpersonal communication and health. In T. L. Thompson, A. M. Doresy, K. I. Miller, & R. Parrott (Eds.), *Handbook of health communication* (pp. 285–313). Mahwah, NJ: Lawrence Erlbaum.

Daniels, M. J., & Parrott, R. L. (1996). Prenatal care from the woman's perspective: A thematic analysis of the newspaper media. In R. L. Parrott & C. M. Condit (Eds.), *Evaluating women's health messages: A resource book* (pp. 222–233). Thousand Oaks, CA: Sage.

DeSantis, A. D. (2002). Smoke screen: An ethnographic study of a cigar shop's collective rationalization. *Health Communication, 14,* 167–198.

DeSantis, A. D., & Morgan, S. E. (2003). Sometimes a cigar [magazine] is more than just a cigar [magazine]: Pro-smoking arguments in *Cigar Aficionado,* 1992–2000. *Health Communication, 15,* 457–480.

Diaz, J. A., Griffith, R. A., Ng, J. J., Reinert, S. E., Friedmann, P. D., & Moulton, A. W. (2002). Patients' use of the Internet for medical information. *Journal of General Internal Medicine, 17,* 180–185.

Diem, S. J., Lantos, J. D., & Tulsky, J. A. (1996). Cardiopulmonary resuscitation on television: Miracles and misinformation. *New England Journal of Medicine, 334,* 1578–1582.

DiFranza, J. R., Richards, J. W., Paulman, P. M., Wolf-Gillispie, N., Fletcher, C., Jaffe, R. D., et al. (1991). RJR Nabisco's cartoon camel promotes camel cigarettes to children. *Journal of the American Medical Association, 266,* 3149–3153.

Dindia, K., & Allen, M. (1992). Sex differences in self-disclosure: A meta-analysis. *Psychological Bulletin, 112,* 106–124.

Duck, S. W. (2007). *Human relationships* (4th ed.). London: Sage.

du Pre, A. (2005). *Communicating about health: Current issues and perspectives* (2ⁿᵈ ed.). New York: McGraw-Hill.

Fischer, P. M., Schwartz, M. P., Richards, J. W., Jr., Goldstein, A. O., & Rojas, T. H. (1991). Brand logo recognition by children aged 3 to 6 years: Mickey Mouse and Old Joe Camel. *Journal of the American Medical Association, 266,* 3145–3148.

Fox, S. (2004, October 10). *Prescription drugs online.* Washington, DC: Pew Internet & American Life Project.

Fox, S. (2005, May 17). *Health information online.* Washington, DC: Pew Internet & American Life Project.

Fox, S. (2006, October 29). *Online health search 2006.* Washington, DC: Pew Internet & American Life Project.

Frost, S. K., Frank, E., & Maibach, E. (1997). Relative risk in the news media: A quantification of misrepresentation. *American Journal of Public Health, 87,* 842–845.

Hall, J. A., Irish, J. T., Roter, D. L., Ehrlich, C. M., & Miller, L. H. (1994). Gender in medical encounters: An analysis of physician and patient communication in a primary care setting. *Health Psychology, 13,* 384–392.

Hall, J. A., & Roter, D. L. (1995). Patient gender and communication with physicians: Results of a community-based study. *Women's Health: Research on Gender, Behavior, and Policy, 1,* 77–95.

Hilton-Morrow, W., & McMahan, D. T. (2003). *The Flintstones* to *Futurama*: Networks and primetime animation. In C. A. Stabile & M. Harrison (Eds.), *Prime time animation: Television animation and American culture* (pp. 74–88). London: Routledge.

Hoek, J., Gendall, P., & Calfee, J. (2004). Direct-to-consumer advertising of prescription medicines in the United States and New Zealand: An analysis of regulatory approaches and consumer responses. *International Journal of Advertising, 23,* 197–227.

Hoffman-Goetz, L., Gerlach, K. K., Marino, C., & Mills, S. L. (1997). Cancer coverage and tobacco advertising in African-American women's popular magazines. *Journal of Community Health, 22,* 261–270.

Hooper, E. M., Comstock, L. M., Goodwin, J. M., & Goodwin, J. S. (1982). Patient characteristics that influence physician behavior. *Medical Care, 20,* 630–638.

Kaplan, S. H., Gandek, B., Greenfield, S., Rogers, W., & Ware, J. E. (1995). Patient and visit characteristics related to physicians' participatory decision-making style. *Medical Care, 33,* 1176–1187.

Kinsella, J. (1989). *Covering the plague: AIDS and the American media.* New Brunswick, NJ: Rutgers University Press.

Kline, K. N. (2003). Popular media and health: Images, effects, and institutions. In T. L. Thompson, A. M. Doresy, K. I. Miller, & R. Parrott (Eds.), *Handbook of health communication* (pp. 557–581). Mahwah, NJ: Lawrence Erlbaum.

Lester, G. W., & Smith, S. G. (1993). Listening and talking to patients: A remedy for malpractice suits? *Western Journal of Medicine, 158,* 268–272.

Moyer, A., Greener, S., Beauvais, J., & Salovey, P. (1995). Accuracy in health research reported in the popular press: Breast cancer and mammography. *Health Communication, 7,* 147–161.

Parrott, R. L., & Condit, C. M. (1996). Introduction: Priorities and agendas in communicating about women's health. In R. L. Parrott & C. M. Condit (Eds.), *Evaluating women's health messages: A resource book* (pp. 1–11). Thousand Oaks, CA: Sage.

Parsons, T. (1951). *The social system.* Glencoe, IL: Free Press.

Petronio, S. (2002). *Boundaries of privacy: Dialectics of disclosure.* Albany: State University of New York Press.

Pingree, S., Boberg, E., Patten, C., Offord, K., Gaies, M., Schenskey, A., et al. (2004). Helping adolescents quit smoking: A needs assessment of current and former teen smokers. *Health Communication, 16,* 183–194.

Pratt, C. A., & Pratt, C. B. (1996). Nutrition advertisements in consumer magazines: Health implications for African Americans. *Journal of Black Studies, 26,* 504–523.

Reeves, P. M. (2000). Coping in cyberspace: The impact of Internet use on the ability of HIV-Positive individuals to deal with their illness. *Journal of Health Communication, 5,* 47–59.

Rosenthal, M., Berndt, R., Donohue, J., Frank, R., & Epstein, A. (2002). Promotion of prescription drugs to consumers. *New England Journal of Medicine, 346,* 498–505.

Roter, D. L., & Hall, J. A. (2006). *Doctors talking with patients/Patients talking with doctors* (2nd ed.). Westport, CT: Praeger.

Roter, D. L., Stewart, M., Putnam, S. M., Lipkin, M., Jr., Stiles, W., & Unui, T. S. (1997). Communication patterns of primary care physicians. *Journal of the American Medical Association, 277,* 350–356.

Secklin, P. L. (2001). Multiple fractures in time: Reflections on a car crash. *Journal of Loss and Trauma, 6,* 323-333.

Seibold, D. R., & Thomas, R. W. (1994). Rethinking the role of interpersonal influence processes in alcohol intervention situations. *Journal of Applied Communication Research, 22,* 177–197.

Shaw, B. R., Hawkins, R., McTavish, F., Pingree, S., & Gustafson, D. H. (2006). Effects of insightful disclosure within computer mediated support groups on women with breast cancer. *Health Communication, 19,* 133–142.

Signorielli, N. (1993). *Mass media images and impact on health: A sourcebook.* Westport CT: Greenwood.

Signorielli, N. (1998). Health images on television. In L. D. Jackson (Ed.), *Health communication research: A guide to developments and directions* (pp. 163–179). Westport, CT: Greenwood.

Street, R. L., Jr. (2003). Communication in medical encounters: An ecological perspective. In T. L. Thompson, A. M. Doresy, K. I. Miller, & R. Parrott (Eds.), *Handbook of health communication* (pp. 63–89). Mahwah, NJ: Lawrence Erlbaum.

Trost, M. R., Langen, E. J., & Kellar-Guenther, Y. (1999). Not everyone listens when you "just say no": Drug resistance in relational context. *Journal of Applied Communication Research, 27,* 120–138.

Turrow, J. (1989). *Playing doctor: Television, storytelling, and medical power.* New York: Oxford University Press.

Turrow, J., & Coe, L. (1993). Curing television's ills: The portrayal of health care. In B. C. Thornton & G. L. Kreps (Eds.), *Perspective on health communication* (pp. 130–145). Prospect Heights, IL: Waveland.

VanLear, C. A., Sheehan, M., Withers, L. A., & Walker, R. A. (2005). AA online: The enactment of supportive computer mediated communication. *Western Journal of Communication, 69,* 5–26.

Wilkes, S., Bell, R. A., & Kravitz, R. L. (2000). Direct-to-consumer prescription drug advertising: Trends, impact, and implications. *Health Affairs, 19,* 110–128.

Wright, K. B., Sparks, L., & O'Hair, H. D. (2008). *Health communication in the 21st century.* Malden, MA: Blackwell.

Young, J. H. (1992). *The medical messiahs: A social history of health quackery in twentieth-century America.* Princeton, NJ: Princeton University Press.

11

Society, Culture, and Communication

I n Chapter 5, we introduced you to the odd term *doing* identity and to the concept of performing rather than being or having your identity. In our relational approach to communication, you always connect to other people through performance. The same connection happens for culture. You don't just have or belong to a culture; you *do* and *perform* it. As a communication student, you can learn what other folks don't know: how people *do culture* without even realizing it. In Chapter 5, we noted that the only way you ever meet "society" is through other people you meet, so here too we stress that your exposure to "culture," whether your own or different, is not exposure to an abstraction. You meet culture when you meet people from a culture doing that culture; you do your own culture when you speak to other people. Society's (and culture's) Secret Agents are the very friends you meet, other people on the streets, human beings you observe, and everyone who communicates with you. Not merely an abstract concept, culture is people *doing* and *saying* things in particular ways.

We usually think of a culture or society as basically geographical or ethnic. Significant differences, of course, exist between societies in different parts of the world, and it is true that they speak different languages; dress differently; observe different customs or place emphasis on time, relationships, or context differently; and use different nonverbal systems. These factors are relevant when talking to people from different countries; however, a better way to see the relationship between culture and language is that culture does not create different communication but different communication creates "culture." From this standpoint, doing or speaking different cultures can happen even within the same nation because *communication creates communities and cultures,* and many subgroups of people have identifiable ways of communicating differently from other people in a nation (for example, auctioneers, bikers, and goths). We could, for example, regard the United States as having Northern and Southern cultures,

Hispanic and Irish American cultures, or men's and women's cultures, if we can find different ways such groups communicate. How cultures and communities represent themselves in the media and their history can also perform culture. Communication scholars focus not on outward differences of skin color, dress, or ethnicity alone but on styles of communication—the first aspect of what this chapter teaches you.

A second lesson of the chapter is that you tend to think of *culture* as something *other* people have—unusual clothes, strange foods, or odd customs like wearing French berets or Japanese geisha clothing, doing strange things with coconuts or tulips, and featuring typical buildings (bamboo huts, Roman temples, Chinese pagodas) or landscapes (deserts, swamps, the bush). *You,* however, also have practices that those from another culture might regard as odd. Acting the way you do just seems normal and natural and right. For example, why do most Americans place such high value on punctuality? Many cultures would find arriving at a very specific time quite strange, utterly obsessive, absurd, and valueless, never stopping to smell the roses. In short, it seems just as normal and natural and right to the Japanese, the Italians, the Serbo Croatians, and the Tutsi to act the way they do as it does to you to do what you do.

An important message of this chapter, then, is that you must learn to ask the question "Who says your culture gets it right all the time?" Believing that your culture is the benchmark for all others is called **ethnocentric bias**: Your own cultural way of acting is right and normal, and all other ways of acting are only variants of the only really good way to act (yours!). As communication students, you must learn to be as detached as possible and to treat your own culture as objectively as you treat others—as far as possible. Everyday communication deeply affects who you are, and a lot of it is cultural. It runs so deep within your routine talk and relational performance that you don't recognize it at first, but this chapter shows you how.

Focus Questions

- What is intercultural/cross-cultural communication?
- What differences in communication patterns and styles are connected to national, ethnic, or local differences?
- How is communication organized to reflect cultural beliefs about time, relationships, conflict, or values?
- What features of a person's "culture" are coded in communication?
- What features of "culture" are transacted by communication?
- How do speech communities make up a small-scale culture?

What Does It Mean to Belong to a Culture?

When you identify yourself as a member of a larger group, such as a culture, to what exactly do you belong?

Culture as Geography or Ethnicity

Let's start by looking at "culture" as a structure, place, and national identity that identifies, for example, Australian, Indian, Japanese, Dutch, or Canadian culture. This way of seeing culture focuses on large-scale differences between nations' styles of religion or belief, ideas of national dreams and goals, or preferred ways of acting. These value systems clearly differentiate, say, "East" and "West" and the communicative differences they display. Usually referred to as cross-cultural or intercultural communication, this style of understanding culture has a long history. **Cross-cultural communication** generally compares the communication styles and patterns of people from very different cultural/social structures, such as nation-states, while **intercultural communication** deals with how people from these cultural/social structures speak to one another and what difficulties or differences they encounter, over and above the different languages they speak (Gudykunst & Kim, 1984). For example, Seki, Matsumoto, and Imahori (2002) looked at the differences in intimacy expression in the United States and Japan. They found, contrary to earlier ethnocentrically biased research, that the Japanese tended to think of intimacy with same-sex friends in relation to such expressive concepts as "consideration/love" and "expressiveness" *more* than did the Americans. The Japanese placed *more* stress than the Americans on *directly* verbalizing their feelings when considering intimacy with mother, father, and same-sex best friend. On the other hand, Americans placed more value than the Japanese on *indirectly* verbalizing their feelings for each other.

A whole area of the communication discipline looks at similar communication questions, treating culture as geography based, and very important research has been done on intercultural communication between nations—seen as cultures (East meets West or Japanese meets U.S. business style, for example; Gudykunst, 2000, 2004).

Later in the chapter, you will see that many different social communities exist in a single society. When you start to look at "cultures" as identifiable racial, geographical, or national groups and to search for their identifying features, you rapidly notice some important points: First, multiple "cultures" exist in one society or national group. Second, multiple *social communities* coexist in a single society and talk amongst themselves as part of their conduct of *membership* (for example, bikers, car mechanics, vegetarians, and ballet dancers).

> In Japan, it is impolite to summon someone with the moving-index-finger gesture as is done in the West to mean "Come here." In Japan, you should hold your palm facing downward and move all your fingers at once.

Transacting Culture

A second answer to the opening question of this section ("What does it mean to belong to a culture?"), then, begins to emerge for communication scholars. The defining element is that you belong to a set of people who share meanings and styles of speaking, systems of beliefs, and customs. You live your life in the context of a communicating set of individuals who transact a universe of thought and behavior that makes possible certain ways of treating other people. For example, goths', punks', and emos' use of symbols like hairstyles, body piercing, cutting, and self-harm along with a relevant music genre and vocabulary

Photo 11.1 What is intercultural communication? What do you think the person on the left is communicating as compared to the one on the right? (See page 315.)

transacts their identity and collectively forms the goth, punk, or emo culture. In part, these groups come together and are recognized once they are labeled and some consistency is observed in their behavior and communication. Similarly, rednecks and redneck culture have been identified and caricatured through particular stories and jokes (for example, by Jeff Foxworthy and Larry the Cable Guy). As Nakayama, Martin, and Flores (2002) point out, White adults and especially "white children do not need to attend to the norms and values of minority groups unless they have direct exposure in their neighborhoods and schools. Minority children, however, are exposed to and compare themselves to [the dominant] white cultural norms through television, books, and other media" (p. 103). Whereas White people can act without knowledge or sensitivity to other cultures' customs in a White society, minority groups are rapidly disciplined for failing to observe White cultural norms.

The structure and discipline of society exert their force through communication and impose beliefs on people through collective values—not in an abstract way but rather by everyday communication and being constantly reminded of those

One minority member points out, "My White friends don't mean to offend me, but they do. How am I supposed to feel when they say 'I think of you as just like me.' They never say they think of themselves as just like me. What they mean is that I seem White enough." (Houston & Wood, 1996)

values by your contacts with other people (Society's/culture's Secret Agents). Your conformity with society's and culture's beliefs and practices is constantly and almost invisibly reinforced in the daily talk that happens informally in the interactions with such agents as your friends, your family, your coworkers, and even strangers. From this point of view, "society" is a way of talking about a **coded system of meaning**, not just a structured bureaucratic machine but a set of beliefs, a heritage, and a way of being that is *transacted* in communication.

The nature of culture and your connection to society is conducted through the specific relationships you have with other individuals whom you meet fairly frequently and with whom you interact daily. From this point of view, then, you can think of culture as a meaning system. If you think of culture as a system of norms, rituals, and beliefs, any group with a system of shared meaning is a culture, so even a friendship or a romance could be a "culture." Farmers at a cattle auction barn, athletes, or members of business organizations could all be considered members of a unique culture. Students and instructors could even be considered two interacting and integrated but separate cultural groups.

Viewing societies and cultures as unique meaning systems provides an opportunity to go beyond traditional structural views of cultures. Although these conventional views can still provide a great deal of valuable information, they tend to overlook numerous, distinct meaning systems within larger structure-based labels, such as nation-states. You cannot legitimately maintain that everyone in America or everyone in India communicates the same way, for example.

Just to identify societies and cultures with nations or races, regions, religions, or ethnicity, unthinkingly or incautiously, is clearly a mistake. The present chapter builds from this point in two ways: First, we examine what you can actually learn from structural perspectives of culture and how that can guide your understanding of culture. Second, we explore what you would miss by taking this approach alone.

Once again, we will emphasize how communication *transacts* culture and how styles of communication serve to include or exclude people from cultural

> **W**hat are some key variations between nations that help us identify "cultural differences" between Europe and Asia, East and West, or one country and another?

communities and groups. We can focus on how, in another curious phrase used by communication scholars, people "speak themselves into culture," or how a membership of, or an allegiance to, a particular culture is done in communication.

Structure-Based Cultural Characteristics

Although we have indicated that it is far too simplistic to equate society *exclusively* with nations, you do need to take into account some very broad differences between nations. Since you are all members of a nation or citizens of a country, you necessarily partake of the customs or beliefs of the nation and its communication patterns and styles. Although broad, such distinctions nevertheless seep down to the individual's way of thinking and are structured into the language terms and meaning systems you use in your everyday talk.

Children learn to view the world in the culturally appropriate way as they learn to speak the corresponding language. For example, small children may be rushed from the store by embarrassed parents who have just been asked loudly, "Why is that man so ugly?" and they will certainly be taught our culture's nonverbal rules: "Look at me when I'm talking to you" and "Don't interrupt when someone is talking." "Remember to say thank you" is another way children are taught our culture's rules about respect and politeness as they learn to talk.

During your childhood and introduction to society (socialization), you learned how to behave, interact, and live with other people *as you learned to communicate*, and these styles of behavior readily became more and more automatic—and hence were automatically included in your later communications—as you grew up. If this did not happen, you could not communicate with other people in your society. Thus, learning the language includes learning the habits of your particular culture or society. Built into such habits of communication are not only ways of demonstrating respect, gratitude, and politeness but many other ideas about time, relationships, and context. For example, different nations, societies, and cultures take different views of the fundamental nature of human beings and whether they control their own destiny or are simply guided by karma, like in the television series *My Name Is Earl*. Another difference is based on the representation of human beings in relation to nature, whether as separate beings—created masters of the beasts of the field and the birds of the air—or as one equal part of an interconnected whole guided by a great spirit.

It makes sense to look at the rich list of differences uncovered among societies—their preferences for particular styles of personality or their national character, for example—even if these sometimes amount to stereotypes that you hold about other nations when representing how people there "typically" act. In doing so, however, we examine how these communication styles are learned and reinforced through interactions with friends, families, and others with whom you share a relationship. In all, we examine the following cross-cultural characteristics: (a) context, (b) collectivism/individualism, (c) time, and (d) conflict.

Context

Some societies, known as **high-context societies** (Samovar & Porter, 2004), place a great deal of emphasis on the total environment or context where speech and interaction take place. In a high-context society, spoken words are much less important than the rest of the context—for example, the relationships between the people communicating. It is much more important for people to indicate respect for one another in various verbal and nonverbal ways than it is for them to pay close attention to the exact words spoken. In such countries as China and Iraq, for example, a person's status in society is extremely important, and people tend to rely on their history and their relationship to the speaker or the audience. In Iraq and some African countries, additional importance may be attached to a person's religious or tribal group to assign meanings to conversation. What someone actually says may be much less important to people in such a society than these contextual background features. Such societies greatly emphasize and give major priority to relationships among family members, friends, and associates. Therefore, it is regarded as ethical to favor one's relatives or as fair to give contracts to friends rather than to the highest bidder because sustaining these relationships is important in the culture. The background knowledge that individuals glean from their relationships is always relevant to what goes on in any instance of interpersonal communication. Everything is connected to this background context of relationships and other personal contexts of status, influence, and personal knowledge.

> Do you think the people in an organization's finance department ("the bean counters") could be classified as high-context or low-context thinkers?

By contrast, in a **low-context society**, the message itself means everything, and it is much more important to have a well-structured argument or a well-delivered presentation than it is to be a member of the royal family or a cousin of the person listening. In a low-context society, therefore, people tend to try to separate their relationships from the messages and to focus on the details and the logic. Detailed information must be given to provide the relevant context, and only the information presented that way counts as relevant to the message.

Although this is supposed to be a broad difference between societies as a whole, it is also possible to differentiate high- and low-context cultures within a particular organization. *Low-context culture in an organization* emphasizes commitment to the job, adherence to plans, concern for others' privacy, emphasis on promptness, and attention to detail. *High-context culture in an organization* emphasizes commitment to people, flexibility in plans, relationships, and open friendliness rather than privacy. Accordingly, there is a tendency within a big-picture approach to base promptness on the relationship itself (doing jobs more quickly for favored customers, for example).

Sometimes used to illustrate this disparity within our own society is the difference between the marketing or sales force in a business and the technicians or engineers who actually make the product. For the marketing and salespeople, it is very important to have good relationships with their customers and with a network of other sales personnel. For the technicians who actually make and service products, it is more important that accurate information be conveyed to customers than that the customers be made to feel good interpersonally. This difference of emphasis sometimes leads to conflict between the same organization's marketing and technical personnel because the technical people feel that marketers will make any promise to keep customers happy, and yet the technical producers and manufacturers recognize that they have physical and engineering limits on what they can actually do. The (low-context) manufacturers, therefore, often feel let down by the (high-context) marketers, who will make wild or technically unrealistic promises to get a sale irrespective of whether the engineers can actually fulfill them.

Collectivism/Individualism

An entire chapter of this book is dedicated to identity (Chapter 5), but the very notion of a personal identity is more of a Western than an Eastern idea. Some cultures stress collectivism/togetherness, and some stress individualism/individuality. As traditionally noted (Gudykunst, 2000; Morsbach, 2004), Eastern societies, such as Japan, tend to be **collectivist**—that is, to stress group benefit and the overriding value of working harmoniously rather than individual personal advancement. Emphasizing the importance of your place in a system—portraying you as just a single bee in a beehive—more than your special and unique qualities as an individual, collectivist societies place greater emphasis on the whole group, stressing common concerns and the value of acting not merely for oneself but for the common good. Western societies, such as the United States, are generally characterized as **individualist**, or focusing on the individual person and his or her personal dreams, goals and achievements, and right to make choices.

Through personal relationships and interactions with others, these characteristics are developed and reinforced in their respective cultures. For instance, within a collective society, an individual who acts to achieve personal rather than collective goals would be viewed as simply selfish and disrespectful, and he or she would be brought back into line and made to understand and accept the value of community and collectivity. Such reprimands, especially made by someone with whom a close relationship is shared, would bolster the prevailing view of society. On the other hand, within individualistic societies, personal achievement is lauded and reinforced through conversations with others. For instance, supervisors may talk with employees about the development of personal goals and post "employee of the month" placards to single out individual achievements. Next time you see such a placard, think of it as an example of American cultural ideas being transacted before your very eyes.

Contrarian Challenge

Some research presents a sharp distinction between individualist and collectivist cultures. Can you think of contrary examples in U.S. culture where the individual is required to subordinate personal goals to the collective good? If you can, does this undercut the whole idea of the great distinction between collectivism and individualism?

Time

Different societies' attitudes toward time diverge as well. In the United States, we know the phrase "time is money" and thus assume it is important not to waste people's time. Therefore, showing up on time helps create a positive impression. Of course, for more relaxed social events, such as parties, being "fashionably late" is OK, but if you are late for an interview without a very good reason, you will probably lose the job. Because cultures differ in how they view time, the importance of brisk punctuality, as opposed to that of leisurely relationship building, is also given different weight. This broad difference of emphasis on activity or relationships in time is labeled as a distinction between **monochronic** and **polychronic societies.**

If you think of time as a straight line from beginning to end, you are thinking in terms of monochronic time, where people do one thing at a time or multitask only because it helps them work toward particular goals with tasks in sequence and communications fitting into a particular order. If you think of time as the rotation of the seasons or something more open ended, you are thinking in terms of polychronic time, where independent and unconnected tasks can be done simultaneously. In a polychronic culture, for example, people often carry out multiple conversations with different people at the same time.

Monochronic cultures, such as the United States, the United Kingdom, or Germany, view time as a valuable commodity and punctuality as very important. People with a monochronic view of time will usually arrive at an appointment a few minutes early as a symbol of respect for the person they are meeting. Polychronic cultures do not hold time in the same reverence; these cultures instead have a much more relaxed attitude toward time. Indeed, as Calero (2005) noted, the predominant U.S. notion of time translates as "childishly impatient" to polychronic cultures. This notion of time is true even in relation to food, specifically in, say, Italy or France where two-course meals can take 3 hours. In polychronic societies, "promptness" is not particularly important, and as long as the person shows up sometime during the right day, that will count as doing what was required. Some Mediterranean and Arab countries do not regard as impolite being late to an appointment or taking a very long time to get down to business. Indeed, placing so much emphasis on time that people's relationships are ignored is regarded as rude and pushy; instead, time should be taken to build

Photos 11.2a and b How do monochronic and polychronic cultures differ in their approach to tasks or meals? (See page 315.)

W hen do you think it is OK to answer a cell phone, and why does it matter where you are, what else you are doing, or whether you are in a conversation with someone else already?

the relationships. In the same way, it is important in some countries not to get to the point too quickly, and a lot of time is spent talking about relational issues or other matters before it is polite to bring up a business question. In the United States (especially the business world), after first establishing a pleasant atmosphere with a few brief courtesies, people will more likely bring up the matter of business fairly early in the conversation.

You can imagine that people with one cultural view of time encountering people with the opposite view can sometimes lead to difficulties! You can also probably tell that polychronic views of time are more likely to be connected with high-context societies and monochronic with low-context societies, but actually a large society, such as the United States, clearly contains the full range of styles.

Although we typically think of Western society as mostly monochronic, note that the increased use of cell phones has tended to alter our perception of time, and it is often accepted that people talking face-to-face will break off their conversation to answer an incoming cell phone call. Willingness to respond to such an interruption is more characteristic of polychronic than of monochronic societies. Our sense of time is being modified by technology such that even societies previously regarded as "monochronic" are actually starting to smudge over into polychronic ways of communicating (Duck, 2007). At least both polychrony and monochrony can coexist in a given society (but perhaps to different degrees and extents). Indeed, people often talk about time shifting, which can be done by, for example, videotaping a television program for watching at a later point or listening to a podcast when it suits you rather than when it was originally made.

Finally, note that societies are different in the way they pay attention to the past, the present, and the future. Different cultures tend to assume that the present is influenced either by one's goals and the future or by past events, and fatalism and preordained destiny tend to control to a greater extent what happens in the present. In the United States, many groups place much greater emphasis on future orientation, particularly in the short term, than on their control over present and future events; some Asian societies, on the other hand, pay more attention to the distant future and, like South American and Mediterranean cultures, tend to assume a greater influence of the past on the present and that destiny or karma affects what happens to us in the present moment (Martin & Nakayama, 2007).

B achen and Illouz (1996) referred to love as "an obsessive theme that proliferates in all imaginable cultural sites from fairy tales and popular songs to prime time TV" (p. 298). Do you agree, and what examples can you find? How does your culture represent the ways "love" is supposed to get done?

Looking at *organizational* cultures, you can see that these differences can be important to the proper functioning of business and even to connect to the presentation of speeches. Polychronic and high-context people, much more concerned with keeping everyone happy than with keeping on time, will focus on the fact that relationships can develop well during business discussions as long as people are not kept too clearly or obsessively focused on the task. By contrast, monochronic and low-context people will want to focus on the agenda and not let time get wasted with people telling funny stories that make them feel good about themselves and each other. (Compare Chapter 8 on socioemotional versus task leaders.)

Conflict

Cultures can also be distinguished according to their understanding of and approach to **conflict**, which involves real or perceived incompatibilities of processes, understandings, and viewpoints between people. Communication scholars Judith Martin and Thomas Nakayama (2007)—drawing from the work of Augsburger (1992)—differentiate two cultural approaches to conflict: *conflict as opportunity* and *conflict as destructive* (pp. 404–413).

    Conflict-as-opportunity cultures tend to be individualist, such as the United States. This approach to conflict is based on the four assumptions listed in Table 11.1 (Martin & Nakayama, 2007, p. 404).

Table 11.1 The Four Assumptions of Conflict-as-Opportunity Cultures

1.	Conflict is a normal, useful process.
2.	All issues are subject to change through negotiation.
3.	Direct confrontation and conciliation are valued.
4.	Conflict is a necessary renegotiation of an implied contract—a redistribution of opportunity, a release of tensions, and a renewal of relationships.

Source: Martin & Nakayama, 2007, p. 404.

    Members of these cultures view conflict as a normal and useful process, an inherent part of everyday life. Naturally experienced when interacting with people, conflict will lead, if handled constructively, to the enhancement of personal and relational life. This cultural view of conflict also understands all issues as subject to change, meaning that all personal or relational processes, goals, or outcomes can be altered. When a person wants to make changes in his or her relationships or personal life, he or she is expected to fully express and work with others to achieve these desires. Finally, members of these cultures view conflict as not only normal and useful but also a necessary requirement for renewing relationships and for achieving personal goals and overall well-being.

    Stressing group and relational harmony above individual needs and desires, **conflict-as-destructive cultures** tend to be collectivist or community-oriented such as many Asian cultures. Religious groups, such as Amish and Quakers, also view conflict as destructive. David's dad attended Quaker meetings as a child and adhered to pacifist ideals even on the playground. He has told stories of other children hitting him, knowing he would not fight back. As instructed in the Bible, he would literally turn the other cheek, and the other children would promptly hit that cheek as well. Nevertheless, David's dad remained steadfast in his culturally based belief in the destructive nature of conflict. As with conflict-as-opportunity cultures, four assumptions guide this approach to conflict, as listed in Table 11.2 (Martin & Nakayama, 2007, p. 406).

Table 11.2 The Four Assumptions of Conflict-as-Destructive Cultures

1.	Conflict is a destructive disturbance of the peace.
2.	The social system should not be adjusted to meet the needs of members; rather, members should adapt to established values.
3.	Confrontations are destructive and ineffective.
4.	Disputants should be disciplined.

Source: Martin & Nakayama, 2007, p. 406.

Contrary to conflict-as-opportunity cultures, this cultural approach does not view conflict as a natural part of everyday experience but rather as unnecessary, detrimental, and to be avoided. Also contrary to conflict-as-opportunity cultures and reflective of collectivist cultures in general, members of conflict-as-destructive cultures do not view individual needs and desires as more important than group needs and established norms. Furthermore, rather than valuing direct confrontation, members consider confrontations futile and harmful to relationships and the group as a whole. Accordingly, those who engage in confrontation should be disciplined to discourage such destructive behaviors since they undo relationships and solidarity.

Of course, conflict occurs in all relationships and among all groups, even those viewing conflict as destructive. However, the management of conflict will also differ among cultural groups. When conflict occurs, people generally engage in one of five styles of conflict management: (1) dominating, (2) integrating, (3) compromising, (4) obliging, and (5) avoiding (Rahim, 1983; Ting-Toomey, 2004).

Dominating

Dominating styles involve forcing one's will on another to satisfy individual desires regardless of negative relational consequences. For example, you and a friend decide to order a pizza, and as you call in the order, your friend mentions a desire for pepperoni. You would rather have sausage and reply, "Too bad. I'm making the call, and we are having sausage."

Integrating

Integrating styles necessitate a great deal of open discussion about the conflict at hand to reach a solution that completely satisfies everyone involved. You and your friend differ on what pizza topping you would like, so you both openly discuss your positions and the options available until you reach a solution that fulfills both of your desires— perhaps getting both toppings or half-sausage and half-pepperoni.

Compromising

Compromising styles are often confused with integrating styles because a solution is reached following discussion of the conflict. However, making a compromise demands that everyone must give something up to reach the solution, and, as a result, people never feel fully satisfied. Returning to the pizza quagmire, you and your friend discuss the conflict and decide to get mushrooms instead of sausage or pepperoni.

Obliging

Obliging styles of conflict management involve giving up one's position to satisfy another's. This style generally emphasizes areas of agreement and deemphasizes areas of disagreement. Using this style of conflict management, as you and your friend discuss what topping to include on your pizza, you probably mention that the important thing is you both want pizza and then agree to order pepperoni instead of sausage.

Avoiding

Finally, avoiding styles of conflict is just that: People avoid the conflict entirely either by failing to acknowledge its existence or by withdrawing from a situation when it arises. So, your friend expresses a desire for pepperoni on that pizza, and even though you really want sausage, you indicate that pepperoni is fine and place the order.

Defining and Performing Membership of a Culture

The preceding section emphasized a set of broad and general differences resulting from seeing culture in structural or geographical terms. Indeed, a lot of *who* you are depends on *where* you are, or at least on where you come *from*, as well as on the groups you belong to and how they expect people to behave. You are not alone: You *belong* and don't always have a choice. Simply being American both constrains and enables certain behaviors and styles. You belong to many groups, some small (groups of friends or neighbors), some large (your citizenship or your ethnic group), some central to your life (family, friends), and some probably peripheral (your tax group, your shoe size). Somewhere in there, somewhere in your sense of yourself, however, is the culture (are the cultures) that you see as yours. However you define the term *culture*, different cultures do things differently. A sense of belonging to a culture brings with it a sense of how to behave, norms of acting, and a host of relational formats. These norms are transacted in communication as respect for elders, permitted degrees of openness and warmth, nonverbal style, degree of deference shown to other people in interaction, and the appropriateness of labels for people.

Identifying Your Culture

These contexts and backgrounds go beyond your immediate networks to a sense of belonging to a larger set of people who include you in their membership. For example, you might start off seeing yourself as a member of a national group (American, English, Italian) or an ethnicity (Caucasian, Pacific Rim, Hispanic/Latino, African). In fact, if you ask people to identify themselves (and when the police issue their "most wanted" descriptions), one of the first references they make is to race or nationality. Certainly geographical locations, nations, races, and religions are important factors in talking about society and cultural identity, but the simple connection or identification of a nationality with a culture is a problem for many reasons. You will find that people use the term *culture* to mean different things in different contexts; a "family," for example, can be seen as a mere family-tree

Ask yourself whether love is crafted outside or inside marriage. Consider whether and in what ways "arranged marriages" are necessarily nonlove marriages. Make a case for the *folly* of relying on the whims and chances of personal emotional experiences of romance rather than on the wise and considered choices of experienced elders as a basis for choosing your marriage partner. In other words, make the case *against* how Western culture typically does romance, courtship, and marriage.

structure, including specific members, or as a set of people—those you feel closest to within the family structure—whose communication patterns transact a sense of membership, community, and connection (see Chapter 7). However, you do not have to think for very long before you start to question whether a nation, an ethnicity, or a religion is the same as a society or a culture. You can tell, for example, that "American" is a very broad category that includes two hemispheres and a large mixture of different cultural groupings, so when someone sports a bumper sticker saying, "Proud to be an American," neither the connections being claimed nor the particular subset of beliefs and characteristics of the larger category being asserted is immediately obvious—at least not from the words alone, though a flag, usually on the sticker, too, gives a fairly substantial hint.

Identifying society and culture in such ways makes the simple mistake of assuming, for example, that everybody from the same nation or country has the same set of assumptions and beliefs. Yet, most countries have regions regarded as different and distinctive (the South, the Midwest, Yorkshire, "the valley"). The belief systems in these small and diverse groups are often recognized as somewhat different and distinct from those within the larger society or nation. Also really obvious in our experience is that a large group like "Americans" can be broken down into smaller groups ("Northern Americans" and "Southern Americans") containing smaller sets of both nations and societies, such as Irish Americans, Southerners, Sioux, African Americans, Iowans, or Republicans. In the same way, such very large nations as the United States are home to citizens originating from all over the world—North Africa, Europe, South America, Asia, the Pacific Rim. So which culture represents the "United States"?

The previous discussion concerning cultural characteristics treated culture very broadly and categorically: If you are a "Westerner," you will behave and communicate in the Western way. Although such broad-brush ideas are very helpful in many circumstances, especially when traveling to other countries, dealing with international relationships, or discussing the clash of cultures and/or diversity, it is important to go beyond the broad ideas and add some finer detail. Consider how your membership in such large categories or broad groups will affect your communication. Only then can you go on to see how communication serves to perform membership of smaller cultures, groups, and networks.

You Belong Without Knowing It

You were born into a society, a nationality, and a heritage; you live some*where;* you follow certain rules that exist in that society (for example, you drive either on the right or on the left); you speak a particular language or set of languages that prevail there; you eat particular foods and can identify "ethnic cuisines" of other nations. That much we can take for granted. The very idea of "homeland security" implies the existence of other, different places from which your homeland needs protection. We often talk in broad terms about "society" and recognize that many large societies, such as the United States, contain a rich diversity of cultures, but from a communication point of view, we must give these concepts a deeper look. How does it all *work?*

> Think carefully about a story we heard where a White professor was told by a student, "You are the only White man I trust." Is it possible to be White and not also be a racist at some level? Does people's very skin communicate the likelihood of certain attitudes, beliefs, and communication styles?

Several cultures may exist within any country, and when talking about such entities, **co-cultures**, or smaller groups of culture within a larger cultural mass (Houston & Wood, 1996), commonly come up in conversation. From the communication studies point of view, however, it is much more interesting to look at how "culture" gets *done,* not only focusing on the physical boundaries that surround it but also exploring how psychological and communicative boundaries get drawn by the habits and practices of communication that occur.

How does society or culture get transacted in the sense introduced in Chapter 1? What other subtleties about "culture" and "society" allow us to identify them in terms of their communication patterns instead of just connecting to or defining them in terms of such features as national dress, flags, or geography? It is important to recognize that, within any given nation or society, many cultures amount to different *relational* groups that transact their business in communicative patterns, codes, and styles.

You are already familiar with the idea that you belong to larger society and to a national group and that you carry out your daily life differently from members of other societies and national groups. Looking at how this is done by everyday communication, however, we examine the larger implications that follow from the basic idea that communication *does* culture.

Of course, you spend your life talking in small- and medium-sized groups. You are born into a family, you go to school (a group of pupils), you have a number of friends and acquaintances, and you work with colleagues who may make up small decision-making groups. You also belong, however, to a larger interacting society that works with you to reinforce norms of behavior and ways of understanding (as well as cooking). We could look at such groups as *communities* that create a *culture* in the sense of sets of beliefs—an organizational culture, the youth culture, the gay community, the student culture, the local community. Some scholars (Philipsen, 1975, 1997) talk about "speech communities" as cultures and define membership in a culture in terms of speaking patterns and styles that reinforce that particular "culture" and make us belong communicatively. We look at this idea next.

You *Do* It Without Knowing It

Your talk indicates or displays your cultural membership. Your culture is written in your voice not only in the language you speak but also in the thoughts you express and the assumptions you make. Obviously, talk accomplishes this in the straightforward sense: French men and women speak French. But they also speak "*being* French." Your two authors, Steve and David, are different. Steve is English; David is American. When

If you do not believe that such speech communities exist and are important, go home for the vacation and try speaking to your parents or off-campus friends as if they are in your student speech community.

we travel in the United States, people say to Steve, "I love your accent," but when we travel in the United Kingdom, they say it to David. So which of us has an accent? No one in either place ever says with marvel to us, "You speak good English," though when we go to France, people might say, "You speak good French" (if we did).

No one says, "I love your man talk" or "You speak good man talk," but a "man's talk" actually exists. Communication scholar Gerry Philipsen (1975) explored the talk in Teamsterville, a pseudonym for a working-class community in Chicago showing a "man's communication style" that occasionally prefers action to words and is based on talking only when power is equal or symmetrical. In this community, a man demonstrates power by punching someone rather than arguing about a problem because speech is regarded as an inappropriate and ineffective way of communicating in situations when demonstrating power. For example, if a man was insulted by a stranger, the culturally appropriate way to deal with the insult would be to inflict physical damage rather than discuss the issue. In Teamsterville, speech in such a situation would be characterized as "homosexual" and weak. On the other hand, when a man in Teamsterville is among friends, his speech is permitted to establish his manliness. If a man's friend made a derogatory remark about the man's girlfriend, the man would either take the remark as a tease or simply tell the friend not to say such things, and violence would not result as it would in the case of strangers saying the same thing. However, in a male offenders' prison, Julia Wood (2004) uncovered a special kind of talk, based on physical strength and the assumed right to control other people, in spouse abusers.

So can we communicate other things as well as "manhood"? Do we talk our age? Our sex? Our historical time? When Lincoln gave the Gettysburg Address, did anyone congratulate him for "speaking good 1860s"? If he was trying to speak "being a good leader," would it have mattered if he had a strong speech impediment and a high, squeaky voice? Perhaps, though, there really is a way to speak "1860s" (or "1960s," come to think of it—watch an *Austin Powers* movie and note the emphasis on outdated styles of talk and thought).

In the United Kingdom, people can tell that Steve is from "the West country," and in the United States, they know David is *not* from "the South." All of them can tell, even on the phone, that we are not ethnic Dutch or Indonesian. They also know we are not women or 5 years old.

Every time we speak, then, other people, whether astute and finely tuned observers or not, know something about our culture. When we see someone wearing "cultural clothes," we assume difference, but we actually wear our culture in our talk and behavior, too. For example, when Steve first met a new colleague (an Eastern European), the conversation lasted only briefly before the colleague said, "You're not American." Steve said, "Oh, the old accent gives me away yet again!" but the colleague said, "No, actually. I'm not a native English speaker, and I can't tell the difference between English and American accents. It was something in your *style* that announced you as 'other.'" So how do we *do* our culture in a way that people can tell we are not at home?

To explore this further, we need to introduce some ideas about the differences people notice in cultures and then see how they show up in talk. Finally, we look at how people do "culture" in many other ways that show the **speech communities** to which we belong and how we even communicate the culture of our times. Watch any movie or TV series from the 1950s, for example, and you will see people treating and talking to each other differently than they do now. Look at how women and men are portrayed in 1950s films, and try not to be amazed.

Communication and Culture

We can summarize what you've learned so far in this chapter in the following ways:

1. If culture is identified with nationality or ethnicity, it becomes too crude a concept.

2. Many cultures can exist within a particular society.

3. How "culture" is used in this chapter represents a specific context for *transacting* beliefs and styles and thus makes "culture" smaller.

Some of these styles will come from a culture's actions, such as its sense of national identity, wearing national costume, carrying out cultural rituals and upholding cultural values, or holding to a particular view, based on individuality or collective membership, of how a self-concept should be seen. Whether you view culture as structural or transacted, these styles of thought will show up in the talk that gets done in the society, culture, or group.

Culture is also transacted by being embedded in networks of others, whose ways of behaving we must recognize and respect in our own individual actions. In part, this explanation recognizes cultures as systems of beliefs but also as dynamic and multiplex—that is, made up of many smaller and interacting groups that connect to one another as speech communities that share nonverbal communication as well as talk, rituals, routines, and beliefs. All of these forms of communication, however, reflect the bigger belief system that makes a culture what it is: Nonverbal styles reflect relationships between people and their different statuses, power, and relationships to other speakers, and rituals are ways of reinforcing certain societal beliefs (for example, Thanksgiving dinner in U.S. society reinforces the importance of family connection).

How Do You Do Culture in Talk?

One characteristic of any culture is what it takes for granted. For example, in a particular culture, certain topics can be talked about and certain ideas are taken for granted, even during persuasion. Kristine Fitch (2003) has written about these taken-for-granted assumptions as "cultural persuadables." Some such assumptions, shared with a particular audience, do not ever need to be stated explicitly, such as the Japanese emphasis on collectivism and community, which makes it unnecessary to say anything directly about community. People just express their arguments in terms of collective goals, and any mention of personal effort comes with the implication that any personal goal is specifically intended to promote community, not the individual. When a Japanese person speaks with individual emphasis on a particular goal, such as wanting to learn something new, then, his or her hope to profit the community by such knowledge is implicit. Therefore, **cultural persuadables** are certain topics that people in a society never bother to persuade anyone else about because their arguments are always raised against a background of common understanding and shared beliefs. In this way, then, various **speech codes**, or a culture's verbalizations of meaning and symbols, tend to have built into them certain ways of understanding the world that guide the particular talk patterns people use in conversation with one another. Always built into every act of persuasion in a particular culture is the set of assumptions that the culture takes for granted.

In addition to his identification of the Code of Honor carried out by the men of Teamsterville as they "do manliness," Philipsen (1997) identified a Code of Dignity, which he identified as characteristic of the "Nacirema" (*American* spelled backward). This code of speech emphasizes relationships, work, communication, and individual/self and is quite easily discovered on TV talk shows and in the broader context of speech in large parts of America. The work by Philipsen and others (e.g., Fitch, 1998) helps us see that speech codes create membership within a given culture. If you do not know how to perform membership of a particular community, you are excluded from it. Your membership in a culture depends on your knowledge of the relevant speech codes not limited to the medical or electronic geek jargon we used as examples in Chapter 2. The important point of this chapter is that *membership of a whole culture* can be represented in and restricted by one's knowledge of speech codes.

A culture works not only as hypertext (the taken-for-granted) but also as a negative hypertext that assumes topics no one needs to speak out loud because everyone already assumes them. In this sense, culture is a way of thought and a set of assumptions taken for granted by everyone who belongs to it; such **culture as code** is what we have in mind when we talk about Society's Secret Agents and how we do culture in talk and relationships—the main theme of this book.

Elaborated and Restricted Codes

Another level of such codes was identified by Basil Bernstein (1971), who detected two different codes in English (restricted code, elaborated code) and described some characteristics of these codes and their users. Restricted code emphasizes authority, for example ("Because I say so!"); elaborated code emphasizes the reasoning behind a command ("Because you must not be unkind to other people"). In a given society, Bernstein argued, everyone has access to a basic **restricted code** in which certain community/cultural orientations are taken for granted in the way that other topics, like cultural persuadables, are taken for granted in relationships and communication. Certain assumptions get made as invisible and unmarked elements of speech—and how audiences understand talk buys into these assumptions, some examples of which have already been discussed, in this chapter, in terms of time, context, and relationships and, in other chapters, in connection with other variables. Bernstein noted that the restricted code emphasizes community relationships, values, and ideas (worlds of meaning) and thus pays more attention to the status of the other person and to collective values, always a part of the taken-for-granted, unspoken background of any communication using this code.

Some people in a culture, Bernstein claimed, have access primarily and almost exclusively to this code and hence tend to emphasize authority, the generality of rules across all situations, and orientation to an external reality that guides behavior ("Rules are rules," "Don't think about it; just do it," "Do it because it's what's right," or "It's the way we do things around here"). In its own way, then, a restricted code emphasizes a conservative and rule-based rather than an individual and conscience-based way of acting in the world. These assumptions are built into how communication happens when this code is used.

By contrast, an **elaborated code** uses speech and language more as a way for people to differentiate their unique personalities and ideas and to express "discrete intent"—that is, their own individuality, purposes, attitudes, and beliefs—than as a way to reinforce collectivity or commonality of outlook. Bernstein stressed that people who primarily use either code, but particularly those using the restricted code, interpret speech from a user of the other code through their own. That is, restricted-code users will treat elaborated-code users as if they are exercising authority and encouraging conformity; elaborated-code users will treat restricted-code users as if they are expressing their own personality. Those who have access

Photo 11.3 How do different speech communities and styles of communication make up cultural differences within a culture? What differences might exist between the cultures of these two men? (See page 315.)

to or have been taught to use the elaborated code, in addition to the commonly available restricted code, tend to emphasize individual conscience, make fewer appeals to authority, and express the importance of individuals making up their own minds about issues in the light of particular circumstances. These styles of thinking come out in the communications people use, and difficulty may occur when one kind of user speaks to someone who uses the other code—just as when someone from a monochronic culture speaks to someone from a polychronic culture.

Bernstein was, at the time, widely perceived as classist because he associated lower educational achievement with use of a restricted code found more frequently in working-class children. However, communication scholar Hank Nicholson (2006) has noted the idea that everyone in a culture has access to a restricted code while only some members of the culture additionally have access to an elaborated code suggests that ability to use elaborated code is a developmental issue: Some learn it; some don't. This point is important for our purposes in this chapter because we have already noted that people learn during childhood not only language but how to be members of their society and therefore the society-appropriate behavioral, emotional, and relational rules.

As an educated member of society for the remainder of your life, you will be confronted with decisions and dilemmas that are based on cultural differences and that require you to understand cultural perspectives. You will need to think carefully and critically about the issue. How will you go about ensuring that you avoid ethnocentric bias and apply a nonjudgmental approach to different ways of performing culture?

As Nicholson (2006) points out, a complete rule contains three parts: an *identifiable situation* (this tells a person when the rule is applicable), a *prescription* (or *proscription)* that indicates whether the rule requires that some behavior should happen (prescription) or be forbidden (proscription), and a *reason for its employment* (indicating the value of the behavior in a particular situation). When a family uses restricted code, it typically omits the *reason* and in some cases the *situation* and therefore focuses only on the prescription/proscription element of a rule. This approach will likely result in children coming to see rules as universals because the specific situations that limit or bound their use have not been identified. This view of rules, in turn, likely means that a child thinks of particular behavior as having less to do with reasoning for oneself than with emotion and the fear of punishment from either the rule teacher or an agent of society (such as the police). In this case, the child learns not to think about subtle differences between situations and events but rather to pay more attention to the authority figure or to the authority dynamics and informal power structure that surround the communication. A community that uses restricted code, therefore, creates a culture where individuals tend to be dogmatic, linguistically powerless, authoritarian, and status oriented. This, in turn, Nicholson asserts, might lead to marginal and perhaps antagonistic relationships with certain cultural and social institutions and their representatives (e.g., school, work), so the individual becomes something of an outsider, suspicious of the power dynamics in the institution, and does not feel commitment to it. Another possibility is that a person using restricted code feels best operating in a culture of rigidly defined roles (e.g., gender roles, where "men are men and women are women") that depend less on the use of verbal skills and more on other ways of communicating and exerting power or control. Certainly consistent with the findings of both Philipsen (1975) and Wood (2004) discussed earlier, these ideas put culture in terms of specific language styles learned in childhood.

Once more, then, we end up back at the theme of the book: Relationships with authority figures, agents of society or culture, or other people are fundamentally transacted in the communication that occurs, and communication transacts one's understanding of and membership in a culture.

Relationships as Culture

This chapter has basically continued our consideration of identity—particularly cultural identity—and indicated that most contact with culture occurs dyadically in that our contacts with such abstract concepts as "society" and "culture" are usually with specific individuals. We have also noted that *otherness* is an essentially relational term recognizing whether and how people belong to or are excluded from membership. Society's Secret Agents work through our daily talk, and the people in our personal networks represent society, which transmits its beliefs, customs, and ideas through dyadic interaction to other people over and above the main media forces that have the same effect more broadly. Of course, people pick up a lot of these ideas in childhood where they are provided with strong and mostly automatic filters for their perceptions so they notice and focus on certain items but not others (Bernstein, 1971). For example, you may attend strongly to age/respect issues, personal achievement, or consensus and happiness in the group as a whole, but you do this more or less automatically. Of course, however, as Nicholson (2006) indicated, "childhood" is not an abstract concept but involves talking to and being influenced by parents, siblings, school peers, teachers, the media, and what we are taught about how "our society" operates. In short, childhood is when we absorb the beliefs of those around us, when we learn to do and value what they do and value. You may value assertiveness, or you may prefer reflective contemplation and subservience to authority. In this way, you *do* your culture by using the filters you learned in your early years without even realizing it, rather like wearing glasses. The lenses, for example, affect what you see to make perception more effective. Most of the time, people are not aware of wearing glasses because of their lenses' "transparency," but nevertheless, they affect what the wearer sees and how he sees it. So too with culture: Though it shapes and to some extent distorts your perceptions and your focus, you are largely unaware of culture and how it affects you.

Focus Questions Revisited

What is intercultural/cross-cultural communication?

Cross-cultural communication involves the comparison of communication behaviors in different cultures usually identified through geographical or ethnic means. Intercultural communication involves the study of communication between two different cultures, again usually identified structurally through geographical or ethnic means. These two forms of communicative scholarship have a very long history, and whole books have been devoted to them (e.g., Gudykunst, 2004; Martin & Nakayama, 2007).

What differences in communication patterns and styles are connected to national, ethnic, or local differences?

Cultures identified at the national, ethnic, or local level demonstrate many communication differences in pattern style and understanding of both verbal and nonverbal communication. At the obvious level, these involve speaking different languages or using different dialects, but we have identified several different ways such communicative differences represent different belief systems about the world. We discussed the goals represented in particular nations' myths and stories.

How is communication organized to reflect cultural beliefs about time, relationships, conflict, or values?

Some cultures focus on individual responsibility; some focus on collective responsibility. Some cultures value maintaining relationships over completing specific tasks; some value completing specific tasks over maintaining relationships. Some cultures tend to focus on accomplishing something within a given time; some take a leisurely approach that allows development of relationships and the demonstration of respect. We identified different approaches to and beliefs about conflict, whether as opportunity or as a destructive influence, and we reported research showing five different ways to manage conflict.

What features of a person's "culture" are coded in communication?
A person's identity is very closely tied to the nature of culture through the speech codes he or she adopts under various sets of circumstances. Speech codes are ways of conveying underlying systems of values with which you feel an affinity and which are shared by a group of other people with whom you claim membership.

What features of "culture" are transacted by communication?
All features of culture are transacted by communication, some at the level of speech codes and some at the level of organized rituals discussed in previous chapters.

How do speech communities make up a small-scale culture?
Speech communities share particular speech codes, which makes them members of the same culture. A couple or dyad may share a unique speech code that differentiates them from everyone else (personal idiom), but in this chapter, we have written more broadly about larger groups that share speech codes. In all cases, the culture is identified from the speech codes the communities employ.

Key Concepts

co-culture   (p. 307)
coded system of meaning   (p. 297)
collectivist   (p. 300)
conflict   (p. 303)
conflict-as-destructive
  cultures   (p. 303)
conflict-as-opportunity
  cultures   (p. 303)
cross-cultural
  communication   (p. 295)
cultural persuadables   (p. 310)
culture as code   (p. 310)

elaborated code   (p. 311)
ethnocentric bias   (p. 294)
high-context society   (p. 298)
individualist   (p. 300)
intercultural
  communication   (p. 295)
low-context society   (p. 299)
monochronic society   (p. 301)
polychronic society   (p. 301)
restricted code   (p. 310)
speech codes   (p. 309)
speech communities   (p. 309)

Questions to Ask Your Friends

- Have your friends tell you about their favorite children's stories, and then discuss the themes demonstrated by those stories and connect them to the cultural ideals.

- How many of your friends are from different cultures? Engage them in conversation about how they carry out annual holiday traditions.

- Do your friends speak in restricted or elaborated codes?

Media Links

- Select and analyze a movie with intercultural themes to show how individuals from different cultures build relationships and develop understanding. Describe how culturally relevant concepts and ideas from this chapter are shown in the movie's characters, plot, setting, script, and acting styles. Some possible examples are *Bend It Like Beckham; My Big Fat Greek Wedding; Amelie; Like Water for Chocolate; In Whose Honor?; Mississippi Masala; Whale Rider; The Fast Runner;* and *Crouching Tiger, Hidden Dragon.*

- How are different cultures represented on television and in movies? Compare current with 30- or 40-year-old shows and movies. What differences do you see, over time? Try comparing some classic Westerns against, for example, *Dances With Wolves.*

- Watch the news on TV or read newspaper stories about other cultures, and show how they are represented. Can you now identify any ethnocentric bias in these reports?

Ethical Issues

- Differences or similarities: Are we all one, all different, or a bit of both?

- Evaluate a problem currently being discussed in this society that grows out of cultural dynamics. Explore at least two possible solutions to, for example, interracial adoption, integration, or racial/ethnic/religious profiling.

- What is the cultural acceptance of routine assumptions and behaviors of everyday life? What are your routine assumptions and behaviors?

Answers to Photo Captions

Photo 11.1 ▪ Intercultural communication is communicating between members of different cultural backgrounds and countries, but the chapter tells us that it also happens *within* a culture. In Photo 11.1, you probably can identify some of the signals that are communicated by the man on the right. He seems relaxed, informal, confident, and in charge. What about the man on the left? What is signified by his headdress, his leg bracelet, and the object he is carrying under his arm? These might be important marks of rank and status in his society.

Photo 11.2a and b ▪ A polychronic society places more emphasis on the relationships between people than on the task, and a monochronic society places emphasis on speed and punctuality plus the rapid and efficient accomplishment of tasks.

Photo 11.3 ▪ Both men appear to be in the same office building outside the elevators and heading to work, yet one is dressed very formally and carries a briefcase, while the other is informally dressed and carries loose papers while texting. Each of them apparently adheres to a different set of standards for dress and the representation of "professionalism in business," and it is likely that they speak differently about these issues.

Student Study Site

Visit the study site at **www.sagepub.com/ciel** for e-flashcards, practice quizzes, and other study resources.

References

Augsburger, D. W. (1992). *Conflict mediation across cultures: Pathways and patterns.* Louisville, KY: Westminster/John Knox.

Bachen, C. M., & Illouz, E. (1996). Imagining romance: Young people's cultural models of romance and love. *Critical Studies in Mass Communication, 13,* 297–308.

Bernstein, B. (1971). *Class, codes, and control.* London: Routledge.

Calero, H. (2005). *The power of nonverbal communication: What you do is more important than what you say.* Los Angeles: Silver Lake.

Duck, S. W. (2007). *Human relationships* (4th ed.). London: Sage.

Fitch, K. L. (1998). *Speaking relationally: Culture, communication, and interpersonal connection.* New York: Guilford Press.

Fitch, K. L. (2003). Cultural persuadables. *Communication Theory, 13*(1), 100–123.

Gudykunst, W. (2000). *Asian American ethnicity and communication.* Thousand Oaks, CA: Sage.

Gudykunst, W. (2004). *Theorizing about intercultural communication.* Thousand Oaks, CA: Sage.

Gudykunst, W. B., & Kim, Y. Y. (1984). *Communicating with strangers: An approach to intercultural communication.* New York: Random House.

Houston, M., & Wood, J. T. (1996). *Gendered relationships.* Mountain View, CA: Mayfield.

Martin, J. N., & Nakayama, T. K. (2007). *Intercultural communication in context* (4th ed.). New York: McGraw-Hill.

Morsbach, H. (2004). *Customs and etiquette of Japan.* London: Global Books.

Nakayama, T. K., Martin, J. N., & Flores, L. A. (Eds.). (2002). *Readings in intercultural communication* (2nd ed.). New York: McGraw-Hill.

Nicholson, H. (2006, April). Bernstein's diamonds. In *Theories mined without success: What went wrong?* Paper presented at panel during Central States Communication Association Convention, Indianapolis.

Philipsen, G. (1975). Speaking "like a man" in Teamsterville: Culture patterns of role enactment in an urban neighborhood. *Quarterly Journal of Speech, 61*(1), 13–22.

Philipsen, G. (1997). A theory of speech codes. In G. Philipsen & T. Albrecht (Eds.), *Developing theories in communication* (pp. 119–156). Albany: State University of New York Press.

Rahim, M. A. (1983). A measure of styles of handling interpersonal conflict. *Academy of Management Journal, 26,* 368–376.

Samovar, L. A., & Porter, R. E. (2004). *Communication between cultures* (5th ed.). Belmont, CA: Wadsworth.

Seki, K., Matsumoto, D., & Imahori, T. T. (2002). The conceptualization and expression of intimacy in Japan and the United States. *Journal of Cross-Cultural Psychology, 33*(3), 303–319.

Ting-Toomey, S. (2004). The matrix of face: An updated face-negotiation theory. In W. Gudykunst (Ed.), *Theorizing about intercultural communication* (pp. 71–92). Thousand Oaks, CA: Sage.

Wood, J. T. (2004). Monsters and victims: Male felons' accounts of intimate partner violence. *Journal of Social and Personal Relationships, 21*(5), 555–576.

12

Technology in Everyday Life

Communication and relationships increasingly center on the use of technology and media. For the sake of organization only, this chapter is primarily concerned with a relational approach to the use of cell phones, iPods, and personal digital assistants (PDAs), as well as to the social uses of the Internet. Chapter 13 is dedicated to the exploration of traditionally labeled "mass" media, such as television, radio, movies, books, video games, newspapers, and the Internet. Even though we are separating these areas into two chapters, we recognize that they are rapidly becoming integrated and will no doubt continue to merge, and both are also merging into relational life. Television, no longer confined to a large-screened unit in such social spaces as your home, waiting rooms, and restaurants, can now be watched wherever you happen to find yourself through cell phones, iPods, and similar technologies. Movies, newspapers, video games, and millions of songs are available for download onto these devices, just waiting to help you accomplish a variety of personal and even relational needs as people pass along cool Web sites, music, and downloads to their friends. As the accessibility of the Internet initially began to grow to its current state, some researchers questioned whether it was a mass medium like television or an interactive technology like traditional land-line telephones (Morris & Ogan, 1996). The Internet is actually both a mass media system and an interactive technology, as are such technologies as cell phones. Accordingly, both chapters will include discussions of the Internet, with this one discussing more of its social and interactive nature and the next chapter discussing it from a mass media perspective.

This separation is still legitimate at the present time but may not be suitable in the future. The continuously changing nature of human communication in general and the use of technology in particular to fulfill relational connections are among the features that make the discipline of communication so intriguing but also challenging. Research and information included in this chapter are based on the present state of technology, but we are writing these words at least a year before you will read them (or listen to them on your iPod). We realize technology will likely have changed even within that relatively brief period of time. Accordingly, you may notice throughout the chapter a recurring theme of technological change and evolution but a constant awareness of their embeddedness in relationships. In fact, we use the term *relational technologies* quite a bit more than just *technology*.

This chapter first explores the use and influence of relational technologies on the construction of personal and relational identities. We examine how the use of these technologies conveys particular meanings to others. We then look at the construction of identity through the Internet, specifically focusing on screen names, e-mail addresses, content creation, social networking sites, and features of Internet activity that impact everyday life. The second half of the chapter is dedicated to the use of technology when interacting with others and how technology influences personal relationships. We first examine the distinct relational features of cell phone interactions and then explore the characteristics of online communication and its influence on relationships and social networks.

Focus Questions

- Why does the use and meaning of relational technologies differ among generations?
- What impact do social networks have on the use and meaning of relational technologies?
- How do technological products and service providers influence the meaning attached to relational technologies?
- What does your screen name and e-mail address tell others about you?
- How are personal Web sites, blogs, and social networking sites impacting the construction of identity and self-disclosure?
- What are the social implications of giving out your cell phone number?
- How do cell phones impact interactions with others?
- What makes online communication different from other forms of communication?
- How is online communication impacting personal relationships and social networks?
- Do people interact with technology like they interact with other people?

How Do People View Technology?

Most people currently conducting research and writing textbooks about technology—including both of your authors—remember a time without cell phones, iPods, or the Internet. You may have heard these technologies referred to as *new* media, because for those writing the textbooks and conduct-ing the research they are new. However, even with growing numbers of nontradi-tional students, the majority of students studying this research and reading these textbooks do not view this technology as new but view it as something that has always been around and that has always been a very significant part of their lives. Accordingly, the term *new media* will not be used when discussing the Internet, cell phones, iPods, and similar devices. Instead, these technologies will be referred to as *relational technologies* in recognition of their truly relational nature.

When college students were asked to name the most popular things on campus as part of a Student Monitor Lifestyle & Media Study, the number-one item on the list was iPods. Beer came in second place, with Facebook, drinking other alcohol, and text messaging rounding out the top five (Snider, 2006).

Beyond the designation of these technologies, the media experience of researchers also influences how technology gets discussed in most current research. Much of what is written about the Internet, cell phones, and other relational technologies frames them as intrusive and threatening, and they are evaluated according to standards and criteria associated with traditional media and technology. Actually an increasingly vital, essen-tial, and beneficial part of everyday life, they should be studied and evaluated according to their own unique standards and norms.

Fears and apprehensions surrounding the latest technology are nothing new and con-cern people other than scholars from previous media generations. The emergence of any new communication technology has historically elicited choruses of concern and anxi-ety, surprisingly similar in nature. People worry about the effects of these technologies on family, community, and, of course, children. While no evidence exists, we imagine focus groups were developed by well-meaning cave people to examine the potentially negative impact of cave drawings on innocent and susceptible cave children. Documented criti-cism of more recent technologies shows people expressed similar fears when radio began appearing in homes in the 1920s, and these were nearly identical to those expressed about television when it began appearing in homes during the 1950s. Actually, many of these criticisms are still being expressed! The even-more-recent introduction of the Internet led to concerns about diminished physical activity and social interaction among its users. Such criticisms are strikingly similar to questions raised in 1926 by the Knights of Columbus Adult Education Committee about telephones in homes, including "Does the telephone make [people] more active or more lazy?" and "Does the telephone break up home life and the old practice of visiting friends?" (as quoted in Fischer, 1992, p. 1).

Of course, the introduction of a new technology is not without its sup-porters, although voices of praise are usually overwhelmed by those of criti-cism. The praise offered for new tech-nologies is often quite similar as well. A public relations announcement by the American Telephone & Telegraph Company (AT&T) had this to say about

The Luddites (named from their leader Ned Ludd) were an early 19th-century British social movement that protested innovations of the Industrial Revolution and were involved in armed conflicts with the British army. Today, Luddite refers to a person who opposes any innovation, especially technology.

telephones: "The telephone is essentially democratic; it carries the voice of the child and the grown-up with equal speed and directness. . . . It is not only the implement of the individual, but it fulfills the needs of all the people" (as quoted in Fischer, 1992, p. 2). These sentiments sound strikingly similar to those surrounding the democratic and equalizing nature of the Internet.

Technologies do impact society and the world in which you live. Regardless of whether its influences are positive or negative, each technology changes how people communicate and interact. The one constant among all technologies, from cave drawings to the Internet to whatever technologies arise next, is that they are all inherently relational in their understanding and use. At the center of all criticism and praise of technologies rest their influence and effect on social interaction and connections among people. This influence is probably why criticism and praise surrounding each emerging technology have sounded so similar; relationships among people have been the one constant throughout all human technological development. Adapted to accomplish and meet relational needs, all technologies have influenced how you interact and relate with others.

Relational Technology and the Construction of Identities

Technological devices do not merely connect you with other people or provide you with information, music, and video. Personal and relational identities are created and maintained through your use of these technologies. We refer to cell phones, iPods, and PDAs as **relational technologies** to emphasize the relational functions and implications of their use in society and within specific groups. Throughout this section of the chapter, we examine how the use of technology creates and conveys information about the self, groups, and relationships.

The Meaning of Relational Technology

The use of relational technologies develops unique meanings for particular social groups. Some groups view the cell phone less as a device to contact others and more as a means of displaying social status and membership (J. Katz, 2006). The social meanings accompanying technologies, along with their significance, vary according to the social system in which they are used. For instance, the meaning and use of these devices often varies among people of different countries (J. Katz & Aakhus, 2002). When cell phones first appeared in the United States, for example, they were marketed as business tools to be used primarily by businesspeople. In the United Kingdom, they were marketed as social relationship tools to be used by everyone. Consequently, cell phones became popular much sooner in the United Kingdom than in the United States. Furthermore, members of business organizations develop shared perspectives governing the use and perceptions of certain technologies (Fulk & Steinfeld, 1990). Members of some organizations may view e-mail as a more appropriate means of communication, while members of other organizations may prefer contact through telephone or face-to-face interactions. The views governing the use of these technologies are developed in large part by how other members of these organizations use and discuss each technology.

Media and Technology Generations

A major influence on your perceptions and use of technology is the generation in which you were born. In fact, media scholars Gary Gumpert and Robert Cathcart (1985) have maintained that the traditional notion of separating generations according to time can be replaced by separating generations according to media experience. What separates generations is not just the chronological era in which they were born but also the media and technology that encompass their world. **Media generations** are differentiated by unique media grammar and media consciousness based on the technological environment in which they are born. Before the introduction of radio, past generations understood the world according to the printed word and standards associated with literacy. Radio generations eventually gave way to television generations, which gave way to digital and Internet generations, which will eventually give way to whatever technology and media generations are on the horizon.

Each technology influences people's thinking, sense of experience, and perceptions of reality in very unique and specific ways. Media generations and societies as a whole consequently develop different standards and methods for evaluating knowledge, experience, and reality (Chesebro, 1984). If you were born into the Internet generation, you think differently and perceive the world differently than someone born before the introduction of the Internet, and vice versa. Furthermore, those born during a particular media era privilege the perspectives or orientations brought about by their dominant technology. Someone in the Internet generation may accept and enjoy an abbreviated podcast or Webcast of a full-length television episode, but someone from a television generation may find it difficult to follow. Likewise, media generations born into a digital world undervalue books and traditional television in favor of the Internet and digital products.

Technology and Social Networks

Your social network is an equally powerful force in guiding perceptions and use of technology. Friends, family, classmates, coworkers, and others with whom you share a particular relationship direct and shape your assumptions about the value of technology and what its use represents both relationally and personally. For example, one study found shared social meanings associated with cell phones among people in regular contact, including cell phone adoption and attitudes about products and services (Campbell & Russo, 2003). The same shared meanings hold true for iPods, PDAs, and other relational technologies.

While generational influence is largely determined by the *availability* of technology, the influence of social networks on your use and perceptions of technology is determined by its actual *use and incorporation* and the social meanings that subsequently develop. Returning to the example involving the introduction of cell phones originally as a business tool in the United States, people soon developed their own understanding and use of this technology based largely on its incorporation by members of their social networks. Friends and families began using cell phones for social interaction, and they subsequently became relational rather than business devices. Cell phone companies

Photo 12.1 What social influence may be impacting the use of media and technology in this picture? (See page 344.)

in the United States, who did not take long to recognize this relational turn, now feature "friends and family" plans and promote the selection of certain individuals within your social network with whom you can share unlimited calling. The incorporation of cell phones as relational tools, however, actually led to this change in marketing strategy.

Your use and incorporation of technology will differ according to the person with whom you are in contact and what you want to achieve through the interaction. You belong to multiple social groups, each of which likely views technology and its use differently. For example, you may be more likely to contact members of one group via e-mail and members of another group through text messages. The technological tendencies of a group may also impact its ability to achieve social status and acceptance. For instance, the use of iPods may be less common in some groups, and owning one may earn you a higher social status. On the other hand, among groups in which these devices are quite common, owning an iPod may not indicate higher social status but establish group membership and acceptance through the common use of this technology. Each social group to which you belong will help shape and mold your view and use of technology, with the group you view as most important for what you wish to achieve personally and relationally likely providing the greatest influence of all.

Technological Products and Service Providers

Somewhat related to the actual use of certain technology discussed above is the use of specific technological products and services. If you are reading this book in public, look around at the cell phones and other relational technologies that people are using. If you are not in a public place or few people are around, examine the devices people are using the next time you go to class. Chances are the majority of people will be using cell phones and other relational technologies that look very similar, a few people will be using devices that appear more modern and advanced, and the remaining few will be using relational technologies that look a bit outdated.

Scholars have long studied the diffusion of innovations, or how new ideas and technologies are spread throughout communities (e.g., E. Katz, Levin, & Hamilton, 1963). Some individuals desire to own the latest relational technology and related accessories as a means of demonstrating technological savvy or social status. Aside from issues associated with cost, those whose technological devices appear dated may care little about possessing the latest products and even purposefully delay adopting new technological devices as a means of conveying technological indifference or mistrust. The majority of people adopt technological devices at relatively the same time, which explains why most of the relational technologies you see look alike. In all three cases of technological adoption, the technological device being used communicates specific attitudes about that technology.

Beyond the speed at which technological devices and services are adopted, specific meanings are associated with the use of particular products and service providers within a social system. The use of these devices allows people to associate themselves with accompanying perspectives and attitudes related to these technological products. One study found that, when purchasing a cell phone, young people are influenced less by quality or available features and more by the image associated with that particular phone. Each style of cell phone is symbolically connected to certain lifestyles, activities, or media personalities, and the use of these phones enables the construction of associated identities. Not limited to the phone model, these connections also include the actual service provider. Individuals in the study linked cell phone networks with specific social features, such as humanitarianism, professionalism, and family. Thus, the use of specific networks facilitates social belonging to groups sharing certain values or orientations (Lobet-Maris, 2003).

Strategic Communication

The medium through which you contact someone can make a difference in his or her reception of your message. The purpose of your message and the technological preferences of the person you are contacting will determine the appropriateness of face-to-face, telephone, or computer-mediated interaction.

Online Activity and the Construction of Identities

Having discussed the influence of relational technologies on the construction of personal and relational identities, we now turn our attention to the Internet. Research concerning the development of online identities has focused on identity construction through chat room discussions. While this line of research has provided valuable insight into Internet activity and personal identity, we would like to focus instead on matters of Internet activity that have received less attention but are continuing to grow in importance in everyday life.

Screen Names

Identity development is accomplished in part through the selection of screen names. Of course, screen names are frequently selected when participating in chat rooms but are also evident when playing MMORPGs (massively multiplayer online role-playing games), uploading videos on YouTube, leaving online comments and evaluations, and

Although former Vice President Al Gore once infamously took credit, no single person can be considered the inventor of the Internet. However, chief among the early major contributors are Leonard Kleinrock and J. C. R. Licklider. Leonard Kleinrock was the first person to publish a paper on packet switching, an essential component of the Internet. J. C. R. Licklider is considered the first person to conceive of a worldwide network of computers, which he labeled a "galactic network."

even selling items on eBay. A person is sometimes known to others only by his or her screen name, which may or may not provide an accurate representation of the person behind the screen. What is known about that individual is often limited to his or her Internet activity, with his or her life beyond the Internet frequently remaining a mystery. A person may also establish a number of screen names and create multiple online identities.

Users may select screen names based on genuine perceived characteristics of the self or uncharacteristic traits they wish to establish online. Such screen names as *shyguy24* or *toughgrl17* may be used by those who view themselves as outgoing or aggressive, as well as by those who see themselves as introverted or passive off-line but who wish to create a unique online persona. People may select a screen name based on genuine characteristics as a natural extension of the self, but they may choose unrepresentative traits as a way to develop untapped aspects of the self and to test these characteristics in what may be an anonymous and nonthreatening environment.

Screen names may represent other aspects of individuals beyond personality traits. Selecting such names as *HawkeyeFreak01*, *TrackStar1756*, or *TennisAce6-0* may symbolize an interest in a particular sport or team. Choosing such names as *FamGuyGeek3564* or *MrknId123* may represent an interest in specific movies, television programs, or other popular-culture products. The screen names that people select may also embody personal relationships (*ProudPapa35*, *JeremiahMom64*, *OlderSister124*, *ILuvJosh74*) or represent people's professions, hobbies, and majors (*CrookedCop104*, *OilPainter23*, *CommStudiesRules73*). Selecting screen names based on these aspects of the self symbolizes their significance in a person's life and overall sense of self. They indicate to others how you view yourself and how you want to be perceived, and they help *perform* your identity (Chapter 5).

E-mail Addresses

Also connected to identity construction, e-mail addresses have three main parts, all of which can convey personal information to others: the username (sometimes a person's screen name), the domain name, and the top-level domain. The username comes before the @ symbol, the domain name comes immediately after the @ symbol, and the top-level domain follows the dot (.).

Usernames

Much of what we discussed concerning screen names also applies to usernames. You can convey multiple aspects of the self through the selection of a username, and other people form impressions of you based on the name you select. We want to caution you that screen names or usernames may create undesired impressions; *2Sexy4U* or *KegLuvver,* for example, may be fine when corresponding and interacting with friends online but not in professional situations. Keep this in mind when creating your résumé. Potential employers may reject a job candidate whose contact information includes an e-mail address beginning *LazyDrunk93*!

Domain Names

The domain name can reveal service provider, profession, or affiliations. Domain names often display a person's Internet service provider, which may be selected based on how people wish to portray themselves to others. For instance, some people may select a relatively small and unfamiliar Internet provider as opposed to a large and recognizable one in an effort to be unique or to display disapproval of large corporations. Individuals wishing to convey Internet experience and capability may use high-speed Internet e-mail addresses with pride. Many of you reading this book have an e-mail account through a school that connects you symbolically to that institution. Some university alumni organizations allow former students to retain their college e-mail addresses after graduation to signify their association with their alma mater.

Top-Level Domain

The top-level material appearing at the end of e-mail addresses also reveals personal information to others. Such codes as *.edu, .gov, .mil,* and *.org* may indicate to others a connection to or an involvement with education, government, military, or an organization, respectively. E-mail addresses originating in countries other than the United States come with a two-digit country code, such as *.uk,* which provides further information about their owners.

Online Content Creation and Identity

The Internet has become both an instrument and a site for self-expression, especially for younger generations. Personal Web pages, blogs, and the posting of original pictures, videos, mash-ups, and other personal creations enable people to share and display their thoughts, interests, and talents and other characteristics of the self. While Internet users of all ages perform these activities, younger people use the Internet for self-expression more than adults. In fact, more than half of online teenagers are considered **content creators**, Internet users who have developed or maintained a Web site or blog or shared their creative work online (Lenhart & Madden, 2005). Looking specifically at blogs, 20% of teenage Internet users report maintaining a blog compared with 8% of adult Internet users (Lenhart & Fox, 2006; Lenhart & Madden, 2005). The disparity in these numbers will likely diminish over time, however, as present-day teenage content creators become adult content creators and as younger generations view content creation and distribution through the Internet as a customary practice.

Personal Web Pages and Blogs

Personal Web pages and blogs—in which the creator discloses only the information he or she wishes—allow for the selective expression of the self and the performance of identity. These sites may be devoted to specific aspects of the self, such as activities involving people, relationships, and interests, or they may display multiple components of the self. People visiting Steve's homepage (http://myweb.uiowa.edu/blastd/) can view the academic area, which includes information about his education, teaching, research, and publication history, as well as the personal area, which provides information about his family, his interests, and the origination of the Duck surname, along with membership in the Hair Club and how to get a Swiss Army knife.

The material and information on personal Web sites and blogs are usually provided for specific reasons. People may incorporate content specifically for personal expression and a desire to share it with others, for example, and they frequently use personal Web pages to maintain connections with their social networks by providing information about the latest events in their lives. The majority of bloggers cite expressing themselves creatively as the primary reason for maintaining a blog, with documenting and sharing personal experiences a close second (see Table 12.1; Lenhart & Fox, 2006). Also a means of exploring identities and expressing aspects of the self that prove difficult through other methods, personal Web pages and blogs in this regard do not function simply as a display and expression of the self but as a means of creating, establishing, and maintaining identities.

Table 12.1 More Blog to Share Experiences Than to Earn Money

Please tell me if this is a reason you personally blog, or not:	Not a reason	Minor reason	Major reason
To express yourself creatively	23%	25%	52%
To document your personal experiences or share them with others	24	26	50
To stay in touch with friends and family	40	22	37
To share practical knowledge or skills with others	35	30	34
To motivate other people to action	38	32	29
To entertain people	39	33	28
To store resources or information that is important to you	52	21	28
To influence the way other people think	49	24	27
To network or to meet new people	50	34	16
To make money	85	8	7

Source: Lenhart & Fox, 2006.

Self-presentation ultimately becomes a fundamental component in the expression and construction of identities through personal Web pages and blogs. The material excluded can become just as significant as the material included. Choice of content along with the

Photo 12.2 What two areas of people's lives are impacted most by social networking sites like Facebook? (See page 344.)

presentation of the material included represents a symbolic display of a person's worldview, providing specific insight into how he or she wishes to be viewed by others. For instance, people use self-presentation strategies frequently in blogs to achieve acceptance and approval and to appear socially competent (Bortree, 2005). People make strategic choices when presenting themselves to others in dyadic or group situations to achieve these same goals; however, they are increasingly doing so digitally and on a much larger and public scale through personal Web pages and blogs.

Social Networking Sites

Social networking sites, such as MySpace and Facebook, allow people to connect with friends, families, and others in an existing social network while establishing new connections and forming relationships with people from around the world. Equally important as establishing and maintaining connections with others, social networking sites are becoming important tools in the display and creation of personal and relational identities, as well as the disclosure of personal information. Self-disclosure is part of relational development, and the self is transacted through relational connections. The sheer breadth and depth of the self-expression and self-disclosure taking place on social networking sites make them unlike any other forum. You might learn more about a person simply by visiting his or her Facebook page than through interacting with him or her over an extended period. In addition, you may have visited pages of coworkers, classmates, friends, or relatives and discovered previously unknown details about them that you may wish you had never learned!

Listen In On Your Life

If you have your own page on a social networking site, what do you believe it conveys to other people about you? How do these perceptions compare with how you view yourself? Do your friends agree about the messages being conveyed?

Self-disclosure taking place on social networking sites leads us to question many classic studies and observations related to disclosure. Communication scholars previously believed that self-disclosure occurs gradually as trust is established in a relationship, but these sites instead provide a tremendous amount of personal information all at once. Peripheral, or relatively minor, information, such as favorite type of ice cream, appears on these sites at the same time as more personal information, such as relationship history and sexual preferences. Scholars also believed that peripheral information about the self would be shared initially; that deeper personal information would be shared later; and, further, that information shared with one person would be different from that shared with another person, depending on the relationships between these individuals. More information, in general, and more personal information, specifically, would be shared with close friends than acquaintances. Unless access is blocked, anyone—regardless of his or her relationship with a creator—can view the information included on most social network pages. You may have heard stories about people being kicked out of school or losing a job because of the content shared on their social networking page. Someone had access to information that he or she would not have gained otherwise. On the other hand, many social networking sites actually require the disclosure of certain information, but the person establishing and maintaining the page freely provides much of the information.

Social networking sites have changed not only the way people think about self-disclosure but also perceptions of social value and belonging. A person's social worth and sense of belonging are often tied to the number of *friends* (or similar designations) established with others using the site, and one may put a great deal of thought and concern into accumulating as many such associations as possible. Of course, long before social networking sites gained such notoriety, evaluations of social worth were often based on the number of friends and acquaintances one possessed. The numbers required to achieve a proper social value, however, are much greater than before. You also will likely never meet or even communicate with those listed as friends or acquaintances on these sites. Further, these sites base group memberships and associations with other people solely on shared interests, locations, and connections with other friends and friends of friends. Just like the accumulation of friends and acquaintances, these connections are not much different from those established long before the development of social networking sites.

Their prevalence and significance in the construction of identity and social belonging, however, are becoming more pronounced. The massive changes in social interactions and the construction of identity resulting from the Internet take us back to the earlier discussion of media generations and the evaluation of technology. Assessment of acceptable social interaction and personal development may vary according to media generation. For instance, people belonging to some media generations may question the value of interactions taking place through the Internet and perceive them as less fulfilling than face-to-face interactions. Some authors have lamented a decline in civic participation (e.g., Putnam, 2000) without fully recognizing that civic participation and community engagement are thriving online. Human interaction and civic participation are changing dramatically but not disappearing. Media generations simply differ on how these activities should appear and take place. Standards for evaluation and techniques for human interaction and civic participation of past media generations do not apply to those of present media generations. For them, human interaction and civic participation are just as meaningful and significant online as they are in any other form.

Relational Technology and Personal Relationships

Having examined the influence of technology on identities, we can now fully explore how technology and relationships are connected and mutually influential. Naturally, these two discussions relate because the construction of identities, often the basis for connections with others, often entails interactions with others through relational technologies or the Internet. For example, instant messaging has been shown to satisfy two major needs for adolescents: maintaining individual friendships and peer group membership. Instant messaging provides a means through which adolescents may interact one-on-one and engage in a similar activity with peers (Boneva, Quinn, Kraut, Kiesler, & Shklovski, 2006, p. 214).

Examining the influence of technology on relationships, Kraut, Brynin, and Kiesler (2006) have observed that on one level changes in technology simply allow people to achieve relatively stable relational goals in new ways. People exchange birthday greetings, for example, through e-cards rather than a traditional card sent through the postal service. Correspondence takes place through phone calls rather than letters. These authors also maintain, however, that more than simply altering how traditional goals are met, technological transformation also changes what can be accomplished, creating new relational goals and norms.

Cell phones, online communication, and other technological advancements are changing how people communicate and form relationships with others, as well as altering established relational goals and norms. This section of the chapter examines the impact of cell phones and other relational technologies on interactions among people. We then examine the characteristics of online communication and its influence on relationships and social networks. Finally, we consider how people interact not only with one another but also with technology itself.

Cell Phones and Personal Relationships

Cell phones have come to represent constant connection to those who possess your number, and how freely people give out their cell phone numbers varies. David rarely gives out his cell phone number, and his wife is the only person who ever calls him on that phone, which for him has become an exclusive symbol of their relationship. Although many colleagues and friends know Steve's U.S. cell phone number, very few people know the number of the cell phone he uses while in Europe—including his coauthor. When returning home to the United Kingdom, Steve becomes symbolically and literally separated from all but a few individuals in his social network. Like many other people, our cell phones have brought about personal and social connotations that dictate their use, including who is able to contact us.

Giving or denying someone access to your cell phone number establishes both the *boundaries* and the *degree of closeness* desired and expected within the relationship. Limiting the

The first public telephone call from a cell phone took place on April 3, 1973, by Martin Cooper, then general manager of Motorola's Communications Systems Division.

availability of contact with a person establishes specific relational boundaries. How that person views and evaluates such limits depends on your relationship. Refusing to provide a cell phone number to a friend may be viewed negatively; therapists not providing clients with their numbers may be viewed as legitimate.

Providing another person with your cell phone number suggests a desire for connection with that individual and perhaps an indication of the type of relationship you wish to establish. For instance, making your number available to an acquaintance could imply a desire to develop a closer type of relationship. As above, the evaluation and meaning of this action generally depends on your relationship with that person. Although it serves to maintain the existence and importance of your relationship, providing a close friend with your cell phone number may be expected. Patients receiving the cell phone number of their doctor along with instructions to call at any time may see this action as more meaningful or consequential because it runs counter to the expectations associated with that relationship.

Constant Connection and Availability

Connection and availability are fully established when calls are actually made and text messages are sent. There are times when the content of these messages is less important than the actual contact itself. Such instances are similar to how seemingly mundane everyday talk keeps relationships going without necessarily adding much in terms of substance. Connecting with another person reestablishes the existence and importance of the relationship, confirming for both parties its existence and value in their lives. At other times the content of these messages is vitally important, especially during the enactment of relational information and other relational maintenance strategies. Of course, letters sent via the Pony Express in 1860 accomplished the same things, so what makes cell phones so different? We are glad you asked!

Cell phones allow people to be in "perpetual contact" with others (J. Katz & Aakhus, 2002). The ability to make instant contact with another person regardless of geographic location creates a symbolic connection unlike that created by any previous communication technology. If you have your cell phone with you, you have your social network with you as well (Duck, 2007). This constant connection with others can provide comfort and security in a relationship or can lead to challenges. Relationships require connections between people, as well as autonomy and independence (Baxter & Montgomery, 1996). While the feeling of constant connection made possible through cell phones can be beneficial, it may decrease feelings of autonomy, equally important and necessary in relationships.

New relational expectations have developed as a result of constant availability through cell phones. When calling someone's cell phone, you expect he or she will be readily available. If he or she does not answer the phone, you generally expect him or her to return the call in a timely manner and provide a plausible excuse for not answering in the first place. The same expectations apply when sending someone a text message. Failure to respond to a text message in a timely manner—or failure to respond, period—can constitute a violation in the relationship (Ling, 2004). Such expectations of contact and promptness do not exist with land-line phones, e-mail, or other forms of communication; however, they may quickly encompass the use of e-mail as it becomes increasingly available through cell phones and other relational technologies.

Shared Experience

We can discuss shared experience derived from the use of cell phones in two ways. First, the actual use of cell phones constitutes shared technological experience. Especially when people correspond through text messages, they engage in the use of the same technology. As discussed earlier in the chapter, particular groups assign great significance and meaning to the use of particular technology, and younger generations adapt more quickly to changing technology. More than simply transmitting information, the act of sending and receiving text messages both announces and establishes shared membership and acceptance into a group.

Cell phones also enable people to engage in shared experience even when physically separated. The immediate transmission of voice, picture, sound, and video provide people with the sense of experiencing an event or occasion together. A person in a disagreement with a romantic partner can be in simultaneous contact with a friend offering guidance and support and subsequently sharing in the experience. Joyous occasions and celebrations can likewise be shared with others who are physically absent. This shared experience seems to parallel that made possible through land-line phones, which are occasionally passed around at parties so someone unable to attend may take part in the occasion. Cell phones, however, allow this shared experience to take place anywhere, and their multimedia capabilities make it increasingly more authentic.

Social Coordination

One of the greatest relational consequences of the cell phone encompasses its use in coordinating physical encounters with others. Face-to-face interactions are created and synchronized through the use of cell phones. The ability to establish the physical location of others while in public creates opportunities for spontaneous physical interaction. If you call a friend while studying in the library only to discover that she is studying in the adjacent building, this discovery could lead to a decision to meet and take a break together. The revelation of proximity made possible through cell phones makes such encounters possible.

Cell phones enable people to synchronize their activities to the point of microcoordination. Making plans to meet someone previously involved establishing a fixed time and physical location for the interaction to occur, but the massive adoption of cell phones has resulted in time and physical location for contact becoming increasingly fluid. **Microcoordination** refers to the unique management of social interaction made possible through cell phones. Rich Ling (2004) has observed three varieties of microcoordination: (1) midcourse adjustment, (2) iterative coordination, and (3) softening of schedules (see Table 12.2).

Online Communication and Personal Relationships

Before discussing the influence of online communication on personal relationships, we want to first consider the unique characteristics of online communication. Recognizing

Table 12.2 Ling's (2004) Three Varieties of Microcoordination

Midcourse adjustment	Involves changing plans once a person has already set out for the encounter—for example, contacting the other person to change locations or to request that he or she pick up someone else on the way.
Iterative coordination	Involves the progressive refining of an encounter. Cell phones have made actually establishing location and time unnecessary. Instead, people increasingly plan to meet without specifying an exact time or location. For instance, friends may agree to meet sometime tomorrow. As a result of progressive calls or messages, they eventually "zoom in on each other" (p. 72).
Softening of schedules	Involves adjusting a previously scheduled time. If you planned to meet a friend for coffee at 3:30 P.M. but a meeting with your adviser took longer than expected and you are running late, cell phones make it much easier to reach your friend and inform him or her of the delay.

Source: Ling, 2004.

Photo 12.3 What type of microcoordination is most likely taking place in this picture? (See page 344.)

that there are a number of unique forms of online communication, such as e-mail, chat rooms, message boards, and instant messaging, we examine the similarities among them.

Characteristics of Online Communication

One characteristic of online communication—and, for that matter, all text-based interactions—is the lack of nonverbal cues available to help determine meaning. Nonverbal communication, such as vocalics and kinesics, is incredibly valuable when crafting and interpreting messages. The number of verbal and nonverbal cues available through a medium or technology determines its **richness**. Face-to-face interactions are considered richer than other types of interaction since verbal communication and a range of nonverbal cues are available to convey and interpret meaning. Phone conversations are less rich since they are limited to verbal communication and vocalics. Online communication is limited to verbal communication, with no nonverbal cues available to assist in conveying and interpreting messages. Accordingly, misunderstandings will more likely occur during online interactions than during telephone conversations or face-to-face interactions. This possibility does not automatically mean that all online interactions will result in misunderstandings, but it does mean that those engaging in online communication must carefully consider the messages they craft and carefully interpret the messages they receive. **Emoticons**, text-based symbols

> The very first "smiley face" emoticon :-) was used at 11:44 A.M. on September 19, 1982, by professor Scott E. Fahlman while contributing to an online bulletin board.

used to express emotions online, often help alleviate problems associated with a lack of nonverbal cues. The general absence of nonverbal cues, however, poses a distinct challenge when interacting online.

In some instances, though, the lack of nonverbal cues may actually be advantageous. People become less concerned with such factors as their appearance and less distracted or troubled by the nonverbal responses of others. Especially beneficial for those who are apprehensive about communicating in other situations, online communication has been found to be more comforting than other forms of interaction and can enhance people's willingness to communicate with others (Freiermuth & Jarrell, 2006). Research also indicates people generally feel they are able to better express themselves online than during off-line interactions (McKenna & Seidman, 2006).

A second characteristic of online communication is its asynchronous nature. In **synchronous communication**—for example, face-to-face interaction—people interact in real time and can send and receive messages at once. In **asynchronous communication**, containing a slight or prolonged delay, the interactants must alternate between sending and receiving. E-mail and even instant messaging represent asynchronous communication. Although some online interactions are close to real time, they still contain a delay, and people must take turns being sender and receiver. The asynchronous nature of online communication provides more time to consider the messages of others and to formulate messages.

While sometimes beneficial, the asynchronous nature of online communication also poses a challenge, especially when it comes to instant messaging. Boneva et al. (2006) have shown that instant messaging provides as much social support as face-to-face interactions and phone conversations, but people using instant messaging report feeling more disconnected from those with whom they use it to interact. While this finding may be the result of diminished nonverbal cues mentioned above, these authors maintain it may actually be the result of multitasking. Specifically, a person may have multiple instant messaging windows open at the same time, while also browsing the Internet, listening to the radio, watching television, and engaging in other activities.

There is some question as to whether this observation results from the nature of instant messaging or how it is being employed. Many face-to-face interactions occur in which one or both of the interactants are engaged in other activities and do not pay close attention to the conversation taking place. In this case, the problem seems to encompass the actual use of instant messaging. On the other hand, interactants in face-to-face encounters may be more likely to pay attention since each person can observe the other's behaviors. Unless a person is using a Webcam, the actual behaviors taking place while instant messaging cannot be observed, and a person may be less likely to

Photo 12.4 In what ways does a Webcam affect the richness and asynchronous nature of online communication? (See page 344.)

focus on the interaction. In this case, the difficulty is derived from the nature of instant messaging. Such questions surround the ensuing debates among academics and the general public concerning the quality of online communication.

Quality of Online Communication

Due in large part to fears associated with new technologies mentioned earlier, many researchers have wrongly positioned face-to-face communication as superior to online communication in quality and influence. Conversely, online communication has been positioned as fraught with challenges and potential harm. Baym, Zhang, and Lin (2004), however, have noted that "face-to-face conversations may not always be the rich, deep, and inherently superior means of communication that it is often presumed to be" (p. 316). Comparing face-to-face, telephone, and online interactions, these authors found the quality of telephone and face-to-face interactions only slightly higher than that of online interactions. Quite often when online communication is evaluated harshly, the norms and practices of other forms of interaction have been used. This type of evaluation is no more legitimate or fair than using norms and practices of online communication to evaluate face-to-face or telephone interactions.

We can make two observations about the quality of online communication and other forms of interaction. First, all forms of interaction have unique benefits and challenges. In this regard, online communication is no different from face-to-face communication, telephone conversations, or any other interaction. Second, as observed with instant messaging, how online communication is used has as much to do with its quality as its actual nature. Again, this use makes it no different from other forms of human communication. What does differentiate online communication is that it is still a relatively new form of interaction for many generations. People's perceptions of quality surrounding online communication are likely associated with their comfort and familiarity with interacting online, and as they continue to integrate online communication into their lives, it will become just as normal and commonplace as face-to-face communication. Many people, especially younger generations, already view online communication in this manner. In fact, research indicates that younger adolescents depend on online interactions to engage in quality communication even more than older adolescents (Peter & Valkenburg, 2006). Perceptions of quality surrounding online communication will most likely continue to change as time goes on.

Personal Relationships and Social Networks

Among the common fears associated with the Internet is that it will diminish social interaction and lead to a disconnection from social networks. Some research has even suggested that the more time a person spends on the Internet, the less time he or she spends with friends, family, and colleagues (Nie, Hillygus, & Erbring, 2002). Other research has suggested that the Internet functions as both a time displacer and a time enhancer (Robinson & De Haan, 2006). As a time displacer, increased time spent using the Internet means decreased time spent engaging in other activities, whether positive, such as interacting with people in your social network, or negative, such as being unproductive in any way. Accordingly, as a time enhancer, Internet use may enable more productive uses of time. For those who use the Internet for social connection, increased time online is associated with decreased use of television (Kraut, Kielser, Boneva, & Schklovski 2006).

Make Your Case

Some people have denounced online communication as inferior to face-to-face communication. Do you believe this evaluation? What are the advantages and disadvantages of both forms of communication? In what ways are online communication and face-to-face communication similar? In what ways are they different?

Online communication enables people to maintain existing relationships, enhance existing relationships, and create new relationships, and it is dramatically changing social networks (Boase, Horrigan, Wellman, & Rainie, 2006). Contrary to fears that the Internet will hinder personal relationships, the majority of Internet users indicate that it has improved the quality of their relationships (Howard, Rainie, & Jones, 2002). In fact, increased use of the Internet allows for increased interaction with friends and family not only online but also face-to-face and over the telephone.

Online communication appears to supplement rather than replace traditional forms of interaction (Boase et al., 2006). Online communication is associated with greater contact with those in social networks. People are not only contacting others more online but also increasing the number of face-to-face interactions, telephone calls, and other interactions. Face-to-face communication remains the dominant mode of interaction among college students, with online and telephone communication used at relatively the same frequency (Baym et al., 2004). The frequency with which people contact others online, face-to-face, or by telephone generally depends on the distance between them (Chen, Boase, & Wellman, 2002). Distance also appears to be associated with the type of online communication used. People use both e-mail and instant messaging, for example, when interacting with others regardless of distance, but they are less likely to use e-mail to contact people who live nearby and more likely to use it to contact long-distant friends and family (Quan-Haase & Wellman, 2002). On the other hand, people are much more likely to use instant messaging to interact with others living nearby (Boneva et al., 2006).

Accessibility of contact is perhaps what makes online communication so useful in maintaining existing relationships and forging new ones. Relationships take a great deal of effort to maintain, the basis of which involves enacting them through regular contact (Duck, 2007). The ease with which contact can be made online may very well increase the likelihood that it will take place at all. Online communication is especially beneficial in maintaining relationships among people not in regular physical contact. Maintaining relationships with people you see on a regular basis is relatively easy compared with maintaining relationships with people you hardly ever see because of distance or other factors (Sahlstein, 2006).

This view of online communication is consistent with research conducted by Cummings, Lee, and Kraut (2006) that may particularly apply to many people reading this book. These authors looked at the role of communication technology in maintaining friendships during the transition from high school to college. The truth is, regardless of how many times "(B)est (F)riends (F)orever" has been written in high school yearbooks, very few relationships last after graduation. In fact, you will never again see many of the people you graduated with, and most will become nothing but a faded memory. We do not want you to worry about losing your close friends from high school because some high school friendships last long after graduation; however, the relationships that do survive after graduation seem to be those in which regular contact is maintained. Cummings et al. (2006) discovered that these relationships maintained through e-mail and instant messaging declined less rapidly than those primarily maintained by phone and even face-to-face contact. The authors speculate that these findings resulted more from increased contact through online communication than from any other factor.

Contacting members of a social network may be especially common among people who spend a lot of time working at a computer, such as students, instructors, and those who use a computer as a part of their employment. It consequently takes little effort to turn that experience into a relational one using the technology directly at hand.

Online communication is dramatically changing the construction and nature of social networks. Boase et al. (2006) have examined online communication's impact on social networks and the development of social capital, or the availability of other people to fulfill needs and provide assistance. Their findings indicate that massive changes in the size and the configuration of social networks are taking place as a result of online communication.

One consequence of online communication is the ability to maintain larger social networks. Internet users report overall larger numbers of people in their social networks than nonusers, made possible in part by how easily contact can be maintained through online communication. As part of their study, Boase et al. (2006, p. 5) distinguished two types of connections in social networks: core ties and significant ties. *Core ties* include people with whom you have a very close relationship and are in frequent contact. You often discuss important matters in life with core ties, and you often seek their assistance in times of need. *Significant ties*, though more than mere acquaintances, represent a somewhat weaker connection. You make less contact with significant ties and are less likely to talk with them about important issues in your life or to seek help from them, but they are still there for you when needed. Boase et al. (2006) found that the number of core ties remains the same regardless of Internet activity, while Internet users report a greater number of significant ties.

Another consequence of online communication involves the configuration of social networks. Traditionally, social networks have developed around geography-based communities. In other words, friends, family, acquaintances, and other people in your social network live in the same town or at least nearby. While physical proximity still plays a large role in the development of social networks, online communication has resulted in more diverse and geographically dispersed networks, allowing people equal access to geographically close and geographically distant members of their social networks (Boase et al., 2006). Some people decry the fact that fewer and fewer people socialize with or even know their neighbors, but this situation does not mean people are antisocial or lack strong social support in times of need. Socialization and social support increasingly come from the Internet rather than next door.

Contrarian Challenge

We have emphasized the positive aspects of online communication. What negative aspects of online communication can you come up with?

The Media Equation

While a great deal of research has focused on technology's impact on relationships between people, one research program has instead looked at relationships between people and technology. Before you start making dinner reservations at a fancy restaurant for you and your computer, this research program has not revealed the co-construction of shared meaning, reality, and other features of human-to-human relationships. It has, however, uncovered something incredibly fascinating: People treat computers, televisions, and other technology systems just like they do other people.

Introduced by Byron Reeves and Clifford Nass (2002), the **media equation** maintains that "media equal life" in such a way that interactions with technology are "fundamentally social and natural" (p. 5). Consequently, interactions with technology are the same as interactions with other people, and people use the same social rules and expectations when interacting with both. You interact with your computer as if it is an actual person.

Reeves and Nass (2002) have noted that many people find the media equation counterintuitive. When they first hear about the media equation, many people deny that they treat technology similarly to people. We often get this response from students when we talk about this concept in class, and it may be your initial impression as well. Consider these possibilities, however, before you fully pass judgment. Have you ever pleaded with your computer to go faster when experiencing a slow connection or yelled at your computer when it crashed? Have you ever yelled at your television when the cable or satellite went out? We suspect you have, at least once before; you may even have talked to or humanized other inanimate objects and technology. Accordingly, it may not be so inconceivable that you interact with computers, television, and other technology like you do with other people, especially given the interactive nature of more recent technological innovations.

To test the media equation, Reeves and Nass (2002) found research involving people-people interaction; erased one of the references to *people* and replaced it with *computer, television,* or another technology; and conducted the study using the same techniques that established the people-people findings. If the study found "people like people who compliment them," they would change this finding to "people like *computers* who compliment them," and then they would test it using the same methods that established the original findings. The results of the people-technology experiments consistently mirrored the results of the original people-people experiment.

Be Nice to Your Computer (Politeness)

When someone asks for your feedback on a project he or she has completed or asks about his or her performance on a task, you generally provide him or her with a positive response. Even in the event that the project was a complete mess or the person's performance was a complete disaster, you will try to find something positive to say. Not necessarily deceitful, you are just not being as negative as you could be because you do not want to hurt his or her feelings. If someone else asked you about that person's performance, your response would be more negative than if that person asked you directly. The same patterns of interaction were found to take place with computers. When asked to evaluate a computer to using the same computer to type their responses, people responded much more positively than when typing their responses on a different computer. They did not want to hurt the computer's feelings. On a personal note, we would like to acknowledge the extraordinary contribution of the computer we are using to type this section of the book—and we hope it does not crash!

Computers Say the Kindest Things (Flattery)

Perhaps one reason evaluations of other people (and evidently computers) are more positive is the finding that people like other people who flatter them. Remember that "brown-noser" or "suck-up" from your high school, the one who always complimented the teachers on their clothing or that "wonderfully crafted and inspirational" examination or assignment? That person knew what he or she was doing. The official term for this behavior is *ingratiation,* and it turns out to be quite effective, whether or not it is genuine or deserved (Gordon, 1996). People like other people who compliment them, and the same evaluative response holds true for computers: People, it was discovered, like computers who offer them praise more than computers that offer no evaluation.

Respect the Authority of Your Television (Specialists)

People evaluate the words and actions of someone with a title more favorably than those of someone without a title. A title increases our perceptions of a person's credibility. As it turns out (and you probably saw this one coming), the same holds true for technology. Participants in one study watched identical programming on three identical television sets. The only difference was one television set was labeled a *generalist* and placed under a sign that read, "News and Entertainment Television," and the other television sets were labeled *specialists* and placed under signs that read "News Television" and "Entertainment Television," respectively. Participants in the study considered the material viewed on the specialist televisions as superior to that viewed on the generalist television, even though it was the exact same material.

I Am Me; I Am My Computer (Personality)

People generally prefer to be around and interact with people who are similar to them more than people who are different. If you have a dominant personality, you will prefer interacting with other people with dominant personalities. Likewise, if you are submissive, you will prefer interacting with other submissive people. People, it turns out, not only perceive computers as having dominant or submissive personalities but also prefer computers whose personality is similar to their own. Furthermore, people are able to recognize that these computers have such similar personalities.

Limitations of the Media Equation

A fascinating line of research, the media equation underscores the pervasiveness and integration of technology in everyday life. However, like all research, it is not without its limitations. First, Reeves and Nass (2002) believe that the media equation exists because people's "old brains" are fooled by new media and technology. Essentially, people's brains have not evolved fast enough to keep pace with advances in technology. We question this assumption, however, and actually believe they have advanced to the exact extent necessary. Technology does not exist externally to your world and sense of reality; it is very much a part of your world and your reality, and your brain treats it as such. People's brains are not lagging behind but keeping pace at exactly the right speed.

Our primary concern with the media equation is that most of the studies used to test it come from psychology. Many traditions in psychology represent human interaction as based on a simple stimulus response (a bell rings and Pavlov's dog salivates, for example, a response extending even to the notion of attraction to other people; Byrne, 1997). As you know from reading this book, the communication discipline generally views human interactions as a much more complex and transactional process in which meaning, relationships, reality, and similarity are co-constructed symbolically. While the media equation corresponds with very basic views of human interaction, it has yet to be applied to the more advanced conceptions of human interactions and relationships (Griffin, 2003).

Despite this criticism, the media equation is fascinating and underscores the impact of technology in everyday life. As technological systems advance and become increasingly powerful and interactive, deeper levels of human-technology interactions will possibly be revealed. In the meantime, cancel those dinner reservations for you and your computer if you already made them, but remember to take your cell phone to lunch!

Focus Questions Revisited

Why does the use and meaning of relational technologies differ among generations?

Media generations develop unique media grammar and media consciousness that impact thinking, sense of experience, and perceptions of reality. Members of these generations develop different standards and methods for evaluating technology and consequently respond to relational technologies in different ways.

What impact do social networks have on the use and meaning of relational technologies?

The actual use and incorporation of relational technology by a social network will determine the social meanings that subsequently develop.

How do technological products and service providers influence the meaning attached to relational technologies?

The speed at which new technologies are adopted will influence the meaning associated with the use of particular products and services. Further, specific meanings are associated with the use of particular products and service providers within a social system.

What does your screen name and e-mail address tell others about you?

The selections of screen names or usernames may inform others of genuine perceived characteristics or characteristics you wish to establish online. E-mail addresses can reveal service providers, professions, affiliations, and other personal information.

How are personal Web sites, blogs, and social networking sites impacting the construction of identity and self-disclosure?

Personal Web pages and blogs allow for the selective expression of the self and the crafting of identities. Web pages, blogs, and social networking sites have led communication scholars to question classic studies and observations related to disclosure. Self-disclosure on these sites does not take place gradually; rather, people provide a tremendous amount of personal information all at once. Furthermore, they reveal relatively minor information at the same time as deeper personal information. Finally, they give the same personal information to everyone instead of disclosing certain information to or hiding certain information from individuals with whom they share a particular relationship.

What are the social implications of giving out your cell phone number?

Cell phones have come to represent constant connection to those who possess your number. Giving someone your cell phone number or denying someone access to your number establishes both the boundaries and the degree of closeness desired and expected within your relationship with that person.

How do cell phones impact interactions with others?

A new relational expectation of constant availability has developed as a result of the constant availability made possible through cell phones. Also, shared experience develops from the actual use of cell phones and from the immediate transmission of voice, picture, sound, and video. Finally, the use of cell phones makes possible the microcoordination of physical social interaction.

What makes online communication different from other forms of communication?
The richness of a medium or technology, determined by the number of verbal and nonverbal cues available, differs among forms of communication. Online communication is considered less rich than face-to-face and telephone interactions. Further, online communication is considered asynchronous, meaning there is either a slight or a prolonged delay of the sending and the receiving of messages. Face-to-face and telephone interactions are considered synchronous, meaning the people involved interact in real time and can be at once senders and receivers.

How is online communication impacting personal relationships and social networks?
Online communication enables people to maintain existing relationships, enhance existing relationships, and create new relationships. Online communication enables people to maintain larger social networks and more geographically diverse social networks.

Do people interact with technology like they interact with other people?
According to the media equation theory, people's interactions with technology are the same as their interactions with other people, using the same social rules and expectations. While the media equation corresponds with basic views of human interaction, it has not yet been applied to the more advanced conceptions of human interaction and relationships examined in communication studies.

Key Concepts

asynchronous communication   (p. 335)
content creators   (p. 327)
emoticons   (p. 335)
media equation   (p. 339)
media generations   (p. 323)

microcoordination   (p. 333)
relational technologies   (p. 322)
richness   (p. 334)
synchronous
   communication   (p. 335)

Questions to Ask Your Friends

- Ask your friends at school how they feel when someone's cell phone rings during class. Do they find it irritating or believe it is acceptable behavior? If you have friends attending another school, ask them how they feel when someone's cell phone rings during class. How do their answers compare with those of friends at your school?

- If you have your own Web site or page on a social networking site, ask your friends to compare how you present yourself on this page to how you present yourself off-line. In what ways are they different and similar?

- Ask your friends about their most recent technology purchase and why they purchased that particular product. Are there any similarities in the products purchased by your friends? Are there any similarities in their reasons for making the purchase?

Media Links

- Examine how characters on television programs use and perform relational technology. Do their use and performance of technology parallel that of your friends, family, coworkers, or classmates?

- When cell phones were introduced in the United States, advertisements stressed their use for business purposes. Early cell phone advertisements in the United Kingdom stressed their use for social connection. Cell phone sales in the United States lagged behind those in the United Kingdom for many years, but cell phone companies in the United States are now featuring relationships in their advertisements. Describe how relationships are featured in the television, print, and Internet advertisements of these companies.

- Visit the official Web sites of various television series and movies. How many of these sites have chat rooms or discussion boards available to connect fans and viewers? How might establishing these relational connections influence the number of people watching these series and films? How might the establishment of these connections influence the interpretation and use of this material?

Ethical Issues

- In many ways, it is easier to fool people in chat rooms or when instant messaging than when talking with them face-to-face. Do you think deceitfulness online is more pardonable than being deceitful when talking with someone face-to-face?

- Students have been suspended from some schools for content on social networking sites. Should schools be allowed to suspend students for this content? Would your assessment change depending on whether the content *did* or *did not* pertain to school-related issues, activities, or people?

- Employers have based hiring decisions on social networking site content. Do you believe these actions are justified? In what ways do employers using social networking sites for the evaluation of job candidates compare and contrast with school officials using these sites for student discipline?

Answers to Photo Captions

Photo 12.1 ▪ The generations in which these gentlemen were born will likely influence their perceptions and use of technology.

Photo 12.2 ▪ Social networking sites are used to establish and maintain relationships, as well as create identities.

Photo 12.3 ▪ The type of microcoordination most likely taking place is iterative coordination, through which people narrow in on one another using cell phones instead of establishing a precise time and location.

Photo 12.4 ▪ Webcams increase the richness of online interaction by increasing the number of nonverbal cues available. They also enable online communication to become more synchronous.

Student Study Site

Visit the study site at **www.sagepub.com/ciel** for e-flashcards, practice quizzes, and other study resources.

References

Baxter, L. A., & Montgomery, B. M. (1996). *Relating: Dialogues and dialectics.* New York: Guilford.

Baym, N. K., Zhang, Y. B., & Lin, M.-C. (2004). Social interactions across media: Interpersonal communication on the Internet, telephone, and face-to-face. *New Media & Society, 6,* 299–318.

Boase, J., Horrigan, J. B., Wellman, B., & Rainie, L. (2006, January 25). *The strength of Internet ties: The Internet and email aid users in maintaining their social networks and provide pathways to help when people face big decisions.* Washington, DC: Pew Internet & American Life Project.

Boneva, B. S., Quinn, A., Kraut, R., Kiesler, S., & Shklovski, I. (2006). Teenage communication in the instant messaging era. In R. Kraut, M. Brynin, & S. Kiesler (Eds.), *Computers, phones, and the Internet: Domesticating information technology* (pp. 201–218). New York: Oxford University Press.

Bortree, D. S. (2005). Presentation of self on the Web: An ethnographic study of teenage girls' weblogs. *Education, Communication & Information, 5,* 25–39.

Byrne, D. (1997). An overview (and underview) of research and theory within the attraction paradigm. *Journal of Social and Personal Relationships, 14,* 417–431.

Campbell, S. W., & Russo, T. C. (2003). The social construction of cell telephony: An application of the social influence model of perceptions and uses of cell phones within personal communication networks. *Communication Monographs, 70,* 317–334.

Chen, W., Boase, J., & Wellman, B. (2002). The global villagers: Comparing Internet users and uses around the world. In B. Wellman & C. Haythornthwaite (Eds.), *The Internet in everyday life* (pp. 74–113). Malden, MA: Blackwell.

Chesebro, J. W. (1984). The media reality: Epistemological functions of media in cultural systems. *Critical Studies in Mass Communication, 2,* 111–130.

Cummings, J. N., Lee, J. B., & Kraut, R. (2006). Communication technology and friendship during the transition from high school to college. In R. Kraut, M. Brynin, & S. Kiesler (Eds.), *Computers, phones, and the Internet: Domesticating information technology* (pp. 265–278). New York: Oxford University Press.

Duck, S. W. (2007). *Human relationships* (4th ed.). Thousand Oaks, CA: Sage.

Fischer, C. (1992). *America calling: A social history of the telephone to 1940.* Berkeley: University of California Press.

Freiermuth, M., & Jarrell, D. (2006). Willingness to communicate: Can online chat help? *International Journal of Applied Linguistics, 16,* 189–212.

Fulk, J., & Steinfeld, C. W. (Eds.). (1990). *Organizations and communication technology.* Newbury Park, CA: Sage.

Gordon, R. A. (1996). Impact of ingratiation on judgments and evaluations: A meta-analytic investigation. *Journal of Personality and Social Psychology, 17,* 45–70.

Griffin, E. (2003). *A first look at communication theory* (5th ed.). New York: McGraw-Hill.

Gumpert, G., & Cathcart, R. (1985). Media grammars, generations, and media gaps. *Critical Studies in Mass Communication, 2,* 23–35.

Howard, P. E. N., Rainie, L., & Jones, S. (2002). Days and nights on the Internet. In B. Wellman & C. Haythornthwaite (Eds.), *The Internet in everyday life* (pp. 45–73). Malden, MA: Blackwell.

Katz, E., Levin, M. L., & Hamilton, H. (1963). Traditions of research on the diffusion of innovations. *American Sociological Review, 28,* 237–252.

Katz, J. E. (2006). *Magic in the air: Cell communication and the transformation of social life.* New Brunswick, NJ: Transaction.

Katz, J. E., & Aakhus, M. A. (Eds.). (2002). *Perpetual contact: Cell communication, private talk, public performance.* Cambridge, UK: Cambridge University Press.

Kraut, R., Brynin, M., & Kiesler, S. (Eds.). (2006). *Computers, phones, and the Internet: Domesticating information technology.* New York: Oxford University Press.

Kraut, R., Kiesler, S., Boneva, B., & Schklovski, I. (2006). Examining the effect of Internet use on television viewing: Details make a difference. In R. Kraut, M. Brynin, & S. Kiesler (Eds.), *Computers, phones, and the Internet: Domesticating information technology* (pp. 70–83). New York: Oxford University Press.

Lenhart, A., & Fox, S. (2006, July 19). *Bloggers: A portrait of the Internet's new storytellers.* Washington, DC: Pew Internet & American Life Project.

Lenhart, A., & Madden, M. (2005, November 2). *Teen content creators and consumers.* Washington, DC: Pew Internet & American Life Project.

Ling, R. (2004). *The cell connection: The cell phone's impact on society.* San Francisco: Morgan Kaufmann.

Lobet-Maris, C. (2003). Cell phone tribes: Youth and social identity. In L. Fortunati, J. E. Katz, & R. Riccini (Eds.), *Mediating the human body: Technology, communication, and fashion* (pp. 87–92). Mahwah, NJ: Lawrence Erlbaum.

McKenna, K. Y. A., & Seidman, G. (2006). Considering the implications: The effects of the Internet on self and society. In R. Kraut, M. Brynin, & S. Kiesler (Eds.), *Computers, phones, and the Internet: Domesticating information technology* (pp. 279–295). New York: Oxford University Press.

Morris, M., & Ogan, C. (1996). The Internet as mass medium. *Journal of Communication, 46,* 39–50.

Nie, N. H., Hillygus, D. S., & Erbring, L. (2002). Internet use, interpersonal relations, and sociability. In B. Wellman & C. Haythornwaite (Eds.), *The Internet in everyday life* (pp. 215–243). Malden, MA: Blackwell.

Peter, J., & Valkenburg, P. M. (2006). Research note: Individual differences in perceptions of Internet communication. *European Journal Communication, 21,* 213–226.

Putnam, R. (2000). *Bowling alone: The collapse and revival of American community.* New York: Simon & Schuster.

Quan-Haase, A., & Wellman, B., with Witte, J. C., & Hampton, K. (2002). Capitalizing on the Internet: Social contact, civic engagement, and sense of community. In B. Wellman & C. Haythornwaite (Eds.), *Internet and everyday life* (pp. 291–324). Malden, MA: Blackwell.

Reeves, B., & Nass, C. (2002). *The media equation: How people treat computers, television, and new media like real people and places.* Stanford, CA: Center for the Study of Language and Information.

Robinson, J. P., & De Haan, J. (2006). Information technology and family time displacement. In R. Kraut, M. Brynin, & S. Kiesler (Eds.), *Computers, phones, and the Internet: Domesticating information technology* (pp. 51–69). New York: Oxford University Press.

Sahlstein, E. M. (2006). The trouble with distance. In D. Kirkpatrick, S. W. Duck, & M. K. Foley (Eds.), *Relating difficulty: The process of constructing and managing difficult interaction* (pp. 119–140). Mahwah, NJ: Lawrence Erlbaum.

Snider, M. (2006, June 8). iPods knock over beer mugs: College kids rank what's most popular. *USA Today,* p. 9D.

13

Relational Uses and Understanding of Media

T hink about the amount of time people actually spend using media each day. How much time do you think the average person spends watching television, listening to music, reading, playing video games, watching movies, and using the Internet?

Before you answer this question, consider why it might be difficult to obtain accurate measurements of any human activity. One reason, of course, it is impossible to measure the exact activities of every single person. Also, people frequently underestimate or overestimate the amount of time spent engaged in particular activities. Plus, people want to be viewed by others (and themselves) in a favorable manner, so their responses may not entirely reflect actual behavior but rather correspond with how they believe they should behave.

The Middletown Media Studies have taken these problems into account when determining the amount of time people spend using media and what media they use (Papper, Holmes, & Popovich, 2004). Comparing the results of telephone surveys, diary records in which people document their own activities, and direct observation in which people were followed and observed during every waking moment of the day, these studies revealed that people actually spend double the amount of time using media than they believe. The Middletown Media Studies also established that people do not use media in isolation but often use two or more media systems simultaneously, an activity referred to as **concurrent media use**. You, for example, may be reading this book while listening to the radio or watching television. Including concurrent media use, the most media-active person observed in these studies spent more than 17 hours using media

The Middletown Media Studies also uncovered that while the majority of media use occurs in the home, 34% of media use occurs outside the home in such locations as businesses, automobiles, school, and work. This percentage will likely increase in the coming years as video, music, and the Internet become more accessible through cell phones and other relational technologies.

each day, and the least media-active person observed spent a bit more than 5 hours using media each day. The average amount of time spent using media daily was nearly 11 hours.

While the sheer amount of time spent using media is reason enough for its importance as an area of study, perhaps more significant is the impact of media on relationships and the impact of relationships on the use of media. Media use at home frequently occurs in the presence of family members, close friends, and romantic partners, while media use outside the home often occurs with those with whom you share more social relationships, such as classmates, coworkers, acquaintances, and even strangers. In fact, the influence of relationships on your use of media is even evident when you are physically alone. The most common medium used concurrently with television was found to be the telephone (Papper et al., 2004). Unless the people in the study were listening to recorded messages and not talking with someone else, their use of television occurred in the context of their relationships.

This chapter first explores early views of media and the media audience. We then position the media audience as active consumers of media products who assign unique meaning to media texts and use media for specific reasons. Next, we discuss the relational uses and functions of media, including how media provide a context for relationships, inform people about relationships, and function as an alternative to relationships. We then examine the use of media in everyday communication, looking specifically at its prevalence as a topic of conversation, its impact in the understanding and dissemination of media messages, and its role in the development of relationships and identities.

Focus Questions

- Why is the term *mass media* inappropriate?
- Why might audience members be considered active consumers of media?
- What are the relational uses and functions of media?
- What functions does talk about media serve in everyday communication?

Is *Mass Media* an Appropriate Term?

Media were originally thought to exert absolute and uniform influence on the lives of "the masses." This view assumed that all media messages were being received and interpreted by members of the audience in the same manner and that they all resulted in the same impact or effect on each audience member. If everyone in your class watched the same episode of a television program, this view would hold that it was received by every member of your class in the exact same way; the episode would mean the exact same thing to everyone in your class and have the exact same effects on each of you. Media were thus seen as powerful agents in shaping opinions and behaviors of a susceptible mass audience in whatever manner desired. This belief in the inescapable and standardized nature of media messages has been characterized as the *hypodermic needle* or *magic bullet* capability of media.

Once actual research was conducted, media scholars quickly debunked as incorrect the notion of all-powerful media exerting unrestricted influence on a susceptible mass audience. The classic view of media also overlooked the profound influence of personal relationships on the reception, interpretation, and impact of media. Remnants of this view are still evident when people blame television, video games, music, movies, or other media for increases in crime, school shootings, or other tragedies that befall society. Media, however, do not exist independently from the cultural, political, and economic systems in which they are embedded (Chesebro & Bertelsen, 1996). Media scholars increasingly recognize that personal and social factors play a huge role in the reception of media messages, how they are interpreted, and their potential impact on opinion and behaviors. Further, as we will soon discuss in more detail, the media audience is viewed no longer as passive receptors but rather as actively engaged users of media. Although people occasionally use terms like *mass media* and *mass audience,* the use of these terms is based more on tradition than on actual conditions.

Increased Availability and Selection of Media

The term *mass* is also indicative of media's ability to reach large numbers of people, an essentially massive audience. However, as the number and availability of media products have increased throughout the years, a less massive audience is receiving the same media product. Think about the changes in the amount and accessibility of media products that have taken place in the past century. For quite some time, people could choose among three broadcast television stations, which meant that on a given evening, television viewers watched one of three different programs. The hundreds of programs now available on demand with the use of DVRs, VCRs, Webcasts, and podcasts increase the number of available options even more. Radio was once limited to the few stations that could be received with a good antenna. Satellite radio has radically increased the number of channels available, and many traditional radio stations worldwide are now available through live Internet feeds. People were once limited to local newspapers. Now hundreds of newspapers—even international ones—are available online, and many newspapers are digitally reproduced and distributed in multiple cities throughout the country.

While the audience of some media still numbers in the millions, comparing present numbers with past illustrates the dramatic drop that has taken place. The highest-rated half-hour television program of all time is "The Giant Jackrabbit" episode of *The Beverly Hillbillies,* which aired on January 8, 1964, with a 65 share. This means that 65% of all television sets in use at that moment were tuned to that episode! Current top-rated programs (see Table 13.1) usually average a third of that number. Furthermore, broadcast television news (ABC, CBS, NBC) once dominated in the ratings, but with Fox News, CNN, MSNBC, and other news outlets now available, the ratings of broadcast news have significantly decreased and continue to decline.

Table 13.1 Nielsen TV Ratings for Network Primetime Series: Top 10 (May 4–10, 2009)

Rank	Program Name	Network	Day	Time	Household Rating/Share	Audience	Viewers
1	AMERICAN IDOL	FOX	Wed	9:00 PM	13.7/21.0	15,685,000	23,574,000
2	AMERICAN IDOL	FOX	Tue	8:00 PM	13.4/21.0	15,319,000	23,414,000
3	DANCING WITH THE STARS	ABC	Mon	8:00 PM	12.6/19.0	14,430,000	20,278,000
4	MENTALIST, THE	CBS	Tue	9:00 PM	10.4/16.0	11,854,000	16,678,000
5	NCIS	CBS	Tue	8:00 PM	10.4/17.0	11,917,000	16,723,000
6	GREY'S ANATOMY	ABC	Thu	9:00 PM	10.3/16.0	11,800,000	15,546,000
7	DANCING W/STARS RESULTS	ABC	Tue	9:00 PM	9.4/14.0	10,763,000	14,556,000
8	CSI	CBS	Thu	9:00 PM	9.2/15.0	10,589,000	14,912,000
9	CRIMINAL MINDS	CBS	Wed	9:00 PM	8.9/14.0	10,176,000	14,128,000
10	CSI: MIAMI	CBS	Mon	10:00 PM	8.7/14.0	9,979,000	13,718,000

Source: http://tvlistings.zap2it.com/ratings/weekly.html

Coupled with and at least partially responsible for the rise in the number of media options available has been an increased tendency to focus a particular media product on specific audiences. Four decades ago, Gary Gumpert (1970) introduced the term **mini-com** to describe the growing tendency to focus media products on specific audience members connected by a common bond. Gumpert perceived media becoming increasingly directed and adapted to multiple "small mass audiences" connected through interest in particular content (p. 286). Connected by their interest in certain hobbies, their political affiliations, or their occupations, these groups seek out media that deal with these areas. A *mass* audience may not be interested in model trains or crocheting, but a *mini* audience interested in these topics will seek out and use media devoted to them. This trend, even more evident now than when it was initially introduced, can be illustrated by the number of magazines now available. National magazines, such as *Life*—which once boasted huge numbers of subscribers—no longer exist. The thousands of magazine titles now available target specific populations, such as croquet players, fishing enthusiasts, and Angus cattle farmers, and feature everything from model trains and crocheting to underwater basket weaving. Someday, a publisher may even aim a magazine called *British and Redneck Professors Monthly* exclusively at us!

Creating Individual Media Experiences

Beyond increased media options and a focus on specific audiences, individual members of an audience have always possessed the ability to create original and distinct media products through their individual and unique use of each media system. As you flip through the channels while trying to find something to watch on television or go back and forth between two or more channels, you create a distinct television product unavailable to people not watching with you. The selection and arrangement of songs on your iPod or MP3 player are distinctive and organized in ways unimaginable by the producers of those songs. Your scanning of headlines and pictures in the newspaper, along with your selection of stories, comics, sports reports, horoscopes, advice columns, letters to the editor, classifieds, and other material, will be unique compared to that of any other reader. When browsing the Internet, you have the ability to create a seemingly infinite number of distinct combinations through your selection of the millions of Web sites available. Visiting a unique combination of sites—for example, espn.com, then myspace.com, then google.com, then sagepub.com, then back to myspace.com, then weather.com, then youtube.com, and then back to myspace.com—provides you with an experience unlike that of any other Internet user. Even if another person happens to follow this same selection pattern, he or she will probably not access the same material, again, which numbers in the millions; nor will he or she spend the same amount of time at each site.

The Active Use of Media

Classic views of the media audience positioned its members as passively receiving media messages without any thought, critical evaluation, or resistance. The current and more accurate conceptualization of media audiences opposes this view of a largely unengaged audience and positions audience members as actively selecting media, interpreting and assigning meaning to media messages in ways unintended and unimagined by the producers of media, and using media for specific and often very relational reasons.

Selecting and Attending to Media

Characterizing audience members as selective users highlights the discriminating nature of the media audience. People do not consume everything available during mediated experiences; nor do they provide their full attention to the media products they use. You may have read the newspaper this morning, but you probably did not read every section or article. Likewise, when you last visited a site on the Internet, you probably used some areas of the site and not others. Not the result of accidentally missing something or being a careless audience member, this manner of consuming media is the result of needing and receiving greater satisfaction from some parts of the media product than from others. You might receive greater satisfaction and enjoyment from the comic section of the newspaper than the advice columns, so you are more likely to read the comic section and skip the advice columns. If you anticipate talking with friends at work about a ballgame that took place the night before, you may read about the game in the morning paper in anticipation of that later conversation.

Photo 13.1 According to the Middletown Media Studies, what type of media use seems to be taking place in this picture? (See page 372.)

Selective Exposure

People generally attend to media that support—and avoid media that counter—existing beliefs, values, and attitudes (Zillmann & Bryant, 1985). You are more likely to listen to radio talk show hosts who support your political views and avoid those hosts who counter your views. A favorite song coming on the radio will likely result in an increase in volume, and a disliked song will lead to changing the station or turning off the radio. As you might imagine, selective exposure research has undergone profound changes resulting from massive increases in the amount of media products available, along with changes in technology, such as recording devices and even the remote control (Bellamy & Walker, 1996).

Personal relationships frequently guide exposure to media. Talk with others, for example, often directs people to certain media. If you are talking with a group of classmates before class and someone mentions a certain Web site, you may visit that site because it sounds interesting or because you will then be able to take part in future conversations about it. Talking with others also influences attitudes toward certain media. Listening to a friend express her dislike for a particular television program may influence your attitude toward that program and lead you to change the channel the next time it comes on.

Attention to Media

In addition to the actual selection of media, the amount of attention audience members provide media will fluctuate. One reason attention fluctuates is that people often do other things while using media. Someone on a bus may glance at passing cars or watch other passengers while reading a book. You may work with the radio on, but it functions primarily as background noise rather than something to which you give your undivided attention. People often talk to one another while watching a television program at home, which decreases their focus on the program being viewed. As we discussed earlier, people often engage in concurrent media use (Papper et al., 2004). Consequently, you may listen to music while using the Internet and vary your degree of concentration on one or the other at any given moment.

A second reason the amount of attention provided to media fluctuates has to do with involvement with the media. Involvement entails getting into or becoming engrossed in the media product or experience (Biocca, 1988). An example of high involvement is really enjoying and becoming engrossed in a movie and feeling a part of the action. An example of low involvement is watching a boring movie at the request of a friend and mentally formulating tomorrow's to-do list instead of paying attention to the action on-screen.

A final reason for fluctuation in the amount of attention paid to media takes us back to their actual selection. If you need the information provided by a particular media product, you will be more likely to focus your attention on it than if you do not. If you are in the market for a new automobile and an automobile commercial comes on the screen, you will likely pay more attention to it than to an advertisement for a product you have little interest in purchasing.

> Commercial breaks may impact your involvement in a television program, but one study suggests that lower involvement is not the only thing that may happen during commercial breaks. People who are really engrossed in a television program will actually respond negatively to products advertised during commercial interruptions (Wang & Calder, 2006). This may lead the makers of Squeaky Clean dish soap to rethink airing a commercial in the middle of *Grey's Anatomy*!

The Polysemic Nature of Media Texts

The polysemic nature of media texts is a fundamental assumption of the active audience approach to media. Words—and all symbols, for that matter—do not have a single meaning but instead are capable of having multiple meanings depending on occasions, circumstances, and how they are used. Media texts, which can include words, visuals, and sounds among other symbolic events, are no different. Rather than having a single meaning, media texts are open to a variety of meanings and are given these multiple meanings by members of the media audience.

A number of factors influence the meaning given to media texts. For instance, one study found that people's understanding and interpretation of television fiction differed significantly according to their cultural backgrounds (Liebes, 1988). An individual's race, ethnicity, gender, economic status, and other demographic and relational variables will influence how he or she interprets a given media text. The variety of circumstances in which that person finds him- or herself and why that particular media text is being consumed will also influence his or her interpretation. For instance, a person listening to a political advertisement of a candidate he or she opposes will naturally interpret the information provided in a different manner than if he or she supported that candidate. Additional media knowledge and experience can also influence how a text is interpreted and understood (Fiske, 1987). For example, listening to DVD commentary while watching a movie will greatly change how you view and experience that movie. Consuming media with others will also impact your interpretation of media text. For instance, laughter from others in a movie theater may lead you to view events on the screen as funnier than you may have otherwise experienced. Talking about media both during the consumption of media texts and after they have been consumed will also influence the meanings people assign to media texts.

The Uses and Gratifications of Media

Research into the selection of media and the attention provided to it, the primary focus of **uses and gratifications** research, has attempted to determine why media systems are used and what audience members gain from their use. Uses and gratifications research originated from the study of radio soap opera audiences conducted in the early 1940s (Herzog, 1944) and grew in prominence during the 1950s and 1960s when researchers sought to determine the effectiveness of media campaigns (Blumler, 1980). Communication scholars James Chesebro and Dale Bertelsen (1996) have summarized the primary findings of this research, as shown in Table 13.2.

Table 13.2 Why People Use Media According to Uses and Gratifications Research

1. Escapism	To avoid ongoing reality systems
2. Reality exploration	To secure basic information and to understand the world in which one exists
3. Character reference	To find suitable models for one's own life
4. Incidental reasons	A kind of miscellaneous category in which it is recognized that each individual may use or be gratified by media for very different, personal, and unique reasons

Source: Chesebro & Bertelsen, 1996, p. 35

While uses and gratifications research has provided us with a more accurate and realistic view of media use by an actively engaged audience, it is not without its limitations. Chesebro and Bertelsen's (1996) characterization of incidental reasons for media underscores the major limitation of uses and gratifications research. Essentially, this research focuses on *individual* uses of media rather than *relational* uses of media. Although some studies recognize the use of media for relational reasons, media research in general de-emphasizes these uses of media. However, a relational view of media is becoming increasingly vital as more and more of the world becomes mediated and interconnected in everyday life with relationships.

Relational Uses and Functions of Media

While often overlooked in the past, media are increasingly viewed as playing an influential role in people's relational lives. We next examine three key areas in which media enable relationships and fulfill social and relational needs.

The Use of Media Is a Shared Relational Activity

The use of media such as television often takes place in the company of others and for specific relational reasons. Most media—especially electronic media—enable interaction to take place and quite frequently are the actual basis for interaction. Print media, such as books, newspapers, and magazines, are more isolating, but, as Bausinger (1984) reminds us, people are still not alone when reading because "it takes place in the context of the family, friends, and colleagues" (p. 350). A sense of connection also exists through shared experience with others through all types of media. In the case of television, regardless of decreases in the amount of people watching the same program and the uniqueness of each viewer's experience, still potentially millions of people watch the same material as you at the exact same time. This phenomenon has led Saenz (1994) to describe television as providing viewers with "the feeling of being present at a 'busy' live cultural site" (pp. 578–579). You often use media in the physical presence of other people, especially those with whom you share personal relationships.

Photo 13.2 Do you think using the Internet as a family will become a shared media experience like watching television as a family? (See page 372.)

Coming Together as a Family

Watching television with family members is a prime example of media as a shared relational activity. Even in media-rich households with multiple television sets, computers, and other media systems, families often come together to watch television, which provides an opportunity for interaction to take place among family members and for enactment of family relationships.

The positive impact of watching television together as a family is being increasingly recognized, but researchers originally viewed television as detrimental to family life and relationships in general. As recently as 1982, the National Institute of Mental Health concluded that television viewing leads to the isolation of and less talk among members of a family (Pearl, Bouthilet, & Lazar, 1982).

Yet, research actually shows that television provides an opportunity for increased social and relational contact and even enhances the communication that occurs. For example, some research indicates that frequent television viewers not only spend more time with their families but also feel better about their family life (Kubey, 1990). Furthermore, viewing television in social and relational contexts has been found to be an active and complex process. We examine discussions about television and other media that take place among family members and those in other sorts of relationships later in the chapter.

Withdrawing From Interactions

While media enable interactions to take place, they also allow us to withdraw from social interaction (Lull, 1980), which is not necessarily harmful for the relationship. Sometimes you want to be around another person and engage in conversation, and other times you do not. If you ever find yourself visiting with someone you do not know well or with whom you have difficulty talking, watching television may enable you to be together without forcing you to talk. Some romantic couples enjoy reading books in the evening, which allows them to be physically together while providing a sense of isolation.

Differentiating Relationships

The shared use of media has even been shown to distinguish particular relationships from others. One study discovered that the most frequent activity shared among spouses that distinguished them from other types of relationships was not eating together, having an intimate conversation, arguing, paying bills, or even lovemaking but watching television together (Argyle & Furnham, 1982). Friends and siblings may play video games together more than those involved in other forms of relationships. Romantic partners or groups of friends may be more likely to watch a movie in a theater. Such media activities become characteristic of those shared within particular relationships.

Enacting and Evaluating Roles

The shared use of media also enables people to establish and enact specific relational roles, expectations, and boundaries (Lull, 1980). How people describe media systems in their lives reflects family dynamics and issues of gender (Livingstone, 1992). Using media together provides an opportunity to discuss and question perceptions and attitudes toward relationships. For instance, television viewing can result in the discussion of relational and family issues, especially when content is relevant to but inconsistent with someone's understanding of relationships (Fallis, Fitzpatrick, & Friestad, 1985). Participation in massively multiplayer online role-playing games (MMORPGs) has been found to enable romantic couples to learn more about one another's personality and worldview. Furthermore, parents who take part in these games with their children find they are able to develop a better understanding of their child's identity and social behavior (Yee, 2006).

Media Inform People About Relationships

Media also inform us about the structure and configuration of relationships, what relationships entail, and how to behave in them, as well as their meaning and value. An abundance of self-help and relationship books, Web sites, talk shows, and call-in radio programs are available to inform and guide people's knowledge of and participation in personal relationships. However, the use of media to inform people about relationships goes beyond this single genre. The majority of media content includes portrayals of relationships. Books, magazines, newspapers, the Internet, movies, songs, and television programs feature both fictional and real social and personal relationships, the depictions of which fluctuate culturally and with the passing of time (LaRossa, 2004).

People base their understanding of relationships and their actions within relationships in part on portrayals in media. People's knowledge of relationships is derived from a variety of sources, such as their own relational experiences and watching others in their social network engage in relationships. Yet a great deal of knowledge and understanding about relationships comes from their depiction and representation in media. In fact, scholars have noted that knowledge of the world and of society is increasingly based on media rather than on socialization by social networks (Cohen & Metzger, 1998). Of course, a variety of sources inform your understanding of relationships, and you can compare the information you gain from one source with the information gained from other sources as you develop your own unique understanding of relationships. Depictions of relationships in media are fundamental to this development in two primary areas.

Media Inform Us How Relationships Should Look

Media representations of relationships provide information about relational roles and demographic characteristics. Essentially, people can learn about what relationships look like and what to expect from them based on their depiction in the media. The relationships depicted on television are not always realistic, however. Multiple races, religions, sexual orientations, socioeconomic categories, and relationship configurations are underrepresented in television and in media as a whole (Dates & Stroman, 2001; Heintz-Knowles, 2001; Robinson & Skill, 2001).

Inaccurate portrayals of relationships in media may create unrealistic expectations. People frequently have the ability to compare relationships depicted in media with relationships observed or enacted in their physical lives, but media representations of relationships may nevertheless create unrealistic expectations and beliefs about how relationships should be enacted and what they should offer (Bachen & Illouz, 1996). For instance, research has shown that viewing romantic genres, such as romantic comedies and soap operas, is associated with unrealistic and overly idealistic expectations about marriage (Segrin & Nabi, 2002). Families do not always look like those portrayed in movies. Role enactment of partners in romantic relationships does not necessarily correspond with that of characters in romance novels.

Even though media representations may lead to inaccurate expectations of relationships, they may be necessary when people are faced with a lack of models in their physical world. For example, children in single-parent households may use depictions of relationships in media to inform them of roles within two-parent households (Hur & Baran, 1979). This use of media has proved critical in the formation of sexual identity among gay teens and adolescents, who frequently encounter a lack of physical life models to inform their sexuality (McKee, 2000; Meyer, 2003). Unfortunately, unrealistic expectations about relationships engendered through media may be especially influential in the absence of physical life comparisons (G. Jones & Nelson, 1996).

Media Inform Us How to Behave in Relationships

The second area in which media inform people about relationships is through the depiction of behaviors and interactions within relationships. Depictions of relationships in media provide models of behavior that inform people about how to engage in relationships. This use of media encompasses the **socialization impact of media**. Through media representations of relationships, people learn how to actually enact the behaviors consistent with various relational roles and how to properly engage in interactions within these relationships. This use of media supplements what people learn by direct experience, as well as by observing and talking with others (McQuail, 1994).

Numerous studies have examined the depiction of family interactions on television and generally observed positive behavior and relational maintenance strategies. B. Greenberg (1980) examined television family interactions as either going toward, going against, or going away, as described in Table 13.3. Going toward actions were found to occur with much greater frequency among television families than the other two actions combined. Subsequent studies have found that television family behavior has changed throughout the decades but generally remains positive (Bryant, Aust, Bryant, & Venugopalan, 2001; Larson, 1993, 2001).

Naturally, this use of media is not limited to families or television. All media systems depict a host of personal and social relationships used to inform us about behavior in relationships along with interaction techniques we might employ. Examples include what might

While the behaviors exhibited on *The Jerry Springer Show* are frequently based on conflict and violence, even this program has been shown to promote positive family behaviors. Through negative audience reaction to the transgressions and misbehavior of guests, Grabe (2002) has argued that the show actually imparts "frequent moral lessons about the virtues of family life in opposition to promiscuous behavior" (p. 314) and "might contribute to the promotion of traditional family values" (p. 326).

Table 13.3 B. Greenberg's (1980) Types of Television Family Interactions

Going toward actions	Positive acts of relationship maintenance, such as sharing or seeking information, showing concern, and overall acceptance
Going against actions	Negative acts such as ignoring, opposing, or attacking others
Going away actions	Acts through which a person distances him- or herself from others either physically or psychologically

Source: B. Greenberg, 1980.

happen on a first date, interactions with friends (Baxter, De Riemer, Landini, Leslie, & Singletary, 1985), interactions with annoying coworkers, and even communication among teachers and students (Freedman, 2003). Incidentally, we are still waiting to hear from Dwayne "The Rock" Johnson and Patrick Dempsey to portray us in case this book is ever turned into a movie! In any case, people use media depictions to inform them of their own relationships. Like relational role and demographic characterizations, media portrayals of relationship interactions and behaviors may not always mirror those in people's physical lives (Brinson, 1992), but they provide a vital source of information that people use in formulating and interacting in their actual relationships.

Media Function as Alternatives to Personal Relationships

Media serve many of the same uses and provide many of the same benefits as personal relationships. Needs and desires gained from personal relationships, such as companionship, information, support, control, intimacy, and entertainment, can be gained from media with the same level of satisfaction and fulfillment. In this sense, media and relationships have been described as "coequal alternatives" (Rubin & Rubin, 1985, p. 39). Notice that the header for this section of the chapter and the description just mentioned both label media as *alternatives* to rather than a *substitution* or *compensation* for personal relationships. Researchers have previously speculated that people might turn to media to compensate for a lack of companionship or substitute media when social and relational interaction is unavailable (Rosengren & Windahl, 1972). While this might be the case in some circumstances, media use has actually been found to enrich already satisfied social and personal lives (Perse & Butler, 2005). Furthermore, words like *substitution* imply an inferior entity is filling in or taking the place of a superior reality. As we will discuss, both personal relationships and media are more effective at fulfilling some needs and desires than others, but neither can be legitimately labeled as superior. Media and personal relationships are equally functional and interchangeable alternatives.

Cohen and Metzger (1998) have observed that many motives for using media correspond with motives for engaging in personal relationships. These authors have specifically compared social and relational needs surrounding feelings of security, such as intimacy, accessibility, control, and relaxation, and noted that social interaction and media both achieve these needs by varying degrees of superiority. For instance, relationships may have the advantage when it comes to *intimacy,* especially intimacy achieved through physical

Photo 13.3 Based on research findings about family interactions on television, what types of interactions would you expect to find in *Family Guy*? (See page 372.)

touch. At the same time, increasingly interactive and emotion-based media, such as those accomplished by digital means, enhance the feelings of intimacy achieved through media. In fulfilling the needs of *accessibility and control,* media seem to have the definite advantage. Except in the event of an errant paper delivery person or a sudden power outage, media always seem to be there for you when you need them. Even the most committed relational partner cannot achieve this level of dependability, even if carrying a cell phone. Furthermore, people have nearly complete control over what they experience through media, which cannot be achieved through relationships and social interaction. Media also seem to have the advantage when it comes to achieving *relaxation.* Perhaps due in part to greater accessibility and control, it is also likely due to the minimum personal investment required when using media. As we will discuss, however, people may become very emotionally invested in media personalities and characters. Furthermore, media can provide both positive and negative experiences.

Companionship and Relational Satisfaction From the Actual Use of Media

The relational and social satisfaction derived from media comes in part from their actual use and position within the home. Research has indicated that some people think of media, such as television or the computer, as a friend or member of the family (Gauntlett & Hill, 1999, pp. 114–119). Watching a movie, reading a book, browsing the Internet, playing a video game, or using any other type of media can provide the same amount of relational satisfaction and experience as going out with a group of friends. In Yee's (2006) study of MMORPGs, 27% of respondents named something that occurred during the game as their most satisfying experience of the past week. The same study found 33% of respondents indicated that their most negative experience of the past week had also occurred while playing the game, which indicates people's emotional investment in media.

Some people may actually prefer the companionship provided by media to that provided by those in their social network. Certainly, on some occasions people would rather use media than be with other people. Think back to a time when you wanted to spend time by yourself reading, watching television, listening to music, or using other media. Whether this use of media served to achieve a sense of companionship or to satisfy another need, you quite possibly enjoyed being away from other people and felt quite satisfied with your mediated experience.

Companionship and Relational Satisfaction From Parasocial Relationships

While media systems themselves can satisfy social and relational needs, many of these needs are met through relationships established with media characters and personalities, known as **parasocial relationships** (Horton & Wohl, 1956). Relationships people form with media characters and personalities have proved just as real and meaningful as those within their physical social networks. People consider and treat movie stars and news anchors just like they do family and friends who live next door.

When first learning about parasocial relationships, students often consider the concept a bit outrageous and often claim they do not form such relationships. They often associate these relationships with stalkers or those who are obsessed with particular characters or media personalities. However, these relationships are actually quite normal and extremely common. In fact, we are fairly confident that you have formed parasocial relationships with media characters and, at a minimum, thought of and talked about fictional characters as if they were actual people.

Parasocial relationships have consistently been found to parallel relationships in physical social networks. Similar to other types of relationships, people are often attracted to media characters and personalities with whom they perceive a certain degree of similarity (Turner, 1993). People use similar cognitive processes when developing parasocial relationships (Perse & Rubin, 1989) and follow the same attachment styles used in physical relationships (Cole & Leets, 1999). Parasocial relationships provide similar levels of satisfaction as other types of relationships (Kanazawa, 2002). As with face-to-face contact, parasocial contact has been shown to lower levels of prejudice (Schiappa, Gregg, & Hewes, 2005). Parasocial relationships, gauged using similar criteria to those used to evaluate other relationships (Koenig & Lessan, 1985), have also been found to follow similar patterns of development, maintenance, and dissolution as relationships with people in physical social networks.

Make Your Case

Research indicates that parasocial relationships are just as meaningful and fulfilling as relationships in our physical world. Nevertheless, some people view these relationships as inferior to those in our physical social networks. Make a case for whichever assessment of parasocial relationships you believe is more accurate.

In fact, when parasocial relationships end (e.g., when a soap opera character "dies"), people experience this loss much in the same manner as they do when losing a close friend (Cohen, 2003).

The Use of Media in Everyday Communication

Media frequently provide the basis for conversation in social and personal relationships. While a definitive number of any topic of conversation is unattainable, reports have indicated that anywhere from 10.5% to half of all conversations involve media to some extent (Alberts, Yoshimura, Rabby, & Loschiavo, 2005; Allen, 1975, 1982; S. Greenberg, 1975). Even using a conservative estimation, these numbers position media as among the most frequent—if not the most frequent—topic of conversation among people. Discussions about media occur both while people are using the media system and while people are away from the media system and engaged in a number of other activities. Conversations about media serve six important functions in social and personal relationships.

Media Provide a General Topic of Conversation

Media have long been recognized as providing people with a general topic of conversation (Berelson, 1949; Boskoff, 1970; Compesi, 1983; Katz, Hass, & Gurevitch, 1973; Lazarsfeld, 1940; Mendelsohn, 1964; Scannell, 1989; Smith, 1975). Much like discussing the weather, the pervasiveness of media enables people to establish a shared topic of discussion that in many cases will not lead to a heated disagreement. As a general topic of conversation, media play a vital social and relational role. Yet, even when media simply appear to provide a topic of conversation, important social and relational work takes place, and other functions of media talk discussed here are ultimately accomplished.

Talk About Media Impacts Its Interpretation and Understanding

Talking about media significantly affects such things as the meanings derived from it as well as emotional responses and attitudes. You may have previously discussed with others the impact or value of certain types of media, such as video games, television, movies, music, and books. Parents might instruct children to stop playing video games and complete their homework. Some people seem to gain absolute pleasure from deriding television, while others are quick to inform you that they never read books. Discussions of media value also involve actual media products and genres. People might tell you they absolutely love a new book just published or tell you about a great Web site they just found. Although not always immediately recognized as such, these discussions of media have influenced your use and understanding of media in some manner.

A more noticeable influence of discussions of media is their impact on the understanding and interpretation of particular media products. Some discussions of media products serve *directional* purposes, such as explaining the plot of a television program to someone who started watching it a few minutes late or describing what happened in a movie to someone who just returned from the restroom. Other examples of this type of media discussion involve repeating dialogue for someone who missed what was said or walking someone through a video game when playing it for the first time. While these examples usually result from requests for clarification or guidance, other directional media talk is offered without prompting.

Discussions of media often bring about new understanding and meaning of media texts and also of relationships (Babrow, 1990; Fiske, 1989; Hodge & Tripp, 1986). Discussions of plot, characters, or actors playing certain roles can change people's interpretation of a movie or a relationship. Talking about a commercial you just heard on the radio can alter its meaning and influence. Alterations in meaning and appreciation of a media product often occur long after it has been consumed. A prime example is discussing what you watched on television the previous evening with friends at work or school the next day. Such discussions of media products can clarify the meanings attached, alter convictions about their significance, and adjust levels of appreciation. These discussions also influence future consumption of media. For instance, a discussion about the background of a musician may change how you interpret her music when listening to it in the future. These are relational consequences of media use.

Talk About Media Impacts the Dissemination and Influence of Media

Media do not have an all-powerful role in people's understanding of the world, knowledge, decisions of value and importance, or behavior, but they do play a significant role in their development. Discussions of media not only aid in the dissemination of media messages but also enhance their impact and are a relational phenomenon.

Even when someone has not watched a program on television, read the latest newspaper, or visited particular Web sites, discussing these media with others can still spread the information contained within them. People often supplement media messages by informing others about things they may have missed in the original message (Klapper, 1960).

The influence of discussions with other people about media content has strong implications for educators and health care advocates. Exposure to television news about science has been found to enhance people's perceived understanding of science and accordingly increase the likelihood that they will discuss scientific issues in everyday conversation (Southwell & Torres, 2006). A media antismoking campaign in Norway used provocative appeals to motivate relational discussion of the material with others (Hafstad & Aaro, 1997). Because of the issues of trust and concern inherent in close relationships, information gained from media but conveyed through a friend, a family member, or another close relationship may quite possibly be considered more significant and valid than information received directly from a media source. For example, you may receive information about the harmful effects of smoking from a public service announcement on the radio and share this information with a friend. Since this information comes from someone with whom your friend shares a close personal relationship, he or she may view it as more meaningful than if he or she had received it by listening to the actual public service announcement. A recent study found that media attempts to promote breast cancer screening influenced middle-aged women more than younger women, who were more influenced by interpersonal discussions with friends, family, and health care providers who often received the information from media sources (K. Jones, Denham, & Springston, 2006).

Talk About Media Promotes the Development of Media Literacy

David's mom likes to tell the story of when he and his younger brother, Kevin, were watching a Bugs Bunny cartoon when they were 6 and 3 years old, respectively. When something outlandish happened in the cartoon, Kevin turned to David and asked, "How did they do that?" David confidently replied, "It's just the magic of television." Perhaps deep inside the recesses of his mind, striving to provide his brother with a better answer may be one of the reasons David started studying communication in the first place—and perhaps the reason he still enjoys watching Bugs Bunny cartoons. Regardless of the accuracy of the original answer, this tale of the McMahan family highlights another consequence of talk about media, specifically the promotion and development of media literacy.

Media literacy entails the learned ability to access, interpret, and evaluate media products. Discussion of media content impacts people's understanding and evaluation of this material, as well as their comprehension of its production and influence. Talking about media with those with whom you share close relationships significantly influences your actual use of media and your development of media literacy.

Discussions regarding the use and interpretation of media, especially television, often occur among family members. Parents and older siblings frequently demonstrate the use of media to young children and guide their understanding of the material both directly and indirectly. Comments about what is being viewed on television by older siblings have been shown to assist younger siblings' understanding of television content (Alexander, Ryan, & Munoz, 1984). Research has indicated that parents greatly influence both what a child learns from television and a child's attitude toward television. There exist both indirect and direct forms of parental influence on children's interpretations of television (Austin, 1993). *Indirect influences* include children's modeling of viewing behaviors exhibited by their parents, as well as general information-seeking patterns resulting from family communication patterns. *Direct influences* include rulemaking and actively mediating children's interpretations of television content

Photo 13.4 What are some things that can happen when a couple talks about media? (See page 372.)

through communication about observations on television. For instance, parents may provide additional information about what is being viewed, comment on behaviors of television characters and personalities, and remark about the connection between television and the physical world (Messaris, 1982; Messaris & Kerr, 1983). Children often ask their parents to explain the narrative techniques, such as why something has (or has not) occurred and what will occur next on a television program (Messaris & Sarett, 1981).

Of course, the promotion of media literacy through discussions of media is not limited to those occurring among family members (Geiger, Bruning, & Harwood, 2001). Some researchers have noted that the ability to evaluate and criticize media is strongly influenced by discussions of media among young children and their incorporation of media in play (Palmer, 1986). Much of what people know about media literacy and their ability to critically evaluate media products has developed from interactions with friends, classmates, professors, coworkers, romantic partners, and others with whom they share a relationship.

Talk About Media Influences Identification and Relationship Development

Talking about media enables people to recognize and promote shared interests, understanding, and beliefs, while also serving to highlight differences among people. A connection or disconnection with others can be based solely on the recognition of shared media experience. Relational connections among soap opera fans are often developed based on their common knowledge and experience from viewing these programs (Whetmore & Kielwasser, 1983). Of course, such connections are not based only on favorite media or developed only among fans. Discussions with a coworker about movies you have both seen may promote feelings of similarity as well. These discussions are influential not only because they allow people to recognize shared media experience but also because they allow people to recognize shared understanding of those experiences. Conversations about media experience can also develop feelings of separation, such as when a classmate talks about a band you have never heard before.

While the actual consumption of media can promote perceptions of similarity and dissimilarity, evaluation of this media plays an important role in the development of these views. For instance, if someone (like one of our relatives) mentions that his or her favorite book of all time is *Communication in Everyday Life* and this happens to be your all-time favorite book, you may feel a sense of connection with that person. Someone else may discuss a new Web site that he finds deplorable, but if you enjoy that Web site, you may feel division or separation from that person. Perceptions of similarity and

Contrarian Challenge

We have emphasized the way in which the use of media can provide a basis for bonding and relational development. However, can you think of examples where media preferences can be a negative influence on relationships?

difference derived from conversations about media are fundamental in the evaluation of others and can play a strong role in the development of relationships. The fact that media are often used as a general topic of conversation when interacting with someone for the first time, as well as that decisions about whether or not to pursue a relationship are often made within the first few moments of an initial interaction, places particular importance on perceptions of media similarity or difference. Imagine how many relationships never materialize just because someone's favorite movie happens to be the *American Idol*–derived epic *From Justin to Kelly*!

Of course, discussions of media content can uncover areas of similarity and difference beyond actual media use and evaluation. For example, discussing a blog entry can lead to the realization that you share certain political views with someone else. Talking about a video on YouTube can bring about recognition of a shared interest comedy. Discussing a social group featured on Facebook can highlight differences of opinion regarding that group. Talking with a romantic partner about a romantic relationship portrayed in a movie can provide a sense of how that person views relationships and whether or not you share such views. The topics included in media are essentially limitless, and thus, so too are the areas of similarity and difference that can be explored through their discussion.

Talk About Media Enables Identity Construction

Media that you use and enjoy are a significant part of who you are as an individual and play a major role in informing people of your identity. Your **media profile**, a compilation of your media preferences and general use of media, informs others about who you are as a person or at least the persona you are trying to project. For instance, David loves watching television, and his favorite shows include, among many others, *The Andy Griffith Show*, *The Simpsons*, *The Dukes of Hazzard*, *The A-Team*, *Married… With Children*, *Night Court*, and *The Golden Girls*. He enjoys most music and especially likes blues, jazz, Southern rock, classic rhythm and blues, music from the '80s, and anything by Eric Clapton and Prince. Thanks to Steve's introduction, David also enjoys listening to the music of Ralph Vaughan Williams but does not care much for Symphony No. 7. His favorite movie of all

Table 13.4 Some Questions to Consider When Creating Your Own Media Profile

1.	Do you like watching television? If so, what are some of your favorite programs?
2.	Do you like listening to music? If so, what are some of your favorite artists and songs?
3.	Do you like watching movies? If so, what are some of your favorite movies?
4.	Do you like to read? If so, what are some of your favorite books, newspapers, magazines, and so forth?
5.	Do you like playing video games? If so, what are some of your favorite games?
6.	Do you like using the Internet? If so, what are some of the sites you visit most often?
7.	What television programs, music, movies, print material, video games, and Internet sites do you dislike?
8.	Do you access television programs, music, movies, and newspapers through the Internet or your cell phone?

time, *The Blues Brothers,* is probably responsible for his initial interest in and enjoyment of blues music. He never reads fiction but will read every newspaper he can get his hands on and frequently reads them online. What does David's media profile inform you about him? What does it tell you about who he is as a person, where and when he grew up, his past experiences, and his additional interests and preferences, along with the beliefs, attitudes, and values he might hold?

Identities constructed through media consumption and subsequent discussions are just as meaningful as other identities (McMahan, 2004). In some cases, this identity construction surrounds the actual use or disuse of particular media systems. Some people wish to portray themselves as never watching television, while others may pride themselves on being voracious readers or gamers. Media identity construction also involves particular media products. These identities, though especially evident among fan cultures (Amesley, 1989; Jenkins, 1992), can occur among all consumers of media. A person may enjoy listening to country music, watching game shows, reading romance novels, or watching action movies, and these preferences and activities become part of this person's identity. Some people may enjoy a particular television program and pride themselves on knowing multiple details about the series. Some people you know may gain pleasure from listening to music acts that few other people have heard of.

Media preferences emerge through everyday communication with others, either through purposeful self-disclosure ("Hello. Nice to meet you. My name is David, and I love watching *The Golden Girls*") or unintentionally through the course of a conversation ("That story reminds me of something that once happened on *The Golden Girls*"). The first example contains a specific reason that David wants to disclose this information, perhaps to create a sense of identification with another fan of the show or someone who enjoys that type of program. Or perhaps the show is such a significant part of David's life that he is disclosing this information to provide a meaningful view of himself for another person. David may not have intentionally mentioned *The Golden Girls* in the second example, but it nevertheless indicates to the other person that David is a fan of the show, watches it occasionally, or has seen at least one episode that was meaningful enough for him to remember.

Discussions of media not only enable us to fully enact those identities related to media but also provide an opportunity to construct other parts of the self. Discussions of media have been shown to perform important roles in the construction of age and gender (Aasebo, 2005). Further, discussions of media can provide a sense of voice and empowerment (Brown, 1994; Jewkes, 2002) and allow media-based identities to be constructed, enacted, and displayed while serving a vital role in the enactment of multiple types of identities.

Focus Questions Revisited

Why is the term *mass media* inappropriate?

The term *mass media* implies that large numbers of people receive the same media product, interpret it in the same way, and are influenced by it in the same way. This characterization ignores personal, social, and relational influences on the interpretation, evaluation, and use of media messages. "Mass" also implies that massive numbers of people receive the same media product. However, while millions of people may have access to media products, the ever-increasing number of media options has resulted in fewer people experiencing the same media product. Finally, individual audience members have the ability to create original and distinct media products through their use of each media system.

Why might audience members be considered active consumers of media?

Rather than passive consumers receiving media messages without any thought, critical evaluation, or resistance, the media audience actively selects media, interprets and assigns meaning to media messages in unique ways, and uses media for specific relational reasons. Members of the audience actively select and attend to certain media, assign a variety of meanings to media texts, and use media for a variety of personal and relational reasons.

What are the relational uses and functions of media?

The use of media is a shared relational activity that enables people to come together, withdraw from relationships, and enact specific relational roles. Media also inform people about how relationships should look and how people should behave in relationships. Media function as coequal alternatives to personal relationships through the actual use of media and the formation and maintenance of parasocial relationships.

What functions does talk about media serve in everyday communication?

Beyond providing a general topic of conversation, talk about media impacts the interpretation and understanding of media. Talk about media also impacts the dissemination and influence of media, promotes the development of media literacy, influences identification and relationship development, and enables identity construction.

Key Concepts

concurrent media use   (p. 349)
media literacy   (p. 366)
media profile   (p. 368)
mini-com   (p. 352)

parasocial relationships   (p. 363)
socialization impact of
  media   (p. 360)
uses and gratifications   (p. 356)

Questions to Ask Your Friends

- Ask your friends to estimate the amount of time they spend using media. How do their responses compare with the average daily media use revealed by the Middletown Media Studies? If there is a significant difference between your friends' estimations and the numbers discovered in the Middletown Media Studies, why do you think this discrepancy exists?

- Ask a few of your friends separately to describe their media profile and then compare their responses once you have compiled a list of these preferences. Do you notice any similarity among their responses? If so, why do you think this similarity exists? What impact would this similarity of media preferences have on the relationships among your friends?

- Ask your friends how often they find themselves talking about media with other people. What media do they discuss most frequently? With whom do they talk about media most often? How have discussions about media influenced their use of media? How have discussions about media influenced their understanding of media?

Media Links

- Examine how relationships are portrayed in the media. What types of relationships are most common? Do media systems (i.e., Internet, books, television, movies) differ on the types of relationships represented? How are these relationships depicted?

- Compare how relationships are portrayed in recent media with their portrayal in media from past decades. What changes do you recognize?

- Visit a newsstand or store that sells magazines and examine the titles available. What does the concept of mini-com tell you about the available collection of magazines? Is the new issue of *British and Redneck Professors Monthly* out yet?

Ethical Issues

- Many concerns about media entail the impact of media on children, which has the potential to be both positive and negative. Who should be most responsible for regulating media used by children: producers of media content or parents?

■ Should people base their perceptions of others on discussions of media? What are the limitations or advantages of using these discussions to evaluate other people?

■ Media content is often shared through digital files, used in mash-ups to create new products, and used in fan-produced Web pages dedicated to media. Many producers of this content discourage these uses of media and frequently take legal action to prevent this behavior. Do you believe the three uses of media content mentioned above should be considered violations of the law? Do you believe any of these uses of media are less of an infraction than the others? If so, why?

Answers to Photo Captions

Photo 13.1 ■ Concurrent media use.

Photo 13.2 ■ Using the Internet as a family appears to be an increasingly common relational experience. Research indicates that over half of Internet users living with a spouse and children go online with others at least a few times each week and an additional 34% do so occasionally (Kennedy, Smith, Wells, & Wellman, 2008).

Photo 13.3 ■ Although Stewie may wish Lois was dead, many episodes of *Family Guy* feature positive feelings among family members. Television family behavior is usually quite positive.

Photo 13.4 ■ Talk about media can provide a couple with a topic of conversation, can promote the development of media literacy, can increase identification, can enable identity construction, and can impact the dissemination and understanding of the media product.

Student Study Site

Visit the study site at **www.sagepub.com/ciel** for e-flashcards, practice quizzes, and other study resources.

References

Aasebo, T. S. (2005). Television as a marker of boys' construction of growing up. *Young: Nordic Journal of Youth Research, 13,* 185–203.

Alberts, J. K., Yoshimura, C. G., Rabby, M., & Loschiavo, R. (2005). Mapping the topography of couples' daily conversation. *Journal of Social and Personal Relationships, 22,* 299–322.

Alexander, A., Ryan, M. S., & Munoz, P. (1984). Creating a learning context: Investigation of siblings during television viewing. *Critical Studies in Mass Communication, 1,* 345–364.

Allen, I. L. (1975). Research report—Everyday conversations about media content. *Journal of Applied Communications Research, 3,* 27–32.

Allen, I. L. (1982). Talking about media experiences: Everyday life as popular culture. *Journal of Popular Culture, 16,* 106–115.

Amesley, C. (1989). How to watch *Star Trek. Cultural Studies, 3,* 323–339.

Argyle, M., & Furnham, A. (1982). The ecology of relationships. *British Journal of Social Psychology, 21,* 259–262.

Austin, E. W. (1993). Exploring effects of active parental mediation of television content. *Journal of Broadcasting & Electronic Media, 37,* 147–158.

Babrow, A. S. (1990). Audience motivation, viewing context, media content, and form: The interactional emergence of soap opera entertainment. *Communication Studies, 41,* 343–361.

Bachen, C. M., & Illouz, E. (1996). Imagining romance: Young people's cultural models of romance and love. *Critical Studies in Mass Communication, 13,* 279–308.

Bausinger, H. (1984). Media, technology and daily life (L. Jaddou & J. Williams, Trans.). *Media, Culture, and Society, 6,* 343–351.

Baxter, R. L., De Riemer, C., Landini, A., Leslie, L., & Singletary, M. W. (1985). A content analysis of music videos. *Journal of Broadcasting & Electronic Media, 29,* 333–240.

Bellamy, R. V., Jr., & Walker, J. R. (1996). *Television and the remote control: Grazing on a vast wasteland.* New York: Guilford Press.

Berelson, B. (1949). What "missing the newspaper" means. In P. F. Lazarsfeld & F. N. Stanton (Eds.), *Communications research 1948–1949* (pp. 111–129). New York: Harper & Brothers.

Biocca, F. A. (1988). Opposing conceptions of the audience. In J. Anderson (Ed.), *Communication yearbook* (Vol. 11, pp. 51–80). Newbury Park, CA: Sage.

Blumler, J. G. (1980). The role of theory in uses and gratifications research. In G. C. Wilhoit & H. DeBock (Eds.), *Mass communication: Review yearbook* Vol. 1, (pp. 201–228). Beverly Hills, CA: Sage.

Boskoff, A. (1970). *The sociology of urban regions* (2nd ed.). Englewood Cliffs, NJ: Prentice Hall.

Brinson, S. L. (1992). TV fights: Women and men in interpersonal arguments on prime-time television dramas. *Argumentation and Advocacy, 29,* 89–104.

Brown, M. E. (1994). *Soap opera and women's talk.* Thousand Oaks, CA: Sage.

Bryant, J., Aust, C. F., Bryant, J. A., & Venugopalan, G. (2001). How psychologically healthy are America's prime-time television families? In J. Bryant & J. A. Bryant (Eds.), *Television and the American family* (2nd ed., pp. 247–270). Mahwah, NJ: Lawrence Erlbaum.

Chesebro, J. W., & Bertelsen, D. A. (1996). *Analyzing media: Communication technologies as symbolic and cognitive systems.* New York: Guilford.

Cohen, J. (2003). Parasocial breakups: Measuring individual differences in responses to the dissolution of parasocial relationships. *Mass Communication & Society, 6,* 191–202.

Cohen, J., & Metzger, M. (1998). Social affiliation and the achievement of ontological security through interpersonal and mass communication. *Critical Studies in Mass Communication, 15,* 41–60.

Cole, T., & Leets, L. (1999). Attachment styles and intimate television viewing: Insecurely forming relationships in a parasocial way. *Journal of Social and Personal Relationships, 16,* 495–511.

Compesi, R. J. (1983). Gratifications of daytime TV serial viewers. *Journalism Quarterly, 57,* 155–158.

Dates, J. L., & Stroman, C. A. (2001). Portrayals of families of color on television. In J. Bryant & J. A. Bryant (Eds.), *Television and the American family* (2nd ed., pp. 207–228). Mahwah, NJ: Lawrence Erlbaum.

Fallis, S. F., Fitzpatrick, M. A., & Friestad, M. S. (1985). Spouses' discussion of television portrayals of close relationships. *Communication Research, 12,* 59–81.

Fiske, J. (1987). *Television culture*. London: Methuen.

Fiske, J. (1989). Moments in television: Neither the text nor the audience. In E. Seiter, H. Borchers, G. Kreutzner, & E. Warth (Eds.), *Remote control: Television, audiences, and cultural power* (pp. 56–78). London: Routledge.

Freedman, D. (2003). Acceptance and alignment, misconception and inexperience: Preservice teacher, representations of students, and media culture. *Critical Studies—Critical Methodologies, 3*, 79–95.

Gauntlett, D., & Hill, A. (1999). *TV living: Television, culture, and everyday life*. London: Routledge.

Geiger, W., Bruning, J., & Harwood, J. (2001). Talk about TV: Television viewers' interpersonal communication about programming. *Communication Reports, 14*, 49–57.

Grabe, M. E. (2002). Maintaining the moral order: A functional analysis of *The Jerry Springer Show*. *Critical Studies in Media Communication, 19*, 311–328.

Greenberg, B. S. (1980). *Life on television: Content analysis of US TV drama*. Norwood, NJ: Ablex.

Greenberg, S. R. (1975). Conversations as units of analysis in the study of personal influence. *Journalism Quarterly, 52*, 128–130.

Gumpert, G. (1970). The rise of mini-com. *Journal of Communication, 20*, 280–290.

Hafstad, A., & Aaro, L. E. (1997). Activating interpersonal influence through provocative appeals: Evaluation of a mass media-based antismoking campaign targeting adolescents. *Health Communication, 9*, 253–272.

Heintz-Knowles, K. E. (2001). Balancing acts: Work-family issues on prime-time television. In J. Bryant & J. A. Bryant (Eds.), *Television and the American family* (2nd ed., pp. 177–206). Mahwah, NJ: Lawrence Erlbaum.

Herzog, H. (1944). What do we really know about daytime serial listeners? In P. Lazarsfeld (Ed.), *Radio research 1942–1943* (pp. 2–23). New York: Duell, Sloan, and Pearce.

Hodge, R., & Tripp, D. (1986). *Children and television: A semiotic approach*. Stanford, CA: Stanford University Press.

Horton, D., & Wohl, R. R. (1956). Mass communication and para-social interaction: Observations on intimacy at a distance. *Psychiatry, 19*, 215–229.

Hur, K. K., & Baran, S. J. (1979). One-parent children's identification with television characters. *Communication Quarterly, 27*, 31–36.

Jenkins, H. (1992). *Textual poachers: Television fans and participatory culture*. New York: Routledge.

Jewkes, Y. (2002). The use of media in constructing identities in the masculine environment of men's prisons. *European Journal of Communication, 17*, 205–225.

Jones, G. D., & Nelson, E. S. (1996). Expectations of marriage among college students from intact and non-intact homes. *Journal of Divorce and Remarriage, 26*, 171–189.

Jones, K. O., Denham, B. E., & Springston, J. K. (2006). Effects of mass and interpersonal communication on breast cancer screening: Advancing agenda setting theory in health contexts. *Journal of Applied Communication Research, 34*, 94–113.

Kanazawa, S. (2002). Bowling with our imaginary friends. *Evolution and Human Behavior, 23*, 167–171.

Katz, E., Hass, H., & Gurevitch, M. (1973). On the use of the mass media for important things. *American Sociological Review, 38*, 164–181.

Kennedy, T. L. M., Smith, A., Wells, A. T., & Wellman, B. (2008, October 19). *Networked families*. Washington, DC: Pew Internet & American Life Project.

Klapper, J. T. (1960). *The effects of mass communication*. New York: Free Press.

Koenig, F., & Lessan, G. (1985). Viewers' relations to television personalities. *Psychological Reports, 57*, 263–266.

Kubey, R. (1990). Television and the quality of family life. *Communication Quarterly, 38,* 312–324.

LaRossa, R. (2004). The culture of fatherhood in the fifties. *Journal of Family History, 29,* 47–70.

Larson, M. S. (1993). Family communication on prime-time television. *Journal of Broadcasting & Electronic Media, 37,* 349–357.

Larson, M. S. (2001). Sibling interaction in situation comedies over the years. In J. Bryant & J. A. Bryant (Eds.), *Television and the American family* (2nd ed., pp. 163–176). Mahwah, NJ: Lawrence Erlbaum.

Lazarsfeld, P. F. (1940). *Radio and the printed page: An introduction to the study of radio and its role in the communication of ideas.* New York: Duell, Sloan, and Pearce.

Liebes, T. (1988). Cultural differences in the retelling of television fiction. *Critical Studies in Mass Communication, 5,* 277–292.

Livingstone, S. M. (1992). The meaning of domestic technologies: A personal construct analysis of familial gender relations. In R. Silverstone & E. Hirsch (Eds.), *Consuming technologies: Media and information in domestic spaces* (pp. 113–130). London: Routledge.

Lull, J. (1980). The social uses of television. *Human Communication Research, 6,* 197–209.

McKee, A. (2000). Images of gay men in the media and the development of self esteem. *Australian Journal of Communication, 27,* 81–98.

McMahan, D. T. (2004). What we have here is a failure to communicate: Linking interpersonal and mass communication. *Review of Communication, 4,* 33–56.

McQuail, D. (1994). *Mass communication theory* (3rd ed.). Thousand Oaks, CA: Sage.

Mendelsohn, H. (1964). Listening to the radio. In L. A. Dexter & D. M. White (Eds.), *People, society, and mass communications* (pp. 239–249). New York: Free Press.

Messaris, P. (1982). Parents, children, and television. In G. Gumpert & R. Cathcart (Eds.), *Intermedia: Interpersonal communication in a media world* (2nd ed., pp. 580–598). New York: Oxford University Press.

Messaris, P., & Kerr, D. (1983). Mothers' comments about TV: Relation to family communication patterns. *Communication Research, 10,* 175–194.

Messaris, P., & Sarett, C. (1981). On the consequences of television-related parent-child interaction. *Human Communication Research, 7,* 226–244.

Meyer, M. D. E. (2003). "It's me. I'm it.": Defining adolescent sexual identity through relational dialectics in *Dawson's Creek. Communication Quarterly, 51,* 262–276.

Palmer, P. (1986). *The lively audience: A study of children around the TV set.* Sydney, Australia: Allen & Unwin.

Papper, R. A., Holmes, M. E., & Popovich, M. N. (2004). Middletown media studies: Media multitasking . . . and how much people really use the media. *International Digital Media & Arts Association Journal, 1,* 4–56.

Pearl, D., Bouthilet, L., & Lazar, J. (Eds.). (1982). *Television and behavior: Ten years of scientific progress and implication for the eighties* (Vol. 1). Rockville, MD: National Institute of Mental Health.

Perse, E. M., & Butler, J. S. (2005). Call-in talk radio: Compensation or enrichment? *Journal of Radio Studies, 12,* 204–222.

Perse, E. M., & Rubin, R. B. (1989). Attribution in social and parasocial relationships. *Communication Research, 16,* 59–77.

Robinson, J. D., & Skill, T. (2001). Five decades of families on television. In J. Bryant & J. A. Bryant (Eds.), *Television and the American family* (2nd ed., pp. 139–162). Mahwah, NJ: Lawrence Erlbaum.

Rosengren, K. E., & Windahl, S. (1972). Mass media consumptions as a functional alternative. In D. McQuail (Ed.), *Sociology of mass communications* (pp. 166–194). Middlesex, UK: Penguin.

Rubin, A. M., & Rubin, R. B. (1985). Interface of personal and mediated communication: A research agenda. *Critical Studies in Mass Communication, 2,* 36–53.

Saenz, M. K. (1994). Television viewing as a cultural practice. In H. Newcomb (Ed.), *Television: The critical view* (pp. 573–586). New York: Oxford University Press.

Scannell, P. (1989). Public service broadcasting and modern public life. *Media, Culture, and Society, 11,* 135–166.

Segrin, C., & Nabi, R. L. (2002). Does television viewing cultivate unrealistic expectations about marriage? *Journal of Communication, 52,* 247–263.

Schiappa, E., Gregg, P. B., & Hewes, D. E. (2005). The parasocial contact hypothesis. *Communication Monographs, 72,* 92–115.

Smith, D. M. (1975). Mass media as a basis for interaction: An empirical study. *Journalism Quarterly, 52,* 44–49, 105.

Southwell, B. G., & Torres, A. (2006). Connecting interpersonal and mass communication: Science news exposure, perceived ability to understand science, and conversation. *Communication Monographs, 73,* 334–350.

Turner, J. R. (1993). Interpersonal and psychological predictors of parasocial interaction with different television performers. *Communication Quarterly, 41,* 443–453.

Wang, A., & Calder, B. (2006). Media transportation and advertising. *Journal of Consumer Research, 33,* 163–172.

Whetmore, E. J., & Kielwasser, A. P. (1983). The soap opera audience speaks: A preliminary report. *Journal of American Culture, 6,* 110–116.

Yee, N. (2006). The psychology of MMORPGs: Emotional investment, motivations, relationship formation, and problematic usage. In R. Schroeder & A. Axelsson (Eds.), *Avatars at work and play: Collaboration and interaction in shared virtual environments* (pp. 187–207). London: Springer-Verlag.

Zillmann, D., & Bryant, J. (Eds.). (1985). *Selective exposure to communication.* Hillsdale, NJ: Lawrence Erlbaum.

14

Public Communication and Personal Influence

M uch influence and persuasion takes place interpersonally and is so common and familiar that people do not even realize it is happening. From "Hey, *buddy,* can you spare a dime?" to *"Dad,* I need a ride to Ellie's at six o'clock tonight" relational claims and reminders are the basis of much persuasion. You do favors for your friends, because that's what friends do. Parents are presumed to have certain responsibilities in relation to their children and vice versa. However, many other forms of persuasion are based on relational themes and implied obligations of friendship or connections among people. This chapter will look at social and personal influence, partly as it has been conceived in previous research on persuasion techniques and partly in terms of the underlying relational assumptions that persuasion basically relies upon. Persuasion can be seen as a relational act, not merely one involving logic or strong arguments, even when it involves persuading larger groups, as in town hall meetings or general civic engagement.

In what follows, we will examine four major areas of public and personal influence: (1) civic engagement and public discourse, (2) sequential persuasion, (3) emotional appeals, and (4) compliance gaining. Exploring civic engagement and public discourse, we will challenge common misconceptions about civic engagement and briefly examine its benefits. We will then discuss public discourse from a relational perspective. We will not discuss specifically how to develop and deliver a presentation but instead discuss the importance of relating to audiences and how to go about analyzing audiences when developing a public presentation. We will also look at various types of persuasive speeches along with using artistic proofs and the social judgment theory when attempting to persuade.

Sequential persuasion will assist you not only when developing a campaign to secure donations or volunteers but also in your everyday life when attempting to influence or being influenced by others. We will introduce various methods of sequential persuasion, discussing why they work and when they work best.

The study of emotions is a growing area of the discipline of communication—and for good reason. Emotions are powerful tools of persuasion, and they frequently lead to successful attempts at influence. In what follows, we will discuss the use of emotional appeals in public and personal influence and then examine two of the most common emotions used in such appeals, fear and guilt, along with some of the lost emotions.

Finally, we will examine compliance gaining, which looks specifically at personal attempts at influence. Compliance gaining differs from other sorts of persuasion in a number of ways, and we will discuss these differences in addition to looking at the importance of relationships when attempting to influence the behavior of people. We will look at the primary and secondary goals of compliance gaining as well as various strategies and why certain strategies may be selected rather than others.

Focus Questions

- What is civic engagement, and what are some common misconceptions people have about it?
- What are the types of persuasive presentations?
- What are the techniques of sequential persuasion?
- Are emotions physical or symbolic and relational, and why should they be included in a chapter on public and personal influence?
- What are the relational influence goals of compliance gaining?
- What are the original five strategies (categories) of compliance gaining?
- What contextual influences impact the selection of compliance gaining strategies?

What Is Civic Engagement?

Civic engagement entails participating in community development, addressing social concerns, and combating injustices. It is a necessary requirement for achieving and sustaining freedom, improving the social world, and being an engaged citizen. Civic engagement has resulted in political transformations of nation-states, the abolishment of slavery, improved working conditions, and the push for equality for African Americans, women, gays and lesbians, and other groups. Political, moral, religious, economic, and social perspectives and approaches have helped shape these changes and events, but they have been fully created and enacted through communication and civic participation. In what follows, we will examine common misconceptions that people have about civic engagement. We will then discuss some of the benefits people gain from participating in civic activities. Next, we will specifically examine communicating in public as a means of civic engagement.

Misconceptions of Civic Engagement

Common misconceptions surround the notion of civic engagement. One misconception is that social and political struggles are concerns of the past and are no longer relevant issues. In reality, many such struggles continue to impact communities, and citizens of the world must strive to recognize and combat injustices and must work to maintain freedom and equality. The issue of equal rights for gays and lesbians, for example, is at the forefront of much civic activity and public discourse. Workers continue to fight for improved working conditions and benefits. Environmental activists struggle to change the ways in which people live and use natural resources. Bigotry and hatred for numerous groups are evident in both speech and law. Inequality and injustices exist throughout the world and demand change. Social and political issues are struggles that are very much concerns of the present.

Another misconception about civic engagement is that participation in such activities is limited to only a few people and does not involve "ordinary" citizens. Beyond the obvious fact that issues of freedom and equality impact everyone, throughout history participants in movements have been largely made up of "ordinary" people rather than members of fringe groups or radicals. In some instances prolonged oppression forces people to act such as in the Watts Riots of 1965 and the Los Angeles Riots of 1992, which

Photo 14.1 Does civic engagement only include protests such as the one pictured here? (See page 413.)

Table 14.1 Benefits of Civic Engagement

Social Change
Civic engagement can lead to changes in society as witnessed in activities involving civil rights, labor movements, environmental measures, gay and lesbian rights, and women's rights among many others.

Social Reinforcement
Civic engagement can lead to the reinforcement of social values. In the United States of America, for example, participation in civic activity itself upholds social values of the country.

Justice
Civic engagement can lead to righting the wrongs of society as well as establishing what society deems right or wrong in the first place. Positions on issues such as stem cell research, abortion, euthanasia, the death penalty, and the treatment of enemy combatants continue to be discussed and evaluated in public forums.

Personal Growth
Civic engagement can result in the development of personal beliefs, values, and attitudes while enhancing social aptitude and belief in one's abilities.

Intellectual Growth
Civic engagement can result in personally developing a better understanding of social issues as well as local and global events.

were sparked by racial injustice; the Stonewall Riots of 1969 in response to police harassment and overall mistreatment of gay men; and the Taxpayer Tea Party Protests and the G20 Riots of 2009. In these cases, most participants did not plan on becoming part of a movement. Furthermore, social movements are not the result of one person but rather the work of many. A single person is often associated with a social issue or movement: for example, Martin Luther King, Jr., (racial equality), Harvey Milk (homosexual rights), Cesar Chavez (labor), and Gloria Steinem (women's rights). However, these people were not singularly responsible for change. Rather, change is the result of countless unknown yet essential people without whom transformation would not occur.

A third misconception is that civic engagement only surrounds *major* issues of national or international importance. While some issues have national or international consequences, many people engaged in civic engagement are dealing with issues of a local nature. Local initiatives such as funding for organizations and public works, zoning, support of community groups, education, and other issues require civic engagement. Students on college campuses are engaged in activities involving student rights, tuition, funding, and general administrative decisions. Although these issues may be perceived by some to be minor issues when compared to issues of genocide, equal rights, or war, they have a tremendous impact on your world and require involvement.

A final misconception is that civic engagement only involves radical actions or activities such as riots and protests. Actually, civic engagement involves a number of activities such as volunteering, membership, fund-raising, petitions, letters, sit-ins, strikes, walkouts, and boycotts, some of which are admittedly more dramatic than others. Public presentations are powerful methods of civic engagement that you will likely experience in your civic life and that will lead to a number of benefits (see Table 14.1).

Public Discourse and Relating to Audiences

At first glance, public speaking—in which both the speaker and the audience play active roles based on and guided through socially established norms and expectations—may appear as merely the enactment of social roles. If public speaking were simply the enactment of social roles, a speaker and an audience would be interchangeable—much like a given customer at a fast-food restaurant and a given cashier. However, public speaking more closely resembles the unique personal relationships that you share with your friends, family, and romantic partners in which the people are irreplaceable; that is, if a speaker or an audience were replaced, the interaction would be totally different. Audience members' characteristics, perceptions, and needs will govern what they expect from a speaker, and public speakers must adapt to each audience accordingly.

Recognition of the relationship between speakers and an audience begins with acknowledging the similarities between public speaking and personal relationships. In personal relationships, people seek to inform, understand, persuade, respect, trust, support, connect, satisfy, and evoke particular responses from one another, and such objectives exist in public speaking situations. In personal relationships, people must adjust to one another just as speakers must adjust to each unique audience to satisfy the goals of a public presentation. People transact their personal relationships though communication and create meaning and understanding that goes beyond the simple exchange of symbols, and the same transactions occur during public presentations.

Relational connections with audiences are often established by noting identification with the audience or how the speaker and the audience are alike (Burke, 1969). People tend to trust and like others whom they perceive as similar to them. Additionally, through identification, the meaning framework of a speaker becomes apparent. People feel as if they understand the way a speaker thinks and views the world because of the similarities between them. Consequently, a speaker's words become more understandable and more believable because the audience members are able to match the speaker's ways of thinking to their own. Ultimately, an audience must perceive a speaker as similar to them in some manner or form, through discussing shared experiences, shared connections with the topic, or shared hopes, fears, joys, and concerns or through using terminology that unites the speaker and an audience in a common endeavor or that is familiar and meaningful to that audience.

Analyzing Audiences

Analyzing audiences and adapting a presentation and its delivery accordingly is fundamental to effective public speaking. Speakers must determine the best way to develop and maintain a positive relationship between themselves and audiences and between audiences and the material. Ultimately, speakers must adapt to an audience all elements of a presentation except one very important factor: what they believe and wish to argue, maintain, or claim. For instance, suppose you are presenting a speech about hunting ordinances before members of your community and want to maintain that hunting is necessary to control certain wildlife populations. Although a large part of your audience opposes the hunting of animals for any reason and will likely disagree with your speech, you should not adjust your beliefs to match the audience's and thus present a speech urging a hunting ban. If you suspect your audience will oppose your speech, however, you will likely provide different evidence, organize and deliver your speech differently, and establish different relational connections with the audience than if you gave a speech to a prohunting audience. You must adjust the speech—that is, how you state your beliefs—to your audience, but do not adjust what you personally believe. In what follows, we discuss various factors that will impact approaches to the audience and provide suggestions and guidelines for developing effective presentations.

Relationship With the Speaker

As mentioned above, speakers must establish and maintain an appropriate relationship with an audience and base all decisions about a speech in part on that relationship. A relationship with an audience may already exist outside the public speaking context. An audience, for example, may consist of colleagues, supervisors, employees, classmates, group members, or community members, and their preexisting relationships with the speaker will impact how they view him or her personally and what they expect from his or her presentation. Identities created in other contexts will influence the public speaking identity created through a presentation, and vice versa. Additionally, the relationships that exist outside the public speaking context will impact the relationship created with the audience through a presentation, and vice versa.

How an audience views a speaker personally has a profound impact on presentations. A speaker's credibility is crucial to the success of a presentation. Think back on times when friends or strangers tried to convince you of something. The most successful individuals were probably (a) those you considered knowledgeable about the topic, (b) those you trusted, and (c) those who seemed most concerned about you. These characteristics touch on the three primary dimensions of credibility: knowledge, trustworthiness, and goodwill (Gass & Seiter, 2007). Speakers must convey to an audience that they are knowledgeable about the topic, that they can be trusted, and that they have the audience's best interest at heart. Notice that these components are often attributed to those with whom you share a personal relationship. In fact, perceptions of credibility are often based largely on the actual relationship shared with someone (i.e., you trust a person because he or she is your *friend,* or you distrust someone because he or she is your *enemy*).

If the audience has no previous knowledge of a speaker's credentials or experience with an issue or perceives the speaker negatively, he or she may need to spend more time explaining his or her credibility and developing a positive relationship with audience members. Also especially important, he or she must provide strong evidence for assertions made throughout the speech along with a clear focus and development of the topic to maintain a strong relational connection. If the audience members already perceive a speaker as credible and view him or her in a positive manner, that speaker will be more easily able to establish a strong relational connection with them, but he or she still must engage in behaviors that will enable full development and maintenance of such a relationship.

Relationship With the Issue and Position

Speakers must also determine an audience's relationship with the issue being addressed or the position being advanced. An audience may have a positive, a negative, or an impartial view of an issue before a speaker even begins to speak. Speakers must take this existing evaluation into consideration when preparing a speech because it will likely impact how the audience receives the presentation and the audience's relationship with the speaker. If the audience opposes a speaker's position, he or she may have to spend additional time establishing his or her credibility, his or her relationship with audience members, and how he or she personally developed the position being supported.

If a speaker anticipates the audience will receive the issue in a positive manner, he or she may spend less time defending and more time clarifying and outlining a position. Also, while establishing credibility and a positive relationship with the audience is always necessary, it will be easier if the audience agrees with the position being advanced. People view individuals whose positions mirror their own as *more* credible than those with opposing beliefs.

Speakers must also adjust their speech if they believe the audience is impartial to the issue, in which case they will probably need to spend more time stressing its importance and its impact on audience members' lives. The audience may not fully understand the issue, so speakers may need to spend more time describing what it entails.

Previous knowledge of the issue by an audience will also impact a presentation. The audience may be very knowledgeable or have little knowledge about the issue, and it is crucial that speakers make an assessment of that before preparing the substance of a speech. The level of audience knowledge and understanding of an issue will influence the depth and intricacy of a speech and what evidence and support material is used, impact the language used and how fully speakers must define and explain terminology used throughout the speech, and dictate how much time must be spent orienting the audience to the topic.

Attitudes, Beliefs, and Values

Determining audience attitudes, beliefs, and values also provides speakers with insight into how an audience may evaluate and respond to an issue and how audience members may view their relationship with them. **Attitudes** are learned predispositions to evaluate something in a positive or negative way that guide thinking and behavior (Fishbein & Ajzen, 1975). For example, you may dislike the taste of liver, which will guide your response to decline eating it should a plateful be passed your way at dinner. Attitudes usually do not change readily but instead remain relatively constant. Generally, the longer you hold an attitude and the more support you discover in its favor, the less likely you will be to change it.

Audiences' attitudes will impact their view of a speaker, the topic, the occasion, and even the evidence provided to develop and support an argument. Some audience members will respond more favorably to statistics while others will respond more favorably to examples or illustrations. Similarly, members of an audience will also possess attitudes regarding the sources of evidence. Some may view the Internet as providing unreliable information while others may view it as providing the most current and accurate information.

Beliefs, or what people hold to be true or false, are formed like attitudes through your direct experience, as well as through media, public and personal relationships, and cultural views of the world. Whereas attitudes are evaluations of something favorable or unfavorable, beliefs are evaluations of something true or false. Like attitudes, your beliefs can change, but they are generally even more stable than attitudes.

Knowing the beliefs of audience members will help speakers determine their attitudes, but the value of this knowledge does not stop there. Knowing the beliefs of an audience can also assist speakers in focusing a presentation. For instance, if you are discussing the problem of illegal immigration, the audience may or may not believe that an illegal immigration problem even exists. If the audience *does not* believe this problem exists, a speaker might focus his or her speech on establishing its existence. If the audience *does* believe that a problem exists with illegal immigration, the speaker may then explore other issues involving this topic.

Knowing the beliefs of an audience will also impact how deeply speakers must support the facts or opinions included in presentations. Depending on an audience's beliefs, some statements or claims of belief may need more or less support. A speaker claiming that "the Earth is round" would feel fairly confident that an audience will not look for proof, and unless that statement is critical to that speaker's argument, he or she would not need to include a great deal of support and development. Statements such as that one would be considered a **given belief**—that is, the majority of people in the audience will hold the same perspective of either true or false. However, saying something like "The issue of illegal immigration has been a problem for decades" might require additional support and development since not all members of an audience may agree with or be aware of this statement of belief. In the majority of cases, it is generally best to support all statements. However, knowing the beliefs of an audience will determine how much development should be included and whether or not the audience will agree with a given statement.

Values are deeply held and enduring judgments of significance or importance that often provide the basis for both beliefs and attitudes. The values that you hold are what you consider most important in this world. When listing values, people often include such things as life, family, truth, knowledge, education, personal growth, health, freedom, and wealth. Although all the items on this list might sound good to you, people do not all agree on their importance. For instance, a person may not view wealth as all that important in life, and not all people believe in the importance of knowledge.

When considering the influence of audience values on a presentation, three points emerge. First, speakers can use values to form an understanding of audience beliefs and attitudes, and vice versa. However, it is not always possible to establish supportive links between these variables. A person may profess to value health but have a positive attitude toward drinking alcohol in excess. Second, speakers can use audience values to determine and successfully convince audience members of their relationship with a topic and why they should listen to a presentation. If audience members value family, a speaker can use the impact the issue has on family life to show them the importance of the issue and why the audience should listen to the presentation. Finally, changing a person's values is very difficult and will take more than a single presentation to accomplish. A speaker might be able to change audience beliefs and attitudes through a single presentation, but values are another story.

Speeches to Convince and Speeches to Actuate

Now that we have discussed connecting to audiences and analyzing audiences, we can turn our attention to the two basic types of persuasive presentations you may deliver as a civically engaged speaker: speeches to convince and speeches to actuate. These types of persuasive speeches are distinguished by their specific purpose. In both cases, though, establishing a positive relationship with the audience is vital to the success of a presentation.

Speeches to Convince

Speeches to convince are delivered in an attempt to impact audience thinking. They encompass a primary claim—essentially, what you are trying to convince your audience to believe. For example, you might want to convince your audience that Puerto Rico should remain a territory of the United States rather than become a state, that tuition increases at your school are detrimental, that a need exists for after-school programs in your community, or that recycling needs will change within the next decade. The four primary types of persuasive claims that can be developed through a speech to convince include (1) policy, (2) value, (3) fact, and (4) conjecture.

Claim of Policy. A **claim of policy** maintains that a course of action should or should not be taken. For example, you may wish to convince the audience to support the development of a school voucher system in your state, that an attendance policy should be instituted at your university, or that automobile manufacturers should follow stricter emissions standards for their products. When supporting a particular policy, a persuasive speaker must demonstrate the need for such a policy, how the policy will satisfy that need, and that the policy can be successfully enacted. A persuasive speaker may also need to prove that the policy advocated is superior to an existing policy or another policy being proposed.

A claim of policy does not have to support a policy. You could also oppose the development of a school voucher system, an attendance policy, or stricter emissions standards. When opposing a policy, a speaker could argue that the need for such a policy does not exist. If a need for such a policy does exist, a speaker might demonstrate that a proposed policy does not satisfy the need, that the policy could not be successfully enacted, or that other policies are superior to the one being presented for consideration. Note that a claim of policy does not necessarily involve individual action but rather involves action of a more collective nature, such as a community, corporation, school, or nation-state. We will talk about persuasive speeches involving individual action (speeches to actuate) later in the chapter.

Claim of Value. A **claim of value** maintains that something is good or bad, beneficial or detrimental, or another evaluative criterion. Claims of value deal largely with attitudes, which were discussed earlier. You may want to convince your audience that George W. Bush was the worst American president or that an exercise regimen is beneficial to child development.

When developing a claim of value, you must let the audience know what criteria you used to determine and judge the value you support. Then, you need to exhibit how the object, person, or idea meets those criteria. You would need to explain to the audience how to determine "the worst president in U.S. history" and how George W. Bush would then be ranked the worst. You would need to explain to your audience what you mean by "beneficial to child development" and why an exercise regimen meets those criteria. Claims of value go beyond simply offering your opinion about something. You must establish criteria and provide evidence to support your claim.

Claim of Fact and Claim of Conjecture. Claims of fact and claims of conjecture are related but have one key distinction. A **claim of fact** maintains that something is true or false. A **claim of conjecture**, though similar to a claim of fact in that something is determined to be true or false, contends what will be true or false in the future (Gouran, Wiethoff, & Doelger, 1994). Examples of claims of fact and conjecture include convincing your audience that decreases in taxes result in increases in consumer spending, that slow drivers cause the majority of traffic fatalities, that banning handguns would lead to an increase in crime, and that education costs will triple within the next 10 years.

Audience Approaches to Speeches to Convince.   Regardless of the type of claim being advanced, an audience's existing beliefs and attitudes will influence what you attempt to achieve with your presentation and the methods you employ. They will also influence how the audience perceives you and your relationship with them.

You may *reinforce an existing way of thinking* to strengthen your audience members' convictions and ensure them of their accuracy and legitimacy. You are not convincing the audience members that their way of thinking is wrong or should be modified, so you can be relatively certain that the audience will support your presentation. Speeches that reinforce an existing way of thinking usually offer additional reasons in support of a particular way of thinking along with new or recent evidence. In these situations, audiences generally view their relationship with the speaker in a very positive manner.

Some situations call for you to *change an existing way of thinking,* in which you essentially tell the audience members that their current way of thinking is wrong or should be modified. This approach does not automatically mean that the audience will be hostile toward you or your position, but audience members will be less supportive of your stance than if you were reinforcing an existing way of thinking. When attempting to bring about this change in members of your audience, do not be too demeaning if discussing their current position. You should strive to develop a very positive relationship with the audience, as well as to enhance audience perceptions of your credibility, particularly of your goodwill. Audience members should recognize that you have their best interests in mind. The degree to which you change audience members' thinking and the extent to which they view your position as close or distant to their own can be determined through the social judgment theory, which we will discuss later in this chapter.

Some audiences have limited or no prior knowledge of your topic, in which case you will not reinforce or change existing ways of thinking but instead *create a new way of thinking.* In these cases, members of your audience will probably be more willing to accept your claim than they would if you attempted to change their position. However, you may need to spend additional time developing the audience members' relationship with the material and stressing the importance of the issue in their lives. You will also need to limit the depth at which you discuss the material. As always, establishing a positive relational connection with your audience will increase your likelihood of success.

Speeches to Actuate

Speeches to actuate are delivered in an attempt to impact audience behavior. You may want members of your audience to join your cause, volunteer with a charitable organization, limit their consumption of natural resources, or vote Quimby for mayor of Springfield. You may end up influencing audience thinking as a consequence of a speech to actuate, but that is not the ultimate goal of such a speech. The ultimate goal of a speech to actuate is to impact the behavior of your audience. You can impact your audience in the four different ways discussed in Table 14.2.

Table 14.2 Impacting Audience Behavior

Reinforcing an existing behavior	In this case, you desire to strengthen audience members' conviction about performing a behavior and ensure that they continue performing it. Reinforcing existing behavior often entails providing new reasons or evidence for enacting this behavior, along with increasing audience confidence and excitement about performing the behavior.
Altering an existing behavior	Here you are not asking the audience to stop performing a certain behavior or to enact a totally new behavior but to modify an existing behavior. It is important that you stress the value of continuing to perform this action and its positive influence in audience members' lives, but you must urge them to perform this action in the more effective or beneficial manner you suggest.
Ceasing an existing behavior	An audience will probably be less supportive of this type of presentation, since you are essentially telling audience members that they are doing something wrong. Be careful not to offend them but be resolute in your support of ceasing that behavior. It is especially important to develop a positive relationship with the audience. Stress that you are doing this for their well-being.
Avoiding a future behavior	When attempting to impact an audience in this manner, you are not necessarily reinforcing an existing behavior but encouraging your audience to avoid a specific new behavior. Such behaviors may be a concern now or in the future. These speeches often require that you provide the audience members with reasons and strategies for avoiding this behavior.

Persuasive Speaking and Artistic Proofs

Each type of persuasive speech can be enhanced through the recognition of the artistic proofs *ethos, pathos,* and *logos.* Aristotle laid out these artistic proofs more than 2,000 years ago, but the ideas behind them remain significant.

Ethos

Ethos involves the use of speaker credibility to impact an audience. We have already talked about the importance of establishing and maintaining your credibility as well as a positive relational connection with an audience. For members of an audience to judge the information provided by a speaker as accurate, valuable, and worthy of their attention and consideration, they must view that speaker as knowledgeable, trustworthy, and concerned about their well-being. Audiences must also perceive a relational connection with the speaker. Audiences' perceptions of speaker credibility and their relationship with the speaker are critical to the success of persuasive attempts. We urge you to consider the great impact that audience perceptions of your credibility will have on the success of your presentations.

Pathos

Pathos involves the use of emotional appeals to impact an audience. The use of such emotions as excitement, sadness, happiness, guilt, and anger can be quite effective when persuading an audience. You may have also witnessed the use of emotional appeals when attending or watching political rallies during which speakers elicit feelings of excitement about a particular candidate and perhaps anger toward political rivals. These emotional appeals are usually quite effective in achieving the desired response. Furthermore, the relational connections necessary for effective presentations often entail certain emotional qualities that will assist speakers persuading an audience. We will discuss emotional appeals later in this chapter.

Logos

Logos involves the use of logic or reasoning to impact an audience. The two primary types of reasoning are inductive reasoning and deductive reasoning. **Inductive reasoning** involves deriving a general conclusion based on specific evidence, examples, or instances. If you go to a restaurant and receive bad service, your friend goes to the same restaurant on another night and receives bad service, and a classmate goes to the restaurant and also reports having received bad service, you may conclude based on these specific instances that this restaurant has bad service. When using inductive reasoning, a sufficient number of examples or instances must exist from which to draw a legitimate conclusion, and these examples or instances must be relevant to the conclusion being established.

Deductive reasoning involves using general conclusions, premises, or principles to reach a conclusion about a specific example or instance. Thus, you may decide that since Duck and McMahan products are generally high in quality, a Duck and McMahan television set would be a high-quality product. Such reasoning frequently takes the form of syllogisms. A **syllogism** is a form of argumentation consisting of a major premise, a minor premise, and a conclusion. The *major premise* of a syllogism is a statement or conclusion of a general nature, while the *minor premise* entails a more specific statement about a particular instance or example. The *conclusion* is then derived from the logical connection between the major and minor premises. This may sound a bit confusing, but examining the following syllogism based on the example above might clear things up for you:

> **Major Premise**: Duck and McMahan products are high in quality.
> (This statement involves a general conclusion about Duck and McMahan products.)
>
> **Minor Premise**: This television is a Duck and McMahan product.
> (This statement involves a specific example connected to the major premise about Duck and McMahan products.)
>
> **Conclusion**: This television is high in quality.
> (The conclusion is based on the major and minor premises. If Duck and McMahan products are high in quality and this television is a Duck and McMahan product, this television must be high in quality.)

This method of reasoning is sometimes presented in a slightly modified form known as an enthymeme. An **enthymeme** is a syllogism that excludes one or two of the three components of a syllogism. An enthymeme may be used when one of the premises is readily understood, accepted as true, or so obvious that it does not even need to be stated. People often use enthymemes when talking with others. If a salesclerk at an electronics store attempted to sell you the Duck and McMahan television, she might exclude both the minor premise and the conclusion in the example syllogism above and simply establish the major premise by saying, "Duck and McMahan products are very high in quality." The fact that this television set is a Duck and McMahan product might be obvious, perhaps as would the natural conclusion. Beyond dealing with the obvious, however, incorporating enthymemes into one's message often seems more natural than speaking in syllogisms. If the salesclerk included all the parts of a syllogism and said, "Duck and McMahan products are high in quality; this television is a Duck and McMahan product; this television is high in quality," you might determine she either is a robot or really needs a coffee break.

As a speaker, you must determine whether it is most appropriate to present the material in the form of a syllogism or an enthymeme. As with other choices involving the development and delivery of a public presentation, this decision will be determined by your analysis of the audience. If your audience is adequately familiar with the material, you could probably use an enthymeme successfully. However, if the audience is unfamiliar with the material or will not readily accept the major or minor premise as true or accurate, you should present the material in the form of a syllogism.

Persuasive Speaking and the Social Judgment Theory

A more recent offering than artistic proofs and also valuable in increasing the effectiveness of persuasive presentations is the theory of social judgment. The **social judgment theory** (M. Sherif & Hovland, 1961; C. Sherif, Sherif, & Nebergall, 1965) explains how people may respond to a range of positions surrounding a particular topic or issue. This theory can be understood as dealing with an audience's relationship with the topic or issue. Using this theory, imagine an audience responding or relating to the various positions connected to a topic or an issue in one of three ways: acceptance, rejection, and noncommitment. These positions can in turn be placed in three types of ranges, referred to as latitudes (see Figure 14.1). The **latitude of acceptance** includes the range of position that the audience deems acceptable. At some point within this latitude of acceptance is the **anchor position**, which represents the preferred or most acceptable position. The **latitude of rejection** includes those positions that the audience deems unacceptable. Finally, the **latitude of noncommitment** includes positions that the audience neither wholly accepts nor wholly rejects.

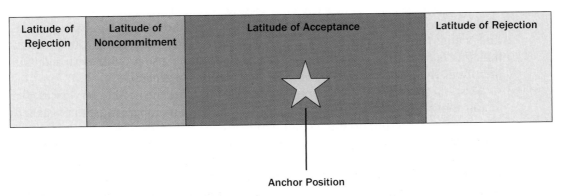

Anchor Position

Figure 14.1 Components of the Social Judgment Theory

T he assimilation effect and contrast effect are similar to a person's relationships with others. Depending on their view of someone, people generally believe they are either more similar to or more different from that person than they actually are.

Variables Impacting Social Judgment

The size of the latitudes is affected by the audience's level of involvement or relationship with the issue. Audience involvement is based on audience members' recognition of the issue's significance and importance in their lives. The greater the significance and importance audience members perceive the issue as having in their lives, the more involved they will be with the issue, and vice versa. As audience members' involvement with an issue increases, so does the size of their latitude of rejection. Audiences highly involved with an issue will have relatively small latitudes of acceptance and noncommitment because people will spend more time thinking about and evaluating the concerns surrounding an issue if they view it as important and meaningful. People will spend less time engaged in those behaviors if they do not view the issue as such. Thus, people highly involved with an issue will have developed a more focused view of what is acceptable.

Audience members will often perceive messages as either closer to or farther away from their position than they actually are. These perceptions are based on the **assimilation effect**, which maintains that if someone advocates a position within your latitude of acceptance, you will view it as closer to your anchor position than it really is, and the **contrast effect**, which maintains that if someone advocates a position within your latitude of rejection, you will view it as farther from your anchor position than it really is. Assimilation and contrast effects are more likely to occur when an actual position is not clear and can thus be minimized by making your position explicit (O'Keefe, 1990). For example, advocating *harsh penalties* for drug dealers is somewhat ambiguous, while advocating the *death penalty* as the punishment for drug dealers is clear and explicit.

Using the Social Judgment Theory to Improve Persuasive Presentations

As you can imagine, determining the social judgment of a group of listeners takes thorough audience analysis. Also true is that various members of the audience will probably hold different anchor positions when it comes to your issue. You will not likely have specific data supporting a precise illustration of audience latitudes. However, you could use audience analysis to provide a rough idea of how the general audience latitudes might appear, which could prove very useful when developing your presentation. Furthermore, elements of the social judgment theory also provide key insight into improving the effectiveness of persuasive presentations in general.

First, the assimilation and contrast effects underscore the need to be very explicit in conveying your goals to the audience. The audience members must know exactly what position you support and want them to accept. When dealing with the contrast effect, if the position you desire is within audience members' latitude of rejection, it may not be as far away from their anchor position as they would assume if you did not explicitly state your position. Audience members may view your position as not even remotely considerable, when in reality it is closer to their anchor position than they realize.

Explicitly stating your position is also necessary when dealing with assimilation effects. Having your audience members believe your position is closer to their anchor position than it actually is might appear to be beneficial. However, this can actually reduce the effectiveness of your presentation. According to O'Keefe (1990), the audience will view you as seeking less change than you actually seek. In fact, "in the extreme case of complete assimilation, receivers may think that the message is simply saying what they already believe—and hence receivers don't change their attitudes at all" (p. 38). Both the assimilation effect and the contrast effect emphasize the need to state your position explicitly.

Second, considering audience perceptions of positions related to your topic will also assist you in determining how to develop your presentation. Audiences with a considerably large latitude of noncommitment may not be particularly involved with the topic or fully aware of its importance in their lives. The size of either the latitude of acceptance or the latitude of rejection may dictate which organizational pattern you use to develop your presentation. People new to public speaking often wonder whether they should include both sides of the issue when presenting a persuasive speech. As with most questions involving presentations, the answer depends on the audience. If you believe the audience will strongly oppose your stance, it might be a good idea to present both sides of the issue to address the limitations of the opposite side. When an audience is neutral or somewhat unopposed to your position, presenting only your side of the issue will usually suffice.

Finally, considering the social judgment of your audience will help you ascertain the degree of change you should seek with your audience. If the anchor position of the audience is far away from the position being advocated, a speaker will be hard-pressed to convince many members of the audience to accept that new position. This reality should not discourage you as a speaker. Rather, you should simply be aware that persuasion is often a continual and gradual process.

Sequential Persuasion

Persuasion as a gradual process is the primary idea behind methods of sequential persuasion. These methods are most commonly used when attempting to secure donations for a community organization or charity but are also evident in everyday interactions with friends, family, and crafty salespeople. Whether you are developing a donation campaign for a local organization, attempting to borrow money from a friend, or trying to increase your monthly sales, sequential methods of persuasion can help. In what follows, we will examine (a) foot in the door, (b) door in the face, and (c) pregiving.

Foot in the Door

The foot-in-the-door technique of persuasion goes back to the days when salespeople went door-to-door selling merchandise—or at least the name does. Two possible derivations of the term exist. First, once a salesperson got into the home, the odds of making a sale dramatically increased. A second derivation is that placing a foot inside the doorway made it impossible for the homeowner to close the door all the way. Whatever the actual origin of the name, the **foot-in-the-door technique** involves making a small request and then following up with a second, larger request. The thinking is that once a person complies with a simple and small request, he or she will be more likely to comply with another, larger request—even one that is much larger than the initial request—even though it is one that would have been rejected outright if it had been asked for at first. So, imagine that we stop by your house collecting donations for the Retired Professors Fund. We ask you to donate $20 to this worthy cause, and you comply by giving us a crisp $20 bill. You are greeted by smiling faces, profound thanks, and assurances of your kindness. Someone else then returns a few days later to further thank you and to let you know that you can do even more to support this worthy group. For only $100 a month, you can "adopt" a needy professor. You will even be sent a picture of your professor and receive periodic updates about your professor. Having previously contributed, you see yourself as the type of person who supports this sort of organization and pledge the $100 a month. According to the foot-in-the-door technique, complying with the initial request greatly increases the chances of compliance with the second, larger request and so saves some deserving professor from destitution, something that would naturally make you feel good about yourself as well.

Why Does Foot in the Door Work?

Two reasons are generally offered to explain why the foot-in-the-door technique tends to work. Daryl Bem's (1972) **self-perception theory** is one explanation. According to this theory, people come to understand their attitudes, beliefs, and values through their actions. If you get a cup of coffee at the Java House coffee shop each day after class, you may come to realize that you have positive attitudes toward drinking coffee and perhaps drinking Java House coffee specifically. The foot-in-the-door technique works because upon contributing (an initially small amount) to a cause, a person begins seeing him- or herself as the type of person who supports a particular organization or worthy causes in general. A second explanation is Leon Festinger's (1957) **cognitive dissonance theory**. According to this theory, people prefer their actions to be consistent with their attitudes, beliefs, and values because inconsistency elicits negative feelings. Thus, people will tend to perform actions that support their attitudes, beliefs, and values while tending to avoid actions that counter their attitudes, beliefs, and values. Bypassing your usual cup of coffee and claiming to your friends that you do not care for the stuff would be inconsistent with known attitudes, beliefs, and values, possibly resulting in negative feelings. From this perspective, the foot-in-the-door technique works because complying with the second request (even though it is larger) would be consistent with previous decisions and would likely prevent the possibility of negative feelings resulting from inconsistency.

Although these theories are traditionally aimed at understanding internal matters, both the self-perception theory and the cognitive dissonance theory can be more fully understood by taking into account *relationships with others*. In the case of the self-perception theory, people may come to understand attitudes, beliefs, and values through their actions, but the continuation and evaluation of those actions and all behavior for that matter are based in large part on the reactions of others. In the case of the cognitive dissonance theory, people also avoid inconsistency because of relational factors. Consistency is expected and comfortable not only for oneself but also for others. If someone behaves in a way that is inconsistent with past behaviors, people tend to notice and may seek to uncover that inconsistency and compel the other person to behave according to expectations. These relational factors also influence internal feelings of discomfort. Knowing that others have certain expectations of you and recognizing that inconsistency may result in their discomfort may lead you to act in a manner consistent with known attitudes, beliefs, and values.

When Is Foot in the Door Most Successful?

The foot-in-the-door technique works best for *prosocial reasons* (Dillard, Hunter, & Burgoon, 1984). So, it would be more effective when seeking donations for a charity, providing volunteer activities for an organization, or supporting another worthy cause. Even though its name is derived from the tactics of salespeople, it is less effective when selling items or for other self-serving reasons.

The foot-in-the-door technique also works best when *different people* make the requests (Chartrand, Pinckert, & Burger, 1999). Complying with a second request made by a different person than the one who made the initial request reinforces attitudes, beliefs, and values. Essentially, a person would be saying that he or she would comply with this sort of request regardless of who was asking. Different people making the requests will also decrease the likelihood of resentment. Especially if a second request is made soon after the original, people may feel as if they are being taken advantage of.

Additionally, the foot-in-the-door technique works best if the initial request is *significant* (Fern, Monroe, & Avila, 1986). The initial request must be large enough that it will be meaningful to the person being asked. A small request may soon be forgotten and have little impact on a person's evaluation of attitudes, beliefs, and values, both of which would undermine the foot-in-the-door strategy.

Finally, the foot-in-the-door technique works best when people are not given *material incentives* to comply (Burger, 1999). Let's go back to our visit to your doorstep while collecting for the Retired Professors Fund. If we offered you an *I Love Professors* T-shirt in exchange for the $20 donation, you would be less likely to comply with the follow-up request for $100 each month for the adoption of a professor. The reason is that you would not necessarily see yourself as the type of person who supports such a cause but instead see yourself as a person who supports such causes when there is something in it for you—in this case a snazzy T-shirt that would make your friends quite envious.

Door in the Face

Unlike the foot-in-the-door technique, the door-in-the-face technique does not aim for compliance with the initial request. In fact, the desire is to be turned down flat and have the "door" slammed in your face. Essentially, the **door-in-the-face technique** involves making a request so large that it will be turned down and then following up with a second, smaller request. The thinking is that people will generally comply with the second, smaller request for a variety of reasons we will discuss below. So, here we come again collecting for the Retired Professors Fund. We ask if you would be willing to donate $200 each month for the adoption of a needy professor. Even though it is a worthy cause, you turn us down since that would be quite a bit of money each month. We then ask if

396 Chapter 14 Public Communication and Personal Influence

you would be willing to donate $100 each month instead. According to the door-in-the-face technique, you will probably comply with this request.

Why Does Door in the Face Work?

There are three primary reasons why the door-in-the-face technique works. The **perceptual contrast effect** maintains that people generally comply with the second request because compared to the initial request it appears much smaller (Miller, Seligman, Clark, & Bush, 1976). If we start out asking for $200 each month, that may seem like a lot of money. However, giving $100 each month may not seem to be as much of a sacrifice compared to giving twice that much. Also you look bad, you think, in turning down what, by comparison, now looks like a reasonable request.

The other two reasons this technique works involve the relationship with the person making the request. The concept of **reciprocal concessions** maintains that people generally comply with the second request because they feel since the person making the request is willing to concede something, they themselves should match the concession and also be willing to concede something (Cialdini et al., 1975). In other words, the person making the request seems willing to give up something, and people feel compelled to accept the second request in order to even things out ("They were willing to give a little, so I should be willing to give a little"). Reciprocal concessions underscores people's desire to have positive relationships with other people, even those with whom they do not share an existing close, personal connection. **Self-presentation** maintains that people are concerned that other people (most notably the person making the request) may view them in a negative light and that complying with the second request might prevent or decrease those negative perceptions (Pendleton & Bateson, 1979).

When Is Door in the Face Most Successful?

As with foot in the door, the door-in-the-face technique works best for *prosocial reasons* (Dillard et al., 1984). However, many salespeople tend to show the high-priced items first and then show more reasonably priced items, perhaps in an attempt to take advantage of the perceptual contrast effect. This technique seems especially true when selling high-ticket items such as automobiles, jewelry, and houses.

Internal perceptions of social responsibility (Tusing & Dillard, 2000) and concerns of guilt (O'Keefe & Figge, 1999) have also been offered as possible explanations of the foot-in-the-door technique. Once again, though, these internal factors are based on external social and relational influences. Relationships come with certain responsibilities, and not accepting these responsibilities would be socially irresponsible and may very well lead to feelings of guilt.

The door-in-the-face technique also works best when the *same person* makes the second request (O'Keefe & Hale, 1998). When the same person makes the request, it is more likely that reciprocal concessions will come into play. Notice this approach is different from the foot-in-the-door technique, which works best when a different person makes the second request.

The door-in-the-face technique also works best when there is a *relatively brief delay* between requests (Fern et al., 1986). In other words, you should not wait too long before making the second request. Delaying the second request will not allow you to take advantage of the perceptual contrast effect. Further, concerns about self-presentation may have diminished if the delay between requests is too long.

Pregiving

Remember that *I Love Professors* T-shirt mentioned above? How would you like one of those for your very own? We would be happy to send you one. By the way, we just happen to be collecting for the Retired Professors Fund; would you care to donate? If you are thinking, "Wow, Steve and David are nice enough to send me a shirt; the least I can do is donate to this worthy cause," then you succumbed to the pregiving technique. Organizations do not send

Photo 14.2 The woman in this photo turned down the volunteer's initial request to become a volunteer herself but did agree to a relatively smaller request to sign a petition. What method of sequential persuasion may have been used here? If she agreed to the second request because she did not want to be viewed in a negative way, what would this be called? (See page 413.)

out return address labels along with a request for donation just because they want to make addressing envelopes easier for people. Free samples at grocery stores are not just a way to have people sample products before buying. Car dealerships do not offer free hotdogs and drinks because purchasing an automobile makes people hungry and thirsty. The **pregiving technique** maintains that when a person is given something or offered favors by someone else, that person is more likely to comply with a subsequent request.

Why Does Pregiving Work?

The primary reason pregiving is thought to work is known as the *norm of reciprocity*, which argues that people comply with requests following receipt of gifts or favors because they want to pay back the person who provided such gifts (Cialdini & Goldstein, 2004). People generally do not like to feel indebted to others, and complying with someone's request enables them to repay the person and even the score—even though a car for a hotdog does not sound like an even trade. More often than not, though, the amount returned is more than what was originally given.

Another possible explanation for the success of pregiving is *increased liking* for the other person. When someone does something for you or gives you something, it is possible that you may view that person more positively. Since people tend to do nice things for people they like, when that person makes a subsequent request, there is an increased chance that you will comply.

When Is Pregiving Most Successful?

The pregiving technique works best when the *same person (or organization)* makes the request. The same person or organization making the request takes advantage of the norm of reciprocity and increased liking that is derived from receiving the gift or favor.

The pregiving technique also works best when there is a *relatively brief delay* between receiving the gift or favor and the request. If the delay is too long, feelings of obligation and increased liking may diminish. You must strike while the iron is hot, so to speak, which is why the product being sampled at the grocery store is nearby and pledge cards are included with those "free" return address labels.

Finally, the pregiving technique works best when the gift or favor is *not seen as a bribe or as having an ulterior motive* (Groves, Cialdini, & Couper, 1992). This finding does not mean that people will not donate to an organization providing address labels, purchase a sampled product, or buy a car after munching on a hotdog. They all work! However, the pregiving technique works better when the gift or favor is seen as an act of kindness rather than a persuasive strategy.

Acts of kindness performed by salespeople are rarely selfless. Indeed, they often represent some form of emotional appeal that creates in the target person some sense of dependence or relational commitment. We will now explore emotional appeals as a special form of persuasion.

Emotional Appeals

When it comes to persuasion and argumentation, the discipline of communication studies has traditionally focused primarily on logic and reasoning. This focus remains an important element within communication and an important component of education. At the same time, there is an increasing awareness of the importance of emotion when studying human behavior in general and when studying human motivation specifically.

If you really think about it, people's actions and the motivation behind them are often more the result of emotional action than the result of logical reasoning. Consider television commercials, which often last no more than 30 seconds with many lasting 15 seconds or less. These brief periods of time do not allow for the construction of a logical argument with strong evidence and sound reasoning. Instead audiences are presented with emotional appeals drawing on such human emotions as fear, guilt, anger, and happiness. A charitable organization urges you to donate money by presenting images of impoverished children with tears in their eyes. A home security company prompts you to purchase an alarm system in case an ax murderer attempts to break into your home. An insurance company encourages you to buy life insurance just in case the alarm system fails to keep out the ax murderer. In these cases and in many others, logical appeals are out, and emotional appeals are in.

Discussing emotion in a communication textbook may initially strike some people as peculiar. Emotions are often considered things that people *feel internally,* which seems far removed from the discussion of symbolic activity. It is true that emotions involve internal activities and feelings. Neuroscientists can even pinpoint changes in the brain when people experience specific emotions. Changes in heart rate, blood pressure, and temperature and a host of other physical changes occur when you experience any emotion.

> Schachter and Singer (1962) demonstrated that physiological arousal itself is not sufficient for people to define their emotions. People need some socially developed label to determine what they are experiencing.

Yet, emotion is also very much a *symbolic activity* and *relational activity*. Symbolically, emotions and the feelings that accompany them are given meaning within a culture or society. Emotions bring about physical change, but this physical change is understood and evaluated according to established meaning. Happiness, sadness, fear, and all other emotions have meaning beyond physical experience or a given instance. Certain emotions are viewed favorably while other emotions are evaluated negatively. Beyond external physical changes such as blushing, sweating, or shaking, people can recognize when other people are experiencing certain emotions through symbolic activities. The display of emotion is evaluated culturally and socially, with some situations warranting the display of certain emotions and behaviors while such displays and behaviors would be considered inappropriate in other situations.

These symbolic characteristics of emotions are learned *relationally*. We are treading lightly here, because we do not want you to think that relationships are just about emotions. People often experience such intense emotions when interacting with certain relational partners (anger when talking with an enemy; happiness when talking with a romantic partner) that there is a tendency to equate relationships with emotions. These intense emotional experiences do not happen all the time, but they are certainly memorable. For instance, your heart may not race whenever your romantic partner walks into the room like it did when you first met, but you probably remember those moments quite vividly. On a personal note—in case they are reading this part of the book—our hearts do still race when our wives walk into the room! But, we digress. Instead of being just about emotions, as we have stressed throughout the book, relationships are about knowledge, connecting symbolically to others, and understanding the world. Accordingly, it is through relationships that people come to understand emotion. Your understanding of emotions and of their appropriate display has developed through everyday communication and interactions with your friends, family, classmates, neighbors, romantic partners, acquaintances, and others with whom you share a relationship. Relationships are not just about emotions, but they are where people learn about them.

So, having discussed what emotions are and their connection with everyday life, we can now examine their use when influencing others. First, we will discuss the use of fear, which is the most researched emotion when it comes to social influence. Next, we will look at the use of guilt. Finally, we will examine some of the "lost" emotions of persuasion.

Fear: Buy This Book and No One Gets Hurt!

If the above header really made people go out and buy this book, the hardworking folks in SAGE marketing would have a much easier job. Although this header may not be very

Photo 14.3 Is the use of emotion something that only involves internal feelings? (See page 413.)

effective, fear appeals often are effective methods of persuasion. Consider the many uses of fear you encounter on a daily basis. Television commercials for high-end home alarm systems warn you that an intruder may be scoping out your residence this very moment. Insurance companies claim they will have you covered if the home alarm system does not work. Politicians exclaim that if a certain package is not passed in Congress then the country will be on the brink of collapse. Billboards caution you that drinking and driving kills, as does texting and driving or reading too many billboards instead of watching the road. Somewhere at this very moment a parent is warning a child to stay in sight; otherwise a stranger may harm him or her. Fear appeals are pervasive persuasive techniques, because they work very well—as long as they are properly implemented.

In all actuality, while often effective, fear appeals do not always work. How many people do you know who have actually bought a high-end home alarm system? When was the last time a billboard convinced you to do or not do something? Somewhere a child has just ignored a parent's warning and is heading over a hill out of sight—thankfully no strangers are lurking about. People do not always perceive the levels of fear anticipated by persuaders, and if they do, they do not always feel as if they are capable of acting. It is not a matter of fear not being an effective tool of persuasion; rather persuaders do not always recognize all the elements connected with fear. Fear is a lot more complicated than expected.

Extended Parallel Process Model

Fortunately, Kim Witte (1992, 1998) has introduced the **extended parallel process model**, which explains the process of fear appeals. Two key elements of this model are *perceived threat* and *perceived efficacy*. The perceived threat entails (a) the extent to which a person believes that he or she is susceptible to the threat and (b) the severity of the threat. A person essentially asks, "How likely is it that this will happen to me, and how bad would it be? What some persuaders fail to do when using a fear appeal is offer people a way out of trouble or make this way out explicit. When a way out is offered, people then determine perceived efficacy. Perceived efficacy entails (a) the extent to which a person believes a recommended course of action will work and (b) whether or not he or she is capable of performing the recommended action. Here, a person essentially asks, "Will this action work, and am I capable of implementing it?"

If a person does not view the perceived threat as severe or does not think personal susceptibility is likely, he or she will likely not act. Research indicates that fear appeals have less impact on younger people than on older people (Mongeau, 1998), and this finding is likely due to younger people not being aware of hardships and problems in life as well as possessing feelings of invulnerability. It may also be a matter of determining what younger people actually fear; they may not fear death, but they may fear being unpopular (Cho & Witte, 2004).

If a person does experience fear as a result of a perceived threat, he or she will likely do something about it. A person will engage in either (a) fear control or (b) danger control, and this choice will be determined by reactions to perceived efficacy. When engaging in *fear control*, people focus on fear itself by denying its existence, not thinking about it, or simply taking deep breaths and hoping it goes away. When engaging in *danger control*, people do something about the threat, likely adopting the measure suggested by the persuasive appeal. As you might imagine, when people do not believe a recommended course of action will work or do not believe they can properly implement the action, they are more likely to engage in fear control. On the other hand, when people believe a course of action will work and believe they can properly implement that action, they are more likely to engage in danger control.

Beyond providing a greater understanding of what happens during a fear appeal process, the extended parallel process model offers insight into successful persuasive attempts. In order for a fear appeal to be effective, the target must perceive the threat as substantial and probable. The target must also perceive the solution as viable and possible. If the threat and solution are not perceived as such, the fear appeal will likely fail.

Guilt: Have You Ever Seen Two Grown Professors Cry?

Although the role of guilt in persuasive attempts has not been studied to the extent of fear, it remains a powerful persuasive tool in personal relationships and persuasive campaigns such as those representing charity organizations. Consider the last time you did something to alleviate negative feelings associated with not doing something you were supposed to do or associated with doing something that countered what you considered proper behavior. Or, perhaps you acted in order to prevent experiencing those feelings in the first place. In either case, you acted due to the experience or anticipation of guilt.

Guilt appeals in advertisements are usually made up of two components: (1) evocation of guilt and (2) path to atonement (O'Keefe, 2002). So, a Retired Professors Fund television commercial might show needy professors with sorrowful eyes staring at the camera while an announcer discusses their horrendous plight. Then, the announcer will discuss how you can help this needy group for less than the price of a latte each day, which in essence will enable you to eliminate feelings of guilt brought on by pictures of professors in need. Naturally, you did not cause this particular tragedy, but since your life appears much better in comparison and you do not like to see people in need, feelings of guilt start to arise. You want to do something about it, so you think that donating to this worthy organization is the way to minimize these feelings.

Most people might think that the more a particular emotion is experienced, the greater the chances of compliance, but this is not always the case. It does appear to be true of fear. Unless people suffer some sort of traumatic breakdown, the more fear one experiences, the more likely he or she will comply. However, this finding does not appear to exist when it comes to guilt. In fact, research indicates that although explicit appeals of guilt do increase feelings of guilt, they do not increase the likelihood of compliance (O'Keefe, 2000). It is possible that other feelings such as anger, annoyance, or resentment may also arise, thereby decreasing the likelihood of compliance. This discovery does not mean that guilt appeals do not work; it means that persuaders need to make sure they do not make people feel too bad.

Of course, advertisements are not the only place where guilt is used in persuasion. Guilt is often used in interactions with others. Like other emotions, guilt is squarely based in relationships with others. A series of studies by Vangelisti, Daly, and Rudnick (1991) uncovered that persuasion was the primary reason for inducing guilt in conversations and that guilt is more likely to be used among those sharing an intimate relationship than among those sharing any other type of relationship. Further, stating relationship obligations, referring to sacrifices, and discussing role obligations were the most common techniques for creating guilt in others. So you are more likely to use guilt when interacting with someone with whom you share a close personal relationship such as a romantic partner, friend, or family member. You are most likely to use guilt when attempting to persuade someone. And when doing so, you are likely to discuss his or her obligations to you as a romantic partner, friend, or family member ("A true friend would do this for me") or discuss your sacrifices (a mother may refer to the 72 hours of labor required to bring someone into the world; the least that person could do is pick up a pair of socks off the floor).

Lost Emotions

Fear and guilt are certainly not the only emotions used in persuasion, but they tend to receive most of the attention from communication scholars. Nevertheless, Robin Nabi (2002) has provided an examination of some of these "lost" emotions. Like fear, *anger* appears positively related to changes in attitude. In other words, the angrier someone gets about an issue, the more likely that person will be persuaded. Of course, you want to ensure that the anger is intentional and is positioned in the appropriate direction. *Disgust* has been found to be negatively correlated with attitude change when it comes to be associated with a position. *Happiness* has often been associated with humor in terms of its persuasive power—people tend to be happy when they find something humorous. Although findings are mixed when trying to determine whether happiness and humor lead to persuasion, they do not hurt matters in many cases. Robert Gass and John Seiter (2007) maintain that humor in particular assists persuasion by gaining attention, through distraction, and by increasing liking for the source. *Hope* is an emotion that may be somewhat familiar in persuasion given a somewhat recent political election. Barack Obama used a great deal of both fear and hope appeals in his presidential campaign. Whether he used more fear or more hope is debated by members from both ends of the political spectrum, but he did address hope on many occasions. In fact, many politicians speak of hope in their campaign messages—so do lottery officials. Yet, in spite of its prevalence, the use of hope in persuasion has received little attention. Like fear appeals, it seems likely that hope would be effective only if audiences found a suggested action to be a viable path to achieving whatever is being hoped for. Emotions are prevalent and influential features in persuasion, and we *hope* more research into their roles in persuasion is soon conducted.

Compliance Gaining

Influence is not just a social phenomenon but is also something that happens in your personal life. Throughout the chapter, we have stressed the relational nature of influence while focusing on public attempts at persuasion and those that may occur while representing an organization. Now, we focus on influence that occurs in actual dyadic (involving two people) relationships.

Consider how many times each day you try to get someone to do something for you or to act a certain way and how many times each day someone tries to get you to do something for him or her or to act a certain way. We are not just talking about making major purchases or donating time and money to a charitable cause—although these experiences may very well make up part of your day. Instead, consider those less dramatic but more prevalent instances such as asking for a ride to class, asking a coworker to switch shifts at work, asking someone to be quiet while studying in the library, or simply asking someone to pass the salt. There are, of course, slightly more significant examples such as asking an instructor for a higher grade on an assignment, asking a supervisor for a raise, or asking a friend to not drive while intoxicated. These issues all deal with what is known as compliance gaining.

Compliance gaining involves interpersonal attempts at influence, especially attempts to influence someone's behavior. Compliance gaining has become one of the most researched areas of persuasion and possesses qualities that make it unique from other areas of research. First, rather than focusing on campaigns or other attempts at mass influence, compliance gaining is focused on relational or dyadic influence. The focus is on what happens among friends, romantic partners, family members, acquaintances, neighbors, and people in other sorts of relationships in everyday life and everyday communication. Second, rather than focusing on the person being persuaded, compliance gaining is more focused on the person doing the persuading. Third—and certainly connected—rather than focusing on which persuasive techniques are most successful, compliance gaining is more concerned with which strategies are most likely to be selected. Moreover, compliance gaining research is concerned with discovering *why* certain strategies are selected in certain situations and when certain interactants (relationships) are involved. Finally, rather than focusing only on the primary goal of compliance, compliance gaining recognizes the existence and importance of secondary goals, which we will discuss below.

Relational Influence Goals

The question that arises pertains to what people are generally trying to achieve by influencing others. Dillard, Anderson, and Knobloch (2002) have observed that while it may seem as if there are numerous reasons why people may attempt to influence others, there

Contrarian Challenge

Changing orientations made the list as a relational influence goal, but what about *reinforcing orientations?* In other words, what if someone already agrees with a position you support and you want to keep it that way? Should reinforcing orientations be included? Are any other goals missing from this list that you believe should be included?

are seven primary goals of influence that tend to emerge. As we discuss these goals, notice that all but one deal directly with *behavior.* When it comes to compliance gaining, changing someone's beliefs, attitudes, and values is rarely the goal and often may not even be a consideration. If you want someone to mow your lawn, for example, it probably does not matter to you if that person's beliefs, attitudes, and values related to lawn mowing are changed. What matters is whether or not you hear the hum of the mower trimming the grass. With this distinction in mind, we can now examine goals of relational influence.

Gaining assistance is a relational influence goal dedicated to obtaining resources. You essentially want someone to do something for you or to give you something. Getting someone to mow your lawn is an example of gaining assistance, then, as is getting someone to loan you $20. *Giving advice* is a relational influence goal dedicated to providing guidance. Dillard et al. (2002) note that giving advice typically involves relationship or health issues, which makes a great deal of sense given our discussion of social network influence on health decisions and lifestyles in Chapter 10. *Sharing activities* is a relational influence goal dedicated to engaging in joint endeavors. For instance, you may want a friend to join you at the theater or to go on a walk with you. *Changing orientations* is a relational influence goal dedicated to changing a person's position on an issue. You might want to change someone's position on an immigration policy, for instance. This goal is the one not directly related to changing behavior, although it could certainly lay the foundation for behavioral change.

Changing relationships is a relational influence goal dedicated to altering the relationship of the interactants. You may wish to break up with someone, or on the other hand you may wish to establish an exclusive dating relationship with that person. In both cases, your goal would be to change the nature of the relationship. *Obtaining permission* is a relational influence goal dedicated to receiving authorization for an action. For instance, a child may ask a parent for permission to go outside and play. Finally, *enforcing rights and obligations* is a relational influence goal dedicated to making someone fulfill a commitment or role. Getting someone to repay a loan by reminding him or her of an earlier promise of repayment is an example of this goal. Reinforcing relational rights also falls into this category. For instance, you might want a friend to go with you to meet someone you met on the Internet because that is something that a friend should do.

Secondary Goals of Compliance Gaining

The primary goal of compliance gaining is to influence someone, especially that person's behavior. Yet, there exist four secondary relational goals that impact how people go about seeking compliance: identity goals, interaction goals, resource goals, and arousal goals (Dillard, 1989; Dillard, Segrin, & Harden, 1989). **Identity goals** of compliance gaining recognize that people desire to act in accordance with the personal and relational identities they attempt to transact and/or the personal and relational identities most appropriate in a given situation. For example, someone wishing to transact a dominant role in a relationship would probably avoid getting down on his or her hands and knees and begging the other person to comply with a request. A student attempting to get a grade increased on a project would probably conform to the identity of respectful student rather than vengeful enemy when visiting an instructor's office—at least if he or she wants to stand a chance—and this example actually highlights the interconnection between the primary and secondary goals.

Connected with identity goals, **interaction goals** of compliance gaining recognize the desire to act appropriately when attempting to gain compliance. There exist appropriate ways of behaving and communicating in certain contexts and especially in certain relational contexts. When attempting to gain compliance, people will generally desire to conform to existing standards of interaction.

Resource goals of compliance gaining recognize the desire to maintain relational resources. When attempting to get someone to comply, people want to avoid doing something that will prevent him or her from being a potential resource in the future. When trying to convince a friend to do something, for instance, you would try to avoid making that person angry and losing him or her as a friend. Consequently, when selecting compliance gaining strategies, people must not only determine what might successfully get someone to comply but also maintain the relationship for future needs.

Finally, **arousal goals** of compliance gaining recognize the desire to keep arousal at an acceptable level. People generally do not wish to appear upset, angry, or nervous or to display other such emotions. At the same time, people may not wish to appear too upbeat, happy, or excited. You might notice how secondary goals not only connect with the primary goal of compliance gaining but also connect with one another. Arousal goals impact identity goals, interaction goals, and resource goals in a number of ways, as do each of the secondary goals of compliance gaining.

Compliance Gaining Strategies

Now that we have introduced compliance gaining and discussed the secondary goals of compliance gaining, we can begin to examine strategies people use to impact the behaviors of others in everyday life. Researchers have offered a number of compliance gaining technique classification systems. In what follows, we will examine typologies and categories of compliance gaining strategies that have been developed. We will then examine contextual factors influencing the strategy selection.

Original Typology

The earliest classification system was provided by Gerald Marwell and David Schmitt in 1967 and set the stage for many subsequent studies. These authors presented a total of 16 compliance gaining strategies but grouped these strategies into five categories: rewarding activities, punishing activities, expertise activities, activation of impersonal commitments, and activation of personal commitments.

Rewarding activities seek compliance through positivity. Someone seeking compliance may make promises, act nicely, or engage in pregiving as discussed above. For example, someone seeking a ride to campus from a classmate might promise to fill the person's car with gas, compliment that person on his or her driving abilities, or provide him or her with lecture notes from a missed class in anticipation of the request.

Punishing activities seek compliance through negativity. Someone seeking compliance may make threats or punish another person. For example, someone wanting a friend to quit drinking might threaten to terminate their relationship, limit the amount of time spent with that friend, or continuously berate him or her.

Expertise activities seek compliance through perceptions of credibility or wisdom. Someone seeking compliance may advise another person to do something based on knowledge of the situation or the ways of the world. This expertise can be either positive or negative. For example, an older relative urging a classmate to stay in school using positive expertise could explain the potential benefits of staying in school such as higher salaries and a sense of accomplishment. Using negative expertise would entail explaining the potential negative consequences of dropping out of school such as limited opportunities for financial advancement and a sense of regret.

Activation of impersonal commitments seeks compliance through the manipulation of internal feelings of obligation and appropriate behavior. Someone seeking compliance may describe positive or negative self-feelings that could result or may engage in positive or negative altercasting. This compliance gaining strategy could be used to get someone to use protection when engaging in sexual activities. Invoking positive self-feelings would entail describing how much better a person would feel about him- or herself after using protection, while invoking negative feelings would entail describing how bad a person would feel about him- or herself after not using protection. Altercasting does not address the person directly, but the point is made nevertheless. Positive altercasting might include comments about how responsible people use protection when engaging in sexual activities, while negative altercasting might include comments about how irresponsible people do not use protection when engaging in sexual activities.

Activation of personal commitments seeks compliance through appealing to obligations to others. Someone seeking compliance using this strategy appeals to relationships. We would actually prefer calling activation of impersonal commitments *personal commitments* and activation of personal commitments *relational commitments,* but Marwell and Schmitt did not

Photo 14.4 This man is attempting to get this woman to comply by reminding her that they are best friends. Which compliance gaining strategy is he using? (See page 413.)

ask us. Still, that might help you distinguish these two categories as long as you remember their actual names should they come up while taking an examination. The basis of activation of personal commitments is the obligation that comes with being in a relationship. For instance, there are certain things a person must do, or is expected to do, for a friend. In Chapter 4, we discussed the *appeal to relationships* fallacy, which occurs when people use relationships to justify behaviors and requests. Appealing to personal commitments is not always justified, but it is often quite effective. Erin Sahlstein (2000) has discussed how relational terms such as *friend, mom,* or *son* are often included in talk when people are seeking compliance ("If you were truly my friend, you would do this for me"). In many ways, relationships serve as the foundation for not only activation of personal commitments but also each of these categories.

Contextual Influences

Compliance gaining may seem fairly straightforward at first (Person A wants to impact the behavior of Person B and selects a strategy to accomplish this goal). However, compliance gaining becomes a bit more complicated when taking into account the many contextual influences that affect a person's selection of the most appropriate and, hopefully, successful category. These contextual elements influence which tactics are used when attempting to gain compliance as well as which tactics are avoided when attempting to gain compliance. In what follows, we will examine seven contextual factors discussed in compliance gaining research (Cody & McLaughlin, 1980; Cody, Woelfel, & Jordan, 1983).

Dominance. **Dominance** is a contextual influence of compliance gaining based on power dimensions within a relationship. You may recall our discussion of power in Chapter 9. French and Raven (1960) noted five bases of power that people use when attempting to influence each other: reward power, coercive power, expert power, legitimate power, and referent power. These power bases continue to be relevant over a half-century after they were first offered. *Reward power* is used when someone has

---

Make Your Case

There is some disagreement in compliance gaining research as to how strategies should be compiled and tested. Some researchers provide study participants with a ready-made list of strategies and ask them to select which ones they would likely use in given situations. Other researchers ask study participants to provide their own strategies rather than selecting them from a ready-made list. These researchers argue that participants may select strategies from ready-made lists that they have never even considered before but mark them because they seem like good ideas. In both cases participants may offer more positive strategies than negative strategies because they want the researcher to see them in a positive manner. Which research methodology do you believe is most appropriate when studying compliance gaining? What other strategies could be used in future compliance gaining research?

something that another person wants or possesses the ability to provide it. With the ability to reward an employee with raises, bonuses, promotions, or time off, an employer might draw upon reward power when attempting to influence an employee. *Coercive power* is used when someone is capable of imposing punishment on another person. Using the above example, with the ability to punish an employee by lowering salaries, preventing promotion, or termination, an employer might also draw upon coercive power when attempting to influence an employee. *Expert power* is used when someone possesses needed knowledge or information. As discussed in Chapter 10, health providers possess this form of power as does anyone with needed expertise. *Legitimate power* is used when someone holds a formal position or role. A supervisor at work could draw upon legitimate power when attempting to influence a subordinate. This form of power is also evident in small groups with formal structure and hierarchy. Finally, *referent power* is used when someone wants to influence another person who wishes to emulate or happens to admire him or her. An older sibling might be able to use this form of power when attempting to influence a younger sibling, for instance.

Intimacy. **Intimacy** is a contextual influence of compliance gaining based on the relational connection among interactants. You would most likely select different compliance gaining strategies when attempting to influence someone with whom you share a close personal relationship such as a friend, a family member, or a romantic partner than you would when attempting to influence a stranger, an acquaintance, or a new neighbor. People generally are more concerned about not upsetting someone with whom they share a close relationship than they are about not upsetting someone with whom they are not close. Further, people who are close to you know intimate details of your life and could potentially use them against you.

Resistance. **Resistance** is a contextual influence of compliance gaining based on anticipated opposition. Your selection of a compliance gaining strategy will be influenced by whether or not you think the other person will go along with your request or will oppose your request. People are generally fairly adept at determining potential resistance, but these assessments are not always accurate. For example, there has probably been an occasion when you were convinced that someone was going to resist your request, spent quite a bit of time determining your strategy, and had already become a bit irritated that the person would even consider denying your wishes only to discover that the person was perfectly agreeable. Of course, the opposite situation has probably happened as well when you were met with unexpected resistance to your request. All in all, though, people are fairly accurate at anticipating opposition, and these perceptions of the situation influence which strategies are selected.

Relational Consequences. **Relational consequences** is a contextual influence of compliance gaining based on the perceived effects a compliance gaining strategy might have on a relationship. Relational consequences can be examined in three different ways. First, attempting to gain compliance comes with the potential of harming a relationship. A negative compliance gaining strategy may cause strife within a relationship, perhaps leading to relational disengagement or disintegration of the relationship in its present form. Second and certainly connected, attempting to gain compliance could result in losing a source of future support and other resources. A negative compliance gaining strategy could be successful at obtaining a desired response from a person at the present time but could result in not being able to come back to that person in the future. Third and finally, attempting to gain compliance could actually lead to the enhancement of a relationship and the reinforcement of a potential source. The negative consequences tend to be addressed more often than the positive consequences, but the positive relational consequences are just as likely. For instance, someone with the potential to use negative compliance gaining strategies but who chooses to use positive compliance gaining strategies may be looked upon more favorably. These actions may thus result in increased liking and dependability.

Personal Benefit. **Personal benefit** is a contextual influence of compliance gaining based on potential personal gain. It is also possible to consider the personal gain of the person being influenced. For instance, if someone is doing something dangerous or placing others in harmful situations, a negative strategy may be selected because compliance is so important that successful influence will outweigh the potential negative consequences. If compliance is simply important for whatever reason, strategies will be selected with decreased regard for relational drawbacks. Any negative consequences would be considered worth it in order to achieve the desired compliance.

Rights. **Rights** is a contextual influence of compliance gaining based on the degree to which the desired outcome seems justified. If a neighbor is playing loud music in the middle of the night, you might feel justified to ask him or her to turn down the music if it is disturbing you. If you think the neighbor's clothes are ugly and wish he or she would change fashions, you might feel less justified in making such a request. Sometimes the right to seek compliance is obvious, but it can get tricky. Relationships frequently inform people of whether or not attempts at compliance are justified, but even then, each unique relationship will vary as to what is considered justified. Asking a neighbor, a coworker, a stranger, or an acquaintance to improve his or her clothing choices may seem less justified than, say, asking the same of a friend, a romantic partner, or a family member, but justification in these relationships may still

People often must take multiple contextual consequences into account. For instance, a friend may be dating someone who is not very good for him or her. You know your friend would benefit from leaving this person, but mentioning this may threaten your friendship. Can you recall a time when you were faced with a situation impacting both relational consequences and personal benefits of a friend? What did you do? What situations justify risking a friendship out of concern for a friend?

be tenuous. Other issues complicate things even more. Consider attempting to get a parent to discipline his or her child, for instance. Certain relationships might increase a person's right to make such a request, but there may nevertheless be disagreement as to whether a person is actually justified. Whatever the case, the extent to which a person does or does not feel justified will influence the selection of compliance gaining strategy.

Apprehension. **Apprehension** is a contextual influence of compliance gaining based on anxiety resulting from the circumstances. Certain compliance gaining situations are more stressful than others—for instance, asking a supervisor for a raise, seeking a higher grade on an assignment from an instructor, or asking someone out on a date. Other compliance gaining situations such as asking someone to pass the salt or asking someone to close a window may be less stressful. Of course, things are never quite as straightforward as they appear, and these examples may or may not lead to apprehension. Contextual factors encompassing the compliance gaining situation offer more accurate predictions of apprehension than the situation itself. Simply glance at the above items for a few prime examples. Each can influence whether or not a situation will lead to apprehension. This is an important point, because it underscores that these contextual influences do not exist in isolation; they exist together and impact one another.

Focus Questions Revisited

What is civic engagement, and what are some common misconceptions people have about it?

Civic engagement entails participating in community development, addressing social concerns, and combating injustices. Common misconceptions about civic engagement include the following: (a) social and political struggles are concerns of the past and are no longer relevant issues; (b) participation in such activities is limited to only a few radical people; (c) it only surrounds major issues of national or international importance; and (d) it only involves radical actions or activities such as riots and protests.

What are the types of persuasive presentations?

The two primary types of persuasive speeches are speeches to convince and speeches to actuate. Speeches to convince are delivered in an attempt to impact audience thinking, and they encompass a primary claim—essentially, what you are trying to convince your audience to believe. The following are the four primary types of persuasive claims that can be developed through a speech to convince: (1) policy, (2) value, (3) fact, and (4) conjecture. Speeches to actuate are delivered in an attempt to impact audience behavior.

What are the techniques of sequential persuasion?

Techniques of sequential persuasion include (a) foot in the door, (b) door in the face, and (c) pregiving. The foot-in-the-door technique involves making a small request and then following up with a second, larger request. The door-in-the-face technique involves making a request so large that it will be turned down and then following up with a second, smaller request. The pregiving technique maintains that when a person is given something or offered favors by someone else, that person is more likely to comply with a subsequent request.

Are emotions physical or symbolic and relational, and why should they be included in a chapter on public and personal influence?

Emotions are both physical and symbolic and relational. Often considered something that people feel internally, emotion is also very much a symbolic and relational activity. Symbolically, emotions and the feelings that accompany them are given meaning within a culture or society. Further, these symbolic characteristics of emotions are learned relationally. When it comes to persuasion, the discipline of communication studies has traditionally focused primarily on logic and reasoning. This focus remains an important element, but there is an increasing awareness of the importance of emotion when studying human behavior in general and when studying human motivation specifically.

What are the relational influence goals of compliance gaining?

There are seven relational influence goals of compliance gaining. *Gaining assistance* is a relational influence goal dedicated to obtaining resources. *Giving advice* is a relational influence goal dedicated to providing guidance. *Sharing activities* is a relational influence goal dedicated to engaging in joint endeavors. *Changing orientations* is a relational influence goal dedicated to changing a person's position on an issue. *Changing relationships* is a relational influence goal dedicated to altering the relationship of the interactants. *Obtaining permission* is a relational influence goal dedicated to receiving authorization for an action. Finally, *enforcing rights and obligations* is a relational influence goal dedicated to making someone fulfill a commitment or role.

What are the original five strategies (categories) of compliance gaining?

Gerald Marwell and David Schmitt's (1967) 16 compliance gaining strategies were grouped into five categories: (1) rewarding activities, (2) punishing activities, (3) expertise activities, (4) activation of impersonal commitments, and (5) activation of personal commitments. Rewarding activities seek compliance through positivity. Punishing activities seek compliance through negativity. Expertise activities seek compliance through perceptions of credibility or wisdom. Activation of impersonal commitments seeks compliance through the manipulation of internal feelings of obligation and appropriate behavior. Activation of personal commitments seeks compliance through appealing to obligations to others.

What contextual influences impact the selection of compliance gaining strategies?

There are seven contextual factors that impact the selection of compliance gaining strategies. Dominance is a contextual influence of compliance gaining based on power dimensions within a relationship. *Intimacy* is based on the relational connection among interactants. *Resistance* is based on anticipated opposition. *Relational consequences* are based on the perceived effects a compliance gaining strategy might have on a relationship. *Personal benefit* is based on potential personal gain. *Rights* are based on the degree to which the desired outcome seems justified. *Apprehension* is based on anxiety resulting from the circumstances.

Key Concepts

activation of impersonal
commitments (p. 406)
activation of personal
commitments (p. 406)
anchor position (p. 391)
apprehension (contextual
influence) (p. 410)
arousal goals (p. 405)
assimilation effect (p. 392)
attitudes (p. 385)
beliefs (p. 385)
civic engagement (p. 380)
claim of conjecture (p. 387)
claim of fact (p. 387)
claim of policy (p. 387)
claim of value (p. 387)
cognitive dissonance
theory (p. 394)
compliance gaining (p. 403)
contrast effect (p. 392)
deductive reasoning (p. 390)
dominance (contextual
influence) (p. 407)
door-in-the-face technique (p. 395)
enthymeme (p. 390)
ethos (p. 389)
expertise activities (p. 406)
extended parallel process
model (p. 400)
foot-in-the-door technique (p. 394)
given belief (p. 386)

identity goals (p. 404)
inductive reasoning (p. 390)
interaction goals (p. 405)
intimacy (contextual
influence) (p. 408)
latitude of acceptance (p. 391)
latitude of noncommitment (p. 391)
latitude of rejection (p. 391)
logos (p. 390)
pathos (p. 389)
perceptual contrast effect (p. 396)
personal benefit (contextual
influence) (p. 409)
pregiving technique (p. 397)
punishing activities (p. 406)
reciprocal concessions (p. 396)
relational consequences (contextual
influence) (p. 409)
resistance (contextual
influence) (p. 408)
resource goals (p. 405)
rewarding activities (p. 405)
rights (contextual influence) (p. 409)
self-perception theory (p. 394)
self-presentation (p. 396)
social judgment theory (p. 391)
speech to actuate (p. 388)
speech to convince (p. 387)
syllogism (p. 390)
values (p. 386)

Questions to Ask Your Friends

- Ask your friends to describe their most recent attempt to influence someone's behavior. What techniques did they use? Were they successful? If so, why do you think they were successful? If not, what do you think would have led to success?

- Ask your friends to describe the most recent attempt by someone to influence their behavior. What techniques did that person use? Was the person successful? If so, why do you think that person was successful? If not, what do you think would have led to success?

- Produce a compliance gaining scenario for your friends such as asking someone to give them a ride. Then ask them to describe how they would go about gaining compliance with a friend, a romantic partner, a colleague/classmate, a neighbor, and an acquaintance. How do their strategies change depending on the relationship?

Media Links

- Watch a series of commercials on television and determine what emotions were used. What emotions are most predominant? Are certain emotions used when selling particular products?

- Look closely at the next mailer you receive from an organization seeking a donation. Is the organization using a technique of sequential persuasion? Do you think it will be successful? If so, what has the organization done correctly? If not, what could it have done differently?

- Try to convince a friend to do something for you while interacting face-to-face. Now try to convince another friend to do the exact same thing; only this time do it through e-mail or text message. What differences did you notice in the two attempts? What similarities did you notice in the two attempts?

Ethical Issues

- Is it ethical to manipulate someone's emotions in order to persuade him or her? Based on how you answered that question, are there any situations or circumstances that would justify the opposite view?

- People frequently comply with requests from others because of their relationship. What are requests you would consider unethical to pose to a friend, even though a friend might comply? How about a romantic partner?

- Dominance exists in relationships, but is it ethical to use dominance to get someone to comply?

Answers to Photo Captions

Photo 14.1 ▪ No. Civic engagement takes many forms such as volunteering, membership, fund-raising, petitions, letters, sit-ins, strikes, walk-outs, boycotts, formal debates, informal discussions, and public presentations just to name a few.

Photo 14.2 ▪ The method of sequential persuasion used by the volunteer would be door in the face. This strategy worked because of self-presentation.

Photo 14.3 ▪ No. Emotion is also a symbolic and relational phenomenon.

Photo 14.4 ▪ The compliance gaining strategy being used is activation of personal commitments.

Student Study Site

Visit the study site at **www.sagepub.com/ciel** for e-flashcards, practice quizzes, and other study resources.

References

Bem, D. J. (1972). Self-perception theory. In L. Berkowitz (Ed.), *Advances in experimental social psychology* (pp. 2–62). New York: Academic Press.

Burger, J. M. (1999). The foot-in-the-door compliance procedure: A multiple process analysis and review. *Personality and Social Psychology Review, 3,* 303–325.

Burke, K. (1969). *A rhetoric of motives.* Berkeley: University of California Press.

Chartrand, T., Pinckert, S., & Burger, J. M. (1999). When manipulation backfires: The effects of time delay and requester on the foot-in-the-door technique. *Journal of Applied Social Psychology, 29,* 211–221.

Cho, H., & Witte, K. (2004). A review of fear-appeal effects. In J. S. Seiter & R. H. Gass (Eds.), *Perspectives on persuasion, social influence, and compliance gaining* (pp. 223–238). Boston: Allyn & Bacon.

Cialdini, R. B., & Goldstein, N. J. (2004). Social influence: Compliance and conformity. *Annual Review of Psychology, 55,* 591–621.

Cialdini, R. B., Vincent, J. E., Lewis, S. K., Catalan, J., Wheeler, D., & Darby, B. L. (1975). Reciprocal concessions procedure for inducing compliance: The door-in-the-face technique. *Journal of Personality and Social Psychology, 37,* 2221–2239.

Cody, M. J., & McLaughlin, M. L. (1980). Perceptions of compliance gaining situations: A dimensional analysis. *Communication Monographs, 47,* 132–148.

Cody, M. J., Woelfel, M. L., & Jordan, W. J. (1983). Dimension of compliance-gaining situations. *Human Communication Research, 9,* 99–113.

Dillard, J. P. (1989). Types of influence goals in personal relationships. *Journal of Social and Personal Relationships, 6,* 293–308.

Dillard, J. P., Anderson, J. W., & Knobloch, L. K. (2002). Interpersonal influence. In M. Knapp & J. A. Daly (Eds.), *Handbook of interpersonal communication* (3rd ed., pp. 425–474). Thousand Oaks, CA: Sage.

Dillard, J. P., Hunter, J. E., & Burgoon, M. (1984). Sequential-request persuasive strategies: Meta-analysis of foot-in-the-door and door-in-the-face. *Human Communication Research, 10,* 461–488.

Dillard, J. P., Segrin, C., & Harden, J. M. (1989). Primary and secondary goals in the production of interpersonal influence messages. *Communication Monographs, 56,* 19–38.

Fern, E. F., Monroe, K. B., & Avila, R. A. (1986). Effectiveness of multiple request strategies: A synthesis of research results. *Journal of Marketing Research, 23,* 144–152.

Festinger, L. (1957). *A theory of cognitive dissonance.* Stanford, CA: Stanford University Press.

Fishbein, M., Ajzen, I. (1975). *Belief, attitude, intention, and behavior: An introduction to theory and research.* Reading, MA: Addison-Wesley.

French, J. R. P., Jr., & Raven, B. (1960). The bases of social power. In D. Cartwright & A. Zander (Eds.), *Group dynamics* (pp. 607–623). New York: Harper & Row.

Gass, R. H., & Seiter, J. S. (2007). *Persuasion, social influence, and compliance gaining* (3rd ed.). Boston: Allyn & Bacon.

Gouran, D. S., Wiethoff, W. E., & Doelger, J. A. (1994). *Mastering communication* (2nd ed.). Boston: Allyn & Bacon.

Groves, R. M., Cialdini, R. B., & Couper, M. P. (1992). Understanding the decision to participate in a survey. *Public Opinion Quarterly, 56,* 475–495.

Marwell, G., & Schmitt, D. R. (1967). Dimensions of compliance gaining behavior: An empirical analysis. *Sociometry, 30,* 350–364.

Miller, G. R., Seligman, C., Clark, N. T., & Bush, M. (1976). Perceptual contrast versus reciprocal concession as mediators of induced compliance. *Canadian Journal of Behavioral Sciences, 8,* 401–409.

Mongeau, P. A. (1998). Another look at fear-arousing appeals. In M. Allen & R. W. Preiss (Eds.), *Persuasion: Advances through meta-analysis* (pp. 53–68). Cresskill, NH: Hampton Press.

Nabi, R. L. (2002). Discrete emotions and persuasion. In J. P. Dillard & M. Pfau (Eds.), *The persuasion handbook: Developments in theory and practice* (pp. 289–308). Thousand Oaks, CA: Sage.

O'Keefe, D. J. (1990). *Persuasion: Theory and research.* Newbury Park, CA: Sage.

O'Keefe, D. J. (2000). Guilt and social influence. In M. E. Roloff (Ed.), *Communication yearbook* (Vol. 23, pp. 67–101). Thousand Oaks, CA: Sage.

O'Keefe, D. J. (2002). Guilt as a mechanism of persuasion. In J. P. Dillard & M. Pfau (Eds.), *The persuasion handbook: Developments in theory and practice* (pp. 329–344). Thousand Oaks, CA: Sage.

O'Keefe, D. J., & Figge, M. (1999). Guilt and expected guilt reduction on door in face. *Communication Monographs, 66,* 312–324.

O'Keefe, D. J., & Hale, S. L. (1998). The door-in-the-face influence strategy: A random effects meta-analytic review. In M. E. Roloff (Ed.), *Communication yearbook* (Vol. 21, pp. 1–33). Thousand Oaks, CA: Sage.

Pendleton, M. G., & Bateson, C. D. (1979). Self-presentation and the door-in-the-face technique for inducing compliance. *Personality and Social Psychology Bulletin, 5,* 77–81.

Sahlstein, E. M. (2000). *Relational rhetorics and RRTs (Relational Rhetorical Terms).* Unpublished manuscript, Iowa City, IA.

Schachter, S., & Singer, J. E. (1962). Cognitive, social, and physiological determinants of emotional state. *Psychological Review, 69,* 379–399.

Sherif, C. W., Sherif, M., & Nebergall, R. (1965). *Attitude and attitude change: The social judgment-involvement approach.* Philadelphia: W. B. Saunders.

Sherif, M., & Hovland, C. I. (1961). *Social judgment: Assimilation and contrast effects in communication and attitude change.* New Haven, CT: Yale University Press.

Tusing, K. J., & Dillard, J. P. (2000). The psychological reality of the door-in-the-face: It's helping not bargaining. *Journal of Language and Social Psychology, 19,* 5–25.

Vangelisti, A. L., Daly, J. A., & Rudnick, J. R. (1991). Making people feel guilty in conversations: Techniques and correlates. *Human Communication Research, 18,* 3–39.

Witte, K. (1992). Putting the fear back into fear appeals: The extended parallel process model. *Communication Monographs, 59,* 330–349.

Witte, K. (1998). Fear as motivator, fear as inhibitor: Using the extended parallel process model to explain fear appeal successes and failures. In P. A. Anderson & L. K. Guerrero (Eds.), *The handbook of communication and emotion: Research, theory, applications, and contexts* (pp. 423–450). San Diego, CA: Academic Press.

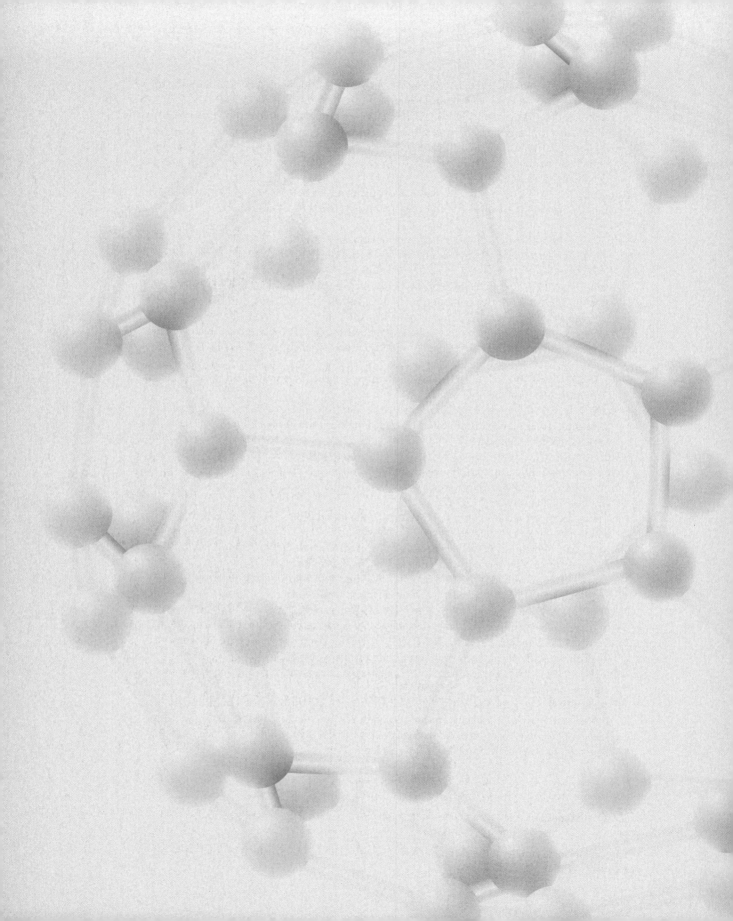

Glossary

accommodation: when people change their accent, their rate of speech, and even the words they use to indicate a relational connection with the person to whom they are talking

accountable self: the aspect of self that allows other people to morally judge a person's performance

accounts: forms of communication that go beyond the facts and offer justifications, excuses, exonerations, explanations, or accusations

action-facilitating support: providing information or performing tasks for others

activation of impersonal commitments: seeking compliance through the manipulation of internal feelings of obligation and appropriate behavior

activation of personal commitments: seeking compliance through appealing to obligations to others

altercasting: how language can impose a certain identity on people (e.g., "Only a *fool* would…"; "The *brightest students* will get this chapter without any trouble") and then burden them with the duty to live up to the description, whether positive or negative

anchor position (social judgment theory): represents the preferred or most acceptable position in an argument

appeal to authority (fallacious argument): when a person's authority or credibility in one area is used to support another area

appeal to people (fallacious argument): claims that something is good or beneficial because everyone else agrees with this evaluation (also called bandwagon appeal)

appeal to relationships (fallacious argument): when relationships are used to justify certain behaviors and to convince others of their appropriateness

apprehension: contextual influence of compliance gaining based on anxiety resulting from the circumstances

argument against the source (fallacious argument): when the source of a message, rather than the message itself, is attacked (also called *ad hominem* argument)

arousal goals: secondary goals of compliance gaining recognizing the desire to keep arousal at an acceptable level

assimilation effect (social judgment theory): maintains that if someone advocates a position within a person's latitude of acceptance, he or she will view it as closer to his or her anchor position than it really is

asynchronous communication: communication in which there is a slight or prolonged delay between the message and the response; the interactants must alternate between sending and receiving messages

attending: the second step in the listening process when stimuli are perceived and focused on

attitude of reflection (symbolic interaction): thinking about how you look in other people's eyes, or reflecting on the fact that other people can see you as a social object from their point of view

attitudes: learned predispositions to evaluate something in a positive or negative way that guide people's thinking and behavior

authority structure: in some families the authority structure stresses the role of one parent as head of the family; others stress equality of all the mature members

autonomy-connectedness: dialectic tension caused by one's desire to retain some independence yet be connected to another person in a relationship

backchannel communication: vocalizations by a listener that give feedback to the speaker to show interest, attention, and/or a willingness to keep listening

back region: a frame where a social interaction is regarded as not under public scrutiny and so people do not have to present their public face (e.g., when servers are in the kitchen or when there are no customers in a restaurant, then servers do not have to behave with dignity or with respect toward customers—and often do not)

beliefs: what a person holds to be true or false

bidirectionality hypothesis: the idea that power can work in two directions; that is, at some points and times it works one way when parents control or influence their young kids, but power also goes the other way and sometimes kids can control or influence parents, for example by throwing temper tantrums

binuclear family: two families based on the nuclear form (e.g., the children's father, their stepmother, and her children, if any, as well as the children's mother and their stepfather and his children, if any)

blended family: when parents adopt nongenetic offspring, divorce, or remarry other partners, then so-called blended families are the result

body buffer zone: a kind of imaginary aura around you that you regard as part of yourself and your personal space

boundary management: focuses on the way marital couples manage talking about private matters with each other and how they coordinate communication boundaries in balancing a need for disclosure with the need for privacy

Burke's pentad: five elements common to all stories and situations: scene, agent, act, agency, and purpose

children-parents (patient-provider relationship): the provider clearly portrays a dominant role of expert while the patient assumes a submissive and dependent role; this view of provider and patient relationships is the most traditional and still most common

chronemics: the study of use and evaluation of time in interactions

civic engagement: participation in community development, addressing social concerns, and combating injustices

claim of conjecture: a claim that something will be true or false in the future

claim of fact: a claim maintaining that something is true or false

claim of policy: a claim maintaining that a course of action should or should not be taken

claim of value: a claim maintaining that something is good or bad, beneficial or detrimental, or another evaluative criterion

co-culture: a smaller group of culture within a larger cultural mass

coded system of meaning: a set of beliefs, a heritage, and a way of being that is transacted in communication

cognitive dissonance theory: people prefer their actions to be consistent with their attitudes, beliefs, and values, because inconsistency elicits negative feelings; explains foot-in-the-door technique

cohesiveness: working in unison

collectivist (culture): one of a culture who subscribes to a belief system that stresses group benefit and the overriding value of working harmoniously rather than individual personal advancement

common purpose: sharing goals and objectives; working toward the same end to achieve a particular result

communication as action: the act of sending messages—whether or not they are received

communication as interaction: an exchange of information between two (or more) individuals

communication as transaction: the construction of shared meanings or understandings between two (or more) individuals

communication privacy management theory: explains how people create and manage privacy boundaries in their relationships

compliance gaining: involves interpersonal attempts at influence, especially attempts to influence someone's behavior

composition fallacy (fallacious argument): argues that the parts are the same as the whole

concurrent media use: use of two or more media systems simultaneously

conflict: real or perceived incompatibilities of processes, understandings, and viewpoints between people

conflict-as-destructive culture: a culture based on four assumptions: that conflict is a destructive disturbance of the peace; that the social system should not be adjusted to meet the needs of members, but members should adapt to established values; that confrontations are destructive and ineffective; and that disputants should be disciplined.

conflict-as-opportunity culture: a culture based on four assumptions: that conflict is a normal, useful process; that all issues are subject to change through negotiation; that direct confrontation and conciliation are valued; and that conflict is a necessary renegotiation of an implied contract—a redistribution of opportunity, a release of tensions, and a renewal of relationships

connotative meaning: the overtones, implications, or additional meanings associated with a word or an object

consistency: whether a message is free of internal contradiction and is in harmony with information known to be true

constitute: create or bring into existence

constitutive approach to communication: communication can create or bring into existence something that has not been there before, such as agreement, a contract, or an identity

consumers (patient-provider relationship): patients viewing themselves as paying providers for specific information and expecting them to carry out their wishes

content creators: Internet users who have developed or maintained a Web site or blog or shared their creative work online

content (representational) listening: obstacle to listening when people focus on the content level of meaning, or literal meaning, rather than the social or relational levels of meaning

continuation of identity: parts of your identity carry over from your normal practices of everyday talk into the workplace, but some parts of your identity are transformed by the workplace

contrast effect (social judgment theory): maintains that if someone advocates a position within a person's latitude of rejection, he or she will view it as farther from his or her anchor position than it really is

convergence: a person moves toward the style of talk used by the other speaker

conversational hypertext: coded messages within conversation that an informed listener will effortlessly understand

counteractive communication: gets the group back on track by reminding group members of the purposes they are there to serve

critical listening: the process of analyzing and evaluating the accuracy, legitimacy, and value of messages

cross-cultural communication: compares the communication styles and patterns of people from very different cultural/social structures, such as nation-states

cultural persuadables: the cultural premises and norms that delineate a range of what may and what must be persuaded (as opposed to certain topics in a society that require no persuasive appeal because the matters are taken for granted)

culture as code: a way of thought and a set of assumptions taken for granted by everyone who belongs to it

cum hoc ergo propter hoc (fallacious argument): argues that if one thing happens at the same time as another, it was caused by the thing with which it coincides; Latin for "with this; therefore, because of this"

decoding: drawing meaning from something you observe

deductive reasoning: using general conclusions, premises, or principles to reach a conclusion about a specific example or instance

denotative meaning: the identification of something by pointing it out ("That is a cat")

Devil terms: powerfully evocative terms viewed negatively in a society (see *God terms*)

dialectic tension: occurs whenever one is in two minds about something because one feels a simultaneous pull in two directions

disruptive communication: diverts a group from its goals and takes it down side alleys

divergence: a talker moves away from another's style of speech to make a relational point, such as establishing dislike or superiority

division fallacy (fallacious argument): argues the whole is the same as its parts

dominance: contextual influence of compliance gaining based on power dimensions within a relationship

door-in-the-face technique: sequential method of persuasion that involves making a request so large that it will be turned down and then following up with a second, smaller request

dyadic process: part of the process of breakdown of relationships that involves a confrontation with a partner and the open discussion of a problem with a relationship

dynamic: elements of nonverbal communication that are changeable during interaction (e.g., facial expression, posture, gesturing; contrast with *static*)

egocentric listening: obstacle to listening when people focus more on their message and self-presentation than on the message of the other person involved in an interaction

elaborated code: speech that emphasizes the reasoning behind a command; uses speech and language more as a way for people to differentiate the uniqueness of their own personalities and ideas and to express their own individuality, purposes, attitudes, and beliefs than as a way to reinforce collectivity or commonality of outlook (contrast with *restricted code*)

emoticons: text-based symbols used to express emotions online, often to alleviate problems associated with a lack of nonverbal cues

emotional support: type of nurturing support enabling people to express their feelings and to have those feelings validated by others

empathy: viewing a problem from the perspective of another person to understand his or her thinking and how he or she is feeling

encoding: putting feelings into behavior through nonverbal communication

engaged listening: making a personal relational connection with the source of a message that results from the source and the receiver actively working together to create shared meaning and understanding

enthymeme: a syllogism that excludes one or two of its three components (see *syllogism*)

environmental distraction: obstacle to listening that results from the physical location where listening takes place

equivocation (fallacious argument): relies on the ambiguousness of language to make an argument

essential function of talk: a function of talk that makes the relationship real and talks it into being, often by using coupling references or making assumptions that the relationship exists

esteem support: type of nurturing support making someone feel competent and valued

ethnocentric bias: believing that the way one's own culture does things is the right and only way to do them

ethos: the use of speaker credibility to impact an audience

experiential superiority: obstacle to listening when people fail to fully listen to someone else because they believe that they possess more or superior knowledge and experience than the other person

expertise activities: seeking compliance through perceptions of credibility or wisdom

extended family: a family that has at its center a nuclear family but also includes grandparents, aunts, cousins, and all other living forms of blood relatives

extended parallel process model: explains the process of fear appeals using the key elements of perceived threat and perceived efficacy

facework: the management of people's dignity or self-respect, known as "face"

factual diversion: obstacle to listening that occurs when so much emphasis is placed on attending to every detail of a message that the main point becomes lost

fallacious argument: an argument that appears legitimate but is actually based on faulty reasoning or insufficient evidence

false alternatives (fallacious argument): occur when only two options are provided, one of which is generally presented as the poor choice or one that should be avoided

family identity: a family identity is a sense of the special or unique features of the family; often revolves around intergenerational storytelling, where the elders talk about dead relatives or relate stories about particular family characters who defined the essence of being "a Threlkeld," for example

family narratives: in the process of storytelling families create a shared sense of meaning about the family experience, whether it is something positive like a birth or an adoption or something negative such as a death or divorce

family of choice: a family created through adoption, or simply the group of people you decide is your "true" family even though there is no genetic connection

family of descent: the whole historical family tree from which you are descended, both living and dead

family of generativity: the family where you are one of the parents of at least one child

family of origin: the family where you are the child of two parents, and in the majority of cases you will have spent some of your life with one or both of them

family storytelling: families have stories about remarkable figures or events in their history that help define the nature of that particular family; telling such stories is a way of bonding and uniting the family as well as identifying some of its key characteristics

foot-in-the-door technique: sequential method of persuasion that involves making a small request and then following up with a second, larger request

formality/hierarchy: creates distance between workers and management and can represent a strain or restraint on relationships as an individual is forced to adopt a professional face rather than a personal identity (Chapter 5) when dealing with people at work

formal power: allocated by a system or group to particular people (e.g., bosses, the police, school principals; compare with *informal power*)

frames: basic forms of knowledge that provide a definition of a scenario, either because both people agree on the nature of the situation or because the cultural assumptions built into the interaction and the previous relational context of talk give them a clue

front region: a place where a social interaction is regarded as under public scrutiny and so people have to be on their best behavior or acting out their professional roles or intended "face" (e.g., the restaurant, where servers have to behave with dignity and with respect toward customers)

given belief: a belief that the majority of people in an audience will view as either true or false

God terms: powerfully evocative terms that are viewed positively in a society (see *Devil terms*)

grave dressing process: part of the breakdown of relationships that consists of creating the story of why a relationship died and erecting a metaphorical tombstone that summarizes its main events and features from its birth to its death

group culture: the set of expectations and practices that a group develops to make itself distinctive from other groups and to give its members a sense of exclusive membership (e.g., dress code, specialized language, particular rituals)

group norms: rules and procedures that occur in a group but not necessarily outside it and that are enforced by the use of power or rules for behavior

group sanctions: punishments for "stepping out of line," speaking out of turn, or failing to accept the ruling of the chair or leader

haptics: the study of the specific nonverbal behaviors involving touch

hasty generalization (fallacious argument): when a conclusion is based on a single occurrence or insufficient data or sample size

hearing: the passive physiological act of receiving sound that takes place when sound waves hit a person's eardrums

high code: a formal, grammatical, and very correct—often "official"—way of talking

high-context society: a culture that places a great deal of emphasis on the total environment (context) where speech and interaction takes place, especially on the relationships between the speakers rather than just on what they say (see *low-context society*)

identity: a person's uniqueness, represented by descriptions, a self-concept, inner thoughts, and performances, that is symbolized in interactions with other people and presented for their assessment and moral evaluation

identity goals: secondary goals of compliance gaining recognizing that people desire to act in accordance with the personal and relational identities they attempt to transact and/or the personal and relational identities most appropriate in a given situation

immediacy: linguistic inclusion (e.g., "Let's…," "we," "us")

indexical function of talk: demonstrates or indicates the nature of the relationship between speakers

individualist: one who subscribes to a belief system that focuses on the individual person and his or her personal dreams, goals and achievements, and right to make choices

inductive reasoning: deriving a general conclusion based on specific evidence, examples, or instances

industrial time: the attention to punctuality and dedication to a task that is connected with the nature of industry (clocking in, clocking out, lunch breaks, etc.)

informal power: operates through relationships and individual reputations without formal status (e.g., someone may not actually be the boss but might exert more influence on other workers by being highly respected; compare with *formal power*)

informational support: type of action-facilitating support providing someone with information in order to increase his or her knowledge and understanding of health issues

instrumental function of talk: when what is said brings about a goal that you have in mind for the relationship, and talk is the means or instrument by which it is accomplished (e.g., asking someone on a date or to come with you to a party)

instrumental goals: are predominant at work and are directed at completion of duties; can also involve a direct assessment of performance

instrumental support: type of action-facilitating support performing tasks for someone

intentionality: a basic assumption in communication studies that messages indicate somebody's intentions or that they are produced intentionally or in a way that gives insight, at the very least, into the sender's mental processes

interaction goals: secondary goals of compliance gaining recognizing the desire to act appropriately when attempting to gain compliance intercultural communication: examines how people from different cultural/social structures speak to one another and what difficulties or conflicts they encounter, over and above the different languages they speak

interdependence: the reliance of each member of a team or group on the other members, making their outcomes dependent on the collaboration and interrelated performance of all members (e.g., a football team dividing up the jobs of throwing, catching, and blocking)

interpreting: the third step in the listening process when meaning is assigned to sounds and symbolic activity

intimacy: contextual influence of compliance gaining based on the relational connection among interactants

intrapsychic process: part of the process of breakdown of a relationship where an individual reflects on the strengths and weaknesses of a relationship and begins to consider the possibility of ending it

introspective units: one of three types of relational continuity constructional units that keep the memory of the relationship alive during the physical separation of the members involved; introspective units are reminders of the relationships during an absence, examples being photographs of a couple, wedding bands, or fluffy toys that one partner gave to another

kin keeping: the act of serving as a reservoir for information about members of the family, which is passed along to the other members of the network

kin networks: the extended relational network of cousins, second cousins, children of cousins, uncles, aunts, and even long-term friends who are considered family, too

kinesics: the study of movements that take place during the course of an interaction

labeling: naming an object or person with a label that the person has to live up to

langue: the formal grammatical structure of language (contrast with *parole*)

latitude of acceptance (social judgment theory): positions in an argument that an audience deems acceptable

latitude of noncommitment (social judgment theory): positions in an argument that an audience neither wholly accepts nor wholly rejects

latitude of rejection (social judgment theory): positions in an argument that an audience deems unacceptable

leadership: the formal position where a specific person has power over the others in the group and is given the responsibility of leading its activities

leakage: unintentional betrayal of internal feelings through nonverbal communication

listening: the active process of receiving, attending to, interpreting, and responding to symbolic activity

logos: the use of logic or reasoning to impact an audience

long-distance relationships (LDRs): relationships characterized by the distance between partners that prevents them from meeting face-to-face frequently (e.g., commuter marriages or relationships where one person lives on the East Coast and one on the West Coast)

low code: an informal and often ungrammatical way of talking

low-context society: assumes that the message itself means everything, and it is much more important to have a well-structured argument or a well-delivered presentation than it is to be a member of the royal family or a cousin of the person listening (see *high-context society*)

machines and mechanics (patient-provider relationship): providers are viewed as competent experts analytically diagnosing a physical problem and then fixing it; patients are passive and allow the expert mechanic to give them a proper tune-up with little or no input or objection

meaning: what a symbol represents

media equation: people use the same social rules and expectations when interacting with technology as they do with other people

media generations: generations that are differentiated by unique media grammar and media consciousness based on the technological environment in which they are born

media literacy: the learned ability to access, interpret, and evaluate media products

media profile: a compilation of a person's media preferences and general use of media

medium distraction: obstacle to listening that results from limitations or problems inherent in certain media and technology, such as mobile phones or Internet connections

message complexity: obstacle to listening when a person finds a message so complex or confusing that he or she stops listening

microcoordination: the unique management of social interaction made possible through cell phones

mini-com: the tendency to focus media products on specific audience members connected by a common bond

monochronic society: a culture that views time as a valuable commodity and punctuality as very important

moral accountability: people are held morally accountable for their actions, statements, or claims and have to explain them as legitimate or reasonable to other people

naming: distinguishing items from other items for which people also have (different) words

narrative: any organized story, report, or talk that has a plot, an argument, or a theme and in which speakers both relate facts and arrange the story in a way that provides an account, an explanation, or a conclusion

negative face wants: the desire not to be imposed upon or treated as inferior (contrast with *positive face wants*)

norm of reciprocity: if one person says something self-disclosing to another person in everyday life, that person should tell the first person something self-disclosing in return

norms: the habitual rules for conducting any family activity

nuclear family: the parents plus their genetically related children

nurturing support: helping people feel better about themselves and the issues they are experiencing

openness-privacy: a dialectic tension caused by people's need to be honest and open yet to retain some privacy and control over information others have about them

parasocial relationships: "relationships" established with media characters and personalities

parole: how people actually use language: where they often speak using kinds of informal and ungrammatical language structure that carry meaning to us all the same (contrast with *langue*)

partners (patient-provider relationship): patients and providers work together to solve a problem and are viewed as equals, each bringing special knowledge to the interaction

past experience with the other: obstacle to listening when previous encounters with a person lead people to dismiss or fail to critically examine a message because the person has generally been right (or wrong) in the past

pathos: the use of emotional appeals to impact an audience

peer culture: the set of attitudes and beliefs that create influence from children or adults of the same age/generation as the target person

perceptual contrast effect: explains door-in-the-face technique; people generally comply with the second request because compared to the initial request it appears much smaller

performative self: a self that is not just a set of characteristics, but the person needs to *do* or *perform* that self appropriately (e.g., needs to act competently when claiming to be a competent person)

personal benefit: contextual influence of compliance gaining based on potential personal gain

personal relationships: relationships that only specified and irreplaceable individuals (such as your mother, father, brother, sister, or very best friend) can have with you personal space: the area around a person that is regarded as part of the person and so the distance at which informal and close relationships are conducted

plausibility: the extent to which a message seems legitimate

polychronic society: a culture that does not see time as linear and simple but complex and made up of many strands, none of which is more important than any other—hence such culture's relaxed attitude toward time

polysemy: multiple meanings for the same word or symbol

positive face wants: the need to be seen and accepted as a worthwhile and reasonable person (contrast with *negative face wants*)

post hoc ergo propter hoc: argues that something is caused by whatever happens before it; Latin for "after this; therefore, because of this"

predicaments: extended embarrassments

pregiving technique: sequential method of persusaion maintaining that when a person is given something or offered favors by someone else, that person is more likely to comply with a subsequent request

presentation: one person's particular version of, or "take" on, the facts or events (contrast with *representation*)

primary groups: groups that share close personal relationships, such as friends (contrast with *secondary groups*)

privacy management: See *boundary management*

professional face: the behaviors, courtesy, and comportment that are appropriate for people to present to others in a workplace

promotive communication: works toward moving the agenda along and keeping people on track

prospective units: one of three types of relational continuity constructional units that keep the memory of the relationship alive during the physical separation of the members involved; prospective units are recognitions that a separation is about to occur, (e.g., "see ya later," "talk soon," or "when shall we three meet again, in thunder, lightning, or in rain?")

provisions of relationships: the deep and important psychological and supportive benefits that relationships provide

proxemics: the study of space and distance in communication

punishing activities: seeking compliance through negativity

receiving: the initial step in the listening process where hearing and listening connect

reciprocal concessions: explains door-in-the-face technique; people generally comply with the second request because they feel since the person making the request is willing to concede something then they themselves should match the concession and also be willing to concede something

red herring (fallacious argument): the use of another issue to divert attention away from the real issue

reflecting (paraphrasing): summarizing what another person has said to convey understanding of the message

regulators: nonverbal actions that indicate to others how you want them to behave or what you want them to do

relational continuity constructional units (RCCUs): small-talk ways of demonstrating that the relationship persists during absence of face-to-face contact (see *introspective*, *prospective*, and *retrospective*)

relational consequences: contextual influence of compliance gaining based on the perceived effects a compliance gaining strategy might have on a relationship

relational goals: typically involve intimacy and support and usually serve recreational or supportive purposes

relational listening: recognizing, understanding, and addressing the interconnection of relationships and communication during the listening process

relational technologies: such technologies as cell phones, iPods, and PDAs whose use has relational functions and implications in society and within specific groups

representation: describes facts or conveys information (contrast with *presentation*)

resistance: contextual influence of compliance gaining based on anticipated opposition

resource goals: secondary goals of compliance gaining recognizing the desire to maintain relational resources

responding: final step in the listening process that entails reacting to the message of another person

restricted code: a way of speaking that emphasizes authority and adopts certain community/cultural orientations as indisputable facts (contrast with *elaborated code*)

resurrection process: part of the breakdown of relationships that deals with how people prepare themselves for new relationships after ending an old one

rewarding activities: seeking compliance through positivity

richness: the characteristics of a message determined by the number of verbal and nonverbal cues available through a medium or technology

rights: contextual influence of compliance gaining based on the degree to which the desired outcome seems justified

rituals: particularly formalized ways for handling, say, the routines of mealtimes or birthday gift giving in a family

rules: rules and norms for "family" that monitor the way in which family life should be carried out

Sapir/Whorf hypothesis: the idea that it is the names of objects and ideas that make verbal distinctions and help you make conceptual distinctions rather than the other way around

secondary groups: groups that represent casual and more distant social relationships, such as the people you meet for discussion section but not for other purposes or at other times (contrast with *primary groups*)

sedimentation: the process by which repeated everyday practices create a "structure" for performance in the future, as a river deposits sediment that alters or maintains its course over time

selective listening: obstacle to listening when people focus on the points of a message that correspond with their views and interests and pay less attention to those that do not

self-concept: a personal, private, and essential core, covered with layers of secrecy, privacy, and convention

self-disclosure: the revelation of personal information that others could not know unless the person *made* it known

self-perception theory: explains foot-in-the-door technique; people come to understand their attitudes, beliefs, and values through their actions

self-presentation: explains door-in-the-face technique; people are concerned that other people (most notably the person making the request) may view them in a negative light and that complying with the second request might prevent or decrease those negative perceptions

semantic diversion: obstacle to listening that occurs when people are distracted by words or phrases used in a message through negative response or unfamiliarity

serial construction of meaning: a model that specifically deals with how two individuals come to understand and appreciate one another through talk, which reveals their shared experiences and leads to a larger understanding that they use the same frameworks/worlds of meaning

sign: a consequence or indicator of something specific, which cannot be changed by arbitrary actions or labels (e.g., "Wet streets are a sign of rain")

single-parent family: family where there are children but only one parent caregiver; singleness may be a choice, a preference, or an unwanted outcome (e.g., as a result of an undesired divorce or unexpected death)

social judgment theory: explains how people may respond to a range of positions surrounding a particular topic or issue

social process: part of the process of breakdown in a relationships that involves telling other people in the network about the problems and either seeking their help to keep the relationship together or seeking support for one's own version of the story of why it has come apart

social relationships: relationships in which the specific people in a given role can be changed and the relationship would still occur (e.g., customer-client relationships are the same irrespective of who is the customer and who is the client on a particular occasion; compare with *personal relationships*)

socialization: the process by which a child comes to understand the way its surrounding culture "does things"—that is, holds certain values to be self-evident and celebrates particular events or festivals

socialization impact of media: depictions of relationships in media provide models of behavior that inform people about how to engage in relationships

source distraction: obstacle to listening that results from auditory and visual characteristics of the message source

speech codes: sets of communication patterns that are the norm for that culture, and only that culture, hence defining it as different from others around it

speech communities: sets of people whose speech codes and practices identify them as a cultural unit, sharing characteristic values through their equally characteristic speech

speech to actuate: a speech delivered in an attempt to impact audience behavior

speech to convince: a speech delivered in an attempt to impact audience thinking; encompasses a primary claim, or essentially what the speaker is trying to convince the audience to believe

static: elements of nonverbal communication that are fixed during interaction (e.g., shape of the room where an interaction takes place, color of eyes, clothes worn during an interview; contrast with *dynamic*)

status of the other: an obstacle to listening when a person's rank, reputation, or social position leads people to dismiss or fail to critically examine a message

structurational approach: to look at how people enact and enable or contain future interactions through their talk

Structuration Theory: points to the regularities of human relationships that act as rules and resources drawn on to enable or constrain social interaction; thus relationships and expectations become a context for future interaction

syllogism: a form of argumentation consisting of a major premise, a minor premise, and a conclusion (see *enthymeme*)

symbol: an arbitrary representation of ideas, objects, people, relationships, cultures, genders, races, etc.

symbolic interaction: how broad social forces affect or even transact an individual person's view of who he or she is

symbolic self: the self that is transacted in interaction with other people; that arises out of social interaction, not vice versa; and hence that does not just "belong to you"

sympathy: expressing an awareness of another person's difficulty or concern

synchronous communication: communication in which people interact in real time and can at once both send and receive messages

Systems Theory: deals with (among other phenomena) family and social events as systems made up of parts but operating as a whole system that can achieve functions that individuals alone cannot and that also creates an environment in which those individuals must exist; the behavior of one part (person) affects the atmosphere and behavior of other parts (persons) of the family

teamwork: when two or more people work together to sustain one another's "face" (e.g., a distressed couple may pretend in the presence of guests that they are getting along fine, and so they act as a team to project the face of their relationship as stable and safe)

turn taking: when one speaker hands over speaking to another person

uses and gratifications: research that has attempted to determine why media systems are used and what audience members gain from their use

values: deeply held and enduring judgments of significance or importance that often provide the basis for both beliefs and attitudes

verifiability: an indication that the material being provided can be confirmed by other sources or means

vocalics (paralanguage): vocal characteristics that provide information about how verbal communication should be interpreted and how the speaker is feeling

vocational anticipatory socialization: the preparation for becoming a worker; takes place from early moments of childhood onward, including through exposure to the media and depiction of the workplace in comedy and other shows

wandering thoughts: an obstacle to listening involving daydreams or thoughts about things other than the message being presented

Photo Credits

Chapter 1

Chapter Opening Photo: © Steve Duck.
Photo 1.1: © Reg Charity/Corbis.
Photo 1.2: © Erel Photography/iStockphoto.
Photo 1.3: © Yvan Dubé/iStockphoto.
Photo 1.4: © Marcus Clackson/iStockphoto.

Chapter 2

Chapter Opening Photo: © Leigh Schindler/
iStockphoto.
Photo 2.1: © Lori Howard/iStockphoto.
Photo 2.2: © Clint Scholz/iStockphoto.
Photo 2.3: © Tina Lorien/iStockphoto.
Photo 2.4: © Leland Bobbé/Corbis.

Chapter 3

Chapter Opening Photo: © Kelvin Murray/
Getty.
Photo 3.1: © Jerry Koch/iStockphoto.
Photo 3.2: © Adrianna Williams/zefa/Corbis.
Photo 3.3: © Galina Barskaya/iStockphoto.
Photo 3.4: © Nancy Brown/The Image Bank/
Getty.

Chapter 4

Chapter Opening Photo: © Shelby Ross/
Getty.
Photo 4.1: © Bruce Ayres/Riser/Getty.
Photo 4.2: © Queerstock/Queerstock/Getty.
Photo 4.3: © Rebecca Ellis/iStockphoto.
Photo 4.4: © Sean Locke/iStockphoto.

Chapter 5

Chapter Opening Photo: © Oleksandr
Gumerov/iStockphoto.

Photo 5.1: © Damon Fourie/Stone/Getty.
Photo 5.2: © Sean Locke/iStockphoto.
Photo 5.3: © Bettmann/Corbis.
Photo 5.1: © Peter Beck/Corbis.

Chapter 6

Chapter Opening Photo: © Andresr/
iStockphoto.
Photo 6.1: © Glenda Powers/iStockphoto.
Photo 6.2: © Slobo Mitic/iStockphoto.
Photo 6.3: © Brad Killer/iStockphoto.
Photo 6.4: © Bonnie Schupp/iStockphoto.

Chapter 7

Chapter Opening Photo: © Simon Marcus/
Corbis.
Photo 7.1: © Donna Elkow-Nash/
iStockphoto.
Photo 7.2: © Elena Korenbaum/
iStockphoto.
Photo 7.3: © digitalskillet/iStockphoto.
Photo 7.4: © Rhienna Cutler/iStockphoto.
Photo 7.5: © Hans Neleman/zefa/Corbis.
Photo 7.6: Brenda Kenneally/Corbis.

Chapter 8

Chapter Opening Photo: © arne thaysen/
iStockphoto.
Photo 8.1: © Kevin C. Cox/Getty Images
Sport/Getty.
Photo 8.2: © Francis Miller/Stringer/
Time & Life Pictures/Getty.
Photo 8.3a: © Maguey Images/ Digital
Vision/Getty.
Photo 8.3b: © Purestock/Purestock/Getty.

Chapter 9

Chapter Opening Photo: © Alex Gumerov/ iStockphoto.
Photo 9.1: © Alex Gumerov/iStockphoto.
Photo 9.2: © Bettmann/Corbis.
Photo 9.3: © Brad Killer/iStockphoto.
Photo 9.4: © Izabela Habur/iStockphoto.

Chapter 10

Chapter Opening Photo: © Todd Pearson/ Getty.
Photo 10.1: © Tom Stewart/Corbis.
Photo 10.2: © David Sucsy/iStockphoto.
Photo 10.3: © Tim Pannell/Corbis.
Photo 10.4: © Ed Kashi/Corbis.

Chapter 11

Chapter Opening Photo: © Robert Churchill/ iStockphoto.
Photo 11.1: © Andrea Booher/ Photographer's Choice/Getty.
Photo 11.2a: © Arctic-Images/Corbis.
Photo 11.2b: © Ariel Skelley/Blend Images/ Getty.
Photo 11.3: © Simon Marcus/Corbis.

Chapter 12

Chapter Opening Photo: © Sophia Tsibikaki/ iStockphoto.
Photo 12.1: © Betsie Van der Meer/Stone/Getty.

Photo 12.2a: © Chris Jackson/Getty Images Entertainment/Getty.
Photo 12.2b: © WIN-Initiative/WIN-Initiative/Getty.
Photo 12.3: © Artiga Photo/Corbis.

Chapter 13

Chapter Opening Photo: © Dave J. Anthony/ Getty.
Photo 13.1: © Image Source Pink/Image Source/Getty.
Photo 13.2: © Aldo Murillo/iStockphoto.
Photo 13.3: © Business Wire/Getty.
Photo 13.4: © Doug Menuez/Photodisc/Getty.

Chapter 14

Chapter Opening Photo: © Will & Deni McIntyre/Getty.
Photo 14.1: © Robert Cianflone/Getty.
Photo 14.2: © Sean Locke/iStockphoto.
Photo 14.3: © Stephen Shugerman/Getty.
Photo 14.4: © Adrian Assalve/iStockphoto.

Throughout Book

Listen In On Your Life icon: © marc brown/ iStockphoto
Contrarian Challenge icon: © Ahmad Hamoudah/iStockphoto.
Strategic Communication icon: © Floortje/ istockphoto
Make Your Own Case icon: © Ieva Geneviciene/iStockphoto

Author Index

Subject Index

Supporting researchers for more than 40 years

Research methods have always been at the core of SAGE's publishing program. Founder Sara Miller McCune published SAGE's first methods book, *Public Policy Evaluation*, in 1970. Soon after, she launched the *Quantitative Applications in the Social Sciences* series—affectionately known as the "little green books."

Always at the forefront of developing and supporting new approaches in methods, SAGE published early groundbreaking texts and journals in the fields of qualitative methods and evaluation.

Today, more than 40 years and two million little green books later, SAGE continues to push the boundaries with a growing list of more than 1,200 research methods books, journals, and reference works across the social, behavioral, and health sciences. Its imprints—Pine Forge Press, home of innovative textbooks in sociology, and Corwin, publisher of PreK–12 resources for teachers and administrators—broaden SAGE's range of offerings in methods. SAGE further extended its impact in 2008 when it acquired CQ Press and its best-selling and highly respected political science research methods list.

From qualitative, quantitative, and mixed methods to evaluation, SAGE is the essential resource for academics and practitioners looking for the latest methods by leading scholars.

For more information, visit **www.sagepub.com**.